Becoming a
Master
Student

DAVE ELLIS

DEBRA DAWSON

Western University

DOUG TOFT

Contributing Editor

⁕ CENGAGE

Australia • Brazil • Canada • Mexico • Singapore • United Kingdom • United States

Becoming a Master Student,
Seventh Canadian Edition
Dave Ellis and Debra Dawson

VP, Product Solutions, K-20: Claudine O'Donnell

Director, Qualitative Publishing: Jackie Wood

Publisher: Carmen Yu

Director of Marketing, Post-Secondary: Jennifer Sutton

Content Manager: Gail Brown

Photo and Permissions Researcher: Jessica Freedman

Rights Project Manager: Lynn McLeod

Production Project Manager: Shannon Martin

Production Service: MPS Limited

Copy Editor: Elspeth McFadden

Proofreader: MPS Limited

Indexer: MPS Limited

Design Director: Ken Phipps

Post-secondary Design Project Manager: Pamela Johnston

Interior Design: Cathryn Mayer

Cover Design: John Montgomery

Cover Image: gilaxia/Getty Images

Compositor: MPS Limited

For product information and technology assistance, contact us at **Canada Support, canadasupport.cengage.com.**

For permission to use material from this text or product, submit all requests online at **www.cengage.com/permissions.**

Library and Archives Canada Cataloguing in Publication:

Ellis, David B., author

Becoming a master student / Dave Ellis, Debra Dawson, Western University ; Doug Toft, contributing editor. – Seventh Canadian edition.

Issued in print and electronic formats.
ISBN 978-0-17-676600-9 (softcover).
—ISBN 978-0-17-688670-7 (PDF)

1. College student orientation.
2. Study skills. I. Dawson, Debra, author II. Toft, Doug, editor III. Title. IV. Title: Master student.

LB2343.3.E44 2019   378.1'98
C2018-905776-9
C2018-905777-7

ISBN-13: 978-0-17-676600-9
ISBN-10: 0-17-676600-6

Cengage Canada
1120 Birchmount Road
Toronto, ON   M1K 5G4
Canada

Cengage is a leading provider of customized learning solutions with employees residing in nearly 40 different countries and sales in more than 125 countries around the world. Find your local representative at **www.cengage.com.**

To learn more about Cengage platforms and services, register or access your online learning solution, or purchase materials for your course, visit **www.cengage.ca.**

Printed in Canada
Print Number: 02   Print Year: 2021

© aprott/iStockphoto

© Hxdbzxy/Shutterstock.com

Brief Table of Contents

Table of Contents

Monkey Business Images/Shutterstock.com

Ammentorp Photography/Shutterstock.com

Chapter **3**

Memory **108**

Chapter **2**

Time **69**

bbernard/Shutterstock.com

Gustavo Frazao/Shutterstock.com

Chapter 7

Thinking 226

Chapter 8

Communicating 264

Chapter 9

Diversity 308

Chapter 10

Money 332

Rawpixel.com/Shutterstock.com

Loveischiangrai/Shutterstock.com

Chapter **11**

Health 359

Chapter **12**

What's Next? **399**

Minerva Studio/Shutterstock.com

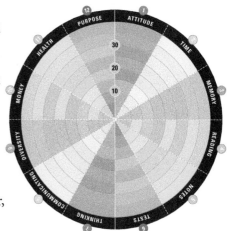

WELCOME TO THE seventh Canadian edition of *Becoming a Master Student*. If you are a student and about to start reading this resource, you will see that the information we provide is designed to support your academic success throughout the coming years. This resource is user-friendly and accessible, with each chapter being composed of a series of short articles. You will find that this new edition contains new critical thinking exercises that help you apply the knowledge and skills you gain from using this resource.

Becoming a Master Student is a different kind of textbook. It functions as a workbook where you read articles and complete short exercises that help you develop the characteristics of successful students and discover more about yourself as a learner. From the first chapter, where you do the *Discovery Wheel* exercise and explore your beliefs about yourself as a learner, to the last chapter, where you repeat this exercise, you will see the changes that have occurred in you.

New to This Edition

In the current edition, we have thoroughly updated the information in the book and placed an emphasis on new and emerging issues that today's students may face (for example, mental health crises). In addition to developing new critical thinking exercises, we have also revised most of the master student profiles to focus on Canadians who exemplify the master student. From environmentalists like Maya Burhanpurkar, to technological innovators such as Ann Makonsinski and Sam Maggs, to change-makers like Brielle Beardy-Linklater and Craig Kielburger, to artists such as Wali Shah and Mariko Tamaki, to extraordinary students like Billy-Ray Belcourt—their stories will inspire you.

Technological tools for student success are no longer isolated in boxes and instead are now woven throughout. You will see more references to apps that you can use to enhance learning, such as those that can help you manage group work or help keep projects on track, and important websites to visit if you want more detailed and topic-specific information. Other changes include a new brief exercise called "do you have a minute?" at the start of each chapter, which is designed to prime students for learning. We have also included the voices of Canadians in the know providing advice to support the success of first-years students in the feature box "Tips for Master Students." Finally, a new feature box called "Did you know that…?" highlights little-known facts about Canada's colleges and universities.

There are many other new highlights for each chapter. The introduction chapter and the first three chapters (*Making Transitions, First Steps, Time, and Memory*) discuss the concepts of growth mindset, grit, and academic tenacity. In these chapters, we emphasize students adopting a growth mindset and developing the resilience that they will need to succeed in school and in life. Chapters 4, 5, and 6—*Reading, Notes*, and *Tests*—discuss the reality of day-to-day school tasks. In these chapters, we have included additional material on using critical thinking to develop metacognitive skills and employing mind

Maya Burhanpurkar
…is an environmental advocate

There's a moment in Maya Burhanpurkar's documentary where she stands next to an ice fjord in Ilulissat, Greenland, realizing what climate change means for the people who live there.

After listening to residents describe how fast the ice is melting, she looks into the camera and says: "I think that I'm going to become a lot more conscientious of the environment when I go about my everyday life because after what I've seen today, the icebergs and now the ice fjord, I really don't want that natural landscape to be destroyed. Every single person counts."

Melting ice changed Burhanpurkar's life and now she's inspiring others around the world with a documentary about climate change.

The film's title, *400 PPM*, refers to the concentration of carbon dioxide in the atmosphere, which now exceeds 400 parts per million, the highest level seen in the history of our species. Burhanpurkar's eye-opening voyage happened when she was invited to tour the Canadian and Greenlandic Arctic aboard the *Sea Adventurer*.

It's impressive enough that this teenager turned her trip into an acclaimed documentary. But that's on top of her previous achievements prototyping "intelligent antibiotics," discovering new properties of a drug to cure Alzheimer's disease, and tracking asteroids.

"I have a scientific background," Burhanpurkar explained. "I'd never done anything creative like this before. It's not really my forte."

She also interviewed prominent Canadians to explain the scientific concepts and social issues, including author Margaret Atwood, former astronaut Col. Christopher Hadfield, anthropologist Dr. Wade Davis, and Nobel laureate Dr. Brad Bass.

Burhanpurkar was among the recipients of the Gloria Barron Prize for Young Heroes for her work on the documentary, which has reached more than 2.2 million students.

"In school we learn facts and figures and that it's going to impact us at some point," Burhanpurkar recalled. "This could not be further from the truth."

"The Arctic is where global warming is changing our planet the fastest," she explains. "It's the canary in the coal mine. It's the Earth's early warning system and its alarm is going off. We need to act now."

"Before I went, I was excited to do the whole ecotourism thing," she said, "but what struck me was meeting the people who are already impacted by climate change."

Farther north, in Uummannaq, Greenland, Burhanpurkar observed that climate change was hurting the Inuit people along with the ice. Thinning glaciers have made ice fishing nearly impossible, devastating the economy and changing the traditional culture.

"It was hardly their fault," she narrated. "It was ours."

Burhanpurkar will take her new awareness with her when she begins college at Harvard.

"I had the opportunity to witness climate change firsthand and it changed my life," Burhanpurkar said.

Source: Shepard, Laura A. (2016, October 5). Teenage scientist captures Arctic ice melt on film. Nexus Media, *Popular Science*. Retrieved from https://www.popsci.com/teenage-scientist-captures-arctic-ice-melt-on-film. Reprinted by permission.

Maya Burhanpurkar (1999–) started her science career in a basement laboratory in her family home at the age of 10. She received a Queen Elizabeth II Diamond Jubilee Medal and has been named one of Canada's Top 20 Under 20. Plus, she has represented Canada in the Intel and Google Science Talent Search Competition.

do you have a minute?

Think of a goal you have for your school year. Write it down. This is not a to-do list. It is a result that you intend to produce by getting one or more items on your to-do list done. Complete this sentence: One thing that I could do to achieve this goal is …

Tips for Master Students

Don't wait until the end of the day to start organizing yourself

I wouldn't wait until the end [of the day] to start organizing—I would take four or five breaks throughout the day and make sure I could jam everything in—and then every night before going to sleep, I would see what's going on for the next day and prepare myself, read up on things. Before every meeting I would look at exactly what I wanted to go in there with and it was constant reminders. I was one of those people who would constantly look at my notes or my phone and be on top of my game.
—Abdullah Snobar, executive director of the DMZ, Ryerson University's technology incubator (*Maclean's*, 2017)

Source: Advice for first-year students from Justin Trudeau (and 27 other people), by *Maclean's*, *Maclean's*, December 1, 2017.

mapping tools to organize notes, as well as new information on effectively preparing for tests, including the use of spaced practice.

The next three chapters present updated material on skills and knowledge which are essential for daily living. *Thinking* now explicitly discusses how to critically evaluate information on the Internet to differentiate what is authentic and credible from what is fabricated or misleading, while *Communicating* discusses blocks to effective listening, and finally *Diversity* includes more on inclusion and power dynamics with a stronger focus on LGBTQQ (lesbian, gay, bisexual, transgendered, and queer or questioning) and Indigenous students.

The final three chapters (*Money, Health,* and *What's Next*) concentrate on important topics for first-year students. In these chapters students will explore issues critical to achieving their long-term goals—from how to access the Canada Student Loan program, to the impact of the use of cannabis on the developing brain, to what supports are available for students with mental health issues and how to successfully network to find a job.

Becoming a Master Student provides the tools for you to be an active and ever-improving participant in your learning journey. As well, this resource will help identify those habits and behaviours that could prevent you from becoming a master student and will also empower you to make the changes needed to succeed—as a student and in life. So, take the time to complete the journal entries and critical thinking exercises, and enjoy reading and learning from the profiles of successful master students.

For Instructors

Downloadable Instructor Supplements

All and other key instructor ancillaries can be accessed through login.cengage.com/instructor, giving instructors the ultimate tools for customizing lectures and presentations.

Test Bank: This resource was revised by Cynthia Mason, Ryerson University. The test bank includes over 150 multiple-choice questions written according to guidelines for effective construction and development of higher-order questions. Also included are a variety of true/false, completion, and short answer questions.

The Test Bank is available in a cloud-based platform. **Testing Powered by Cognero®** is a secure online testing system that allows you to author, edit, and manage test bank content from any place you have Internet access. No special installations or downloads are needed, and the desktop-inspired interface, with its drop-down menus and familiar, intuitive tools, allows you to create and manage tests with ease. You can create multiple test versions in an instant, and import or export content into other systems. Tests can be delivered from your learning management system, your classroom, or wherever you choose. Testing Powered by Cognero for *Becoming a Master Student*, Seventh Canadian Edition, can also be accessed through login.cengage.com. Printable versions of the Test Bank are available by contacting your sales and editorial representative.

PowerPoint: Microsoft® PowerPoint® lecture slides have been created for every chapter. There is an average of 20 slides per chapter, many featuring key figures, tables, and photographs from *Becoming a Master Student*, Seventh Canadian Edition. Principles of clear design and engaging content have been incorporated throughout, making it simple for you to customize the deck for your courses.

Image Library: This resource consists of digital copies of figures, short tables, and photographs used in the book. You may use these jpegs to customize the PowerPoint or create your own presentations.

Instructor's Guide: This resource was revised by Juliet O'Neill Dunphy, Concordia University. It is organized according to the chapters in *Becoming a Master Student* and addresses key educational concerns, such as typical stumbling blocks students face and how to address them.

MindTap

MindTap for *Becoming a Master Student*, Seventh Canadian Edition is a peronalized digital learning solution that guides students to analyze, apply, and elevate thinking, and allows instructors to measure skills and promote better outcomes with ease. A fully online learning solution, MindTap combines all student learning tools—readings, multimedia, activities, and assessments—into a single Learning Path that guides the student through the curriculum. Instructors personalize the experience by customizing the presentation of these learning tools to their students, even seamlessly introducing their own content into the Learning Path.

For Students

MindTap

Stay organized and efficient with *MindTap*—a single destination with all the course material and study aids you need to succeed. Built-in apps leverage social media and the latest learning technology. For example:

- ReadSpeaker will read the text to you.
- Flashcards are pre-populated to provide you with a jump start for review—or you can create your own.
- You can highlight text and make notes in your MindTap Reader. Your notes will flow into Evernote, the electronic notebook app that you can access from anywhere.
- Study tools and self-quizzing allows you to assess your understanding.

Visit www.login.cengage.com to start using **MindTap**. Enter the Online Access Code from the card included with your text. If a code card is not provided, you can purchase instant access at Cengage.ca.

List of Reviewers

Liza Arnason
University of Ontario Institute of Technology

Judith Grad
Concordia University

Christina Lord
Brescia University College

Witty Sandle
The King's University

Nicola Winstanley
Humber College

Acknowledgments

I would like to take this opportunity to thank the many people who have been instrumental in developing this new edition. To begin with, I want to acknowledge the land on which the revisions to this book were done. Western University is situated on the traditional territories of the Anishinaabeg, Haudenosaunee, Lunaapeewak, and Attawandaron peoples, who have longstanding relationships to the land and region of southwestern Ontario and the city of London. The local First Nation communities of this area include Chippewas of the Thames First Nation, Oneida Nation of the Thames, and Munsee Delaware Nation.

The feedback and suggestions from the review panel members were vital to the revisions for this edition and helped to identify what changes were needed in this resource to make our students more successful. Thank you for reading the content so thoroughly and for your insightful feedback.

Next, I would like to thank Content Manager Gail Brown. You were superb at keeping me on track and guiding me through the revision process. I would also like to thank the rest of the team at Cengage Education Ltd.—Leanna MacLean and Carmen Yu, publishers; Jennifer Sutton, Marketing Director; Lynn McLeod, Rights Project Manager; Shannon Martin, Production Project Manager; Nastasia Delmedico, Digital Production Manager; and Jessica Freedman, Permissions Researcher.

Without my research assistant, Rosanne Greene, this book would not have happened—your keen research skills were critical in hunting down key facts for the book. Plus, I appreciated your diligence in helping me seek out Canada's most interesting and accomplished young people for the profiles in this book. I also thank all of the students and instructors I have worked with over the years at Western University. Learning is a reciprocal process, and I learn so much from each of you every time I enter the classroom. Heartfelt gratitude is also expressed to the staff of the Centre for Teaching and Learning and the Student Success Centre, who inspire me with their dedication to enhancing student learning, both inside and outside the classroom.

Finally, to my family, Avery Dawson Dance and Susan Grindrod—thank you so much for putting up with my spending the weekends and our holidays at the computer. I am truly grateful to Avery for reading the book and for talking to me about the complexity of students' lives today and to Susan for her unflagging support, patience, and can-do attitude throughout the writing of this book. You are both blessings in my life.

Debra Dawson
London, Ontario

Western University, Paul Mayne, "Award celebrates her 'oasis of discovery'." Western News, June 8, 2016, http://news.westernu.ca/2016/06/award-celebrates-her-oasis-of-discovery/

About the Canadian Author

Debra Dawson has a PhD in Educational Psychology. She was the founding Director of the Centre for New Students and later the Director of Teaching and Learning Services at Western University. She is currently the Director of the Centre for Research on Teaching and Learning in Higher Education at Western University. Debra is an award-winning teacher, and the 2016 recipient of the Society for Teaching and Learning in Higher Education's Christopher Knapper Lifetime Achievement Award, an honour given to those who have made significant contribution to teaching, learning, and educational development in Canadian higher education.

Making Transitions

© wavebreakmedia/Shutterstock.com

what is included ...

do you have a minute?

Take a minute to make a list of anything you would like to accomplish in the next five years. Here are some possibilities for this list:

1. Projects you'd like to start or finish.
2. Skills you'd like to acquire.
3. Tasks you'd like to complete.
4. New activities that you would like to try.

Save this list and refer to it as you read and work through this chapter. Everything you wrote down is a clue about what's important to you. This chapter is filled with strategies for getting clear about what you want and taking immediate steps to get it.

WHAT if ...

I could use the ideas in this Introduction to master any transition in my life?

WHY the Introduction matters ...

You can ease your transition to higher education and set up a lifelong pattern of success by following the strategies described here.

HOW you can use this Introduction ...

Discover a way to interact with the book that multiplies its value. Use a journal to translate personal discoveries into powerful new behaviours. Connect with people and organizations that support your success.

Postsecondary education—
WHY IT MATTERS

Students often wonder if it is really worth it to go to college or university. You bet it is. The research of Ernest Pascarella and Patrick Terrenzini (2005) over three decades shows that going to college has big payoffs even beyond the skills and knowledge you will acquire. Sure, you are growing up as you go through school, but beyond getting older it turns out that school makes a positive impact on many dimensions of your life.

Postsecondary education adds value to your life by increasing or significantly enhancing many facets of your life:

Your Psychosocial Skills
- Self-esteem
- Leadership skills
- Independence
- Interpersonal skills

Your Attitudes and Values
- Civic and community engagement
- Openness to diversity
- Support for gender equality

Your Career and Economic Outcomes
- Job satisfaction
- Earnings
- Occupational status
- Job search abilities and skills
- Employment and career mobility

Your Quality of Life
- Good health
- How long you will live
- Feelings of well-being
- Interest in lifelong learning
- Better consumer choices
- Savings

Of course, how much you get out of your postsecondary experience depends on what you choose to do both inside and outside the classroom. Inside the classroom you want to be as engaged in learning as you can. According to Laurie Schreiner (2010a), this means being truly involved in what is going on in class—asking questions, participating in discussions with other students, and vigorously exploring ideas. You also want to try to connect what you learn in the classroom to the real world. By the way, if you do this, not only will you get more out of school, but you'll also get higher grades too and be more likely to graduate.

Getting involved in activities outside class will also serve to enhance the benefits of your postsecondary experience. Take the time to explore new interests—try to take a broad range of courses so that you can fully develop your options. Even if you took a similar course in high school, try it again at university or in college; courses tend to be taught differently and the opportunities to take the conversation to a greater depth are more likely at this point. Our hobbies and other interests often give us vital clues about our passions in life, clues that can point us in the direction of careers we might explore. So use this time to join new clubs, participate in volunteer activities, and try out as many new "hats" as possible. As most of us are likely to have multiple careers throughout our lives, it just makes sense to try to develop the broadest possible toolkit of skills and knowledge. You never know what you will need in the future.

We will explore more about the value of higher education in Chapter 1, "First Steps." ✳

Source: How College Affects Students, Vol. 2, A Third Decade of Research, by Pascarella, Ernest T., and Patrick T. Terenzini. Copyright © 2005 John Wiley & Sons. Used with permission of John Wiley & Sons, Inc.

REWRITE THIS BOOK

Some books should be preserved in pristine condition. This isn't one of them.

Something happens when you interact with your book by writing in it. *Becoming a Master Student* is about learning, and learning is an active pursuit, not a passive one. When you make notes in the margin, you can hear yourself talking with the author. When you doodle and underline, you can see the author's ideas taking shape. You can even argue with the author and come up with your own theories and explanations. In all of these ways, you become a coauthor of this book. You rewrite it to make it yours.

While you're at it, you can create symbols or codes that will help when reviewing the text later on, such as "Q" for questions or exclamation points for important ideas. You can also circle words to look up in a dictionary.

Remember, if you try out an idea in this book and it doesn't work for you, you can rewrite it. Change the exercises to fit your needs. Create a new technique by combining several others. Create a technique out of thin air!

Find something you agree or disagree with on this page and write a short note in the margin about it. Or draw a diagram. Better yet, do both. Let creativity be your guide. Have fun.

Begin rewriting now. ✳

practising
CRITICAL THINKING

I-1

Textbook reconnaissance

Start becoming a master student this moment by doing a 15-minute "textbook reconnaissance." Here's how.

First, read this book's Table of Contents. Do it in three minutes or less. Next, look at every page in the book. Move quickly. Scan headlines. Look at pictures. Notice forms, charts, and diagrams.

A textbook reconnaissance shows you where a course is going. It gives you the big picture. That's useful because brains work best when going from the general to the specific. Getting the big picture before you start makes it easier to recall and understand details later on.

Look for ideas you can use. When you find one, write the page number and a short description on a separate sheet of paper. Or use sticky notes to flag the pages that look useful. (If you are reading *Becoming a Master Student* as an e-book, you can flag pages electronically.) You could even use notes in different colours to signal priority, such as green for ideas to use right away and yellow for those to apply later. The idea behind this technique is simple: It's easier to learn when you're excited, and it's easier to get excited about a course if you know it's going to be useful, interesting, or fun.

How to succeed in your first year

Students often ask me what it takes to be successful in my first-year course, thinking that there must be a "trick" or secret. There is no secret. Most students forget that if they were "good enough" to be admitted to their postsecondary program, they have already indicated that they have what it takes to succeed at college or university. The skills that make you a successful student are really the same ones that lead to success in any aspect of life—all success takes is time on task. Quite simply, the more time and effort you put into school, the more you get out of it. Nonetheless, here are a few suggestions from actual students that may help.

Relax . . . don't get stressed out. You need to put everything in perspective and take a deep breath from time to time. If you let stress build up, it will interfere with your ability to succeed.

Ask for help if you need it. Students often wait too long before they ask for any kind of help. Don't do this. Speak to your professor or TA, see the counselling centre, ask for academic advice. All of these services are in place to help you, so use them.

Keep up with your readings and make notes before coming to class. In most courses, there is a lot of reading that you will be expected to do on your own. Lectures are not intended to cover everything in a course and reading/note-taking is a very important skill you must master in your time at school. Making notes based on your reading before class provides you with a guide to what will be discussed in class. You will be better prepared to actually listen to the instructor if you have some idea where she or he is going.

Attend class. In most courses, attendance is optional. However, classes are offered for a reason: Class provides an important "value added" component to the course material. Take advantage of this. Research consistently shows that the vast majority of students who come to class end up doing better on the exams than those who do not (Moore, 2006).

If you approach it as you would any other exciting opportunity, college or university can be one of the best times of your life. Work hard and challenge yourself, and your higher education career will be very rewarding.

Courtesy of Michael Atkinson

Dr. Mike Atkinson, Introductory Psychology Professor & 3M National Teaching Fellow, Western University

The DISCOVERY and INTENTION JOURNAL ENTRY SYSTEM

ONE WAY TO become a better student is to grit your teeth and try harder. There is another way. Using familiar tools and easily learned processes, the Discovery and Intention Journal Entry system can help increase your effectiveness by showing you how to focus your energy.

The Discovery and Intention Journal Entry system is a little like flying a plane. Airplanes are seldom exactly on course. Human and automatic pilots are always checking positions and making corrections. The resulting flight path looks like a zigzag. The plane is almost always flying in the wrong direction, but because of constant observation and course correction, it arrives at the right destination.

A similar system can be used by students. Most Journal Entries throughout this book are labelled as either Discovery Statements or Intention Statements; some are Discovery/Intention Statements. Each Journal Entry will contain a short set of suggestions that involve writing.

Through **Discovery Statements**, you can assess "where you are." These statements are a record of what you are learning about yourself as a student—both strengths and weaknesses. Discovery Statements can also be declarations of your goals, descriptions of your attitudes, statements of your feelings, transcripts of your thoughts, and chronicles of your behaviour.

Sometimes Discovery Statements chronicle a light bulb moment—a flash of insight that results when a new idea connects with your prior experiences, your preferred styles of learning, or both. Perhaps a solution to a long-standing problem suddenly occurs to you, or a life-changing insight wells up from the deepest recesses of your mind. Don't let such moments disappear. Capture them in Discovery Statements.

Intention Statements can be used to alter your course. They are statements of your commitment to do a specific task or take a certain action. An intention arises out of your choice to direct your energy toward a particular goal. While Discovery Statements promote awareness, Intention Statements are blueprints for action. The two processes reinforce each other.

The purpose of this system is not to get you pumped up and excited to go out there and try harder. Rather, Discovery and Intention Statements are intended to help you focus on what you want to accomplish and how you plan to achieve your goals.

The Journal Entry process is a cycle. First, you write Discovery Statements about where you are now and where you want to be. Next, you write Intention Statements about the specific steps you will take to get there. Then, you follow up with Discovery Statements about whether you completed those steps and what you learned in the process, followed by more Intention Statements, and so on. Sometimes a statement will be long and detailed. Usually, it will be short—maybe just a line or two. With practice, the cycle will become automatic.

Don't panic when you fail to complete an intended task. Straying off course is normal. Simply make the necessary corrections. Miraculous progress might not come immediately. Do not be concerned. Stay with the cycle. Use Discovery Statements to get a clear view of your world and what you want out of it. Then use Intention Statements to direct your actions. When you notice progress, record it.

That's the system in a nutshell. Discovery leads to awareness. Intention leads to commitment, which naturally leads to focussed action.

The following statement might strike you as improbable, but it is true: It often takes the same amount of energy to get what you want in school as it takes to get what you don't want. Sometimes getting what you don't want takes even more effort. An airplane burns the same amount of fuel flying away from its destination as it does flying toward it. It pays to stay on course. Similarly, you can put as much energy into finding ways to procrastinate as you would studying for an exam and getting an A. One approach leads to success; the other does not.

You can use the Discovery and Intention Journal Entry system to stay on your own course and get what you want out of school. Consider the guidelines that follow, and then develop your own style. Once you get the hang of it, you might discover you can fly. ✳

DISCOVERY AND INTENTION
Statement guidelines

Writing journal entries helps you to develop self-awareness, self-direction, and other master student qualities. Use the following guidelines as a checklist. Consider removing this page from the book and posting it in a prominent place where you'll typically be writing your responses to the Journal Entries.

Discovery Statements

1 Record the specifics about your thoughts, feelings, and behaviour. We talk to ourselves constantly in our heads. When internal chatter gets in the way, write down what you are telling yourself. If this seems difficult at first, just start writing. The act of writing can trigger a flood of thoughts.

Thoughts also include mental pictures. These are especially powerful. Picturing yourself flunking a test is like a rehearsal to do just that. One way to take away the power of negative images is to describe them in detail.

Notice how you feel when you function well. Use Discovery Statements to pinpoint exactly where and when you learn most effectively.

In addition, observe your actions and record the facts. If you spent 90 minutes chatting online with a favourite cousin instead of reading your anatomy text, write about it and include the details. Record your observations quickly, as soon as you make them.

2 Use discomfort as a signal. When you approach a daunting task, such as a difficult math problem, notice your physical sensations. Feeling uncomfortable, bored, or tired might be a signal that you're about to do valuable work. Stick with it. Tell yourself you can handle the discomfort just a little bit longer. You will be rewarded with a new insight.

3 Suspend judgment. When you are discovering yourself, be gentle. Suspend self-judgment. If you continually judge your behaviours as "bad" or "stupid," your mind will rebel. For your own benefit, be kind.

4 **Tell the truth.** Suspending judgment helps you tell the truth about yourself. "The truth will set you free" is a saying that endures for a reason. The closer you get to the truth, the more powerful your Discovery Statements will be. And if you notice that you are avoiding the truth, don't blame yourself. Just tell the truth about it.

Intention Statements

1 **Make intentions positive.** The purpose of writing intentions is to focus on what you want rather than what you don't want. Instead of writing "I will not fall asleep while studying accounting," write "I intend to stay awake when studying accounting."

Also avoid the word *try*. Trying is not doing. When we hedge our bets with *try*, we can always tell ourselves, "Well, I *tried* to stay awake." We end up fooling ourselves into thinking we succeeded.

2 **Make intentions observable.** Experiment with an idea from educational trainer Robert Mager (1975), who suggests that goals be defined through behaviours that can be observed and measured. Rather than writing "I intend to work harder on my history assignments," write "I intend to review my class notes, and I intend to make summary sheets of my reading." Then, when you review your progress, you can determine more precisely whether you have accomplished what you intended.

3 **Make intentions small and achievable.** Break large goals into small, specific tasks that can be accomplished quickly. If you want to get a high mark in biology, ask yourself, "What can I do today?" You might choose to study biology for an extra hour. Make that your intention.

When setting your goals, anticipate self-sabotage. Be aware of what you might do, consciously or unconsciously, to undermine your best intentions; for example, you might go online to chat just ten minutes before you intend to study, but ten minutes is likely to stretch to much longer. Also, be careful of intentions that depend on others. If you write that you intend that your study group complete an assignment by Monday, then your success depends on the other students in the group. Likewise, you can support your group's success by following through on your stated intentions.

4 **Set timelines that include rewards.** Timelines can focus your attention. For example, if you are assigned to write an essay, break the assignment into small tasks and set a precise due date for each one. You might write "I intend to select a topic for my essay by 9 a.m. Wednesday."

When you meet your goal on time, reward yourself. Rewards that are an integral part of a goal are powerful. External rewards, such as a movie or an afternoon in the park, are valuable, too. These rewards will work only if you're willing to withhold them. If you plan to take a nap on Sunday afternoon whether or not you've finished your English assignment, the nap is not an effective reward.

5 **Move from intention to action.** Intention Statements are of little use until you act on them. If you want new results in your life, then take action. Life responds to what you *do*. Discover the joy of "baby steps." Even simple changes in behaviour can produce results. If you find yourself procrastinating, then promise to read for five minutes and then take a break—you'll be surprised at how fast those five minutes stretch into ten. Even tiny steps make a difference.

Look for prompts for action throughout this book. In addition to Journal Entries, there are numerous critical thinking exercises that you should try. These are suggestions for specific actions based on the text. ✳

journal entry   I-1

Discovery Statement

Recalling Excellence

Welcome to the first Journal Entry in this book. You'll find Journal Entries in every chapter, all with a similar design that allows space where you can write.

In the space below, write a description of a time in your life when you learned or did something well. This experience does not have to be related to school. Describe the details of the situation, including the place, time, and people involved. Describe how you felt about it, how it looked to you, how it sounded. Describe the physical sensations you associate with the event. Also describe your emotions.

I discovered that . . .

_____

_____

_____

_____

_____

_____

Characteristics of
A MASTER STUDENT

This book is all about helping you to be successful in post-secondary education. To be successful you need to develop the characteristics of a master student. As you open the door to higher education, many opportunities will be presented to help you grow and become a better student. Treat every Journal Entry or critical thinking exercise as a chance to improve your skills and become a master student.

Mastery requires effort and attention. We are all learning machines but that doesn't mean that learning happens effortlessly. The flawless presentation only becomes that way when you rehearse many nights in advance. The well-written paper requires rigorous editing days in advance of the due date.

Below are some of the characteristics of a master student. Take a moment to reflect and assess how developed this characteristic is in you. Put a checkmark by the characteristics you have already got down pat. Put an exclamation point by the ones that are still in development. Don't worry if you still need to acquire some of these characteristics. That's what this book is all about. Mastery requires time. Each chapter in this book can place you on the next rung of the ladder to becoming a master student.

Engage in learning

Master students realize that lots of learning happens both inside and outside the classroom. In class they are fully engaged in class activities. They join in all class activities like debates, simulations, or role plays. In large classes, they seize opportunities to get to know their profs by being a class representative. They actively participate in groups, and contribute to group projects. They know you only get out of class what you are willing to put into it.

Master students get involved in a variety of extracurricular activities including campus clubs. They try new activities and find out what they like to do best. They know they can always say no to activities that fail to create value for them. They join new groups because the activity piques their interest or because they always wanted to try out a new sport or activity, not because they feel guilty or obligated.

Monkey Business Images/Shutterstock.com

Manage out-of-class time

Master students have superb time management skills. By being good time managers, master students control their stress level, and they are unlikely to be surprised about upcoming quizzes, tests, or assignment deadlines. They recognize that getting a big picture of the year ahead makes it easier to get assignments done on time and erases the need for all-night study sessions.

They know that what they do outside class matters as much as—or even more than—what they do in class. They schedule at least two hours of study time for each hour that they spend in class.

Actively participate in class

Learning is not a spectator sport, so master students are willing to actively participate in class. They recognize that we learn by doing, and by hands-on participation in learning activities. Master students speak up in class and focus on what's happening in class. They are both mentally and physically involved in class activities. Master students come to class ready to actively participate.

Be tech savvy

A master student defines *technology* as any tool that's used to achieve a human purpose. From this point of view, computers become tools for deeper learning, higher productivity, and greater success. When faced with a task to accomplish, the master student chooses effectively from the latest options in hardware and software. He doesn't get overwhelmed with unfamiliar technology. Instead, he embraces learning about the new technology and finding ways to use it to help him succeed at the given task. He also knows when to go "offline" and fully engage with his personal community of friends, family members, classmates, instructors, and coworkers.

Self-regulate learning

Psychologists use the term **self-regulation** to describe people who set specific goals, monitor their progress toward those goals, and regularly change their behaviour to produce the desired results. Master students have a clear idea of their academic objectives and their own capabilities. They embrace the opportunities to meet the obstacles in reaching those objectives.

Adopt a growth mindset

Master students believe that success in school is determined more by their effort than it is by intelligence alone (Dweck, 2006). They have developed what is called a **growth mindset**. They recognize that learning is often challenging and see setbacks as opportunities to learn. They are flexible in the learning strategies they adopt to solve problems and have a can-do attitude. They look at failure as just another piece of information. They see lack of success as the need to try a new learning strategy or to approach the problem from a different perspective.

We will discuss more in Chapter 1, "First Steps," about why having a growth mindset is so important for your success.

Nurture grit

Having **grit** is also key to academic success for master students. Grit is a combination of both perseverance and passion that leads individuals to take on long-term goals and never give up no matter what obstacles they face (Duckworth, 2016). Your passion for your goals gives you a single-minded determination that nothing can derail, and you feel tremendous satisfaction when you succeed in reaching your valued goals (Duckworth & Eskreis-Winkler, 2013). To measure your grit, go to *angeladuckworth.com/grit-scale*.

Developing the characteristics of a master student

Review the items that you put an exclamation mark beside; these are the characteristics that you want to see develop over the coming year. Here are a couple of ideas to get you started.

To foster engagement in learning, write a Discovery Statement to yourself about what new activity you will try next. Commit to trying something new this week. Master students are engaged students.

Start being a better time manager by copying all your assignment and test due dates into your calendar. The first step to being on time is knowing when things are due.

Active learning requires your participation in class. Keep a log of all the times you raised your hand in class this week and then increase your participation in classes where your participation was low.

To become more tech savvy, consider attending any technology workshops offered on campus. Commit to downloading a new app that helps you manage your work each week. Start with a time management tool like *Remember the Milk*. It's only by using such tools that you will start to see the possibilities.

Developing your growth mindset will happen if you are willing to take on challenging tasks, like learning a new language, and if you stay focussed on the process rather than the outcome of this activity. Ask yourself to accept feedback on learning openly and without being defensive. Doing challenging tasks will allow your growth mindset to expand.

Grit is all about determination, so find role models—other "gritty" people, and see how they behave. A significant part of grit is sticking with tasks. Look for a learning task you find difficult and then just keep practising until you master the new task.

Becoming a Master Student promotes self-regulation through the ongoing cycle of discovery, intention, and action. Write Discovery Statements to monitor your progress toward your long-term goals and evaluate the results you're currently creating in life. Based on your discoveries, create Intention Statements for this term and in the next two years. Describe exactly what you will do to create new results in each time frame. Then follow through with each action. In this way, you take charge of your transition to higher education, starting now.

Growth mindset, **academic tenacity**, and grit are all non-cognitive factors that are highly related to achievement in school and in life. Your likelihood of success will be enhanced if you are able to tolerate frustration and to regulate your own behaviour, and if you feel that you belong. Although passion for your long-term goals is important, higher education offers you the opportunity to explore your interests and abilities before committing to your lifelong goals. Moreover, some students come to college or university with a growth mindset while others may develop one over time. Commit to trying an activity that has often challenged you in the past. By building up your ability to handle frustration, you will be enhancing your growth mindset and developing your academic tenacity.

Remember that grit, like anything else, is open to change. To nurture grit, pursue your interest, determine your long-term goals, and surround yourself with others who have grit. Find a role model with grit and speak to them about how they developed the courage to pursue their goals even in the light of adversity. Recognize that success takes time and the belief that with practice you will succeed. ✳

Get the most out of
THIS BOOK

Get used to the look and tone

This book looks different from many other traditional textbooks. *Becoming a Master Student* presents major ideas in magazine-style articles. You will discover lots of lists, blurbs, one-liners, pictures, charts, graphs, illustrations, and even a joke or two.

Even though this book is loaded with special features, you'll find some core elements. For example, the two pages that open each chapter include a "lead" article, which is followed up with an introductory exercise. And at the end of each chapter you'll find features to help you reflect on and apply what you've learned in the chapter: a Power Process, a Put it to Work article, a chapter quiz, and Skills Snapshot, as well as a Master Student Profile—all noted in a toolbar at the top of the page.

Rip 'em out or go online

The pages of the print version of *Becoming a Master Student* are perforated because some of the information here is too important to leave in the book (and some your instructor might want to see). For example, Journal Entry I-3 asks you to list some important things you want to get out of your education. To keep yourself focussed, you could rip that page out and post it where you'll see it several times a day. Or if you purchased the ebook, you can make notes and journal entries on your phone or other device so you'll always have them to refer to.

Skip around

You can use this book in several different ways. Read it straight through. Or pick it up, turn to any page, and find an idea you can use. Look for ideas you can use right now. For example, if you are about to choose a program of study or are considering changing schools, skip directly to the articles on these topics in Chapter 7, "Thinking," and Chapter 12, "What's Next?" respectively.

Use what works

If it doesn't work, lose it. If there are sections of the book that don't apply to you at all, skip them—unless, of course, they are assigned. Then see if you can gain value from these sections anyway. When you are committed to getting value from this book, even an idea that seems irrelevant or ineffective at first can turn out to be a powerful tool.

Own this book

Right now, put your name, address, and related information on the inside cover of this book, and don't stop there. Determine what you want to get out of school and create a record of how you intend to get it by reading the Power Process and completing the Journal Entries in this introduction. Every time your pen touches a page or you create notes in the ebook, you move closer to mastery of learning.

Practise critical thinking

Throughout this book are Practising Critical Thinking activities. Their purpose is to reinforce contemplation and problem-solving. Other aspects of the text, including Journal Entries and Skills Snapshots also promote critical thinking.

Practising
CRITICAL THINKING 1-1

Becoming Self-aware

One of the first keys to developing metacognitive skills is becoming self-aware. Here are some key questions you need to ask yourself. Think about ONE specific course you are taking when you write your responses.

1. How many hours do you spend studying for your course? _____
2. Are you up to date on course assignments and readings? _____
3. How do you take notes or study while reading the textbook? _____
4. How do you take notes in class? _____
5. Do you review your notes? _____ When? _____ How? _____
6. Do you stop periodically to check to see if you understand the material? _____

(Svinicki & McKeachie, 2014, p. 294)

Review your answers periodically to see if you are making adjustments to how you learn based on the feedback you receive on class tests and assignments. Checking in periodically with yourself is an important step to becoming self-aware.

From McKeachie/Svinicki, McKeachie's Teaching Tips, 14E. © 2014 South-Western, a part of Cengage, Inc. Reproduced by permission. www.cengage.com/permissions

---

Find out learning styles

Check out the Learning Style Inventory and related articles in Chapter 1. This material will help you to discover your preferred learning style and allow you to explore new styles. Then, throughout the rest of the book, you will find suggestions for applying your knowledge of learning styles. The modes of learning can be accessed by asking four basic questions: *What if? Why? How?* and *What.* You can use this four-part structure to effectively learn anything.

Experience the power of the Power Processes

A Power Process is a suggestion to shift your perspective or try a new behaviour. Look for this feature near the end of each chapter. Users of *Becoming a Master Student* often refer to these articles as their favourite part of the book. Approach them with a sense of play and possibility. Start with an open mind, experiment with the ideas, and see what works.

■ POWERPROCESS

Ideas Are Tools

There are many ideas in this book. When you first encounter them, don't believe any of them. Instead, think of them as tools.

For example, you use a hammer for a purpose—to drive a nail. When you use a new hammer, you might notice its shape, its weight, and its balance. You don't try to figure out whether the hammer is "right." You just use it. If it works, you use it again. If it doesn't work, you get a different hammer.

People have plenty of room in their lives for different kinds of "hammers," but they tend to limit themselves. A new idea, at some level, is a threat to their very being—unlike a new hammer, which is simply a new hammer.

Most of us have a built-in desire to be right. We think our ideas represent us. Imagine someone defending a hammer. Picture this person holding up a hammer and declaring, "Oh, hammer, we stand on guard for thee. There are only two kinds of people in this world: people who believe in this hammer and people who don't."

That ridiculous picture makes a point. This book is not a manifesto. It's a toolbox, and tools are meant to be used.

If you read about a tool in this book that doesn't sound "right" or one that sounds a little goofy, remember that the ideas here are for using, not necessarily for believing in. Suspend your judgment. Test the idea for yourself. If it works, use it. If it doesn't work, don't use it.

Any tool—whether it's a hammer, a computer program, or a study technique—is designed to do a specific job. A master mechanic carries a variety of tools because no single tool works for all jobs. If you throw a tool away because it doesn't work in one situation, you won't be able to pull it out later when it's just what you need. So if an idea doesn't work for you and you are satisfied that you gave it a fair chance, don't throw it away. File it away instead. The idea might come in handy soon.

And remember, this book is not about figuring out the "right" way. Even the "ideas are tools" approach is not "right." It's a hammer... or maybe a saw.

Galpi/Shutterstock.com

Read the feature boxes

Look for feature boxes—highlighted material such as additional information, resources, and useful strategies—throughout this book. Take notice of the Tips for Master Students boxes. These short pieces offer insight that might transform your experience of postsecondary education.

Use the modes to learn from *any* instructor

Students who experience difficulty in school might say, "My teacher doesn't get me" or "In class, we never have time for questions" or "The instructor doesn't teach to my learning style."

Such statements can become mental crutches—a set of beliefs that prevent you from taking responsibility for your education. To stay in charge of your learning, consider adopting attitudes such as the following:

I will look for the potential value in learning this information.

I can learn something useful in any situation, even if I don't like it at first.

No matter who's teaching a course, I am responsible for what I learn.

I will master this subject by using several modes of learning.

Remember that you can take action on such statements even if you don't fully agree with them yet. One way to change your attitudes is to adopt new behaviours, see how they work, and watch for new results in your life. This approach can be adapted to each mode:

To develop Mode 1, ask questions that help you understand why it is important for you to learn about a specific topic. You might also want to form a study group.

To develop Mode 2, ask questions that help you gather enough information to understand the main points and key facts. Also, learn a new subject in stages. For example, divide a large reading assignment into sections and then read each section carefully before moving on to the next one.

To develop Mode 3, ask questions about how a theory relates to daily life. Also, allow time to practise what you learn. You can do experiments, conduct interviews, create presentations, find a relevant work or internship experience, or even write a song that summarizes key concepts. Learn through hands-on practice.

To develop Mode 4, ask questions about ways to apply what you have just learned to several situations. Also, seek opportunities to demonstrate your understanding. You could coach a classmate about what you have learned, present findings from your research, explain how your project works, or perform a song that someone else created.

Even when teachers don't promote all four modes of learning, you can take charge of the way you learn. In the process, you consciously direct your growth and create new options.

Take this book to work

With a little tweaking in some cases, you can apply nearly all the techniques in this book to your career. For more details, see the Put it to Work articles in each chapter. Use them to make a seamless transition from success in school to success on the job. ✳

Commitment

This book is worthless unless you actively participate in its activities and exercises. One powerful way to begin taking action is to make a commitment. Conversely, without commitment, sustained action is unlikely, and the result is again a worthless book. Therefore, in the interest of saving your valuable time and energy, this exercise gives you a chance to declare your level of involvement up front. From the choices below, choose the sentence that best reflects your commitment to using this book. Write the number in the space provided at the end of the list.

1. "Well, I'm reading this book right now, aren't I?"

2. "I will skim the book and read the interesting parts."

3. "I will read the book and think about how some of the techniques might apply to me."

4. "I will read the book, think about it, and do the exercises that look interesting."

5. "I will read the book, do some exercises, and complete some of the Journal Entries."

6. "I will read the book, do some exercises and Journal Entries, and use some of the techniques."

7. "I will read the book, do most of the exercises and Journal Entries, and use some of the techniques."

8. "I will study this book, do most of the exercises and Journal Entries, and use some of the techniques."

9. "I will study this book, do most of the exercises and Journal Entries, and experiment vigorously with most of the suggestions in order to discover what works best for me."

10. "I will use this book as if the quality of my education depends on it—doing all the exercises and Journal Entries, experimenting with most of the techniques, inventing techniques of my own, and planning to reread this book in the future."

Enter your commitment level and today's date here:

Commitment level _____ Date _____

If you selected commitment level 1 or 2, you might consider passing this book on to a friend. If your commitment level is 9 or 10, you are on your way to terrific success in school. If your level is somewhere in between, experiment with the techniques and learning strategies in this book. If you find that they work, consider returning to this exercise and raising your level of commitment.

Here's the sales pitch

The purpose of this book is to help you make a successful transition to higher education by setting up a pattern of success that will last the rest of your life. However, you're unlikely to take action and use the ideas in this book until you believe you have something to gain.

Before you stiffen up and resist this pitch, remember you have already bought this book. To get value for your money, commit to becoming a master student. Here's what is in it for you.

Get full value for your money. Your postsecondary education is expensive—when you add up tuition, books, and living expenses, you might be paying $100.00 to sit in class. So, why not get the most out of it? As you'll see, the higher your education level the more you will earn more and the healthier you will be (Statistics Canada, 2017a).

Get suggestions from thousands of students. The ideas and techniques in this book are here not just because educators and psychologists say they work. They're here because tens of thousands of students have used them and say they work.

Get a tested product. Previous editions of this book have been found to be successful for millions of students. In particular, students with successful histories have praised the techniques in this book.

Making the transition to
POSTSECONDARY EDUCATION

Monkey Business Images/Shutterstock.com

YOU SHARE ONE thing in common with other students at your college or university: Entering postsecondary education represents a major change in your life. You've joined a new culture with its own set of rules, both spoken and unspoken.

Whether they've just graduated from high school or have been out of the classroom for decades, students new to higher education immediately face many differences between secondary and postsecondary education. The sooner you understand these differences, the sooner you can deal with them. Here are some examples:

- *New academic standards.* Often there are fewer tests in postsecondary education than in high school, and getting good marks might be tougher. You'll probably find that instructors expect you to study more than you did in high school. At the same time, your instructors will give you less guidance about what or how to study, and less feedback about how you are doing.

- *Responsibility for your own learning.* In postsecondary education, it is up to you to seek help if you need it. Although your instructors will be helpful if you tell them you are having difficulty learning, they expect you to take the first steps to ask for assistance. They are also less likely to give reminders about due dates for assignments or upcoming quizzes or to hand out study sheets before tests. Particularly in large classes, instructors are far less likely to contact you if your grades are a problem than your teachers would be in high school.

- *Differences in teaching styles.* Instructors at colleges and universities are often steeped in their subject matter. Many did not take courses on how to teach, and some professors might seem more focussed on research than on teaching.

- *A larger playing field.* The institution you've just joined might seem immense, impersonal, and even frightening. The sheer size of the campus, the variety of courses offered, the large number of departments—all of these can add up to a confusing array of options.

- *More students and more diversity.* The educational institution you're attending right now might enrol hundreds or thousands more students than your high school. Think of the possibilities to get to know so many new people.

There's an opportunity that comes with all of these changes: a greater degree of freedom. Postsecondary education presents you with a new world of choices. You are now responsible for deciding what classes to take, how to structure your time, and with whom to associate. Perhaps more than ever before, you'll find that your education is your own creation. To start on the road to academic success, keep the following in mind.

Decrease the unknowns

Before classes begin, get a map of the school property and walk through your first day's schedule, perhaps with a classmate or friend. Visit the classrooms and sit down in a seat and imagine yourself taking notes the next day. Anything you can do to get familiar with the new routine will help.

Admit your feelings—whatever they are

Postsecondary school can be an intimidating experience for new students. Anyone can feel anxious, isolated, homesick, or worried about doing well academically. Students such as international students, mature students, commuters, Indigenous students, and people with disabilities can feel especially isolated.

Those emotions are common among new students, and there's nothing wrong with them. Simply admitting the truth about how you feel—to yourself and to someone else—can help you cope. And you can almost always do something constructive in the present moment, no matter how you feel; for example, you might talk to your residence assistant or visit your centre for new students.

If your feelings about this transition make it hard for you to carry out the activities of daily life—going to class, working, studying, and relating to people—then get professional help. Start with a counsellor at the student health services or counselling service on your campus. The mere act of seeking help can make a difference.

Allow time for transition

You don't have to master the transition to higher education right away. Going to school often means moving away from home, friends, and familiar routines. Give it some time. Also, plan your academic schedule with your needs for transition in mind. Balance time-intensive courses with others that don't make as many demands.

Access resources

You can make a powerful difference in your education by using all of the resources available to students. Your supports include people, clubs and organizations, and school and community services. Perhaps more than ever before, you'll find that your education is your own creation.

Of all resources, people are the most important. You can isolate yourself, study hard, and get a good education. When you make the effort to establish relationships with instructors, staff members, fellow students, and employers, you can get a great education.

Build a network of people who will personally support your success in school.

Accessing resources is especially important if you are the first person in your family to enter higher education.

As a first-generation student, you are having experiences that people in your family may not understand. Talk to your family about your activities at school. If they ask how they can help you, give specific answers. Also, ask your advisor about programs for first-generation students on your campus.

Furthermore, if you used services for students with disabilities in high school, make sure you contact the campus disabilities office before classes begin. If you need academic accommodation for your classes or examinations, the staff at this office will make those arrangements for you. Remember, there are many people on campus to support your success, but you need to reach out to them.

Meet with your academic counsellor

One person in particular can help you access resources and make the transition to higher education—your

journal entry   I-2

Intention Statement

Plan for Transition

As a way to ease your transition to higher education, consider setting a goal to meet at least one new person each week for the next month. You could introduce yourself to someone in each of your classes, for example. You could also see your teachers during office hours and meet with your academic advisor.

List your ideas for ways to meet people in the space below.

_____

_____

_____

I intend to…

_____

_____

_____

_____

_____

academic counsellor or advisor. Meet with this person regularly. Counsellors generally have a big picture of course requirements, options for choosing programs of study, and the resources available at your institution. If your school has a first-year peer mentor program, get involved.

Learn the language of postsecondary education

Terms such as grade point average (GPA), prerequisite, corequisite, antirequisite, matriculation, registrar, and syllabus might be new to you. Ease your transition to higher education by checking your school calendar for definitions of these words and others that you don't understand. Also ask your academic advisor for clarification.

Experiment with new ways to study

You can cope with increased workloads and higher academic expectations by putting all of your study habits on the table and evaluating them. Don't assume the learning strategies you used in the past will automatically transfer to your new role in higher education. Keep the habits that serve you, drop those that hold you back, and adopt new ones to promote your success. Go

to the sessions offered in your school by your learning skills counsellors or the advisors in your student success centre. On every page of this book, you'll find helpful suggestions to help you study. ✳

Are you the typical student enrolled in postsecondary education in Canada?

If you are, then you are more likely to

- be female (56 percent, versus 44 percent male)
- be Canadian (89.1 percent, versus 10.9 percent international)
- be studying business, management, and public administration (18.4 percent), humanities (15 percent), or social and behavioural sciences and law (13.4 percent)
- have a parent who has completed at least some postsecondary education (73 percent)

(Statistics Canada, 2017b, 2017c, 2017d; Charbonneau, 2014)

Classroom civility—
WHAT'S IN IT FOR YOU

THE TOPIC OF this article might seem like a lesson in common sense, yet some students forget the simple behaviours that create a sense of safety, mutual respect, and community.

Consider an example: A student arrives 15 minutes late to a lecture and lets the door slam behind her. She pulls a fast-food burger out of a paper bag. Then her cellphone rings at full volume—and she answers it. Behaviours like these send a message to everyone in the room: "I'm ignoring you."

Without civility, you lose

Even a small problem with classroom civility creates problems for everyone. Learning gets interrupted. Trust breaks down. Your tuition dollars go down the drain. You invest hundreds of hours and thousands of dollars in getting a degree. You deserve to enter classrooms that are free of discipline problems and bullies.

Many schools have formal policies about classroom civility in their student code of conduct. Find out what policies apply to you. The consequences for violating them can be serious and may include expulsion or legal action.

With civility, you win

When you treat instructors and other students with respect, you're more likely to be treated that way in return. A respectful relationship with an instructor could turn into a favourable reference letter, a mentorship, a job referral, or a friendship that lasts for years after you graduate. Politeness pays.

Classroom civility does not mean that you have to be passive or insincere. You can present your opinions with passion and even disagree with an instructor in a way that leaves everyone enriched rather than threatened.

Lack of civility boils down to a group of habits. Like any habits they can be changed. The following suggestions reflect simple common sense, and they make an uncommon difference.

- *Be on time.* And if you have to leave class early, let the instructor know at the start of the class.
- *Participate fully.* Join in discussions and turn off your electronic devices. Find out your instructor's policy about the use of laptops in the classroom.
- *Communicate respect to your instructors and your classmates.* Call your instructors *Professor* or *Doctor* both in person and in email correspondence. Combine your passion for your opinion with respect for the opinions of others whether you are talking in class or online. If you work in groups, set group rules to stop misunderstandings.
- *Discuss grade disagreements in private.* Make an appointment to discuss your concerns at the instructor's office. During the meeting state your concerns respectfully and then focus on finding solutions. Find out if your school has a policy covering the issue by checking in with your school ombudsperson.

See civility as a contribution

Every class you enter has the potential to become a community of people who talk openly, listen fully, share laughter, and arrive at life-changing insights. Part of civility is staying open to the value that other people have to contribute. Embrace the diversity that your school has to offer. Master students embrace diversity and civility both inside and outside the classroom. ✳

Succeeding in higher
EDUCATION—AT ANY AGE

BEING AN ADULT learner puts you on a strong footing. With a rich store of life experience on which to draw, you can ask meaningful questions and more easily make connections between course work and daily life.

Any skills that you've developed to work on teams, manage projects, meet deadlines, and solve problems are assets. Many instructors will enjoy the expertise you will bring to their classrooms.

wavebreakmedia/Shutterstock.com

Following are some suggestions for returning mature students. Even if you don't fit into this category, you can look for ways to apply these ideas.

Acknowledge your concerns

Adult learners are often worried about issues like being the oldest person in class, paying tuition, and having the time they need to balance working with going to school and having a family life.

Those concerns are understandable. Now consider some facts. If you're returning to school after a long break from the classroom, you are part of a growing trend in Canadian postsecondary education. Recently, Livingstone and Raykov (2013) reported that the percentage of Canadian adults (in the 25 to 64 age range) enrolled in some type of adult education course increased from just over 50 percent in 1998 to over 60 percent by 2010. Most individuals are there to advance their careers. If you are returning to school, look for orientation programs and clubs for mature students. The supports are out there, but you need to get involved.

Meet with an academic advisor

In talking about what is important for mature students in postsecondary education, many people point to academic advisors as being key for student success (McLaren, 2009). Advisors can check to see if past credits for college-level courses will be counted. Even if you've never attended a postsecondary institution, you may still be eligible for credits due to your life experiences. Some schools offer prior learning assessment where you can receive credit for the experiential learning or skills you have developed through work or hobbies. Ask advisors about what financial aid is available for mature students.

Plan your week

Many mature learners report that their number one problem is time. One solution is to plan your week. By planning ahead, a week at a time, you get a bigger picture of your multiple roles as a student, an employee, and a family member. In selecting courses, consider workload like the amount of reading or writing you have to do. Consider going part-time to make it easier to balance work and school—but be careful this doesn't affect your financial aid package. Build leisure time into your schedule so you have the opportunity to recharge your batteries.

For more suggestions on managing time, see Chapter 2, "Time."

Delegate tasks

If you have children, delegate some of the chores to them. Or start a meal exchange in your neighbourhood. Cook dinner for yourself and someone else one night each week. In return, ask that person to furnish you with a meal on another night. A similar strategy can apply to child care and other household tasks.

Find common ground with traditional students

Traditional and non-traditional students have many things in common. They seek to gain knowledge and skills for their chosen careers. They desire financial stability and personal fulfillment. You share a central goal with younger students: succeeding in school. It's easier to get past the generation gap when you remember this. Consider pooling resources with younger students. Share notes, form study groups, or edit each other's essays.

Get to know other returning students

Introduce yourself to other mature learners. Being in the same classroom gives you an immediate bond. Build a network of mutual support. Find other mature students through contacting your mature student centre or club. Many postsecondary institutions offer special orientation programs just for mature and non-traditional students.

Enlist your employer's support

Let your employer in on your educational plans. Point out how the skills you gain in the classroom will help you meet work objectives. You might find that your company reimburses its employees for some tuition costs or even grants time off to attend classes.

Look for child care

For some students, returning to class means looking for child care outside the home. Many schools offer childcare facilities at reduced rates for students.

Review your subjects before you start classes

If, for example, you've registered for trigonometry and you haven't taken a math class since high school, consider brushing up on the subject before classes begin. Check online for review materials, from old exams to online courses in different subject areas. Also, talk with future instructors about ways to prepare for their classes.

Prepare for an academic environment

Many courses you take will include some online component, so it is important for you to feel comfortable in a blended learning environment. Free online courses are a great way to improve your comfort in this new environment.

Faculty members might take a little longer to return your calls or emails than you're used to, especially during holidays and summer breaks. Knowing the rhythm of academic life can help you plan around these possibilities.

Integrate class work with daily experiences

According to psychologist Malcolm Knowles (1984), mature learners in particular look for ways to connect classroom experience with the rest of their lives. This approach can promote success in school for students of any age. You can start by remembering two words: *why* and *how*. *Why* prompts you to look for a purpose and benefit in what you're learning. For example, your psychology instructor lectures about Abraham Maslow's ideas on the hierarchy of human needs. Maslow (1971) stated that the need for **self-actualization** is just as important as the need for safety, security, or love. This term is about your desire to live up to your fullest potential in life; to be the best that you can be.

Ask yourself why this concept, self-actualization, would make a difference in your life. Perhaps your reason for entering postsecondary education is connected to your own quest for self-actualization, that is, for maximizing your fulfillment in life and living up to your highest potential. The theory of self-actualization could clarify your goals and help you get the most out of school.

How means looking for immediate application. Invent ways to use and test concepts in your daily life—the sooner, the better. For example, how could you restructure your life for greater self-actualization? What would you do differently on a daily basis? What would you have that you don't have now?

"Publish" your schedule

After you plan your study and class sessions for the week, hang your schedule in a place where others who live with you will see it. Designate open slots in your schedule where others can sign up for "appointments" to see you. Give your family members access to your online calendar so they know your schedule too.

Enrol family and friends in your success

School can cut into your social life. Prepare your support network by discussing this issue ahead of time. Share your reason for getting a degree, and talk about what your whole family has to gain from this change in your life. Encourage your friends and family to attend social events at school with you. ✳

practising
CRITICAL THINKING

I-3

Get to know the Indigenous origins of your new school

As you make the transition to your new school, take the time to get to know on whose traditional land your school is located. The preface to this book mentions that the revisions to this book were done on the traditional territories of the Anishinaabeg, the Haudenosaunee, the Lunaapeewak, and the Attawandaron peoples. The territorial or land acknowledgment demonstrates our respect and recognition of the Indigenous peoples of North America. You will hear your school's land acknowledgement spoken often at the beginning of classes, conferences, or meetings on your campus. Take a moment to write down the territorial acknowledgment in the space provide below:

_____

_____

_____

_____

_____

_____

_____

_____

_____

_____

If your school doesn't yet have a formal land acknowledgement, you can find out whose land you are on by visiting your school's Indigenous student services or going online to *www.caut .ca/content/guide-acknowledging-first-peoples-traditional-territory*

STUDYING IN CANADA
—what international students need to know

If you are an international student, you have made an excellent choice in choosing to attend higher education in Canada. You are joining the close to 500,000 international students who chose to study in Canada in 2017 (CBIE, 2018). China is the most common country of origin of international students to Canada with 28 percent, followed by India at 25 percent (CBIE, 2018). However, Canada is the destination of choice for students from a wide range of countries, from Brazil to Japan. We offer a high-quality education system with lots of supports in place to ensure your success. Canadians value equality and generally feel everyone is equal in our society. No matter who you are or where you come from, Canadians try to treat everyone the same. Tolerance is a value we hold dear. There are, however, a few things you might want to consider to get the most out of your postsecondary experience in Canada. Canadians, like people everywhere, are varied in their beliefs so there will always be exceptions to the comments below.

Adjust to Canadian society

Canadians feel it is essential to be on time—this is true about getting to class on time, handing in assignments, or going to appointments. If you know that you are going to be late, it is important to let others know.

We are a fairly informal society. Don't be surprised that students in your classes feel quite comfortable asking questions of their instructors and even disagreeing with them. Good students ask good questions, and instructors look favourably on this behaviour.

There is a strong focus on the individual in Canadian society, so people often tend to focus more on themselves than on the group or family. Their decision-making will emphasize their individual needs rather than the needs of the group, such as what their family wants them to do. This may be quite different from what you have experienced before.

Connect to resources

It's normal to find your transition to your new country and new school sometimes frustrating. Typically international students experience some form of culture shock, which may make you feel alienated from your fellow students at times. This is a normal part of the adjustment process. You may go from feeling very excited about your new experiences, to feeling irritated and depressed about how things feel so different than they did at home; but hang in there and things will get better. Eventually you may even laugh about some previous misunderstandings; you will adapt to your new

Courtesy of Debra Dawson

environment. (For example, why do Canadians say "sorry" about everything, even things like the weather they clearly have no control over? Who knows? But just try throwing in a lot of "sorry" into your conversations and see how fast everyone starts to think you must be Canadian too.) To help with this cultural transition, give yourself time to adjust, and learn as much as you can about Canadian customs, culture, and etiquette. Keep in touch with family from home but reach out to new friends too. The wider your network of support, the easier you will find your transition.

Connect to international student services. There are counsellors there to talk to if you find it hard going. They will help you settle in to your new environment and provide needed advice on everything from what to wear in winter to medical insurance. They will be your go-to place for all questions about Canada.

If you are considering immigrating to Canada after you complete your schooling, Arthur and Flynn (2013) suggest you make sure you get some Canadian work experience through internships or field placements while you are still in school. They also suggest that it is important to begin to build your employment networks at this time. Again, services for international students should be able to tell you more about what is involved in getting permanent residency in Canada.

For Canadian students, there is a big advantage to having students from so many different countries in your classes. They provide you with the opportunity to broaden your perspectives without even leaving home. ✳

Did you **know that …?**

Centennial College, the oldest publicly funded community college in Ontario, is home to close to 100 ethnocultural cultural groups with 80 different languages being spoken by its students ("50 little-known facts", 2017).

ENROL YOUR INSTRUCTOR
in your education

Monkey Business Images/Shutterstock.com

Faced with an instructor you don't like, you have two basic choices. One is to label the instructor a "dud" and let it go at that. When you make this choice, you get to endure class and complain to other students. This choice puts you at the mercy of circumstance. It gives your instructor sole responsibility for the quality of your education and the value of your tuition payments.

There is another option. Don't give away your power. Instead, take responsibility for your education.

The word *enrol* in this headline is a play on words. Usually, we think of students as the people who enrol in school. Turn this idea on its head. See if you can enlist instructors as partners in getting what you want from higher education.

Research the instructor

There are formal and informal sources of information you can turn to before you register for class. One is your institution's calendar. Most schools have formal evaluations of instructors available in paper form or on the Web. You can also talk to students who have taken courses from the instructor.

Or introduce yourself to the instructor. Set up a visit during office hours and ask about the course. This can help you get the flavour of the class, as well as clues to the instructor's teaching style.

Show interest in class

Students give instructors moment-by-moment feedback in class. That feedback comes through posture, eye contact, responses to questions, and participation in class discussions. If you find a class boring, transform the instructor through a massive display of interest. Ask lots of questions. Show enthusiasm through nonverbal language—sit up straight, make eye contact, take detailed notes. Your enthusiasm might enliven your instructor. If not, you are still creating a more enjoyable class for yourself.

Take responsibility for your attitude

Maybe your instructor reminds you of someone you don't like—your annoying Aunt Edna, a rude store clerk, or the Grade 5 teacher who kept you after school. Your attitudes are in your own head and beyond the instructor's control.

An instructor's beliefs about politics, religion, or feminism are not related to teaching ability. Likewise, using a formal or informal lecture style does not indicate knowledge of subject matter. Being aware of such things can help you let go of negative judgments.

Separate liking from learning

Remember, you don't have to like an instructor to learn from one. Even in this situation, you can still create value. The idea is to accept your feelings and take responsibility for what you learn. In fact, learning to take ownership of your own learning is what master students do.

Personal preferences regarding an instructor's clothes, hairstyle, political views, accents, or mannerisms can get in the way, too. One of the best parts of higher education is that you will get to be taught by the best from around the world. Don't let this opportunity pass you by.

Form your own opinion about each instructor

You might hear conflicting reports about instructors from other students. The same instructor could be described as a riveting speaker or as completely lacking in charisma. Decide for yourself.

Seek alternatives

You might feel more comfortable with another instructor's style or method of organizing course materials.

Consider changing instructors, or attending an additional section taught by a different instructor. You can also learn from other students, courses, tutors, and study groups, or from online material. You can be a master student, even when you have instructors you don't like. Your education is your own creation.

Submit professional work

Prepare papers and projects as if you were submitting them to an employer. Pay attention to form. Instructors often grade hundreds of papers during a term. Your neat, orderly, well-organized paper can lift an instructor's spirits after a long night of deciphering gibberish.

Accept criticism

Learn from your instructors' comments about your work. It is an instructor's job to give feedback. Don't take it personally. Sometimes students ignore these comments and then get penalized on the next assignments for making the same mistakes. When you get a paper back, read the comments and then wait 24 hours to read them again. If you don't understand the comment or you disagree with the feedback, make an appointment to see your instructor. When you meet with the instructor or teaching assistant, ask him or her to explain the comments; then, ask how you can improve next time, and what are the critical elements to which you need to pay attention.

Use office hours to get to know your instructors

Instructors will offer hours when they are available in their office to see you, and they usually let you know what these office hours are during the first class. Note your instructor's office hours and follow these tips for making the most of your instructor's (and your) time.

- Come prepared with a list of questions and any materials you'll need. During the meeting, take notes on the instructor's suggestions.
- Show the instructor your class notes to see if you're capturing essential material.
- Get feedback on outlines that you've created for papers.
- Ask about ways to prepare for upcoming exams.
- Ask about the possibilities of declaring a major in in the course subject area it if interests you, and ask what careers are associated with that major.
- Avoid questions that might offend your instructor—for example, "I missed class on Monday. Did we do anything important?"
- Ask if your instructor is willing to answer occasional short questions via email or a phone call. Ask how

Tips for **Master Students**

Give feedback to your professors

Talk to your profs! They are invested in your success, and care about your learning. So go and see them, not just for help on homework or essays, but for advice and guidance. Most profs love to talk about their own work, so stop by in office hours and ask what they do and why they do it.

—Dr. S. L. Wismath, professor, department of mathematics and computer science, and liberal education program, at the University of Lethbridge; 2017 3M National Teaching Fellow (*Maclean's*, 2017)

Source: Advice for first-year students from Justin Trudeau (and 27 other people), by *Maclean's*, *Maclean's*, December 1, 2017.

often they respond to email—some instructors only respond to student email once a day whereas others may be available 24/7.

- Thank your instructor for making time for you when the meeting is over.

Use course evaluations

In many classes you'll have an opportunity to evaluate the instructor. When you're asked to do so, respond honestly and seriously. Student evaluations are often the basis of faculty performance appraisals. Formal evaluations often come late in the course, after final tests and assignments. This might lead you to gloss over evaluations or give only vague feedback. If you want your feedback to make a difference, treat this evaluation as you would an assignment. Write about the aspects of the class that did not work well for you. Offer specific ideas for improvement. Also note what *did* work well.

Take further steps, if appropriate

Sometimes severe conflict develops between students and instructors. In such cases, you might decide to file a complaint or ask for help from a third party, such as the department chair or an administrator. If you don't know to whom to complain, check to see if you have an ombudsperson (a neutral individual who provides unbiased counsel to students).

Be prepared to document your case in writing. When talking about the instructor, offer details. Describe specific actions that created problems for the class. Stick to the facts; cite events that other class members can verify. Your school probably will have a formal appeal procedure to use in these cases. Before you act, understand what the policies are. You have a right and a responsibility to complain if you think you have been treated unfairly. ✳

Connect to school
RESOURCES

Monkey Business Images/Shutterstock.com

When you entered postsecondary education, you also signed up for a world of student services. Any of them can help you succeed in school.

Following are a few examples of school resources. Check your school calendar, newspaper, and website for the specific resources available to you. Your student fees pay for them, so use them.

Academic counsellors or advisors can help you with selecting courses, choosing programs, planning your career, and adjusting in general to the culture of post-secondary education.

Arts resources can include museums, galleries, special libraries, and music and film recording and editing equipment. Music practise rooms are often available to all students.

Athletic facilities and *recreation centres* often include open weight rooms, swimming pools, indoor tracks, basketball courts, and racquet-sport courts available to all students.

Multi-faith centres are open to students of any religion. They are quiet places to pray or meditate in peace.

Child care is sometimes made available to students at a reasonable cost through on-site daycares or preschools.

Counselling services help students deal with the emotional pressures of school life, usually for free. Support is also provided for lesbian, gay, bisexual, transgendered, queer, and questioning students (LGBTQQ). If you need help that is not available on campus, ask for a referral to an appropriate agency off campus.

Staff of the *financial aid, assistance*, or *awards office* can help students find a combination of loans, scholarships, and bursaries. These centres often help with counselling on how to manage your budget. It is not necessary for students to drop out of school for financial reasons when financial assistance is available.

Career services offer assistance in planning your career. Career counsellors can also help you find part-time employment while you are a student and a job after you graduate. Get to know career services in first year, when you have time to explore what this service has available to support your goals.

Hotlines can save your life during a crisis. Professionals or trained volunteers are often available to help 24 hours a day, whether the situation involves a mental health issue, physical abuse, HIV/AIDS, sexual assault, potential suicide, or another emergency. Go online to check for local providers.

Indigenous services are offered on most campuses and provide assistance with supporting the academic success of First Nations, Inuit, or Métis students. They also provide opportunities for non-Indigenous students to learn more about their community.

Learning management system (LMS) is a software package used at most schools to provide students with supplementary course materials such as quizzes or course syllabi. Usually, you can access your LMS only after you have enrolled in a specific course.

Learning skills and effective writing centres are there for everyone, not just for students who are having difficulty in their courses. If you want a competitive edge to improve your academic standing, make use of these services before your first exam or assignment is due. For students whose first language is not English, making use of such centres may be essential to success.

Libraries are a key resource for student success. Academic librarians can point you toward resources that will assist in your academic research and writing. Check out your library's website to see what information and services are offered.

The Ombudsperson provides safe, confidential counselling if you feel you are being treated unfairly in some way or you are having a conflict with an instructor. The Ombudsperson can tell you the appeal procedures for grades and suggest good techniques for problem-solving.

The *Registrar's office* handles information about transcripts, marks, changing programs, transferring

Do you have a minute?

Sometimes the hardest part of meeting a goal is simply getting started. To get past this obstacle, take a "baby step" right away. In 60 seconds or less, you can often do something right away that takes you in your desired direction.

Review the following table for examples. Then plan a few baby steps of your own.

If you want to...	Then take a minute to...
Exercise every day right after getting up in the morning.	Lay out your exercise clothes and shoes the night before.
Communicate more effectively with your instructors.	Write down three questions you'd like to ask one of your instructors during an office hour.
Express gratitude to the key people in your life.	Send one person a short text with a specific thank you.
Get started on a writing assignment.	Brainstorm a list of 5 possible ideas for a topic.
Reduce the amount of time you spend sitting every day.	Stand up for a minute right now. Stand up whenever you answer the phone.
Manage stress more effectively.	Take 60 seconds to scan your body for tension and relax those muscles.
Protect your privacy online.	Create a password that's stronger than one of your current ones. Then go online to test password security: *howsecureismypassword.net*

credits, and dropping or adding classes. It also serves as a focal point for information and advice often provided both in person and through a student portal. You'll probably contact this office after you graduate when employers or other schools ask to receive transcripts of your courses and marks.

The **school calendar** lists course descriptions, requirements for graduation, and information on everything from the school's history to its marking practices.

School security services can tell you what's safe and what's not. They can also provide information about parking, bicycle regulations, and traffic rules. Many provide a foot patrol to escort students back to their residence or to their cars at night.

Services for students with disabilities have staff members who specialize in helping students with a wide variety of disabilities make the adjustment to college or university.

Specialty clubs and organizations promote everything from public speaking (Toastmasters) to conservation (Greenpeace) and are likely to be found on campus or in your local community.

Student government can help you develop skills in leadership and teamwork. If you have experience with student government, many employers will take notice.

Wellness Centres connect students with health and wellness resources. They provide interactive resources to support your well-being on topics from nutrition to sexual violence. They are usually connected or part of student health services.

Student health services often provide treatment for a wide variety of problems. Many offer health and wellness programs and information on alcohol and drug abuse and addiction. Staff are typically available to provide the care you need.

Student organizations present an opportunity to explore service clubs, religious groups, sports clubs, political groups, sororities, fraternities, and programs for special populations. The last might include centres for women; students with disabilities; and gay, lesbian, transgendered, and bisexual students. As almost 11 percent of the students enrolled in postsecondary education come from countries outside Canada (Statistics Canada, 2016), many schools will have an international student centre. For Canadian-born students, getting involved in such centres is a great way for you to connect to new people with diverse backgrounds.

Student unions are hubs for social activities, special programs, and free entertainment. Clubs and organizations often meet there, too.

Tutoring can help, even if you think you are hopelessly stuck in a course. It is available through academic departments, or through counselling and learning skills services. ✳

Resources

This week take the time to check out some of the resources your school has both in person and online. For example, it may be the student success centre or financial aid department. Come up with a list of five places that you will visit in the next few weeks. Tell why this resource is something you need to connect with and where it is located.

Resource	Why do you need to visit it?	Where is it located?
1.		
2.		
3.		
4.		
5.		

Extracurricular activities:
REAP THE BENEFITS

Many students in higher education are busier than they've ever been before. Often that's due to the variety of extracurricular activities available to them: athletics, student newspapers, debate teams, study groups, political action groups, and many more.

With this kind of involvement come potential benefits. People involved in extracurricular activities are often excellent students. Such activities help them bridge the worlds inside and outside the classroom. Through student organizations, they develop new skills, explore possible careers, build contacts for jobs, and add experiences to their resumés. They make new friends among students and faculty, work with people from other cultures, and sharpen their skills at conflict resolution. Involvement in campus activities can ease the transition to postsecondary education.

During your orientation week, you will probably hear about Shinerama, Canada's largest postsecondary fundraiser, which raises money to help people with Cystic Fibrosis. It started at Wilfrid Laurier University in 1961

© Rob Esselment

and now has more than 35,000 college and university students involved in volunteering for this fundraising project ("50 little-known facts", 2017). Shine on!

Many schools offer an Alternative Spring Break program where students have a hands-on community

Tips for **Master Students**

service learning experience during reading week that allows them to experience new cultures, apply the knowledge they've been learning in class, and work with different service agencies on a wide variety of social issues.

Getting involved in such organizations comes with some risks as well. When students don't balance extracurricular activities with class work, their success in school can suffer. They can also compromise their health by losing sleep, neglecting exercise, skipping meals, or relying on fast food. These costs are easier to avoid if you keep a few suggestions in mind:

- *Make conscious choices* about how to divide your time between schoolwork and extracurricular activities.

Decide up front how many hours each week or month you can devote to student organizations. Leave room in your schedule for relaxing and for unplanned events. For more ideas, see Chapter 2, "Time."

- *Look to the future* when making commitments. Write down three or four of the most important goals you'd like to achieve in your lifetime. Then choose extracurricular activities that directly support those goals.

- *Create a career plan* that includes a list of skills needed for your next job. Then choose extracurricular activities to develop those skills. If you're unsure of your career choice, then get involved in campus organizations or visit the career centre to explore your options.

- *Recognize reluctance* to follow through on a commitment. You might agree to attend meetings and find yourself forgetting them or consistently showing up late. If that happens, write a Discovery Statement about the way you're using time. Follow that with an Intention Statement about ways to keep your agreements—or consider renegotiating your agreements.

- *Check out the rules* before joining any student organization. Ask about dues and attendance requirements.

- *Do a trial run* by attending one or two meetings of an organization. Explain that you want to find out what the group is about before making a commitment. ✳

Make the
CAREER CONNECTION

THE SUGGESTIONS IN this book can help you succeed both inside and outside the classroom. Apply the techniques you gain from this course to any learning situation you encounter, whether at home, at school, or at work.

Staying current in the job market means continually expanding your knowledge and skills. You will probably change careers several times during your working life—a possibility that calls for continuous learning. As a master

student, you can gain favour with employers by getting up to speed quickly on new jobs and new projects.

Starting now, read this book with a mental filter in place. Ask yourself: How can I use this idea to meet my career goals? How can I apply this technique to my current job or the next job I see for myself? The answers can help you thrive in any job, whether you work full- or part-time. To stimulate your thinking, look for the Put it to Work article located in each chapter. In addition, invent techniques of your own based on what you read and test them at work. There's no limit to the possibilities.

For example, you can use the Discovery and Intention Journal Entry system while you're in the workforce. Write Discovery Statements to note your current job skills as well as areas for improvement. Also use Discovery Statements to describe what you want from your career.

Follow up with Intention Statements that detail specifically what you want to be doing one year, five years, and ten years or more from today. Write additional Intention Statements about specific actions you can take right now to meet those career goals.

Below is a textbook reconnaissance that lists articles in this book with workplace applications. These are just a few examples. As you read, look for more.

- The skills you learn as you are *Making the transition to postsecondary education* (Introduction) can help you make the transition to a new job. For example, you can decrease unknowns by working for a company on a temporary, part-time, or contract basis or you might have the opportunity to job shadow an employee for a day. These activities can lead to an offer of full-time employment. If that happens, you'll already know a lot about the company.

- The article *23 ways to get the most out of now* (Chapter 2, "Time") is packed with ideas you can transfer to the workplace. For example, tackle difficult tasks first in the day, or at any other time when your energy peaks. Also find five-minute tasks that you can complete while waiting for a meeting to start.

- The article *15 memory techniques* (Chapter 3, "Memory") will come in handy as you learn the policies and procedures for a new job.

- Techniques presented in *Remembering names* (Chapter 3) can help as you meet people during your job search and as you are being introduced to new co-workers.

- Use *Muscle Reading* (Chapter 4, "Reading") to keep up with journals and books in your field. This set of techniques can also help you scan websites for the information you want, keep up with ever-increasing volumes of email, and reduce mountains of inter-office memos to manageable proportions.

- The article *Record* (Chapter 5, "Notes") explains different formats for taking notes—mind maps, concept maps, the Cornell format, and more. These are tools you can use to document what happens at work-related meetings.

- Adapt the ideas mentioned in *Cooperative learning: Studying in groups* (Chapter 6, "Tests") in order to cooperate more effectively with members of a project team.

- Use the thinking skills presented in *Gaining skill at decision-making* (Chapter 7, "Thinking") when it comes time to choose a career, weigh job offers, or make work-related decisions.

- Ideas from *Managing conflict* (Chapter 8, "Communicating") can help you defuse tensions among co-workers.

- The suggestions in *Building relationships across cultures* (Chapter 9, "Diversity") can assist you in adapting to the culture of a new job. Each company, large or small, develops its own culture—a set of shared values and basic assumptions. Even if you are self-employed, you can benefit by discovering and adapting to a client's corporate culture.

- Return to *Create your career now* (Chapter 12, "What's Next?") at any time in the future when you're redefining the kind of work that you want to do. Then hone your job-hunting skills with *Build an irresistible resumé* and *Use job interviews to "hire" an employer* (also in Chapter 12).

- The only job security available today is the ability to transfer skills from one position to another. *Now that you're done—begin* (Chapter 12) opens up pathways to lifelong learning. Use these suggestions to continually update your job skills and explore new areas for personal development. ✳

Discovery Statement

Choosing Your Purpose

Success is a choice—your choice. To *get* what you want, it helps to *know* what you want. That is the purpose of this Journal Entry, which has two parts.

You can begin choosing success right now by setting a date, time, and place to complete this Journal Entry. Write your choices here, then block out the time on your calendar.

Date: _____

Time: _____

Place: _____

Part 1

Select a time and place when you know you will not be disturbed for at least 20 minutes. (The library is a good place to do this.) Relax for two or three minutes, clearing your mind. Next, complete the following sentences—and then keep writing.

When you run out of things to write, stick with it just a bit longer. Be willing to experience a little discomfort. Keep writing. What you discover might be well worth the extra effort.

What I want from my education is . . .

_____

_____

_____

_____

When I complete my education, I want to be able to . . .

_____

_____

_____

I also want . . .

_____

_____

_____

_____

_____

Part 2

After completing Part 1, take a short break. Reward yourself by doing something that you enjoy. Then come back to this Journal Entry.

Now, review the above list of things that you want from your education. See if you can summarize them in a one-sentence, polished statement. This will become a statement of your purpose for taking part in higher education.

Allow yourself to write many drafts of this Purpose Statement, and review it periodically as you continue your education. With each draft, see if you can capture the essence of what you want from higher education and from your life. State it in a vivid way—a short sentence that you can easily memorize, one that sparks your enthusiasm, and makes you want to get up in the morning.

You might find it difficult to express your purpose statement in one sentence. If so, write a paragraph or more. Then look for the sentence that seems most charged with energy for you.

Following are some sample purpose statements:

- My purpose for being in school is to gain skills that I can use to contribute to others.
- My purpose for being in school is to live an abundant life that is filled with happiness, health, love, and wealth.
- My purpose for being in school is to enjoy myself by making lasting friendships and following the lead of my interests.

Write at least one draft of your purpose statement below:

_____

_____

_____

_____

_____

_____

_____

_____

_____

_____

_____

© aprott/iStockphoto

Discover What You Want

Imagine a person who walks up to a counter at the airport to buy a plane ticket for his next vacation. "Just give me a ticket," he says to the reservation agent. "Anywhere will do."

The agent stares back at him in disbelief. "I'm sorry, sir," he replies. "I'll need some more details. Just minor things—such as the name of your destination city and your arrival and departure dates."

"Oh, I'm not fussy," says the would-be vacationer. "I just want to get away. You choose for me."

Compare this with another traveller who walks up to the counter and says, "I'd like a ticket to Ixtapa, Mexico, departing on Saturday, March 23, and returning Sunday, April 7. Please give me a window seat, first class, with vegetarian meals."

Now, ask yourself which traveller is more likely to end up with a vacation that he'll enjoy.

The same principle applies in any area of life. Knowing where we want to go increases the probability that we will arrive at our destination. Discovering what we want makes it more likely that we'll attain it. Once our goals are defined precisely, our brains reorient our thinking and behaviour to align with those goals—and we're well on the way there.

The example of the traveller with no destination seems far-fetched. Before you dismiss it, do an informal experiment: Ask three other students what they want to get out of their education. Be prepared for hemming and hawing, vague generalities, and maybe even a helping of à la mode pie-in-the-sky.

What you will hear will be amazing, considering the stakes involved. Our hypothetical vacationer is about to invest a couple of weeks of his time and hundreds of dollars—all with no destination in mind. Students routinely invest years of their lives and tens of thousands of dollars

with an equally hazy idea of their destination in life.

Now suppose that you ask someone what she wants from her education and you get this answer: "I plan to get a degree in journalism with double minors in earth science and Portuguese so that I can work as a reporter covering the environment in Brazil." Chances are you've found a master student. The details of a person's vision offer a clue to mastery.

Discovering what you want greatly enhances your odds of succeeding in postsecondary education. Many students quit school simply because they are unsure about what they want from it. With well-defined goals in mind, you can look for connections between what you want and what you study. The more connections you discover, the more likely you'll stay in school—and the more likely you'll benefit from postsecondary education. For maximum clarity, write down what you want. Goals that reside strictly in your head can remain fuzzy. Writing them down brings them into sharper focus.

As you write about what you want, expand your imagination to different time frames. Define what you want to be, do, and have next week, next month, and next year. Write about what you want five years from now—and five minutes from now.

To move into action, use this book. It's filled with places to state what you want to accomplish and how you intend to go about it. Every Journal Entry and exercise exists for this purpose. Fill up those pages. With your dreams and new behaviours in hand, you might find that events fall into place almost magically. Start telling people about what you want, and you'll eventually find some who are willing to help. They might offer an idea or two or suggest a person to call or an organization to contact. The sooner you discover what you want, the sooner you can create the conditions that transform your life.

Name_____   Date____/____/____

1. List three common differences between secondary and postsecondary education.

2. According to the text, one way to master the transition to postsecondary education is to remind yourself that you already know how to study. True or False? Explain your answer.

3. List two arguments for regularly attending classes in postsecondary education.

4. Give two examples of how to enhance civility in the classroom.

5. Define the term *self-regulation*.

6. The purpose of the Discovery and Intention Journal Entry system is to increase the amount of effort you put into succeeding in postsecondary education. True or False? Explain your answer.

7. Describe in your own words the necessary steps to complete a textbook reconnaissance.

8. List at least two benefits of discovering what you want from your education.

9. List five examples of school resources that could help you get the most from postsecondary education.

10. Beyond a higher income, what are three other benefits to postsecondary education?

Monkey Business/Fotolia

First Steps

do you have a minute?

Take a minute to write down a "baby step"—a task that takes 60 seconds or less—that can help you move toward completing a current project or assignment. For example, brainstorm a list of topics for a paper that you plan to write. If you can spare another minute, then do that task immediately.

WHAT if...

I could start to create new outcomes in my life by accepting the way I am right now?

WHY this chapter matters...

Success starts with telling the truth about what is working—and what isn't—in your life right now.

HOW you can use this chapter...

Skim this chapter for three techniques that you'd like to use in school or in your personal life during the upcoming week. Make a note to yourself or mark the pages where the strategies that you intend to use are located in the chapter.

FIRST STEP:
Truth is a key to mastery

The first step technique is simple: Tell the truth about who you are and what you want. End of discussion.

Well, it's not *quite* that simple.

The First Step is one of the most valuable tools in this book. It magnifies the power of all the other techniques. It is a key to becoming a master student. To succeed in school, tell the truth about what kind of student you are and what kind of student you want to become. Success starts with telling the truth about what is working—and what is not working—in your life right now. Urging you to tell the truth sounds like pie-in-the sky moralizing, but there is nothing moralizing about a First Step. It is a practical, down-to-earth way to change behaviour.

When we acknowledge our strengths, we gain an accurate picture of what we can accomplish. When we admit that we have a problem, we are free to find a solution. Ignoring the truth, on the other hand, can lead to problems that stick around for decades.

First Steps are universal

When you see a doctor, the First Step is to tell the truth about your current symptoms. That way you can get an accurate diagnosis and effective treatment plan. This principle is universal. It works for just about any problem in any area of life. First Steps are used by millions of people who want to turn their lives around. No technique in this book has been field-tested more often or more successfully—or under tougher circumstances. For members of Gamblers Anonymous, the First Step is acknowledging that they are compulsive gamblers. Their First Step is admitting how frequently they gamble. When people go for credit counselling, their First Step is telling the truth about how much money they earn, how much they spend, and how much they owe. People dealing with a variety of other challenges—including troubled relationships with food, drugs, sex, and work—also start by telling the truth. They use First Steps to change their behaviour, and they do it for a reason: First Steps work.

First Steps are judgment free

It's not easy to tell the truth about ourselves. Many of us approach a frank evaluation of ourselves about as enthusiastically as we'd treat a call from the bank about being overdrawn. However, we could think of self-evaluations as an opportunity to solve problems and take charge of our lives. In fact, the most successful people tend to be those who are most willing to look at their flaws and then make a change.

It might seem natural to judge our own shortcomings and feel bad about them. Some people believe that such feelings are necessary in order to bring about change. Think again. There is an alternative. We can discover a way to gain skill without negative feelings about the past. By taking a First Step, we can change the way things *are* without having to be upset about the way things *have been*.

First Steps point us toward goals

Master students get the most value from a First Step by turning their perceived shortcomings into goals. "I don't exercise enough" turns into "I will walk briskly for 30 minutes at least three times per week." The key is to state First Steps in a way that allows for new possibilities in the future. Use language in a way that reinforces your freedom to change. For example, "I can't succeed in math" is better stated like this: "During math courses, I tend to get confused early in the term and find it hard to ask questions. I could be more assertive in asking for help right away." Telling the truth about what we don't want gives us more clarity about what we *do* want.

First Steps include strengths

For some of us, it's even harder to recognize our strengths. Finding out our strengths is important as strengths—such as having hope, zest, love, and gratitude—are uniquely related to greater life satisfaction (Park, Peterson, & Seligman, 2004). Maybe we don't want to brag. Maybe we're attached to our poor self-images. The reasons don't matter. The point is that using the First Step technique in *Becoming a Master Student* means telling the truth about our positive qualities, too.

First Steps are specific

Whether written or verbal, First Steps are more powerful when they are specific. For example, if you want to improve your note-taking skills, you might write, "I am an awful note-taker." It would be more effective to write, "I can't read

80 percent of the notes I took in Introduction to Psychology last week, and I have no idea what was important in that class." Be just as specific about what you plan to achieve. You might declare, "I want to take legible notes that help me predict what questions will be on the final exam."

Completing the exercises and Journal Entries in this chapter can help you tap resources you never knew you had. For example, do the Discovery Wheel to get a big picture view of your personal effectiveness, and complete the Learning Styles Inventory and read the articles on multiple intelligences, metacognition, and growth mindset to find out more about how you perceive and process information. You might be surprised at what you find out about yourself and you might even disagree with the results of an exercise. Use your disagreement as another opportunity for self-discovery and exploration. All of these activities are First Steps. It's just that simple. The truth has power. ✳

practising
CRITICAL THINKING
1-1

Taking the First Step

The purpose of this exercise is to give you a chance to discover and acknowledge your own strengths, as well as areas for improvement. For many students, this is the most difficult exercise in the book. To make the exercise worthwhile, do it with courage.

Some people suggest that looking at areas for improvement means focussing on personal weaknesses. They view it as a negative approach that runs counter to positive thinking. Well, perhaps. Positive thinking is a great technique. So is telling the truth, especially when we see the whole picture—the negative aspects as well as the positive ones.

If you admit that you can't add or subtract and that's the truth, then you have taken a strong, positive First Step toward learning basic math. On the other hand, if you say that you are a terrible math student and that's not the truth, then you are programming yourself to accept unnecessary failure.

The point is to tell the truth. This exercise is similar to the Discovery Statements that appear in every chapter. The difference is that in this case, for reasons of confidentiality, you won't write down your discoveries in the book.

You are likely to disclose some things about yourself that you wouldn't want others to read. You might even write down some truths that could get you into trouble. Do this exercise on separate sheets of paper; then hide or destroy them. Protect your privacy.

To make this exercise work, follow these suggestions:

Be specific. It is not effective to write "I can improve my communication skills." Of course you can. Instead, write down precisely what you can *do* to improve your communication skills; for example, "I can spend more time really listening while the other person is talking, instead of thinking about what I'm going to say next."

Look beyond the classroom. What goes on outside of school often has the greatest impact on your ability to be an effective student. Consider strengths and weaknesses that you may think have nothing to do with school.

Be courageous. This exercise is a waste of time if it is done half-heartedly. Be willing to take risks. You might open a door that reveals a part of yourself that you didn't want to admit was there. The power of this technique is that once you know what is there, you can do something about it.

Part 1

Time yourself, and for 10 minutes write as fast as you can, completing each of the following sentences at least 10 times with anything that comes to mind. If you get stuck, don't stop. Just write something—even if it seems crazy.

- I never succeed when I...
- I'm not very good at...
- Something I'd like to change about myself is...

Part 2

When you have completed the first part of the exercise, review what you have written, crossing off things that don't make any sense. The sentences that remain suggest possible goals for *becoming a master student*.

Part 3

Here's the tough part. Time yourself, and for 10 minutes write as fast as you can, completing the following sentences with anything that comes to mind. As in Part 1, complete each sentence at least 10 times. Just keep writing, even if it sounds silly.

- I always succeed when I...
- I am very good at...
- Something I like about myself is...

Part 4

Review what you have written and circle the things that you can fully celebrate. This is a good list to keep for those times when you question your own value and worth.

Discovery/Intention Statement

Create Value from This Chapter

Take five minutes to skim the Discovery Wheel exercise on the next page. Find one statement that describes a skill you already possess—a personal strength that will promote your success in school. Write that statement here:

_____

_____

_____

_____

The Discovery Wheel might also prompt some thoughts about skills you want to acquire. Describe one of those skills by completing the following sentence:

I discovered that . . .

_____

_____

_____

_____

_____

Now, skim the appropriate chapter in this book for at least three articles that could help you develop this skill. For example, if you want to take more effective notes, turn to Chapter 5, "Notes." List the names of your chosen articles here and a time when you will read them in more detail.

I intend to . . .

_____

_____

_____

_____

_____

_____

_____

The Discovery Wheel

The Discovery Wheel is another opportunity to tell the truth about the kind of student you are and the kind of student you want to become.

This is not a test. There are no trick questions, and the answers will only have meaning for you.

Here are two suggestions to make this exercise more effective. First, think of it as the beginning of an opportunity to change. There is another Discovery Wheel at the end of this book. You will have a chance to measure your progress, so be honest about where you are now. Second, lighten up. A little laughter can make self-evaluations a lot more effective.

Here's how the Discovery Wheel works. By the end of this exercise, you will have filled in a circle similar to the one in Figure 1.1. The Discovery Wheel is a picture of how you see yourself as a student. The closer the shading comes to the outer edge of the circle, the higher the evaluation of a specific skill. In the example to the right, the student has rated her reading skills as low and her note-taking skills as high.

The terms *high* and *low* are not meant to reflect judgment. The Discovery Wheel is not a permanent picture

of who you are. It is a picture of how you view your strengths and weaknesses as a student today. To begin this exercise, read the following statements and award yourself points for each one, using the point system described below. Then add up your point total for each section and shade the Discovery Wheel in Figure 1.2 to the appropriate level.

5 points	This statement is always or almost always true of me.
4 points	This statement is often true of me.
3 points	This statement is true of me about half the time.
2 points	This statement is seldom true of me.
1 point	This statement is never or almost never true of me.

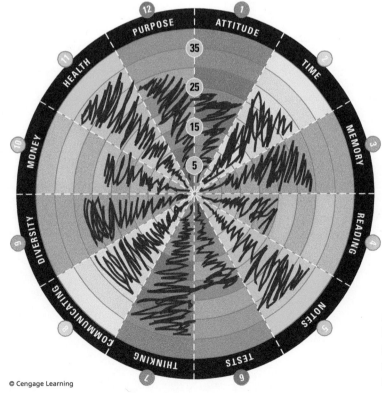

© Cengage Learning

Figure 1.1 Sample Discovery Wheel. Notice how this student has rated her reading skills low and her note-taking skills high.

① Attitude

_____ I enjoy learning.

_____ I understand and apply the concept of multiple intelligences.

_____ I connect my courses to my purpose for being in school.

_____ I make a habit of assessing my personal strengths and areas for improvement.

_____ I am satisfied with how I am progressing toward achieving my goals.

_____ I use my knowledge of learning styles to support my success in school.

_____ I am willing to consider any idea that can help me succeed in school—even if I initially disagree with that idea.

_____ I regularly remind myself of the benefits I intend to get from my education.

_____ **Total score: Attitude**

② Time

_____ I set long-term goals and periodically review them.

_____ I set short-term goals to support my long-term goals.

_____ I write a plan for each day and each week.

_____ I assign priorities to what I choose to do each day.

_____ I plan regular recreation time.

_____ I adjust my study time to meet the demands of individual courses.

_____ I have adequate time each day to accomplish what I plan.

_____ I plan review time so I don't have to cram before exams.

_____ **Total score: Time**

③ Memory

_____ I am confident of my ability to remember.

_____ I can remember people's names.

_____ At the end of a lecture, I can summarize what was presented.

_____ I apply techniques that enhance my memory skills.

_____ I can recall information when I'm under pressure.

_____ I remember important information clearly and easily.

_____ I can jog my memory when I have difficulty recalling.

_____ I can relate new information to what I've already learned.

_____ **Total score: Memory**

④ Reading

_____ I preview and review reading assignments.

_____ When reading, I ask myself questions about the material.

_____ I underline or highlight important passages when reading.

_____ When I read textbooks, I am alert and awake.

_____ I relate what I read to my life.

_____ I select a reading strategy to fit the type of material I'm reading.

_____ I take effective notes when I read.

_____ When I don't understand what I'm reading, I note my questions and find answers.

_____ **Total score: Reading**

5 **Notes**

_____ When I am in class, I focus my attention.

_____ I take notes in class.

_____ I am aware of various methods for taking notes and choose those that work best for me.

_____ I distinguish important material and note key phrases in a lecture.

_____ I copy down material that the instructor writes on the board.

_____ I can put important concepts into my own words.

_____ My notes are valuable for review.

_____ I review class notes within 24 hours.

_____ **Total score: Notes**

6 **Tests**

_____ I use techniques to manage stress related to exams.

_____ I manage my time during exams so that I am able to complete them.

_____ I am able to predict test questions.

_____ I adapt my test-taking strategy to the kind of test I'm taking.

_____ I understand what essay questions ask and can answer them completely and accurately.

_____ I start reviewing for tests at the beginning of the term.

_____ I continue reviewing for tests throughout the term.

_____ My sense of personal worth is independent of my test scores.

_____ **Total score: Tests**

7 **Thinking**

_____ I have flashes of insight and often think of solutions to problems at unusual times.

_____ I use brainstorming to generate solutions to a variety of problems.

_____ When I get stuck on a creative project, I use specific methods to get unstuck.

_____ I see problems and tough decisions as opportunities for learning and personal growth.

_____ I am willing to consider different points of view and alternative solutions.

_____ I can detect common errors in logic.

_____ I construct viewpoints by drawing on information and ideas from many sources.

_____ As I share my viewpoints with others, I am open to their feedback.

_____ **Total score: Thinking**

8 **Communicating**

_____ I am candid with others about who I am, what I feel, and what I want.

_____ Other people tell me that I am a good listener.

_____ I can communicate my upset and anger without blaming others.

_____ I can make friends and create valuable relationships in a new setting.

_____ I am open to being with people I don't especially like in order to learn from them.

_____ I can effectively plan and research a large writing assignment.

_____ I create first drafts without criticizing my writing, then edit later for clarity, accuracy, and coherence.

_____ I know ways to prepare and deliver effective speeches.

_____ **Total score: Communicating**

9   Diversity

_____ I build rewarding relationships with people from backgrounds different from my own.

_____ I use critical thinking to overcome stereotypes.

_____ I point out examples of discrimination and sexual harassment and effectively respond to them.

_____ I am constantly learning ways to thrive with diversity in school and/or the workplace—attitudes and behaviours that will support my success.

_____ I can effectively resolve conflict with people from other cultures.

_____ My writing and speaking are free of sexist and homophobic expressions.

_____ I take diversity into account when assuming a leadership role.

_____ I use technology in a way that enriches my life and supports my success.

_____ **Total score: Diversity**

10   Money

_____ I am in control of my personal finances.

_____ I can access a variety of resources to finance my education.

_____ I am confident that I will have enough money to complete my education.

_____ I take on debts carefully and repay them on time.

_____ I have long-range financial goals and a plan to meet them.

_____ I make regular deposits to a savings account.

_____ I pay off the balance on credit card accounts each month.

_____ I can have fun without spending money.

_____ **Total score: Money**

11   Health

_____ I have enough energy to study and still fully enjoy other areas of my life.

_____ If the situation calls for it, I have enough reserve energy to put in a long day.

_____ The food I eat supports my long-term health.

_____ The way I eat is independent of my feelings of self-worth.

_____ I exercise regularly to maintain a healthy weight.

_____ My emotional health supports my ability to learn.

_____ I notice changes in my physical condition and respond effectively.

_____ I am in control of any alcohol or other drugs I put into my body.

_____ **Total score: Health**

12   Purpose

_____ I see learning as a lifelong process.

_____ I relate my studies to what I plan to do for the rest of my life.

_____ I learn by contributing to others.

_____ I have a written career plan and update it regularly.

_____ I am gaining skills to support my success in the workplace.

_____ I take responsibility for the quality of my education—and my life.

_____ I live by a set of values that translates into daily actions.

_____ I am willing to accept challenges even when I'm not sure how to meet them.

_____ **Total score: Purpose**

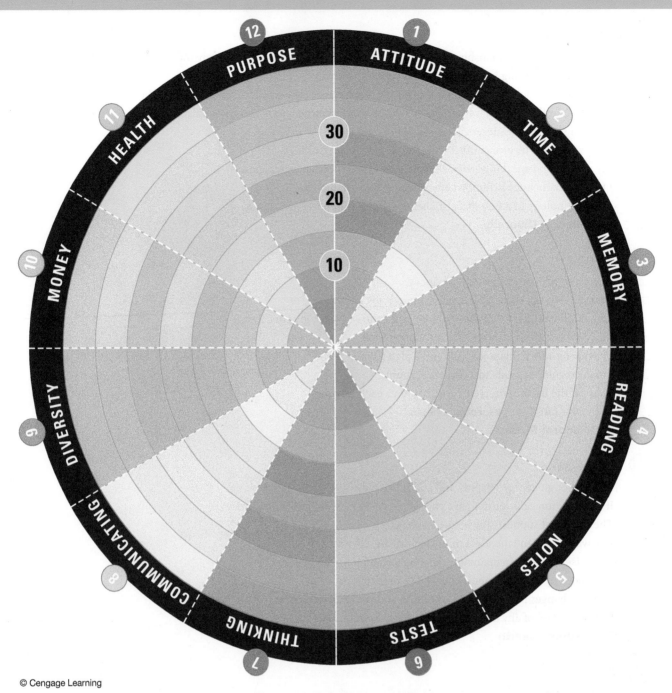

Figure 1.2 Your Discovery Wheel.

Filling in your Discovery Wheel.

Using the total score from each category, shade in each section of the Discovery Wheel.
Use different colours, if you want. For example, you could use green to denote areas you want to work on.
When you have finished, complete the Journal Entry that follows.

Discovery/Intention Statement

Roll Your Discovery Wheel

Now that you have completed your Discovery Wheel, spend a few minutes with it. Get a sense of its weight, shape, and balance. Can you imagine running your hands around it? If you could lift it, would it feel light or heavy? How would it sound if it rolled down a hill? Would it roll very far? Would it wobble? Make your observations without judging the wheel as good or bad. Simply be with the picture you have created.

After you have spent a few minutes studying your Discovery Wheel, complete the following sentences in the space below. Don't worry if you can't think of something to write. Just put down whatever comes to mind. Remember, this is not a test.

Overview

This wheel is an accurate picture of my ability as a student because...

_____

_____

My self-evaluation surprises me because...

_____

_____

Strengths

The two areas in which I am strongest are...

_____

_____

Goals

The areas in which I want to improve are...

_____

_____

I want to concentrate on improving these areas because...

_____

_____

To meet my goals for improvement, I intend to...

_____

_____

Note: You'll get at opportunity to reflect on your progress when you do the Discovery Wheel exercise again in Chapter 12.

LEARNING STYLES:
Discovering how you learn

Right now, you are investing substantial amounts of time, money, and energy in your education. What you get in return for this investment depends on how well you understand the process of learning and use it to your advantage.

If you don't understand learning, you might feel bored or confused in class. After getting a low grade, you might have no idea how to respond. Over time, frustration can mount to the point where you question the value of being in school.

Some students answer that question by dropping out of school. These students lose a chance to create the life they want. Society loses the contributions of educated workers.

Start by understanding the different ways that people create meaning from their experience and change their behaviour. In other words, learn about *how* we learn.

We learn by perceiving and processing

Experiential learning theory suggests that learning is a process of meaning making where we develop understanding of new concepts through interactions with our environment. Learning is seen as a cyclical process where we develop new ideas, test them out, receive feedback, and then further refine our ideas and beliefs as a result of experiences (Kolb & Kolb, 2005). When we learn well, says psychologist David Kolb (1984), two things happen. First, we *perceive*; that is, we notice events and take in new experiences. Second, we *process*, or deal with, experiences in a way that helps us make sense of them. Our **learning style** is how we prefer to perceive and process information.

Some people especially enjoy perceiving through *concrete experience* (feeling). They like to absorb information through their five senses. They learn by getting directly involved in new experiences. When solving problems, they rely on intuition as much as intellect. These people typically function well in unstructured classes that allow them to take initiative.

Other people favour perceiving by *abstract conceptualization* (thinking). They take in information best when they can think about it as a subject separate from themselves. They analyze, intellectualize, and create theories. Often these people take a scientific approach to problem-solving and excel in traditional classrooms.

People also process experiences differently. Some people favour processing information by *reflective observation* (watching). They prefer to stand back, watch what is going on, and think about it. They consider several points of view as they attempt to make sense of things and generate many ideas about how something happens. They value patience, good judgment, and a thorough approach to learning.

Other people like to process experience by *active experimentation* (doing). They prefer to jump in and start doing things immediately. These people do not mind taking risks as they attempt to make sense of things; risk-taking helps them learn. They are results oriented and look for practical ways to apply what they have learned.

Perceiving and processing—an example

Suppose that you get a new cellphone. It has more features than any phone you've used before. You have many options for learning how to use it. For example, you could do any of the following:

- Just get your hands on the phone right away, press some buttons, and see if you can dial a number or send a text message.

- Read the instruction manual and view help screens on the phone before you try to make a call.

- Recall experiences you've had with phones in the past and what you've learned by watching other people use their cellphones.

- Ask a friend who owns the same type of phone to coach you as you experiment with making calls and sending messages.

These actions illustrate the different ways of perceiving and processing:

- Getting your hands on the phone right away and seeing if you can make it work is an example of learning through *concrete experience*.

- Reading the manual and help screens before you use the phone is an example of learning through *abstract conceptualization*.

- Recalling what you've experienced in the past is an example of learning through *reflective observation*.
- Asking a friend to coach you through a hands-on activity with the phone is an example of learning through *active experimentation*.

In summary, your learning style is the unique way you blend feeling, thinking, watching, and doing. You tend to use this approach in learning anything from cellphones to algebra to English composition. Knowing your learning style may provide you with a useful framework from which to consider how or under what conditions you learn best. Kolb and Kolb (2005) propose that although you may have a preferred way of learning, your learning style is not fixed or unchangeable. Reading the next few pages and doing the recommended activities will help you to explore your learning style in more detail. ✳

journal entry 1-3

Discovery Statement

Prepare for the Learning Style Inventory

As a warmup for the LSI and articles that follow, spend a minute or two thinking about times in the past when you felt successful at learning. Underline or highlight any of the following statements that describe those situations:

- I was in a highly structured setting, with a lot of directions about what to do and feedback on how well I did at each step.
- I was free to learn at my own pace and in my own way.
- I learned as part of a small group.
- I learned mainly by working alone in a quiet place.
- I learned in a place where there were a lot of activities going on.
- I learned by forming pictures in my mind.
- I learned by *doing* something—moving around, touching something, or trying out a process for myself.
- I learned by talking to myself or explaining ideas to other people.
- I got the "big picture" before I tried to understand the details.
- I listened to a lecture and then thought about it after class.
- I read a book or article and then thought about it afterward.
- I used a variety of media—such as a video, audio recording, or computer—to assist my learning.
- I went beyond taking notes and wrote in a personal journal.
- I was considering where to attend school and knew I had to actually set foot on each campus before choosing.
- I was shopping for a car and paid more attention to how I felt about test driving each one than to the sticker prices or fuel efficiencies.
- I was thinking about going to a movie and carefully read the reviews before choosing one.
- Review the list for any patterns in the way you prefer to learn. If you see any patterns, briefly describe them on a seperate piece of paper.

Directions for completing the Learning Style Inventory

To help you become more aware of learning styles, David Kolb developed the Learning Style Inventory (LSI). This inventory is included on the next several pages. Responding to the items in the LSI can help you discover a lot about the ways you learn. Following the LSI are suggestions for using the LSI results to promote your success.

The LSI is not a test. There are no right or wrong answers. Your goal is simply to develop a profile of your current learning style. So, take the LSI quickly. You might find it useful to recall a recent time when you learned something new at school, at home, or at work. However, do not agonize over your responses.

Note that the LSI consists of 12 sentences, each with four different endings. Read each sentence, and then rank each ending using the following scale:

4 = Most like you

3 = Second most like you

2 = Third most like you

1 = Least like you

Use each number only one time for each sentence. This is a forced-choice inventory, so you must rank each ending. *Do not leave any endings blank.* Read the instructions at the top of the LSI. When you understand example A, you are ready to begin.

Learning Style Inventory

Read the first sentence and its four possible endings. Put a 4 next to the ending that best describes the way you currently learn. Then continue ranking the other endings with a 3, 2, and 1, which represents the ending that is least like you. Do this for each sentence. Use the following example as a guide:

A. When I learn: __2__ I am happy. __3__ I am fast. __4__ I am logical. __1__ I am careful.

Remember: 4 = Most like you   3 = Second most like you   2 = Third most like you   1 = Least like you

Do not leave any endings blank. Use each number only once for each question.

1. When I learn:	__1__ I like to deal with my feelings.	__2__ I like to think about ideas.	__4__ I like to be doing things.	__3__ I like to watch and listen.
2. I learn best when:	__3__ I listen and watch carefully.	__2__ I rely on logical thinking.	__1__ I trust my hunches and feelings.	__4__ I work hard to get things done.
3. When I am learning:	__2__ I tend to reason things out.	__3__ I am responsible about things.	__4__ I am quiet and reserved.	__1__ I have strong feelings and reactions.
4. I learn by:	__1__ feeling.	__4__ doing.	__2__ watching.	__3__ thinking.
5. When I learn:	__1__ I am open to new experiences.	__2__ I look at all sides of issues.	__3__ I like to analyze things, break them down into their parts.	__4__ I like to try things out.
6. When I am learning:	__3__ I am an observing person.	__1__ I am an active person.	__2__ I am an intuitive person.	__4__ I am a logical person.
7. I learn best from:	__3__ observation.	__1__ personal relationships.	__2__ rational theories.	__4__ a chance to try out and practice.
8. When I learn:	__4__ I like to see results from my work.	__2__ I like ideas and theories.	__3__ I take my time before acting.	__1__ I feel personally involved in things.
9. I learn best when:	__2__ I rely on my observations.	__1__ I rely on my feelings.	__4__ I can try things out for myself.	__3__ I rely on my ideas.
10. When I am learning:	__1__ I am a reserved person.	__4__ I am an accepting person.	__3__ I am a responsible person.	__2__ I am a rational person.
11. When I learn:	__2__ I get involved.	__3__ I like to observe.	__4__ I evaluate things.	__1__ I like to be active.
12. I learn best when:	__2__ I analyze ideas.	__3__ I am receptive and open-minded.	__1__ I am careful.	__4__ I am practical.

Scorecard

Brown F　　Total　19

Teal W　　Total　30

Purple T　　Total　31

Orange D　　Total　40

Grand Total　120

Scoring Your Inventory

Now that you've finished taking the LSI, you probably have some questions about what it means. You're about to discover some answers!

STEP 1 First, copy your numbers from the Learning Style Inventory to the corresponding lines on this page. When you've finished, add up all of the numbers you gave to the items marked with brown F letters. Then write down that total on your Scorecard next to "**Brown F**." Next, add up all of the numbers for "Teal W," "Purple T," and "Orange D." Write down those totals in the Scorecard box as well.

STEP 2 Add the four totals to arrive at a **Grand Total** and write down that figure in the Scorecard box. (*Note:* The grand total should equal 120. If you have a different amount, go back and re-add the colored letters. It was probably just an addition error.)

	First Column Ranking	Second Column Ranking	Third Column Ranking	Fourth Column Ranking
1. When I learn:	1 F	2 T	4 D	3 W
2. I learn best when:	3 W	2 T	1 F	4 D
3. When I am learning:	2 T	3 D	4 W	1 F
4. I learn by:	1 F	4 D	2 W	3 T
5. When I learn:	1 F	2 W	3 T	4 D
6. When I am learning:	3 W	1 D	2 F	4 T
7. I learn best from:	3 W	1 F	2 T	4 D
8. When I learn:	4 D	2 T	3 W	1 F
9. I learn best when:	2 W	1 F	4 D	3 T
10. When I am learning:	1 W	4 F	3 D	2 T
11. When I learn:	2 F	3 W	4 T	1 D
12. I learn best when:	2 T	3 F	1 W	4 D

Learning Style Graph

STEP 3 Transfer your totals from Step 2 to the lines on the Learning Style Graph below. On the brown (F) line, find the number that corresponds to your "**Brown F**" total from your Scorecard. Then write an X on this number. Do the same for your "**Teal W**," "**Purple T**," and "**Orange D**" totals. The graph on this page is for you to keep. The graph on the page about "Developing all four modes of learning" is for you to turn in to your instructor if required to do so.

STEP 4 Now draw four straight lines to connect the four X's. Then shade in the area to form a "kite." *This is your learning*

style profile. (For an example, see the illustration below.) Each X that you placed on these lines indicates your preference for a different aspect of learning as described here.

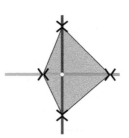

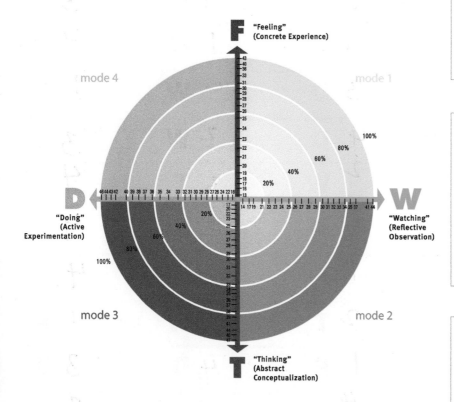

F: Feeling
Concrete Experience

The number where you put your X on this line indicates your preference for learning things that have personal meaning. The higher your score on this line, the more you like to learn things that you feel are important and relevant to yourself.

W: Watching
Reflective Observation

Your number on this line indicates how important it is for you to reflect on the things you are learning. If your score is high on this line, you probably find it important to watch others as they learn about an assignment and then report on it to the class. You probably like to plan things out and take the time to make sure that you fully understand a topic.

T: Thinking
Abstract Conceptualization

Your number on this line indicates your preference for learning ideas, facts, and figures. If your score is high on this line, you probably like to absorb many concepts and gather lots of information on a new topic.

D: Doing
Active Experimentation

Your number on this line indicates your preference for applying ideas, using trial and error, and practicing what you learn. If your score is high on this line, you probably enjoy hands-on activities that allow you to test out ideas to see what works.

Interpreting Your Learning Style Graph

When you examine your completed Learning Style Graph, you will notice that your learning style profile (the "kite" that you drew) might be located primarily in one part of the graph. This will give you an idea of your preferred mode of learning—the kind of behaviors that feel most comfortable and familiar to you when you are learning something.

Using the descriptions below and the sample graphs, identify your preferred learning mode.

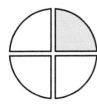

Mode 1 blends feeling and watching.
If the majority of your learning style profile is in the upper right-hand corner of the Learning Style Graph, you probably prefer Mode 1 learning. You seek a purpose for new information and a personal connection with the content. You want to know why a course matters and how it challenges or fits in with what you already know. You embrace new ideas that relate directly to your current interests and goals.

Mode 2 blends watching and thinking.
If your learning style profile is mostly in the lower right-hand corner of the Learning Style Graph, you probably prefer Mode 2 learning. You are interested in knowing what ideas or techniques are important. You seek a theory to explain events and are interested in what experts have to say. You enjoy learning lots of facts and then arranging these facts in a logical and concise manner. You break a subject down into its key elements or steps and master each one in a systematic way.

Mode 3 blends thinking and doing. If most of your learning style profile is in the lower left-hand corner of the Learning Style Graph, you probably prefer Mode 3 learning. You hunger for an opportunity to try out what you're studying. You get involved with new knowledge by testing it out. You investigate how ideas and techniques work, and you put into practice what you learn. You thrive when you have well-defined tasks, guided practice, and frequent feedback.

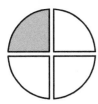

Mode 4 blends doing and feeling. If most of your learning style profile is in the upper left-hand corner of the Learning Style Graph, you probably prefer Mode 4 learning. You get excited about going beyond classroom assignments. You like to take what you seek ways to apply this newly gained skill or information at your workplace or in your personal relationships.

It might be easier for you to remember the modes if you summarize each one as a single question:

> Mode 1 means asking, *Why* learn this?

> Mode 2 means asking, *What* is this about?

> Mode 3 means asking, *How* does this work?

> Mode 4 means asking, *What if* I tried this in a different setting?

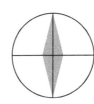

Combinations
Some learning style profiles combine all four modes. The profile to the left reflects a learner who is focused primarily on gathering information—*lots* of information! People with this profile tend to ask for additional facts from an instructor, or they want to know where they can go to discover more about a subject.

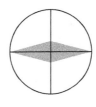

The profile to the left applies to learners who focus more on understanding what they learn and less on gathering lots of information. People with this profile prefer smaller chunks of data with plenty of time to process it. Long lectures can be difficult for these learners.

The profile to the left indicates a learner whose preferences are fairly well balanced. People with this profile can be highly adaptable and tend to excel no matter what the instructor does in the classroom.

Developing All Four Modes of Learning

Each mode of learning represents a unique blend of feeling, watching, thinking, and doing. No matter which of these you've tended to prefer, you can develop the ability to use all four modes:

- **To develop Mode 1,** ask questions that help you understand *why* it is important for you to learn about a specific topic. You might also want to form a study group.

- **To develop Mode 2,** ask questions that help you understand *what* the main points and key facts are. Also, learn a new subject in stages. For example, divide a large reading assignment into sections and then read each section carefully before moving on to the next one.

- **To develop Mode 3,** ask questions about *how* a theory relates to daily life. Also allow time to practice what you learn. You can do experiments, conduct interviews, create presentations, find a relevant work or internship experience, or even write a song that summarizes key concepts. Learn through hands-on practice.

- **To develop Mode 4,** ask *what-if* questions about ways to use what you have just learned in several different situations. Also, seek opportunities to demonstrate your understanding. You could coach a classmate about what you have learned, present findings from your research, explain how your project works, or perform your song.

Developing all four modes offers many potential benefits. For example, you can excel in many types of courses and find more opportunities to learn outside the classroom. You can expand your options for declaring a major and choosing a career. You can also work more effectively with people who learn differently from you.

In addition, you'll be able to learn from instructors no matter how they teach. Let go of statements such as "My teachers don't get me" and "The instructor doesn't teach to my learning style." Replace those excuses with attitudes such as "I am responsible for what I learn" and "I will master this subject by using several modes of learning."

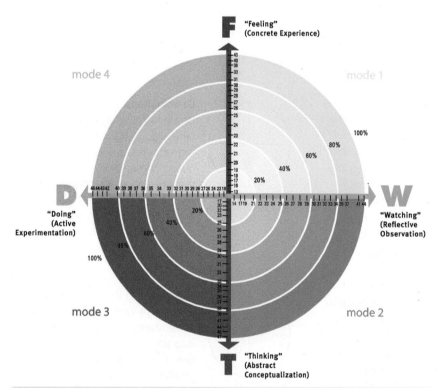

The graph on this page is here for you to turn in to your instructor if required to do so.

Balancing Your Preferences

The chart below identifies some of the natural talents people have, as well as challenges for people who have a strong preference for any one mode of learning. For example, if most of your "kite" is in Mode 2 of the Learning Style Graph, then look at the lower right-hand corner of the following chart to see whether it gives an accurate description of you.

After reviewing the description of your preferred learning mode, read all of the sections that start with the words "People with other preferred modes." These sections explain what actions you can take to become a more balanced learner.

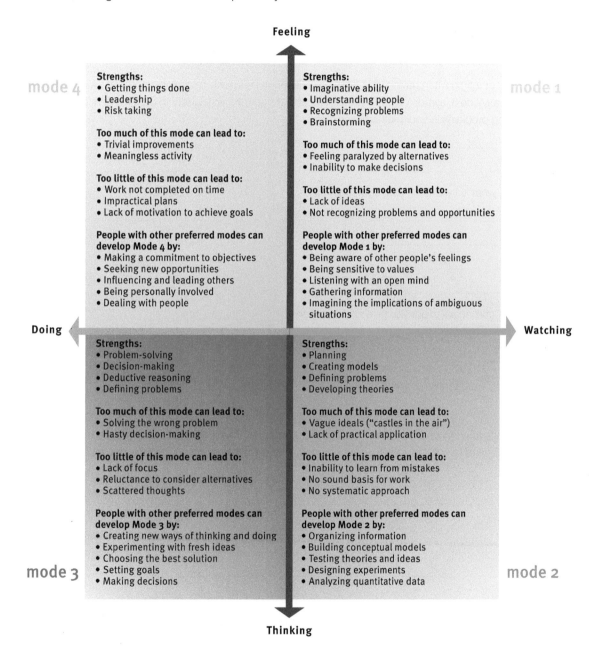

Feeling

mode 4

Strengths:
• Getting things done
• Leadership
• Risk taking

Too much of this mode can lead to:
• Trivial improvements
• Meaningless activity

Too little of this mode can lead to:
• Work not completed on time
• Impractical plans
• Lack of motivation to achieve goals

People with other preferred modes can develop Mode 4 by:
• Making a commitment to objectives
• Seeking new opportunities
• Influencing and leading others
• Being personally involved
• Dealing with people

mode 1

Strengths:
• Imaginative ability
• Understanding people
• Recognizing problems
• Brainstorming

Too much of this mode can lead to:
• Feeling paralyzed by alternatives
• Inability to make decisions

Too little of this mode can lead to:
• Lack of ideas
• Not recognizing problems and opportunities

People with other preferred modes can develop Mode 1 by:
• Being aware of other people's feelings
• Being sensitive to values
• Listening with an open mind
• Gathering information
• Imagining the implications of ambiguous situations

Doing / **Watching**

Strengths:
• Problem-solving
• Decision-making
• Deductive reasoning
• Defining problems

Too much of this mode can lead to:
• Solving the wrong problem
• Hasty decision-making

Too little of this mode can lead to:
• Lack of focus
• Reluctance to consider alternatives
• Scattered thoughts

People with other preferred modes can develop Mode 3 by:
• Creating new ways of thinking and doing
• Experimenting with fresh ideas
• Choosing the best solution
• Setting goals
• Making decisions

mode 3

Strengths:
• Planning
• Creating models
• Defining problems
• Developing theories

Too much of this mode can lead to:
• Vague ideals ("castles in the air")
• Lack of practical application

Too little of this mode can lead to:
• Inability to learn from mistakes
• No sound basis for work
• No systematic approach

People with other preferred modes can develop Mode 2 by:
• Organizing information
• Building conceptual models
• Testing theories and ideas
• Designing experiments
• Analyzing quantitative data

mode 2

Thinking

Take your time to absorb all this material. Be willing to read through it several times and ask questions.

Your efforts will be rewarded. In addition to discovering more details about *how* you learn, you'll gain a set of strategies for applying this knowledge to your courses. With these strategies, you can use your knowledge of learning styles to succeed in school.

Above all, aim to recover your natural gift for learning as a master student. Rediscover a world where the boundaries between learning and fun, between work and play, all disappear. While immersing yourself in new experiences, blend the sophistication of an adult with the wonder of a child. This is a path that you can travel for the rest of your life.

Discovery/Intention Statement

Put Your Learning Style into Practice

Now that you have taken the Learning Style Inventory, let's think about how you can put into practice the new knowledge you have gained about how you perceive and process information. On the line below, write down what mode your "kite" most closely resembles.

_____

_____

Take a moment to think of a time when having your learning style mode may have helped you complete work on a project. For instance, if you are a Mode 3 learner, perhaps you can recall a time where your ability to perform deductive reasoning really helped with solving problems in your mathematics class.

_____

_____

Now, given your mode, what do you think your strengths will be in working on a group project?

_____

_____

_____

_____

Given your mode, what challenges might you face in working on a project with others?

_____

_____

_____

_____

If you had the opportunity to pick two other group members to work on a project with you, what modes would you want those individuals to have, and how might their talents be beneficial to successfully completing the project?

_____

_____

_____

_____

_____

The next time you work in a group, try to use this new knowledge of learning styles to understand both your own behaviour and the behaviour of others.

Using your learning style profile to
SUCCEED

Develop all four modes of learning

Each mode of learning highlighted in the Learning Style Inventory represents a unique blend of concrete experience, reflective observation, abstract conceptualization, and active experimentation. You can explore new learning styles simply by adopting new habits related to each of these activities. Recent research suggests that a *Balanced Learning Style,* one that assimilates all four modes of learning, may be the best to have, as it makes you the most adaptive to learning in any situation (Kolb & Kolb, 2005). Consider the following suggestions as places to start expanding your current learning style. Also remember that any idea about learning styles will make a difference in your life only when it leads to changes in your behaviour.

To gain concrete experiences:

- See a live demonstration or performance related to your course content.
- Engage your emotions by reading a novel or seeing a video related to your course.
- Interview an expert in the subject you're learning or a master practitioner of a skill you want to gain either in person or virtually.
- Conduct role-plays, exercises, or games based on your courses.
- Conduct an informational interview with someone in your chosen career or shadow that person for a day on the job.
- Look for a part-time job, internship, or volunteer experience that complements what you do in class.
- Deepen your understanding of another culture and extend your foreign language skills by studying abroad.

To become more reflective:

- Keep a personal journal or blog and write about connections among your courses.
- Form a study group online or in person to discuss and debate topics related to your courses.

- Create analogies to make sense of concepts; for instance, see if you can find similarities between career planning and putting together a puzzle.
- Visit your course instructor during office hours to ask questions.
- During social events with friends and relatives, briefly explain what your courses are about.

To develop abstract thinking:

- Take notes on your reading in outline form; consider using word-processing software with an outlining feature.
- Supplement assigned texts with other books, magazine and online newspaper articles, and related websites.
- Attend lectures given by your current instructors and others who teach the same subjects or watch a TED talk related to your courses.
- Take ideas presented in the text or lectures and translate them into visual form—tables, charts, diagrams, and maps (see Chapter 5, "Notes").
- Create visuals and use computer software to re-create them with more complex graphics and animation.

To become more active:

- Conduct laboratory experiments or field observations.
- Go to settings where theories are being applied or tested.
- Make predictions based on theories you learn, and then see if events in your daily life confirm your predictions.
- Try out a new behaviour described in a lecture or reading, and observe its consequences in your life.

Look for examples of the modes in action

To understand the modes of learning, notice when they occur in your daily life. You are a natural learner, and this means that the modes are often at work. You use them when you solve problems, make choices, and experiment with new ideas.

Suppose that your family asks about your career plans. You've just enrolled for your first semester of classes, and you think it's too early to think about careers. Yet you choose to brainstorm some career options anyway. If nothing else, it might be fun, and you'll have some answers for when people ask you what you're going to do after college. This is an example of Mode 1: You asked, "Why learn about career planning?" and came up with an answer.

During the next meeting of your psychology class, your instructor mentions the career planning centre on campus. You visit the centre's website and discover its list of services. While you're online, you also register for one of the centre's workshops because you want more information about writing a career plan. This illustrates Mode 2: You asked, "What career planning options are available?" and discovered several answers.

In the workshop, you learn about the role that internships and extracurricular activities play in career planning. All of these are ways to test an early career choice and discover whether it appeals to you. You enjoy being with children, so you choose to volunteer at a campus-based child care centre. You want to discover how this service learning experience might help you choose a career. This is Mode 3: You asked, "How can I use what I learned in the workshop?" This led you to working with children.

Your experience at the centre leads to a work study assignment there. On the basis of this new experience, you choose to declare a major in early childhood education. This is an example of Mode 4: You asked, "What if this assignment points to a new direction for my future?" The answer led to a new commitment.

Use the modes while choosing courses

Remember your learning style profile when you're thinking about which classes to take and how to study for each class. Look for a fit between your preferred mode of learning and your course work.

If you prefer Mode 1, for example, look for courses that sound interesting and seem worthwhile to you. If you prefer Mode 2, consider classes that centre on lectures, reading, and discussion. If you prefer Mode 3, choose courses that include demonstrations, lab sessions, role-playing, and other ways to take action. And if you enjoy Mode 4, look for courses that could apply to many situations in your life—at work, at home, and in your relationships.

You won't always be able to match your courses to your learning styles. View those situations as opportunities to practise becoming a flexible learner. The more balanced you are in the four modes, the easier it will be for you to adapt to different learning situations. By developing your skills in all four modes, you can excel in many types of courses. Also, see the sidebar "Use the modes to learn from *any* instructor" for specific strategies to make the most out of all your classes, regardless of your learning style.

Use the modes to explore your career

Knowing about learning styles becomes especially useful when planning your career.

People who excel at Mode 1 are often skilled at tuning in to the feelings of clients and co-workers. These people can listen with an open mind, tolerate confusion, be sensitive to people's feelings, open up to problems that are difficult to define, and brainstorm a variety of solutions. If you like Mode 1, you may be drawn to a career in counselling, social services, the ministry, or another field that centres on human relationships. You might also enjoy a career in the performing arts.

People who prefer Mode 2 like to do research and work with ideas. They are skilled at gathering data, interpreting information, and summarizing, arriving at the big picture. They may excel at careers that centre on science, math, technical communications, or planning. Mode 2 learners may also work as college teachers, lawyers, technical writers, or journalists.

People who like Mode 3 are drawn to solving problems, making decisions, and checking on progress toward goals. Careers in medicine, engineering, information technology, or another applied science are often ideal for them.

People who enjoy Mode 4 like to influence and lead others. These people are often described as "doers" and "risk takers." They like to take action and complete projects. Mode 4 learners often excel at managing, negotiating, selling, training, and teaching. They might also work for a government agency.

Remember, any career can attract people with a variety of learning styles. For instance, the healthcare field is large enough to include people who prefer Mode 3 and become family physicians *and* people who prefer Mode 2 and become medical researchers.

Keep in mind that there is no strict match between learning styles and certain careers. Learning is essential to success in all careers.

Expect to encounter different styles

As higher education and the workplace become more diverse and technology creates a global marketplace, you'll meet people who differ from you in profound ways. Your fellow students and co-workers will behave in ways that express a variety of preferences for perceiving information, processing ideas, and acting on what they learn. Consider, for example, a study group member who always takes the initiative, manages the discussion, delegates any work involved, and follows up with everyone; that student probably prefers active experimentation.

Differences in learning style can be a stumbling block—or an opportunity. When differences intersect, there is the potential for conflict, as well as for creativity. Succeeding with peers often means seeing the classroom and workplace as a laboratory for learning from experience. Resolving conflict and learning from mistakes are all part of the learning cycle.

Look for specific clues to another person's style

You can learn a lot about other people's styles of learning simply by observing them during the workday. Look for clues such as these:

Approaches to a task requiring learning

Some people process new information and ideas by sitting quietly and reading or writing. When learning to use a piece of equipment, such as a new printer, they'll go online to watch an instruction video first. Others will skip the video, unpack all the boxes, and start setting up equipment. And others might ask a more experienced colleague to guide them in person, step by step.

Word choice

Some people like to process information visually. You might hear them say, "I'll look into that" or "Give me the big picture first." Others like to solve problems verbally: "Let's talk through this problem." In contrast, some people focus on body sensations ("This product feels great") or action ("Let's run with this idea and see what happens").

Body language

Notice how often co-workers or classmates make eye contact with you and how close they sit or stand next to you. Observe their gestures, as well as the volume and tone of their voices.

Process preferences

Look for patterns in the way your co-workers and classmates meet goals. When attending meetings, for example, some of them might stick closely to the agenda and keep an eye on the clock. Other people might prefer to go with the flow, even if it means working an extra hour or scrapping the agenda.

Accommodate differing styles

Once you've discovered differences in styles, look for ways to accommodate them. As you collaborate on projects with other students or co-workers, keep the following suggestions in mind:

Remember that some people want to reflect on the big picture first

When introducing a project plan, you might say, "This process has four major steps." Before explaining the plan

in detail, talk about the purpose of the project and the benefits of completing each step.

Allow time for active experimentation and concrete experience

Offer people a chance to try out a new product or process for themselves—to literally get the feel of it.

Allow for abstract conceptualization

When leading a study group or conducting a training session, provide handouts that include plenty of visuals and step-by-step instructions. Visual learners and people who like to think abstractly will appreciate these handouts. Also schedule periods for questions and answers.

When planning a project, encourage people to answer key questions

Remember the four essential questions that guide learning. Answering *Why?* means defining the purpose and desired outcomes of the project. Answering *What?* means assigning major tasks, setting due dates for each task, and generating commitment to action. Answering *How?* means carrying out assigned tasks and meeting regularly to discuss things that are working well and ways to improve the project. And answering *What if?* means discussing what the team has learned from the project and ways to apply that learning to the whole class or larger organization.

When working on teams, look for ways the members can complement one another's strengths

If you're skilled at planning, find someone who excels at doing. Also, seek people who can reflect on and interpret the team's experience. Pooling different styles allows you to draw on everyone's strengths.

Resolve conflict with respect for styles

When people's styles clash in educational or work settings, you have several options. One is to throw up your hands and resign yourself to personality conflicts. Another option is to recognize differences, accept them, and respect them as complementary ways to meet common goals. Taking that perspective allows you to act constructively. You might do one of the following:

Resolve conflict within yourself

In your mental pictures of classrooms and workplaces, are people all supposed to have the same style? If you have such ideas, let them go. If you *expect* to find differences in styles, you can more easily respect those differences.

Let people take on tasks that fit their learning styles

People gravitate toward the kinds of tasks they've succeeded at in the past, and that's fine. Remember, though, that learning styles are both stable and dynamic. People can broaden their styles by tackling new tasks to reinforce different modes of learning.

Accept change—and occasional discomfort

Seek out chances to develop new modes of learning. If your instructor asks you to form a group to complete an assignment, avoid joining a group where everyone shares your learning style. Get together with people who both complement and challenge you. You are more likely to be successful on the project if you bring different skill sets to the table. It may not always be comfortable, but discomfort is a natural part of the learning process. By choosing to move through discomfort, you consciously expand your ability to learn in new ways. ✳

Use the modes to learn from *any* instructor

Students who experience difficulty in school might say, "My teacher doesn't get me" or "In class, we never have time for questions" or "The instructor doesn't teach to my learning style."

Such statements can become mental crutches—a set of beliefs that prevent you from taking responsibility for your education. To stay in charge of your learning, consider adopting attitudes such as the following:

I will look for the potential value in learning this information.

I can learn something useful in any situation, even if I don't like it at first.

No matter who's teaching a course, I am responsible for what I learn.

I will master this subject by using several modes of learning.

Remember that you can take action on such statements even if you don't fully agree with them yet. One way to change your attitudes is to adopt new behaviours, see how they work, and watch for new results in your life. This approach can be adapted to each mode:

To develop Mode 1, ask questions that help you understand why it is important for you to learn about a specific topic. You might also want to form a study group.

To develop Mode 2, ask questions that help you gather enough information to understand the main points and key facts. Also, learn a new subject in stages. For example, divide a large reading assignment into sections and then read each section carefully before moving on to the next one.

To develop Mode 3, ask questions about how a theory relates to daily life. Also, allow time to practise what you learn. You can do experiments, conduct interviews, create presentations, find a relevant work or internship experience, or even write a song that summarizes key concepts. Learn through hands-on practice.

To develop Mode 4, ask questions about ways to apply what you have just learned to several situations. Also, seek opportunities to demonstrate your understanding. You could coach a classmate about what you have learned, present findings from your research, explain how your project works, or perform a song that someone else created.

Even when teachers don't promote all four modes of learning, you can take charge of the way you learn. In the process, you consciously direct your growth and create new options.

Connecting your mode of learning to Canadian employers' wish list

Canadian employers want individuals from all four learning modes. Your learning style will influence not just how you prefer to learn in class but how you act in the workplace. In fact, the strengths identified in each of the modes match up well with the key employability skills identified by *The Conference Board of Canada in 2000* (2010). The Conference Board identifies three primary sets of skills they suggest you need to be successful in the workplace regardless of whether you work on your own or as part of a larger organization. First, you need to have what they call *fundamental skills*, which they see as essential to progress in the

(Continued)

workplace. These include communication skills, and your ability to manage information, use numbers, think critically, and solve problems. The next set of skills they call *personal management skills*, which they see as the skills, attitudes, and behaviour that will help you develop to your full potential. Finally, *teamwork skills* are needed to enhance the outcomes of any teamwork or project. These include skills that allow you to work well with others and to fully assist with tasks or projects that must be completed. Although we will talk more about those skills later in this book (see Chapter 12, "What's Next?"), let's take a quick look at some of those skills now and see how they match up with your preferred learning style. Keep in mind that developing your skills at using all four modes is likely to be important for success in the world of work.

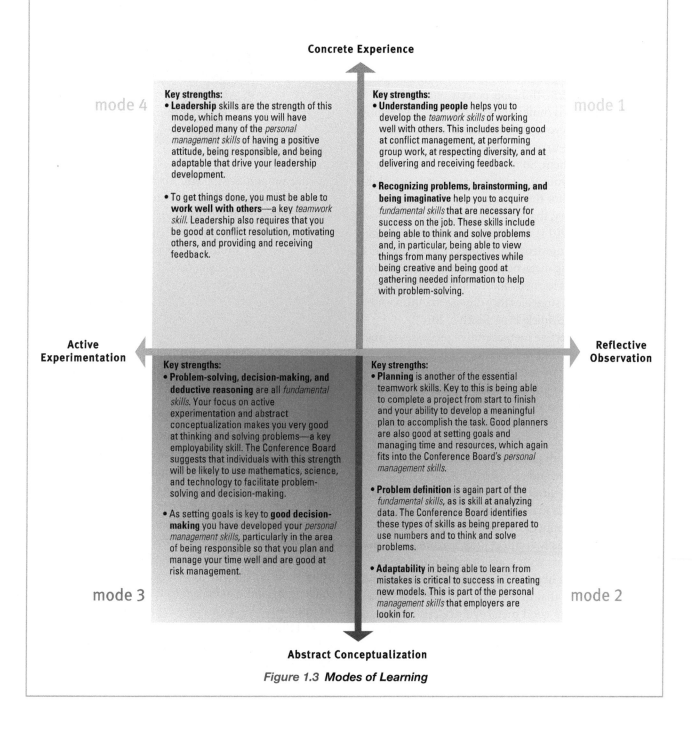

Concrete Experience

mode 4

Key strengths:
- **Leadership** skills are the strength of this mode, which means you will have developed many of the *personal management skills* of having a positive attitude, being responsible, and being adaptable that drive your leadership development.

- To get things done, you must be able to **work well with others**—a key *teamwork skill*. Leadership also requires that you be good at conflict resolution, motivating others, and providing and receiving feedback.

mode 1

Key strengths:
- **Understanding people** helps you to develop the *teamwork skills* of working well with others. This includes being good at conflict management, at performing group work, at respecting diversity, and at delivering and receiving feedback.

- **Recognizing problems, brainstorming, and being imaginative** help you to acquire *fundamental skills* that are necessary for success on the job. These skills include being able to think and solve problems and, in particular, being able to view things from many perspectives while being creative and being good at gathering needed information to help with problem-solving.

Active Experimentation

Reflective Observation

Key strengths:
- **Problem-solving, decision-making, and deductive reasoning** are all *fundamental skills*. Your focus on active experimentation and abstract conceptualization makes you very good at thinking and solving problems—a key employability skill. The Conference Board suggests that individuals with this strength will be likely to use mathematics, science, and technology to facilitate problem-solving and decision-making.

- As setting goals is key to **good decision-making** you have developed your *personal management skills*, particularly in the area of being responsible so that you plan and manage your time well and are good at risk management.

Key strengths:
- **Planning** is another of the essential teamwork skills. Key to this is being able to complete a project from start to finish and your ability to develop a meaningful plan to accomplish the task. Good planners are also good at setting goals and managing time and resources, which again fits into the Conference Board's *personal management skills*.

- **Problem definition** is again part of the *fundamental skills*, as is skill at analyzing data. The Conference Board identifies these types of skills as being prepared to use numbers and to think and solve problems.

- **Adaptability** in being able to learn from mistakes is critical to success in creating new models. This is part of the personal *management skills* that employers are lookin for.

mode 3

mode 2

Abstract Conceptualization

Figure 1.3 *Modes of Learning*

The magic of
METACOGNITION

Vladgrining/Shutterstock.com

It's pronounced "metta-cog-ni-shun." "Meta" means *beyond* or *above*, **cognition** refers to everything that goes on inside your brain—thinking, perceiving, and learning. **Metacognition** is thinking about thinking or learning about learning. It's your ability to stand "above" your mental processes—to observe them and to take conscious control of them. So metacognition is both your understanding of your thinking practices and your ability to accurately monitor those practices and then make changes, if necessary, that lead to deeper learning (Larmar & Lodge, 2014). Learning to effectively recognize the limits of your knowledge takes time, practice, and effort. Students with strong metacognitive skills have knowledge about themselves as learners, and about different types of academic tasks and strategies they can use to solve a variety of academic tasks (Svinicki & McKeachie, 2014).

Developing effective metacognitive processes is one of the main benefits of higher education. Mastering these skills allows you to learn anything you want, at any time. Students with good metacognitive skills have higher academic success and are less likely to drop out than those who lack these skills. Also, metacognitive skills are an essential component of graduate employability. Students with good metacognitive skills tend to be more productive and creative (Bain, 2012).

Why is metacognition so important? Having good metacognitive skills makes learning easier as you are able to make meaning of the world around you; you are able to more easily connect prior learning with new knowledge. Students with good metacognitive skills are therefore more likely to be engaged in learning and to apply strategies that lead to effective learning. So, in essence, developing good metacognitive capital is a key ingredient of student success (Larmar & Lodge, 2014).

Monitoring your behaviour

Strong students tend to be confident but not overly confident about their ability to succeed. They recognize that being overconfident about their metacognitive skills can lead them to be ineffective at monitoring their own behaviour. Being overconfident may stop you from noticing that you are having problems with

learning and it may stop you from making the effort necessary to succeed. Unfortunately, students who are not as competent at self-monitoring tend to be unaware that they are not as skilled as their colleagues; they are therefore be overconfident about their likelihood of success (Brown, Roediger, & McDaniel, 2014). Students with better metacognitive skills will have good alignment between beliefs about their academic performance and their ability to successfully complete academic tasks. And because there is congruence between their beliefs and performance, they actually have higher achievement than students who are overconfident about their skills (Elliot, Dweck, & Yeager, 2017).

Developing a variety of learning skills

Students with strong metacognitive skills have a variety of learning strategies they can apply and are willing to learn new ones when presented with new academic tasks. They know that applying the same learning strategies to each academic task is not likely to lead to success. "Practice, practice, practice" is also one of their mantras with the focus on practising, revising strategy, and then practising again. One key to developing good metacognitive skills is exposure to new academic tasks that are challenging and that engage you as a learner. Without building your metacognitive capital over time, your critical thinking is diminished, your motivation to learn will decrease, and your academic success will be hampered (Larmar & Lodge, 2014).

Among other things, metacognition includes these abilities:

- *Planning*—the ability to determine your purpose, choose from alternative behaviours, predict their consequences, and monitor your progress in meeting your goals

- *Analysis*—the ability to separate a whole subject into its parts
- *Synthesis*—the ability to combine parts to form a meaningful whole
- *Application*—the ability to transfer new concepts and skills from one life situation to another

Connecting metacognitive thinking with your mode of learning

Each aspect of metacognition dovetails nicely with a mode of learning. Mode 1 involves planning—connecting the content of a course to your personal interests and goals. In Mode 2, you analyze by taking key ideas apart, separating skills into their component steps, and learning each step in turn. In Mode 3, you synthesize—that is, combine all of the separate ideas, facts, and skills you learned to see how they work in a real-life situation. And in Mode 4, you take what you have learned in one course and apply it in other courses and outside the classroom. Again, you can see that developing a more balanced learning style can help you get more out of your education as you will have more tools and resources to apply to a wide variety of academic tasks.

Students who master metacognition can

- state the ways that they'll benefit from learning a subject;
- develop the ability to critically reflect on their own learning;
- make accurate statements about their current abilities;
- monitor their behaviour and change their habits;
- choose and apply various strategies for reading, writing, speaking, listening, managing time, and related tasks; and
- modify strategies so that they work in several contexts.

Becoming more aware about your own learning goals and then reflecting on your performance is the key to academic success (Svinicki & McKeachie, 2014). You can improve your own metacognitive skills through

- self-checking your homework before handing it in,
- evaluating your likelihood of success frequently,
- assessing how confident you are that you got the answers right on your homework or quizzes,
- reflecting on your experience when you get homework or a quiz back,
- trying academic tasks that are challenging for you and that require you to learn new strategies for success,
- being more aware of the limits of your knowledge, and
- embracing setbacks in learning as an opportunity to learn more about yourself as a learner.

With metacognition, you can view any course as one step along the path to learning what you want to learn. The magic of metacognition is that you become your own best teacher. ✳

Practising
CRITICAL THINKING   1-2

Becoming self-aware

One of the first keys to developing metacognitive skills is becoming self-aware. Here are some key questions you need to ask yourself. Think about ONE specific course you are taking when you write your responses.

1. How many hours do you spend studying for your course? _____

2. Are you up to date on course assignments and readings? _____

3. How do you take notes or study while reading the textbook? _____

4. How do you take notes in class? _____

5. Do you review your notes? _____When? _____ How? _____

6. Do you stop periodically to check to see if you understand the material? _____

(Svinicki & McKeachie, 2014, p. 294)

Review your answers periodically to see if you are making adjustments to how you learn based on the feedback you receive on class tests and assignments. Checking in periodically with yourself is an important step to becoming self-aware.

Creating a mindset
FOR ACHIEVEMENT

Have you ever wondered why some students seem to thrive on challenges while others just give up at the first roadblock to learning a new skill? What is the **mindset** or set of assumptions, values, and beliefs that guides your thinking about what contributes to success or failure in life? Growth mindset, a concept we first discussed in the Introduction, is the idea that success in life is determined more by effort and the strategies you use to support success than by intelligence or talent alone (Dweck, 2006). Research done by Carol Dweck and her associates indicates that when students have a growth mindset they are more likely to persist in the face of obstacles, and see failures as a call to action, unlike students who have a **fixed mindset**, who see intelligence or talents as fixed traits that can't be altered (Dweck, Walton, & Cohen, 2014). Believing that intelligence is malleable and capable of change is critical to developing a growth mindset.

Having the ability to stick with difficult tasks and pursue long-term goals leads to academic tenacity (a term we discussed briefly in the Introduction), an essential ingredient for academic success. Students with academic tenacity like learning challenges, feel engaged with school both academically and socially, and are willing to give up short-term pleasures, like going to a movie, to achieve long-term goals, like becoming a lawyer or carpenter.

One of the goals of higher education is to help you develop characteristics for success like growth mindset and academic tenacity.

Growth versus fixed mindset

Those with a growth mindset believe that change is possible over time if you work hard or engage in new learning strategies. Therefore, even if you do poorly on one test, you are not condemned to always do poorly in school (Dweck, 2006). Students with a fixed mindset tend to believe that success in school is attributable to being intelligent so that if they do poorly on a test they believe their results are because they are just not smart enough. They become overly concerned about their innate ability to succeed rather focussing their attention on what they could do better next time. As a result, those with a fixed mindset tend to give up when they meet obstacles rather than putting more effort into studying or trying other strategies to succeed.

Fixed mindset students see effort as something only students with little ability need to use and are hesitant to try activities that would show their shortcomings. They tend to have perfectionist tendencies and they view setbacks as an indicator that they aren't good enough. They avoid tasks that challenge them and that might help them grow.

Students with a growth mindset are more likely to experience challenging tasks as enjoyable and as an opportunity to put their skills, knowledge, and creativity to the test. They are more willing to get out of their comfort zone when placed in a learning situation. They thrive on challenges rather than struggle just to survive. You feel lousy when you get a bad grade but it is what you do with the results of an assessment that really counts. Growth mindset individuals review their study strategies to try to determine what they did wrong, whereas fixed mindset individuals are likely to be paralyzed by the results and do nothing. Students with a growth mindset have good metacognitive skills as they regularly reflect on their own learning and see feedback as information needed for learning (Elliot, Dweck, & Yeager, 2017).

Significantly, research has found that those with a growth mindset are likely to have higher achievement scores (Dweck, 2006). The good news is that you can change your mindset, which is just a set of beliefs that you can alter. The First Step to changing your mindset is learning about growth mindset so you are already starting to change the way you think about academic success (Dweck et al., 2014). Once you start to believe that change is possible, it is easier to keep on trying when the going gets tough. We will talk more about how to develop a growth mindset in Chapter 2, "Time." To help determine your mindset, see Carol Dweck's online inventory at *www.mindsetonline.com/testyourmindset/step1.php*. ✳

Traps of the fixed mindset

Dweck (2006) suggests there are several traps that you can fall into with a fixed mindset that will hinder learning. Read these traps and see if any apply to you. Next time you fall into one of these traps consider what you can do to change from feeling hopeless about learning to being engaged.

1. *"I deserve it, no matter what."* Feelings of entitlement can prevent you from even trying. When you aren't picked for the team, others are to blame, not you. Unfortunately, blaming others seldom leads to success. Instead next time try to determine why others were selected. Did they come out earlier for practices or try harder to succeed? Starting to see how effort fits into your success and then beginning to make more effort yourself will help you to switch to a growth mindset. Recognize that you may have to try and try again before success occurs. As you see others less as adversaries, they are more likely to want to support your goals.

2. *"Everything is going perfectly."* Individuals with a fixed mindset are often in denial about potential problems and therefore sometimes ignore red flags that the things aren't going well. When the team dumps you as their leader, you feel hurt and judged. Instead you need to approach team leadership as a time to hone your communication skills. Learning to really listen to others is important and is crucial for success in working with others. This is also another important step to developing a growth mindset.

3. *"I'll never succeed at anything."* When setbacks occur and you immediately feel that no matter what you do you are doomed to failure, you are engaging in a form of duality thinking that is part of the fixed mindset trap. Events that occur in your life are viewed as great or terrible, good or bad, strong or weak. Instead, when events don't go as you expected, it is important not to give in to those overwhelming thoughts; rather, take a deep breath, take a walk, and then try to look at the situation from multiple perspectives. Is it really the end of the world? Try and think of a variety of strategies that you can use the next time you are in that situation. With a growth mindset, you can learn that every setback doesn't indicate failure but rather an opportunity to try something new next time.

Claim your
MULTIPLE
INTELLIGENCES

People often think that being smart means the same thing as having a high IQ, and that having a high IQ automatically leads to success. However, psychologists are finding that IQ scores do not always foretell which students will do well in academic settings—or after they graduate (Bernstein, Penner, Clarke-Stewart, & Roy, 2006).

Centre: © Tanya Constantine/Getty Images, clockwise from bottom left: spiber.de/Shutterstock.com, © Tim Laman/Getty, smolaw/Shutterstock.com, © Vladimir Godnik/Getty, © Meg Takamura, © Doug Menuez/Getty, Ondrej Prosicky/Shutterstock .com, © George Doyle/Getty, collage by Walter Kopec

Psychologist Howard Gardner (1993) believes that no single measure of intelligence can tell us how smart we are. Instead, Gardner defines intelligence in a flexible way as "the ability to solve problems, or to create products, that are valued within one or more cultural settings." He also identifies several types of intelligence, as described below and in Table 1-1. Similar to learning style theory, Gardner believes that people will start their learning journey at different points depending upon the strength of their **multiple intelligences**.

People using *verbal/linguistic intelligence* are adept at language skills and learn best by speaking, writing, reading, and listening. They are likely to enjoy activities such as telling stories and doing crossword puzzles.

Those using *mathematical/logical intelligence* are good with numbers, logic, problem-solving, patterns, relationships, and categories. They are generally precise and methodical, and are likely to enjoy science.

When people learn visually and by organizing things spatially, they display *visual/spatial intelligence*. They think in images and pictures, and understand best by seeing the subject. They enjoy charts, graphs, maps, mazes, tables, illustrations, art, models, puzzles, and costumes.

People using *bodily/kinesthetic intelligence* prefer physical activity. They enjoy activities such as building things, woodworking, dancing, skiing, sewing, and crafts. They are generally coordinated and athletic, and would rather participate in games than just watch.

Those using *musical/rhythmic intelligence* enjoy musical expression through songs, rhythms, and musical instruments. They are responsive to various kinds of sounds, remember melodies easily, and might enjoy drumming, humming, and whistling.

People using *intrapersonal intelligence* are exceptionally aware of their own feelings and values. They are generally reserved, self-motivated, and intuitive.

Outgoing people show evidence of *interpersonal intelligence*. They do well with cooperative learning and are sensitive to the feelings, intentions, and motivations of others. They often make good leaders. This type of intelligence is associated with **emotional intelligence**—the ability to recognize feelings and respond to them appropriately. This form of intelligence is talked about in greater detail in Chapter 8, "Communicating."

Those using *naturalist intelligence* love the outdoors and recognize details in plants, animals, rocks, clouds, and other natural formations. These people excel in observing fine distinctions among similar items.

Each of us has multiple intelligences to some degree. And each of us can learn to enhance the ones we don't favour. Experiment with learning in ways that draw on a variety of intelligences—including those that might be less familiar. When we acknowledge all of our intelligences, we can constantly explore new ways of learning. ✶

Practising
CRITICAL THINKING

1-3

Develop your Multiple Intelligences

Gardner's theory of multiple intelligences complements the discussion of different learning styles in this chapter. The main point is that there are many ways to gain knowledge and acquire new behaviours. You can use Gardner's concepts to explore a range of options for achieving success in school, work, and relationships.

Table 1.1 summarizes Gardner's theory of multiple intelligences and suggests ways to apply the main ideas. Instead of merely glancing through this table, get active. Place a check mark next to any of the characteristics that possibly describe you. Also check off the learning strategies that you intend to use. Finally, underline or highlight any of the possible careers that spark your interest. Follow up with Discovery Statements about how these possibilities align with your interests, connect to your career plans, and align with your choice of a major.

Remember that Table 1-1 is *not* an exhaustive list or a formal inventory. Take what you find merely as points of departure. You can invent strategies of your own to cultivate different intelligences.

Table 1.1 Multiple Intelligences

Type of intelligence	Possible characteristics	Possible learning strategies	Possible careers
Verbal/linguistic	❑ You enjoy writing letters, stories, and papers. ❑ You prefer to write directions rather than draw maps. ❑ You take excellent notes from textbooks and lectures. ❑ You enjoy reading, telling stories, and listening to them.	❑ Highlight, underline, and write other notes in your textbooks. ❑ Recite new ideas in your own words. ❑ Rewrite and edit your class notes. ❑ Talk to other people often about what you're studying	Librarian, lawyer, editor, journalist, English teacher, radio or television announcer
Mathematical/logical	❑ You enjoy solving puzzles. ❑ You prefer math or science class to English class. ❑ You want to know how and why things work. ❑ You make careful step-by-step plans.	❑ Analyze tasks into a sequence of steps. ❑ Group concepts into categories and look for underlying patterns. ❑ Convert text into tables, charts, and graphs. ❑ Look for ways to quantify ideas—to express them in numerical terms.	Accountant, auditor, tax preparer, mathematician, computer programmer, statistician, economist, math or science teacher
Visual/spatial	❑ You draw pictures to give an example or clarify an explanation. ❑ You understand maps and illustrations more readily than text. ❑ You assemble things from illustrated instructions. ❑ You especially enjoy books that have a lot of illustrations.	❑ When taking notes, create concept maps, mind maps, and other visuals (see Chapter 5, "Notes"). ❑ Code your notes by using different colours to highlight main topics, major points, and key details. ❑ When your attention wanders, bring it into focus by sketching or drawing. ❑ Before you try a new task, visualize yourself doing it well.	Architect, commercial artist, fine artist, graphic designer, photographer, interior decorator, engineer, cartographer
Bodily/kinesthetic	❑ You enjoy physical exercise. ❑ You tend to avoid sitting still for long periods of time. ❑ You enjoy working with your hands. ❑ You use a lot of gestures when talking.	❑ Be active in ways that support concentration; for example, pace as you recite, read while standing up, and create flash cards. ❑ Carry materials with you and practise studying in several different locations. ❑ Create hands-on activities related to key concepts; for example, create a game based on course content. ❑ Notice the sensations involved with learning something well.	Physical education teacher, athlete, athletic coach, physical therapist, chiropractor, massage therapist, yoga teacher, dancer, choreographer, actor

(Continued)

Table 1.1 Multiple Intelligences (continued)

Type of intelligence	Possible characteristics	Possible learning strategies	Possible careers
Musical/rhythmic	❏ You often sing in the car or shower. ❏ You tap your foot to the beat of a song. ❏ You play a musical instrument. ❏ You feel most engaged and productive when music is playing.	❏ During a study break, play music or dance to restore energy. ❏ Put on background music that enhances your concentration while studying. ❏ Relate key concepts to songs you know. ❏ Write your own songs based on course content.	Professional musician, music teacher, music therapist, choral director, musical instrument sales representative, musical instrument maker, piano tuner
Intrapersonal	❏ You enjoy writing in a journal and being alone with your thoughts. ❏ You think a lot about what you want in the future. ❏ You prefer individual projects to group projects. ❏ You take time to think things through before talking or taking action.	❏ Connect course content to your personal values and goals. ❏ Study a topic alone before attending a study group. ❏ Connect readings and lectures to a strong feeling or significant past experience. ❏ Keep a journal that relates your course work to events in your daily life.	Minister, priest, rabbi, professor of philosophy or religion, counselling psychologist, creator of a home-based or small business
Interpersonal	❏ You prefer group work to working alone. ❏ You have plenty of friends and regularly spend time with them. ❏ You enjoy talking and listening more than reading or writing. ❏ You thrive in positions of leadership.	❏ Form and conduct study groups early in the term. ❏ Create flash cards and use them to quiz study partners. ❏ Volunteer to give a speech or to lead group presentations on course topics. ❏ Teach the topic you're studying to someone else.	Manager, school administrator, salesperson, teacher, counselling psychologist, arbitrator, police officer, nurse, travel agent, public relations specialist, creator of a mid-size to large business
Naturalist	❏ As a child, you enjoyed collecting insects, leaves, or other natural objects. ❏ You enjoy being outdoors. ❏ You find that important insights occur during times you spend in natural surroundings. ❏ You read books and magazines on nature-related topics.	❏ During study breaks, take walks outside. ❏ Post pictures of outdoor scenes where you study and play recordings of outdoor sounds while you read. ❏ Invite classmates to discuss coursework while taking a hike or going on a camping trip. ❏ Focus on careers that hold the potential for working outdoors.	Environmental activist, park ranger, recreation supervisor, historian, museum curator, biologist, criminologist, mechanic, woodworker, construction worker, construction contractor or estimator

© Dana Heinemann/Shutterstock

MOTIVATION—
I'm just not in the mood

In large part, this chapter is about your motivation to succeed in school. And a First Step in creating motivation is getting some definitions straight.

The terms **self-discipline**, **willpower**, and **motivation** are often used to describe something missing in ourselves. We say things like "If I were more motivated, I'd get more involved in school" or "Of course she got an A. She has self-discipline" or "If I had more willpower, I'd lose weight." It seems that certain people are born with lots of motivation, while others miss out on it.

An alternative is to stop assuming that motivation is mysterious, determined at birth, or hard to come by. Perhaps what we call *motivation* is something that you already possess—or simply a habit that you can develop with practice. We are motivated to act by many things—by external rewards or punishments, by our interests, and by our internalized pressures to act. However, certain types of goals are more likely to lead to academic tenacity, and perseverance in the face of challenges (Dweck, Walton, & Cohen, 2014). Academic tenacity is fostered by having **intrinsic motivation** rather than by **extrinsic motivation**. You are more likely to be intrinsically motivated if the goals you set satisfy internal goals such as the satisfaction you feel with a job well done. When you are intrinsically motivated, the rewards you receive when you

complete a task are intrinsic to the activity itself, such as the feeling of satisfaction from completing a ten-kilometre race or the photograph you took of a sunrise. When we are extrinsically motivated, the goals we set are external to the activity itself such as receiving $100 for getting an A in a course or cleaning your room just so your parents don't yell at you. You are more likely to continue to engage in difficult learning activities, such as studying for your math test, if your goal is to have subject mastery than if your goal is to ensure that your name gets posted on the honour roll for others to see.

Learning to see the long-term relevance of what you are studying in terms of **intrinsic goals** will help make it easier to persevere when you encounter obstacles. Framing your studies in terms of intrinsic goals—for example, how what you are studying will help you to create meaningful relationships with others or to contribute to society—will increase the likelihood that you will stay the course when learning gets tough.

To have intrinsic motivation requires that three primary needs are met. Specifically, that you have a sense of

1. autonomy, and feel a choice about your actions so that you feel you are engaged in learning because the activities relate to your own interests and values;

2. belonging, and feel connected to others in secure and close relationships;

3. competence, and feel the need to put your skills to the test. (Rudow, 2017)

Those with a growth mindset are far more likely to be intrinsically motivated than those with an extrinsic motivation. If you work at developing your growth mindset, when you engage in learning tasks where setbacks occur, if you are intrinsically motivated, you don't view these setbacks as failure but rather as just another opportunity to try again.

Promise it

Motivation can come simply from making a commitment, from being clear about your goals and sharing those goals with others. If you want to start a study group, you can commit yourself to inviting people and setting a time and place to meet. Promise your classmates that you'll do this, and ask them to hold you accountable.

Befriend your discomfort

Sometimes keeping your word means doing a task you'd rather put off, such as reading a chapter in a statistics book or proofreading an essay. In the face of such discomfort, we can procrastinate. Or we can use this barrier as a means to get the job done.

Begin by investigating the discomfort. Notice the thoughts running through your head and speak them out loud: "I'd rather walk on a bed of coals than do this." Also observe what's happening with your body. For example, are your shoulders tight? Do you feel any tension in your stomach?

Once you're in contact with your mind and body, stay with the discomfort a few minutes longer. Don't judge it as good or bad. Accepting the thoughts and body sensations robs them of power. They might still be there, but in time they can stop being a barrier for you.

Discomfort can be a gift—an opportunity to do valuable work on yourself. On the other side of discomfort lies mastery.

Change your mind—and your body

You can also get past discomfort by planting new thoughts in your mind or changing your physical stance. For example, instead of slumping in a chair, sit up straight or stand up. Notice what happens to your discomfort.

Work with thoughts, too. Replace "I can't stand this" with "I'll feel great when this is done."

Turn down the pressure

The mere thought of starting a huge task can induce anxiety. To get past this feeling, turn down the pressure by taking "baby steps." Divide a large project into small tasks. In 30 minutes or less, you could preview a book,

Did you **know that …?**

The term *stress* was invented by an endocrinologist at McGill University, named Dr. Hans Selye. He was the first to start doing research in this new field, which focussed on the effects of biological stress on people ("50 little-known facts, 2017). Students often talk about being "stressed out" by school. Recent research shows that students who are successful academically are good at focussing their attention so that they stay on task and focus on long-term goals; they are actually happier and therefore better able to control stress (Barseghian, 2013).

create a rough outline for a paper, or solve two or three math problems. Careful planning can help you discover many such steps to make a big job doable.

Ask for support

Other people can become your allies in overcoming procrastination. You might want to form a support group and declare what you intend to accomplish before each meeting. Then ask members to hold you accountable. If you want to begin exercising regularly, ask another person to walk with you three times weekly. People in support groups ranging from Alcoholics Anonymous to Weight Watchers know the power of this strategy.

Adopt a model

One strategy for succeeding at any task is to hang around the masters. Find someone you consider successful and spend time with her. Observe this person and use her as a model for your own behaviour. You can "try on" this person's actions and attitudes. This person can become a mentor for you.

Compare the payoffs to the costs

Behaviours such as cramming for exams or neglecting exercise have payoffs. Cramming might give us more time that's free of commitments. Neglecting exercise can give us more time to sleep.

However, you need to determine the costs of putting things off. For example, skipping a reading assignment can give you time to go to the movies. However, you might be unprepared for class and have twice as much to read the following week.

Maybe there is another way to get the payoff (going to the movies) without paying the cost (skipping the reading assignment). With some thoughtful weekly planning, you might choose to give up a few hours of television and end up with enough time to read the assignment *and* go to the movies.

Comparing the costs and benefits of any behaviour can fuel our motivation. We can choose new behaviours because they align with what we want most. ✳

What's stopping you from getting started on your schoolwork?

All of us sometimes have difficulty getting work done or find a million reasons to put off beginning a new task. If you have difficulty getting going on your homework or being prepared for tests, you are in good company. About 70 percent of students report having chronic problems with **procrastination** (Pychyl, 2010)—putting things off until it is too late to get the task done properly. We all procrastinate, but when our behaviour starts to interfere with our success, we need to consider why. Why do we sometimes delay getting started on our essay until we don't have enough time to do a good job? Researchers have suggested a variety of reasons. In the next chapter, we will talk about strategies you can use to overcome procrastination; but for now consider if any of these reasons for procrastination might apply to you.

- You give in to the immediate impulse of wanting to feel better now. You want immediate gratification. Dr. Tim Pychyl suggests that this failure to self-regulate or control our own behaviour to achieve our goals interferes with many activities, from starting to exercise to stopping overeating. As he suggests, it is easy to "give in to feel good" (2010, p. 27) and avoid aversive activities like starting to study for finals. Unfortunately, you feel lousy and more stressed out later when you realize that the delay in getting to your school work means there isn't enough time to do a good job; the short-term gain actually harms you in the long term (Sirois & Pychyl, 2013).
- You fear failure and are pessimistic about the test outcome—the more you procrastinate, the more anxious you become as deadlines loom. This is the most common reason given for procrastination (Brownlow & Reasinger, 2000).

- To protect your self-image, you create actual barriers to your own success—this is called self-handicapping (Brownlow & Reasinger, 2000). You avoid studying so that any poor test performance you suffer can be attributed to your lack of effort rather than lack of ability (Beck, Koons, & Milgrim, 2000).
- You have a low level of self-esteem and just don't believe you can get it right (Brownlow & Reasinger, 2000).
- You are a perfectionist. If you can't get the paper done perfectly, you won't finish it at all. Or as a perfectionist, you may set unrealistic goals for an assignment, then feel overwhelmed in meeting those goals. Students with a fixed mindset often have perfectionist tendencies (Dweck, 2006).
- You have a hard time with what the task requires of you, such as a challenging new topic or having to use unfamiliar skills.
- You have a hard time setting goals or pursuing the goals you have.

Why does procrastination matter?

Research suggests that procrastination

- causes lower grades (Brownlow & Reasinger, 2000)
- impacts your health (Pychyl, Morin, & Salmon, 2000)
- makes you more dissatisfied with your courses (Brownlow & Reasinger, 2000)
- leads to higher rates of course withdrawal (Pychyl et al., 2000)
- makes you feel more negative in general (Pychyl, 2010)

So the next time you find yourself putting off studying, try to think about why that is and put into action some of the steps listed in the last article.

© Tim Pychyl and Paul Mason

Ideas Are Tools

There are many ideas in this book. When you first encounter them, don't believe any of them. Instead, think of them as tools.

For example, you use a hammer for a purpose—to drive a nail. When you use a new hammer, you might notice its shape, its weight, and its balance. You don't try to figure out whether the hammer is "right." You just use it. If it works, you use it again. If it doesn't work, you get a different hammer.

People have plenty of room in their lives for different kinds of "hammers," but they tend to limit themselves. A new idea, at some level, is a threat to their very being—unlike a new hammer, which is simply a new hammer.

Most of us have a built-in desire to be right. We think our ideas represent us.

Imagine someone defending a hammer. Picture this person holding up a hammer and declaring, "Oh, hammer, we stand on guard for thee. There are only two kinds of people in this world: people who believe in this hammer and people who don't."

That ridiculous picture makes a point. This book is not a manifesto. It's a toolbox, and tools are meant to be used.

If you read about a tool in this book that doesn't sound "right" or one that sounds a little goofy, remember that the ideas here are for using, not necessarily for believing in. Suspend your judgment. Test the idea for yourself. If it works, use it. If it doesn't work, don't use it.

Any tool—whether it's a hammer, a computer program, or a study technique—is designed to do a specific job. A master mechanic carries a variety of tools because no single tool works for all jobs. If you throw a tool away because it doesn't work in one situation, you won't be able to pull it out later when it's just what you need. So if an idea doesn't work for you and you are satisfied that you gave it a fair chance, don't throw it away. File it away instead. The idea might come in handy soon.

And remember, this book is not about figuring out the "right" way. Even the "ideas are tools" approach is not "right."

It's a hammer... or maybe a saw.

Gelpi/Shutterstock.com

Put it to WORK

To get more value from *Becoming a Master Student*, make the career connection. Think about how you can use the strategies from this chapter to find the job you want and do the work you love. Following are ways to get started.

Remember learning styles during job interviews

You probably feel more comfortable with a person when you feel you have something in common—this is called rapport. When meeting with a job interviewer, look for clues to the person's learning style. Then see if you can establish rapport by matching that person's style in a small, significant way.

For example, mirror the interviewer's *word choice*. Some people like to process information visually. You might hear them say, "I'll look into that" or "Give me the big picture first." Those who like to solve problems verbally might say, "Let's talk through this problem" or "I hear you!" In contrast, some interviewers express themselves using body sensations ("This product feels great") or action ("Let's run with this idea and see what happens").

Kinesthetic preferences are also expressed in posture. Notice whether the job interviewer is sitting with arms crossed and legs crossed or open. If you can mirror that position in a natural way, do so.

As you look for ways to establish rapport, be subtle. The goal is not to manipulate but to find common ground.

Discover your co-workers' learning styles

Once you are at work, remember that people constantly express their preferences for learning. Look for clues such as these:

- The worker who's continually on the move might prefer concrete experience over memos and meetings. She likes to learn by *doing*.
- The person who's usually on the phone with customers and clients makes it a priority to build relationships. She learns by *feeling*.

Phovoir/Shutterstock.com

- You might have a supervisor who enjoys working with concepts as much as working with people and who also has detailed plans and goals. This person has a preference for *thinking*.
- During a training session, a co-worker might do a lot of observation before they are willing to practise a new skill. He prefers to learn by *watching*.

Now create a career connection of your own

Spend five minutes reviewing this chapter. Look for a suggestion you will commit to use when you are working or applying for a job. In a sentence or two, describe your new behaviour and the benefit you want to gain from it. For example, "I will think about people's preferences for learning rather than getting into an argument with co-workers because they are not approaching a problem the way I would." Describe your planned behaviour on a separate piece of paper.

QUIZ

Name_____   Date____/____/____

1. Explain three ways that you can use knowledge of your learning styles to succeed in school.

2. Tell why employers value Mode 1 thinking in their employees.

3. The First Step technique refers only to telling the truth about your areas for improvement. True or False? Explain your answer.

4. Compare and contrast the concepts of growth mindset and fixed mindset (explain how they are similar and different).

5. Briefly describe how being aware of your own multiple intelligences can help you thrive in higher education.

6. According to the Power Process, "Ideas are tools." If you want the ideas in this book to work, you must believe in them. True or False? Explain your answer.

7. Define the word *metacognition* and give an example of it that relates to how you read a textbook.

8. Explain several reasons why we all might procrastinate on occasion. List three strategies you can use to overcome it.

9. Give an example of the difference between intrinsic and extrinsic motivation.

10. State two reasons why having perfectionist tendencies can stop you from being an engaged learner.

Skills **SNAPSHOT**

The Discovery Wheel in this chapter includes a section labelled *Attitude*. For the next 10 to 15 minutes, go beyond your initial responses to that exercise. Consider your beliefs about yourself as a learner as they exist today, after reading and doing this chapter.

Begin by reflecting on some recent learning experiences. Then take another step toward mastery by choosing to follow up on your reflections with a specific action.

SELF-AWARENESS

Three things I do well as a student are...

Three areas in which I'd like to improve as a student are...

STYLES

If asked to describe my learning style in one sentence, I would say that I am...

To become a more flexible learner, I could...

FLEXIBILITY

When I disagree with what someone else says, my first response is usually to...

In these situations, I could be more effective by...

NEXT ACTION

I'll know that I've adopted new attitudes to support my success when I'm able to say...

To reach that level of mastery, the most important thing I can do next is to...

MASTER STUDENT
PROFILE

David Simmonds
... is motivating

Western University, Crystal Lamb

David's commentary can be found in a variety of media including the *Toronto Star*, *The Globe and Mail*, and *CBC News: The National*, where he has served as a regular news contributor. In 2015, the Diversity Advancement Network named David to their list of the Top 100 Black Canadians in the Role Model category.

When David Simmonds was searching for his voice, he found it as a student on Western's campus. Simmonds, BA'07 (Political Science), grew up in the Toronto (GTA). In his current role as Vice-President of Public Affairs at McKesson Canada, he manages corporate marketing, public policy and communications for the large health company. He knew from the moment he first crossed over University Drive Bridge on a campus visit with his parents that Western had the atmosphere he was looking for in a university.

"The student voice is important at Western. When I was a student, I found myself having a role to play in offering that voice—and it just never stopped," he said.

"I became passionate about telling stories early in my family life. You had to tell stories to get fed in a family with six kids," he laughed. "And then I learned to tell stories in a powerful and persuasive way in the liberal arts program. My experiences at Western gave me tools in my toolkit I use to this day."

Simmonds quickly found himself "immersed in the culture" as a student, becoming involved on campus in residence life, intramurals, and students' council, as well as off campus by helping organizations around the city.

"I felt very supported. Back then, not a lot of students really looked like me. As a young black man from a different community, I had a different perspective. But I was supported to be my full self. I remember the first time I met a faculty member who was black and what that did for me. It was a small moment, a small interaction, but it was important because it showed me Western was a place where I could bring my full self to the classroom. If I can play a role in some way to help others now, how can I not?"

Following graduation, Simmonds completed a master's degree in education at the University of Toronto and a master's degree in communications and media studies from Royal Roads University. In addition to his role at McKesson, he is an instructor in the post-graduate certificate program in marketing, communications, and public relations at the University of Toronto, and works as a public speaker. He also volunteers for a number of organizations, including Toronto's specialty HIV/AIDS hospital, Casey House, and the Canadian Club of Toronto.

"If you have a good idea, you have to express it to make change," he says. "Every time I come to campus, no matter how much it changes, when I walk past a tree or hear a bird chirp, it reminds me of something that happened when I was on campus that had an impact on me. It's a reminder about the transformative power this institution has on people's lives."

Source: Lamb, C. (2016, June 23). New president to help alumni find their voices. *Western News*. Retrieved from http://news.westernu.ca/2016/06/new-president-help -alumni-find-voices/. Reprinted by permission.

Master Student Profiles

Each chapter of this text profiles a person who embodies several qualities of a master student. As you read about these people and others like them, ask yourself: How can I apply this? Look for the timeless qualities in the people you read about. Many of the strategies used by master students from another time or place are tools that you can use today.

The master students in this book were chosen because they demonstrate unusual and effective ways to learn. Remember that these are just 12 examples of master students. Reflect on other master students you've read about or know personally. As you meet new people, look for those who excel at learning. The master student is not a vague or remote ideal. Rather, master students are among us.

In fact, there's one living inside your skin.

Time

chapter 2

Alex Staroseltsev/Shutterstock.com

what is included ...

do you have a minute?

Think of a goal you have for your school year. Write it down. This is not a to-do list. It is a result that you intend to produce by getting one or more items on your to-do list done. Complete this sentence: One thing that I could do to achieve this goal is ...

WHAT if ...

I could develop my self-esteem?
I could meet my goals with time to spare?
I could develop my growth mindset?

WHY this chapter matters ...

Procrastination and lack of planning can quickly undermine your success in school, and in life.

HOW you can use this chapter ...

Discover the details about how you currently use time. Set goals that help you to develop your growth mindset. Know exactly what to do today, this week, and this month to achieve your goals. Reduce or even eliminate procrastination.

You've got the
TIME

The words *planning* and *time management* can call forth images of restriction and control. You might visualize a prune-faced scrooge hunched over your shoulder, stopwatch in hand, telling you what to do every minute. Bad news.

Good news: You do have enough time for the things you want to do. All it takes is learning to plan.

Time is an equal opportunity resource. No matter how newsworthy we are, no matter how rich or poor, we get 168 hours to spend each week—no more, no less. Time is also an unusual commodity. It cannot be saved. You can't stockpile time like wood for the stove or food for the winter. It can't be seen, felt, touched, tasted, or smelled. You can't sense time directly. Even scientists and philosophers find it hard to describe. Because time is so elusive, it is easy to ignore. That doesn't bother time at all. Time is perfectly content to remain hidden until you are nearly out of it. And when you are out of it, you are out of it.

Time is a non-renewable resource. If you're out of wood, you can chop some more. If you're out of money, you can earn a little extra. If you're out of love, there is still hope. If you're out of health, it can

often be restored. But when you're out of time, that's it. When this minute is gone, it's gone.

Time seems to pass at varying speeds. Sometimes it crawls and sometimes it's faster than the speed of light. On Friday afternoons, classroom clocks can creep. After you've worked a 10-hour day, reading the last few pages of an economics assignment can turn minutes into hours. A year in school can stretch out to an eternity. At the other end of the spectrum, time flies. There are moments when you are so absorbed in what you're doing that hours disappear like magic.

When you say you don't have enough time, you might really be saying that you are not spending the time you *do* have in the way that you want.

Everything written about time management can be reduced to three main ideas:

1. **Discover exactly *what* you want.** State your wants as clear, specific goals. And put them in writing.

2. **Know *how* to get what you want.** Determine what you'll do *today* to get what you want in the future. Put those intentions in writing as well.

---

journal entry   2-1

Discovery/Intention Statement

Create Value from This Chapter

Think back to a time during the past year when you rushed to finish a project or when you did not find time for an activity that was important to you. List one thing you did to contribute to this outcome.

I discovered that I . . .

_____

_____

Take a few minutes to skim this chapter. Find three to five articles that might help you avoid such outcomes in the future and list them below.

Title   Number

_____

_____

_____

_____

If you don't have time to read these articles in depth right now, schedule a time to do so.

I intend to . . .

_____

_____

_____

3. **Follow up with an action.** Begin the First Steps of achieving your goals. Do what you intend to do.

When we forget these principles, we can easily spend most of our time responding to interruptions, last-minute projects, and emergencies. Life feels like a scramble to just survive. We're so busy achieving someone else's goals that we forget about getting what *we* want.

According to Stephen R. Covey (1990), the purpose of planning is to carve out space in your life for things that are not urgent but are truly important. Examples are exercising regularly, reading, praying or meditating, spending quality time alone or with family members and friends, travelling, and cooking nutritious meals. Each of these contributes directly to our personal goals for the future and to the overall quality of our lives in the present.

Yet when schedules get tight, we often drop important activities. We postpone them for that elusive day when we'll finally "have more time." Learning time management techniques has been found to be critical for student learning. Students who have good long-term planning techniques have better academic outcomes (van der Meer, Jansen, & Torenbeek, 2010). Don't wait for that time to come. *Make* the time. Use the activities in this chapter to empower yourself. Spend your most valuable resource in the way you choose. ✳

practising
CRITICAL THINKING
2-1

The Time Monitor/Time Plan process

The purpose of this exercise is to transform time into a knowable and predictable resource. To do this, monitor your time in 15-minute intervals, 24 hours a day, for seven days. Record how much time you spend sleeping, eating, studying, attending lectures, travelling to and from class, working, on social media, playing video games, listening to music, taking care of the kids, running errands—everything.

If this sounds crazy, hang on for a minute. This exercise is not about keeping track of the rest of your life in 15-minute intervals. It is an opportunity to become conscious of how you spend your time, and your life. Use the Time Monitor/Time Plan process only for as long as it is helpful to do so. When you know how your time is spent, you can make choices with open eyes.

You can plan to spend more time on the things that are most important to you and less time on the unimportant. Monitoring your time puts you in control of your life. To do this exercise, complete the following steps.

Step 1
Look at the sample Time Monitor/Time Plan in Figure 2.1. On Monday, the student got up at 6:45 a.m., showered, and got dressed. He ate breakfast from 7:15 to 7:45. It took him 15 minutes to walk to class (7:45 to 8:00), and he attended classes from 8:00 to 11:00.

List your activities in the same way. When you begin an activity, write it down next to the time you begin. Round off to the nearest 15 minutes. If, for example, you begin eating at 8:06, enter your starting time as 8:00.

Step 2
Fill out your Time Monitor. Now it's *your* turn. Using the blank Time Monitor in Figure 2.2, choose a day to begin monitoring your time. On that day, start filling out your Time Monitor. Keep it with you all day and use it for one full week. Take a few moments every couple of hours to record what you've done. Or enter a note each time that you change activities.

Step 3
After you've monitored your time for one week, group your activities together into categories. List them in the "Category" column in Figure 2.3, which includes the categories "Sleep," "Class," "Study," and "Meals." Think of other categories to add. "Grooming" might include showering, putting on makeup, and getting dressed. "Travel" could include walking, taking the bus, and riding your bike. Other categories might be "Exercise," "Video games," "Work," "Social Media," and "Children." Write in the categories that work for you.

Step 4
List your estimated hours for each category of activity. Guess how many hours you *think* you spent on each category of activity. List these hours in the "Estimated" column in Figure 2.3.

Then, list your *actual* hours for each category of activity. Add up the figures from your daily time monitoring. List these hours in the "Actual" column in the same figure. Make sure that the grand total of all categories is 168 hours.

MONDAY 9 / 12

Monitor	Plan
6:45 Get up	
Shower	
7:00 ———	7:00
7:15 Breakfast	
7:30	
7:45 Walk to class	
8:00 Econ 1	8:00
8:15	
8:30	
8:45	
9:00	9:00
9:15	
9:30	
9:45	
10:00 Bio 1	10:00
10:15	
10:30	
10:45	
11:00	11:00
11:15 Study	
11:30	
11:45	
12:00	12:00
12:15 Lunch	
12:30	
12:45	
1:00	1:00
1:15 Eng. Lit	
1:30	
1:45	
2:00	2:00
2:15 coffee shop	
2:30	
2:45	
3:00	3:00
3:15	
3:30	
3:45	
4:00	4:00
4:15 Study	
4:30	
4:45	
5:00	5:00
5:15 Dinner	
5:30	
5:45	
6:00	6:00
6:15	
6:30 social media	
6:45	
7:00	7:00

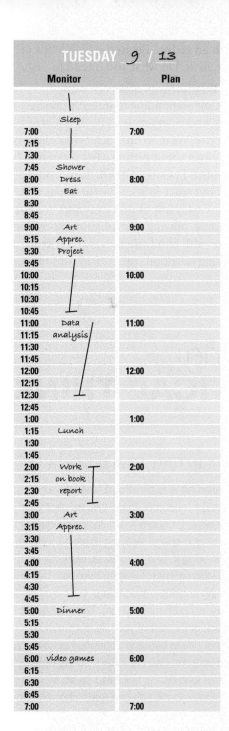

TUESDAY 9 / 13

Monitor	Plan
Sleep	
7:00	7:00
7:15	
7:30	
7:45 Shower	
8:00 Dress	8:00
8:15 Eat	
8:30	
8:45	
9:00 Art	9:00
9:15 Apprec.	
9:30 Project	
9:45	
10:00	10:00
10:15	
10:30	
10:45	
11:00 Data	11:00
11:15 analysis	
11:30	
11:45	
12:00	12:00
12:15	
12:30	
12:45	
1:00	1:00
1:15 Lunch	
1:30	
1:45	
2:00 Work	2:00
2:15 on book	
2:30 report	
2:45	
3:00 Art	3:00
3:15 Apprec.	
3:30	
3:45	
4:00	4:00
4:15	
4:30	
4:45	
5:00 Dinner	5:00
5:15	
5:30	
5:45	
6:00 video games	6:00
6:15	
6:30	
6:45	
7:00	7:00

Figure 2.1 Sample Time Monitor

Step 5

Reflect on the results of this exercise. Compare the "Estimated" and "Actual" columns. You might feel disappointed or even angry about where your time goes. Use those feelings as motivation to make different choices. Think about how you would complete these sentences:

I was surprised at the amount of time I spent on . . .
I want to spend more time on . . .
I want to spend less time on . . .

Step 6

Repeat this exercise. Do this exercise as many times as you want. The benefit is developing a constant awareness of your activities. With that awareness, you can make informed choices about how to spend the time of your life.

MONDAY ___ / ___ / ___ /

Monitor	Plan
7:00	7:00
7:15	
7:30	
7:45	
8:00	8:00
8:15	
8:30	
8:45	
9:00	9:00
9:15	
9:30	
9:45	
10:00	10:00
10:15	
10:30	
10:45	
11:00	11:00
11:15	
11:30	
11:45	
12:00	12:00
12:15	
12:30	
12:45	
1:00	1:00
1:15	
1:30	
1:45	
2:00	2:00
2:15	
2:30	
2:45	
3:00	3:00
3:15	
3:30	
3:45	
4:00	4:00
4:15	
4:30	
4:45	
5:00	5:00
5:15	
5:30	
5:45	
6:00	6:00
6:15	
6:30	
6:45	
7:00	7:00
7:15	
7:30	
7:45	
8:00	8:00
8:15	
8:30	
8:45	
9:00	9:00
9:15	
9:30	
9:45	
10:00	10:00
10:15	
10:30	
10:45	
11:00	11:00
11:15	
11:30	
11:45	
12:00	12:00

TUESDAY ___ / ___ / ___ /

Monitor	Plan
7:00	7:00
7:15	
7:30	
7:45	
8:00	8:00
8:15	
8:30	
8:45	
9:00	9:00
9:15	
9:30	
9:45	
10:00	10:00
10:15	
10:30	
10:45	
11:00	11:00
11:15	
11:30	
11:45	
12:00	12:00
12:15	
12:30	
12:45	
1:00	1:00
1:15	
1:30	
1:45	
2:00	2:00
2:15	
2:30	
2:45	
3:00	3:00
3:15	
3:30	
3:45	
4:00	4:00
4:15	
4:30	
4:45	
5:00	5:00
5:15	
5:30	
5:45	
6:00	6:00
6:15	
6:30	
6:45	
7:00	7:00
7:15	
7:30	
7:45	
8:00	8:00
8:15	
8:30	
8:45	
9:00	9:00
9:15	
9:30	
9:45	
10:00	10:00
10:15	
10:30	
10:45	
11:00	11:00
11:15	
11:30	
11:45	
12:00	12:00

WEDNESDAY ___ / ___ / ___ /

Monitor	Plan
7:00	7:00
7:15	
7:30	
7:45	
8:00	8:00
8:15	
8:30	
8:45	
9:00	9:00
9:15	
9:30	
9:45	
10:00	10:00
10:15	
10:30	
10:45	
11:00	11:00
11:15	
11:30	
11:45	
12:00	12:00
12:15	
12:30	
12:45	
1:00	1:00
1:15	
1:30	
1:45	
2:00	2:00
2:15	
2:30	
2:45	
3:00	3:00
3:15	
3:30	
3:45	
4:00	4:00
4:15	
4:30	
4:45	
5:00	5:00
5:15	
5:30	
5:45	
6:00	6:00
6:15	
6:30	
6:45	
7:00	7:00
7:15	
7:30	
7:45	
8:00	8:00
8:15	
8:30	
8:45	
9:00	9:00
9:15	
9:30	
9:45	
10:00	10:00
10:15	
10:30	
10:45	
11:00	11:00
11:15	
11:30	
11:45	
12:00	12:00

Adapted from © Cengage Learning

(Continued)

Figure 2.2 *Your Time Monitor*

THURSDAY ___ / ___ / ___ /		FRIDAY ___ / ___ / ___ /		SATURDAY ___ / ___ / ___ /	
Monitor	Plan	Monitor	Plan	Monitor	Plan
7:00	7:00	7:00	7:00		
7:15		7:15			
7:30		7:30			
7:45		7:45			
8:00	8:00	8:00	8:00		
8:15		8:15			
8:30		8:30			
8:45		8:45			
9:00	9:00	9:00	9:00		
9:15		9:15			
9:30		9:30			
9:45		9:45			
10:00	10:00	10:00	10:00		
10:15		10:15			
10:30		10:30			
10:45		10:45			
11:00	11:00	11:00	11:00		
11:15		11:15			
11:30		11:30			
11:45		11:45			
12:00	12:00	12:00	12:00		
12:15		12:15			
12:30		12:30			
12:45		12:45			
1:00	1:00	1:00	1:00		
1:15		1:15			
1:30		1:30			
1:45		1:45			
2:00	2:00	2:00	2:00		
2:15		2:15			
2:30		2:30			
2:45		2:45			
3:00	3:00	3:00	3:00		
3:15		3:15			
3:30		3:30			
3:45		3:45			

THURSDAY (cont.)		FRIDAY (cont.)		SUNDAY ___ / ___ / ___ /	
Monitor	Plan	Monitor	Plan	Monitor	Plan
4:00	4:00	4:00	4:00		
4:15		4:15			
4:30		4:30			
4:45		4:45			
5:00	5:00	5:00	5:00		
5:15		5:15			
5:30		5:30			
5:45		5:45			
6:00	6:00	6:00	6:00		
6:15		6:15			
6:30		6:30			
6:45		6:45			
7:00	7:00	7:00	7:00		
7:15		7:15			
7:30		7:30			
7:45		7:45			
8:00	8:00	8:00	8:00		
8:15		8:15			
8:30		8:30			
8:45		8:45			
9:00	9:00	9:00	9:00		
9:15		9:15			
9:30		9:30			
9:45		9:45			
10:00	10:00	10:00	10:00		
10:15		10:15			
10:30		10:30			
10:45		10:45			
11:00	11:00	11:00	11:00		
11:15		11:15			
11:30		11:30			
11:45		11:45			
12:00	12:00	12:00	12:00		

Adapted from © Cengage Learning

Figure 2.2 *Your Time Monitor*

WEEK OF ___ / ___ / ___ /		
Category	Estimated Hours	Actual
Sleep		
Class		
Study		
Meals		

Adapted from © Cengage Learning

Figure 2.3 *Your Estimated and Actual Hours*

practising
CRITICAL THINKING 2-2

Seeing where all the time goes

You've probably heard people say, "I just don't know where my time goes." Well, this chapter offers ways to find out.

First, discover the details about how you spend your lifetime by completing the Time Monitor/Time Plan in Figure 2.2.

Next, get a big picture of those results—literally. Create a chart, diagram, or some other visual way to show the categories of activity that take up most of your time. Consider creating a pie chart like the example shown below.

Using a pie chart to display your activities is useful for at least two reasons. First, a circle is a fixed shape. It reinforces the idea that you have only a fixed amount of time to work with—24 hours per day, 168 hours per week. Second, seeing your life represented on the chart can help you adjust the size of each slice in the pie—that is, each category of activity.

After looking at the example in Figure 2.4, fill in the first blank circle with your totals from the "Estimated Hours" column in Figure 2.3.

Label this pie chart "Estimated hours." Then fill in the second blank circle with the totals from your "Actual" column on that page. Label this pie chart "Actual."

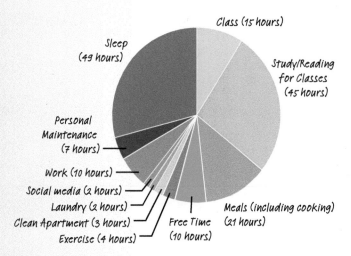

Figure 2.4 **Sample Pie Chart of Activities**

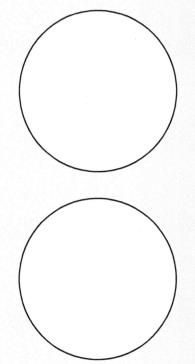

Figure 2.5 **Pie Chart of Your Activities**

Developing
SELF-EFFICACY

ShutterDivision/Shutterstock.com

THE CHALLENGE of postsecondary education often puts self-esteem at risk. The rigours of class work, financial pressures, and new social settings can test your ability to adapt and change.

Self-esteem can erode in ways that are imperceptible. Over time, you can gradually buy into a reduced sense of your own possibilities in life. This orientation makes it less likely that you'll take risks, create a vision for the future, and accomplish your goals.

During the past 30 years, psychologists have produced several key studies about **self-efficacy**. This term refers to your belief in your ability to determine the outcomes of events—especially outcomes that are strongly influenced by your own behaviour. A strong sense of self-efficacy allows you to tackle problems with confidence, set long-term goals, and see difficult tasks as creative challenges rather than potential disasters.

While self-esteem refers to an overall impression of your abilities, self-efficacy is more exact, pointing to specific factors that influence the ways you think, feel, and act. According to Bandura (1984), self-efficacy has several sources. You can use specific strategies to strengthen it.

Set up situations in which you can win

Start by planning scenarios in which you can succeed. Bandura calls these "mastery situations." For example, set yourself up for success by breaking a big project down into small, doable tasks. Then tackle and complete the first task. This accomplishment can help you move on to the next task with higher self-efficacy. Success breeds more success.

Set goals with care

If you want to boost self-efficacy, be picky about your goals as well. According to the research, goals that you find easy to meet will not boost your self-efficacy. Instead, set goals that call on you to overcome obstacles, make persistent effort, and even fail occasionally. At the same time, it's important to avoid situations in which you are *often* likely to fail. Setting goals that you have little chance to meet can undermine your self-efficacy. Ideal goals are both challenging *and* achievable. A strong sense of self-efficacy allows you to tackle problems with confidence, set long-term goals, and see difficult tasks as creative challenges rather than potential disasters.

Adopt a model

Find a model, someone who has succeeded where you want to succeed. Look for people with whom you have a lot in common—and who have mastered the skills that you want to acquire. Besides demonstrating strategies

---

Notable failures: Persisting at goals

Einstein was four years old before he could speak and seven before he could read.

Beethoven's music teacher once said of him, "As a composer he is hopeless."

When Star Trek went off the air in 1969, it was deemed a flop. It wasn't until 1973 when the first Star Trek movie appeared that **William Shatner's** name became equated with the name of James T. Kirk—a role he remains famous for to this day.

Michael J. Fox did poorly in school and wasn't tall enough to play his favourite sport, hockey. Luckily drama class intrigued him and by the age of 15 he had starred in his first professional role on TV.

Walt Disney was fired by a newspaper editor because "he lacked imagination and had no good ideas."

Decca Records turned down a recording contract with the **Beatles** with an unprophetic evaluation: "We don't like their sound. Groups of guitars are on their way out."

"I've missed more than 9,000 shots in my career," **Michael Jordan** said. "I've lost almost 300 games. Twenty-six times I've been trusted to take the game winning shot . . . and missed. I've failed over and over and over again in my life. That is why I succeed."

After **Carl Lewis** won the gold medal for the long jump in the 1996 Olympic games, he was asked to what he attributed his longevity, having competed for almost 20 years. He said, "Remembering that you have both wins and losses along the way. I don't take either one too seriously."

Spike Lee applied for graduate study at the two top film schools in the U.S. Due to his scores on the Graduate Record Exam, both schools turned Lee down.

Sometimes you feel that no matter how hard you try, you are doomed to fail. However, keep in mind that many famous people did not meet with success initially, but later went on to fame and fortune. The adage "If at first you don't succeed, try, try again" has a lot of merit. It is often from our failures that we learn the most. So, the next time you get a poor grade on a test or don't make the team you want, keep in mind that that event just might be your First Step to success. In fact, failure is an important part of developing your growth mindset: When you fail and then take steps to improve, you increase your grit and resiliency.

Source: Adapted from Gillett, R., Feloni, R., & Lutz, A.(2016, October 27). But They Did Not Give Up. http://www.des.emory.edu/mfp/OnFailingG .html 33 famous people who failed before they succeeded. *Business Insider*. Retrieved from http://www.businessinsider.com/famous-people -who-failed-before-they-succeeded-2016-10/

and techniques for you to use, these people hold out a real possibility of success for you.

Change the conversation about yourself

Monitor what you say and think about yourself. Whether you are fully aware of them or not, your thoughts and words can make or break your sense of self-efficacy.

Pay close attention and notice when you speak or think negatively about yourself. Telling the truth about your weaknesses is one thing. Consistently underrating yourself is another. Be balanced. Tell the truth about the times you set a goal and miss it. Also take the time to write and speak about the goals you meet and what works well in your life.

People with a strong sense of self-efficacy attribute their failures to skills that they currently lack—but that they can acquire in the future. This approach chooses not to look on failures as permanent, personal defects. Rather than saying "I just don't have what it takes to become a skilled test-taker," say "I can adopt techniques to help me remember key facts even when I feel stressed."

Compare yourself to yourself

When we're unsure of ourselves, we can look in any direction and see people who seem more competent and more confident than we do. When we start the comparison game, we open the door to self-doubt.

There is a way to play the comparison game and win: Instead of comparing yourself to others, compare yourself to yourself. Measure success in terms of self-improvement rather than of triumphs over others. Take time to note any progress you've made over time toward your goals. Write Discovery Statements about that progress. Celebrate your success in any area of life, no matter how small that success might seem.

Instead of deflecting compliments ("It was nothing"), fully receive the positive things that others say about you ("Thank you"). Also take public credit for your successes. "Well, I was just lucky" can change to "I worked hard to achieve that goal." ✳

Setting **GOALS** and developing your **GROWTH MINDSET**

Many of us have vague, idealized notions of what we want out of life. These notions float among the clouds in our heads. They are wonderful, fuzzy, safe thoughts such as "I want to be a good person," "I want to be financially secure," or "I want to be happy."

Such outcomes are great possible goals. Left in a generalized form, however, these goals can leave us confused about ways to actually achieve them, and years can pass without our getting any closer to them. If you really want to meet a goal, translate it into specific, concrete behaviours. Make your goal as real as a hammer. And use your time in specific ways to move yourself closer to your goal.

There is nothing vague or fuzzy about hammers. You can see them, feel them, and hear them. They have a clear function. Goals can be every bit as real and useful.

Consider the type of goal you want to accomplish

In the last chapter we talked about the importance of developing a growth mindset. Dweck et al. (2014) suggest that students with a fixed mindset, those who believe intelligence, not effort, determines outcomes and are perfectionist about their work, are more likely to pursue **performance goals**. These are goals where your primary interest is how you will be judged by others rather than what you learned (Elliot, Dweck & Yeager, 2017). Getting an A on your French test to impress other students in your class is a performance goal. These goals might sound good in the short term but are unlikely to keep you motivated for the long haul. The problem with performance goals is that you are likely to choose tasks where you have a high likelihood of success and where failure is unlikely to occur. Growth mindset students are more likely to choose **learning** or **mastery goals** where the task is to develop competence and master new skills to your own satisfaction (Elliot, Dweck & Yeager, 2017). Students with a growth mindset are interested in pursuing academic projects from which they learn, even if academic setbacks occur. A learning goal for your French course would be becoming fluent in the language.

Learning goals combined with persistence lead to academic tenacity. You may have a mixture of learning and performance goals depending upon the nature of the academic tasks you have to perform; but if the only goals you set for yourself are ones where you avoid failure, you are not stretching yourself. The problem with performance goals is that by avoiding tasks that might lead to failure we may also be avoiding the opportunity to learn.

Create long-term goals

To develop a growth mindset, you also need to believe that learning is important. If you have a "who cares" attitude to learning, it will be hard to get excited about anything going on in school. This means that you need to develop some long-term learning goals. What do you want to get out of your higher education experience? What purpose does it serve for you?

If you have a meaningful long-term goal, then it will be easier to be engaged in your own learning and to stay the course when learning gets tough. The goal must be specific and meaningful to you personally (Dweck et al.,

2014), so if you are studying engineering it could be that you are interested in learning mathematics so that you can ensure that better automobiles are built that prevent accidents. That's a goal worth investing time and energy in. Even if you don't have a fully formed idea of what you want to get out of your postsecondary education, starting to come up with an answer will put you on the path for getting the most out of your education. Developing a meaningful long-term goal will help you to become the person you want to be. Learning just to pass the test will soon become boring if you don't have a higher goal in store.

Develop academic tenacity and grit

Duckworth, Peterson, Mathews, and Kelly (2007) performed research that showed that grit or academic perseverance is essential to your ability to pursue long-term goals. Grit and a focus on long-term goals are required for academic achievement. Many academic goals take a long time to be complete, and require commitment, passion, and sustained effort. Having grit and a growth mindset will help see your dreams come true. Developing self-control will allow you to stay the course even when things get difficult, and to navigate setbacks when they occur.

Long-term academic goals are more likely to be achieved when you develop the self-control needed to not to put aside studying for activities like playing video games or chatting online, which are in no way linked to achievement. Ducksworth and Seligman (2005) did research that found that self-discipline was a stronger predictor of student academic success

Be SMART about your goals

Consider whether your goals are Specific, Measurable, Attainable, Relevant, and Time-bound, or SMART. Edwin Locke (2004) suggests that when we use SMART goals we are more likely to achieve the results we want.

- Ensure that your goals have clarity. This is very important and by being specific, measurable, and time-bound you are more likely to have clear goals.

- For goals to be relevant, they need to be sufficiently challenging and rewarding.

- Get feedback on your goals. This allows you to clarify any uncertainties along the way and make adjustments when necessary.

Suppose that one of your goals is to become a better student by studying harder. You're headed in a powerful direction; now go for the specifics. Translate that goal into a concrete action, such as "I will study two hours for every hour I'm in class." Specific goals make clear what actions are needed or what results are expected. Consider these examples:

Vague goal	SMART goal
Get a good education	Graduate with a B.Sc. degree in engineering, with honours, by 2023
Enhance my spiritual life	Meditate for 15 minutes daily for a month
Get control of my expenses	Bring lunch to school everyday for a semester

than IQ scores. Why did this happen? It turned out that students with good self-discipline spent more time studying and less time on distracting activities. Academic success is therefore determined by having a growth mindset, developing long-term goals, and developing self-regulatory behaviours like effective time management strategies.

Write down your goals

Writing down your goals exponentially increases your chances of meeting them. Having clear goals is a remedy for procrastination. When you write your goals down, you put in writing what is important to you and then it is harder to avoid tasks that will help you to achieve your own goals. Writing exposes undefined terms, unrealistic time frames, and other symptoms of fuzzy thinking. If you've been completing Intention Statements as explained in the Introduction to this book, then you've already had experience writing goals. Goals and Intention Statements both address changes you want to make in your behaviour, your values, your circumstances—or all of these. To keep track of your goals, put a reminder on your phone to reflect on your goals periodically.

Develop a realistic plan

Of course, having a goal is just the First Step. Next you need to come up with a realistic plan to achieve it. This realistic plan should help you not to waste the time you're given in your higher education career.

Dweck (2006) suggests that a good plan must include three essential components. *When* will you begin to implement your plan? *Where* and *how* will you implement your plan? Remember that baby steps are often necessary to achieve success. If your goal is to become a world-class speed skater, what do you need to do? First, begin to skate daily, starting today (*When*); find out where speed skaters train (*Where*); and talk to some about how they learned to be exceptional athletes (*How*). Consider any obstacles that might be in your path to success and how you could overcome them. For instance, if the best speed skating oval is in another town, you could talk to your academic counsellor about the possibility of doing an exchange at another institution where there are better opportunities for practising speed skating. Once you can specify these concrete steps, the chances of success for your plan will increase and you are beginning to develop a growth mindset plan. You are a growth mindset individual if you stick with the plan over the long haul. ✳

What can you do to develop a growth mindset?

1. Challenge yourself with hard problems or tasks from which you can learn.
2. Learn and apply a variety of study strategies to academic tasks.
3. Monitor your performance with a goal to evaluating effectiveness of the study strategies you chose rather than judging yourself .
4. Choose mastery or learning goals rather than performance goals; if you choose to do only tasks you know you are already good at how can you grow?
5. Once you think of a good learning goal, think carefully about the steps necessary to achieve it.
6. Try to anticipate potential obstacles to achieving your goal and then consider various strategies you might use to overcome those roadblocks.
7. Try to choose projects that align with your interests and long-term goals.
8. Brainstorm new solutions to your problem.
9. If you find yourself slipping into a fixed mindset of judging yourself negatively for your academic performance, try to think of obstacles as just bumps in the road. Let that negative feeling go and concentrate on what successful strategies you can try next time to improve the outcome.
10. Most importantly, don't give up. Your ability to try, fail, and then try again is the most essential thing you can do to develop a growth mindset.

Creating plans for success

One way to make goals effective is to develop realistic plans. That's what this exercise is about. Using a process of brainstorming and reflection, you can break a long-term goal into smaller segments until you have created a plan for action. When you analyze a goal to this level of detail, you're well on the way to meeting it.

For this exercise, you will use a pen, extra paper, and a timer like your phone. Timing is an important part of the brainstorming process, so follow the stated time limits. This entire exercise takes about 50 minutes.

Part one: Long-term goals

Brainstorm. Begin with an eight-minute brainstorm. For eight minutes, write down everything you think you want in your life. Write as fast as you can and write whatever comes into your head. Leave no thought out. Don't worry about accuracy. The objective of a brainstorm is to generate as many ideas as possible. Use a separate sheet of paper for this part of the exercise.

Reflect. After you have finished brainstorming, spend the next six minutes looking over your list. Analyze what you wrote. Read the list out loud. If something is missing, add it. Look for common themes or relationships between goals. Do your learning or mastery goals align with your long-term goals? Look for a "fit" between all of your goals and your purpose for taking part in postsecondary education, as well as your overall purpose in life. Consider the satisfaction you'll gain in attaining your objectives. If you don't feel a significant emotional connection with a written goal, consider letting it go or filing it away to review later.

Then circle the three long-term goals that are most important to you—goals that will take many years to achieve.

Before you continue, take a minute to reflect on the process you've used so far. What criteria did you use to select your top three goals? For example, list some of the core values (such as happiness) or character strengths (such as hope, zest for life, gratitude, and love) underlying these goals.

Part two: Creating a plan

Brainstorm. Read out loud the three long-term goals you selected in Part One. Choose one of them. Then brainstorm a list of all the mini steps that would lead to the accomplishment of that one long-term goal. Keep in mind the three essential steps of a good plan: *when, where, and how*.

Spend eight minutes on this brainstorm. Remember, neatness doesn't count.

When...

Where...

How...

Reflect. What are potential obstacles that may stop you from achieving your plan? Spend 5 minutes writing down potential roadblocks to success. Now spend 10 minutes brainstorming looking for workable solutions. Record the roadblocks and the solutions below.

Obstacles...

Solutions ...

Part three: Review and plan small steps

Review your plan including possible obstacles and solutions and then modify the plan as needed. Select one step you will take today to start moving your plan forward.

_____

_____

This helps you link goal setting to time management.

Decide on a list of small, achievable steps you can take right away to help you accomplish your long-term goals.

_____

_____

Write these small steps down on a daily to-do list or keep the to-do list on your phone.

If you want to accomplish some of them by a certain date, enter them in a calendar that you consult daily or have your phone or electronic calendar give you periodic reminders. Then, over the coming weeks, review your to-do list and calendar. Take note of your progress and celebrate your successes.

The more you practise developing plans for success, the more effective you can be at choosing goals that have meaning for you. You can repeat this exercise, employing the other long-term goals you generated or creating new ones. By using this brainstorm and reflection process, you can make goals come to life in the here and now.

The ABC daily
TO-DO LIST

chrupka/Shutterstock.com

ONE OF THE MOST effective ways to stay on track and actually get things done is to use a daily to-do list. While the Time Monitor/Time Plan gives you a general picture of the week, your daily to-do list itemizes specific tasks you want to complete within the next 24 hours.

One advantage of keeping a daily to-do list is that you don't have to remember what to do next. It's on the list. A typical day in the life of a student is full of separate, often unrelated tasks—reading, attending lectures, reviewing notes, working at a job, writing papers, researching special projects, running errands. It's easy to forget an important task on a busy day. When that task is written down, you don't have to rely on your memory.

The following steps present one method for to-do lists. Experiment with these steps, modify them as you see fit, and invent new techniques that work for you.

Step 1 Brainstorm tasks

To get started, list all of the tasks you want to get done tomorrow. Each task will become an item on a to-do list. Don't worry about putting the entries in order or scheduling them yet. Just list everything you want to accomplish on a sheet of paper or a planning calendar, or in a notebook.

Step 2 Estimate time

For each task you wrote down in Step 1, estimate how long it will take you to complete it. This can be tricky. If you allow too little time, you end up feeling rushed. If you allow too much time, you become less productive. For now, give it your best guess. Your estimates will improve with practice. Now pull out your calendar or Time Monitor/Time Plan. You've probably scheduled some hours for activities such as classes or work. This leaves the unscheduled hours for tackling your to-do lists.

Add up the time needed to complete all your to-do items. Also add up the number of unscheduled hours

in your day. Then compare the two totals. The power of this step is that you can spot overload in advance. If you have eight hours' worth of to-do items but only four unscheduled hours, that's a potential problem. To solve it, proceed to Step 3.

Step 3 Rate each task by priority

To prevent overscheduling, decide which to-do items are the most important given the time you have available. One suggestion for doing this comes from the book *How to Get Control of Your Time and Your Life* by Alan Lakein (1996): Simply label each task A, B, or C.

The As on your list are those things that are the most critical. These are assignments that are coming due or jobs that need to be done immediately. Also included are activities that lead directly to your short-term goals.

The Bs on your list are important, but less so than the As. Bs might someday become As. For the present, these tasks are not as urgent as As. They can be postponed, if necessary, for another day.

The Cs do not require immediate attention. C priorities include activities such as "shop for a new blender" and "research genealogy on the Internet." Cs are often small, easy jobs with no set timeline. These, too, can be postponed.

Once you've labelled the items on your to-do list, schedule time for all of the As. The Bs and Cs can be done randomly during the day when you are between tasks and are not yet ready to start the next A.

Step 4 Cross off tasks

Keep your to-do list with you at all times, crossing off activities when you finish them and adding new ones when you think of them. Crossing off tasks can be

> **Don't wait until the end of the day to start organizing yourself**
>
> *I wouldn't wait until the end [of the day] to start organizing—I would take four or five breaks throughout the day and make sure I could jam everything in—and then every night before going to sleep, I would see what's going on for the next day and prepare myself, read up on things. Before every meeting I would look at exactly what I wanted to go in there with and it was constant reminders. I was one of those people who would constantly look at my notes or my phone and be on top of my game.*
> —Abdullah Snobar, executive director of the DMZ, Ryerson University's technology incubator (*Maclean's,* 2017)
>
> Source: Advice for first-year students from Justin Trudeau (and 27 other people), by *Maclean's, Maclean's,* December 1, 2017.

fun—a visible reward for your diligence. This step fosters a sense of accomplishment.

Step 5 Evaluate

At the end of the day, evaluate your performance. Look for A priorities you didn't complete. Look for items that repeatedly turn up as Bs or Cs on your list and never seem to get done. Consider either changing these to As or dropping them altogether. Similarly, you might consider changing an A that didn't get done to a B or C priority. When you're done evaluating, start on tomorrow's to-do list. Be willing to admit mistakes. You might at first rank some items as As only to realize later that they are actually Cs. Some of the Cs that lurk at the bottom of your list day after day might really be As. When you keep a daily to-do list, you can adjust these priorities before they become problems.

The ABC system is not the only way to rank items on your to-do list. Some people prefer the "80-20" system. This is based on the idea that 80 percent of the value of any to-do list comes from only 20 percent of the tasks on that list. So, on a to-do list of 10 items, find the two that will contribute most to your life, and complete those tasks without fail.

Or you can develop your own style for to-do lists. You might find that grouping items by categories such as "errands" or "reading assignments" works best. Be creative.

Keep in mind the power of planning a whole week or even two weeks in advance. Planning in this way can make it easier to put activities in context and see how your daily goals relate to your long-term goals. Weekly planning can also free you from feeling that you have to polish off your whole to-do list in one day. Instead, you can spread tasks out over the whole week.

In any case, make starting your own to-do list an A priority. ✳

practising
CRITICAL THINKING

2-4

Creating your own ABC daily to-do list

Create an ABC daily to-do list in the table below. Remember the five steps: Step 1, brainstorm tasks you need to do today; Step 2, estimate the time for the task; Step 3, rate the priority of the task; Step 4, cross off tasks as you complete them; and Step 5, evaluate your performance. Try doing this exercise on paper or even with the Reminder app on your iPhone or *Google Keep* on your Android. There are also lots of other to-do apps, such as *Wonderlist: To-Do List & Tasks* or *Remember the Milk*; check out what you can find online and see what works best for you.

When using the ABC priority method, you might experience an ailment common to students: C fever. This is the uncontrollable urge to drop that A task and begin crossing Cs off your to-do list. If your history paper is due tomorrow, you might feel compelled to vacuum the rug, call your third cousin in Tulsa, and make a trip to the store for shoelaces. The reason C fever is so common is that A tasks are usually more difficult or time-consuming to achieve, with a higher risk of failure.

If you notice symptoms of C fever, ask yourself this: Does this job really need to be done now? Do I really need to organize my music collection, or might I better use this time to study for tomorrow's accounting exam? Use your to-do list to keep yourself on task, working on your As. Don't panic or berate yourself when you realize that in the last six hours, you have completed 11 Cs and not a single A. Calmly return to the As.

Step 1: Brainstorm all tasks	Step 2: Estimate time for each task	Steps 3 & 4: Rate all tasks as A=Most important B= Less important C= No immediate action needed Next, cross off tasks as you complete them	Step 5: Evaluate
1.			
2.			
3.			
4.			

Make time-maximizing choices about
MULTITASKING

Oleksiy Mark/Shutterstock.com

When we get busy, we get tempted to do several things at the same time. It seems like such a natural solution: Watch a show on Netflix *and* read a textbook. Talk on the phone *and* outline a paper. Write an email *and* listen to a lecture. These are examples of multitasking.

There's a problem with this strategy: Multitasking is much harder than it looks. If you multitask too much or do it unwisely, you will be wasting more time than you are saving. Despite the awe-inspiring complexity of the human brain, research reveals that we are basically wired to do one thing at a time (Lien, Ruthruff, & Johnston, 2005). One study found that people who interrupted work to check email or surf the Internet took up to 25 minutes to get back to their original task (Thompson, 2005). It turns out that managing two or more tasks requires significant attention; dividing your attention just doesn't work. More importantly students who multitask with social media take longer to complete learning activities and have poorer comprehension of the new material they are being taught (Law & Stock, 2017). In the classroom if you are watching movies on your laptop or accessing material that is not related to the class activity,

not only is your learning compromised but students who can see your screen also have their comprehension of class material impaired—so your multitasking has implications for others (Sana, Weston, & Cepeda, 2013).

And it is not just laptops that interfere with learning, students who text during lectures have significant problems taking notes. Why does this happen? If you are distracted by the phone, it should be no surprise that your notes are less complete and that will impact test-taking at a later date (Chen & Yan, 2016). Similarly, accessing social media during class has been shown to have a negative impact on learning (Chen &Yan, 2016). In fact, recent research even suggests that multitasking particularly with media may even have long-term implications for how we learn (Rosen, 2008; Sana et al, 2013). So why do we do it? We switch tasks, particularly while doing school work, for the immediate pleasure given by the media-related activity, like YouTube or Facebook; we haven't enough self-control to stop such impulsive behaviour (Meier, Reinecke, & Meltzer, 2016).

The solution is an old-fashioned one: Whenever possible, take life one task at a time. Develop a key quality of master students—focussed attention. Then add the following strategies to your toolbox.

Capture fast-breaking ideas with minimal interruption

Your brain is an expert nagger. After you choose to focus on one task, it might issue urgent reminders about 10 more things you need to do. Keep a pen and paper handy to write down those reminders. You can take a break later and add them to your to-do list. Your mind can quiet down once it knows that a task has been captured in writing.

Monitor the moment-to-moment shifts in your attention

Whenever you're studying and notice that you're distracted by thoughts of doing something else, make a tally mark on a sheet of paper. Simply being aware of your tendency to multitask can help you reclaim your attention.

Handle interruptions with care

Some breaking events are so urgent that they call for your immediate attention. When this happens, note what you were doing when you were interrupted. For example, write down the number of the page you were reading, or the name of the computer file you were creating. When you return to the task, your notes can help you get up to speed again.

Multitask by conscious choice

If multitasking seems inevitable, then do it with skill. Pair one activity that requires concentration with another activity that you can do almost automatically. For example, studying for your psychology exam while doing laundry is a way to reduce the disadvantages of multitasking. Pretending to listen to your children while looking at Facebook is not.

Align your activities with your passions

Our attention naturally wanders when we find a task to be trivial, pointless, or irritating. At those times, switching attention to another activity becomes a way to reduce discomfort.

Handling routine tasks is a necessary part of daily life. But if you find that your attention frequently wanders throughout the day, ask yourself: Am I really doing what I want to do? Do my work and my classes connect to my interests?

If the answer is no, then the path beyond multitasking might call for a change in your academic and career plans. Determine what you want most in life. Then use the techniques in this chapter to set goals that inspire you. Whenever an activity aligns with your passion, the temptation to multitask loses power. ✳

THERE IS AN APP FOR THAT:
Using technology for time management

Time management tools generally fall into two major categories, no matter which system or set of techniques you use:

- *Lists* of goals and planned actions for meeting those goals (to-do items).
- *Calendars* for scheduling appointments and keeping track of due dates.

Today you can choose from hundreds of online applications that fill these functions. Many are Web-based and synchronize with apps for smart-phones and tablets. A few options are described here. To find more, search online, using the key words *calendar apps*, *goal setting apps*, *time management apps*, and *to-do list managers*.

Many time management applications are aimed directly at students (see Table 2.1). For instance, *Lifehack* lists 18 top apps and tools for time management (*www.lifehack.org/articles/technology/top-15-time-management-apps-and-tools.html*). There are some great free apps for students: *Office Lens* by Microsoft allows you to take pictures of whiteboards in class and save as a PDF, Word, or PowerPoint® file so you can annotate the file later; *Dragon Dictation* allows you to dictate your homework and then paste the file into any application using your phone's clipboard; and *myHomework Student Planner* helps you to keep track of your course schedule and homework and even sends you reminders about due dates. Search for *best student apps* for other tools that you might find helpful.

What to consider before you choose an app

You'll be spending a lot of time with your calendar, list manager, and other apps. Choose carefully and be willing to read reviews and test-drive several before making a final choice. Be sure to consider aspects such as ease of use and options for backing up your data.

Price is not always a major factor as many free apps will meet your needs. Also remember that all of these tools are optional. People lived organized lives long before computers were invented. Even today, there are plenty of people who plan effectively with pencil and paper. The goal is to actually get stuff done. Keep it simple, make it easy, and do what works. ✳

Table 2.1 *Time Management Tools*

Purpose	Application	Uses
Calendar	*Google Calendar* (*www.google.com/calendar*)	Keep track of scheduled events and share them with other people; use Tasks for your to-do list; coordinate your data with other Google online applications
Calendar	*30 Boxes* (*30boxes.com*)	Keep track of scheduled events, and share them with other people
File-syncing	*Dropbox* (*www.dropbox.com*)	Keep your files in one place so there is no need to email yourself backups
Goal setting	*Goals on Track* (*www.goalsontrack.com*)	List SMART goals, and track your progress toward achieving them
Lists	*Gubb* (*www.gubb.net*)	Create and edit lists (including to-do lists), check off completed items, assign due dates to items, and send lists via email or text messaging
Lists	*Todoist* (*www.todoist.com*)	Access tasks and projects anywhere. Collaborate with others.
Lists	*Remember the Milk* (*www.rememberthemilk.com*)	Create and manage tasks online and offline, and send yourself reminders
Lists	*IRUNURUN* (*www.irunurun.com*)	See your daily, weekly progress on goals and get support from a community of people.
Multipurpose	*OneDrive* (*onedrive.live.com/about/en-ca/*)	Create and share files and photos. Access files on and offline
Multipurpose	*Google Drive* (*docs.google.com*)	Gives you free access to create and share documents, spreadsheets, presentations, and forms
Multipurpose	*Office Online* (*products.office.com/en-us/office -online/documents-spreadsheets -presentations-office-online*)	Gives you free access to Word, PowerPoint®, Excel, and OneNote

PLANNING
sets you free

Planning sets you free. When you set goals and manage time, your life does not just happen by chance. You are on equal terms with the greatest sculptor, painter, or playwright. More than creating a work of art, you are designing a life.

Without planning, we simply "dig in." We forget the difference between being busy and being productive. Planning replaces this behaviour with clearly defined outcomes and action steps. As we focus on our most important activities, we are free to let go of everything else. We can actually end up doing less and being more effective at the same time. Turns out that super-productive people are all planners; they schedule everything—even down time (Brenza, 2016).

An effective plan is flexible, not carved in stone. You can change your plans frequently and still preserve the advantages of planning—choosing your overall direction and taking charge of your life. And even when other people set the goal, you can choose how to achieve it.

Planning is a creative venture that lasts for a lifetime. Following are suggestions that flow directly from this point of view.

Back up to a bigger picture

When choosing activities for the day or week, step back for a few minutes and consider your longer-range goals—what you want to accomplish in the next six months, the next year, the next five years, and beyond.

Ask whether the activities you're about to schedule actually contribute to those goals. If they do, great. If not, ask whether you can delete some items from your calendar or to-do list to make room for goal-related activities. See if you can free up at least one hour each day for doing something you love instead of putting it off to a more "reasonable" or "convenient" time. Staying open-minded about what you can achieve can lead to a future you never dreamed was possible. It's also part of having a growth mindset.

Look for what's missing—and what to maintain

Goals often arise from a sense of what's missing in our lives. Goal setting is fuelled by problems that are not resolved, projects that are incomplete, relationships we want to develop, and careers we still want to pursue.

However, not all planning has to spring from a sense of need. You can set goals to maintain things that you already have, or to keep doing the effective things that you already do. If you exercise vigorously three times each week, you can set a goal to keep exercising. If you already have a loving relationship with your spouse, you can set a goal to nurture that relationship for the rest of your life.

Return to the present

Once you've stated your longest-range goals, work backward until you can define a next step to take. Suppose your 30-year goal is to retire and maintain your present standard of living. Ask yourself, "To do that, what financial goals do I need to achieve in 20 years? In 10 years? In 1 year? In 1 month? In 1 week?" Put the answers to these questions in writing. Some people refer to this as "backward planning." It's a way to drill down to details after thinking forward into the future.

Schedule fixed blocks of time first

When planning your week, start with class time and work time. These time periods are usually determined in advance, so other activities must be scheduled around them. Then schedule essential daily activities such as sleeping and eating. In addition, schedule some time each week for actions that lead directly to one of your written goals.

Set clear starting and stopping times

Tasks often expand to fill the time we allot to them. "It always takes me an hour just to settle into a reading assignment" might become a self-fulfilling prophecy.

Try scheduling a certain amount of time for a reading assignment—set a timer on your phone, and stick to it. This technique is called time boxing. Instead of working on the task until it's done, commit to work on it just for that specific amount of time. Set your timer, and get to work. In effect, you're placing the task inside a definite "box"—a specific space on your daily calendar.

Time boxing is one way to overcome resistance to a task, focus your attention, and make a meaningful dent in large projects. The amount of time you choose can be relatively small—even 10 minutes. You can start with short periods, and gradually increase them. Feeling rushed or sacrificing quality is not the goal here. The point is to push yourself a little and discover what your time requirements really are.

Schedule for flexibility and fun

Recognize that unexpected things will happen, and allow for them. Leave some holes in your schedule. Build in blocks of unplanned time. Consider setting aside time each week marked "flex time" or "open time." Use these hours for emergencies, spontaneous activities, errands, catching up, or seizing new opportunities.

Also make room for fun. Fun is important. Brains that are constantly stimulated by new ideas and new challenges need time off to digest them. Take time to browse aimlessly through the library, stroll with no destination, ride a bike, or do other things you enjoy. It's important to "waste" time once in a while.

To maintain flexibility and fun, be realistic. Don't set yourself up for failure by telling yourself you can do a four-hour job in two hours. There are only 168 hours in a week. If you schedule 169 hours, you're sunk.

Plan for changes in your workload

You might find yourself with a lighter load of assignments to complete during the first few days or weeks of any course. This typically happens when instructors give an overview of the subject or take time to review material that you already know from another course. However, don't let your homework slide. Once the term gets going, courses often switch to a much faster pace with profs increasing the readings and assignments.

To stay on top of your workload over the entire term, plan for such a change of pace. Stay on top of your assignments right from the start. Whenever possible, work ahead. This tactic gives you an edge when the load for a course gets heavier, or when big assignments for several courses are due during the same week.

Tips for Master Students

Read your syllabi and map out your semester

You can normally anticipate lots of work around midterms and the end of the semester. If you take a few moments to make a plan, you won't get caught off-guard or forget an assignment, and can use your time wisely for both work and fun.

—Tim O'Connell, professor of recreation and leisure studies at Brock University; 2017 3M National Teaching Fellow. (*Maclean's*, 2017)

Source: Advice for first-year students from Justin Trudeau (and 27 other people), by *Maclean's*, *Maclean's*, December 1, 2017.

Start the day with your most important task

Review your to-do list and calendar first thing each morning. Then visualize the rest of your day as a succession of tasks. Your most important task would be the A task on your ABC to-do list. This is the thing that you want to complete today without fail. Behold your Most Important Task (MIT). Do it as early in the day as possible and put effort into doing this task well.

The time management cycle: Pulling it all together

These steps reflect the time management cycle illustrated in Figure 2.6. By thinking through each step of your plan, you are more likely to achieve your goals and reduce the stress that school (and life) can bring. ✳

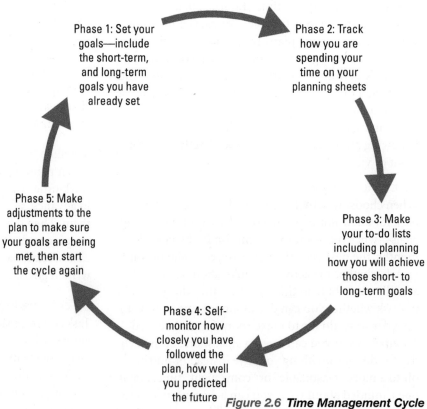

Phase 1: Set your goals—include the short-term, and long-term goals you have already set

Phase 2: Track how you are spending your time on your planning sheets

Phase 3: Make your to-do lists including planning how you will achieve those short- to long-term goals

Phase 4: Self-monitor how closely you have followed the plan, how well you predicted the future

Phase 5: Make adjustments to the plan to make sure your goals are being met, then start the cycle again

Figure 2.6 **Time Management Cycle**

Stop **PROCRASTINATION** now

Consider a bold idea: The way to begin to stop procrastinating is to choose to stop procrastinating. Giving up procrastination is actually a simple choice; people make it complicated.

Test this idea for yourself. Think of something that you've been putting off. Choose a small, specific task—one that you can complete in five minutes or less. Then do that task today. Procrastination is both about *starting* and *finishing* tasks (Mann, 2016).

So, tomorrow, choose another task and do it. Repeat this strategy each day for one week. Notice what happens to your habit of procrastination.

If the above suggestion just doesn't work for you, then experiment with any strategy from the list below. (Just don't put it off.)

Discover the costs

Find out if procrastination keeps you from getting what you want. Clearly seeing the side effects of procrastination can help you kick the habit.

Be wary of social media

Recognize that giving in to the short-term "feel good" of quickly checking Facebook can have a long-term impact on getting the work done. Many students say that when they participate in social media they just lose track of time and this causes a delay in getting the work done (Meier, Reinecke, & Meltzer, 2016). They also end up feeling more stressed than ever. Check the result of the exercise in Practising Critical Thinking 2-2, "Seeing Where All the Time Goes," to see how much time you are spending on social media. Are you controlling your time on social media, or are you letting it control you?

Find out if you are a procrastinator

You probably already have an idea about whether or not you are a procrastinator, but one way to find out is to do a simple inventory online. Keep in mind that we all procrastinate at times. Delaying action is only a problem when it interferes with your successfully completing your goals. Complete this online inventory and you just might be surprised: *www.psychologytoday.com/tests /career/procrastination-test-abridged*

Discover your procrastination style

Psychologist Linda Sapadin (1997) identifies different styles of procrastination. For example, *dreamers* have big

AnemStyle/Shutterstock.com

goals that they seldom translate into specific plans. *Worriers* focus on the worst-case scenario and are likely to talk more about problems than about solutions. *Defiers* resist new tasks or promise to do them and then don't follow through. *Overdoers,* also known as *pleasers*, create extra work for themselves by refusing to delegate tasks and neglecting to set priorities. And *perfectionists* put off tasks for fear of making a mistake.

Awareness of your procrastination style is a key to changing your behaviour. If you exhibit the characteristics of an overdoer, for example, then say no to new projects. Also ask for help in completing your current projects.

To discover your procrastination style, observe your behaviour. Avoid judgments. Just be a scientist: Record the facts. You can also do an online quiz to identify your style at *www.beatprocrastinationcoach.com/faq/Quiz.htm.*

Write Discovery Statements about specific ways you procrastinate. Follow up with Intention Statements about what to do differently.

Trick yourself into getting started

If you have a 50-page chapter to read, then grab the book and say to yourself, "I'm not really going to read this chapter right now. I'm just going to flip through the pages and scan the headings for 10 minutes."

Tricks like these can get you started on a task you've been dreading.

Let feelings follow action

If you put off exercising until you feel energetic, you might wait for months. Instead, get moving now. Then watch your feelings change. After five minutes of brisk walking, you might be in the mood for a 20-minute run. This principle—action generates motivation—can apply to any task that you've put on the back burner.

Choose to work under pressure

Sometimes people thrive under pressure. As one writer puts it, "I don't do my *best* work under deadline. I do my *only* work under deadline." Used selectively, this strategy might also work for you.

Put yourself in control. If you choose to work with a due date staring you right in the face, then schedule a big block of time during the preceding week. Until then, enjoy!

Think ahead

Use the monthly calendar in Figure 2.8 or the long-term planner in Figure 2.10 to list due dates for assignments in all your courses or set reminders in your phone. Using these tools, you can anticipate heavy demands on your time and take action to prevent last-minute crunches. Make *Becoming a Master Student* your home base—the first place to turn in taking control of your schedule.

The 7-step day antiprocrastination plan

Listed here are seven strategies you can use to reduce or eliminate many sources of procrastination. The suggestions are tied to the days of the week to help you remember them. Use this list to remind yourself that each day of your life presents an opportunity to stop the cycle of procrastination.

MONDAY Make it meaningful. What is important about the task you've been putting off? List all the benefits of completing it. Look at it in relation to your short- or long-term goals. Be specific about the rewards for getting it done, including how you will feel when the task is completed. To remember this strategy, keep in mind that *meaningful* starts with the letter *M*, like the word *Monday*.

TUESDAY Take it apart. Break big jobs into a series of small ones you can do in 15 minutes or less. If a long reading assignment intimidates you, divide it into two-page or three-page sections. Make a list of the sections and cross them off as you complete them so you can see your progress. Even the biggest projects can be broken down into a series of small tasks. This strategy *Take it apart* starts with the letter *T*, so mentally tie it to *Tuesday*.

WEDNESDAY Write an Intention Statement. For example, if you can't get started on a term paper, you might write, "I intend to write a list of at least 10 possible topics by 9:00 p.m. I will reward myself with an hour of guilt-free recreational reading." Write your intention on an index card and carry it with you, or post it in your study area where you can see it often. In your memory, file the first word in this strategy—*write*—with *Wednesday*.

THURSDAY Tell everyone. Publicly announce your intention to get a task done. Tell a friend that you intend to learn 10 irregular French verbs by Saturday. Tell your spouse, roommate, parents, and children. Include anyone who will ask whether you've completed the assignment or who will suggest ways to get it done. Make the world your support group. Associate *tell* with *Thursday*.

FRIDAY Find a reward. Construct rewards for yourself carefully. Be willing to withhold them if you do not complete the task. Don't pick a movie as a reward for studying biology if you plan to go to the movie anyway. And when you legitimately reap your reward, notice how it feels. Remember that *Friday* is a fine day to *find* a reward. (Of course, you can find a reward on any day of the week. Rhyming *Friday* with *fine day* is just a memory trick.)

SATURDAY Settle it now. Do it now. The minute you notice yourself procrastinating, plunge into the task. Imagine yourself at a cold mountain lake, poised to dive. Gradual immersion would be slow torture. It's often less painful to leap. Then be sure to savour the feeling of having the task behind you. Link *settle* and *savour* with *Saturday*.

SUNDAY Say no. When you keep pushing a task into a low-priority category, re-examine your purpose for doing it at all. If you realize that you really don't intend to do something, quit telling yourself that you will. That's procrastinating. Just say no. Then you're not procrastinating. You don't have to carry around the baggage of an undone task. *Sunday*—the last day of this seven-day plan—is a great day to finally let go and just *say* no.

Play with antiprocrastination apps

There are apps for everything these days, including procrastination. Many of these are based on the Pomodoro Technique (*pomodorotechnique.com*). This method is simple (a key benefit for procrastinators): Set a timer for 25 minutes. During that period, get started on just one task that you've been putting off. Then take a five-minute break.

The beauty of this technique is twofold. First, you can do just about anything for 25 minutes—especially when you know a break is coming up. Second, 25 minutes is enough to actually accomplish something. It might even make you interested in going for another 25 minutes. Find apps for the Pomodoro Technique by searching the Web. Even simpler: Use a kitchen timer or the alarm on your smartphone.

Create goals that draw you forward

A goal that grabs you by the heartstrings is an inspiration to act now. If you're procrastinating, then set some goals that excite you. Then you might wake up one day and discover that procrastination is part of your past. ✳

practising
CRITICAL THINKING

2-5

1. List five areas of your life in which you procrastinate, and describe them briefly in the first column below.

2. Look back at the articles you just read about procrastination, and pick a procrastination tool that you think might work to help you overcome each of your five procrastination areas. Write that tool in the second column.

3. In the third column, describe specifically how you will implement the procrastination tool.

Example:

Procrastination area	Potential tool	Specific plan
1. Not starting my research project.	Take It Apart	Break down the project as follows:
		Topic/thesis statement (week 1)
		Preliminary research (week 2)
		In-depth research (week 3)
		First draft (week 4)
		Revision for final version (week 5)

_____

_____

_____

_____

_____

_____

_____

_____

_____

_____

_____

_____

23 WAYS TO GET
the most out of now

THE FOLLOWING time-management techniques are about
- Choosing your time
- Choosing your place
- Getting focussed when you study
- Questions that keep you focussed

Don't feel pressured to use all of the techniques listed below or to tackle them in order. As you read, note the suggestions you think will be helpful. Pick one technique to use now. When it becomes a habit, come back to this article and select another one. Repeat this cycle and enjoy the results as they unfold in your life.

Ammentorp Photography/Shutterstock.com

Choosing your time

1 Study difficult (or "boring") subjects first. If your chemistry problems put you to sleep, get to them first, while you are fresh. We tend to give top priority to what we enjoy studying, yet the courses we find most difficult often require the most creative energy. With that task out of the way, the rest of the day can be a breeze. Save your favourite subjects for later.

Continually being late with course assignments indicates a trouble area. Further action is required. Clarify your intentions about the course by writing down your feelings in a journal, talking with an instructor, or asking for help from a friend or counsellor. Consistently avoiding study tasks can also be a signal to re-examine your course program or major.

2 Be aware of your best time of day. Many people learn best in daylight hours. If this is true for you, schedule study time for your most difficult subjects before nightfall.

Others experience the same benefits by staying up late. They flourish after midnight. If you aren't convinced,

then experiment. When you're in a time crunch, get up early or stay up late. You might even see a sunrise.

3 Use waiting time. Five minutes waiting for a bus, 20 minutes waiting for the dentist, 10 minutes between classes—waiting time adds up fast. Have short study tasks ready to do during these periods. For example, you can carry a notebook with facts, formulas, or definitions and pull it out anywhere.

A mobile phone with an audio recording app can help you use commuting time to your advantage. Make recordings of yourself reading your notes or find out if your instructor has made a podcast of the last class session. Then play these in the car stereo as you drive, or listen through your headphones as you ride on the bus or subway.

4 Study two hours for every hour you're in class. Students in higher education are regularly advised to allow two hours of study time for every hour spent in class. If you are in class 15 hours each week, then plan to spend 30 hours a week studying. That adds up to 45 hours each week for school—more than a full-time job. The benefits of thinking in these terms will be apparent at exam time.

You can be flexible about spending more time on one course you find challenging than on courses you find easier, but just make sure that at the end of week you keep to the "two to one rule for studying." Start by looking at your Time Monitor/ Time Plan to see how much time you currently spend studying; then look to see what adjustments are needed to get in the required study time.

Keep in mind that the quality of your study time counts as much as the quantity. Being focussed is the key to successful studying. Just being at your desk is not enough if your time is spent watching YouTube videos or daydreaming.

5 **Monitor how much time you spend online.** Avoid spending your time on high-tech time-wasters like responding to social media or email notifications. Turn off the email alerts and plan to check your emails only during breaks in studying. Most super-productive people only check email a couple of times a day (Brenza, 2016). Review your Time Monitor/Time Plan to see how much time you spend on social media or video games and then make a conscious choice about how you want to spend your time. Dr. Pychyl (2010) warns that we need to beware of push technologies that remind us of incoming emails and text messages. It is just too easy to give in to the impulse to read these messages when they are literally being pushed at us. Turn off those functions on your phones and devices to help resist the temptation to respond. Staying on constant alert for a new text, Tweet, or Facebook update distracts you from achieving your goals.

Choosing your place

6 **Use a regular study area.** Your body and your mind know where you are. Using the same place to study, day after day, helps train your responses. Study where you'll be alert—not, for instance, in an easy chair or in bed. In bed, your body gets a signal. For most students, that signal is more likely to be "Time to sleep!" than "Time to study!" Just as you train your body to be alert at your desk, you also train it to slow down near your bed. For that reason, don't study where you sleep. If you live in residence, there is probably a study hall. Try studying there rather in close proximity to your bed in your dorm room. Learning requires energy so put yourself in a situation that supports this message.

Libraries are designed for learning. The lighting is perfect. The noise level is low in quiet study areas. Entering a library is a signal to focus the mind and get to work. Many students can get more done in a shorter time frame at the library than anywhere else. Experiment for yourself.

Getting focussed when you study

7 **Set limits on screen time.** Access to the Internet and wireless technologies offers easy ways to procrastinate. In his book *Crazy Busy: Overstretched, Overbooked, and About to Snap*, Edward Hallowell (2006) coined a word to describe these activities when they're done too often—*screensucking*. To get an accurate picture of your involvement in playing computer games, accessing social media, and participating in other online activity, use the Time Monitor exercise included earlier in this chapter. Then make conscious choices about how much time you want to spend online.

These activities can have a definite impact on meeting your academic goals. A recent survey of college students by the American College Health Association (2016) found that 19.8 percent said that their Internet use and computer gaming had interfered with their academic performance, such as causing a lower grade on an exam or assignment.

While using your laptop or tablet, consider applications such as *Freedom* (*freedom.to*), *SelfControl* (*self-controlapp.com*), and *Cold Turkey* (*getcoldturkey.com*). These limit or block Internet access for an amount of time that you determine in advance.

8 **Pay attention to your attention.** Breaks in concentration are often caused by internal interruptions. Your own thoughts jump in to divert you from your studies. When this happens, notice these thoughts and let them go. Perhaps the thought of getting something else done is distracting you. One option is to handle that other task now and study later. Or you can write yourself a note about it or schedule a specific time to do it.

9 **Agree with living mates about study time.** This includes roommates, partners, and children. Make the rules clear and be sure to follow them yourself. Explicit agreements—even written contracts—work well. Hang a "Do not disturb" sign on your door. Using signs can relieve you of the need to deal with each interruption—a time-saver in itself.

10 **Turn off your devices and stop checking your messages.** The phone is the ultimate interrupter. People who wouldn't think of distracting you in person might text or call you at the worst times because they can't see that you are studying. You don't have to be a phone victim. If a simple "I'm busy, I'm studying" doesn't work, use dead silence or don't respond to the message. Turns out that even if you don't answer the phone just hearing it buzz interferes with your ability to do your work and causes your problem-solving skills to decrease (Carr, 2017). Set your smartphone to "airplane mode" to disable texts and calls.

11 Learn to say no. This is a timesaver and a valuable life skill for everyone. Some people feel it is rude to refuse a request. But saying no can be done effectively and courteously. Others want you to succeed as a student. When you tell them that you can't do what they ask because you are busy educating yourself, most people will understand.

12 Get ready the night before. Completing a few simple tasks just before you go to bed can help you get in gear the next day. If you need to make some phone calls first thing in the morning, look up those numbers, write them on a sticky note it and set it near the phone. If you plan to spend the next afternoon writing a paper, get your materials together: notes, outline, paper, pencil, flash drive, laptop—whatever you will need. Pack your lunch or put gas in the car. Organize the baby's diaper bag and your messenger bag or backpack.

13 Avoid noise distractions. To promote concentration, avoid studying in front of a screen and turn off your music too. Many students insist that they study better with background noise, and this might be true. Some students report good results with carefully selected and controlled music. For many others, silence is the best form of music to study by.

At times, noise levels might be out of your control. Your neighbours might decide to find out how far they can turn up their music before the walls crumble. Schedule study sessions during periods when your living environment is usually quiet. If you live in residence, ask if study rooms are available. Or go somewhere else where it's quiet, such as the library.

14 Manage interruptions. Sometimes interruptions happen. Create a system for dealing with them. Try to make sure you get back on track as fast as possible. One option is to write a quick note to remind about what you're doing the moment an interruption occurs. As soon as possible, return to the note and pick up the task where you left off.

Questions that keep you focussed

15 Ask: What is one task I can accomplish toward achieving my goal? This is a helpful technique to use when faced with a big, imposing job. Pick out one small accomplishment, preferably one you can complete in about five minutes; then do it. The satisfaction of getting one thing done can spur you on to get one more thing done. Meanwhile, the overall job gets smaller.

16 Ask: Am I being too hard on myself? If you are feeling frustrated with a reading assignment, if your attention wanders repeatedly, or if you've fallen behind on math problems that are due tomorrow, take a minute to listen to the messages you are giving yourself. Are you scolding yourself too harshly? Lighten up. Allow yourself to feel a little foolish and then get on with the task at hand. Don't add to the problem by berating yourself.

Labelling and generalizing weaknesses are other ways people are hard on themselves. Being objective and specific will help eliminate this form of self-punishment and will likely generate new possibilities. An alternative to saying, "I'm terrible in algebra," is to say, "I don't understand factoring equations." This rewording suggests a plan to improve.

17 Ask: Is this a piano? Carpenters who construct rough frames for buildings have a saying they use when they bend a nail or accidentally hack a chunk out of a piece of wood: "Well, this ain't no piano." It means that perfection is not necessary. Ask yourself if what you are doing needs to be perfect. Perhaps you don't have to apply the same standards of grammar to lecture notes that you would apply to an essay. If you can complete a job 95 percent perfectly in two hours and 100 percent perfectly in four hours, ask yourself whether the additional 5 percent improvement is worth doubling the amount of time you spend.

Sometimes, though, it *is* a piano. A tiny miscalculation can ruin an entire lab experiment. A misstep in solving a complex math problem can negate hours of work. Computers are notorious for turning little errors into nightmares. Accept lower standards only when appropriate.

A related suggestion is to weed out low-priority tasks. The to-do list for a large project can include dozens of items, not all of which are equally important. Some can be done later, while others could be skipped altogether, if time is short.

18 Ask: Can I do just one more thing? Ask yourself this question at the end of a long day. Almost always you will have enough energy to do just one more short task. The overall increase in your productivity might surprise you.

19 Ask: Am I making time for things that are important but not urgent? If we spend most of our time putting out fires, we can feel drained and frustrated. According to Covey (1990), this happens when we forget to take time for things that are not urgent but are truly important. Examples include exercising regularly, reading, spending quality time alone or with family members and friends, and cooking nutritious meals. Each of these can contribute directly to our long-term goals. Yet when schedules get tight, we often forgo these things, waiting for that elusive day when we'll "finally have more time."

That day won't come until we choose to make time for what's truly important. Knowing this, we can use some of the suggestions in this chapter to free up more time.

20 Ask: How did I just waste time? Notice when time passes and you haven't accomplished what you had planned to do. Take a minute to review your actions and note the specific ways you wasted time. We tend to operate by habit, wasting time in the same ways over and over again. When you are aware of things you do that drain your time, you are more likely to catch yourself in the act next time. Observing one small quirk might save you hours. But keep this in mind: Asking you to notice how you waste time is not intended to make you feel guilty. The point is to increase your skill by getting specific information about how you use time.

21 Ask: "Can I delegate this?" Instead of slogging through complicated tasks alone, you can draw on the talents and energy of other people.

You can apply the same principle in your life. Instead of doing all the housework or cooking by yourself, for example, you can assign some of the tasks to family members or room-mates. All of these tactics can free up extra hours for studying. It's not practical or ethical to delegate certain study tasks, such as writing term papers. However, you can still draw on the ideas of others in completing such tasks. For instance, you might form a writing group to edit and critique papers, brainstorm topics or titles, and develop lists of sources. If you are involved with a group project, assign each member a different role or task so that you don't end up doing the lion's share of the work by yourself.

22 Ask: "Could I find the time if I really wanted to?" The way people speak often rules out the option of finding more time. An alternative is to speak about time with more possibility. The next time you're tempted to say, "I just don't have time," pause for a minute. Question the truth of this statement. Could you find four more hours this week for studying? Suppose that someone offered to pay you $10,000 to find those four hours. Suppose too that you will get paid only if you don't lose sleep, call in sick for work, or sacrifice anything important to you. Could you find the time if vast sums of money were involved? Remember that when it comes to school, vast sums of money *are* involved

23 Ask: Am I willing to promise it? This might be the most powerful time-management idea of all. If you want to find time for a task, promise yourself—and others—that you'll get it done.

To make this technique work, do more than say that you'll try or that you'll give it your best shot. Take an oath, as you would in court. Give it your word.

One way to accomplish big things in life is to make big promises. There's little reward in promising what's safe or predictable. No athlete promises to place seventh in the Olympic Games. Chances are that if we're not making big promises, we're not stretching ourselves. Promises can work magic. When our word is on the line, it's possible to discover reserves of time and energy we didn't know existed. Promises can push us to exceed our expectations.

For more helpful tips on how to resist procrastination, go to *www.procrastination.ca/*. On this website, Dr. Tim Pychyl talks about his recent research on this topic and provides links to his blog, comics, and podcasts. Listening to his podcasts on the way to school might just be what you need to do to get things done. ✳

© Tim Pychyl and Paul Mason

BEYOND TIME MANAGEMENT:
Stay focussed on what matters

OPOLJA/Shutterstock.com

ASK SOME PEOPLE about managing time, and a dreaded image appears in their minds.

They see a person with a 50-item to-do list clutching a calendar chock full of appointments. They imagine a robot who values cold efficiency, compulsively accounts for every minute, and has no time for people.

These stereotypes about time management hold a kernel of truth. Sometimes people fixate so much on time management that they fail to appreciate what they are doing. Time management becomes a burden, a process that prevents them from actually enjoying the task at hand. At other times, people who pride themselves on efficiency are merely keeping busy. In their rush to check items off a to-do list, they might be fussing over activities that create little value in the first place.

It might help you to think beyond time management to the larger concept of *planning*. The point of planning is not to load your schedule with obligations. Instead, planning is about getting the important things done and still having time to be human. An effective planner is productive and relaxed at the same time.

Focus on outcomes

You might feel guilty when you occasionally stray from your schedule and spend two hours napping or watching reality TV. But if you're regularly meeting your goals and leading a fulfilling life, there's probably no harm done. Managing time and getting organized are not ends in themselves. It is possible to be efficient, organized, and miserable. Larger outcomes such as personal satisfaction and effectiveness count more than the means used to achieve them.

Visualizing the desired outcome can be as important as having a detailed action plan. Here's an experiment. Write a list of goals you plan to accomplish over the

next six months. Then create a vivid mental picture of yourself attaining them and enjoying the resulting benefits. Visualize this image several times in the next few weeks. File the list away, making a note on your calendar to review it in six months. When six months have passed, look over the list and note how many of your goals you have actually accomplished.

Focus on your own well-being first

Whatever you need to do to stay healthy both mentally and physically, schedule that in first, whether that involves going to the gym regularly, doing yoga, or spending time with elders or friends. Bresciani, Duncan, and Hui Cao (2010) suggest that this is the best way to ensure that key activities that relate to our own well-being actually occur. They suggest that you ask yourself, "How can I plan those well-being activities so there is the least likelihood of them being displaced by other tasks?" Good question. And if you don't know what those well-being activities are, they recommend starting with developing your sense of humour and including some belly laughs in each day.

Do less

Planning is as much about dropping worthless activities as about adding new and useful ones. See whether you can reduce or eliminate activities that contribute little to your values. When you add a new item to your schedule or to-do list, consider dropping a current one.

Slow down

Sometimes it's useful to hurry, such as when you're late for a meeting or about to miss a train. At other times, haste is a choice that serves no real purpose. If you're speeding through the day like a launched missile, consider what would happen if you got to your next destination a little bit later than planned. Rushing to stay a step ahead might not be worth the added strain.

Handle it now

A long to-do list can result from postponing decisions and procrastinating. An alternative is to handle a task or decision immediately. Answer that letter now. Make that phone call as soon as it occurs to you. Allen (2001) suggests finding those things you can do in two minutes or less and do them now. Then you don't have to add the task to your calendar or to-do list.

Remember people

Few people on their deathbed ever say, "I wish I'd spent more time at the office." They're more likely to say, "I wish I'd spent more time with my family and friends." Life is about relationships. Make connections to all sorts of people who cross your path in the day, from your instructors, to friends, to your coach. It turns out that having multiple roles in life is one of the keys to well-being, so don't neglect the people who you value in your life (Bresciani et al., 2010).

OPOLJA/Shutterstock.com

Forget about time

Schedule "downtime"—a period when you're accountable to no one else and have nothing to accomplish—into every day. Even a few minutes spent in this way can yield a sense of renewal. Strictly speaking, time cannot be managed. The minutes, hours, days, and years simply march ahead. What we can do is manage ourselves with respect to time. A few basic principles can help us do that as well as a truckload of cold-blooded techniques. ✳

practising
CRITICAL THINKING

2-6

Master monthly calendar

This exercise will give you an opportunity to step back from the details of your daily schedule and get a bigger picture of your life. The more difficult it is for you to plan beyond the current day or week, the greater the benefit of this exercise.

Your basic tool is a one-month calendar. Use it to block out specific times for upcoming events, such as study group meetings, due dates for assignments, review periods before tests, and other time-sensitive tasks.

To get started, you might want to copy the blank monthly calendar on the next page onto both sides of a sheet of paper. Or make several copies of these pages and tape them together so that you can see several months at a glance.

Alternatively, you can create a calendar from a template in your word processor, download a free calendar online, or use the calendar on your phone.

Also, be creative. Experiment with a variety of uses for your monthly calendar. For instance, you can note day-to-day changes in your health or moods, list the places you visit while you are on holiday, or circle each day that you practise a new habit. For examples of filled-in monthly calendars, see the pages below.

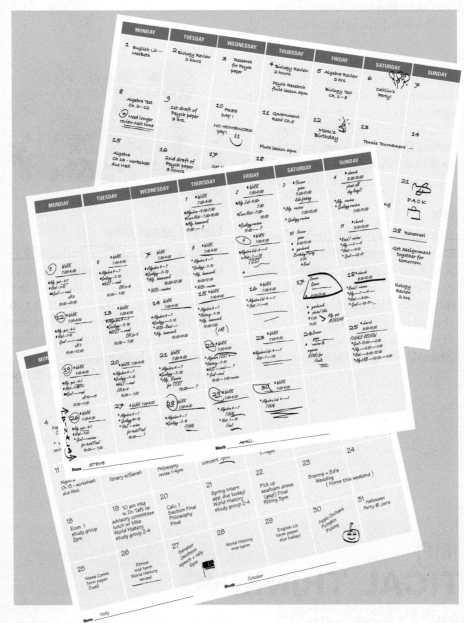

Adapted from © Cengage Learning

Figure 2.7 Sample Calendar of Events

MONDAY	TUESDAY	WEDNESDAY	THURSDAY	FRIDAY	SATURDAY	SUNDAY

Name ______________________ **Month** ______________________

Adapted from © Cengage Learning

Figure 2.8 ***Your Monthly Calendar***

GEARING UP:
Using a long-term planner

PLANNING A DAY, a week, or a month ahead is a powerful practice. Using a long-term planner—one that displays an entire quarter, a session, or a year at a glance—can yield even more benefits.

With a long-term planner, you can eliminate a lot of unpleasant surprises. Long-term planning allows you to avoid scheduling conflicts—the kind that obligate you to be in two places at the same time three weeks from now. You can also anticipate busy periods, such as final exams, and start preparing for them now. Good-bye, all-night cram sessions. Hello, serenity.

Find a long-term planner, or make your own
Buy a planner or be creative and make your own long-term planner. A big roll of newsprint pinned to a bulletin board or taped to a wall will do nicely. There are numerous apps for this too such as *Week Calendar, Touch Calendar or aCalendar*.

Enter scheduled dates that extend into the future
Use your long-term planner to list commitments that extend beyond the current month. Enter test dates, lab sessions, days that classes will be cancelled, and other events that will take place over this term and next term.

Create a master assignment list
Find the syllabus for each course you're currently taking. Then, in your long-term planner, enter the due dates for all of the assignments in all of your courses. This can be a powerful reality check.

The purpose of this process is not to make you feel overwhelmed by all the things you have to do. Rather, its aim is to help you take a First Step toward recognizing the demands on your time. Armed with the truth about how you use your time, you can make more accurate plans.

Include non-academic events
In addition to tracking academic commitments, you can use your long-term planner to mark significant events in your life outside of school. Include birthdays, doctor's appointments, concert dates, credit card payment due dates, and car maintenance schedules.

Use your long-term planner to divide and conquer
For some people, academic life is a series of last-minute crises punctuated by periods of exhaustion. You can avoid that fate. One trick is to set due dates for yourself *before* the final due date. Another trick is to break down big assignments and projects into smaller assignments and subprojects, each with their own due date.

Week of	Monday	Tuesday	Wednesday	Thursday	Friday	Saturday	Sunday
9 / 5							
9 / 12		English quiz					
9 / 19			English paper due		Speech #1		
9 / 26	Chemistry test					Skiing at the lake	
10 / 3		English quiz		Speech #2			
10 / 10			Geography project due				
10 / 17			--- No classes ---				

Adapted from © Cengage Learning

*Figure 2.9 **Sample Long-Term Planner***

Name _____

LONG-TERM PLANNER ___ / ___ / ___ to ___ / ___ / ___

Week of	Monday	Tuesday	Wednesday	Thursday	Friday	Saturday	Sunday
__ / __							
__ / __							
__ / __							
__ / __							
__ / __							
__ / __							
__ / __							
__ / __							
__ / __							
__ / __							
__ / __							
__ / __							
__ / __							
__ / __							
__ / __							
__ / __							
__ / __							
__ / __							
__ / __							
__ / __							
__ / __							
__ / __							
__ / __							
__ / __							
__ / __							
__ / __							
__ / __							
__ / __							
__ / __							
__ / __							

Adapted from © Cengage Learning

Figure 2.10 **Your Long-Term Planner**

When planning to write an important essay, for instance, enter the final due date in your long-term planner. Then set individual due dates for each milestone in the writing process—creating an outline, completing your research, finishing a first draft, editing the draft, and preparing the final copy. By meeting these interim due dates, you make steady progress on the assignment throughout the term. That sure beats trying to crank out all those pages at the last minute. ✳

POWERPROCESS

Persist

Most students enter school with a desire to graduate. Ask them what it takes to success and you'll get a lot of great ideas. What students sometimes forget is the power of persistence—doing the gritty and unglamorous things that really work, day after day.

This is how habits pay off. For instance, exercising for better health is a great idea. And exercising is likely to fail if you only go to the gym once. Networking is highly recommended for finding a job. And pointless if you stop after talking to one person. These are just a couple of examples. The point is the power of any strategy or habit emerges only if you persist.

Research indicates that it takes about 10,000 hours of deliberate practice for athletes, musicians, and other performers to win international competitions (Ericsson, Prietula, & Cokely, 2007). Look into the profiles of the Master Students profiled in this book and you'll find many examples of deliberate practice—a fancy term for persistence.

The manuscripts for the Harry Potter books were rejected by multiple editors. Author J.K.Rowling persisted until she eventually found a publisher. She went on to sell 450 million books.

In 2006, a young student named Stefani Germanotta signed a deal with Def Jam Records. In three months, the company decided her style was not a good fit and cancelled her contract. After that Germanotta spent a couple of years playing in small clubs, making little money, and crafting her performance skills. People noticed. Finally, there was another record deal and a new name for her act: Lady Gaga.

The willingness to persist unleashes many qualities of a master student: competence, courage, self-direction, and more. To make this Power Process work, remember four things. First, persistence is not about positive thinking. Persistence works better when you tell the truth about your current abilities. Accepting who you are—with all your strengths and weaknesses—makes it easier to take setbacks in stride, learn from your mistakes, and move back into action.

Second, persistence is not about blind determination. If a strategy fails to produce the results you want, then feel free to give it up and try another one. Keep your eyes on the prize, and stay flexible about how to achieve it. If plan A fizzles out, then move on to plan B or C.

Third, persistence is not about going it alone. Life is not a solo act. We are social creatures and find strength in community. One key to persistence is to find people who have already achieved what you want. Seek out and spend time with those people. Ask them for guidance. They are living reminders that getting what you want is possible—if you persist.

Finally, persistence calls on you to give up the desire for instant gratification. This can be tough when we see so many advertisements and self-help books telling us we can turn our lives around in just a few days.

Master students harness their critical thinking skills to cut through the hype. They know that they are in the game for the long haul and that there are no quick fixes. They know that getting a degree is a marathon, not a sprint. Every class attended, and every assignment handed in is one small step on the way to a big victory.

Becoming a Master Student is about getting what you ultimately want. There is nothing mysterious about the process of doing this: Discover the outcomes you want to achieve. Make it your intention to do what it takes to produce those outcomes. Than act on your intentions.

And persist.

Put it to WORK

Being skilled at managing time will serve you in any career you choose. Here are some ways to transfer techniques from this chapter to the workplace.

LightField Studios/Shutterstock.com

Monitor work time

Use the Time Monitor/Time Plan process to analyze the way you currently use your time at work. With this awareness, you can minimize downtime and boost your productivity. Look for low-value activities to eliminate. Also note your peak periods of energy during the workday and schedule your most challenging tasks for these times.

Use a long-term planner to manage major projects at work

Besides scheduling a due date for the final product, set interim due dates—what you'll produce at key points leading up to that final date. For example, you're planning to launch a new in-house training program in one year. Set individual due dates for finishing each major component of the program—such as manuals, websites, and videos.

Avoid the perils of multitasking

Our effectiveness often decreases when we try to do several things at once, such as talking on a mobile phone while driving. When you get busy at work, you might feel tempted to multitask. Yet studies indicate that multi-tasking reduces metabolic activity in the brain, lowers the ability to complete tasks efficiently, and increases the number of errors made in following a procedure (Bresciani et al., 2010). Plan your workday as a succession of tasks. Then give each task your full attention. Use the ABC priority system to weed out tasks of lower importance. This can give you more time to focus on the As.

Overcome procrastination

This problem is as widespread in the workplace as it is on any campus. Apply the suggestions from "Stop procrastination NOW" and "The 7-day antiprocrastination plan" to work tasks as well as academic tasks.

Calculate the cost of attending meetings

Meetings are a way of life for countless people in the workplace. In fact, if you're in a management or supervisory position, meetings can take up most of your workday. See if you can to calculate what it costs you to attend a one-hour business meeting. With this data in hand, write an Intention Statement about how you plan to get the most value out of the meetings you will attend in the future.

Use a lifeline to chart your career path

Your career plan can extend decades into the future. Below are some possible lifeline entries for a person focussing on a career in education.

May 2024	Graduate with a teaching degree
August 2025	Begin teaching high school art
September 2032	Apply to go on a savings plan to fund a personal sabbatical
September 2034	Return to school for a graduate degree in school administration
September 2035	Begin career as a high school principal
September 2039	Take a one-year sabbatical to live in New Zealand
September 2040	Return to job as a high school principal
January 2044	Begin a home-based consulting business, advising teachers and principals about ways to avoid career burnout

Do long-term planning for your organization or your chosen career. The strategies for long-term planning in this chapter can help you set goals that extend well into the future. For example, create a lifeline for your work life, listing specific outcomes to achieve during each of the next five years.

QUIZ

Name_____   Date____/____/____

1. Name three ways you can control interruptions when you study.

2. Rewrite the statement "I want to study harder" so that it becomes a specific time-oriented goal.

3. The text suggests that long-term goals are important. Write one example of a long-term goal.

4. Give an example of a performance goal and a learning or mastery goal. Why does it matter which type of goal you aim to reach?

5. What are at least 5 of the 23 ways to get the most out of now?

6. Explain why multitasking is not an effective way to get work done.

7. Define "C fever" as it applies to the ABC priority method.

8. Scheduling marathon study sessions once in a while is generally an effective strategy. True or False? Explain your answer.

9. Describe at least three strategies for overcoming procrastination.

10. Why is persisting at difficult tasks important to academic tenacity?

Skills SNAPSHOT

The Discovery Wheel in Chapter 1 includes a section labelled "Time." For the next 10 to 15 minutes, go beyond your initial responses to that exercise. Take a snapshot of your skills as they exist today, after reading this chapter and completing the exercises in it.

Begin by reflecting on some recent experiences. Then take the next step in your mastery of time by choosing the strategy you'd like to experiment with next.

GOALS

I would describe my ability to set specific goals as . . .

The most important goal for me to achieve during this school year is . . .

DAILY PLANNING

When setting priorities for what to do each day, the first thing I consider is . . .

I keep track of my daily to-do items by . . .

PROCRASTINATION

The kinds of tasks on which I tend to procrastinate include . . .

My strategies for overcoming procrastination currently include . . .

BALANCE

My ability to balance recreation with working and studying can be described as . . .

If I sense that I'm not making enough time for family and friends, I respond by . . .

NEXT ACTION

I'll know that I've reached a new level of mastery with time management and planning when . . .

To reach that level of mastery, the most important thing I can do next is to . . .

Ann Makosinski
... uses her time creatively

Susie Mesure, The Independent,
January 16, 2016

Ann Makosinski (b. 1997) became an inventor at an early age and was named to the *Time* magazine Top 30 Under 30 in 2013. Her inventions aim to improve the life of people worldwide. She studies English literature at UBC to get a balance between the arts and science.

Being told to put down their smartphone and live in the moment is nothing new to most teenagers. But how many teens are the ones doing the telling?

Ann Makosinski is urging thousands of people to ditch their devices and do something else instead with their time. The [then]18-year-old Canadian university student does not even own a smartphone and never has done.

Makosinski, who has won global acclaim for inventing a torch powered solely by the heat from your hand, was speaking at TEDx Teen, a youth-orientated offshoot of the TED Talks programme, held in London. "The main moral of my talk is, next time you pick up your phone, think about all the possibilities off it."

She wants to encourage children—and adults—to be more creative, which requires independent thinking. She described how as a child her parents would refuse to give her toys or let her watch television. And she was never allowed a mobile phone. "My parents didn't want me distracted and playing games on it, because that would be wasting time," she recalls. "So to entertain myself I made my own toys. Not being given everything encourages you to create. . . . That was one of the first steps for me learning to invent things."

Makosinski already has a string of high-profile international awards for her own inventions. As well as the torch, which she came up with for a friend in the Philippines who didn't have electricity at home so couldn't study, she has designed a phone-charging travel mug; she won $50,000 from Shell Canada for her prototype, which uses heat from hot water to funnel electricity to mobile devices. She appreciates the irony, given her antipathy, but says: "It'll appeal to the masses." Despite shunning smartphones Makosinski is no technophobe. She has started making YouTube videos and has an iPod Touch, which she uses to contact her boyfriend via Facebook Messenger.

She also has an analogue "flip phone," which she bought before starting at the University of British Columbia, where she studies arts and science. She laughs, remembering how she had bought a phone with a touch screen but made her father double back to the shop so she could switch it for her analogue handset. She warns that constant fiddling with your phone adds up. "The overall interaction every day is huge. . . . You need to put it down. Just for a day! Try it and see what happens."

Not having a phone in school made her more sociable, she adds. "With everyone texting in high school, I had to interact with people so I didn't look like that awkward person standing in the corner not saying anything." Now she'll ring up for an actual chat. "People nowadays are so afraid of talking on the phone it's ridiculous. They're like, 'I'd rather text'. But if they don't want to talk to you . . . then that's probably a sign that they don't value you as a friend. Or they have issues that they need to deal with!"

Her favourite social media is YouTube; she likes nothing better than making a snack and a cup of hot chocolate and settling down to watch vloggers—Zoella or Tyler Oakley, say—on her laptop. She avoids Facebook, Twitter and Instagram where possible, but admits they are useful for promoting her nascent YouTube channel.

Source: Mesure, S. (2016, January 16). Ann Makosinski: Teenage inventor uses TEDx talk to call on young people to ditch their smartphones. *The Independent.* Retrieved from *http://www.independent.co.uk/life-style/ ann-makosinski-teenage-inventor-uses-tedx-teen-talk -to-call-on-young-people-to-ditch-their-a6816626.html.* Reprinted with permission.

Soul wind/Shutterstock.com

Memory

WHAT if . . .

I could use my memory to its full potential?

WHY this chapter matters

Learning memory techniques can boost your skills at test-taking, reading, note-taking, and many other tasks.

HOW you can use this chapter

Focus your attention.

Make conscious choices about what to remember.

Recall facts and ideas with more ease.

do you have a minute?

Take action to make sure that you remember the important commitments in your academic life right now. Take a minute to pull out your calendar and enter due dates for your current assignments.

Your memory and your brain—
4 KEY PRINCIPLES

SHARPENING YOUR memory starts with understanding how memory depends on that organ in your head—your brain.

Following are four key things to understand about how you remember and learn. They will introduce you to ideas and suggestions that are presented in more detail in the rest of this chapter.

Principle 1: See memory as something you *do*, not something you have

Once upon a time, people talked about human memory as if it were a closet. You stored individual memories there like old shirts and stray socks. Remembering something was a matter of rummaging through all that stuff. If you were lucky, you found what you wanted.

This view of memory creates some problems. For one thing, closets can get crowded; things too easily disappear. Even with the biggest closet, you eventually run out of space. If you want to pack some new memories in there—well, too bad. There's no room. Brain researchers have shattered this image to bits. Memory is not a closet. It's not a place or a thing. Instead, memory is a *process*.

On a conscious level, memories appear as distinct and unconnected mental events: words, sensations, images. They can include details from the distant past—the smell of cookies baking in your grandmother's kitchen or the feel of sunlight warming your face through the window of your Grade 1 classroom. On a biological level, each of those memories involves millions of nerve cells, or **neurons**, firing chemical messages at each other. If you could observe these exchanges in real time, you'd see regions of cells all over the brain glowing with electrical charges at speeds that would put a computer to shame.

When a series of brain cells connects several times in a similar pattern, the result is a memory. Canadian psychologist Donald Hebb (2001) uses the aphorism "Neurons which fire together, wire together" to describe this principle. This means that memories are not really "stored." Instead, remembering is a process in which you **encode** information as links between active neurons that fire together and **decode**, or reactivate, neurons that wired together in the past. Memory is the probability that certain patterns of brain activity will occur again in the future. In effect, you re-create a memory each time you recall it.

Scientists tell us that the human brain is "plastic." Whenever you efficiently encode and decode, your brain changes physically. You grow more connections between neurons. The more you learn, the greater the number of connections. For all practical purposes, there's no limit to how many memories your brain can process. Knowing this allows you to step out of your crowded mental closet into a world of infinite possibilities. There's a lot you can do to wire those neural networks into place. That's where the memory techniques described in this chapter come into play.

Principle 2: Remember that the memory process works in stages

The memory process consists of a series of events. To make the most of your memory, apply an appropriate memory strategy when one of these events takes place:

Pay attention to sense experiences
Memories start as events that we see, hear, feel, touch, or taste. Memory strategies at this stage are about choosing where to focus your attention.

Move sense experiences to short-term memory
Sensory memories last for only a few seconds. If you don't want them to disappear, then immediately apply a strategy for moving them into short-term memory, such as reciting the information to yourself several times. Short-term memory is a place where you can "hold" those fleeting sensory memories for up to several minutes but only while you are actively working with memory. **Working memory** helps you to plan and carry

out behaviour such as following the steps in a recipe. You want to get the steps in the right order to make a successful pie but not necessarily memorize the steps for life. Having a good working memory has been found to be highly correlated with both intelligence and academic achievement (Burmester, 2017).

Encode for long-term memory

If you want to recall information for more than a few minutes, then wire the new neural connections in a more stable way. This calls for a more sophisticated memory strategy—one that allows you to refire the connections for days, weeks, months, or even years into the future. Working memory is typically regarded as the entry point to long-term memory. If you rehearse and elaborate on information long enough, it is more likely to become part of your long-term memory, where permanent changes occur to your neurons and strengthen the connections between them (Burmester, 2017).

Decode important information on a regular basis

The more often you recall information, the more stable the memory becomes. To remember it, retrieve it.

Principle 3: Choose strategies for encoding

Mastery in encoding involves making choices about *what* to remember and *how* to remember it. This in turn makes it easier for you to decode, or recall, the material at a crucial point in the future—such as during a test.

Say that you're enjoying a lecture in introduction to psychology. It really makes sense. In fact, it's so interesting that you choose to just sit and listen, without taking notes. Two days later, you're studying for a test and wish you'd made a different choice. You remember that the lecture was interesting, but you don't recall much else. In technical terms, your decision to skip note-taking was an **encoding error**.

So, you decide to change your behaviour and take extensive notes during the next psychology lecture. Your goal is to capture everything the instructor says. This too has mixed results—a case of writer's cramp and 10 pages of dense, confusing scribbles. Oops. Another encoding error.

Effective encoding is finding a middle ground between these two extremes. As you listen and read, you make moment-to-moment choices about what you want to remember. You distinguish between key points, transitions, and minor details. You predict what material is likely to appear on a test. You also stay alert for ideas you can actively apply. These are things you capture in your notes.

You might consider drawing mind map summaries of your readings and lecture notes. Include visual images. Put main ideas in larger letters and brighter colours.

Or try to connect what you are learning now to what you have learned in the past. Ask yourself, "How do these new ideas relate to what I already know?"

Principle 4: Choose strategies for decoding

You've probably experienced the "tip of the tongue" phenomenon. You know that the fact or idea that you want to remember is just within reach—so close that you can almost feel it. Even so, the neural connections stop just short of total recall. This is an example of a decoding glitch.

No need to panic. You have many options at this point. These are known as decoding strategies. For example:

Relax—your mood affects your memory

The information that you want to recall is less likely to appear if you're feeling overly stressed. Taking a long, deep breath and relaxing muscles can work wonders for your body and your brain.

Let it go for the moment

When information is at the tip of your tongue, one natural response is to try hard to remember it. However, this can just create more stress that in turn interferes with decoding. Another option is to stop trying to decode and to do something else for the moment. Don't be surprised if the memory you were seeking suddenly pops into your awareness while you're in the midst of an unrelated activity.

Recall something else

Many encoding strategies are based on associations—finding relationships or connections between something you already know and something new that you want to remember. This means that you can often recall by taking advantage of those associations. Say you're taking a multiple-choice test and can't remember the answer to a question. Instead of worrying about it, just move on. You might latter come across a question on the same topic that triggers the answer to the earlier question. This happens when a key association is activated.

Recreate the original context

Encoding occurs at specific times and places. If a fact or idea eludes you at the moment, then see whether you can recall where you were when you first learned it. Think about what time of day that learning took place and what kind of mood you were in. Sometimes you can decode the information merely by remembering where you first saw the information on the whiteboard or where on the page you saw it in a book.

There are many other strategies you can use to effectively encode and retrieve memories, and we will cover more of them later in this chapter. ✳

Discovery/Intention Statement

Create Value from This Chapter

Write a sentence or two describing the way you feel when you want to remember something but have trouble doing so. Think of a specific incident in which you experienced this problem, such as trying to remember someone's name or a fact you needed during a test.

I discovered that I . . .

_____

_____

_____

_____

_____

Now spend five minutes skimming this chapter and find three to five memory strategies you think could be helpful. List the strategies below and note the page numbers where they are explained. Then write an Intention Statement scheduling a time to study them in more detail.

Strategy   **Page number**

_____

_____

_____

_____

_____

I intend to . . .

_____

_____

_____

_____

_____

_____

_____

_____

_____

_____

The memory JUNGLE

THINK OF YOUR MEMORY as a vast, overgrown jungle. This memory jungle is thick with wild plants, exotic shrubs, twisted trees, and creeping vines. It spreads over thousands of kilometres—dense, tangled, forbidding. _The more often you recall information, and the more often you put the same information into your memory, the easier it is to find._

© Michael Atkinson

Imagine that the jungle is surrounded on all sides by towering mountains. There is only one entrance to the jungle: a small meadow that is reached by a narrow pass through the mountains.

In the jungle there are animals, millions of them. The animals represent all of the information in your memory.

Imagine that every thought, mental picture, or perception you ever had is represented by an animal in this jungle. Every single event ever perceived by any of your five senses—sight, touch, hearing, smell, or taste—has also passed through the meadow and entered the jungle. Some of the thought animals, such as the colour of your Grade 7 teacher's favourite sweater, are well hidden. Other thoughts, such as your cellphone number or the position of the reverse gear in your car, are easier to find.

There are two rules of the memory jungle. Each thought animal must pass through the meadow at the entrance to the jungle. And once an animal enters the jungle, it never leaves.

The meadow represents **short-term memory**. You use this kind of memory when you look up a telephone number and hold it in your memory long enough to make a call. Short-term memory appears to have a limited capacity (the meadow is small) and disappears fast (animals pass through the meadow quickly). Your ability to chunk pieces of information together lets you increase the capacity of your short-term memory. Lots of things can lead to information not being transferred from short-term memory. For instance, just after your friend tells you his new phone number, your conversation is interrupted. If you don't have time to rehearse the new number, chances are it won't pass into long-term memory.

The jungle itself represents **long-term memory**. This is the kind of memory that allows you to recall information from day to day, week to week, and year to year. Remember that thought animals never leave the long-term memory jungle. The trick, though, is that although thought animals never leave long-term memory, you may not be able to access a specific thought animal (or memory) when you want to. The following visualizations can help you recall useful concepts about memory.

Visualization #1: A well-worn path

Imagine what happens as a thought—in this case we'll call it an elephant—bounds across short-term memory and into the jungle. The elephant leaves a trail of broken twigs and hoof prints that you can follow. Brain research suggests that thoughts can wear paths in the brain (Brown, Roediger, & McDaniel, 2014). These paths are called **neural traces**. The more well-worn the neural trace, the easier it is to retrieve (recall) the thought. In other words, the more often the elephant retraces the path, the clearer the path becomes. The more often you recall information, and the more often you put the same information into your memory, the easier it is to find. Practising retrieval is the key to memory. For example, when you buy a new car, the first few times you try to find reverse, you have to think for a moment. After you have found reverse every day for a week, the path is worn into your memory. After a year,

© Michael Atkinson

the path is so well-worn that when you dream about driving your car backward, you even dream the correct motion for putting the gear in reverse.

Visualization #2: A herd of thoughts

The second picture you can use to your advantage is the picture of many animals gathering at a clearing—like thoughts gathering at a central location in the memory. It is easier to retrieve thoughts that are grouped together, just as it is easier to find a herd of animals than it is to find a single elephant.

Pieces of information are easier to recall if you can associate them with similar information. So, the organization of material is a key to successful recall

© Michael Atkinson

of information. For example, you can more readily remember a particular player's batting average if you can associate it with other baseball statistics.

Visualization #3: Turning your back

Imagine releasing the elephant into the jungle, turning your back, and counting to 10. When you turn around, the elephant is gone. This is exactly what happens to most of the information you receive.

Generally, we can recall only 50 percent of the material we have just read. Within 24 hours, most of us can recall only about 20 percent. This means that 80 percent

© Debra Dawson

© Michael Atkinson

of the material has not been meaningfully encoded and is wandering around, lost in the memory jungle.

The remedy is simple: Review quickly. Do not take your eyes off the thought animal as it crosses the short-term memory meadow, and review it soon after it enters the long-term memory jungle. Wear a path in your memory immediately.

Visualization #4: You are directing the animal traffic

The fourth picture is one with you in it. You are standing at the entrance to the short-term memory meadow, directing herds of thought animals as they file through the pass, across the meadow, and into your long-term memory. You are taking an active role in the learning process. You are paying attention. You are doing more than sitting on a rock and watching the animals file past into your brain. See what type of animal it is—think about whether you have seen it before or whether it is something new. Try to categorize the thought animals—compare with animals you have seen before (Svinicki, 2004). Connecting these new animals to those you have seen before increases the odds you will recognize them the next time you see them in the memory jungle. Practise getting the animals out of the jungle—what types of animals did you see? (Karpicke & Blunt, 2011). As you engage in this process, you have taken control of your memory. ✳

15 MEMORY TECHNIQUES

EXPERIMENT WITH THESE techniques to develop a flexible, custom-made memory system that fits your style of learning.

The 15 techniques are divided into four categories, each of which represents a general principle for improving memory. Briefly, these are the categories:

1. **Organize it.** Organized information is easier to find.
2. **Use your body.** Learning is an active process; get all of your senses involved.
3. **Use your brain.** Work *with* your memory, not *against* it.
4. **Recall it.**

   This is easier when you use the other principles efficiently to notice and elaborate on incoming information.

The first three categories, which include techniques 1 through 12, are about storing information effectively. Most memory battles are won or lost here.

To get the most out of this article, first survey the following techniques by reading each heading. Then read the techniques. Next, skim them again, looking for the ones you like best. Mark those and use them.

Organize it

1 Be selective. There's a difference between gaining understanding and drowning in information. During your stay in higher education, you will be exposed to thousands of facts and ideas. No one expects you to memorize all of them. To a large degree, the art of memory is the art of selecting what to remember in the first place.

As you dig into your textbooks and notes, make choices about what is most important to learn. Imagine that you are going to create a test on the material and consider the questions you would ask.

When reading, look for chapter previews, summaries, and review questions. Pay attention to anything printed in bold type. Also notice visual elements—tables, charts, graphs, and illustrations. All of these are clues pointing to what's important. During lectures, notice what the instructor emphasizes. Anything that's presented visually—on the board, on overheads, or with PowerPoint® slides—is probably crucial.

2 Make it meaningful. You remember things better if they have meaning to you. One way to create meaning is to learn from the general to the specific. Before you begin your next reading assignment, skim it to locate the main idea. You can use the same techniques you learned in the practising critical thinking exercise "Textbook reconnaissance" in the introductory chapter. If you're ever lost, step back and look at the big picture. The details might make more sense.

You can organize any list of items—even random ones—in a meaningful way to make them easier to remember. In his book *Information Anxiety*, Richard Saul Wurman (1989) proposes five principles for organizing any body of ideas, facts, or objects as outlined in Table 3.1.

3 Create associations. The data already encoded in your neural networks are arranged according to a scheme that makes sense to you. When you introduce new data, you can remember the details more effectively if you associate them with similar or related data.

Think about your favourite courses. They probably relate to subjects that you already know something about. If you know a lot about the history of 20th-century music, you'll find it easier to remember facts about music recorded since 1900. And if you've already passed an advanced algebra course, you're primed to remember calculus formulas.

Table 3.1 Principles for Organizing Ideas, Facts, or Objects

Principle	Example
Organize by **time**	Events in history or in a novel flow in chronological order.
Organize by **location**	Addresses for a large company's regional offices are grouped by province and city.
Organize by **category**	Nonfiction library materials are organized by subject categories.
Organize by **continuum**	Products rated in *Consumer's Guide* are grouped from highest in price to lowest in price, or highest in quality to lowest in quality.
Organize by **alphabet**	Entries in a book index are listed in ABC order.

Even when you're tackling a new subject, you can build a mental store of basic background information—the raw material for creating associations. Preview reading assignments, and complete those readings before you attend lectures. Before taking advanced courses, master the prerequisites. Trying to recall discrete pieces of information increases the memory load and makes it more difficult to recall at a later date. The more associations you form between what you already know (prior knowledge) and what you are trying to learn, the easier it will be for you to recall that info at a later date.

Use your body

4 Learn actively. Action is a great memory enhancer. You can test this theory by studying your assignments with the same energy that you bring to the dance floor or the basketball court.

You can use simple, direct methods to infuse your learning with action. When you sit at your desk, sit up straight. Sit on the edge of your chair, as if you were about to spring out of it and sprint across the room.

Also experiment with standing up when you study. It's harder to fall asleep in this position. Some people insist that their brains work better when they stand.

Pace back and forth and gesture as you recite material out loud. Use your hands. Get your whole body involved in studying.

This technique illustrates the practical advantage of knowing about learning styles. In Chapter 1, the article "Learning styles: Discovering how you learn" explains four aspects of learning: concrete experience, abstract conceptualization, active experimentation, and reflective observation. Many courses in higher education lean heavily toward abstract conceptualization, emphasizing lectures, essays, and textbook assignments. These courses might not give you the chance to act on ideas, to experiment with them, and to test them in situations outside the classroom.

So get involved in activities outside of the classroom that allow you to test what you are learning in class. For example, if you are interested in the environment, get involved with a club that takes you out into nature and see how well the theories hold up in the real world. Bring those experiences back into the classroom.

Your English instructor might tell you that one quality of effective writing is clear organization. To test this idea, examine the texts you come in contact with daily—newspapers, popular magazines, websites, and textbooks. Look for examples of clear organization *and* unclear organization. Then write Intention Statements about ways to organize your own writing more clearly.

Your sociology class might include a discussion about how groups of people resolve conflict. See if you can apply any of these ideas to resolving conflict in your own family or residence. Then write Discovery Statements about your experiences.

The point behind each of these examples is the same: To remember an idea, go beyond thinking about it. *Do* something with it.

5 **Recite and repeat.** When you repeat something out loud, you anchor the concept in two different senses. First, you get the physical sensation in your throat, tongue, and lips when voicing the concept. Second, you hear it. The combined result is synergistic, just as it is when you create pictures. That is, the effect of using two different senses is greater than the sum of their individual effects.

The "out loud" part is important. Reciting silently in your head can be useful—in the library, for example— but it is not as effective as making noise. Your mind can trick itself into thinking it knows something when it doesn't. Your ears are harder to fool.

The repetition part is important, too. Repetition is a common memory device because it works. It is particularly useful when you want to memorize facts—unrelated bits of information, like the capitals of the provinces or types of rocks. However, it leads to what we think of as **shallow processing**—where the information is stored according to its surface features like the shape of the letters or the sound of the words—information that does not really connect to the meaning of the information. So although this can be a very successful strategy for memorizing some types of information, when you can learn pieces of information without learning the meaning, this is not as effective at getting information into long-term memory. Remembering information word for word means you are not getting the in-depth understanding required for **deep learning**. You may have difficulty on a test if the instructor rewords the concept. To get the in-depth understanding required, learn the connections between the concepts. So rather than learning just the names of different rocks, try to learn why and how they differ from one another. Repetition blazes a trail through the pathways of your brain, making the information easier to find. Repeat a concept out loud until you know it, then say it five more times.

Recitation works best when you recite concepts in your own words. For example, if you want to remember that the acceleration of a falling body due to gravity at sea level equals 9.8 metres per second, you might say, "Gravity makes an object accelerate 9.8 metres per second faster for each second that it's in the air at sea level." Putting it in your own words forces you to think about it.

Have some fun with this technique. Recite by writing a song about what you're learning. Sing it in the shower. Use any style you want ("Country, jazz, hip hop, or rap—when you sing out loud, learning's a snap!").

Or imitate someone. Imagine your textbook being read by a celebrity or comedian like John Oliver or Arnold Schwarzenegger ("Talk to the hand. Make my density equal mass over volume.").

Recite and repeat. It's a technique you can use anywhere.

6 **Create pictures.** Draw diagrams. Make cartoons. Use these images to connect facts and illustrate relationships. Associations within and among abstract concepts can be "seen" and recalled more easily when they are visualized. The key is to use your imagination.

For example, Boyle's law states that at a constant temperature the volume of a confined ideal gas varies inversely with its pressure. Simply put, cutting the volume in half doubles the pressure. To remember this concept, you might picture someone "doubled over" using a bicycle pump. As she increases the pressure in the pump by decreasing the volume in the pump cylinder, she seems to be getting angrier. By the time she has doubled the pressure (and halved the volume) she is boiling ("Boyle-ing") mad.

Another reason to create pictures is that visual information is associated with a part of the brain that is different from the part that processes verbal information. When you create a picture of a concept, you are anchoring the information in a second part of your brain. This increases your chances of recalling that information.

To visualize abstract relationships effectively, create an action-oriented image, such as the person using the pump. Make the picture vivid, too. The person's face could be bright red. And involve all of your senses. Imagine how the cold metal of the pump would feel and how the person would grunt as she struggled with it.

Use your brain

7 **Overlearn.** One way to fight mental fuzziness is to learn more than you need to know about a subject simply to pass a test. You can pick a subject apart, examine it, add to it, and go over it until it becomes second nature.

This technique is especially effective for problem-solving. Do the assigned problems, and then do more problems. Many textbooks have study guides attached to them. Do the problems in the guides. Look up additional problems from a reputable source online. Find another textbook and work similar problems. Then

practising
CRITICAL THINKING

3-1

Solidifying your memory

Brown, Roediger, and McDaniel, the authors of *Make It Stick: The Science of Successful Learning* (2014), suggest that engaging in reflection after each lecture or reading assignment helps you solidify your memory by getting you to practise retrieval and to rephrase what you have learned in your own words. After class today, take a few minutes to answer the following five questions. Answering these five questions after every lecture will get you to move from taking a surface approach to learning where you focus on direct recall of facts, to a deeper approach to learning where you are able to apply what you have learned to a variety of situations and to improve your academic performance.

What were the key ideas or concepts?

_____

_____

What are some examples of these key ideas?

_____

_____

How do these ideas relate to what I have already learned?

_____

_____

What concepts or ideas are new to me?

_____

_____

What is my definition for these new ideas or terms?

_____

_____

make up your own problems and solve them. Practice testing is one of the most highly effective strategies for learning, particularly when you space out your testing over a period of time (Brown, Roediger, & McDaniel, 2014). When you pretest yourself in this way, the potential rewards are speed, accuracy, and greater confidence at final exam time.

8 **Escape the short-term memory trap.** Short-term memory is different from the kind of memory you'll need during final exams. For example, most of us can look at an unfamiliar phone number once and remember it long enough to dial it. See if you can recall that number the next day.

Short-term memory can fade after a few minutes, and it rarely lasts more than several hours. At the end of class, take a few minutes to write down the most important points you learned in class today. It's too easy to be writing notes and copying the PowerPoint® slides in class without really thinking about what the instructor is saying. If you know you are going to have to summarize your notes at the end of class, you will pay more attention. Similarly, a short review within minutes or hours of a study session can move material from short-term memory into long-term memory. That quick mini review can save you hours of study time when exams roll around.

9 **Use your times of peak energy.** Study your most difficult subjects during the times when your energy peaks. Many people can concentrate more effectively during daylight hours. The early morning hours can be especially productive, even for those who hate to get up with the sun. Observe the peaks and valleys in your energy flow during the day and adjust study times accordingly. However, be careful not to fall into the trap of waiting to feel energy before you start to study. Sometimes you just have to do it.

10 **Distribute learning.** Literally hundreds of studies in psychology have found that cramming for exams doesn't work (Dunlosky, Marsh, Rawson, Nathan, & Willingham, 2013; Kang, 2016). More than worrying about the number of hours you study, pay more attention to how you space out your studying over the weeks prior to your exam. It has been consistently shown that repeated interactions with your study material lead to better academic performance than mass studying right before the exam. Turns out the old adage "practice makes perfect" really does apply to enhancing learning but only when you distribute your study sessions over a period of time.

With **spaced practice** there are more opportunities to practise retrieving information from long-term memory. Spaced practice also positively impacts transfer of learning so that you are more likely to be able to apply what you know to a new situation during your exam or test.

Learning transfer is important because this is what allows you to relate what you have learned to new tasks, new courses of study, and to the workplace (Scharff et al., 2017). To be effective at learning transfer requires that you become aware of what you know and don't know and then take corrective action to solve any knowledge or skill gaps. Therefore, to enhance learning transfer effects, make sure you intersperse your studying with quizzes on the material to be learned. Doing practice quizzes gives you more opportunities to practise retrieval of information and to apply what you have learned to a new context; it also benefits your development of metacognitive skills.

11 **Take regular breaks.** You can get more done if you take regular breaks. You can even use the breaks as mini rewards. After a productive study session, give yourself permission to check your email, listen to a song, or play 10 minutes of hide-and-seek with your kids. Set a timer to remind yourself to get back on track.

Distributing your learning is a brain-friendly thing to do. You cannot absorb new information and ideas during all of your waking hours. If you overload your brain, it will find a way to shut down for a rest—whether you plan for it or not. By taking periodic breaks while studying, you allow information to sink in. During these breaks, your brain is taking the time to literally rewire itself by growing new connections between cells. Psychologists call this process **consolidation** (Siegel, 2001). Learning occurs when you effectively recode and consolidate new material and that material moves from short-term memory to long-term memory. But be careful to get back on task—it is easy to become so engaged with social media that you don't realize your 20-minute break has stretched to an hour.

12 **Elaborate.** According to Harvard psychologist Daniel Schacter (2001), all courses in memory improvement are based on a single technique—elaboration. **Elaboration** means consciously encoding new information. Current brain research indicates that elaboration is more effective than simply repeating information or rehearsal for successfully enhancing long-term memory (Brown, Roediger, & McDaniel, 2014).

One way to elaborate is to ask yourself questions about incoming information: "Does this remind me of something or someone I already know?" "Is this similar to a technique that I already use?" and "Where and when can I use this information?" The more you can connect what you are learning to what you previously learned, the more effective elaboration is likely to be. In other words, the greater your prior knowledge of a subject the easier it will be to use elaboration as a memory technique.

When you learned to recognize Italy on a world map, your teacher probably pointed out that the country is shaped like a boot. This is a simple form of elaboration.

The same idea applies to more complex material. When you meet someone new, for example, ask yourself, "Does she remind me of someone else?" Or when reading this book, preview the material in the chapter opener.

Two other common elaborative study strategies are **graphic organizers** and **concept maps**. One example of a graphic organizer is a *topic–point–details* chart. At the top of this chart, write the main topic of a lecture or reading assignment. In the left column, list the main points you want to remember. And in the right column, list key details related to each point. See Figure 3.1 for the beginning of a chart based on this article.

You could use a similar chart to prompt critical thinking about an issue. Express that issue as a question, and write the question at the top. In the left column, note the opinion about the issue. In the right column, list notable facts, expert opinions, reasons, and examples that support each opinion. Figure 3.2 illustrates this using the issue of tax cuts as a strategy for stimulating the economy.

Sometimes you'll want to remember the main actions in a story or historical event. Create a timeline by drawing a straight line. Place points in order on that line to represent key events. Place earlier events toward the left end of the line and later events toward the right.

Figure 3.3 shows the start of a timeline of events relating to the history of Afghanistan since 1933.

When you want to compare or contrast two things, play with a Venn diagram. Represent each thing as a circle. Draw the circles so that they overlap. In the overlapping area, list characteristics that the two things share. In the outer parts of each circle, list the unique characteristics of each thing. Figure 3.4 compares the two types of Journal Entries included in this book—Discovery Statements and Intention Statements.

The graphic organizers described here are just a few of the many kinds available. To find more examples, do an Internet search. Have fun, and invent graphic organizers of your own.

Another variation on the graphic organizer is the concept map. Concept mapping, pioneered by Joseph Novak and D. Bob Gowin (1984), is a tool you can use to display the organization underlying lectures, discussions, and reading materials. A subject that you study in school might include dozens or even hundreds of concepts that you need to learn. However, learning the subject relies on a simple, underlying process: You take one new concept at a time and link it to a concept that you already understand, creating a new **proposition** that states a relationship between two or more concepts.

MEMORY TECHNIQUES

Point	Details
1. Be selective	Choose what not to remember. Look for clues to important material.
2. Categorize	Organize by time, location, category, continuum, or alphabet.
3. Create associations	Link new facts with facts you already know.
4. Learn actively	Sit straight. Stand while studying. Recite while walking. Test those theories in the real world.
5. Relax	Release tension. Remain alert.

Figure 3.1 Topic–Point–Details Chart

STIMULATE THE ECONOMY WITH CORPORATE TAX CUTS?

Opinion	Support
Yes	Savings from tax cuts allow businesses to invest money in new equipment.
	Tax cuts encourage businesses to expand and hire new employees.
No	Least efficient way to create jobs and increase growth in the economy.
	Tax cuts create budget deficits.
Maybe	Tax cuts might work in some economic conditions.
	Budget deficits might be only temporary.

Source: Adapted from © Cengage Learning.

Figure 3.2 Question–Opinion–Support Chart

CHRONOLOGY OF AFGHANISTAN BEGINNING WITH INDEPENDENCE FROM BRITAIN IN 1919

1933	1973	1978-1979	1989-1996	2001-2011	2011-2014
Zahir Shah rules as king for the next 4 decades.	Coup led by Mohammed Daud. Declares country a republic.	Daud is overthrown. Power struggles occur. Soviet forces enter country.	Soviet forces leave but civil war continues. Taliban seize control of Kabul.	US, Britain launch air strikes, Taliban deposed from government, Canada joins mission, Karzai elected PM twice.	Canadian military involvement formally ends. New election held in which the incumbent Karzai is not eligible to run.

Source: Adapted from © Cengage Learning.

Figure 3.3 *Time Line*

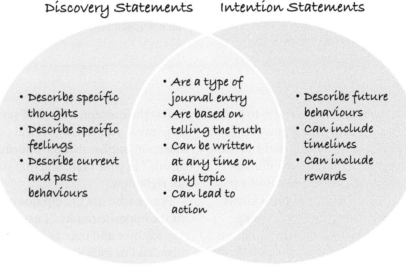

Discovery Statements — Intention Statements

- Describe specific thoughts
- Describe specific feelings
- Describe current and past behaviours

- Are a type of journal entry
- Are based on telling the truth
- Can be written at any time on any topic
- Can lead to action

- Describe future behaviours
- Can include timelines
- Can include rewards

Source: Adapted from © Cengage Learning.

Figure 3.4 *Venn Diagram*

Concept maps take this process out of your head and put it on paper in a visual format. You list concepts and arrange them in a meaningful order. Then you explicitly state the relationships between concepts, forming meaningful propositions.

Concept maps also promote critical thinking. Creating a concept map can alert you to gaps in your understanding—where you are missing concepts, or concepts with illogical links. Concept mapping is an elaborative study strategy that we know supports effective encoding (Svinicki, 2004), particularly when they are developed along with materials you are trying to learn.

Why do they work? Both concept maps and graphic organizers lead to deeper processing of material and therefore better encoding of information in memory. When you enrich the material, you are learning by focussing on the meaning of ideas or concepts; when you organize that information, you create multiple ways to access the information at a later date. This goes way

beyond recognizing a word by its surface features, such as how it is spelled. Try creating a concept map for yourself the next time you are studying and see if this works for you. Elaborative study techniques such as concept maps have been shown to lead to higher course grades than more basic study strategies like rehearsal (Pintrich, Smith, Garcia, & McKeachie, 1993), so give it a go.

Recall it

13 Use it before you lose it. Practise retrieval of information frequently. Even information encoded in long-term memory becomes difficult to recall when we don't use it regularly. The pathways to the information become faint with disuse. Research has consistently found that practice testing is an extremely effective memory strategy (Dunlosky et al., 2013), and that it works best when practice testing is distributed over time rather than having testing sessions back to back.

This points to a powerful memory technique. To remember something, access it repeatedly. Read it, write

How to create a concept map

1. **List the key concepts in the text.** Aim to express each concept in three words or less. Most concept words are nouns, including terms and proper names. At this point, you can list the concepts in any order. For ease in ranking the concepts later, write each one on a single Post-it® note.

2. **Rank the concepts so that they flow from general to specific.** On a large sheet of paper, write the main concept at the top of the page. Place the most specific concepts near the bottom. Arrange the rest of the concepts in appropriate positions throughout the middle of the page. Circle each concept.

3. **Draw lines that connect the concepts.** On these connecting lines, add words that describe the relationship between the concepts. Again, limit yourself to the fewest words needed to make an accurate link—three words or less. Linking words are often verbs, verb phrases, or prepositions.

4. **Finally, review your map.** Look for any concepts that are repeated in several places on the map. You can avoid these repetitions by adding more links between concepts. Also look for accurate linking words and missing concepts.

As you gain facility with concept maps, you might wish to create them on your devices. Apps like *Inspiration* or *Simple Mind Free* are visual thinking and learning tools that are specifically designed to create concept maps.

---

it, speak it, listen to it, apply it. Find some way to make contact with the material regularly. Each time you do so, you widen the neural pathway to the material and make it easier to recall the next time. To retrieve information, you need to have effective cues, which is why it is so important to connect new learning to prior knowledge. Context matters. We have a limitless learning capacity; it is retrieval that is sometimes the problem. Recent research shows that, although using good study techniques like elaboration are important for learning, practising organized retrieval of information is the key to significant gains in learning (Karpicke & Blunt, 2011; Brown, Roediger, & McDaniel, 2014)! One way to combine the two techniques of elaboration and retrieval is to practise creating concept maps *without* having the study materials present.

Another way to make contact with the material is to teach it. Teaching demands mastery. When you explain the function of the pancreas to a fellow student, you discover quickly whether you really understand it yourself.

Study groups are especially effective because they put you on stage. The friendly pressure of knowing that you'll teach the group helps focus your attention.

14 Adopt the attitude that you never forget. You might not believe that an idea or a thought never leaves your memory. That's OK. In fact, it doesn't matter whether you agree with the idea or not. It can work for you anyway.

Test the concept. Instead of saying, "I don't remember," you can say, "It will come to me." The latter statement implies that the information you want is encoded in your brain and that you can retrieve it—just not right now.

People who use the flip side of this technique often get the opposite results. "I never remember anything," they say over and over again. "I've always had a poor memory. I'm such a scatterbrain." That kind of negative talk is self-fulfilling.

Instead, use positive affirmations that support you in developing your memory: "I recall information easily and accurately." "At any time I choose, I will be able to recall key facts and ideas." "My memory serves me well."

15 Combine techniques. All of these memory techniques work even better in combination. Choose two or three techniques to use on a particular assignment and experiment for yourself. For example, after you take a few minutes to get an overview of a reading assignment, you could draw a quick concept map to represent the main points. Or you could overlearn a chemistry equation by singing a jingle about it all the way to work. If your attitude is that calculus is difficult, you could acknowledge that. Then you could distribute your study time in short, easy-to-handle sessions. Combining memory techniques involves using sight, sound, and touch when you study. The effect is synergistic. ✳

practising
CRITICAL THINKING

Using a concept map

Use a concept map as a tool to interpret and evaluate a piece of writing. First, list the key concepts from a chapter (or section of a chapter) in a textbook you're reading. Then connect these concepts with linking words. Create your concept map on a separate sheet of paper. Then take a few minutes to assess the author's presentation as reflected in your concept map. Pay special attention to the links between concepts. Are they accurate? Do they reveal false assumptions or lack of evidence? Write your evaluation of your concept map here.

_____

_____

_____

_____

_____

_____

_____

_____

_____

_____

_____

_____

_____

_____

_____

_____

_____

_____

_____

_____

_____

_____

_____

_____

_____

_____

_____

_____

_____

_____

Use flash cards to reinforce memory

One memory strategy you might find useful involves a special kind of flash card (see Figure 3.5).

To create a standard flash card, you write a question on one side of an index card and its answer on the other side. Flash cards have a question on *both* sides. Here's the trick: The question on each side of the card contains the answer to the question on the other side. You can also create flash cards online by going to *studyblue.com* or *quizlet.com*

The questions you write on flash cards can draw on both **lower-** and **higher-order thinking skills**. Lower-order thinking skills deal primarily with the recall of facts, whereas higher-order thinking skills require you to manipulate information or ideas in order to come up with an answer. Writing these questions forces you to encode material in different ways. You activate more areas of your brain and burn the concepts even deeper into your memory.

For example, say that you want to remember the subject of Bill 101, which made French the official language of the province of Québec. On one side of an index card, write a lower-order question: *What bill made French the official language of the province of Québec?* Turn the card over and write a higher-order question: *What was the impact of Bill 101 on language acquisition?*

To get the most from flash cards:

- Add a picture to each side of the card. This helps you learn concepts faster and develop a more visual learning style.

- Read the questions and recite the answers out loud. Two keys to memory are repetition and novelty, so use a different voice whenever you read and recite. Whisper the first time you go through your cards, then shout or sing the next time. Doing this develops an auditory learning style.

- Carry flash cards with you and pull them out during waiting times. To develop a kinesthetic learning style, handle your cards often.

- Create flash cards for each new and important concept within 24 hours after attending a class or completing an assignment. This is your *active stack* of cards. Keep answering the questions on these cards until you learn each new concept.

- Create flash card decks for each of your courses. Mix up your reviews of different courses. These are your *review stacks*. Mixing the cards up makes learning more challenging, but when learning is difficult it leads to deeper learning and improved performance on your tests.

- Get started creating flash cards using blank index cards right now.

- Start by creating a flash card about remembering how to use flash cards! Or use an app like *Quizlet* or *StudyBlue* to create flash cards.

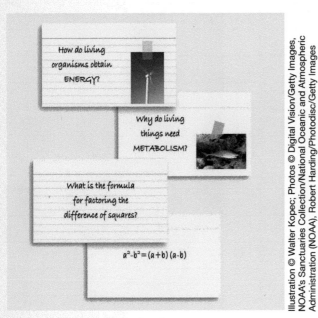

Illustration © Walter Kopec; Photos © Digital Vision/Getty Images, NOAA's Sanctuaries Collection/National Oceanic and Atmospheric Administration (NOAA), Robert Harding/Photodisc/Getty Images

Figure 3.5 *Using Flash Cards*

Set a trap for
YOUR MEMORY

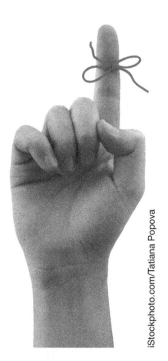

WHEN YOU WANT to remind yourself to do something, link this activity to another event you know will take place. The key is to "trap" your memory by picking events that are certain to occur.

Say that you're walking to class and suddenly remember that your accounting assignment is due tomorrow. Switch your watch to the opposite wrist. Now you're "trapped." Every time you glance at your wrist and remember that you have switched your watch, it becomes a reminder that you were supposed to remember something else. (You can do the same with a ring.)

If you empty your pockets every night, put an unusual item in your pocket in the morning to remind yourself to do something before you go to bed. For example, to remember to call your younger sister on her birthday, pick an object from the playpen—a teething toy, perhaps—and put it in your pocket. When you empty your pocket that evening and find the teething toy, you're more likely to make the call.

Everyday rituals that are seldom neglected, such as feeding a pet, listening to the weather report, and unlacing shoes, provide opportunities for setting traps. For example, tie a triple knot in your shoelace as a reminder to set the alarm for your early morning study group meeting.

You can even use imaginary traps. To remember to do your laundry, picture your laundry bag hanging on the front door. In your mind, create the feeling of reaching for the doorknob and grabbing the laundry bag instead. When you get home, and reach to open the front door, the image is apt to return to you. To remember to pay your phone bill, visualize a big, burly bill collector knocking on your front door to talk to you about how much you owe. The next time you arrive at your front door, you'll be glad that you got there before he did. You still have time to make your payment!

Mobile devices work well for setting memory traps. To remind yourself to bring your textbook to class, for example, set an alarm on your cellphone to go off

10 minutes before you leave the house. Visualize yourself picking up the book when the alarm goes off. Link two activities together, and make the association unusual. ✳

Did you **know that …?**

> Part of Albert Einstein's brain is being used for neuroscience research at McMaster University. They have discovered differences in the way his brain is structured that they think may be related to his brilliance at spatial and mathematical thinking ("50 little-known facts", 2017). More than 60 years after his death, there is still a lot to learn from Einstein.

journal entry   3-2

Discovery Statement

Revisit Your Memory Skills

Take a minute to reflect on the memory techniques in this chapter. You probably use some of them already without being aware of it. In the space below, list at least three techniques you have used in the past and describe how you used them.

_____

_____

_____

_____

_____

Remembering
NAMES

New friendships, job contacts, and business relationships all start with remembering names. Here are some techniques to help you remember them.

Recite and repeat in conversation

When you hear a person's name, repeat it. Immediately say it to yourself several times without moving your lips. You could also repeat the name out loud in a way that does not sound forced or artificial: "I'm pleased to meet you, Camille."

Ask the other person to recite and repeat

You can let other people help you remember their names. After you've been introduced to someone, ask that person to spell the name and pronounce it correctly for you. Most people will be flattered by the effort you're making to learn their names.

Visualize

After the conversation, construct a brief visual image of the person. For a memorable image, make it unusual. For example, imagine the name painted in hot pink fluorescent letters on the person's forehead.

Admit you don't know

Admitting that you can't remember someone's name can actually put people at ease. Most of them will sympathize if you say, "I'm working to remember names better. Yours is right on the tip of my tongue. What is it again?"

Introduce yourself again

Most of the time we assume introductions are one-shot affairs. If we miss a name the first time around, our hopes for remembering it are dashed. Instead of giving up, reintroduce yourself: "Hello, again. We met earlier. I'm Jesse. Please tell me your name again."

Use associations

Link each person you meet with one characteristic that you find interesting or unusual. For example, you could make a mental note: "Vicki Chan—long, black hair" or "Vincent Cote—round glasses."

Rawpixel.com/Shutterstock.com

Limit the number of new names you learn at one time

Occasionally, we find ourselves in situations where we're introduced to many people at the same time: "Dad, these are all the people in my school choir." "Let's take a tour so you can meet all 32 people in this department."

When meeting a group of people, concentrate on remembering just two or three names. Free yourself from feeling obligated to remember everyone. Few of the people in mass introductions expect you to remember their names. Another way to avoid memory overload is to limit yourself to learning just first names. Last names can come later.

Ask for photos

In some cases, you might be able to get photos of all the people you meet. For example, a small business where you apply for a job might have a brochure with pictures of all the employees. Ask for individual or group photos and write in the names if they're not included. You can use these photos as "flash cards" as you drill yourself on names. Or take a picture with your phone when you add someone to your contacts. If you get business cards, enter phone numbers, email addresses, and other contact information as well. It will be a lot easier to recall their names later with the visual cues.

Go early

Consider going early to conventions, parties, and classes. Sometimes just a few people show up on time at these occasions. That's fewer names for you to remember. And as more people arrive, you can overhear them being introduced to others—an automatic review for you.

Make it a game

In situations where many people are new to one another, consider pairing up with another person and staging a contest. Challenge each other to remember as many new names as possible. Then choose an "award"—such as a movie ticket or free meal—for the person who wins.

Intend to remember

The simple act of focussing your attention at key moments can do wonders for your memory. Test this idea for yourself. The next time you're introduced to someone, direct 100 percent of your attention to hearing that person's name. Do this consistently and see what happens to your ability to remember names.

The intention to remember can be more powerful than any single memory technique. Recalling names is not just important in school; it is also an important skill on the job. As the section later in this chapter called *Put It to Work* suggests, many of the ideas in this chapter are essential for career success. So practise learning names now—it's a skill you will use for a lifetime. ✻

MNEMONIC
devices

PRONOUNCED "NE-MON'-IK," this word refers to tricks that can increase your ability to recall everything from grocery lists to speeches.

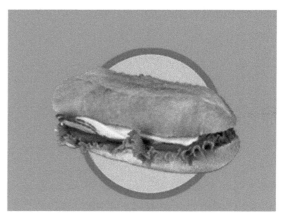
Photo: © magicoven/Shutterstock; illustration: © Walter Kopec

Some entertainers use **mnemonic devices** to perform "impossible" feats of memory, such as recalling the names of everyone in a large audience after hearing them just once. Waiters use mnemonics to take orders from several tables without the aid of pad and pencil. Using mnemonic devices, speakers can go for hours without looking at their notes. The possibilities for students are endless. They provide ways for you to organize learning, particularly of arbitrary material, and help you to cue learning for retrieval.

There is a catch. Mnemonic devices have three serious limitations:

1. They don't always help you understand or digest material. Instead of encouraging critical thinking skills, mnemonics rely only on rote memorization.

2. The mnemonic device itself is sometimes complicated to learn and time-consuming to develop. It might take more energy to create such a device than to memorize something by using a more traditional memory technique, such as repetition.

3. Mnemonic devices can be forgotten. Recalling a mnemonic device might be as hard as recalling the material itself.

In spite of their limitations, mnemonic devices can be powerful. There are five general categories: new words, creative sentences, rhymes and songs, the loci system, and the peg system.

New words

Acronyms are words created from the initial letters of a series of words. Examples include CSIS (Canadian Security Intelligence Service), radar (radio detecting and ranging), scuba (self-contained underwater breathing apparatus), and laser (light amplification by stimulated emission of radiation). You can make up your own acronyms to recall series of facts.

A common mnemonic acronym is Roy G. Biv, which has helped thousands of students remember the colours of the visible spectrum (red, orange, yellow, green, blue, indigo, and violet). IPMAT helps biology students remember the stages of cell division (interphase, prophase, metaphase, anaphase, and telophase). OCEAN helps psychology students recall the five major personality factors: open-mindedness, conscientiousness, extraversion, agreeableness, and neuroticism. (You can also use CANOE for this list.) The acronym HOMES helps people remember the names of the Great Lakes: Huron, Ontario, Michigan, Erie, and Superior. There's also FOIL, which helps algebra students remember the order for multiplying elements in a binomial equation: first, outer, inner, last. Using mnemonic devices involves you using elaborative rehearsal and therefore facilitates moving information from working memory to long-term memory (Burmester, 2017).

Creative sentences

Acrostics are sentences that help you remember a series of letters that stand for something. For example, the first letters of the words in the sentence "Every good boy does fine" (E, G, B, D, and F) are the music notes of the lines of the treble clef staff. In biology, you might be required to memorize the major categories of living things in the animal world:

kingdom

phylum

class

order

family

genus

species

variety

Believe it or not, there's a creative sentence for that: *Kings play cards on fairly good soft velvet.*

Rhymes and songs

Advertising executives spend billions of dollars a year on commercials designed to burn their messages into your memory. You are programmed to remember rhymes and songs from the time you watched *Sesame Street.*

Rhymes have been used for centuries to teach children basic facts. Here's one that has helped many a student on spelling tests: "I before E except after C." To remember how many days are in each month of the year, you can say, "Thirty days hath September, April, June, and November . . . ."

The loci system

The word **loci** is the plural of *locus,* a synonym for *place* or *location.* Use this system to create visual associations with familiar locations (see Figure 3.6). Unusual associations are the easiest to remember.

Example 1

The loci system is an old one. Ancient Greek orators used it to remember long speeches. For example, if an

Photo: © magicoven/Shutterstock; illustration: © Walter Kopec

Figure 3.6 *Mnemonic device: The peg system*

orator's position was that road taxes must be raised to pay for school equipment, his loci visualizations might have looked like the following.

First, as he walks in the door of his house, he imagines a large *porpoise* jumping through a hoop. This reminds him to begin by telling the audience the *purpose* of his speech.

Next, he visualizes his living room floor covered with paving stones, forming a road leading into the kitchen. In the kitchen, he pictures dozens of schoolchildren sitting on the floor because they have no desks.

Now it's the day of the big speech. The Greek politician is nervous. He is perspiring, and his toga sticks to his body. He stands up to give his speech, and his mind goes blank. Then he starts thinking to himself:

I am so nervous that I can hardly remember my name. But no problem—I can remember the rooms in my house. Let's see, I'm walking in the front door and— wow! I see the porpoise. That reminds me to talk about the purpose of my speech. And then there's that road leading to the kitchen. Say, what are all those kids doing there on the floor? Oh, yeah, now I remember—they have no desks! We need to raise taxes on roads to pay for their desks and the other stuff they need in classrooms.

Example 2

The loci system can also be based on parts of your body. When studying biology, for instance, use the loci system to memorize the order of structures of living things.

Start with your toes, the lowest points of your body. Associate them with the lowest structure of living things—*atoms.*

The top of your head is the highest point on your body. So associate it with the highest order of living things—*biosystems*, or groups of species.

Then associate the intermediate structures with points on your body between your head and toes.

Link *molecules* to your feet.

Link *cells* to your ankles.

Link *tissues* with your knees.

Link *organs* with your waist.

Link *organ systems* with your chest.

Link *organisms* with your neck.

The peg system

This technique employs key words that are paired with numbers. Each word forms a "peg" on which you can "hang" mental associations. This is a good method to use to memorize lists of items—like your grocery list. To use this system effectively, learn the following peg words and their associated numbers well:

1-bun	6-sticks
2-shoe	7-heaven
3-tree	8-gate
4-door	9-wine
5-hive	10-hen

Believe it or not, you can use the peg system to remember the capital cities of Canada. Let's see: one-bun–Toronto (picture the CN tower sticking out of a bun), two-shoe—Québec City (picture the snowmen of Carnival all wearing high heel shoes), and three-tree—Charlottetown (picture the fathers of confederation all climbing a tree). Since we remember pictures longer than words, it may be easier to recall these weird scenes than you would believe and, more importantly, the names of the capitals. In fact, the more bizarre the imagery, the more likely you are to recall the list of words. Try to use this technique today to remember your grocery list while studying for a test. ✳

practising
CRITICAL THINKING

3-4

Get creative

Construct your own mnemonic device for remembering some of the memory techniques in this chapter. Make up a poem, jingle, acronym, or acrostic, or use another mnemonic system. Describe your mnemonic device in the space below.

_____

_____

_____

_____

_____

_____

_____

_____

_____

_____

_____

practising CRITICAL THINKING 3-5

Remember enjoyment

Take five minutes to remember a time when you enjoyed learning something. In the space below, describe that experience in a sentence or two. Then make a brief list of the things you found enjoyable about that experience.

Within the next 24 hours, compare your list with those of other classmates. Look for similarities and differences in the descriptions of your learning experiences.

Based on your comparison, form a tentative explanation about what makes learning enjoyable for people. Summarize your explanation here:

Pulling it
ALL TOGETHER

Throughout this chapter you've heard about

- Strategies such as elaboration that you can use to help with encoding information into long-term memory

- The importance of practising retrieval of information from storage

- Memory tricks called mnemonics that are useful for memorizing facts or lists

But it is important to keep in mind that, to be a successful learner, along with these memory strategies you also need to develop the metacognitive and goal-setting skills discussed in Chapters 1, "First Steps," and Chapter 2, "Time." These include the following:

- Setting goals for yourself and making plans to achieve them

- Monitoring your own understanding of texts, and of problems or tasks you are assigned

- Adjusting or regulating your own learning to respond to the task demands; for instance, slowing down your reading rate when you have difficulty understanding the text

You also need to think about how you manage your studying resources:

- How you organize your time and your study environment

- How you persist with difficult or boring tasks

- When you seek help from friends

Take a moment to consider the following questions and write down your answers.

1. How often do you check to see if you understand what you are reading? What do you do when you find you don't understand something?

_____

_____

_____

2. What do you do when faced with a boring assignment?

_____

_____

_____

3. How do you decide whether to use a shallow or deep processing technique? For instance, when should you use recital and when might you want to create a graphics organizer?

_____

_____

_____

Finally, one strategy that would help you become a better learner is to become more self-regulated. Marilla Svinicki (2004), a renowned psychologist, has developed a GAMES model that works well with her students to develop good study behaviour.

G is for goal-oriented behaviour—when you sit down to study, what goal do you set? Good learners go farther than just saying they will read three chapters. Instead, they set out goals, such as key questions they want answers to by the time they finish studying.

A is for active studying and involves doing something with the material. Come up with your own examples of the concepts that you have covered in a chapter rather than just colouring the page yellow with highlighting.

M is for meaningful studying. How often do you try to connect what you are learning to what you already know? Connecting what you learn to prior knowledge significantly increases how much you will learn. This is where developing concept maps or graphics organizers can really make a difference.

E is for explaining what you have learned to others. Have you tried to explain what you learned to members of your study group or students in your class? Once you can explain ideas to others—putting what you have read in your own words—you will find it much easier to recall those ideas during a test.

S is for self-monitoring. How often do you check while you are reading to see if you really understand the material? Self-monitoring is where you check to make sure you got the answers correct to those questions you set out to answer at the start of your studying. Svinicki suggests trading questions with students in your study group to make sure you are understanding what you are reading. One key to self-monitoring is to do it continuously while you are learning new material. Don't wait until the night before an exam to check on your comprehension.

So, the next time you are studying, consider putting GAMES into action. ✴

Source: Adapted from *Learning and Motivation in the Postsecondary Classroom*, by Marilla D. Svinicki. Copyright © 2004 Anker Publishing. Reproduced with permission of John Wiley & Sons, Inc.

POWERPROCESS

Love Your Problems (and Experience Your Barriers)

We all have problems and barriers that block our progress or prevent us from moving into new areas. Often, the way we respond to our problems puts boundaries around our experiences. We place limitations on what we allow ourselves to be, do, and have.

Our problems might include fear of speaking in front of a group, anxiety about math problems, or reluctance to sound ridiculous when learning a foreign language. We might have a barrier about looking silly when trying something new. Some of us even have anxiety about being successful.

Problems often work like barriers. When we bump up against one of our problems, we usually turn away and start walking along a different path. And all of a sudden—bump!—we've struck another barrier. And we turn away again. As we continue to bump into problems and turn away from them, our lives stay inside the same old boundaries. Inside these boundaries, we are unlikely to have new adventures. We are unlikely to improve or to make much progress.

If we respond to problems by loving them instead of resisting them, we can expand the boundaries in which we live out lives.

The word *love* might sound like an overstatement. In this Power Process, the word means to accept your problems, to allow and permit them, to embrace them. The more we deny or resist a problem, the stronger it seems to become. When we accept the fact that we have a problem, we are more likely to find effective ways to deal with it.

Suppose one of your barriers is being afraid of speaking in front of a group. You could get up in front of the group and pretend that you're not afraid. Or you could tell yourself, "I'm not going to be scared," and then try to keep your knees from knocking. Generally, these strategies don't work.

A more effective approach is to love your fear. Go to the front of the room, look out into the audience, and say to yourself, "I am scared. I notice that my knees are shaking and my mouth feels dry, and I'm having a rush of thoughts about what might happen if I say the wrong thing. Yes, I'm scared, and I'm not going to fight it. I'm going to give this speech anyway."

The beauty of this Power Process is that you continue to take action—giving your speech, for example—no matter what you feel. You walk right up to the barrier and then *through* it. You might even find that if you totally accept and experience a barrier, such as fear, it shrinks or disappears. Even if that does not happen right away, you still open up to new experiences and gain new chances to learn.

Loving a problem does not need to stop us from solving it. In fact, fully accepting and admitting a problem usually helps us take effective action—which can free us of the problem once and for all.

iStockphoto.com/Miroslav Ferkuniak/Studio1One

Put it to WORK

You can use strategies in *Becoming a Master Student* to succeed at work. Get started by reflecting on the following case study.

© Stephen Coburn/Shutterstock

Paula Chang is a nurse at a large urban hospital. Paula just joined the staff in the cardiology department, which includes 40 nurses, doctors, and other healthcare workers. She was hired two months after graduating with a nursing degree from a nearby university.

Among Paula's goals for her new career was to learn the names of her colleagues by the end of the first week on the job. She succeeded.

One afternoon, the department head, Dr. Frank Rangel, invited Paula into his office for an informal chat. Frank had heard several colleagues talking about Paula's ability to remember names. He wanted to congratulate her—and learn a thing or two about memory techniques from his youngest team member.

"You're the first person on my staff who's ever managed to learn so many names so quickly," said Frank. "What's your secret?"

"No secrets, honest," Paula replied. "It's all about attitude, I guess. I simply made it a priority to remember names. I remember a teacher I had in college who had anywhere from 50 to 100 students in his lecture classes. On the first day of class, he went around the room and asked each of us for our name. It took a lot of time, but then he called us by name for the rest of the semester. I remember feeling so touched by that. I promised I would do the same thing when I started my first job."

Frank smiled and said, "That's impressive. Memorizing so many names so quickly is a neat trick. But I'm just wondering: Does it really make a difference?"

"Yes, I think so," Paula said. "For one thing, I feel more confident right away about my surroundings. I feel more comfortable asking questions when I remember names."

Paula also shared an idea with Frank for future new employees. As a visual learner, she learns better by seeing photos of people and associating pictures with names. So Paula volunteered to take pictures of her colleagues to help everyone learn names.

Paula applied several strategies from this chapter:
- Create pictures.
- Engage your emotions.
- Intend to remember.

List more memory strategies that Paula could use:

_____

_____

_____

_____

_____

Also consider the following suggestions when you want to sharpen your memory for names in the workplace. You can adapt these techniques to remembering any kind of detailed, factual information.

- Think of someone you already know who has the same first name as a new co-worker. Visualize these two people standing side by side. Look for strong differences or similarities between them.
- Use rhymes or alliteration (the repetition of sounds). If Tim is slim or Sandra wears a scarf, you've got a natural "hook" for remembering their names.
- Use a new person's name every chance you get. In a meeting, for example, refer to "Sanjay's idea" or "Susan's question."
- Make small talk with people when you first meet them. Associate one key fact—such as a person's hometown or favourite hobby—with an image of the person's face.

QUIZ

Name_____   Date_____/_____/_____

1. Which is a more effective memory technique for long-term retention—recitation or elaboration?

2. Give a specific example of "setting a trap" for your memory.

3. Describe a visualization that can help you remember Boyle's law.

4. Define learning transfer and give an example of how you can enhance learning transfer when studying.

5. What is the difference between deep and surface learning? Name at least one technique that you can use to deepen your learning.

6. Create an acronym that you could use to recall a series of facts in one of your courses.

7. Mnemonic devices are tricks that can increase your ability to
   (a) learn complicated pieces of information
   (b) memorize mathematical equations
   (c) memorize facts and ideas
   (d) learn difficult concepts

8. Briefly describe at least three memory techniques.

9. What is self-monitoring?

10. Define the term *graphic organizer* and give two examples.

Skills SNAPSHOT

Use this exercise to monitor the Master Student qualities that you're developing—especially those related to memory.

Begin by reflecting on some recent experiences. Then take the next step toward memory mastery by committing to a specific action in the near future.

DISCOVERY

My score on the Memory section of the Discovery Wheel in Chapter 1 was . . .

Recalling key facts more quickly and accurately could help me be more effective in the following situations: . . .

Memory techniques that I already use include . . .

INTENTION

I'll know that I've reached a new level of mastery with remembering ideas and information when . . .

To reach that level of mastery, the most important thing I can do next is to . . .

Stated as a goal, my intention is . . .

ACTION

To achieve the goal I just wrote, the most important thing I can do next is to . . .

At the end of this course, I would like my Memory score on the Discovery Wheel to be . . .

chapter 3

■ Put it to Work
■ Quiz
■ Skills Snapshot
▶ ▶ ▶ ▶

MASTER STUDENT
PROFILE

Maya Burhanpurkar
...is an environmental advocate

Courtesy of Maya Burhanpurkar

Maya Burhanpurkar (1999–) started her science career in a basement laboratory in her family home at the age of 10. She received a Queen Elizabeth II Diamond Jubilee Medal and has been named one of Canada's Top 20 Under 20. Plus, she has represented Canada in the Intel and Google Science Talent Search Competition.

There's a moment in Maya Burhanpurkar's documentary where she stands next to an ice fjord in Ilulissat, Greenland, realizing what climate change means for the people who live there.

After listening to residents describe how fast the ice is melting, she looks into the camera and says: "I think that I'm going to become a lot more conscientious of the environment when I go about my everyday life because after what I've seen today, the icebergs and now the ice fjord, I really don't want that natural landscape to be destroyed. Every single person counts."

Melting ice changed Burhanpurkar's life and now she's inspiring others around the world with a documentary about climate change.

The film's title, *400 PPM*, refers to the concentration of carbon dioxide in the atmosphere, which now exceeds 400 parts per million, the highest level seen in the history of our species. Burhanpurkar's eye-opening voyage happened when she was invited to tour the Canadian and Greenlandic Arctic aboard the *Sea Adventurer*.

It's impressive enough that this teenager turned her trip into an acclaimed documentary. But that's on top of her previous achievements prototyping "intelligent antibiotics," discovering new properties of a drug to cure Alzheimer's disease, and tracking asteroids.

"I have a scientific background," Burhanpurkar explained. "I'd never done anything creative like this before. It's not really my forte."

She also interviewed prominent Canadians to explain the scientific concepts and social issues, including author Margaret Atwood, former astronaut Col. Christopher Hadfield, anthropologist Dr. Wade Davis, and Nobel laureate Dr. Brad Bass.

Burhanpurkar was among the recipients of the Gloria Barron Prize for Young Heroes for her work on the documentary, which has reached more than 2.2 million students.

"In school we learn facts and figures and that it's going to impact us at some point," Burhanpurkar recalled. "This could not be further from the truth."

"The Arctic is where global warming is changing our planet the fastest," she explains. "It's the canary in the coal mine. It's the Earth's early warning system and its alarm is going off. We need to act now."

"Before I went, I was excited to do the whole ecotourism thing," she said, "but what struck me was meeting the people who are already impacted by climate change."

Farther north, in Uummannaq, Greenland, Burhanpurkar observed that climate change was hurting the Inuit people along with the ice. Thinning glaciers have made ice fishing nearly impossible, devastating the economy and changing the traditional culture.

"It was hardly their fault," she narrated. "It was ours."

Burhanpurkar will take her new awareness with her when she begins college at Harvard.

"I had the opportunity to witness climate change firsthand and it changed my life," Burhanpurkar said.

Source: Shepard, Laura A. (2016, October 5). Teenage scientist captures Arctic ice melt on film. Nexus Media. *Popular Science*. Retrieved from *https://www.popsci .com/teenage-scientist-captures-arctic-ice-melt-on-film*. Reprinted by permission.

Reading

what is included...

do you have a minute?

Find a tool for building your vocabulary. For example, test your web browser to see if it will display definitions when you control-click on a word. You could also search for a dictionary app and download it to your mobile phone or tablet.

wavebreakmedia/Shutterstock.com

WHAT if ...

I could finish my reading with time to spare and easily recall the key points?

WHY this chapter matters ...

Higher education requires extensive reading of complex material.

HOW you can use this chapter ...

Analyze what effective readers do and experiment with new techniques. Increase your vocabulary and adjust your reading speed for different types of material. Comprehend difficult texts with more ease.

Muscle
READING

When you have reading to do for school, where do you usually do it? In a chair? On your bed?

What do you do when you realize that you didn't understand something you have read?

Do you test yourself on what you are learning while you are reading a chapter in your textbook?

If you underline your textbook when studying, how much of the page is coloured in?

Take some time to think of the answers to these questions before you start reading this chapter. There is a way you could actually spend less time on your reading and get more out of it—the process is called Muscle Reading. It is an energizing technique designed to increase your comprehension of what you've read.

Picture yourself sitting at a desk, a book in your hands. Your eyes are open, and it looks as if you're reading. Suddenly your head jerks up. You blink. You realize your eyes have been scanning the page for 10 minutes, and you can't remember a single thing you have read.

Or picture this: You've had a hard day. You don't get to your books until 8 p.m. You begin a reading assignment on something called "the equity method of accounting for common stock investments." I am preparing for the future, you tell yourself, as you plod through two paragraphs and begin the third. Suddenly, the clock reads 11:00 p.m. Say good-bye to three hours.

Sometimes the only difference between a sleeping pill and a textbook is that the textbook doesn't have a warning on the label about operating heavy machinery.

Contrast this scenario with the image of an active reader. This person does the following:

- Stays alert, poses questions about what she reads, and searches for the answers

- Recognizes levels of information within the text, separating the main points and general principles from supporting details

- Quizzes himself about the material, makes written notes, and lists unanswered questions

- Instantly spots key terms and takes the time to find the definitions of unfamiliar words

- Thinks critically about the ideas in the text and looks for ways to apply them

That sounds like a lot to do. Yet, skilled readers routinely accomplish all these things and more—while enjoying reading (Bohart, 2005). Master students actively engage with the material and wrestle meaning from the pages. They write questions in the margins and annotate their texts to make them their own. Master students are committed to practising information literacy; they ask themselves what is the source of the material I'm reading? Is the source credible—should I trust it? How can I apply this information? What other facts do I need to draw a conclusion?

Keep in mind that reading textbooks is different from reading the comics in a newspaper and that reading may have different purposes in

---

journal entry 4-1

Discovery/Intention Statement

Discover What You Want from This Chapter

Recall a time when you encountered problems with reading, such as words you didn't understand or paragraphs you paused to reread more than once. Sum up the experience and how you felt about it by completing the following statement.

I discovered that I...

_____

_____

_____

Now list three to five specific reading skills you want to gain from this chapter.

I intend to...

_____

_____

_____

_____

different courses. In anatomy you may be trying to memorize key concepts while in English you may be more concerned about how the author applies the ideas presented.

We are in a knowledge-based economy so you are going to be reading a lot, not just in class, but on the job; so learning how to get the most out of what you're reading is important.

One way to experience success in reading is to approach reading using the Muscle Reading process.

You can use Muscle Reading to avoid mental mini-vacations and reduce the number of unscheduled naps during study time, even after a hard day.

This is not to say that Muscle Reading will make your education a breeze. Muscle Reading might even look like more work at first. Effective textbook reading is an active, energy-consuming, purposeful business. Like all learning, it requires self-control and for you to exercise self-regulation over your behaviour. It takes effort. That's why this strategy is called Muscle Reading. ✳

How Muscle Reading **WORKS**

Muscle reading is a three-phase technique you can use to extract the ideas and information you want.

Phase 1 includes steps to take *before* you read.

Phase 2 includes steps to take *while* you read.

Phase 3 includes steps to take *after* you read.

Each phase has three steps. See Figure 4.1.

PHASE ONE:
  Before you read
  Step 1: **Preview**
  Step 2: **Outline**
  Step 3: **Question**

PHASE TWO:
  While you read
  Step 4: **Focus**
  Step 5: **Reflect**
  Step 6: **Answer**

PHASE THREE:
  After you read
  Step 7: **Recite**
  Step 8: **Review**
  Step 9: **Review again**

Figure 4.1 Muscle Reading Steps

g-stockstudio/Shutterstock.com

To assist your recall of Muscle Reading strategies, memorize three short sentences:

P$_{ry}$ O$_{ut}$ Q$_{uestions.}$

F$_{ocus,}$ R$_{eflect,}$ and seek A$_{nswers\ to}$ questions.

R$_{ecite,}$ R$_{eview,}$ and R$_{eview\ again.}$

These three sentences correspond to the three phases of the Muscle Reading technique. Each sentence is an acrostic. The first letter of each word stands for one of the nine steps listed above.

Take a moment to invent images for each of those sentences.

For Phase 1, visualize or feel yourself prying out questions from a text. These are questions you want answered based on a brief survey of the assignment. Make a mental picture of yourself scanning the material, spotting a question, and reaching into the text to pry it out. Hear yourself saying, "I've got it. Here's my question." Then for Phase 2, get your brain involved. Feel yourself looking through a pair of binoculars trying to find an elusive bird. Reflect on which one it is, looking up images in the text that reflect what you are seeing through the lenses. Finally, you enter Phase 3. Hear your voice reciting what you have learned. Listen to yourself making a speech or singing a song about the material as you review it.

To jog your memory, write the first letters of the Muscle Reading acrostic in a margin or at the top of your notes. Then check off the steps you intend to follow. Or write the Muscle Reading steps on index cards and then use them for bookmarks.

Muscle Reading might take a little time to learn. At first you might feel it's slowing you down. That's natural when you're gaining a new skill. Mastery comes with time and practice. ✳

PHASE 1: BEFORE YOU READ
Preview, Outline, Question

Step 1 Preview

Before you start reading, preview the entire assignment. You don't have to memorize what you preview to get value from this step. Previewing sets the stage for incoming information by warming up a space in your mental storage area.

If you are starting a new book, look over the table of contents and flip through the text page by page. If you're going to read one chapter, flip through the pages of that chapter. Even if your assignment is merely a few pages in a book, you can benefit from a brief preview of the table of contents.

Keep an eye out for summary statements. If the assignment is long or complex, read the summary first. Many textbooks have summaries in the introduction or at the end of each chapter.

Read all chapter headings and subheadings. Like the headlines in a newspaper, these are usually printed in large, bold type. Often headings are brief summaries in themselves.

When previewing, seek out familiar concepts, facts, or ideas. These items can help increase comprehension by linking new information to previously learned material. Look for ideas that spark your imagination or curiosity. Inspect drawings, diagrams, charts, tables, graphs, and photographs. Imagine what kinds of questions will show up on a test. Previewing helps to clarify your purpose for reading. Ask yourself what you will do with this material and how it can relate to your long-term goals. Are you reading just to get the main points? Key supporting details? Additional details? All of the above? Your answers will guide what you do with each step that follows.

Keep the preview short. If the entire reading assignment will take less than an hour, your preview might take five minutes. Previewing is also a way to get started when an assignment looks too big to handle. It is an easy way to step into the material.

Step 2 Outline

With complex material, take time to understand the structure of what you are about to read. Outlining actively organizes your thoughts about the assignment and can help make complex information easier to understand.

If your textbook provides chapter outlines, spend some time studying them. When an outline is not provided, sketch a brief one in the margin of your book or at the beginning of your notes on a separate sheet of paper. Later, as you read and take notes, you can add to your outline.

Headings in the text can serve as major and minor entries in your outline. For example, the heading for this article is "Phase 1: Before you read," and the subheadings list the three steps in this phase. When you outline, feel free to rewrite headings so that they are more meaningful to you.

The amount of time you spend on this step will vary. For some assignments, a 10-second mental outline is all you might need. For other assignments (fiction and poetry, for example), you can skip this step altogether.

Step 3 Question

Before you begin a careful reading, determine what you want from an assignment. Then write down a list of questions, including any that resulted from your preview of the materials.

Another useful technique is to turn chapter headings and subheadings into questions. For example, if a heading is "Transference and suggestion," you can ask yourself, "What are *transference* and *suggestion*? How does *transference* relate to *suggestion*?" Make up a quiz as if you were teaching this subject to your classmates. If there are no headings, look for key sentences and turn these into questions. These sentences usually show up at the beginnings or ends of paragraphs and sections.

Have fun with this technique. Make the questions playful or creative. You don't need to answer every question that you ask. The purpose of making up questions is to get your brain involved in the assignment. Take your unanswered questions to class, where they can be springboards if there is class discussion.

Demand your money's worth from your textbook. If you do not understand a concept, write specific questions about it. The more detailed your questions, the more powerful this technique becomes. ✳

PHASE 2: WHILE YOU READ
Focus, Reflect, Answer

Step 4 Focus

You have previewed the assignment, organized it in your mind, and formulated questions. Now you are ready to begin reading.

It's easy to fool yourself about reading. Just having an open book in your hand and moving your eyes across a page doesn't mean that you are reading effectively. Reading takes mental focus.

As you read, be conscious of where you are and what you are doing. When you notice your attention wandering, gently bring it back to the present moment. Being mindful about your reading is essential to stop you from turning pages without paying attention to what you are reading. Reading for school is not like reading for leisure. If you skip a few pages

of a magazine, there are no long-term consequences; but missing an important definition in the middle of the paragraph may impact your understanding of key concepts in the chapter, as well as the results on your next test.

To begin, get in a position to stay focussed. There's a saying about corporation presidents: They usually wear out the front of their chairs first. Approach your reading assignment like a company president. Sit up. Keep your spine straight. Use the edge of your chair. And avoid reading in bed—except for fun.

Avoid marathon reading sessions. Schedule breaks and set a reasonable goal for the entire session. Then reward yourself with an enjoyable activity for five or 10 minutes every hour or two.

For difficult passages, set more limited goals for focussed reading. Read for a half-hour and then take a break. Most students find that shorter periods of reading distributed throughout the day and week can be more effective than long sessions.

You can use the following five techniques to stay focussed as you read:

1. Read the material out loud, especially if it is complicated. Some of us remember better and understand more quickly when we hear an idea.

2. Adjust the speed with which you are reading to the difficulty of the material. Experts monitor their comprehension as they read, asking themselves, Do I understand this passage? They read slowly when they encounter new material. They are willing to reread passages for comprehension when they have to, and they keep a specialized dictionary close by to look up new terms.

3. Visualize the material. Form mental pictures of the concepts as they are presented. If you read that a voucher system can help control cash disbursements, picture a voucher handing out dollar bills. Using visual imagery in this way can help deepen your understanding of the text, while allowing information to be transferred into your long-term memory.

4. Keep a specialized dictionary handy, if necessary. Many disciplines are jargon heavy. You need to understand their jargon in order to understand their text. For instance, in Psychology they often talk about something being statistically significant. Saying the word "significant" in psychology doesn't just mean it is important; it means that the results of a study are not due to chance alone. You can see how confusing this can be to those not used to the jargon of a discipline. So just because you are familiar with a term in everyday language does mean that you will understand the term in a disciplinary context. This is where those specialized dictionaries, like the *Oxford Dictionary of Psychology*, can really come in handy.

5. Predict how the author will answer the key questions you have identified. Then read to find out if your predictions were accurate.

Step 5 Reflect

As you read, seek out the answers to your questions. You are a detective, watching for every clue. Reflect on whether or not you are truly understanding what you are reading. When you do find an answer, flag it so that

it stands out on the page. Deface your books. Have fun. Flag answers by writing comments, highlighting, filling in your outline, or marking up pages in any other way that helps you. Indulge yourself as you never could with your secondary school books.

Reflect about the purpose of your reading. Are you looking for important concepts? Write a note to yourself. "This idea is important because…" or "this word means…". The purpose of marking up a book is to call out important concepts or information that you will need to review later. As you reflect on what you are reading, you are already taking an important step to later being able to recall material you have read and apply the concepts you are learning on your next test.

As you reflect on what you are reading, consider these questions:

■ Do you understand what you are reading? Mark passages you don't understand and write questions to ask in class.

■ Are the topics covered in the text also emphasized in class? If yes, this suggests this is material you particularly need to pay attention to for your next test or assignment.

■ Do you know the definitions of key terms? Using your own words, write short definitions.

■ Do you understand key terms? Try to come up with your own examples. If you don't understand a term, circle it and any other words to look up later in a dictionary.

■ Do you agree with the author? Write personal comments—points of agreement or disagreement—in the margin.

■ Do you know which sections of the reading are most important? Stick Post-it® notes on critical sections and label them for quick referral.

■ Do you comprehend what you have read? Rewrite chapter titles, headings, and subheadings so that they're more meaningful to you.

Step 6 Answer

As you read, seek out the answers to your questions and write them down. Fill in your outline. Write summaries by listing the main points or key events covered in a chapter. Write mini-indexes in the margin; mini-indexes contain the numbers of other pages in the book where the same topic is discussed. In science-related subjects, it may be useful to draw diagrams or pictures that help you organize and integrate textual material in visual terms. The more accurate the drawing, the greater the benefit in using it as a study tool.

Jot down any new questions and note when you don't find the answers you are looking for. Use these notes to ask questions in class, or see your instructor personally.

When you read, create an image of yourself as a person in search of the answers. You are a detective, watching for every clue, sitting erect in your straight-back chair, demanding that your textbook gives you what you want—the answers. ✳

Five smart ways to use metacognitive self-regulation to making highlighting effective

Step 5 in Muscle Reading mentions a powerful tool—highlighting. This strategy is powerful but it also presents a danger—the ever-present temptation to highlight too much text. If you highlight too much of what you are reading, you are not discriminating between important and unimportant ideas in the text (Bell & Limber, 2010). In fact, research has found that excessive highlighting is no more successful a reading strategy than simply reading the text alone (Leopold & Leutner, 2015). So how can you make highlighting an effective reading strategy for you? In a nutshell, by intentionally monitoring your understanding of the text as you read. Consciously controlling your behaviour is what self-regulation is all about and master students use this skill to be better readers. Remember, good learners have strong metacognitive skills (see Chapter 1, "Time"): They set goals (*I will read 10 pages of my text today*), they monitor their progress towards that goal (*I've read and understood the first five pages I read*), and they change their strategies when goals aren't being met (*I didn't understand what I just read. I better read that paragraph again and look up the new terms in a dictionary*).

Let's start with the five simple steps to highlighting:

1. **Read carefully first.** Read an entire chapter or section at least once before you begin highlighting. Don't be in a hurry to mark up your book. Get to know the text first. Make two or three passes through difficult sections before you highlight.

2. **Circle important words or concepts.** Select words or concepts that you think are the important points in the chapter you have just read.

3. **Reread the chapter.** As you reread the chapter, highlight additional information you think is important to understand the text. Try to connect what you are reading to your prior knowledge. Ask yourself, How does this relate to what I previously knew? When you highlight, remember to look for passages that directly answer the questions you posed during Step 3 of Muscle Reading. Within these passages, highlight individual words, phrases, or sentences rather than whole paragraphs. The important thing is to choose an overall strategy before you put highlighter to paper.

4. **Use side notes.** As you reread the chapter, consider whether the paragraph is presenting a new concept or idea or simply providing an example of a concept or idea. Write notes in the margin about the purpose of the paragraph.

5. **Use highlighting to monitor your reading comprehension.** After you finish reading the chapter, reflect on your ability to implement this strategy. Did you perform all the steps for effective highlighting? For highlighting to be a successful learning strategy, you need to check your comprehension of the material you read. Stop reading periodically and look back over the sentences you've highlighted. See if you are making accurate distinctions between main points and supporting material. Highlighting too much—more than 10 percent of the text—can be a sign that you're not making this distinction and that you don't fully understand what you're reading. Being able to consciously monitor your understanding is the key to effectively using highlighting as a reading strategy. When highlighting, you're making moment-by-moment decisions about what you want to remember from a text. You're also making inferences about what material might be included on an exam. Research shows that it is the combination of highlighting with checking reading comprehension that makes a significant difference in your ability to succeed on tests (Leopold & Leutner, 2015). If you find that highlighting along with monitoring your own comprehension is not an effective strategy for reading difficult material, see the article "When reading is tough" later in this chapter for some tips that can help.

PHASE 3: AFTER YOU READ
Recite, Review, Review Again

Step 7 Recite

Talk to yourself about what you've read. Or talk to someone else. When you're finished with a reading assignment, make a speech about it. When you recite, you practise an important aspect of metacognition—**synthesis**, or combining individual ideas and facts into a meaningful whole.

One way to get yourself to recite is to look at each highlighted point. Note what you marked, then put the book down and start talking out loud. Explain as much as you can about that particular point.

To make this technique more effective, do it in front of a mirror. It might seem silly, but the benefits can be enormous. Reap them at exam time. A related technique is to stop reading periodically and write a short, free-form summary of what you just read. In one study by Karpicke and Blunt (2011), this informal "retrieval practice" helped students recall information better than other study techniques.

Classmates are even better than mirrors. Form a group and practise teaching each other what you have read. One of the best ways to learn anything is to teach it to someone else.

In addition, talk about your reading whenever you can. Tell friends and family members what you're learning from your textbooks.

Talking about your reading reinforces a valuable skill—the ability to summarize. To practise this skill, pick one chapter (or one section of one chapter) from any of your textbooks. State the main topic covered in this chapter. Then state the main points that the author makes about this topic.

For example, the main topic up to now in this chapter is Muscle Reading. The main point about this topic is that Muscle Reading includes three phases—steps to take before you read, while you read, and after you read. For a more detailed summary, you could name each of the nine steps.

Note: This "topic–point" method does not work so well when you want to summarize short stories, novels, plays, and other works of fiction. Instead, focus on action. In most stories, the main character confronts a major problem and takes a series of actions to solve it. Describe that problem and talk about the character's key actions—the turning points in the story.

Muscle Reading—a leaner approach

Keep in mind that Muscle Reading is an overall approach, not a rigid, step-by-step procedure. Here's a shorter variation that students have found helpful. Practise it with any chapter in this book:

- **Preview and question.** Flip through the pages, looking at anything that catches your eye—headings, subheadings, illustrations, photographs. Turn the title of each article into a question. For example, "How Muscle Reading works" can become "How does Muscle Reading work?" List your questions on a separate sheet of paper, or write each question on an index card.

- **Read to answer your questions.** Read each article, then go back over the text and underline or highlight answers to the appropriate questions on your list.

- **Recite and review.** When you're done with the chapter, close the book. Recite by reading each question—and answering it—out loud. Review the chapter by looking up the answers to your questions. (It's easy—they're already highlighted.) Review again by quizzing yourself one more time with your list of questions.

Extending Muscle Reading to Web pages and ebooks

You can still use the three phases of Muscle Reading when accessing a web page or ebook on your devices. Muscle your way into reading from screens by using features that are not available with printed books. Though features on digital devices vary, see if you can do the following.

Phase 1: Before you read   For more readable text, adjust the font size or zoom in on a page. You can also change the contrast between the text and background. It is useful to change those settings when you are in a place with dim lighting. In addition, cut the clutter: Web pages abound with ads, pop-up windows, and animations. Getting rid of all that stuff makes it easier to avoid time-wasting distractions and focus your attention on the core content of the page. There are ad blockers like *Mercury Reader* for Chrome that do just that. Many Web browsers such as Safari and Firefox also come with a built-in "reader" mode that does much the same thing.

Phase 2: While you read

Find navigation tools. To flip electronic pages, look for *previous* and *next* buttons or arrows on the right and left borders of each page. Many ebooks also offer a *go to page* feature that allows you to key in a specific page number.

Access the Table of Contents. For a bigger picture of the text, look for a table of contents that lists chapter headings and subheadings. Note that charts, illustrations, photos, tables, diagrams, and other visuals might be listed separately.

Search the text. Look for a search box that allows you to enter key words and find all the places in the text where those words are mentioned.

Look for links to related information. Many ebook readers will supply a definition of any word in the text. All you need to do is highlight a word and click on it. Also find out if your ebook reader will connect you to websites related to the topic of your ebook.

Highlight, annotate, and reflect. Look for ways to electronically underline or highlight text. You can annotate the book by keying in your own notes tied to specific pages. You might be able to tag each note with a key word and then sort your notes into categories. Take time to reflect and monitor your comprehension of what you have read.

Stay focussed. It's easier to get distracted when you use your devices to read text. Research reports that students reading ebooks are more likely to get distracted by social media, emails, and messaging than those reading from print materials (Subrahmanyam, Michikyan, Clemmons, Carrillo, Uhls, & Greenfield, 2013). So, turn off your alerts and keep focussed on your reading.

Print. See if you can connect your ebook device to a printer. You might find it easier to study difficult passages or to look at large illustrations or charts on paper as they don't translate well to the small screen.

Phase 3: After you read   You still want to recite and review material to aid in moving information to long-term memory. Some ebooks can create instant summaries of your highlighted passages—check out Amazon Kindle. Just remember that it is reflecting on learning and monitoring your comprehension of what you have read that makes the difference for later recall.

Step 8 Review

Plan to do your first complete review within 24 hours of reading the material. This point is critical: A review within 24 hours moves information from your short-term memory to your long-term memory.

Review within one day. If you read it on Wednesday, review it on Thursday. During this review, look over your notes and clear up anything you don't understand. Recite some of the main points again.

This review can be short. You might spend as little as 15 minutes reviewing a difficult two-hour reading assignment. Investing that time now can save you hours later when studying for exams.

Step 9 Review again

The final step in Muscle Reading is the weekly or monthly review. This step can be very short—perhaps only four or five minutes per assignment. Simply go over your notes. Read the highlighted parts of your text. Recite one or two of the more complicated points.

The purpose of these reviews is to keep the neural pathways to the information open and to make them more distinct. That way, the information can be easier to recall. You can accomplish these short reviews anytime, anywhere, if you are prepared.

Conduct a five-minute review while you are waiting for a bus, for your laundry to dry, or for the water to boil. Write ideas, formulas, concepts, and facts on a notepad or keep track of them on your laptop or mobile device and carry them with you. These short review periods can be effortless and fun.

Sometimes longer review periods are appropriate. For example, if you found an assignment difficult, consider rereading it. Start over, as if you had never seen the material before. Sometimes a second reading will provide you with surprising insights. But be careful when rereading not to give in to the illusion of knowing (Brown, Roediger, & McDaniel, 2014). This is where you mistake fluency with a text with comprehension. So, make an effort to ask yourself, What is the text all about? and try to answer that question in your own words.

Decades ago, psychologists identified the **primacy–recency effect** that suggests that we remember most easily the first and last items in any presentation (Pineño & Miller, 2005). Previewing and reviewing your reading can put this theory to work for you. ✳

Discovery/Intention Statement

Experimenting with Muscle Reading

After reading the steps included in Muscle Reading, reflect on your reading skills. Are you a more effective reader than you thought you were? Less effective? Record your observations below.

_____

_____

_____

_____

_____

_____

_____

_____

_____

_____

_____

_____

_____

Many students find that they only do the "Focus" step with their textbooks. You've just read about the advantages of eight additional steps you should perform. Depending on the text, reading assignment, your available time, and your commitment level to the material, you may discover through practice which additional steps work best for you. Right now, make a commitment to yourself to experiment with all or several of the additional Muscle Reading steps by completing the following Intention Statement.

I intend to use the following Muscle Reading steps for the next two weeks in my _____ class:

❏ Preview

❏ Outline

❏ Question

❏ Focus

❏ Reflect

❏ Answer

❏ Recite

❏ Review

❏ Review again

WORD POWER:
Expanding your vocabulary

© Shahrul Azman/Shutterstock

Having a large vocabulary makes reading more enjoyable and increases the range of materials you can explore. In addition, building your vocabulary gives you more options for self-expression when speaking or writing. When you can choose from a larger pool of words, you increase the precision and power of your thinking.

Strengthen your vocabulary by savouring words. Look up unfamiliar words. Pay special attention to words that arouse your curiosity.

Students regularly use two kinds of dictionaries: the desk dictionary (the one you typically have in your home) and the unabridged dictionary (a large dictionary that provides complete information about words; typically found in the library). Or you may prefer to use one of the many free online dictionaries. Just be sure to check one that spells words using Canadian English, such as *dictionary.canadaspace.com*. If you want to keep learning new words, there are many apps that will give you a word of the day that you can listen to on your mobile device. Try learning new words to broaden your vocabulary while you are travelling to school on public transit.

Construct a word stack

When you come across an unfamiliar word in class or when you are reading, write it down in a note pad or keep a list of new words on your computer. Below the word, copy the sentence in which it was used. You can look up each word immediately, or you can look up the words later. Write the definition of each word on the back of the index card, adding the diacritical marks that tell you how to pronounce it.

Divide words into parts

Another suggestion is to divide an unfamiliar word into syllables and look for familiar parts. This works well if you make it a point to learn common prefixes (beginning syllables) and suffixes (ending syllables). For example, the suffix *-tude* usually refers to a condition or state of being. Knowing this makes it easier to conclude that *habitude* refers to a usual way of doing something and that *similitude* means being similar or having a quality of resemblance. See an unabridged dictionary for more examples of word parts.

Infer the meaning of words from their context

You can often deduce the meaning of an unfamiliar word simply by paying attention to its context—the surrounding words, phrases, sentences, paragraphs, or images. Later you can confirm your deduction by consulting a dictionary.

Practise looking for context clues:

- *Definitions.* A key word might be defined right in the text. Look for phrases such as *defined as* or *in other words*. These often introduce definitions.

- *Examples.* Authors often provide examples to clarify a word meaning. If the word is not explicitly defined, then study the examples. They're often preceded by the phrases *for example, for instance,* or *such as.*

- *Lists.* When a word is listed in a series, pay attention to the other items in the series. They might define the unfamiliar word through association.

- *Comparisons.* You might find a new word surrounded by synonyms—words with a similar meaning. Look for synonyms after words such as *like* and *as.*

- *Contrasts.* A writer might use a word together with its antonym—a word or phrase with the opposite meaning. Look for phrases such as *on the contrary* and *on the other hand.* ✳

Get SPUNKI with your reading

After finishing a book chapter or article for one of your classes, take a few minutes to complete the following sentences in writing:

What I found *surprising* in this reading is…

What I found *puzzling* in this reading is…

What I found *useful* in this reading is…

What I found *new* in this reading is…

What I already *knew* in this reading is…

What I found *interesting* in this reading is…

These questions provide a good way for you to organize your notes and can help make reading more fun. They also provide cues for you to monitor your comprehension of what you read. You can use the acronym SPUNKI to remember the key words in each of the six questions: **s**urprising, **p**uzzling, **u**seful, **n**ew, **k**new, **i**nteresting. Go on—get SPUNKI with your reading!

When reading is
TOUGH

wavebreakmedia/Shutterstock.com

SOMETIMES ORDINARY READING
methods are not enough. It's easy to get bogged down in a murky reading assignment. The solution starts with a First Step: When you are confused, tell the truth about it.

Successful readers monitor their understanding of reading material. They do not see confusion as a mistake or a personal shortcoming. Instead, they take it as a cue to change reading strategies and process ideas at a deeper level. Somehow, students get the idea that reading means opening a book and slogging through the text in a straight line from the first word until the last. Actually, this is an ineffective way to read. Consider the following suggestions.

Feel free to shake up your routine
Make several passes through any reading material. During a preview, for example, just scan the text to look for key words and highlighted material. Next, skim the entire chapter or article again, spending a little more time and taking in more than you did during your preview. Finally, read in more depth, proceeding word by word through some or all of the text.

Look for essential words

If you are stuck on a paragraph, mentally cross out all of the adjectives and adverbs and read the sentence without them. Find the important words. These will usually be verbs and nouns.

Create a concept map

To help you organize complex ideas create a concept map. In Chapter 3, "Memory," we talked about how to create concept maps—two-dimensional maps of key ideas and connecting links to show how those ideas are related. Generating concept maps will get you actively involved in information processing and deepen your learning (Leopold & Leutner, 2015). Create a concept map of a chapter you have read and then compare your map with a friend in the same course. Discuss why your maps are similar or different and why you linked specific ideas or concepts together. Reflecting on your map construction is a key component of this reading strategy. Well-designed concepts maps are also a great tool to study from later.

Talk to your instructor or teaching assistant

When you are stuck, admit it and make an appointment with your instructor. Most teachers welcome the opportunity to work individually with students. Be specific about your confusion. Point out the paragraph that you found toughest to understand.

Become engaged with the text

If you find the textbook boring, it is hard to be excited about reading. To overcome this, you need to find a personal reason for doing the reading that goes beyond "Because I have a test coming up." Try to connect what you are reading to your prior knowledge—what have you heard about this topic before. This also will increase the likelihood that you will be able to recall the information you read later.

Skip around

Jump immediately to the end of the article or chapter. You might have lost the big picture, and sometimes simply seeing the conclusion or summary is all you need to put the details in context. Retrace the steps in a chain of ideas and look for examples. Absorb facts and ideas in

Did you **know that ...?**

> There once was a funeral for a textbook on a Canadian campus? A student named Lou McMann from the University of Prince Edward Island finally passed his introductory math course after taking the course seven times. Now that is determination to succeed no matter what. To celebrate, his colleagues had a funeral for his math textbook ("50 little-known facts, 2017).

whatever order works for you—which may be different than the author's presentation.

Take a workshop from your learning skills or student success centre

Most schools provide free workshops to students on all aspects of learning including textbook reading. These services are part of your tuition fee, so make good use of them. It is often the top students who use these services the most, as they are ones seeking that competitive edge in terms of grades. So be like the best and seek help—even if you don't really think you need it.

Use another text

Find a similar text in the library or related information online. Sometimes a concept is easier to understand if it is expressed another way.

Ask, "What's going on here?"

When you feel stuck, stop reading for a moment and diagnose what's happening. At these stop points, mark your place in the margin of the page with a penciled "S" for "Stuck." If you see a pattern to your marks over several pages, this might indicate a question you want to answer before going further. Or you might discover a reading habit you'd like to change.

Stop reading

When none of the above suggestions work, do not despair. Admit your confusion and then take a break. Catch a movie, go for a walk, study another subject, or sleep on it. The concepts you've already absorbed might come together at a subconscious level as you move on to other activities. Allow some time for that process. When you return to the reading material, you will see it with fresh eyes (Bohart, 2005). ✳

Reading science texts

Reading science texts can be a particular challenge to many students. Why? Because the writing style is so different than what you usually read, like novels or Web pages. Science writing tends to adopt a fairly authoritative position, have a denser structure, and be presented in an impersonal way (Hodges, 2015). Sometimes just trying to follow the sentence structure is enough for the meaning of what you are reading to get lost. Another challenge is that the reading often assumes you have already learned information necessary to understand the text.

In addition, the mental effort it can take to read science texts can be overwhelming as it often requires that you focus on more than one idea at a time. This can make it difficult for you to realize what you know and don't know. Finally, sometimes students assume that the purpose of doing the reading is just to learn the facts. Not true! Even though the text is presented in an authoritative manner, your task is still to question what you read and analyze and evaluate what you are reading.

So, what can you do to improve your understanding of science texts?

- Keep asking yourself, What is this reading about? This means you need to try to evaluate whether or not the text makes sense given what you already know. So continuously monitoring your comprehension is key; and when you don't understand what you've read, you need to change your reading strategy to improve your comprehension (see the section on When Reading is Tough for other strategies) rather than skipping over the section and hoping it will all become clearer at a later date. To test your comprehension, try to summarize the text to a classmate and then ask your partner to ask you questions about why you think what you think about what you read.

- Recognize that you will have to learn a whole new vocabulary to understand science fully and that words you may be familiar with in everyday reading may have a different meaning in your science text. For instance, the word "temperature" means how hot or cold something is in everyday language but in chemistry it indicates "the direction that energy flows (as heat) when two objects come in thermal contact." So, to make you sure you understand what you're reading, check the meanings of words with a science dictionary.

- Don't skip over graphics, formulae, symbols, and equations in your texts. Often students may jump over graphs and tables in favour of learning from the textual material. Learning to understand the graphics and formulae is part of the language of science. Your ability both to understand graphic representations and also to be able to take textual information and convert it to graphs is essential for understanding the process and content of science.

- Do the readings before class. Although your professor may be easier to understand than the textbook, if the first time you hear a new term is in class, your understanding of the material will not be as deep as if you have already started to consider what a term might mean before class. Reading the textbook before class will also help to lessen the cognitive load in learning new material. If you haven't read the material before class, it will be difficult to connect what you are learning to prior knowledge and to start to forge those new neural connections in your brain, connections which are what meaningful learning is all about (Hodges, 2015).

Developing
INFORMATION LITERACY

Rawpixel.com/Shutterstock.com

Master students are able to find information from appropriate sources. They recognize that in addition to reading their textbooks they are also going to be required to search out information for their assignments. They must also be able to assess the accuracy of those sources.

Information literacy is a set of skills to use whenever you want to answer questions or find information. For example, you might want to develop a topic for a paper or assignment. Or you might want to learn more about a product, a service, a vacation spot, or a potential job. You might want to follow up on something you heard on the radio or saw on the Web. Or you need information for a speech. All of these require information literacy.

An important quality of master students is curiosity. To answer questions, master students find information from appropriate sources, evaluate the information, organize it, and use it to achieve a purpose. Information literacy is the ability to do this in a world where data is literally at your fingertips.

Discover your purpose

One of the early steps in Muscle Reading involves asking questions. Research means asking questions as well.

Discover your main question. This is the thing that sparked your curiosity in the first place. Answering it is your purpose for doing research.

Your main question will raise a number of smaller, related questions. These are supporting questions, and they also call for answers.

Suppose that your main question is this: What led the federal government in 2017 to change the laws regarding cannabis possession in Canada?

Here are some possible supporting questions:

How was cannabis previously treated under the *Controlled Drugs and Substances Act*?

How do provincial governments vary in their laws regarding the distribution and wholesaling of cannabis?

What are the risks for youth consuming cannabis?

Listing your main and supporting questions can save hours of time. If you ever feel overwhelmed or get sidetracked, pull out your list of questions. When the information you're finding answers one of those questions, then you're on track. If you're wading through material that's not answering your questions, then it's time to find another source of information or revise your questions.

Distinguish between primary and secondary sources of information

As a researcher, you can distinguish between primary and secondary sources. Primary sources can lead to information treasures. Primary sources are firsthand materials—personal journals, literary works, letters, speeches, government documents, scientific experiments, field observations, interviews with recognized experts, archeological digs, artifacts, and original works of art. Primary sources can also include scholarly publications such as the *Canadian Journal for the Scholarship of Teaching and Learning*. One clue that you're dealing with primary source is the title. If it includes the word "journal," then you're probably reading a primary source. Signs of scholarly articles include

- Names of authors with their credentials and academic affiliations
- A brief abstract (summary) of the article, along with a section on research methods (how the authors tested their ideas and reached their conclusions)
- Conclusions based on an extensive review of relevant publications, survey research, data collected in a laboratory experiment, or a combination of these
- Extensive bibliographies or references to the work of other scholars

If you pick up a magazine with pages of full-colour advertisements and photos of celebrities, you're not reading a scholarly journal.

Though many kinds of publications can be useful, scholarly journals are unmatched in depth and credibility. Journal articles are usually peer reviewed. This means that other experts in the field read and review the articles to make sure that they are accurate.

Secondary sources summarize, explain, and comment on primary sources. Examples that can be helpful to you in your research include most scholarly journals, popular but reliable periodicals like *MacLean's*, and general reference works such as the *Encyclopaedia Britannica* or the *Oxford Companion to English Literature*. Secondary sources are useful places to start your research. Use them to get an overview of your topic.

Get to know your library

Speaking to a reference librarian can save you hours. So, if you can't find what you want, go ask a librarian. Take a tour of your library and do a virtual tour of your library's website.

Libraries—from the smallest one in your hometown to the Library and Archives Canada—consist of just three basic elements:

- *Catalogues*—online databases that list all of the library's accessible sources
- *Collections*—materials, such as periodicals (magazines and newspapers), books, pamphlets, audiovisual materials, and materials available from other collections via interlibrary loan. Many of these materials will be available to you online through your library website.
- *Technological resources*—Internet access to specialized resources, such as databases stored online that allow you to look at full-text articles from magazines, journals, and newspapers. These are often available from your home via a computer or other mobile device with a password. Also ask about ebooks that can be delivered straight to your computer.

Before you start your next research project, take some time to investigate all three elements of your school's library. The library catalogue available on your library website is a database that lists all available materials, both print and online. To find materials, do a keyword search—much like using a search engine on the Internet.

Search the subject guides

Use the library website to view the wide array of research guides by subject. Generally, library research guides have been developed to provide an overview of subject areas such as anthropology, history, biology, civil engineering, etc. These subject guides provide information on the major reference sources available for individual subject areas. You will become aware of the main encyclopedias, critical works, biographies, almanacs, dictionaries, statistics, and major online databases and indexes for your field of study. These reference tools will be invaluable when conducting research for assignments and tests.

Search for information with key words

One crucial skill for information literacy is using key words. Key words are the most important terms in your main and supporting questions. These are the words that you enter into a library database or online search box. Your choice of key words determines the quality of results that you get from Internet search engines such as google.com and from library catalogues. For better search results, here are some guidelines:

- *Use specific key words.* "Reading strategies or note-taking strategies" will get more specific results than "study strategies." Do not type in your whole research question as a sentence. The search engine will look for each word and give you a lot of useless results.
- *Use unique key words.* Whenever possible, use proper names. Enter "Beatles" or "Coldplay" rather than "British rock bands." If you're looking for nearby restaurants, enter "restaurant" and your postal code rather than the name of your city.
- *Use quotation marks if you're looking for certain words in a certain order.* "Audacity of hope" will return a list of pages with that exact phrase.
- *Search within a site.* If you're looking only for articles about college tuition from *The Globe and Mail*, then add "globe and mail" or "*globeandmail.com*" to the search box.
- *Remember to think of synonyms.* For example, "hypertension" is often called "high blood pressure."
- *When you're not sure of a key word, add a wild card character.* In most search engines, that character is the asterisk (*). If you're looking for the title of a film directed by Sarah Polley and just can't remember the name, enter "sarah polley directed *."
- *Look for more search options.* Many search engines also offer advanced search features and explain how to use them. Look for the word "advanced" or "more" on the site's home page, and click on the link. If in doubt about how to use your library's search engines, ask a librarian for help.

Evaluate information

Some students assume that anything that's published in print or on the Internet is true. Unfortunately, that's not the case. Some sources of information are more reliable than others, and some published information is misleading or mistaken.

Before evaluating any source of information, make sure that you understand what it says. Use the techniques of Muscle Reading to comprehend an author's message. Then think critically about the information. Chapter 7, "Thinking," offers many suggestions for doing this. Here are some things you should be sure to look for:

Relevance. Look for sources that deal directly with your research questions. If you're in doubt about the relevance of a particular source, ask yourself, "Will this material help me achieve the purpose of my research and support my thesis?"

Currency. Notice the publication date of your source material. If your topic is time-sensitive, set some guidelines about how current you want your sources to be; for example, that they were published during the last five years.

Credibility. Scan the source for biographical information about the author. Look for education, training, and work experience that qualifies this person to publish on the topic.

Bias. Determine what the website or other source is "selling"—the product, service, or point of view it promotes. Political affiliations or funding sources might colour the author's point of view.

Evaluate Internet sources with extra care

Ask the following questions:

- *Who pays for the site?* Carefully check information from an organization that sells advertising. Look for an "About This Site" link—a clue to sources of funding.

- *Who runs the site?* Look for a clear description of the person or organization responsible for the content. If the sponsoring person or organization did not create the site's content, then find out who did.

- *How is the site's content selected?* Look for a link that lists members of an editorial board or other qualified reviewers.

- *Does the site separate fact from opinion?* Reliable sites often follow a newspaper model, which separates reports about current events from editorials.

- *Does the site support claims with evidence?* Credible sites base their editorial standards on expert opinion and facts from scientific studies. Look for references to primary sources. If you find grandiose claims supported only by testimonials, beware. When something sounds too good to be true, it probably is.

- *Does the site link to other sites?* Think critically about these sites as well.

- *How can readers connect with the site?* Look for a way to contact the site's publisher with questions and comments. See whether you can find a physical address, email address, and phone number. Sites that conceal this information might conceal other facts. Also inspect reader comments on the site to see whether a variety of opinions are expressed.

Many websites from government agencies and non-profit organizations have strict and clearly stated editorial policies. These sites are often good places to start your research.

Use information

Take careful notes on your sources using the techniques explained in Chapter 5, "Notes." Remember to keep a list of all your sources of information and avoid plagiarism. Be prepared to cite your sources in footnotes or endnotes, and a bibliography or references page.

Also make time to digest all the information you gather. Ask yourself these questions:

- Do I have answers to my main question?
- Do I have answers to my supporting questions?
- What are the main ideas from my sources?
- Do I have personal experiences that can help me answer these questions?
- On what points do my sources agree?
- On what points do my sources disagree?
- Do I have statistics and other facts that I can use to support my ideas?
- What new questions do I have?

The beauty of these questions is that they stimulate your thinking. Discover the pleasures of emerging insights and sudden inspiration. You just might get hooked on the adventure of information literacy. ✳

practising
CRITICAL THINKING

4-2

Information literacy

Using two different search engines, go online and get three references from each search engine, for an upcoming assignment in one of your courses.

Enter the same key words into each search engine.

    List key words: _____

Search Engine A) _____

    Reference 1) _____
    Reference 2) _____
    Reference 3) _____

Search Engine B) _____

    Reference 4) _____
    Reference 5) _____
    Reference 6) _____

Did you get the same references?

_____

Explain why you used the specific key words to find the resources.

_____
_____
_____
_____
_____
_____
_____
_____
_____
_____

Evaluate EACH of the three sources for

a. currency

_____
_____
_____

b. credibility

_____
_____
_____

c. bias

_____
_____
_____

Explain why you would be likely to use each of the sources for your upcoming assignment, or why not.

_____
_____
_____
_____
_____
_____
_____

Staying literate in
THE DIGITAL AGE

"Read for pleasure when I can't keep up with my course reading?! Why would I?" It turns out that reading books for pleasure is strongly linked to success in school and in the workplace. Skilled readers generally go on to higher-paying jobs and have more opportunities to advance in their careers.

Recent research published by Life Literacy Canada (2018) found that

- Those with higher levels of prose literacy are more likely to have higher paying jobs, better health, and higher levels of involvement with community groups.
- The Conference Board of Canada states that work-place literacy is important for creating a workforce that is better at decision-making and at teamwork, and is more productive.
- But the study also found that
- More than four out of ten adult Canadians (48%) have low levels of literacy—they have less than high school level of prose literacy.

If you'd like to begin or increase your leisure reading, here are a few suggestions for how to get started.

Read for pleasure

Look for fun things to read—books that are not required for your classes or job and that reflect your personal interests. Scan websites like *Good Reads or Oprah's Book Club* to get ideas. Check out the books that have been nominated for Canada's Giller prize (worth a $100,000) or read the books on the list for the CBC annual "battle of the books," Canada Reads. Many schools hold similar competitions to Canada Reads, and they host author readings of novels and public debates on their merits. Making reading social is a great way to get more out of reading. Join a book club—book clubs are a great way to meet new people, to share ideas, and have fun. There are book clubs that focus on LGBTQ authors, nonfiction work, mysteries, etc. Put the key words "book clubs local" in your browser to find a club near you. Or start your own club; for helpful hints on how to join or start your own book club, go to *www .bookclubcentral.org/about.*

Make time to read

Keep track of how much time you spend in front of screens playing games or being on social media. Consider trading some of that time for pleasure reading.

Let books read to you

Comb your local library for audiobooks. Many are available as digital downloads.

Slow down and reflect

When you read for pleasure, forget about speed-reading. Take in the words at your own pace.

In addition, look up from the page once in a while to think about what you've just read, or write a journal entry. In a Discovery Statement, list the main points or events that you want to remember. Also note what surprised you or led to a flash of insight. Whenever you disagree, argue with the author in writing.

In an Intention Statement, describe any follow-up action you want to take. Perhaps what you've read suggests a goal for you to achieve or an idea that you may want to use. Describe it in more detail. List the next action you could take to get started. ✳

English as a
SECOND LANGUAGE

IF YOU GREW UP speaking a language other than English, or if you grew up speaking a dialect of English that is termed nonstandard—such as a Caribbean dialect of English— you're probably called a student of English as a Second Language (ESL) or an English Language Learner (ELL). Your cultural background as a whole might differ greatly from many of your fellow students. You might also speak several languages in addition to English.

Knowing a language other than English offers advantages. You can think thoughts that are not possible in English and see the world in ways that are unique to people who speak your native language.

If you are having difficulties mastering English, experiment with the following suggestions to learn English with more success.

Many ESL/ELL students feel insecure about using English in social settings, including the classroom. Choosing not to speak, however, can delay your mastery of English and isolate you from other students.

As an alternative, make it your intention to speak up in class. List several questions beforehand, and plan to ask them. Also schedule a time to meet with your instructors during office hours to discuss any material that you find confusing. These strategies can help you build relationships while developing English skills.

In addition, start a conversation with at least one native speaker of English in each of your classes. For openers, ask about their favourite instructors or ideas for future courses to take.

Celebrate mistakes

English is a complex language. Whenever you extend your vocabulary and range of expression, the likelihood of making mistakes increases. The person who wants to master English yet seldom makes mistakes is probably being too careful. Do not look upon mistakes as a sign of weakness. Mistakes can be your best teachers—if you are willing to learn from them.

Remember that the terms "English as a Second Language" and "English Language Learner" describe a difference—not a deficiency. The fact that you've entered a new culture and are mastering another language gives you a broader perspective than people who speak only one language. And if you currently speak two or more languages, you've already demonstrated your ability to learn.

Analyze errors in using English

To learn from your errors, first make a list of the errors that are common to you. Ask an instructor or an English-speaking friend to help you. Next to the error, write a corrected version. For examples, see Table 4.1.

Table 4.1 ***Error Correction***

Error	Correction
Sun is bright.	The sun is bright.
He cheerful.	He is cheerful.
I enjoy to play chess.	I enjoy playing chess.
Good gifts received everyone.	Everyone received good gifts.
I knew what would present the teachers.	I knew what the teachers would present.
I like very much burritos.	I like burritos very much.
I want that you stay.	I want you to stay.
Is raining.	It is raining.
My mother she lives in Manitoba.	My mother lives in Manitoba.
I gave the paper to she.	I gave the paper to her.
They felt safety in the car.	They felt safe in the car.
He has three car.	He has three cars.
I have helpfuls family members.	I have helpful family members.
She don't know nothing.	She knows nothing.

Learn by speaking and listening

You probably started your English studies by using textbooks. Writing and reading in English are important, but to gain greater fluency, make it your goal to hear and speak English.

For example, listen to radio talk shows or podcasts. Imitate the speaker's pronunciation by repeating phrases and sentences that you hear. During conversations, notice the facial expressions and gestures that accompany certain English words and phrases.

If you speak English with a heavy accent, do not be concerned. Many people speak accented yet clear English. Work on neutralizing your accent only if you can't be understood easily.

Take advantage of opportunities to read and hear English at the same time. For instance, turn on English subtitles when watching a film. Also, search your library for audiobooks. Check out the printed book, and follow along as you listen.

Use technology resources

There are numerous apps to help you learn English on your phone, tablet, or computer (and incidentally many will help you learn other languages too). They include *busuu* (*www.busuu.com/en/mobile*), *Speaking-PalEnglish Tutor* (*www.speakingpal.com/products*), or *MyWordBook* (*www.britishcouncil.org/english/business/apps/mywordbook-2*). These apps have tools like flashcards, podcasts, and quizzes to help you master speaking English. To find out more, put "best mobile apps for ESL students" in your browser—you will be surprised at what you will find.

Gain skills in note-taking and testing

When taking notes, remember that you don't have to capture everything that an instructor says. To a large extent, the art of note-taking consists of choosing what *not* to record. Listen for key words, main points, and important examples. Remember that instructors will often repeat these things. You'll have more than one chance to pick up on the important material. When you're in doubt, ask for repetition or clarification. For additional suggestions, see Chapter 5, "Notes."

Taking tests is a related challenge. You may find that certain kinds of test questions—such as multiple-choice items—are more common in Canada than in your native country. Don't leave answers blank unless there is a penalty for wrong answers. Guessing is better than not

answering at all. Chapter 6, "Tests," can help you master these and many other types of tests.

When in doubt, use expressions you understand

Native speakers of English use many informal expressions that are called *slang*. You are more likely to find slang in conversations than in written English.

Native speakers also use *idioms*—colourful expressions with meanings that are not always obvious. Idioms can often be misunderstood. For instance, a "fork in the road" does not refer to an eating utensil discarded on a street; it refers to a choice you have to make.

Learning how to use slang and idioms is part of gaining fluency in English. However, these elements of the language are tricky. If you mispronounce a key word or leave one out, you can create a misunderstanding. In important situations—such as applying for a job or meeting with a teacher—use expressions you fully understand.

Create a community of English learners

Learning as part of a community can increase your mastery. For example, when completing a writing assignment in English, get together with other people who are learning the language. Read each other's papers and suggest revisions. Plan on revising your paper a number of times based on feedback from your peers.

You might feel awkward about sharing your writing with other people. Accept that feeling—and then remind yourself of everything you have to gain by learning from a group. In addition to learning English more quickly, you can raise your grades and make new friends.

Native speakers of English might be willing to assist your group. Ask your instructors to suggest someone. This person can benefit from the exchange of ideas and the chance to learn about other cultures. Most schools offer international student services, and these typically have English conversation classes. Effective writing programs can also be very helpful with your written submissions. Make sure you investigate the resources available on your campus.

Celebrate your gains

Every time you analyze and correct an error in English, you make a small gain. Celebrate those gains. Taken together over time, they add up to major progress in mastering English as a second language. ✳

Getting past
ROADBLOCKS TO READING

Even your favourite strategies for reading can fail when you're dealing with bigger issues. Those roadblocks to getting your reading done can come from three major sources:

- Finding enough time to keep up with your reading
- Making choices about what to read once you find the time
- Getting interrupted by other people while you're reading

For solutions to each of these problems, read on.

Scheduling time for reading

Planning dispels panic (*I've got 300 pages to read before tomorrow morning!*) and helps you finish off your entire reading load for a term. Creating a reading plan is relatively simple if you use the following steps:

Step 1. Estimate the total number of pages that you'll read

To arrive at this figure, check the course syllabus for each class that you're taking. Look for lists of reading assignments. Based on what you find, estimate the total number of pages that you'll read for all your classes.

Step 2. Estimate how many pages you can read during one hour

Remember that your reading speed will be different for various materials. It depends on everything from the layout of the pages to the difficulty of the text. To give your estimate some credibility, base it on actual experience. During your first reading assignment in each course, keep track of how many pages you read per hour.

Step 3. Estimate your total number of reading hours

Divide the total number of pages from Step 1 by your pages-per-hour from Step 2. For example, look at this calculation:

600 (total pages for all courses this term) ÷ 10 (pages read per hour) = 60 (total reading hours needed for the term)

LightField Studios/Shutterstock.com

The result is the total number of hours you'll need to complete your reading assignments this term. Remember to give yourself some "wiggle room." Allow extra hours for rereading and unplanned events. Consider taking your initial number of projected hours and doubling it. You can always back off from there to an estimate that seems more reasonable.

Step 4. Schedule reading time

Take the total number of hours from Step 3 and divide it by the number of weeks in your current term. That will give you the number of hours to schedule for reading each week.

60 (total reading hours needed for the term) ÷ 16 (weeks in the term) = 3.75 (hours per week to schedule for reading)

Now, go to your calendar or long-term planner and reflect on it for a few minutes. Look for ways to block out those hours next week. For ideas, review Chapter 2, "First Steps."

Step 5. Refine your reading plan

Scheduling your reading takes time. The potential benefits are beyond calculation. With a plan, you can be more confident that you'll actually get your reading done. Even if your estimates are off, you'll still go beyond blind guessing or leaving the whole thing to chance. Your reading matters too much for that.

Making choices about what to read

Books about time management often mention the "80/20" principle. According to this principle, 80 percent of the value created by any group derives from only 20 percent of its members. If you have a to-do list of 10 items, for example, you'll get 80 percent of your desired results by doing only two items on the list.

The point is not to take these figures literally but to remember the underlying principle: *Focus on what creates the most value.* Look at your reading in light of the 80/20 principle. For instance:

- In a 10-paragraph article, you might find 80 percent of the crucial facts in the headline and first paragraph. (In fact, journalists are *taught* to write this way.)

- If you have a 50-page assignment, you may find that the most important facts and ideas are in 10 pages of that total.

- If you're asked to read five books for a course, you may find that most exam questions come from just one of them.

A caution is in order here. The 80/20 principle is not a suggestion to complete only 20 percent of your reading assignments. That choice can undermine your education. To find the most important parts of anything you read, first get familiar with the whole. Only then can you make sound choices about where to focus.

Skilled readers constantly make choices about what to read and what *not* to read. They realize that some texts are more valuable for their purposes than others and that some passages within a single text are more crucial than the rest. When reading, they instantly ask, "What's most important here?"

The answer to this question varies from assignment to assignment, and even from page to page within a single assignment. Pose this question each time that you read, and look for clues to the answers. Pay special attention to the following:

- Any readings that your instructor refers to in class
- Readings that are emphasized in a class syllabus
- Readings that generate the most questions on quizzes and tests
- Parts of a text that directly answer the questions you generated while previewing
- Chapter previews and summaries (usually found at the beginning and end of a chapter or section)

Dealing with interruptions

Sometimes the people you live with and care about the most—a friend, roommate, spouse, or child—can become a temporary roadblock to reading.

The following strategies can help you stay focussed on your reading:

Attend to people first

When you first come home from school, keep your books out of sight. Spend some time with your roommates or family members before you settle in to study. Make small talk and ask them about their day. Give the important people in your life a short period of full, focussed attention rather than a longer period of partial attention. Then explain that you have some work to do. Set some ground rules for the amount of time you need to focus on studying. You could be rewarded with extra minutes or hours of quiet time.

Plan for interruptions

It's possible that you'll be interrupted even if you set up guidelines for your study time in advance. If so, schedule the kind of studying that can be interrupted. For instance, you could write out or review flash cards with key terms and definitions. Save the tasks that require sustained attention for more quiet times.

Use "pockets" of time

See whether you can arrange a study time in a quiet place at school before you come home. If you arrive at school 15 minutes earlier and stay 15 minutes later, you can squeeze in an extra half hour of reading that day. Also look for opportunities to study on campus between classes.

When you can't read everything, read something

Even if you can't absorb an entire chapter while your roommates are blasting music, you can skim a chapter. Or you can just read the introduction and summary. When you can't get it *all* done, get *something* done.

Caution: If you always read this way, your education will be compromised. Supplement this strategy with others from this chapter so that you can get your most important reading done.

Read with children underfoot

It is possible to have both effective study time and quality time with your children. The following suggestions come mostly from students who are also parents. The specific strategies you use will depend on your schedule and the ages of your children.

- *Find a regular playmate for your child.* Some children can pair off with close friends and safely retreat to their rooms for hours of private play. You can check on them occasionally and still get lots of reading done.

- *Create a special space for your child.* Set aside one room or area of your home as a play space. Childproof this space. The goal is to create a place where children can roam freely and play with minimal supervision. Consider allowing your child in this area *only* when you study. Your homework time then becomes your child's reward. If you're cramped for space, just set aside some special toys for your child to play with during your study time.

- *Use electronic devices responsibly*. Whenever possible, select educational programs that keep your child's mind active and engaged. Also see whether your child can use headphones while watching television or on a device. That way, the house stays quiet while you study.

- *Schedule time to be with your children when you've finished studying*. Let your children in on the plan:

"I'll be done reading at 7:30. That gives us a whole hour to play before you go to bed."

- *Ask other adults for help*. Getting help can be as simple as asking your spouse, partner, neighbour, or fellow student to take care of the children while you study. Offer to trade child care with a neighbour: You will take his kids and yours for two hours on Thursday night if he'll take them for two hours on Saturday morning.

- *Find community activities and services*. Ask whether your school provides a daycare service. In some cases, these services are available to students at a reduced cost. ✳

practising
CRITICAL THINKING

4-3

Read an editorial in a newspaper or magazine. Analyze this editorial by taking notes in the three-column format below. Use the first column for listing major points, the second for supporting points, and the third for key facts or statistics that support the major or minor points. For example:

Major point	Supporting point	Key fact
Organic farming is good for the environment.	Neither conventional farming nor organic farming production methods are done exactly the same by all farmers, so it is difficult to really compare these two methods.	The lack of use of synthetic pesticides prevents harm to local wildlife.

Major point	Supporting point	Key fact

Ask another student to do this exercise with you. Then compare and discuss your notes. See if you identified the same main points.

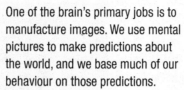

POWERPROCESS

Notice your Pictures and Let Them Go

Philip and Karen Smith/Iconica/Getty Images

One of the brain's primary jobs is to manufacture images. We use mental pictures to make predictions about the world, and we base much of our behaviour on those predictions.

Pictures can sometimes get in our way. Take the student who plans to attend a school he hasn't visited. He chose this school for its strong curriculum and good academic standing, but his brain didn't stop there. In his mind, the campus has historic buildings with ivy-covered walls and tree-lined avenues. The professors, he imagines, will be as articulate as Justin Trudeau and as entertaining as Ryan Reynolds. The cafeteria will be a cozy nook serving everything from delicate quiche to strong coffee. He will gather there with fellow students for hours of stimulating, intellectual conversation. The library will have every book, while the computer lab will boast the newest technology.

The school turns out to be four grey buildings downtown next to the bus station. The first class he attends is taught by an overweight, balding professor wearing a purple and orange bird-of-paradise tie. The cafeteria is a nondescript hall with machine-dispensed food, and the student's room is barely large enough to accommodate his roommate's tuba. This hypothetical student gets depressed. He begins to think about dropping out of school.

It's no wonder that pictures have this kind of power. Your brain is incredibly efficient at processing images. In a matter of seconds, for example, you can recognize a familiar face and "read" it for signs of that person's emotional state. If the emotion is not what you expected, then you could find yourself bracing for conflict. The reason: Reality has failed to match up with one of your precious mental pictures.

The problem with pictures is that they can prevent us from seeing what is really there. That is what happened to the student in this story. His pictures prevented him from noticing that his school is in the heart of a culturally vital city—close to theatres, museums, government offices, clubs, and all kinds of stores. The professor with the weird tie is not only an expert in his field but also a superior teacher. The school cafeteria is skimpy because it can't compete with the variety of inexpensive restaurants in the area.

Our pictures often lead us to becoming angry or disappointed. We set up expectations of events before they occur. Sometimes we don't even realize that we have these expectations. The next time you discover you are angry, disappointed, or frustrated, look to see which of your pictures isn't being fulfilled.

When you notice that pictures are getting in your way, in the gentlest manner possible, let your pictures go. Let them drift away like wisps of smoke picked up by a gentle wind.

This Power Process can be a lifesaver when it comes to reading. Some students enter higher education with pictures about all the reading they'll be required to do before they graduate. They see themselves feeling bored, confused, and worried about keeping up with assignments. If you have such pictures, be willing to let them go. This chapter can help you recreate your whole experience of reading, which is crucial to your success.

Sometimes when you let go of old pictures, it's helpful to replace them with new, positive pictures. These new images can help you take a fresh perspective. The new pictures might not feel as comfortable and genuine as your old ones, but it's important to let those old pictures go. No matter what picture is in your head, you can still be yourself.

Put it to **WORK**

You can use strategies you learn in *Becoming a Master Student* to succeed in your career.

You can use research and reading skills to discover employers that interest you and make the best impression on them during your job search. Once you've got a job, use reading skills to gain skills and advance your career.

bbernard/Shutterstock.com

Use information literacy for effective job hunting

Get to know the reference librarians at your school library and public library. These specialists are your allies in discovering who's hiring in your area and what kinds of skills they want to see in new employees. Uncovering this kind of information usually calls for going beyond company websites. Librarians can help.

Develop information literacy for the work world

Your supervisor might ask, "Have we priced our products above or below the going rate in our region?" or "What's unique about our line of services, compared to our competitors?" Use the research skills suggested in "Developing information literacy" to answer those questions quickly and accurately.

This is another area where reference librarians can help. Some specialize in doing research for certain types of businesses and non-profit organizations.

Expand your literacies for the digital age

Employers also now expect that you will have other forms of literacy. They may expect you to have tech tool literacy, so that you know how to use apps such as Skype, Padlet, Pinterest; data literacy, so that you are familiar with Canadian data sets (*http://open.canada.ca/en*) or Google's *Public Data Explorer* (*www.google.com/publicdata/directory*); and digital literacy, so you are knowledgeable about things like Creative Commons usage (*https://creativecommons.org/*) or how to start a professional learning network.

Expand your vocabulary

One key to workplace success is expanding your vocabulary. Learn the key terms used by people in your industry or profession. Find out which publications and websites are popular with your co-workers. Start reading these sources, making special note of words and concepts that are new to you.

Read with a purpose

At work, you're probably reading in order to produce an outcome. Determine your purpose in reading each document and extract what you need to effect that outcome. Look for executive summaries at the front of long documents. Everything you want to know might be there, all in a few pages.

Read with a bias toward action

Your reading might include passages that call for action on your part. Mark these passages with an appropriate symbol in the margin. For example, write a big letter "A" for *action* next to the relevant paragraph. Or draw a small box there and check off the box after taking the appropriate action. Another option is to enter actionable items directly in your calendar or add them to your to-do list.

Create "read anytime" files

Many of the paper-based documents that people get at work consist of basic background material. Often these items are important to read but not urgent. Place these documents in a folder and dig into them when you have a few spare moments.

Now create a career connection of your own

Commit to using a suggestion from this chapter at work. Also describe the benefit you want to gain; for example, "I will regularly read the business section of *The Globe and Mail* and the *National Post* looking for news about companies that I'd like to work for someday."

State your strategy and desired benefit in the space below:

_____
_____
_____
_____

QUIZ

chapter 4

■ Put it to Work
◄ ◄ ◄ ◄
■ Skills Snapshot
■ Master Student Profile

Name_____   Date____/____/____

1. Name the acrostic that can help you remember the steps of Muscle Reading.

2. You must complete all nine steps of Muscle Reading to get the most out of any reading assignment. True or False? Explain your answer.

3. Describe at least three strategies you can use to preview a reading assignment.

4. Explain why self-regulation is important for reading.

5. In addition to underlining and highlighting, there are other ways to mark up a text. List three possibilities.

6. To get the most benefit from marking a book, underline at least 25 percent of the text. True or False? Explain your answer.

7. Explain at least three techniques you can use when reading is tough.

8. What is the difference between a primary and secondary source of information. Give an example of each.

9. Define the "topic–point" method of summarizing.

10. An active reader does all of the following EXCEPT
    (a) Looking up unfamiliar terms and concepts
    (b) Testing herself on the material
    (c) Reading quickly, focussing in on the sound of the words
    (d) Checking for main points and supporting points

Skills SNAPSHOT

Now that you've learned about Muscle Reading, review the *Reading* section of the Discovery Wheel on in Chapter 1. Think about whether that evaluation of your reading skills is still accurate. After studying this chapter, you might want to make some major changes in the way you read. Or, perhaps you are a more effective reader than you thought you were.

In either case, take a snapshot of your current reading skills by completing the following sentences.

BEFORE YOU READ

If someone asked me how well I keep up with my assigned reading, I would say that . . .

To get the most out of a long reading assignment, I start by . . .

WHILE YOU READ

To focus my attention while I read, I . . .

When I take notes on my reading, my usual method is to . . .

AFTER YOU READ

When it's important for me to remember what I read, I . . .

When I don't understand something that I've read, I overcome confusion by . . .

NEXT ACTION

I'll know that I've reached a new level of mastery with reading when . . .

To reach that level of mastery, the most important thing I can do next is to . . .

MASTER STUDENT
PROFILE

chapter 4

■ Put it to Work
■ Quiz
■ Skills Snapshot
◄ ◄ ◄ ◄

Mariko Tamaki
…is collaborative

Mariko Tamaki, Toronto-born graphic author and comic book writer, knows what it's like to be the odd one out. *Skim*, her best-known and award-winning graphic novel, is a window into the experience of being an outsider in high school.

"I was a teenage girl who was queer that went to an all-girls private school. So, I've been that person and I know that place really well, and I obviously typically want to start writing from a place that feels really familiar," she explains at WordsFest.

Tamaki thinks telling these kinds of stories about minorities is important. She adds, "I certainly think as a queer, Asian, chubby teenager I did not see a lot of queer, Asian chubby teenagers hanging out in my library." She also wants to see stories of immigration and what it means to be First Nations as a greater part of Canadian literature.

Her experience of growing up in Toronto also shaped the stories she tells. It was there that she explored collaborative methods of art, something she continues now. Most of her graphic novels, including *Skim* and *This One Summer* are created in partnership with someone else. "I get a real kick out of creating a story with somebody else and creating a world with somebody else, and conspiring with somebody on the details of what will make that world," she says.

Tamaki's novels, which are mostly collaborative works, are mainly about the experiences of teenage girls. She says, "I think there is something about adolescence that I've always found fascinating because it's a time when you're deciding

who you're going to be in a much more obvious way."

"I always say that high school, being a teenager, is almost a form of drag. Really, you're sort of trying on these different personas of femininity or masculinity or whatever it is," she adds.

Now, though, she's writing about a whole different set of people—namely Supergirl and the Hulk. For her, comics have more constraints than graphic novels, but she disagrees with the notion "that creativity can only happen when you're completely untethered and there's no boundaries."

In fact, the boundaries involved make her focus on making the best work she can. Tamaki also discusses recent criticism of how female superheroes are portrayed. "It's funny because on the one hand, as a feminist I think about it all the time, and on the other [h]and I'm just trying to get work done. I think it's really important that people speak out … [but] you can't just listen to a bunch of people. You have to create what makes sense to you," Tamaki says.

And Tamaki continues to create what makes sense to her. She has recently written a new *Hulk* series for Marvel Comics and *Supergirl: Being Super* for DC Comics, as well as the graphic novel, *Laura Dean Keeps Breaking Up With Me* with Rosemary Valero-O'Connell, which tells the story of a messy teenage relationship.

Source: Tombs, Jen. (2016, November 7). Mariko Tamaki tries to diversify the graphic novel scene. *The Gazette*. Retrieved from *https://www.westerngazette .ca/culture/mariko-tamaki-tries-to-diversify-the -graphic-novel-scene/article_4a9b4fb4-a51f-11e6-a3a0 -239f4668607a.html*. Reprinted by permission.

Blackwood, Maailah, Western Gazette

Mariko Tamaki (1975–) is an award-winning writer, playwright, and performer. She is launching a new *Hulk* series, *She-Hulk* for Marvel Comics.

Notes

Dragon Images/Shutterstock.com

do you have a minute?

Look at the notes you made from a class you attended today. Do they make sense to you now? Look up any new terms you learned today in your textbook and see how well you captured the instructor's ideas in your own words. Add any additional material you need to better understand your notes.

WHAT if ...

I could take notes that remain informative and useful for weeks, months, or even years to come?

WHY this chapter matters ...

Note-taking helps you remember information and influences how well you do on tests and assignments.

HOW you can use this chapter ...

Experiment with several formats for note-taking. Create a note-taking format that works especially well for you. Take effective notes in special situations—such as while reading and when instructors talk fast.

The note-taking
PROCESS FLOWS

One way to understand note-taking is to realize that taking notes is just one part of a process. Effective note-taking consists of three parts: observing, recording, and reviewing. First, you observe an "event"—a statement by an instructor, a lab experiment, a slide show of an artist's work, or a chapter of required reading. Then you record your observations of that event; that is, you "take notes." These can be recorded in a variety of formats—paragraphs, outlines, diagrams, and more. Finally, you review what you have recorded. You memorize, reflect, apply, and rehearse what you're learning. This step lifts ideas off the page and stores them in a working part of your mind.

Each part of the process is essential, and each depends on the others. Your observations determine what you record. What you record determines what you review. And the quality of your review can determine how effective your next observations will be. For example, if you review your notes on the Sino-Japanese War of 1894, the next day's lecture on the Boxer Rebellion of 1900 will make more sense.

Legible and speedy handwriting is useful when taking notes. A knowledge of outlining is handy, too. A nice pen, a new notebook, and a laptop computer are all great note-taking devices. But they're all worthless— unless you participate as an energetic observer *in* class and regularly review your notes *after* class. If you take those two steps, you can turn even the most disorganized chicken scratches into a powerful tool.

Note-taking is a well-researched aspect of student success in higher education. Study after study points to the benefits of taking notes. High-achieving students typically approach note-taking in the same way they do other aspects of self-regulated learning (Bonner & Holliday, 2006). They set goals and create strategies to ensure that they stay on task and monitor their comprehension of what they are hearing.

With good note-taking, you create a set of materials that refreshes your memory and helps you prepare for tests. Taking summary notes prompts you to listen effectively during class. You translate new ideas or concepts into your own words and images. You impose a personal and meaningful structure on what you see, read, and hear. You move from passive observer to active participant (Brazeau, 2006). It's not that you take notes so that you can learn from them later. Instead, you learn *while* taking notes.

Although typing your notes on a computer seems like a good way to get down key concepts during a lecture, recent research shows that this may not be an effective strategy for learning and retention. Mueller and Oppenheimer (2014) compared students who took notes using long hand with those taking notes on a laptop. They found that when students were asked to directly recall factual material both groups did equally well; but when students had to apply what they learned and answer conceptual questions, the students who had handwritten notes significantly outperformed those who took notes on the computer. Other researchers have found that laptop use leads to grades being about half a grade lower for those who used a computer versus those who don't (Patterson & Patterson, 2017). That's the difference between getting a C+ rather than a B on a test.

Why might this be the case? Sometimes note-taking looks like a passive affair, especially in large lecture classes. One person at the front of the room does most of the talking. Everyone else is seated and silent, taking notes. The lecturer seems to be doing all of the work. However, effective note-taking requires active engagement with the material. You may find it easier to get all the material recorded on your laptop compared to writing by hand, but typing makes it easy not to stop and process the material. On the other hand, if you are taking notes by hand, you probably can't get it all down so you need to listen, summarize what you are hearing, and pay attention to the important details. This leads to better encoding of material in memory and helps enhance recall at a later date. There may be reasons to take notes on a computer, such as if you have a particular learning disability; but for most students taking notes by hand is the better choice.

Using a tablet might create the best of both worlds—you can take notes and draw a concept map where you capture the ideas being presented in the lecture. If you do use a laptop in class, try to summarize material being presented rather than just recording the instructor word for word.

Students who take notes by hand listen for levels of ideas and information, make choices about what to record, and compile materials to review. In higher education, you might spend hundreds of hours taking notes. Making them more effective is a direct investment in your success in college and beyond. Think of your notes as a textbook that *you* create—one that's more current and more in tune with your learning preferences than any textbook you could buy. ✳

journal entry   5-1

Discovery/Intention Statement

Get What You Want from This Chapter

Think about the possible benefits of improving your skills at note-taking. Recall a recent incident in which you had difficulty taking notes. Perhaps you were listening to an instructor who talked fast, or you got confused and stopped taking notes altogether. Describe the incident in the space below.

_____

_____

_____

_____

_____

_____

_____

_____

_____

Now preview this chapter to find at least five strategies that you can use right away to help you take better notes. Sum up each of those strategies in a few words and note page numbers where you can find out more about each suggestion.

Strategy   Page number

_____

_____

_____

_____

_____

_____

_____

_____

Reflect on your intention to experiment actively with this chapter. Describe a specific situation in which you might apply the strategies you listed above. If possible, choose a situation that will occur within the next 24 hours.

I intend to …

_____

_____

_____

_____

_____

_____

OBSERVE
The note-taking process flows

Monkey Business Images/Shutterstock.com

Sherlock Holmes, a fictional master detective and student of the obvious, could track down a villain by observing the fold of his scarf and the mud on his shoes. In real life, a doctor can save a life by observing a mole—one a patient has always had—that undergoes a rapid change. A student can save hours of study time by observing that she gets twice as much done at a particular time of day.

Keen observers see facts and relationships. They know ways to focus their attention on the details, then tap their creative energy to discover patterns. To sharpen your classroom observation skills, experiment with the following techniques and continue to use those that you find most valuable.

Observation starts with preparation. Arrive early, and then put your brain in gear by reviewing your notes from the previous class. Scan your reading assignment. Look at the sections you have underlined or highlighted. Review assigned problems and exercises. Note questions you intend to ask. To further sharpen your classroom observation skills, try out the following techniques, and continue to use those that you find most valuable. Many of these strategies can be adapted to the notes you take while reading.

Set the stage

Complete outside assignments. Nothing is more discouraging (or boring) than sitting through a lecture about the relationship of Le Châtelier's principle to the principle of kinetics if you've never heard of Henri Louis Le Châtelier or kinetics. Instructors usually assume that students complete assignments, and they construct their lectures accordingly. The more familiar you are with a subject, the more easily you can understand important information during class lectures.

Bring the right materials

"Can I borrow a pen?" Sound familiar? A good pen does not make you a good observer, but the lack of a pen or a notebook can be distracting enough to take the fine edge off your concentration. Make sure you have a pen, pencil, notebook, and any other materials you will need.

Bring your textbook to class, especially if the lectures relate closely to the text.

If you are consistently unprepared for a class, you are indicating something about your intentions concerning the course. Find out if it is. The next time you're in a frantic scramble to borrow pen and paper 37 seconds before the class begins, notice the cost. Use the borrowed pen and paper to write a Discovery Statement about your lack of preparation. Consider whether you intend to be successful in the course.

Ask your instructor if you are allowed to use a laptop in class. Using a laptop may allow you to access other material the instructor has provided for the course like the PowerPoint® presentation or other course materials available through your course website. However, make sure you are only using your laptop for course-related activities, not to check your social media sites.

Sit front and centre

Students who get as close as possible to the front and centre of the classroom often do better on tests, for several reasons. The closer you sit to the lecturer, the more likely you are to pay attention and the fewer distracting classmates are likely situated between you and the instructor. Material on the board is easier to read from up front. Also, the instructor can see you more easily when you have a question.

In addition, sitting closer increases your ability to hear and take effective notes. Get close to the source of the sound—your instructor. Get close to the energy. While some instructors can project their energy to a large audience, some cannot. If you can't hear your professors, particularly in large lecture halls, ask them to use a microphone if one is available.

Sitting close to the front is a way to commit yourself to getting what you can out of school. One reason students gravitate to the back of the classroom is that they think the instructor is less likely to call on them. Sitting in back can signal a lack of commitment, and instructors do notice. When you sit up front, you are declaring your willingness to take a risk and participate.

"Be here now" in class

Refocus your wandering mind

Don't fight daydreaming. When you notice your mind wandering during class, look at this as an opportunity to refocus your attention. If thermodynamics is losing out to beach parties, let go of the beach.

Notice your writing

When you discover yourself slipping into a fantasyland, feel the weight of your pen in your hand. Notice how your notes look. Paying attention to the act of writing can bring you back to the here and now.

You can also use writing in a more direct way to clear your mind of distracting thoughts. Pause for a few seconds and write those thoughts down. If you're distracted by thoughts of errands you need to run after class, record them on a pad of paper or your mobile device. Or simply put a symbol, such as an arrow or asterisk, in your notes to mark the places where your mind started to wander. Once your distractions are out of your mind and safely stored on paper, you can gently return your attention to taking notes.

Be with the instructor

In your mind, put yourself right up front with the instructor. Imagine that you and the instructor are the only ones in the room and that the lecture is a personal conversation between the two of you. Pay attention to the instructor's body language and facial expressions. Look the instructor in the eye.

Remember that the power of this suggestion is immediately reduced by digital distractions—checking your Facebook site, browsing the Internet, or text messaging. Patterson and Patterson (2017) speculate that "cyber slacking" is another reason grades are lower for those who take notes on their laptops. Your digital devices are also a distraction to the students sitting near you. Taking notes by hand is a way to stay more focussed. The physical act of taking notes signals your mind to stay in the same room as the instructor. When you become aware of yourself daydreaming, bring yourself back to class by paying attention to the temperature in the room, the feel of your chair, or the quality of light coming through the window. Listen to the sound of the instructor's voice. Be in that environment. Once your attention is back in the room, you can focus on what's happening in class.

Postpone debate

When you hear something you disagree with, note your disagreement and let it go. Don't allow your internal dialogue to drown out subsequent material. Internal debate can prevent you from absorbing new information. It is okay to absorb information you don't agree with. Just absorb it with the mental tag "My instructor says …, and I don't agree with this."

Let go of judgments about lecture styles

Human beings are judgment machines. We evaluate everything, especially other people.

Don't let your attitude about an instructor's lecture style, habits, or appearance get in the way of your education. You can decrease the power of your judgments if you become aware of them but choose to let them go.

You can even let go of judgments about rambling, unorganized lectures. Turn them to your advantage. Take the initiative and organize the material yourself. While taking notes, separate the key points from the examples and supporting evidence. Note the places where you got confused and make a list of questions to ask.

Participate in class activities

Ask questions. Volunteer for demonstrations. Be willing to take a risk or look foolish, if that's what it takes for you to learn. Chances are, the question you think is "dumb" is also on the minds of several of your classmates. Remember, learning is an active, not a passive, activity. The more you do with the material in class, the more likely you are to recall it later. So, join in class discussions; don't treat being in class as if you are watching a movie. Get active.

Relate the class to your goals

If you have trouble staying awake in a particular class, write at the top of your notes how that class relates to a specific goal. Identify the reward or payoff for reaching that goal.

Think critically about what you hear

This might seem contrary to the previously mentioned technique, "Postpone debate." This is the time to list questions or write down your agreements and disagreements. After class, look up answers in your text or visit your instructor during office hours to review the material.

Watch for clues

Be alert to repetition

When an instructor repeats a phrase or an idea, make a note of it. Repetition is a signal that the instructor thinks the information is important.

Listen for introductory, concluding, and transition words and phrases

These include phrases such as "the following three factors," "in conclusion," "the most important consideration," "in addition to," and "on the other hand." These phrases and others signal relationships, definitions, new subjects, conclusions, cause and effect, and examples. They reveal the structure of the lecture. You can use these phrases to organize your notes.

Watch the board or PowerPoint® presentation

If an instructor takes the time to write something down, consider the material to be important. Copy all diagrams and drawings, equations, names, places, dates, statistics, and definitions that the instructor puts on the board. But check first to see if any complicated diagrams are posted on the course website or are in your textbook.

Watch the instructor's eyes

If an instructor glances at her notes and then makes a point, it is probably a signal that the information is especially important. Anything she reads from her notes is a potential test question.

Highlight the obvious clues

Instructors will often tell students point-blank that certain information is likely to appear on a test or an exam. Make stars or other special marks in your notes next to this information. Instructors are not trying to hide what's important. ✳

journal entry   5-2

Discovery/Intention Statement

Create More Value from Lectures

Think back to the last few lectures you have attended. How do you currently observe (listen to) lectures? What specific behaviours do you have as you sit and listen? Briefly describe your responses in the space below.

I discovered that I …

_____

_____

_____

Now write an Intention Statement about any changes you want to make in the way you respond to lectures.

I intend to …

_____

_____

_____

What to do when you miss a class

In most courses, you'll benefit by attending every class session. If you miss a class, try to catch up as quickly as possible.

Clarify policies on missed classes   On the first day of classes, find out about your instructors' policies on absences. See if you can make up assignments, quizzes, and tests. Also inquire about doing extra-credit assignments. If you know in advance that you'll miss some classes, let your instructor know as soon as possible. Create a plan for staying on top of your coursework.

Contact a classmate   Early in the semester, identify a student in each class who seems responsible and dependable. Exchange email addresses and phone numbers. If you know you won't be in class, contact this student ahead of time. When you notice that your classmate is absent, pick up extra copies of handouts, make assignments lists, and offer copies of your notes. But don't rely too heavily on other people's notes. There is no guarantee that their notes are as good as yours.

Contact your instructor   If you miss a class, contact your instructor. Ask if he has another section of the same course that you could attend so you won't miss the lecture information. Check the course website for handouts or important information you might have missed and ask the instructor if there were any handouts in class. Don't ask him if you missed anything important! Professors tend to feel that everything in class is important.

Consider technology   If there is a course website, check it for assignments and the availability of handouts you missed. Free online services such as *NoteMesh* allow students to share notes with one another. These services use wiki software, which allows you to create and edit Web pages with any browser. Other great note-sharing apps include *OneNote* and the perennial student favourite *Evernote*. These last two software applications let you do even more than note sharing—you can record audio to your notes, bring images into your notes, save Web links, and even directly draw on notes with a stylus. Before using such tools, check with instructors for their policies on note sharing.

RECORD
The note-taking process flows

The format and structure of your notes are more important than how fast you write or how elegant your handwriting is. The following techniques can improve the effectiveness of your notes.

General techniques for note-taking

Use key words

An easy way to sort the extraneous material from the important points is to take notes using key words. Key words or phrases contain the essence of communication. They include

- concepts, technical terms, names, and numbers
- linking words, including words that describe action, relationship, and degree (e.g., *most*, *least*, and *faster*).

Key words evoke images and associations with other words and ideas. They trigger your memory. That makes them powerful review tools. One key word can initiate the recall of a whole cluster of ideas. A few key words can form a chain from which you can reconstruct an entire lecture.

To see how key words work, take yourself to an imaginary classroom. You are now in the middle of an anatomy lecture. Picture what the room looks like, what it feels like, how it smells. You hear the instructor say:

OK, what happens when we look directly over our heads and see a piano falling out of the sky? How do we take that signal and translate it into the action of getting out of the way? The first thing that happens is that a stimulus is generated in the neurons—receptor neurons—of the eye. Light reflected from the piano reaches our eyes. In other words, we see the piano. The receptor neurons in the eye transmit that sensory signal, the sight of the piano, to the body's nervous system. That's all they can do, pass on information. So we've got a sensory signal coming into the nervous system. But the neurons that initiate movement in our legs are effector neurons. The information from the sensory neurons must be transmitted to effector neurons, or we will get squashed by the piano. There must be some kind of interconnection between receptor and effector neurons. What happens between the two? What is the connection?

Key words you might note in this example include *stimulus, generated, receptor neurons, transmit, sensory signals, nervous system, effector neurons,* and *connection.* You could reduce the instructor's 163 words to these 12 key words. With a few transitional words, your notes might look as shown in Figure 5.1.

> Stimulus (piano) generated in receptor neurons (eye)
>
> Sensory signals transmitted by nervous system to effector neurons (legs)
>
> What connects receptor to effector?

Figure 5.1 *Using Key Words for Note-taking*

Note the last key word of the lecture above—*connection*. This word is part of the instructor's question and leads to the next point in the lecture. Be on the lookout for questions like this. They can help you organize your notes and are often clues for test questions.

Use pictures and diagrams

Make relationships visual. Copy all diagrams from the board and invent your own.

A drawing of a piano falling on someone who is looking up, for example, might be used to demonstrate the relationship of receptor neurons to effector neurons. Label the eyes "receptor" and the feet "effector." This picture implies that the sight of the piano must be translated into a motor response (see Figure 5.2). By connecting the explanation of the process with the unusual picture of the piano falling, you can link the elements of the process together.

Adapted from © Cengage Learning

Figure 5.2 *Using Pictures and Diagrams for Note-taking*

Write notes in paragraphs

When it is difficult to follow the organization of a lecture or to put information into outline form, create a series of informal paragraphs. These paragraphs will contain few complete sentences. Reserve complete sentences for precise definitions, direct quotations, and important points that the instructor emphasizes by repetition or other signals—such as the phrase, "This is an important point." For other material, apply the suggestions in this article for using key words.

Copy material from the board or PowerPoint® presentation

Record all formulas, diagrams, and problems that the instructor writes down. Copy dates, numbers, names, places, and other facts. If it's on the board or in the presentation, put it in your notes. You can even use your own signal or code to flag that material. Anything the instructor presents can appear on a test. Ask your instructor if the presentation software slides are available to you on the course website. Some instructors provide full slides to you while others will give you partial slides or an outline of the day's lesson that you need to fill in class.

Use only one side of a piece of paper

When you use one side of a page, you can review and organize all your notes by spreading them out side by side. Most students find the benefit well worth the cost of the paper. Perhaps you're concerned about the environmental impact of consuming more paper. If so, you can use the blank side of old notes and use recycled paper.

Keep your own thoughts separate

For the most part, avoid making editorial comments in your lecture notes. The danger is that when you return to your notes, you might mistake your own idea for that of the instructor. If you want to make a comment—either a question to ask later or a strong disagreement—clearly label it as your own. Pick a symbol or code and use it in every class.

Use an "I'm lost" signal

No matter how attentive and alert you are, you might get lost and confused in a lecture. If it is inappropriate to ask a question, record in your notes that you were lost. Invent your own signal—for example, a circled question mark. When you write down your code for "I'm lost," leave space for the explanation or clarification that you will get later. The space will also be a signal that you missed something. Later, you can speak to your instructor or ask to see a fellow student's notes. As long as you are honest with yourself when you don't understand, you can stay on top of the course.

Label, number, and date all notes

Develop the habit of labelling and dating your notes at the beginning of each class. Number the page, too. Sometimes the sequence of material in a lecture is important. Write your name and phone number in each notebook in case you lose it. Class notes become more and more valuable as a term or session progresses.

Tips for Master Students

Pick up a pen and learn to take good notes

Learn to take good notes during lectures. This may sound like a small matter, but it's not. Note-taking should not be confused with copying. Note-taking is not stenography. Neither should it be confused with audio recording. Good notes are not a verbatim record of everything the professor says. Good note-takers are thinking, comparing and questioning... Put away the laptop and cellphone and pick up your pad of paper and pen. If it feels like that is a lot more work, you're right. But you'll be happy you did it.

—James Compton, associate professor, faculty of information and media studies at the University of Western Ontario, and president of the Canadian Association of University Teachers (*Maclean's*, 2017)

Source: Advice for first-year students from Justin Trudeau (and 27 other people), by *Maclean's*, *Maclean's*, December 1, 2017.

Use standard abbreviations

Be consistent with your abbreviations. If you make up your own abbreviations or symbols, write a key explaining them in your notes. Avoid vague abbreviations. When you use an abbreviation such as *comm.* for *committee*, you run the risk of not being able to remember whether you meant *committee, commission, common, commit, community, communicate,* or *communist.*

One way to abbreviate is to leave out vowels. For example, *talk* becomes *tlk, said* becomes *sd, Canadian* becomes *Cdn.*

Leave blank space

Notes tightly crammed into every corner of the page are hard to read and difficult to use for review. Give your eyes a break by leaving plenty of space.

Later, when you review, you can use the blank spaces in your notes to clarify points, write questions, or add other material. Instructors often return to material covered earlier in the lecture.

Take notes in different colours

You can use colours as highly visible organizers. For example, you can signal important points with red. Or use one colour of ink for notes about the text and another colour for lecture notes. Notes that are visually pleasing can be easier to review.

Use graphic signals

The following ideas can be used with any note-taking format.

- Use brackets, parentheses, circles, and squares to group information that belongs together.
- Use stars, arrows, and underlining to indicate important points. Flag the most important points with double stars, double arrows, or double underlines.
- Use arrows and connecting lines to link related groups and to replace words such as *leads to, becomes,* and *produces.*
- Use equal signs and greater- and less-than signs to indicate compared quantities.
- Use question marks for their obvious purpose. Double question marks can signal tough questions or especially confusing points.

To avoid creating confusion with graphic symbols, use them carefully and consistently. Write a "dictionary" of your symbols in the front of your notebooks, such as the one shown in Figure 5.3.

Use recorders effectively

There are persuasive arguments for not using a digital recorder. Here are the main ones.

When you record a lecture, there is a strong temptation to daydream. After all, you can always listen to the lecture again later on. Unfortunately, if you let the

$[\ ],\ (\ ),\ \bigcirc,\ \square$ = info that belongs together

$*,\ \searrow,\ \underline{\quad}$ = important

$**,\ \searrow\searrow,\ \equiv,\ !!!$ = extra important

$>$ = greater than $\quad <$ = less than
$=$ = equal to

$\longrightarrow$ = leads to, becomes
Ex: school $\rightarrow$ job $\rightarrow$ money

$?$ = huh?, lost

$??$ = big trouble, clear up immediately

Figure 5.3 *Dictionary of Symbols*

recorder do all of the work, you are skipping a valuable part of the learning process. Actively participating in class can turn a lecture into a valuable study session.

There are more potential problems. Listening to recorded lectures can take a lot of time—more time than reviewing written notes. Recorders can't answer the questions you didn't ask in class. Also, recording devices malfunction.

With those warnings in mind, some students use a recorder effectively. For example, you can use recordings as backups to written notes. Turn the recorder on, then take notes as if it weren't there. Recordings can be especially useful if an instructor speaks fast. Remember to check with your instructor first. Some prefer not to be recorded.

You could also record yourself after class, reading your written notes. Teaching the class to yourself is a powerful review tool. Instead of taping all of your notes, for example, you might record only the key facts or concepts.

Check with your instructor to see if they make podcasts of their lectures. They can be great tools for review if you listen to them on your electronic devices while traveling on the bus or just walking around campus.

The Cornell format

A note-taking system that has worked for students around the world is the *Cornell format* (Pauk & Owens, 2005). Originally developed by Walter Pauk at Cornell University during the 1950s, this approach is now taught and used in many countries.

The cornerstone of this system is what Pauk calls the *cue column*—a wide margin on the left-hand side of the paper. The cue column is the key to the Cornell format's many benefits. Here's how to use the Cornell format.

Format your paper

On each sheet of your notepaper, draw a vertical line, top to bottom, about two inches from the left edge of the paper. This line creates the cue column—the space to the left of the line.

Take notes, leaving the cue column blank

As you read an assignment or listen to a lecture, take notes on the right-hand side of the paper. Fill up this column with sentences, paragraphs, outlines, charts, or drawings. Do not write in the cue column. You'll use this space later, as you do the next steps.

Condense your notes in the cue column

Think of the notes you took on the right-hand side of the paper as a set of answers. In the cue column, list potential test questions that correspond to your notes. Write one question for each major term or point (see Figure 5.4).

As an alternative to questions, you can list key words from your notes. Yet another option is to pretend that your notes are a series of articles on different topics. In the cue column, write a newspaper-style headline for each "article." In any case, be brief. If you cram the cue column full of words, you defeat its purpose—to reduce the number and length of your notes.

Write a summary

Pauk recommends that you reduce your notes even more by writing a brief summary at the bottom of each page. This step offers you another way to engage actively with the material. It can also make your notes easier to review for tests.

Use the cue column to recite

Cover the right-hand side of your notes with a blank sheet of paper. Leave only the cue column showing.

Cue column	Notes
What are the goals of the Integrated Pan-Canadian Healthy Living Strategy?	The goals are: — to improve overall health outcomes for all Canadians. — to reduce health disparities between Canadians. — to emphasize healthy eating and physical activity to the Canadian public. — to address other healthy living priorities. Source: Health Canada, 2003.
Who is developing this strategy?	The federal, provincial, and territorial governments, together with their partners (NGOs, health specialists, First Nations, Métis and Inuit people, and others) are working together to develop the Healthy Living Strategy.

Summary
The federal and provincial/territorial governments plan to improve the health of Canadians by supporting them in making positive health choices through the Integrated Pan-Canadian Living Strategy.

Figure 5.4 **Cue Column**

Then look at each item you wrote in the cue column and talk about it. If you wrote questions, answer each question. If you wrote key words, define each word and talk about why it's important. If you wrote headlines in the cue column, explain what each one means and offer supporting details. After reciting, uncover your notes and look for any important points you missed. Repeat this cycle of reciting and checking until you've mastered the material.

Word template for Cornell notes

If you take notes on your computer, there actually is a Word template you can use. This may be much simpler than bringing rulers and pads of paper to class. Just search online for Cornell template; it is easy to find.

Mind mapping

This system, developed by Tony Buzan (1993), can be used in conjunction with the Cornell format. In some circumstances, you might want to use **mind maps** exclusively. Mind maps are great ways to organize your notes or an essay you might have to do.

To understand mind maps, first review the features of traditional note-taking. Outlines (explained in the next section) divide major topics into minor topics, which, in turn, are subdivided further. They organize information in a sequential, linear way.

This kind of organization doesn't reflect certain aspects of brain function, a point that has been made in discussions about left brain and right brain activities. People often use the term *right brain* when referring to creative, pattern-making, visual, intuitive brain activity. They use the term *left brain* when talking about orderly, logical, step-by-step characteristics of thought. Writing instructor Gabrielle Rico (1983) uses another metaphor. She refers to the left-brain mode as our "sign mind" (concerned with words) and the right-brain mode as our "design mind" (concerned with visuals).

A mind map uses both kinds of brain functions. Mind maps can contain lists and sequences and show relationships. They can also provide a picture of a subject. Mind maps are visual patterns that can serve as a framework for recalling information. They work on both verbal and nonverbal levels.

Mind mapping is also a great way to support metacognitive thinking, as it requires you to reflect on your thinking to identify key concepts in a lecture or article you are reading and to capture that reflection in visual–verbal image (Sweet, Blythe, & Carpenter, 2017). Reflection as you know is a key component of metacognition. Mind mapping also requires you to analysis what you are hearing in a lecture or reading in an article and therefore leads to deeper thinking.

One benefit of mind maps is that they quickly, vividly, and accurately show the relationships between ideas. Also, mind mapping helps you think from general to specific. By choosing a main topic, you first focus on the big picture, then zero in on subordinate details. And by using only key words, you can condense a large subject into a small area on a mind map. You can review more quickly by looking at the key words on a mind map than by reading notes word for word. See Figure 5.5 for a sample mind map.

You can create mind maps on a piece of paper, or another option is to use software such as *FreeMind*, *Coggle*, or *MindMaple*, which allow you to draw flow charts or diagrams on your device. If you are involved in group projects, then there are several other mind mapping tools that will let you work share your results with others. Two common tools are *Mindomo* or *MindMeister*. Mind mapping is a great way to explore ideas and to see things visually.

Outlining

An outline shows the relationship between major points and supporting ideas. One benefit of taking notes in the outline format is that doing so can totally occupy your attention. You are recording ideas and also organizing them. This can be an advantage if the material has been presented in a disorganized way. Perhaps you've had negative experiences with outlining in the past. Instructors might have required you to use complex, rigid outlining formats based exclusively on Roman numerals or on some unfamiliar system. By playing with variations, you can discover the power of outlining to reveal relationships between ideas. You can create outlines on paper or use technology to create good outlines. Examples of a few good outline apps are *WorkFlowy*, *Checkvist*, or Microsoft *OneNote*.

practising
CRITICAL THINKING   5-1

Create a mind map of a recent lecture

1. *Give yourself plenty of room.* Use legal or even ledger size blank paper. If that's not available, turn regular notebook paper on its side so that you can take notes in a horizontal format. You can also do this on your device if that works better for you. You can create a simple mind map in Word using shapes and text boxes.

2. *Determine the main concept of the lecture.* Write that concept in the centre of the paper and circle it, underline it, or highlight it with colour. Record concepts related to the main concept on lines that radiate outward from the centre. An alternative is to circle these concepts.

3. Use key words only. Whenever possible, reduce each concept to a single word per line or circle in your mind map. Try to summarize and condense ideas to their essence. Key words are usually nouns and verbs that communicate the bulk of the speaker's ideas. Choose words that are rich in associations and that can help you re-create the lecture.

4. *Jazz it up.* Use colour to organize your mind map. If there are three main subjects covered in the lecture, you can record each subject in a different colour. Add symbols and other images as well.

5. *Create links.* One mind map doesn't have to include all of the ideas in a lecture or an article. Instead, you can link mind maps. For example, draw a mind map that sums up the five key points in your lecture today, and then make a separate, more detailed mind map for each of those key points. Within each mind map, include references to the others. This helps explain and reinforce the relationships among many ideas. (Some students pin several mind maps next to each other on a bulletin board or tape them to a wall. This allows for a dramatic—and effective—look at the big picture).

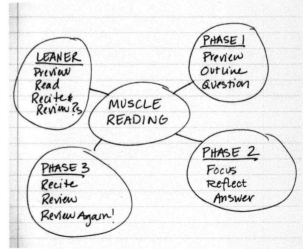

© Cengage Learning

Figure 5.5 Sample Mind Map

Technically, each word, phrase, or sentence that appears in an outline is called a *heading*. These are arranged in different levels:

- In the first or "top" level of headings, note the major topics that are presented in a lecture or reading assignment.

- In the second level of headings, record the key points that relate to each topic in the first-level headings.

- In the third level of headings, record specific facts and details that support or explain each of your second-level headings. Each additional level of subordinate heading supports the ideas in the previous level of heading.

Roman numerals offer one way to illustrate the difference between levels of headings; see Figure 5.6. You can also use other heading styles, as illustrated in Figure 5.7.

Combining formats

Feel free to use different note-taking systems for different subjects, and don't be afraid to combine formats. Do what works for you.

Distinguish levels with indentations only:

First-level heading
　　Second-level heading
　　　　Third-level heading
　　　　　　Fourth-level heading

Distinguish levels with bullets and dashes:

FIRST-LEVEL HEADING
　• Second-level heading
　　– Third-level heading

Distinguish headings by size:

FIRST-LEVEL HEADING
Second-level heading
Third-level heading

Figure 5.7 **Outline B: Other Heading Styles**

For example, combine mind maps along with the Cornell format. You can modify the Cornell format by dividing your paper in half, reserving one half for mind maps and the other for linear information, such as lists, graphs, and outlines, as well as equations, long explanations, and word-for-word definitions. You can incorporate a mind map into your paragraph-style notes whenever you feel one is appropriate. Mind maps are also useful for summarizing notes taken in the Cornell format.

John Sperry, a teacher at Utah Valley State College, developed the following note-taking system that includes all of the formats discussed in this article:

- Fill up a three-ring binder with fresh paper. Open your notebook so that you see two blank pages—one on the left and one on the right. Plan to take notes across this entire two-page spread.

- During class or while reading, write your notes only on the left-hand page. Place a large dash next to each main topic or point. If your instructor skips a step or switches topics unexpectedly, just keep writing.

- Later, use the right-hand page to review and elaborate on the notes that you took earlier. This page is for anything you want. For example, add visuals such as mind maps. Write review questions, headlines, possible test questions, summaries, outlines, mnemonics, or analogies that link new concepts to your current knowledge.

- To keep ideas in sequence, place appropriate numbers on top of the dashes in your notes on the left-hand page. Even if concepts are presented out of order during class, they'll still be numbered correctly in your notes. ✱

The Integrated Pan-Canadian Healthy Living Strategy Will Improve the Health of All Canadians

First-level heading

I. The goal of the Integrated Pan-Canadian Healthy Living Strategy is to improve overall health outcomes for all Canadians.

Second-level heading

A. Its aim is to reduce health disparities between groups of Canadians.

B. It emphasizes healthy eating and physical activity, and their relationship to healthy weights.

II. The Healthy Living Strategy is a joint venture of the federal, provincial, and territorial governments working together with outside partners.

A. Partners include NGOs, health specialists, First Nations, Métis and Inuit people, community leaders, business people, and others.

B. All these partners have important perspectives on how best to encourage and support healthy living for Canadians. Their input has been gathered in the following ways.

Third-level heading

1. Consultation meetings with all partners.

2. Strategic roundtables with government officials and partners.

3. Written reports on the results of these consultations.

4. A national symposium on healthy living.

Figure 5.6 **Outline A: Level of Headings**

REVIEW
The note-taking process flows

Think of reviewing as an integral part of note-taking rather than as an added task. To make new information useful, encode it in a way that connects to your long-term memory. The key is reviewing.

General techniques for reviewing

Review within 24 hours

Reviewing your notes within 24 hours of taking them might be the most powerful note-taking technique you can use. It can save you hours of review time later in the term.

Many students are surprised that they can remember the content of a lecture in the minutes and hours after class. They are even more surprised by how well they can read the sloppiest of notes. Unfortunately, short-term memory deteriorates quickly. The good news is that if you review your notes soon enough, you can move that information from short-term to long-term memory (see Figure 5.8). And you can do it in just a few minutes—often 10 minutes or less.

The sooner you review your notes, the better, especially if the class was difficult. In fact, you can start reviewing during class. When your instructor pauses

Absodels/Getty Images

to set up the overhead projector or erase the board, scan your notes. Dot the *i*s, cross the *t*s, and write out unclear abbreviations. Another way to use this technique is to get to your next class as quickly as you can. Then use the four or five minutes before the lecture begins to review the notes you just took in the previous class. If you do not get to your notes immediately after class, you can still benefit by reviewing later in the day. A review right before you go to sleep can also be valuable.

Think of the day's unreviewed notes as leaky faucets, constantly dripping, losing precious information until you shut them off with a quick review. Remember, Ebbinghaus showed that it's possible to forget up to 80 percent of the material within 24 hours—unless you review.

Edit notes

During your first review, fix words that are illegible. Write out abbreviated words that might be unclear to you later. Make sure you can read everything. If you can't read something or don't understand something you *can* read, mark it, and make a note to ask your instructor or another student. Check to see that your notes are labelled with the date and class and that

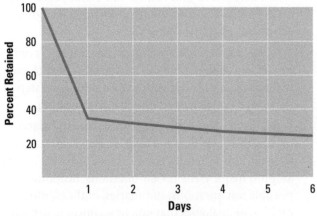

Figure 5.8 *The Ebbinghaus Forgetting Curve*
To study the process of memory and forgetting, Hermann Ebbinghaus devised a method for testing memory. The results, shown here in what has come to be known as the Ebbinghaus forgetting curve, demonstrate that forgetting occurs most rapidly shortly after learning and then gradually declines over time.

the pages are numbered. You can edit with a different coloured pen or pencil if you want to distinguish between what you wrote in class and what you filled in later.

Fill in key words in the left-hand column

This task is important if you are to get the full benefit of using the Cornell format. Using the key word principles described earlier in this chapter, go through your notes and write key words or phrases in the left-hand column.

These key words will speed up the review process later. As you read your notes and focus on extracting important concepts, your understanding of the lecture is further reinforced.

Use your key words as cues for review

With a blank sheet of paper, cover your notes, leaving only the key words in the left-hand margin showing. Take each key word in order and recite as much as you can about the point. Then uncover your notes and look for any important points you missed.

Conduct short weekly review periods

Once a week, review all of your notes again. The review sessions don't need to take a lot of time. Even a 20-minute weekly review period is valuable. Some students find that a weekend review, say, on Sunday afternoon, helps them stay in continuous touch with the material. Scheduling regular review sessions on your calendar helps develop the habit.

As you review, step back to see the larger picture. In addition to reciting or repeating the material to yourself, ask questions about it: "Does this relate to my goals? How does this compare to information I already know, in this field or another? Will I be tested on this material? What will I do with this material? How can I associate it with something that deeply interests me? Am I unclear on any points? If so, what exactly is the question I want to ask?"

Create summaries

Mind mapping is an excellent way to make summary sheets. After drawing your map, look at your original notes and fill in anything you missed. This system is fun to use. It's quick, and it gives your brain a hook on which to fasten the material (see Figure 5.9).

Another option is to create a "cheat sheet." There's only one guideline: Fit all your review notes on a single sheet of paper. Use any note-taking format that you want—mind map, outline, Cornell method, or a combination of all of them. The beauty of this technique is that it forces you to pick out main ideas and key details. There's not enough room for anything else!

If you're feeling adventurous, create your cheat sheet on a single index card. Start with the larger sizes and then work down to a regular sized index card.

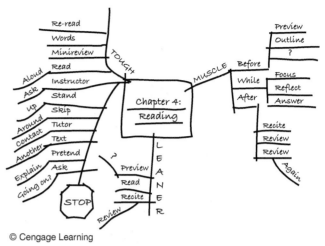

© Cengage Learning

Figure 5.9 *A Sample Mind Map Summary*

Some instructors might let you use a summary sheet during an exam. But even if you can't use it, you'll benefit from creating one while you study for the test. Summarizing is a powerful way to review. ✳

journal entry   5-3

Discovery Statement

Reflect on Your Review Habits

Think about the way you have conducted reviews of your notes in the past. Respond to the following statements by checking "Always," "Often," "Sometimes," "Seldom," or "Never" after each.

I review my notes immediately after class.
_____ Always _____ Often _____ Sometimes
_____ Seldom _____ Never

I conduct weekly reviews of my notes.
_____ Always _____ Often _____ Sometimes
_____ Seldom _____ Never

I make summary sheets of my notes.
_____ Always _____ Often _____ Sometimes
_____ Seldom _____ Never

I edit my notes within 24 hours.
_____ Always _____ Often _____ Sometimes
_____ Seldom _____ Never

Before class, I conduct a brief review of the notes I took in the previous class.
_____ Always _____ Often _____ Sometimes
_____ Seldom _____ Never

Turn PowerPoint® presentations into **POWERFUL NOTES**

PowerPoint® presentations are common. They can also be lethal for students who want to master course content or those who simply want to stay awake.

Some students stop taking notes during a PowerPoint® presentation. This choice can be hazardous to your academic health for three major reasons:

- *PowerPoint® presentations don't include everything.* Instructors and other speakers use PowerPoint® to organize their presentations. Topics covered in the slides make up an outline of what your instructor considers important. Slides are created to flag the main points and signal transitions between points. However, speakers usually add examples and explanations that don't appear on the slides. In addition, slides will not include any material from class discussion, including any answers that the instructor gives in response to questions.

- *You stop learning.* Taking notes forces you to capture ideas and information in your own words. Also, the act of writing things down helps you remember the material. If you stop writing and let your attention drift, you can quickly get lost.

- *You end up with major gaps in your notes.* When it's time to review your notes, you'll find that material is missing. This can be a major pain at exam time.

- To create value from PowerPoint® presentations, take notes on them. Continue to observe, record, and review. See PowerPoint® as a way to *guide* rather than to *replace* your own note-taking. Even the slickest, smartest presentation is no substitute for your own thinking.

Experiment with the following suggestions. They include ideas about what to do before, during, and after a PowerPoint® presentation.

Before the presentation

Sometimes instructors make PowerPoint® slides available before a lecture. Download these files. Scan the slides, just as you would preview a reading assignment.

Consider printing out the slides and bringing them along to class. (If you own a copy of PowerPoint®, then choose the "handouts" option when printing, which generates lines on which to write your notes next to each slide. This will save paper and ink.) You can take notes directly on the pages that you print out as shown in Figure 5.10. Be sure to add the slide numbers if they are missing.

If you use a laptop computer for taking notes during class, then you might not want to bother with printing. Just open up the PowerPoint® file and type your notes

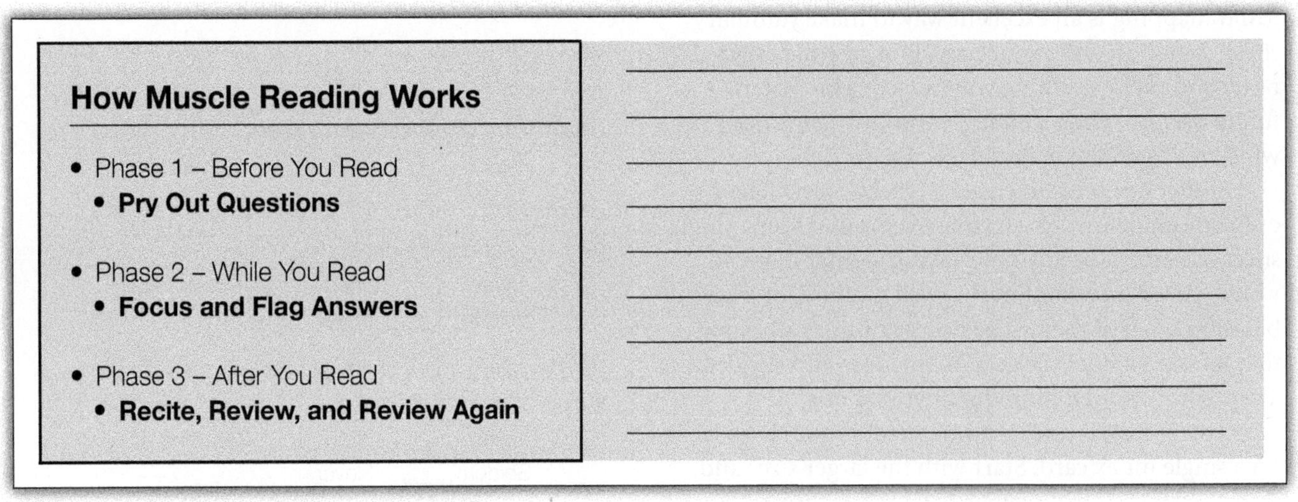

How Muscle Reading Works

- Phase 1 – Before You Read
  - **Pry Out Questions**

- Phase 2 – While You Read
  - **Focus and Flag Answers**

- Phase 3 – After You Read
  - **Recite, Review, and Review Again**

_____
_____
_____
_____
_____
_____
_____
_____

Figure 5.10 PowerPoint® Slides "Handout"

in the window that appears at the bottom of each slide. After class, you can print out the slides in note view. This will show the original slides plus any text that you added.

During the presentation

In many cases, PowerPoint® slides are presented visually by the instructor *only during class*. The slides are not provided as handouts, and they are not available online for students to print out.

This makes it even more important to take effective notes in class. Capture the main points and key details as you normally would. Use your preferred note-taking strategies.

Be selective in what you write down. Determine what kind of material is on each slide. Stay alert for new topics, main points, and important details. Taking too many notes makes it hard to keep up with a speaker and separate main points from minor details.

In any case, go *beyond* the slides. Record valuable questions and answers that come up during a discussion, even if they are not a planned part of the presentation.

After the presentation

If you printed out slides before class and took notes on those pages, then find a way to integrate them with the rest of your notes. For example, add references in your notebook to specific slides. Or create summary notes that include the major topics and points from readings, class meetings, and presentation slides.

Printouts of slides can provide review tools. Use them as cues for review. Cover up your notes so that only the main image or words on each slide are visible. See whether you can remember what else appears on the slide, along with the key points from any notes you added.

Also consider "editing" the presentation. If you have the PowerPoint® file on your computer, make another copy of it. Open up this copy, and see whether you can condense the presentation. Cut slides that don't include anything you want to remember. Also rearrange slides so that the order makes more sense to you. Remember that you can open up the original file later if you want to see exactly what your instructor presented. ✳

When your instructor
TALKS FAST

Take more time to prepare for class
Familiarity with a subject increases your ability to pick up on key points. If an instructor lectures quickly or is difficult to understand, conduct a thorough preview of the material to be covered.

Be willing to make choices
When an instructor talks fast, focus your attention on key points. Instead of trying to write everything down, choose what you think is important. Occasionally, you will make a wrong choice and neglect an important point. Worse things could happen. Stay with the lecture, write down key words, and revise your notes immediately after class.

Share notes with classmates
Your fellow students might write down something you missed. At the same time, your notes might help them. Exchanging notes can fill in the gaps.

Leave large empty spaces in your notes
Leave plenty of room for filling in information you missed. Use a symbol that signals you've missed something, so you can remember to come back to it.

See the instructor after class
Take your class notes with you and show the instructor what you missed.

Use a digital recorder
Recording a lecture gives you a chance to hear it again whenever you choose. Some recorders allow you to vary the speed of the recording. With this feature, you can perform magic and actually slow down the instructor's speech. Again, remember to seek permission before you record anybody's voice.

Before class, take notes on your reading assignment
You can take detailed notes on the text before class. Leave plenty of blank space. Take these notes

with you to class and simply add your lecture notes to them.

Go to the lecture again
Many classes are taught in multiple sections. That gives you the chance to hear a lecture at least twice—once in your regular class and again in another section of the class.

Ask questions—even if you're totally lost
Many instructors have an exam review session. This is the time to ask about the points you missed.

There might be times when you feel so lost that you can't even formulate a question. That's okay. One option is to report this fact to the instructor or teaching assistant. She can often guide you to a clear question. Another option is to ask a related question. This might lead you to the question you really wanted to ask.

Ask the instructor to slow down
This is the most obvious solution. If asking the instructor to slow down doesn't work, ask him to repeat what you missed. ✳

practising
CRITICAL THINKING

5-2

Taking notes under pressure

With note-taking, as with other skills, the more you practise the better you become. You can use online news broadcasts and videos to practise listening for key words, writing quickly, focussing your attention, and reviewing. Programs that feature speeches and panel discussions work well for this purpose. So do documentary films.

The next time you watch or listen to such a program, use pen and paper to jot down key words and information. If you fall behind, relax. Just leave a space in your notes and return your attention to the program or broadcast. If a program includes commercial breaks, use them to review and revise notes. At the end of the program, spend five minutes reviewing all of your notes. Create a mind map of a few news stories, then sum up the news of the day for a friend.

This exercise will help you develop an ear for key words. Since you can't ask questions or request that the speaker slow down, you train yourself to stay totally in the moment.

Don't be discouraged if you miss a lot the first time around. Do this exercise several times and observe how your mind works.

You can also ask a classmate to do this exercise with you. Compare your notes and look for any points that either of you missed.

Taking notes
WHILE READING

Taking notes while on school- or work-related reading requires the same skills that apply to class notes: observing, recording, and reviewing. Use these skills to take notes for review and for research.

Review notes

Review notes will look like the notes you take in class. Take review notes when you want more detailed notes than writing in the margin of your text allows. You might want to single out a particularly difficult section of a text and make separate notes. Or you might want to make summaries of overlapping lecture and text material. You can't underline or make notes in library books, so these sources will require separate notes, too.

To take more effective review notes, follow these suggestions:

- *Use a variety of formats.* Translate text into Cornell notes, mind maps, or outlines. Combine these formats to create your own. Translate diagrams, charts, and other visual elements into words. Then reverse the process by translating straight text into visual elements.

- *Don't let the creation of formats get in your way.* Even a simple list of key points and examples can become a powerful review tool.

- *Condense a passage to key quotations.* Authors embed their essential ideas in key sentences. As you read, continually ask yourself, "What's the point?" Then see if you can point to a specific sentence on the page to answer your question. Look especially at headings, subheadings, and topic sentences of paragraphs. Write these key sentences word for word in your notes, and put them within quotation marks. Copy as few sentences as you can and still retain the core meaning of the passage.

- *Condense by paraphrasing.* Pretend that you have to summarize a chapter, article, or book on a postcard. Limit yourself to a single paragraph—or a single sentence—and use your own words. This is a great way to test your understanding of the material.

- *Take a cue from the table of contents.* Look at the table of contents in your book. Write each major heading on a piece of paper, or key those headings into a word-processing file on your computer. Include page numbers. Next, see if you can improve on the table of contents. Substitute your own headings for those that appear in the book. Turn single words or phrases into complete sentences, and use words that are meaningful to you.

- *Note special concepts in math and science.* When you read mathematical, scientific, or other technical materials, copy important formulas or equations. Re-create important diagrams, and draw your own visual representations of concepts. Also write down data that might appear on an exam.

Research notes

Take research notes when preparing to write a paper or deliver a speech. One traditional method of research is to take notes on index cards. You write one idea, fact, or quotation per card. The advantage of limiting each card to one item of information is that you can easily arrange cards according to the sequence of your outline—and ongoing changes in your outline. You can also do the same thing on your computer using presentation software such as PowerPoint® or Keynote®. Each idea this time is put on a separate slide. Similar to the index cards, you can re-organize the slides easily when you do your outline.

You can also take advantage of the software features of your word processing program that help you create tables of contents, indexes, graphics, and other elements you might want to use in your project later on.

No matter which method you use, your research notes will fall into two main categories.

The first category is information about your sources. Use tools like the citation management software mentioned later in this chapter to document your sources and it will be a snap. You'll need such information later in the writing process as you create a formal list of your sources—especially sources of quotations or paraphrased material that is included in the body of your paper or presentation. By keeping track of your sources as you conduct research, you create a working bibliography. Ask your instructor about what style guide you should follow in creating your bibliography—APA, MLA, or Chicago. Check your library website for more information on style guides. When recording your own ideas, simply note the source as "me."

The second category of research notes includes the actual ideas and facts that you will use to create the content of your paper or presentation. Again, if you're using index cards, write only *one* piece of information on each information card—a single quotation, fact, or concept. Doing so makes it easier for you to sort cards later.

Be sure to avoid plagiarism. When people take words or images from a source and present them as their own, they are committing **plagiarism**. Even when plagiarism is accidental, the consequences can be harsh. For essential information on this topic, see "Academic integrity: Avoiding plagiarism" in Chapter 8, "Communicating."

If you're taking notes on a computer and using online sources, be especially careful to avoid plagiarism. When you copy text or images from a website, separate those notes from your own ideas. Use a different font for copied material, or enclose it in quotation marks.

Schedule time to review all the information and ideas that your research has produced. By allowing time for

rereading and reflecting on all the notes you've taken, you create the conditions for genuine understanding.

Start by summarizing major points of view on your topic. Note points of agreement and disagreement among your sources.

Also see if you can find direct answers to the questions that you had when you started researching. These answers could become headings in your paper.

Look for connections in your material, including ideas, facts, and examples that occur in several sources. Also look for connections between your research and your life—ideas that you can verify based on personal experience.

Adapt to special cases

The style of your notes can vary according to the nature of the material. If you are assigned a short story or poem, read the entire work once without taking any notes. On your first reading, simply enjoy the piece. When you finish, write down your immediate impressions. Then go over the piece and make brief notes on characters, images, symbols, settings, plot, point of view, or other aspects of the work.

Normally, you would ask yourself questions *before* you read an assignment. When you read fiction or poetry, however, ask yourself questions *after* you have read the piece. Then reread it (or skim it, if it's long) to get answers. Your notes can reflect this question-and-answer process. ✳

Using citation management software to keep track of references

Documenting your sources of information is a key skill to enhancing your information literacy and to getting an A on your paper. Keeping track of everything you've read for an essay or project could be a time-consuming and frustrating process. Luckily, citation management software has been developed that will help you to organize and record all the information sources you are using in an easily accessible format. The software allows you to record your sources while you research rather than you scrambling to create the reference list when your project is complete and finding out that bibliographic information is incomplete or missing. There are many tools available free or at low cost, such as *Zotero*, *Mendeley*, or *EndNote Basic*. These tools are great at helping you record

bibliographic information from books, scholarly articles, and other sources. You can import the information directly from bibliographic databases such as *PsycInfo*, *PubMed*, *Scopus*, *Web of Science*, the library catalogue, and other Web pages. Plus, citation information like author, title, year of publication can be manually entered and edited. You can organize your work by creating a separate folder for each project. Some tools even allow you to share your citation list with others, a feature which is useful if you are doing a collaborative project. When you are finished your project, the software will automatically generate your bibliography, in-text citations, endnotes, and footnotes. To find out more about these tools, check with a librarian at your school.

Taking effective notes for
ONLINE COURSEWORK

If you are taking an online course or a course that is heavily supported by online materials, note-taking could be a new challenge. You can use a variety of strategies to succeed.

Do a trial run with technology

Verify your access to course websites, including online tutorials, PowerPoint® presentations, readings, quizzes, tests, assignments, and discussion boards. Ask your instructors for website addresses, email addresses, and passwords. Work out any bugs when you start the course and well before that first assignment is due.

If you're planning to use a computer lab on campus, find one that meets course requirements. Different computer labs will have specialized software for your courses; find the one that works best for you.

Develop a contingency plan

Murphy's Law of Computer Crashes states that technology tends to break down at the moment of greatest inconvenience. You might not believe this piece of folklore, but it's still wise to prepare for it:

- Find a "technology buddy" in each of your classes—someone who is tech savvy, someone you can contact to get help with computer problems.

- Every day, make backup copies of files created for your courses. Most schools give you access to cloud storage such as *One Drive*, or *Google Drive* or *Dropbox*. The beauty of cloud storage is that you can access your files anywhere, anytime you have Web access.

- Take notes right on course materials. You can print out anything that appears on a computer screen, from course materials to presentation slides. Remember that one potential problem with having printed course materials, though, is that you might skip the note-taking process altogether. ("I can just print out everything!") You would then miss the chance to internalize a new idea by restating it in your own words—a principal benefit of note-taking. Result: Material passes from computer to printer without ever intersecting with your brain.

Syda Productions/Shutterstock.com

- To prevent this problem, find ways to engage actively with online materials. Take review notes in Cornell, mind map, concept map, or outline format. Write Discovery and Intention Statements to capture key insights from the materials and to state ways you intend to apply them. Also talk about what you're learning. Recite key points out loud, and discuss what you read online with other students. Of course, it's fine to print out online material. If you do, treat your printouts like textbooks, and apply the steps of Muscle Reading explained in Chapter 4. In addition, consider the following ways to create the most value from course content that's delivered online.

Get actively involved with the course

If your course has a "coffee lounge," share info about your hobbies and other out-of-class activities there. The more you get to know your classmates, the easier it will be to ask for help when you need it, just as you would in a face-to-face course.

Your online or blended course will include a page that lists homework assignments and test dates. That's only the beginning. Look for ways to engage with the material by submitting questions, participating actively in discussion forums, completing assignments, and interacting with the instructor and other students. This is different than your face-to-face classes in that you may have to communicate through written text—so be prepared to spend more time reading and writing online than you would in a regular class.

Set up folders and files for easy reference

Create a separate folder for each class on your computer's hard drive. Give each folder a meaningful name, such as *biology–spring 2019*. Place all files related to a course in the appropriate folder. Doing this can save you from one of the main technology-related time wasters: searching for lost files. To help you organize your files, you might want to try using technology too. For instance, *Google Keep* is a free note-taking app that allows you to organize your files by colour, share notes with others, and look for everything with a good search engine; it is linked to your Google account.

Take responsibility

If you register for an online course with no class meetings, you might miss the motivating presence of an instructor and classmates. Instead, manufacture your own motivation. Online classes force you to be a self-directed learner even more than face-to-face classes. If staying on task is a challenge for you, this might not be the best way for you to learn. Be clear about what you'll gain by doing well in the course. Relate course content to your major and your career goals. Don't wait to be contacted by your classmates and instructor. Initiate that contact on your own. Be prepared to spend as much time online as you would in a traditional course—a minimum of six hours a week. That doesn't include extra time you will spend working on class projects or preparing for tests.

If you feel confused about anything you're learning, ask for help right away. This is especially important when you don't see the instructor in class. Some students simply drop online courses rather than seek help. Email or call the instructor before you make that choice. If the instructor is on campus, you might be able to arrange for a meeting during office hours.

Manage time and tasks carefully

Courses that take place mostly or totally online can become invisible in your weekly academic schedule. This tendency reinforces the temptation to put off dealing with these courses until late in the term. You can avoid this fate by considering these suggestions:

- Early in the term, create a detailed schedule for online courses. In your calendar, list a due date for each assignment, as you would for your other courses. Break big assignments into smaller steps, and schedule a due date for each step. Use assignment apps like *myHomework Student Planner* to keep you on track.

- Consider scheduling times in your daily or weekly calendar to complete online course work. Give these scheduled sessions the same priority as regular classroom meetings. At these times, check for online announcements relating to assignments, tests, and other course events.

- When you receive an online assignment, email any questions immediately. Keep in mind that just because the course is online doesn't mean the instructor is available 24/7. Find out when is the best time to contact them and how long it will take for a response. Remember to check the course website for frequently asked questions.

- Download or print out online course materials as soon as they're posted on the class website.

- If possible, submit online assignments early. But a reminder in your device so you don't lose track of due dates. Staying ahead of the game will help you avoid an all-nighter at the computer during finals week.

Ask for feedback

To get the most from online learning, request feedback from your instructor via email. When appropriate, also ask for conferences by phone or in person.

Sharing files offers another source of feedback. For example, Microsoft *Word* has a Track Changes feature that allows other people to insert comments into your documents and make suggested revisions. These edits are highlighted on the screen. Use such tools to get feedback on your writing from instructors and peers.

Note: Be sure to check with your instructors to see how they want students enrolled in their online courses to address and label their emails. Many teachers ask their online students to use a standard format for the subject area so they can quickly recognize emails from them.

Contact other students

Make personal contact with at least one other student in each of your classes—especially classes that involve lots of online course work. Create study groups to share notes, quiz each other, critique papers, and do other learning tasks. This kind of support can help you succeed as an online learner. ✳

Why online learning might work well for you—what students have to say

Four students sat down with a group of instructors to talk about their experiences with learning online or in blended learning classroom. Kate, Simon, Richard, and Mirella have had a variety of online experiences from participating in MOOCS, taking all or part of their degree online, to experiencing the flipped classroom.

What does it take to succeed in learning online?   Mirella found out she needed to be a **self-directed learner**. She suggested it is easy to slip behind and not watch the lectures online when you don't have to be in class at a particular time. Kate agreed that students can feel a lack of accountability for learning when they don't have to "attend" class and that this can be a barrier to success. One strategy that Kate used to overcome this problem was to schedule in a regular time each week to do her online work as if it were a face-to-face class.

What do you like about online learning?   Simon found that online learning often includes different modes of presentation of the material—videos, PowerPoint® presentations, online discussions—so he thought it actually targeted more diverse ways of learning and was in fact more responsive to individual differences among students. Both Kate and Simon liked reviewing material at their own pace. Simon would take the material the instructor had posted and add in his own material for learning, like a YouTube clip. Kate found she had multiple ways of finding answers to questions when she got stuck on a concept or idea. She could look up material in the text, ask a peer a question, or review the lecture one more time—that just isn't possible in traditional classes. Conversely, she could skip over sections she was already familiar with. She also appreciated that the discussions in the online forums allowed more student voices and perspectives to be heard than often happened in the face-to-face classes.

Mirella noticed that when she took a first-year class online many of the students were actually in an upper year. The first-year students were often initially intimidated about learning in an online environment—worrying that they couldn't succeed. However, they all commented after a few weeks that in fact the online environment actually offered them more support for learning than their other classes by providing the material in a variety of formats and giving them the freedom to review the course at their leisure. Mirella found that the weekly quizzes in her course helped her to keep up with the material and facilitated learning. Finally, Richard commented how much easier it was to organize and do group and collaborative work in an online environment—you didn't need for instance to try to find a time and place to meet outside of class and working online gave them an easily accessible common space to share learning.

Overall the discussion suggested that to succeed in an online course, you needed to follow these guidelines:

- Schedule time to do online work as if it were a regular class.

- Limit your online distractions—no one will be there to check if you are spending your study time on social media rather than course work, so be self-disciplined.

- Think about how you learn best—reading, watching, or actively problem-solving—and try to integrate that into your online learning.

- Share good material you find online with the rest of the class.

- Ask questions in the discussion forums—chances are if you have a question about a topic so do many other students in the class.

- Don't be afraid to ask your instructor for help.

- Participate in the discussion forums; your online anonymity can actually make speaking up in class easier than it would be in your face-to-face classes.

- Be organized—have a calendar of due dates of assignments and tests.

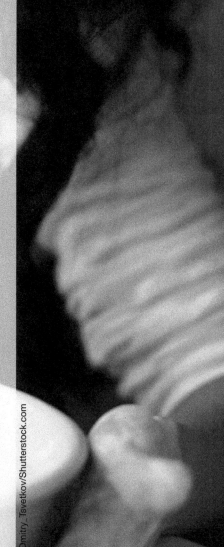

I Create It All

This article describes a powerful tool for times of trouble. In a crisis, "I create it all" can lead the way to solutions. "I create it all" means treating experiences, events, and circumstances in your life as if you created them.

"I create it all" is one of the most unusual and bizarre suggestions in this book. It certainly is not a belief. Use it when it works. Don't when it doesn't.

Keeping that in mind, consider how powerful this Power Process can be. It is really about the difference between two distinct positions in life: being a victim or being responsible.

A victim of circumstances is controlled by outside forces. We've all felt like victims at one time or another. Sometimes we felt helpless.

In contrast, we can take responsibility. Responsibility is "response-ability"—the ability to choose a *response* to any event. You can choose your *response* to any event, even when the event itself is beyond your control.

Many students approach grades from the position of being victims. When the student who sees the world this way gets an F, she reacts something like this: "Another F! That teacher couldn't teach her way out of a wet paper bag. She can't

teach English for anything. And that text-book—how boring!"

The problem with this viewpoint is that in looking for excuses, the student is robbing herself of the power to get any grade other than an F. She's giving all of her power to a bad teacher and a boring textbook.

There is another way. By *taking responsibility*, you recognize that you choose your grades by choosing your actions. Then you are the source, rather than the result, of the grades you get. The student who got an F could react like this:

"Another F! Oh, shoot! Well, hmmm.... What did I do to create it?"

Now, that's power. By asking, "How did I contribute to this outcome?" you are no longer the victim. This student might continue by saying, "Well, let's see. I didn't review my notes after class. That might have done it." Or "I went out with my friends the night before the test. Well, that probably helped me fulfill some of the requirements for getting an F."

The point is this: When the F is the result of your friends, the book, or the teacher, you probably can't do anything about it. However, if you *chose* the F, you can choose a different grade next time. You are in charge.

Dmitry_Tsvetkov/Shutterstock.com

Put it to WORK

Developing the ability to take useful notes during meetings is one way to make yourself valued in the workplace. It might even help you get promoted. With this in mind, look for ways to apply suggestions from this chapter at work.

LightField Studios/Shutterstock.com

Hanae Niigata is a part-time office manager for a large cardiovascular clinic. Her responsibilities include handling incoming calls, scheduling patient visits, maintaining medical records, and completing other tasks assigned by physicians and nurses.

Hanae's career focus is healthcare. She has worked as a home health aide and is currently enrolled in school. Her goal is to obtain a degree in nursing and work as a registered nurse.

Hanae has a reputation as a hard worker. Even in a noisy environment with frequent interruptions, she completes tasks that require attention to detail and sustained concentration. She catches errors on medical records that her co-workers tend to miss. In addition, Hanae is often the first person in the office to whom people turn when they have a problem to solve. Even in the most difficult circumstances, she can generate a list of options—including solutions that occur to no one else.

Recently, Hanae attended a two-hour course on a new telephone system soon to be installed in her office. She was told to take detailed notes so she could teach the system to several receptionists. Hanae was shocked that the old system was being replaced. In her opinion, it was user-friendly.

As the training session began, Hanae diligently attempted to write down almost everything the instructor said. While doing so, she repeatedly found herself distracted by the thought that her manager was replacing a perfectly good phone system with some "sure-to-be-a-nightmare, high-tech garbage."

After completing the course, Hanae sat down with her manager to fill him in on the new system. As she thumbed through her notes, she realized they didn't make much sense to her, even though she had just finished writing

them. She couldn't recall much of the course from memory, either, leaving her with little information to share with her manager.

Hanae routinely applies strategies from this book to many areas of her work. For example, she is a creative thinker and problem-solver, using several strategies you will learn in Chapter 7, "Thinking." But when it came to the training session, she didn't apply any of the book's note-taking strategies. Create a list of strategies that Hanae could have used to take more effective notes on the training session that she attended.

When you are at a work meeting, consider using the three "As" when you take notes. Record key details about the following:

- *Attendance.* Notice who shows up. Your employer might expect meeting notes to include a list of attendees.

- *Agreements.* The purpose of most meetings is to reach an agreement about something—a policy, project, or plan. Note each agreement. If you're not sure whether an agreement was reached, ask for clarification.

- *Actions.* During meetings, people often commit to take some type of action in the future. Record each proposed follow-up action and who agreed to do it.

Skilled meeting planners often put an agenda in writing and distribute it in advance. You can use this agenda as a way to organize your notes. However, be prepared for times when people depart from the agenda and introduce new topics.

QUIZ

Name_____ Date____/____/____

1. What are the three major steps of effective note-taking, as explained in this chapter? Summarize each step in one sentence.

2. Techniques you can use to "set the stage" for note-taking do NOT include
   (a) Completing outside assignments.
   (b) Bringing the right materials.
   (c) Setting aside questions in order to concentrate.
   (d) Conducting a short pre-class review.
   (e) Sitting front and centre.

3. What is an advantage of sitting in the front and centre of the classroom?

4. Describe why mind mapping might help to improve your metacognitive skills.

5. An effective method to postpone debate during a lecture is to ignore your own opinions and passively record the instructor's words. True or False? Explain your answer.

6. Do this when using the Cornell system of note-taking (circle all that apply):
   (a) Write the main point on a line or in a box, circle, or any other shape.
   (b) Use only Roman numerals in an outline form.
   (c) Copy each new concept on a separate index card.
   (d) Remember never to combine it with mind mapping.
   (e) Draw a vertical line about two inches from the left edge of the paper.

7. Explain how key words can be used when taking notes. Then select and write down at least five key words from this chapter.

8. Reviewing within 24 hours assists short-term memory only. Long-term memory requires reviews over a longer period of time. True or False? Explain your answer.

9. Describe at least three strategies for reviewing notes.

10. Briefly define the word *responsibility* as it is used in the Power Process, "I Create It All."

Skills SNAPSHOT

The Discovery Wheel in Chapter 1 includes a section labelled *Notes*. For the next 10 to 15 minutes, go beyond your initial responses to that exercise. Take a snapshot of your skills as they exist today, after reading and doing this chapter.

Begin by reflecting on some of your recent experiences with note-taking. These experiences can include classroom notes, as well as notes on your reading assignments. Then take the next step toward mastery by committing to a specific action in the near future.

OBSERVING

If my attention wanders while taking notes, I refocus by . . .

When I strongly disagree with the opinion of a speaker or author, I respond by . . .

RECORDING

The formats I usually use to take notes are . . .

A new note-taking format that I'd like to experiment with is . . .

REVIEWING

If asked to rate the overall quality of the notes that I've taken in the last week, I would say that . . .

In general, I find my notes to be most useful when they . . .

NEXT ACTION

I'll know that I've reached a new level of mastery with note-taking when . . .

MASTER STUDENT PROFILE

Sam Maggs
… embraces her geekdom

George Pimentel/WireImage/Getty Images

Sam Maggs earned her stripes as a "geek girl" navigating the virtual worlds of *Doom* and *Myst*. But it was her Millennium Falcon-like maneuvering of the very real D. B. Weldon Library at her alma mater that provided the pop culture authority with the skills she needed to turn her love of sensation fiction into a sensational career.

In just a few short years since completing her university studies, Maggs has become the funny feminist face of geekdom—no easy task when you consider fictional places like Westeros, Jakku and Osiris are so often dominated by males both in portrayal and creation.

Winner of Cineplex Entertainment's Casting Call contest in 2014, before moving to Edmonton to start her dream job as a writer for best-selling video game developer, BioWare.

She was initially influenced by her mother and father—the couple saw the original *Star Wars* 20 times in the theatre—and, later, English and Writing Studies professor Christopher Keep.

"Having a professor and a mentor like Professor Keep, who believed in my writing even when I was not so confident in it, was really invaluable and gave me the skills and the confidence I needed to go on to a master's degree and book publishing," explained Maggs

Maggs has logged hundreds, if not thousands, of hours gaming since she was a tween. The chance to work for the company behind such mega-hits as *Mass Effect, Dragon Age*, and *Star Wars: The Old Republic* was a no-brainer for the young woman considered by many as the living embodiment of "a strong female character."

"It's just really cool to come to work every day to a place where you sit down in a writer's room and talk about things like diversity and representation."

"We still have a long way to go in terms of diversity and representation

and a lot of work to do. But the amount of change I have seen, in even the last five years, is honestly extraordinary," Maggs said. "That's in large part because of the prominence of social media. Women have always been involved in geekdom; we've always liked sci-fi and TV and comic books. But we haven't traditionally felt welcome in the spaces in which these things are discussed. But now with social media, there are so many of us. There is this influx and we have been able to form these communities and find each other online and speak out about the things that we don't think represent us well."

And video games aren't the only thing Maggs is writing. The author of *The Fangirl's Guide to the Galaxy*, considered the ultimate handbook for ladies living the nerdy life, Maggs' has also written a book titled *Wonder Women*. In *Wonder Women*, Maggs profiles inventors and trailblazers who changed history without history taking notice.

"So many women contributed to so many incredible discoveries and inventions through history that I feel very humbled to be able to bring their stories to the world and tell people about the really radical stuff that they did. I can't wait for people to learn about them."

Source: Renaud, Jeffrey. (2016, Fall). Multimedia maven Sam Maggs is the First Lady of Geek. *Western Alumni* (Alumni Gazette). Retrieved from *www.alumni .westernu.ca/alumni-gazette/fall-2016/millennial -falcon.html?referrer=https://www.google.ca/*. Reprinted with permission.

Tests

what is included . . .

do you have a minute?

Write a study checklist for the next test in a course that you're taking right now. Include reading assignments and dates for class notes on which the test will be based.

© Robert Kneschke/Shutterstock.com

WHAT if …

I could let go of anxiety about tests—or anything else?

WHY this chapter matters …

Adopting a few simple techniques can make a major difference in how you feel about tests, and how you perform on them.

HOW you can use this chapter …

Predict test questions and use your study time more effectively. Harness the power of cooperative learning by studying with other people. Gain strategies for raising your scores on tests. Separate your self-image from your test scores.

DISARM TESTS

On the surface, tests don't look dangerous, yet sometimes we treat them as if they were land mines. Suppose a stranger walks up to you on the street and asks, "Does a finite abelian P-group have a basis?" Will you break out in a cold sweat? Will your muscles tense up? Will your breathing become shallow?

Probably not. Even if you have never heard of a finite abelian P-group, you are likely to remain coolly detached. However, if you find the same question on a test and if you have never heard of a finite abelian P-group, your hands might get clammy.

Grades (A to F) are what we use to give power to tests. And there are lots of misconceptions about what grades are. Grades are not a measure of intelligence or creativity. They are not an indication of our ability to contribute to society. Grades are simply a measure of how well we do on tests. Some people think that a test score measures what a student has accomplished in a course. This is false. A test score is a measure of what a student scored on a test. If you are anxious about a test and blank out, the mark cannot measure what you've learned. The reverse is also true: If you are good at taking tests and a lucky guesser, the score won't be an accurate reflection of what you know.

Grades are not a measure of self-worth. Yet we tend to give test scores the power to determine how we feel about ourselves. Common thoughts include "If I fail a test, I am a failure" or "If I do badly on a test, I am a bad person." The truth is that if you do badly on a test, you are a person who did badly on a test. That's all. Carrying around misconceptions about tests and marks can put undue pressure on your performance.

If you experience test anxiety, then you might find this line of reasoning hard to swallow. Test anxiety is a common problem among students. And it can surface in many ways, masquerading as a variety of emotions. Here are some examples:

- *Anger:* "The teacher never wanted me to pass this stupid course anyway."

- *Blame:* "If only the class were not so boring."

- *Fear:* "I'll never have enough time to study."

Believing in any of these statements leaves us powerless. We become victims of things that we don't control—the teacher, the textbook, or the wording of the test questions.

Another option is to ask, What can *I* do to experience my next test differently? How can I prepare more effectively? How can I manage stress before, during, and after the test? When you answer such questions, you take back your power.

It is easier to do well on exams if you don't put too much pressure on yourself. Don't give the test some magical power over your personal worth as a human being. Academic tests are not a matter of life and death. Even scoring badly on an important test—an entrance test for medical school or the bar exams, for example—usually only means a delay in your plans.

Whether the chance of doing poorly is real or exaggerated, worrying about it can become paralyzing. The way to deal with tests is to keep them in perspective. ✳

What to do
BEFORE the test

Philipp Nemenz/Cultura/Getty Images

STUDENTS LIKE TO SAY that they plan to *study* for a test. There's a big problem with that term: It doesn't always have a clear definition. "Study" might mean "read," "write," or "recite." It could mean all of those things—or something else entirely.

One way to save hours of wasted study time is to look on each test as a performance. From this point of view, preparing for a test means *rehearsing*. Study for a test in the way that a musician rehearses for a concert or an actor prepares for opening night—by simulating the physical and psychological conditions you'll encounter when you actually enter the exam room.

Review

Rehearsing means doing the kind of tasks that you'll perform during a test—answering questions, solving problems, composing essays. Start this process with regular reviews of course content. Test preparation comes down to answering questions about your self-awareness (What do I know?), task awareness (What do I have to learn?), and strategy awareness (How can I close the gap between what I know and what I don't know?). Answering these questions means managing your review time, creating review tools, and planning your test-taking strategy.

Long before the test, ask your instructor what form the test will take. If the exam is mainly essay questions, then practise making up questions and answering those questions. Similarly, if the test is likely to be multiple-choice, see if old exams are available or do the practice questions in your study guide.

It is good to rehearse for the test using the same methods that will actually be used on the test. You'll recall from Chapter 4, "Reading," that retrieval practice is one of the most effective learning strategies that you can do to prepare for a test and one that is way more effective than simple rereading the text (Brown, Roediger, & McDaniel, 2014). As you review, start every session with affirmations such as "I study with energy and efficiency" or "I am smart and prepared to do well on this test." Keep these statements simple and to the point. This powerful technique can help you stay positive.

Schedule your practice sessions

A key to successful test preparation is managing review time. Schedule specific times in your calendar for practice sessions before the test. The biggest benefit of early review is that facts have time to roam around in your head, you have more opportunity to connect what you are learning to prior knowledge, and therefore memories are more likely to be consolidated into long-term memory. Use short daily review sessions to prepare the way for major review sessions.

Do daily reviews

Daily reviews include the short pre- and post-class reviews of lecture notes suggested in Chapter 5, "Notes." Research indicates that this is an effective tool for moving ideas from short-term to long-term memory (see Chapter 3, "Memory"). Also conduct brief daily reviews when you read. Before reading a new assignment, scan your notes and the sections you underlined in the previous assignment. Use the time you spend waiting for the bus or doing the laundry to conduct short reviews. Concentrate daily reviews on two kinds of material: material you have just learned, either in class or from your reading, and material that involves simple memorization (equations, formulas, dates, definitions). During a lull in class, go over the notes you just took.

Conduct short daily reviews several times throughout the day. To make sure you do, include them on your daily to-do list. Write down reminders, such as "5 min. review of biology" or "10 min. review of economics," and give yourself the satisfaction of crossing them off your list.

Do weekly reviews

Weekly reviews are longer—about an hour per subject. They are also more structured than short daily reviews. When a subject is complex, the brain requires time to dig into the material. Review each subject at least once a week. Weekly sessions include reviews of assigned reading and lecture notes. During your weekly reviews, try studying for 20 minutes and then taking a 10-minute break (take a walk or chat with a friend). Set your timer on your phone so the 10-minute break doesn't stretch to 20. During the break, consider whether you truly understood what you were just reviewing and how easy it was to focus on the material for 20 minutes. If it was easy to focus for 20 minutes, lengthen the study session to a half hour before you take a break. It's easier to commit to studying if you know when the breaks will be.

Do major reviews

Major reviews are usually conducted the week before final exams or other critical exams. They help integrate concepts and deepen understanding of the material presented throughout the term. These are longer review periods—two to five hours at a stretch, punctuated by sufficient breaks. (You have probably noticed that the effectiveness of your review begins to drop after an hour or so unless you give yourself a short rest.)

After a certain point, short breaks every hour might not be enough to refresh you. That's when it's time to quit. Learn your limits by being conscious of the quality of your concentration. During long review sessions, study the most difficult subjects when you are the most alert, at the beginning of the session.

Don't cram

It is tempting to think that you can just cram it all in on the day or two leading up to your test, but research has shown this is just not a positive study strategy (Brown, Roediger, & McDaniel, 2014). Spaced practice, where you space or distribute your practice over time (such as doing five practice sessions over five days), leads to a better performance than **massed practice** (such as completing five practice sessions in one day). Massed practice relies more heavily on short-term memory which you will recall from Chapter 3 is a limited-capacity system. Spaced practice, on the other hand, helps implant memories in your long-term memory store, which is much larger. Having some breaks between practice sessions means that in all likelihood a little forgetting will have occurred by the time you try to remember information; but by having to work harder to retrieve the correct response, you build your habit strength. (The term *habit strength* refers to the fact that the likelihood of correctly answering a question increases the more you practise.) You also want to ensure that practice doesn't become mindless or rote in nature. Spacing out the time between study sessions leads to a deeper memory bond being formed so it increases the odds you will be able to retrieve critical information when you need to on the test.

Give memory a chance to consolidate by making sure you have the time to practise mental rehearsal and other processes that facilitate memory consolidation.

Do interleaved practice

Interleaved practice occurs when you vary the task you do when studying; rather than doing 15 of the same problem type when you study math, you intersperse different problem types when you study. Interleaving helps you to discriminate later between different types of problem sets and apply the correct solutions. You can also interleave your practice by moving back and forth between different subjects you are studying—moving from your math homework, to English reading, to psychology research, then back to math.

Interleaved practice makes learning harder initially; but when learning is difficult, recall improves (Brown, Roediger, & McDaniel, 2014). Effortful retrieval is a key component of effective learning. Learning that requires effort changes the brain with new neural connections being formed. That's good news! Because of the neuroplasticity of the brain, our intellectual abilities are determined to a large extent by the effort we put into learning new skills and knowledge.

Interleaved practice turns out to be better than **blocked practice**—where you solve similar problems repeatedly—at helping you acquire motor skills, learn new concepts, and not surprisingly learn math problem-solving. Interleaved practice requires you to switch back and forth in the strategies you need to apply to problems or situations and leads to greater learning gains. Having to switch strategies improves your discriminatory abilities and therefore success in a real-world setting (Brown, Roediger, & McDaniel, 2014).

Find or create practice materials

Create mind map summary sheets

There are several ways to make a mind map as you study for tests. Start by creating a map totally from memory. You might be surprised by how much you already know. Mind maps release floods of information from the brain because the mind works by association. Each idea is linked to many other ideas. You think of one and other associations come to mind.

Let the associations flow. If one seems to go someplace else, simply start another branch on your map. After you have gone as far as you can using recall alone, go over your notes and text and fill in the rest of the map.

Another way to create a mind map summary is to go through your notes and pick out key words. Then, without looking at your notes, create a mind map of everything you can recall about each key word. Finally, go back to your notes and fill in material you left out. You can also start a mind map using underlined sections from your text.

Use flash cards

Create flash cards that include both what you just learned with what you learned weeks ago. In Chapter 3, "Memory," we talked about how to create flash cards either on index cards or using an app like *Tinycards*. Use flash cards for formulas, definitions, theories, key words from your notes, axioms, dates, foreign language phrases, hypotheses, and sample problems. Remember that self-quizzing helps you improve retrieval from memory on your tests. You can create self-quizzes from study guides, or better yet write your own questions. Mix up the questions with each review. Before you check your answers, try to predict how confident you

are that you got the correct answer. This will teach you how to self-monitor your learning, a vital component of metacognition. Remember that the harder it is to recall, the deeper the learning—therefore you will be more likely to answer similar questions on your test or exam. But, don't forget to check your answers!

Self-quizzing is a far more effective strategy than rereading or highlighting the material. Just because you have become familiar with the material doesn't mean you will be able to retrieve it or apply the information to a new context during the test. Self-quizzing helps you to determine what you truly know or don't know. This self-knowledge is important, as everyone is susceptible to the **illusion of knowing**—when you are so familiar with a passage you have read that you feel like you know it. Self-quizzing helps you to put that judgment to the test. Students who do not self-quiz enough are more likely to overestimate their mastery of new material (Brown, Roediger, & McDaniel, 2014).

Get copies of old exams

Check your school's policy about making past tests and exams available to students. Some might not allow it.

Find out if practice quizzes are available on your course website. Copies of previous exams for the course might be available from the instructor, the instructor's department, the library, or the counselling office. Old tests can help you plan a review strategy and give you practice in applying what you learned to new examples. One caution: If you rely exclusively on old tests, you might gloss over material the instructor has added since the last test.

Create review tools

Create study checklists

You can use study checklists the way a pilot uses a preflight checklist. Pilots go through a standard routine before they take off. They physically mark off each item: test flaps, check magnetos, check fuel tanks, adjust instruments, check rudder, etc. They use a written list to be absolutely certain they don't miss anything. Once they are in the air, it's too late, and the consequences of failing to check thoroughly could be drastic. Taking an exam is like flying a plane. Once the test begins, it's too late to memorize that one equation you forgot to include in your review.

Make a checklist for each subject. List reading assignments by chapters or page numbers. List dates of lecture notes. Write down various types of problems you will need to solve. Write down other skills you must master. Include major ideas, definitions, theories, formulas, and equations.

A study checklist is not a review sheet; it is a to-do list. Checklists contain the briefest possible description of each item to study.

Instead of a checklist, you may want to use a test prep plan. This written plan goes beyond a study checklist to include the following:

- The date and time of each test, along with the name of the course and instructor.

- The location of the test—in large classes, tests are often written in a different room than your classroom. If there are multiple sections of a course, the test or exam may be in several different classrooms

so be careful to find out where you are writing your specific test.

- The type of items—such as essay or multiple choice—that are likely to appear on each test.

- Specific dates and times that you intend to study for each test (which you then enter on your calendar).

- Specific strategies that you intend to use while studying for each test.

practising
CRITICAL THINKING

6-1

Creating your own study checklist

For this exercise, you will need to indicate the chapter you are studying, pages covered, class dates, and key concepts covered in class and your readings, plus any other skills you are developing. This will provide you with a quick study checklist for you to review before your test. To determine the concepts being covered in your reading, do a quick overview of the chapter looking at large headings—particularly those that are new to you. After each class, write down any of the key concepts or terms covered that day.

Here is a sample table.

Course: Student Success   **Test: January 22**

Chapter	# of pages	Date of classes associated with each chapter	Key concepts covered in the chapter and classes	Other skills being developed
6	28	Jan. 6 & 10	Interleaved practice Retrieval practice	Studying for multiple-choice exams, studying for online quizzes

Pick one of your courses to create a study checklist for your next test. Fill in the table below.

Course:_____ Test Date_____

Chapter	# of pages	Date of classes associated with each chapter	Key concepts covered in the chapter and classes	Other skills being developed

If you have a friend taking the same class, compare checklists to see if you both have identified the same key concepts or terms and skills to be mastered.

Revise your checklist as needed.

All your test prep plans should include sleeping at least eight hours the night before your exam—a well-rested mind is one the best ways to ensure academic success.

Monitoring your reviews

Each day that you prepare for a test, assess what you have learned and what you still need to learn. See how many items you've covered from your study checklist. Look at the tables of contents in your textbooks and write an X next to the sections that you've summarized. Using a monitoring system can help you gauge the thoroughness of your reviews and alert you to areas that still need attention.

Plan a test-taking strategy

Do a dry run

Write up your own questions and take this "test" several times before the actual exam. If the exam will include mainly true/false or short-answer questions, brainstorm a list of such questions—a mock test—and do a dry run. You might type up this "test" so that it looks like the real thing. If possible, take your practice test in the same room where you will take the actual test.

Meet with your instructors to go over your mock test. Ask whether your questions focus on appropriate topics and represent the kind of items you can expect to see on the actual test. ✳

WAYS TO PREDICT
test questions

Predicting test questions can do more than get you a better mark. It can also keep you focussed on the purpose of a course and help you design your learning strategies. Making predictions can be fun, too—especially when they turn out to be accurate.

Ask about the nature of the test

Eliminate as much guesswork about tests as possible. Ask your instructor to describe upcoming tests. Do this early in the term so you can be alert for possible test questions throughout the course. Many instructors are happy to answer such questions directly. Here are some questions you might want to ask:

- What course material will the test cover—readings, lectures, lab sessions, or a combination?

- Will the test be cumulative, or will it cover just the most recent material you've taught?

- Will the test focus on facts and details or major themes and relationships?

- Will the test call on me to solve problems or apply concepts?

- What types of questions will be on the test—true/false, multiple choice, short-answer, essay?

- Will I have choices about which questions to answer?

- Will your instructor write and score the test—or will a teaching assistant perform those tasks?

Note: In order to study appropriately for essay tests, find out how much detail the instructor wants in your answers. Ask how much time you'll be allowed for the test and how long the essay answers should be (number of pages or word limit). Having that information before you begin studying will help you gauge the depth to which you must know the material.

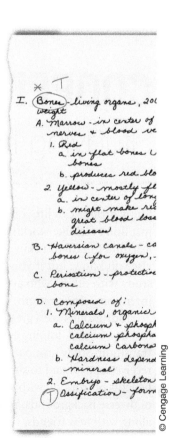

Put yourself in your instructor's shoes

If you were teaching the course, what information would you want students to take away? What kinds of questions would you put on an exam? Make up practice test questions and then answer them. You can also brainstorm test questions with other students—a great activity for study groups.

Look for possible test questions in your notes

Have a separate section in your notebook labelled "Test questions." Add several questions to this section after every lecture and assignment. You can also create your own code or graphic signal—such as a *T!* in a circle—to flag possible test questions in your notes.

See the article "Words to watch for in essay questions" later in this chapter. Use it as a guide to turn the key words in your notes into questions.

Look for clues in your textbook chapters such as chapter overviews and summaries, headings, list of key words, and review questions. The textbook may have a related website where you can take practice tests.

Look for clues to possible questions during class

During lectures you can predict test questions by observing what an instructor says and how he says it. Instructors often give clues. For example, they might repeat important points several times, write them on the board, or return to them in subsequent classes.

Certain gestures can indicate critical points. For example, your instructor might pause, look at notes, or read passages word for word.

Notice whether your instructor has any strong points of view on certain issues. Questions on those issues are likely to appear on a test. Also pay attention to questions the instructor poses to students, and note questions that other students ask.

When material from reading assignments is covered extensively in class, it is likely to be on a test. In science courses and other courses involving problem-solving, work on sample problems using different variables.

Save all quizzes, papers, lab sheets, and marked materials of any kind

Quiz questions have a way of reappearing, in slightly altered form, on final exams. If copies of previous exams and other marked materials are available, use them to predict test questions.

Apply your predictions

To get the most value from your predictions, use them to guide your review session.

Remember the obvious

Be on the lookout for these words: *This material will be on the test.* ✳

COOPERATIVE LEARNING:
Studying in groups

Study groups can lift your mood on days when you just don't feel like working; they can help making learning fun. If you skip a solo study session, no one else will know; but if you declare your intention to study with others who are depending on you, your intention gains strength.

Study groups are a great way to ease the stress of being in a new school. Joining a study group can help ease the transition. Study groups can be a great way to give and receive support and to share talents. To multiply the benefits of working with study groups, seek out people of diverse backgrounds. You can get a new perspective, along with new friends.

© Andersen Ross/Blend Images/ageFotostock

Form a study group

Choose a focus for your group

Many students assume that the purpose of a study group is to help its members prepare for a test. That's one valid purpose—and there are others.

Through his research on cooperative learning, psychologist Joe Cuseo (2003) has identified several kinds of study groups. For instance, members of *test review* groups meet after tests to compare answers and help each other discover sources of errors. *Note-taking* groups focus on comparing and editing notes, often meeting directly after the day's class. *Research* groups meet to help each other find, evaluate, and take notes on background materials for papers and presentations. *Reading* groups can be useful for courses in which test questions are based largely on textbooks; these groups meet to compare the passages individual members have highlighted and the notes they have made in the margins.

Look for dedicated students

Find people you are comfortable with and who share some of your academic goals. Look for students who pay attention, ask questions, and take notes during class, and invite them to join your group.

Another way to form a study group is to post a note on a discussion board on your course website, asking interested students to contact you. This is a good way to meet new people, but you will have less control over who applies to join the group.

Limit groups to four people. Research on cooperative learning indicates that four people is an ideal group size (Cuseo, 2003). Larger ones can be unwieldy.

Studying with close friends is fine, but if your common interests are pizza and jokes, you might find it hard to focus.

Hold a planning session

Ask people to get together for a snack and talk about group goals, meeting times, and other logistics. Get group members to agree to come prepared for meetings so that everyone's time isn't being wasted and to discourage social loafing. You don't have to make an immediate commitment. Test the group first by planning a one-time session. If that session works, plan another. After a few successful sessions, schedule regular meetings. As you look for a place to meet, make sure you pick a quiet place, such as a study room in your library or a study hall in your residence. Plan on only meeting for two to three hours max—longer sessions tend to be unproductive and shorter ones can be too rushed.

Conduct your study group

Ask your instructor for guidelines on study group activity

Many instructors welcome and encourage study groups. However, they have different ideas about what kinds of collaboration are acceptable. Some activities—such as sharing test items or writing papers from a shared outline—are considered cheating and can have serious consequences. Let your instructor know that you're forming a group, and ask for clear guidelines.

Set an agenda for each meeting

Set an agenda for each meeting including objectives and activities to meet those objectives. Ideas for activities can be found later in this article. Set approximate time limits for each agenda item and determine a quitting time. Finally, end each meeting with assignments for all members.

Assign roles

To make the most of your time, ask one member to lead each group meeting. The leader's role is to keep the discussion focussed on the agenda and ask for contributions from all members. Assign another person to act as recorder. This person will take notes on the meeting, recording possible test questions, answers, and main points from group discussions. Rotate both of these roles so that every group member takes a turn.

Test each other by asking questions

Group members can agree to bring five to 10 sample test questions to each meeting. Then you can all take the test made up from these questions.

Practise teaching each other

Teaching is a great way to learn something. Turn the material you're studying into a list of topics and assign a specific topic to each person, who will then teach it to the group. When you teach something, you naturally assume an instructor's attitude ("I know this"), as opposed to a student's attitude ("I still have to learn this"). The vocalization involved in teaching further reinforces the concepts.

Create a testing group

Often there are ideas or concepts you are having trouble understanding. Send one member of your group to the whiteboard and have the individual try to explain the concept to the others. The role of the other students in the group is to ask questions that relate to the larger concept being studied. Each member of the group will likely have some information necessary to explore the concept; working together you can create a better understanding of the concept. You should ask questions without opening your textbooks.

Compare notes

Make sure that you all heard the same thing in class and that you all recorded the important information. Ask others to help explain material in your notes that is confusing to you.

Brainstorm test questions

Set aside 5 to 10 minutes of each study session to use brainstorming techniques (described in detail in

Chapter 7, "Thinking") to create test questions. You can add these to the "Test questions" section of your notebook.

Ask each member to contribute

Recognize signs that group members are not contributing in equal ways. For instance, someone in your group might consistently fail to prepare for meetings or feel that he has nothing to contribute. Other members might dominate the group discussions.

As a group, brainstorm ways to get unprepared members involved. Reel in a dominating member by reminding him of the importance that everyone's voice be heard.

Work in groups of two at a computer to review a course

One person can operate the keyboard while the other person dictates summaries of lectures and assigned readings. Together, both group members can check facts by consulting textbooks, lecture notes, and class handouts.

Create wall-sized mind maps or concept maps to summarize a textbook or series of lectures

Work on large sheets of butcher paper, or tape together pieces of construction paper. When doing a mind map, assign one branch of the mind map to each member of the study group. Use a different coloured pen or marker for each branch. (For more information on concept maps, see Chapter 3, "Memory." Mind maps were discussed in Chapter 5, "Notes.")

Monitor effectiveness

On your meeting agenda, include an occasional discussion about your group's effectiveness. Are you meeting consistently? Is the group helping members succeed in class?

To resolve conflict among group members, keep the conversation constructive. Focus on solutions. Move from vague complaints ("You're never prepared") to specific requests ("Will you commit to bringing 10 sample test questions next time?"). Asking a "problem" member to lead the next meeting might make an immediate difference.

Use technology to organize your work

Web-based applications allow you to create virtual study groups and collaborate online. For example, create and revise documents with sites such as *Google Docs*, *One Drive*, and *Zoho Writer*. You can also create and share PowerPoint® and Keynote® presentations with tools such as *SlideShare* (www.slideshare.net) and *Prezi* (www.prezi.com).

Project management apps like *Redbooth*, *Trello*, *Asana*, *Basecamp* , or *5 pm* are a great way to coordinate group projects. You can share files, create a group calendar, assign tasks, chat online, post messages, and track progress toward milestones such as key due dates. ✳

Students offering support

Want to combine help with your studying with your quest for social justice? Then *Students Offering Support* (SOS) might just be the group for you. SOS is a national charitable organization founded in 2004 by Greg Overholt who was a student at that time at Wilfrid Laurier University. This organization provides tutoring sessions at low cost to groups of students and uses the money raised to support charities. The study group sessions are led by top-notch student volunteers. Each chapter of the organization raises money for a different group. For example, in 2007,

the Laurier chapter built a school in Belize. Since 2004, Laurier students have raised over $240,000 for sustainable development projects in Africa and Latin America, while student volunteers tutored over 5000 students in exam study sessions. So if you want to help raise your marks and change the world, get involved with your school's SOS chapter. If your school doesn't have a chapter, consider starting one yourself.

Go to *www.studentsofferingsupport.ca* to find out more about Students Offering Support.

What to do
DURING THE TEST

ESB Professional/Shutterstock

Prepare yourself for the test by arriving early. That often leaves time to do a relaxation exercise. While you're waiting for the test to begin and talking with classmates, avoid the question "How much did you study for the test?" This question might fuel anxious thoughts. When you enter the room, try to choose a seat near a wall and near a clock so that you have something to look at during the exam. In a large test hall, it can be difficult to look anywhere without the instructor thinking you are trying to look at other students' papers.

As you begin

Ask the instructor, proctor, or invigilator if you can use scratch paper during the test. If you use a separate sheet of paper without permission, you might appear to be cheating. If you do get permission, use this paper to jot down memory aids, formulas, equations, facts, or other material you know you'll need and might forget. An alternative is to make quick notes in the margins of the test sheet. Similarly, find out the rules for having any electronics on your desk. Although students can sometimes bring calculators, most schools ban mobile devices even if you are using them just to know the time. Plan on wearing a watch or use the clock in the exam room.

Pay attention to verbal directions given as a test is distributed. Then scan the whole test immediately. Evaluate the importance of each section. Notice how many marks each part of the test is worth and estimate how much time you'll need for each section, using its value as your guide. For example, don't budget 20 percent of your time for a section that is worth only 10 percent of the marks.

Read the directions slowly. Then reread them. It can be agonizing to discover that you lost marks on a test merely because you failed to follow the directions. When the directions are confusing, ask to have them clarified.

Now you are ready to begin the test. If necessary, allow yourself a minute or two of "panic" time. Notice any tension you feel, and apply one of the techniques explained in the article "Let Go of Test Anxiety" later in this chapter.

Answer the easiest, shortest questions first. This gives you the experience of success. It also stimulates associations and prepares you for more difficult questions. Pace yourself and watch the time. If you can't think of an answer, move on. Follow your time plan.

If you are unable to determine the answer to a test question, keep an eye out throughout the test for context clues that may remind you of the correct answer, or provide you with evidence to eliminate wrong answers.

Multiple-choice questions

- *Answer each question in your head first.* Do this before you look at the possible answers. Circle key words in the question. Think about where in the textbook or your lecture notes the questions come from. If you come up with an answer that you're confident is right, look for that answer in the list of choices.

- *Test each possible answer.* Remember that multiple-choice questions consist of two parts: the question stem (an incomplete statement or question at the beginning) and a list of possible answers. Each answer, when combined with the stem, makes a complete statement or question-and-answer pair that is either true or false. When you combine the stem with each possible answer, you are turning each multiple-choice question into a small series of true/false questions. Choose the answer that makes a statement true.

- *Read all possible answers before selecting one.* Check to see if the stem includes negatives like the word NOT or NEVER. If it does, circle the word so that you pay attention to it when you try to select your response. Sometimes two answers will be similar but only one will be correct, so read the answers slowly and pay attention to subtle differences in the answers. You might want to try determining which is the best answer if two answers are similar.

- *Don't be fooled by distractors.* These are extra pieces of information that literally distract you from finding the correct answer. Instead, look for the key points and strike out the distractors.

- *Eliminate incorrect answers.* Cross off the answers that are clearly not correct. The answer you cannot eliminate is probably the best choice.

- *Don't rely on recognition.* Just because a fact seems to be true doesn't mean it is the answer to that question. Don't be fooled by familiarity in answering questions. Check to see if the answer matches the question being asked.

- *Review your answers.* If you have time, review your answers. Only change your responses if you can logically justify making the switch. Your first guess is usually your best guess unless you read the question incorrectly.

- *Check your time.* Periodically check to see if your pace with answering questions is in line with the time left for the test. If you get stuck on a question, skip it and come back to it later.

True/false questions

- *Read the entire question.* Separate the statement into its grammatical parts—individual clauses and phrases—and then test each one. If any part is false, the entire statement is false.

- *Look for qualifiers.* These include words such as *all, most, sometimes,* or *rarely.* Absolute qualifiers such as *always* or *never* generally indicate a false statement.

- *Find the devil in the details.* Double-check each number, fact, and date in a true/false statement. Look for numbers that have been transposed or facts that have been slightly altered. These are signals of a false statement.

- *Watch for negatives.* Look for words such as *not* and *cannot.* Read the sentence without these words and see if you come up with a true or false statement. Then reinsert the negative words and see if the statement makes more sense. Watch especially for sentences with two negative words. As in math operations, two negatives cancel each other out: *We cannot say that Chekov never succeeded at short story writing* means the same as *Chekov succeeded at short story writing.*

Computer-graded tests

- Make sure that the answer you mark corresponds to the question you are answering.

- Check the test booklet against the answer sheet whenever you switch sections and whenever you come to the top of a column.

- Watch for stray marks; they can look like answers.

- If you change an answer, be sure to erase the wrong answer completely, removing all pencil markings.

Open-book tests

- Carefully organize your notes, readings, and any other materials you plan to consult when writing answers. Don't be misled by thinking open-book tests are easy when they are often the most difficult. The fact that you can bring many pieces of material with you to the test means organization is the key.

- Write down any formulas you will need on a separate sheet of paper.

- Bookmark the table of contents and index in each of your textbooks. Place Post-it® notes and index flags or paper clips on other important pages of books (pages with tables, for instance).

- Create an informal table of contents or index for the notes you took in class.

- Predict which material will be covered on the test and highlight relevant sections in your readings and notes.

Short-answer/fill-in-the-blank tests

- Concentrate on key words and facts. Be brief.

- Over-learning material can really pay off. When you know a subject backward and forward, you can answer this type of question almost as quickly as you can write.

Matching tests

- Begin by reading through each column, starting with the one with fewer items. Check the number of items in each column to see if they're equal. If they're not, look for an item in one column that you can match with two or more items in the other column.

- Look for any items with similar wording and make special note of the differences between these items.

- Match words that are similar grammatically. For example, match verbs with verbs and nouns with nouns.

- When matching individual words with phrases, first read a phrase. Then look for the word that logically completes the phrase.

- Cross out items in each column when you are through with them.

Essay questions

Managing your time is crucial to answering essay questions. Note how many questions you have to answer and monitor your progress during the exam period. Writing shorter answers and completing all of the questions on an essay test will probably yield a better score than leaving some questions blank.

Find out what an essay question is asking—precisely

If a question asks you to *compare* the ideas of Sigmund Freud and Karl Marx, no matter how eloquently you *explain* them, you are on a one-way trip to No Credit City. See the article "Words to watch for in essay questions" in this chapter.

Before you write, make a quick outline

An outline can help speed up the writing of your detailed answer, you're less likely to leave out important facts, and if you don't have time to finish your answer, your outline could win you some points. To use test time efficiently, keep your outline brief. Focus on key words to use in your answer.

Introduce your answer by getting to the point

General statements such as "There are many interesting facets to this difficult question" can cause acute irritation for instructors marking dozens of tests.

One way to get to the point is to begin your answer with part of the question. Suppose the question is "Discuss how increasing the city police budget might or might not contribute to a decrease in street crime." Your first sentence might be "An increase in police expenditures will not have a significant effect on street crime for the following reasons." Your position is clear. You are on your way to an answer.

When you expand your answer with supporting ideas and facts, start out with the most solid points. Be brief and avoid filler sentences.

Write legibly

Marking essay questions is in large part a subjective process. Sloppy, difficult-to-read handwriting might actually lower your mark.

Write on one side of the paper only

If you write on both sides of the paper, writing will show through and obscure the writing on the other side. If necessary, use the blank side to add points you missed. Leave a generous left-hand margin and plenty of space between your answers, in case you want to add to them later.

Finally, if you have time, review your answers for grammar and spelling errors, clarity, and legibility.

Online tests

If the test is going to be online, in advance of the test ask the instructor if the test is open book or not. Ask whether you can go back to a question if you skip it.

Also ask if you can review all the questions before you begin to fill in your answers. If you must answer each question before you move on to the next question, this could be stressful to you and you will need to prepare even more thoroughly for the exam than for one that is paper based. If your instructor has not done so already, ask him to put up sample quizzes on your course management system so that you can practise completing the test online. During the actual test, you will also need to monitor your time even more carefully to ensure that you are able to answer all the test questions.

Finally, ask your instructor if it is possible to change your answers, and if you can print out the test and your answers before you submit the test. The printed tests are good for you to review prior to the final exam.

If your test is online, consider your test space. If it is your residence room, make sure you place a big "Do not disturb" sign on the door and that the space is quiet enough so that you can focus on the test. As with a paper-based test, have all the tools you will need to complete the test—such as pens, calculators, or a water bottle—out on your desk prior to beginning the test. ✳

Words to watch for in essay questions

The following words are commonly found in essay test questions. If you want to do well on essay tests, study this page thoroughly. Know these words backward and forward. To heighten your awareness of them, underline the words when you see them in a test question.

Analyze: Break into separate parts and discuss, examine, or interpret each part. Then give your opinion.

Compare: Examine two or more items. Identify similarities *and* differences.

Contrast: Show differences. Set in opposition.

Criticize: Make judgments. Evaluate comparative worth. Criticism often involves analysis.

Define: Explain the exact meaning—usually, a meaning specific to the course or subject. Definitions are usually short.

Describe: Give a detailed account. Make a picture with words. List characteristics, qualities, and parts.

Discuss: Consider and debate or argue the pros and cons of an issue. Write about any conflict. Compare and contrast.

Enumerate: List the main parts or features in a meaningful order, and briefly describe each one.

Evaluate: Make judgments about accuracy, quality, or both (similar to *criticize*).

Explain: Make an idea clear. Show logically how a concept is developed. Give the reasons for an event.

Illustrate: Clarify an idea by giving examples of it. Read the test directions to see whether the question requires you to include an actual illustration (like a diagram).

Interpret: Explain the meaning of a new idea or event by showing how it relates to more familiar ideas or events. Interpretation can involve evaluation.

List: Write a series of concise statements (similar to *enumerate*).

Outline: List the main topics, points, features, or events and briefly describe each one. (This does not necessarily mean creating a traditional outline with Roman numerals, numbers, and letters.)

Prove: Support with facts, examples, and quotations from credible sources (especially those presented in class or in the text).

Relate: Show the connections between ideas or events. Provide a larger context for seeing the big picture.

State: Explain precisely and clearly.

Summarize: Give a brief, condensed account of a longer text. Include the overall main idea and major point including the conclusions. Avoid unnecessary details.

Trace: Show the order of events or the progress of a subject or event.

If some of these terms are still unclear to you, consult your unabridged dictionary. A thorough knowledge of these words helps you answer essay questions in a way that best demonstrates your understanding of the course content.

The high costs of
CHEATING

Lucky Business/Shutterstock.com

CHEATING ON TESTS can be a tempting strategy. It offers the chance to get a good grade without having to study.

Instead of studying, you could spend more time watching TV, partying, sleeping, or doing anything that seems like more fun. Another benefit is that you could avoid the risk of doing poorly on a test—which could happen even if you *do* study.

But before you rush out to make cheating a habit, remember that cheating carries costs. Here are some consequences to consider:

You risk failing the course or getting expelled from your school

The consequences for cheating are serious. Cheating can result in failing the assignment, failing the entire course, getting suspended, or getting expelled from college or university entirely. Documentation of cheating may also prevent you from being accepted to other postsecondary institutions as academic misconduct may be listed on your transcript.

You learn less

While you might think that some courses offer little or no value, it is more likely that you can create value from any course. If you look deeply enough, you can discover some idea or acquire some skill to prepare you for future courses or your career after graduation.

You lose money and time

Getting an education costs a lot of money. Cheating sabotages your purchase. You pay full tuition without getting full value for it. You shortchange yourself and possibly your future co-workers, customers, and clients. Think about it: You probably don't want a surgeon who cheated in medical school to operate on you.

Fear of getting caught promotes stress

When you're fully aware of your emotions about cheating, you might discover intense stress. Stress can compromise your physical health and overall quality of life. Even if you're not fully aware of your emotions, you're likely to feel some level of discomfort about getting caught.

Cheating on tests can make it easier to violate your integrity again

Human beings become comfortable with behaviours that they repeat. Cheating is no exception.

Think about the first time you drove a car. You might have felt excited—even a little frightened. Now driving is probably second nature, and you don't give it much thought. Repeated experience with driving has created familiarity, which has lessened the intense feelings you had during your first time at the wheel.

You can experience the same process with almost any behaviour. Cheating once will make it easier to cheat again. And if you become comfortable with compromising your integrity in one area of life, you might find it easier to compromise in other areas. It is a slippery slope to leading a less than ethical life.

Cheating lowers your self-esteem

Whether or not you are fully aware of it, cheating sends you the message that you are not smart enough or responsible enough to make it on your own. You deny yourself the celebration and satisfaction of authentic success.

In the end it is about the value of your degree. Cheating lowers that value and you end up cheating yourself out of your own education. So, think twice even if you think, "Well, everyone is doing it, so who does it harm?" An effective alternative to cheating is to become a master student. Ways to do this are described on every page of this book. ✳

Perils of high-tech cheating

Digital technology offers many blessings, but it also expands the options for cheating during a test. For example, one student loaded class notes into a Sidekick (a hand-held device) and tried to read them. Another student dictated his class notes into files stored on his iPod and tried to listen to them. At one school, students used cellphones to take photos of test questions. They sent the photos to classmates outside the testing room, who responded by text-messaging the answers (Glater, 2006).

All of these students were caught. Schools are becoming sophisticated about detecting high-tech cheating. Some install cameras in exam rooms. Others use software that monitors the programs running on students' computers during tests. And most schools simply ban all digital devices during tests. The bottom line: If you cheat on a test or assignment, you are more likely than ever before to get caught.

There's no need to learn the hard way—through painful consequences—about the high costs of high-tech cheating. Using the suggestions in this chapter can help you succeed on tests *and* preserve your integrity.

THE TEST ISN'T OVER UNTIL . . .

Many students believe that a test is over as soon as they turn in the answer sheet. Consider another point of view: You're not done with a test until you know the answer to any question that you missed—and why you missed it.

This point of view offers major benefits. Tests in many courses are cumulative. In other words, the content included on the first test is assumed to be working knowledge for the second test, mid-term, or final exam. When you discover what questions you missed and understand the reasons for lost points, you learn something—and you greatly increase your odds of achieving better scores later in the course.

To get the most value from any test, take control of what you do at two critical points: the time immediately following the test, and the time when the test is returned to you.

Immediately following the test

After finishing a test, your first thought might be to nap, snack, watch a movie online, or go out with friends to celebrate. Restrain those impulses for a short while so that you can reflect on the test. The time you invest now carries the potential to raise your marks in the future.

To begin with, sit down in a quiet place and take a few minutes to write some Discovery Statements related to your experience of taking the test. Doing this while the test is still fresh in your mind increases the value of this technique. Describe how you felt about taking the test, how effective your review strategies were, and whether you accurately predicted the questions that appeared on the test.

Follow up with an Intention Statement or two. State what, if anything, you will do differently to prepare for the next test. The more specific you are, the better. If the test revealed any gaps in your knowledge, list follow-up questions to ask in class.

When the test is returned

When a returned test includes an instructor's comments, view this document as a treasure trove of intellectual gold. It is only by carefully reviewing your tests that you can improve upon your performance next time. Review and reflection are critical elements of being a self-regulated learner. So the next time you get a test back, don't just look at the mark; thoroughly review the test to see what you can do better next time.

Ask these questions:

- On what material did the instructor base test questions—readings, lectures, discussions, or other class activities?

- Were there questions from specific chapters that you missed more than others? If yes, then it will be important to reread those chapters and ask your instructor more questions before the final exam.

- What types of questions appeared in the test— objective (e.g., matching items, true/false questions, or multiple-choice), short-answer, or essay?

- What types of questions did you miss?

- Can you learn anything from the instructor's comments that will help you prepare for the next test?

- What strategies did you use to prepare for this test? What would you do differently to prepare for your next test?

- Are there specific skills or study habits that you need to change before the next test?

Also see if you can correct any answers that lost points. To do this, carefully analyze the source of your errors and find a solution (see some examples in Table 6.1). Consult the following chart for help. If you can't determine why you got the answer wrong make an appointment to review the test with your professor or teaching assistant. ✳

Table 6.1 **Examples of Errors and Solutions**

Source of test error	Possible solutions
Study errors—studying material that was not included on the test, or spending too little time on material that did appear on the test	• Ask your instructor about specific topics that will be included on a test. • Practise predicting test questions. • Form a study group with class members to create mock tests.
Careless errors, such as skipping or misreading directions	• Read and follow directions more carefully–especially when tests are divided into several sections with different directions. • Set aside time during the next test to proofread your answers.
Concept errors—mistakes made when you do not understand the underlying principles needed to answer a question or solve a problem	• Look for patterns in the questions you missed. • Make sure that you complete all assigned readings, attend all lectures, and show up for laboratory sessions. • Ask your instructor for help with specific questions.
Application errors—mistakes made when you understand underlying principles but fail to apply them correctly	• Rewrite your answers correctly. • When studying, spend more time on solving sample problems. • Predict application questions that will appear in future tests and practise answering them.
Test mechanics errors—missing more questions in certain parts of the test than others, changing correct answers to incorrect ones at the last minute, leaving items blank, miscopying answers from scratch paper to the answer sheet	• Set time limits for taking each section of a test and stick to them. • Proofread your test answers carefully. • Look for patterns in the kind of answers you change at the last minute. • Change answers only if you can state a clear and compelling reason to do so.

Discovery/Intention Statement

Preparing for the Next Test

Review a recent test or quiz you wrote and try to see what you could do differently next time. In particular, consider how much time you spent studying and what strategies you used to answer questions you did poorly on. For instance, if the test was multiple-choice, did you consider each possible answer as a true/false question and use logic to eliminate distractors? Have your attended a study skills workshop or exam review sessions? Were you part of a study group?

Part A

1. For the next test or quiz I promise to study _____ hours for each chapter on the test.

2. To improve my test score next time, I will _____ _____

Part B

Make a commitment to develop a mastery goal for your next quiz or test in that course.

3. My goal for the next test is to _____ _____

Part C

Review your responses with a partner in class to see if he has any suggestions for improving your test performance next time. Share study strategies that have worked for you.

LET GO
of test anxiety

IF YOU FREEZE during all kinds of tests and flub questions when you know the answers, you might be suffering from test anxiety.

Pormezz/Shutterstock.com

A little tension before a test is good. That tingly, butterflies-in-the-stomach feeling you get from extra adrenalin can sharpen your awareness and keep you alert. You can enjoy the benefits of a little tension while you stay confident and relaxed.

If your level of tension interferes with your daily life and consistently prevents you from doing your best in school, you might be experiencing anxiety. Symptoms of anxiety include not being able to concentrate, sweating, insomnia, shortness of breath, and stomach ache (Mayo Clinic, 2007). Anxiety has three elements: mental, physical, and emotional. The mental element includes your thoughts, including predictions of failure. The physical component includes physical sensations, such as shallow breathing and muscle tension. The emotional element occurs when thoughts and physical sensations combine. The following techniques can help you deal with these elements of anxiety in *any* situation.

Dealing with thoughts

Yell "Stop!"

When you notice that your mind is consumed with worries and fears, and your thoughts are spinning out of control, mentally yell, "Stop!" If you're in a situation that allows it, yell it out loud. This action is likely to bring your focus back to the present moment and allow you to redirect your thoughts.

Once you've broken the cycle of worry or panic, you can use any of the following techniques.

Accept your feelings

Telling someone who's anxious about a test to "just calm down" is like turning up the heat on a pan that's already boiling over: The "solution" simply worsens the problem. If you take such advice to heart, you can end up with two problems. First, there's your worry about the test. Second, there's your worry about the fact that you're worried!

There's a way to deal with both problems at the same time: Simply accept your feelings, whatever they are. Fear and anxiety tend to increase with resistance. The more you try to suppress them, the more intensity the feelings gain.

As an alternative, stop resisting. See anxiety as a cluster of thoughts and body sensations. Watch the thoughts as they pass through your mind. Observe the sensations as they wash over you. Let them arise, peak, and pass away. No feeling lasts forever. The moment you accept fear, you pave the way for its release.

Dispute your thoughts

You can take the previous technique one step further. Do some critical thinking. Anxiety about tests often boils down to this statement: *Getting a low grade on a test is a disaster*. Do the math, however: A four-year degree often involves taking about 40 courses (10 courses per year over four years for a full-time student). This means that your final grade on any one course amounts to about only 4 percent of your total grade point average.

Also consider that your final grade in any one course is usually based on much more than one test. This means that a single test score is not going to make or break your college career.

This argument is not meant to convince you to stop preparing for tests. It *is* an argument to keep each test in perspective—and to dispute thoughts that only serve to create anxiety.

Visualize success

Most of us live up—or down—to our own expectations. If we spend a lot of time mentally rehearsing what it will be like to fail a test, our chances of doing so increase. Instead, you can take time to rehearse what it will be like to succeed. Be specific. Create detailed pictures, actions, and even sounds as part of your visualization. If you are able to visit the room where you will take the test, mentally rehearse while you are actually in this room.

Over-prepare for tests

One way that performing artists prepare for auditions where they know they will be anxious is to over-prepare. Simple as this sounds, this is one of the best techniques that you can use to overcome anxiety on test day. The more you practise the more confident you will be when you walk into your test. Keep preparing for your test with self-quizzes or flashcards until the day of the test, and it will feel like just one more day of practising retrieval.

Just start

When the test begins, just dive in. The blank page can fuel anxiety, so to get the ball rolling, quickly read the test. When you see something you can answer, put down the first answer that comes to mind—you can always change your answer later. Answering some questions will fuel your self-confidence.

Focus

Focus your attention on a specific object. During an exam, take a few seconds to listen to the sounds of concentration—the squeaking of chairs, the scratching of pencils, the muted coughs. Touch the surface of your desk and notice the texture. Concentrate all of your attention on one point. Don't leave room in your mind for anxiety-related thoughts.

Praise yourself

Talk to yourself in a positive way. Many of us take the first opportunity to belittle ourselves: "Way to go, dummy! You don't even know the answer to the first question on the test." We wouldn't dream of treating a friend this way, yet we do it to ourselves.

An alternative is to give yourself some encouragement. Treat yourself as if you were your own best friend. Consider telling yourself, "I am very relaxed. I am doing a great job on this test."

Consider the worst

Rather than trying to put a stop to your worrying, consider the very worst thing that could happen. Take your fear to the limit of absurdity.

Imagine the catastrophic problems that might occur if you were to fail the test. You might say to yourself, "Well, if I fail this test, I might fail the course, lose my scholarship, and get kicked out of school. Then I won't be able to get a job, so the bank will repossess my car, and I'll start drinking." Keep going until you see the absurdity of your predictions. After you stop laughing, you can backtrack to discover a reasonable level of concern.

Dealing with the physical sensations of anxiety

Breathe

You can calm physical sensations within your body by focussing your attention on your breathing. Concentrate on the air going in and out of your lungs. Experience it as it passes through your nose and mouth.

Do this for two to five minutes. If you notice that you are taking short, shallow breaths, begin to take longer and deeper breaths. Imagine your lungs to be a pair of bagpipes. Expand your chest to bring in as much air as possible. Then listen to the plaintive chords as you slowly release the air.

Train yourself to tense and relax your muscles

Sit comfortably with your eyes closed. Slowly scan your body for tension in your muscles. Starting with the muscles in your feet, notice if they are relaxed. Tense the muscles in your feet and then relax. Slowly repeat this same procedure on your ankles, then calves, thighs, and so on, telling each group of muscles to tense and relax, slowly moving up your body. Pay particular attention to the muscles in your neck, shoulders, and jaw—these are parts of the body we often hold tension in. If you are aware of a particularly tense part of your body or if you discover tension when you're scanning your body, you can release this tension with this tense–relax method. For instance, if your shoulders are tense, pull them back, arch your back, and tense your shoulder muscles even more tightly. Then relax. The net result is that you can be aware of the relaxation and allow yourself to relax even more.

Clench your fists, tighten your jaw, straighten your legs, and tense your abdomen all at once. Then relax and pay close attention to the sensations of relaxation. By paying attention, you can learn to re-create these sensations whenever you choose.

Use guided imagery

Relax completely and take a quick fantasy trip. Close your eyes, free your body of tension, and imagine yourself in a beautiful, peaceful, natural setting. Create as much of the scene as you can. Be specific. Use all of your senses.

For example, you might imagine yourself at a beach. Hear the surf rolling in and the sea gulls calling to each other. Feel the sun on your face and the hot sand between your toes. Smell the sea breeze. Taste the salty mist from the surf. Notice the ships on the horizon and the rolling sand dunes. Use all of your senses to create a vivid imaginary trip.

Some people find that a mountain scene or a lush meadow scene works well. You can take yourself to a place you've never been or re-create an experience out of your past. Find a place that works for you and practise getting there. When you become proficient, you can return to it quickly for trips that might last only a few seconds.

With practice, you can use this technique even while you are taking a test.

Describe sensations

Focus your attention on your anxiety. If you are feeling nauseated or if you have a headache, concentrate on that feeling. Describe it to yourself. When you completely experience a physical sensation, it will often disappear. People suffering from chronic pain have used this technique successfully (Kabat-Zin, 2001).

Be with it

As you describe your anxiety in detail, don't resist it. A recent study of students who were anxious found that those who spent 10 minutes before the test writing about their fears actually did better in terms of achievement than those who just relaxed before the test. It appears that by writing about it, students were able to get rid of their fears ahead of the test and so were able to relax and better concentrate during the test (Taylor, 2011).

Care for your body as much as your mind

Being well rested and fed on exam day won't guarantee a higher test score. However, preparing for a test physically as well as mentally can reduce stress. Exercise regularly, particularly the day before your test; do something aerobic like riding your bike or going for a run. Because sleep deprivation can affect memory, avoid all-nighters as a study strategy. Also moderate your use of mood-altering chemicals, including caffeine, cannabis, and alcohol.

Dealing with emotions: practise detachment

To *detach* means to step back from something and see it as separate from ourselves. When we detach from an emotion, we no longer identify with it. We no longer say, "*I* am afraid" or "*I* am sad." We say something like "There's fear again" or "I feel sadness right now." Using language such as this offers us a way to step back from our internal experiences and keep them in perspective.

Before a test, you might find it especially useful to detach from your thoughts. Borrow some ideas from acceptance and commitment therapy, which is used by a growing number of therapists (Hayes, 2004). Take an anxiety-producing thought—such as *I always screw up on tests*—and do any of the following:

- Repeat the thought over and over again out loud until it becomes just a meaningless series of sounds.
- Repeat the thought while using the voice of a cartoon character such as Donald Duck or Homer Simpson.
- Rephrase the thought so that you can sing it to the tune of a nursery rhyme or the song "Happy Birthday."

- Preface the thought with "I'm having the thought that . . ." (*I'm having the thought that I always screw up on tests.*)
- Talk back to your mind by saying, "That's an interesting thought, mind; thanks a lot for sharing." Or simply say, "Thanks, mind."

For more information about this technique, see "Power Process: Detach" at the end of the chapter.

Get help

When these techniques don't work, when anxiety is serious, get help. If you become withdrawn, have frequent thoughts about death or suicide, get depressed and stay depressed for more than a few days, or have prolonged feelings of hopelessness, see a counsellor or doctor.

Depression and anxiety are common among students. Suicide is the second leading cause of death among young adults between the ages of 15 and 25. This is tragic and unnecessary. Most schools have counsellors and doctors available through student services or student health services. If not, the student health service or another office can refer you to community agencies that provide free or inexpensive counselling. You can also get emergency assistance over the phone. More information about good mental health websites can be found in Chapter 11, "Health." ✳

Have some FUN!

Contrary to popular belief, finals week does not have to be a drag.

In fact, if you have used techniques in this chapter, exam week can be fun. You will have done most of your studying long before finals arrive.

When you are well prepared for tests, you can even use fun as a technique to enhance your performance. The day before a final, go for a run or play a game of basketball. Take in a movie or a concert. A relaxed brain is a more effective brain. If you have studied for a test, your mind will continue to prepare itself even while you're at the movies.

Get plenty of rest, too. There's no need to cram until 3:00 a.m. when you have reviewed material throughout the term.

On the first day of finals, you can wake up refreshed, have a good breakfast, and walk into the exam room with a smile on your face. You can also leave with a smile on your face, knowing that you are going to have a fun week. It's your reward for studying regularly throughout the term.

practising
CRITICAL THINKING   6-2

20 things I like to do

One way to relieve tension is to mentally yell "Stop!" and substitute a pleasant daydream for the stressful thoughts and emotions you are experiencing. In order to create a supply of pleasant images to recall during times of stress, conduct an eight-minute brainstorm about things you like to do. Your goal is to generate at least 20 ideas. Time yourself and write as fast as you can in the space below.

When you have completed your list, study it. Pick out two activities that seem especially pleasant and elaborate on them by creating a mind map. Write down all of the memories you have about that activity.

You can use these images to calm yourself in stressful situations.

Intention Statement

Notice Your Excuses and Let Them Go

Do a timed, four-minute brainstorm of all the reasons, rationalizations, justifications, and excuses you have used to avoid studying. Be creative. List your thoughts in the space below by completing the following Discovery Statement.

I discovered that I . . .

_____

_____

_____

_____

_____

_____

Next, review your list, pick the excuse that you use the most, and circle it. In the space below, write an Intention Statement about what you will do to begin eliminating your favourite excuse. Make this Intention Statement one that you can keep, with a timeline and a reward.

I intend to . . .

_____

_____

_____

_____

_____

_____

_____

_____

_____

Discovery Statement

Explore Your Feelings About Tests

Complete the following sentences.

As exam time gets closer, one thing I notice that I do is . . .

_____

_____

_____

When it comes to taking tests, I have trouble . . .

_____

_____

The night before a test, I usually feel . . .

_____

_____

The morning of a test, I usually feel . . .

_____

_____

During a test, I usually feel . . .

_____

_____

_____

_____

When I get a test score, I usually feel . . .

_____

_____

_____

_____

Getting ready for
MATH TESTS

© EtiAmmos/Shutterstock

Many students who could succeed in math shy away from the subject. Some had negative experiences in past courses. Others believe that math is only for gifted students.

At some level, however, math is open to all students. There's more to this subject than memorizing formulas and manipulating numbers. Imagination, creativity, and problem-solving skills are important, too.

Consider a three-part program for math success. Begin with strategies for overcoming math anxiety. Next, boost your study skills. Finally, let your knowledge shine during tests.

Overcome math anxiety

Many schools offer courses in overcoming math anxiety. Visit student services or your academic counsellor to find out about resources on your campus. Also experiment with the following suggestions.

Connect math to life

Think of the benefits of mastering math courses. You'll have more options for choosing a major and a career. Math skills can also put you at ease in everyday situations—calculating the tip for a waiter, balancing your chequebook, working with a spreadsheet on a computer. If you follow baseball statistics, cook, do construction work, or snap pictures with a camera, you'll use math. And speaking the language of math can help you feel at home in a world driven by technology.

Pause occasionally to get an overview of the branch of math that you're studying. What's it all about? What basic problems is it designed to solve? How do people apply this knowledge in daily life? For example, many architects, engineers, and space scientists use calculus daily.

Take a first step

Math is cumulative. Concepts build upon each other in a certain order. If you struggled with algebra, you may have trouble with trigonometry or calculus.

To ensure that you have an adequate base of knowledge, tell the truth about your current level of knowledge and skill. Before you register for a math course, locate assigned texts for the prerequisite courses. If the material in those books seems new or difficult for you, see the instructor. Ask for suggestions on ways to prepare for the course. Also, there are many free mathematics tutorials available online that you can use to brush up on your math skills if they feel rusty.

Remember that it's okay to continue your study of math from your current level of ability, whatever that level might be.

Change your conversation about math

When students fear math, they often say negative things to themselves about their abilities in this subject. Many times this self-talk includes statements such as *I'll never be fast enough at solving math problems* or *I'm good with words, so I can't be good with numbers.*

Get such statements out in the open, and apply some emergency critical thinking. You'll find two self-defeating assumptions lurking there: *Everybody else is better at math and science than I am* and *Since I don't understand a math concept right now, I'll never understand it.* Both of these statements are illogical.

Replace negative beliefs with logical, realistic statements that affirm your ability to succeed in math: *Any confusion I feel now can be resolved. I learn math without comparing myself to others. And I ask whatever questions are needed to aid my understanding.*

Choose your response to stress

Math anxiety is seldom just "in your head." It can also register as sweaty palms, shallow breathing, tightness in the chest, or a mild headache. Instead of trying to ignore these sensations, just notice them without judgment. Keep breathing. Over time, simple awareness decreases their power.

In addition, use stress management techniques. "Let go of test anxiety" in the previous section offers a bundle of them.

Boost study skills for math

Take math courses back to back

Approach math in the same way that you learn a foreign language. If you take a year off in between French I and French II, you won't gain much fluency. To master a language, you take courses back to back. It works the same way with math, which is a language in itself.

Form a study group

During the first week of each math course, organize a study group. Ask each member to bring five problems to group meetings, along with solutions. Also exchange contact information so that you can stay in touch via email, phone, and text messaging.

Avoid short courses

Courses that you take during summer school or another shortened term are condensed. You might find yourself doing far more reading and homework each week than you do in longer courses. If you enjoy math, the extra intensity can provide a stimulus to learn. But if math is not your favourite subject, give yourself extra time. Enrol in courses spread out over more calendar days. Give your brain the extra time it needs to absorb the information and skills.

Participate in class

Success in math, as in other subjects, depends on your active involvement. Attend class regularly. Complete homework assignments *when they're due*—not just before the test. If you're confused, get help right away from an instructor, tutor, or study group. Instructors' office hours, free on-campus tutoring, and classmates are just a few of the resources available to you. Make daily contact with math.

Try to solve problems before you go to class

Attempting to solve problems before you are taught a solution strategy turns out to be a great way to prime your brain for learning (Brown, Roediger, & McDaniel, 2014). By puzzling through how you might solve a particular problem type, you become more receptive to new learning. This strategy is called **generation**. So, before your professor teaches you how to solve a problem, spend a few minutes before class wrestling with the new problem type—when you are taught the solution, you will see that your classroom learning is stronger.

Prepare for several types of tests

Math tests often involve lists of problems to solve. Ask your instructor about what type of tests to expect. Then prepare for the tests using strategies from this chapter.

Ask questions fearlessly

It's a cliché, and it's true: In math, there are no dumb questions. Ask whatever questions will aid your understanding. Keep a running list of them, and bring the list to class.

Make your text top priority

Math courses are often text driven. Class activities closely follow the book. This fact underscores the importance of completing your reading assignments. Master one concept before going on to the next, and stay current with your reading. Be willing to read slowly and reread sections as needed.

Do homework consistently

Students who succeed in math do their homework daily—from beginning to end, and from the easy problems all the way through the hard problems. If you do homework consistently, you're not likely to be surprised on a test.

When doing homework, use a common process to solve similar problems. There's comfort in rituals, and using familiar steps can help reduce math anxiety.

Read actively

To get the most out of your math texts, read with paper and pencil in hand. Work out examples. Copy diagrams, formulas, and equations. Use chapter summaries and introductory outlines to organize your learning.

From time to time, stop, close your book, and mentally reconstruct the steps in solving a problem. Before you memorize a formula, understand the basic concepts behind it.

Practise solving problems

To get ready for math tests, work *lots* of problems. Find out if practice problems or previous tests are on file in the library, in the math department, or with your math instructor. Go online and search for practise problems—there are tons out there.

Isolate the types of problems that you find the most difficult. Practise them more often. Be sure to get help with these kinds of problems *before* exhaustion or frustration sets in.

To prepare for tests, practise working problems fast. Time yourself. This activity is a great one for math study groups.

Approach problem-solving with a three-step process, as shown in Figure 6.1. During each step, apply an appropriate strategy.

Practise mixing up problem types

Earlier in the chapter we talked about interleaving practice or switching between problem types when you are studying. This is particularly important in studying math. Although the temptation is to solve one problem type until you get it down perfectly, the research shows

1: Prepare	2: Compute	3: Check
• Read each problem two or three times, slowly and out loud whenever possible. • Consider creating a chart with three columns labelled *What I already know, What I want to find out,* and *What connects the two.* The third column is the place to record a formula that can help you solve the problem. • Determine which arithmetic operations (addition, subtraction, multiplication, division) or formulas you will use to solve the problem. • See if you can estimate the answer before you compute it.	• Reduce the number of unknowns as much as you can. Consider creating a separate equation to solve each unknown. • When solving equations, carry out the algebra as far as you can before plugging in the actual numbers. • Cancel and combine. For example, if the same term appears in both dividend and divisor, they will cancel each other out. • Remember that it's OK to make several attempts at solving the problem before you find an answer.	• Plug your answer back into the original equation or problem and see if it works out correctly. • Ask yourself if your answer seems likely when compared with your estimate. For example, if you're asked to apply a discount to an item, that item should cost less in your solution. • Perform opposite operations. If a problem involves multiplication, check your work by division; add, then subtract; factor, then multiply; find the square root, then the square; differentiate, then integrate. • Keep units of measurement clear. Say that you're calculating the velocity of an object. If you're measuring distance in metres and time in seconds, the final velocity should be in metres per second.

© Cengage Learning

Figure 6.1 **Three-Step Process for Solving Math Problems**

that students who interleave their problem types rather than working through a problem set that was clustered by problem type do better on the exam. It is tougher studying this way and learning feels slower BUT it pays off. The research is conclusive that you are more likely to have long-term retention of material and to achieve mastery if you interleave your practice (Brown, Roediger, & McDaniel, 2014).

Use tests to show what you know

Practise test-taking

Part of preparing for any math test is rehearsal. Instead of passively reading through your text or scanning class notes, do practice tests:

- Print out a set of practice problems, and set a timer for the same length of time as your testing period.
- Whenever possible, work practice problems in the same room where you will take the actual test.
- Use only the kinds of supporting materials—such as scratch paper or lists of formulas—that will be allowed during the test.

Engage in self-reflection

After you complete your practice test, reflect on your problem-solving strategy:

How much time did you spend studying?

How many practice problems did you do prior to the quiz?

How did you prepare for the quiz?

What study strategies did you use?

Which strategies helped or hindered your learning?

You also should explore how confident you were in your answers, and how accurately you could predict your success. Keep in mind that the illusion of knowing can lead you to overestimate how well you will do. If your problem-solving strategy was not successful, what other strategy could you try with similar problems? If you don't know why you got a particular question wrong, ask another student in your class or your instructor. Research has demonstrated that engaging in such self-reflections is a key component of being a self-regulated learner and that it leads to greater academic success (Elliot, Dweck, & Yeager, 2017).

Ask appropriate questions during the test

If you don't understand a test item, ask for clarification. The worst that can happen is that an instructor or proctor will politely decline to answer your question.

Write legibly

Put yourself in the instructor's place. Imagine the prospect of grading stacks of illegible answer sheets. Make your answers easy to read. If you show your work, underline key sections and circle your answer.

Do your best

There are no secrets involved in getting ready for math tests. Master some stress management techniques, do your homework, get answers to your questions, and work sample problems. If you've done those things, you're ready for the test and deserve to do well. If you haven't done all those things, just do the best you can.

Did you **know that ...?**

Alex Trebek, the host of the TV show *Jeopardy*, studied philosophy at the University of Ottawa. Creating jeopardy cards of your course materials (where you put the answer on one side of the card and the question on the other) is a great way to liven up your studying. Think about doing this in your study group ("50 little-known facts, 2017).

Remember that your personal best can vary from test to test, and even from day to day. Even if you don't answer all test questions correctly, you can demonstrate what you *do* know right now.

During the test, notice when solutions come easily. Savour the times when you feel relaxed and confident. If you ever feel math anxiety in the future, these are the times to remember. ✳

practising
CRITICAL THINKING

6-3

Multiple-choice strategies

Create a short multiple-choice test on a topic in a course you're taking right now. Ask several people from the class to take this exam.

Then, as a group, discuss the answer you chose for each question. Also talk about *why* and *how* you chose each answer. The purpose is to identify the strategies that different people use when answering a multiple-choice question—especially when they are unsure of the correct answer.

You might discover some test-taking strategies that you would use in the future. List those strategies in the space below.

_____

_____

_____

_____

_____

_____

_____

_____

_____

_____

_____

Repeat this exercise by creating and discussing tests in other formats: short-answer, true/false, and essay.

Studying across the
CURRICULUM

Think for a moment about the range of subjects that you're asked to study in higher education. Schools offer courses in everything from algebra to zoology, and you'll sample a variety of them. The challenge is to shift intellectual gears so that you can succeed in all those different subjects.

Some of the subjects you'll study in higher education share a single purpose—to *propose theories based on observations*. Physics, biology, and chemistry offer theories to explain and predict events in the natural world. Social sciences, such as psychology and sociology, offer theories to predict and explain events in the human world.

Other subjects go beyond theory to *define problems and offer solutions*. Their subjects range from the abstract problems of pure mathematics to the practical problems of engineering and computer science.

Courses in the arts do not propose carefully reasoned theories. Nor do they focus on solving problems. Instead, they *teach through vicarious experience*. When you read a novel, see a play, or watch a film, you view the world through another human being's eyes. Just as you learn from your own experience, you can learn from the experience of others.

To deal with all those differences in subjects, pull out a full toolbox of strategies. When preparing for tests in specific subjects, consider the suggestions in Table 6.2. Then create more strategies of your own.

Succeeding in science courses

Many of the strategies that help you prepare for math tests can also help you succeed in science courses. For example, forming small study groups can be a fun way to learn these subjects. Relating science to your career interests and daily life is also important. People in many professions—from dentists to gardeners—rely on science to do their jobs. And even if you don't choose a science-driven career, you will live in a world that's driven by technology. Understanding how scientists observe, collect data, and arrive at conclusions can help you feel more at home in this world. In addition, use some strategies that are unique to succeeding in science courses.

Prepare for variety

Remember that the word *science* refers to a vast range of subjects—astronomy, biology, chemistry, physics, physiology, geology, ecology, geography, and more. Most of these subjects include math as one of their tools. Beyond that, however, there are key differences. You can take advantage of this variety. Choose courses in a science that matches your personal interests and comfort level for technical subjects.

Prepare for lab sessions

Laboratory work is crucial to many science classes. To get the most out of these sessions, be prepared. Complete required reading before you enter the lab. Also gather the materials you'll need ahead of time. ✳

Table 6.2 Cross-Curriculum Study Strategies

Subject area	Strategies for test preparation
Humanities: English, literature, public speaking, history, religion, philosophy, fine arts	• Deepen your reading skills by previewing and reviewing each assignment (see Chapter 4, "Reading"). • Keep a dictionary handy, and create an updated list of new words and their definitions. • Experiment with several different formats for taking notes (see Chapter 5, "Notes"). • Keep a personal journal in which you practise writing and make connections between the authors and ideas that you're studying. • Take part in class discussions, and welcome chances to speak in front of groups.
Math and natural sciences: algebra, geometry, calculus, chemistry, biology, physics	• Before registering for a course, make sure that you are adequately prepared through prior course work. • In your notes, highlight basic principles—definitions, assumptions, and axioms. • Learn concepts in the sequence presented by your instructor. • If you feel confused, ask a question immediately. • Attend all classes, practise solving problems every day, and check your work carefully. • Translate word problems into images or symbols; translate images and symbols into words. • Balance abstract ideas with concrete experiences, including laboratory sessions and study groups. • Take math courses back to back so you can apply what you learn in one level of a math course immediately to the next level.
Social sciences: sociology, psychology, economics, political science, anthropology, geography	• Pay special attention to theories—statements that are used to explain relationships between observations and to predict events. • Expect to encounter complex and contradictory theories, and ask your instructor about ways to resolve disagreements among experts in the field. • Ask your instructor to explain the scientific method and how it is used to arrive at theories in each of the social sciences. • Ask about current issues in the social sciences. • Ask for examples of a theory, and look for them in your daily life.
Foreign languages: learning to speak, read, and write any language that is new to you	• Pay special attention to the "rules"—principles of grammar, noun forms, and verb tenses. For each principle, list correct and incorrect examples. • Spend some time reading, writing, or speaking the language every day. • Welcome the opportunity to practise speaking in class, where you can get immediate feedback. • Start or join a study group in each of your language classes. • Spend time with people who are already skilled in speaking the language. • Travel to a country where the language is widely spoken. • Take your language courses back to back to ensure fluency.

Celebrate
MISTAKES

THE TITLE OF THIS article is no mistake. But no, you should not make mistakes on purpose. Rather, the goal here is to shine a light on mistakes so that we can examine them, fix them, and learn from them. Mistakes that are hidden cannot be corrected; conversely, mistakes that are identified are often worth celebrating.

Gustavo Frazao/Shutterstock.com

Mistakes are valuable feedback

Mistakes are part of the learning process. In fact, mistakes are often more interesting and more instructive than are successes. If you interpret an F on a test as a failure, you don't get to change anything. But if you interpret F as feedback, you can change your thinking and behaviour in ways that promote your success. This is adopting a growth mindset.

You can choose a new learning strategy, or let go of an excuse about not having the time to study. Getting prompt and meaningful feedback on your performance is a powerful strategy for learning anything.

Mistakes demonstrate that we're taking risks

People who play it safe make few mistakes. Making mistakes can be evidence that we're stretching to the limit of our abilities—growing, risking, and learning. Fearing failure and therefore not taking risks stops us from taking steps that are necessary for academic success. Having grit and resilience is essential so that we continue to strive for success even in the face of adversity. It's an important component of having a growth mindset and what master students do.

Mistakes are often key turning points on the road to mastery

Figuring out that learning is a struggle is a key element of future success. There is a myth that learning should be easy. In fact, people who view learning as hard, that it

does involve making mistakes, are more likely to persist in the face of challenges. Learning to see mistakes as lessons rather than failure sets you on the road to future success.

Celebrating mistakes gets them out into the open

When we celebrate a mistake, we remind ourselves that the person who made the mistake is not bad—just human. Everyone makes mistakes. This is not a recommendation that you purposely set out to make mistakes. Mistakes are not an end in themselves. Rather, their value lies in what we learn from them. When we admit to a mistake, we can correct it.

Tips for Master Students

Experience failure now and then

If you go into your first year accepting that you won't win every competition you enter, ace every class or have an ideal relationship with every friend and every member of your family, it's okay! When you experience failure now and then, try to remember that there is no better way to learn about yourself and about getting the most out of life than stumbling now and then. Be resilient. Believe it will get better. Listen and be true to yourself—this is really where your path starts.

—Robert Herjavec, CEO of global IT security firm Herjavec Group and cast member of ABC's *Shark Tank*. He has a double degree in political science and English from the University of Toronto. (*Maclean's*, 2017)

Source: Advice for first-year students from Justin Trudeau (and 27 other people), by *Maclean's*, *Maclean's*, December 1, 2017.

Mistakes happen only when we're committed to making things work

Imagine a school where teachers usually come to class late. Residence halls are never cleaned, and scholarship cheques are always late. The administration is in chronic debt, students seldom pay tuition on time, and no one cares. In this school, the word *mistake* would have little meaning. Mistakes become apparent only when people are committed to quality. ✱

journal entry   6-5

Reviewing Strategies for Success

From chapters 3, 4, 5, and 6 we have laid out the steps it takes to learn and apply what you have learned in tests. Many of these ideas are reinforced in the research by Brown, Roediger, and McDaniel (2014). They suggest that successful students do the following:

1. *Own their learning* and realize they need to be active, not passive, participants in their own educational experience.

2. *Embrace challenging learning experiences* and see setbacks as a sign of effort, not failure.

3. *Space out their study sessions* rather than cramming. New material needs to be reviewed more frequently and then you can wait days or even weeks before reviewing again.

4. *Use self-quizzes* to improve their learning and enhance their metacognitive skill development.

5. *Use mnemonic devices* when learning arbitrary material.

6. *Elaborate on what they have learned* by connecting what they are learning to prior knowledge or explaining what they are learning to others using their own words.

7. Take time to *reflect on their own learning* and to assess what they have learned well and what other strategies they might need to engage in next time.

Review these statements and determine which one you still need to work on to be a master student. Write a specific step you will take to achieve this goal in the coming week.

This week I will....

EB Adventure Photography/Shutterstock.com

POWERPROCESS

Detach

This Power Process helps you release the powerful, natural student within you. It is especially useful whenever negative emotions are getting in your way.

Attachments are addictions. When we are attached to something, we think we cannot live without it, just as a drug addict feels he cannot live without drugs. We believe our well-being depends on maintaining our attachments.

We can be attached to just about anything: beliefs, emotions, people, roles, objects. The list is endless.

One person, for example, might be so attached to his car that he takes an accident as a personal attack. Pity the poor unfortunate who backs into this person's car. He might as well have backed into the owner himself.

Another person might be attached to her job. Her identity and sense of well-being depend on it. She could become really depressed if she got fired.

When we are attached and things don't go our way, we can feel angry, sad, afraid, or confused.

Suppose you are attached to getting an A on your physics test. You feel as though your success in life depends on getting that A. As the clock ticks away, you work harder on the test, getting more stuck. That voice in your head gets louder: "I must get an A. I MUST get an A. I MUST GET AN A!"

Now is a time to detach. Practise observer consciousness. See if you can just *observe* what's going on, letting go of all your judgments. When you just

observe, you reach a quiet state above and beyond your usual thoughts. This is a place where you can be aware of being aware. It's a tranquil spot, apart from your emotions. From here, you can observe yourself objectively, as if you were someone else. Pay attention to your thoughts and physical sensations. If you are confused and feeling stuck, tell yourself, "Here I am, confused and stuck." If your palms are sweaty and your stomach is one big knot, admit it. Practise perspective by putting current circumstances into a broader perspective. View your personal issues within the larger context of your community, nation, or even planet. Breathe. Calm your mind and body with relaxation techniques.

Practise detaching before the big test. The key is to let go of automatic emotional reactions when you don't get what you want.

Caution: Giving up an *attachment* to being an A student does not mean giving up *being* an A student. Giving up an attachment to a job doesn't mean giving up the job. When you detach, you get to keep your values and goals. However, you know that you will be OK even if you fail to achieve a goal. You are more than your goals. You are more than your thoughts and feelings. These things come and go. Meanwhile, the part of you that can *just observe* is always there and always safe, no matter what happens.

Behind your attachments is a master student. Release that mastery. Detach.

Put it to WORK

You can apply many of the techniques discussed in this chapter directly to common situations in the workplace. For example, use the test-taking strategies when you take licensing exams, certification exams, and other tests in your career field. In addition, consider the following suggestions.

Seize opportunities to learn cooperatively

Forming study groups or committees helps you develop important workplace skills. Almost every job is accomplished by the combined efforts of many people. For example, manufacturing a single car calls for the contributions of designers, welders, painters, electricians, marketing executives, computer programmers, and many others.

Perhaps you prefer to complete your assignments by working independently. However, teamwork is often required in the workplace. Joining study groups now, while you are in school, can help you expand your learning styles and succeed in the workplace.

Apply your cooperative learning skills to working on project teams

To create a successful project team at work, combine the individual skills of team members in complementary ways. There are many important tasks in any project:

- *Planning*—defining the desired outcomes, setting due dates for each task, and generating commitment to action.
- *Doing*—carrying out assigned tasks.
- *Reflecting*—meeting regularly to discuss what's working well and ways to improve the next phase of the project.
- *Interpreting*—discussing what the team has learned from the project and ways to apply that learning to the whole organization.

Many people are drawn to one of these tasks more than the others. Assign tasks to people based on their strengths and preferences.

One potential trap of working in teams is that one person ends up doing most of the work. This person might feel resentful and complain. If you find yourself in this situation, transform your complaint into a request. Instead of scolding team members for being lazy, request help. Ask team

wavebreakmedia/Shutterstock.com

members to take over tasks that you've been doing. Delegate specific jobs.

Manage job stress

The same techniques that help you manage test anxiety can help you manage stress at work. Apply techniques for managing the mental and physical aspects of stress while interviewing for a job, making a presentation, doing a performance review, or carrying out any task that raises your anxiety level.

Celebrate mistakes

Recall a mistake you made at work and then write about it. In a Discovery Statement, describe what you did to create a result you didn't want ("I discovered that I tend to underestimate the number of hours projects take"). Then write an Intention Statement describing something you can do differently in the future ("I intend to keep track of my actual hours on each project so that I can give more accurate estimates").

Go for fun

Finally, see if you can adapt suggestions from "Have some FUN!" to cultivate enjoyment at work. One benefit of career planning (see Chapter 12, "What's Next?") is finding a job that allows you to follow your interests—in other words, to have fun. Successful people often eliminate the distinction between work and play in their lives. You're more likely to excel professionally when you're having a blast at your job.

QUIZ

chapter 6

■ Put it to Work
◄ ◄ ◄ ◄
■ Skills Snapshot
■ Master Student Profile

Name_____   Date____/____/____

1. Preparing for tests can include creating review tools. Name at least two of these tools.

2. When answering multiple-choice questions, it is better to read all of the possible answers before answering the question in your head. True or False? Explain your answer.

3. The presence of absolute qualifiers, such as *always* or *never*, generally indicates a false statement. True or False? Explain your answer.

4. Briefly explain the differences between a daily review and a major review.

5. Define the term *study checklist,* and give three examples of what to include on such checklists.

6. Describe how using the Power Process "Detach" differs from giving up.

7. Choose one technique for taking math and science tests, and explain how it, or some variation of it, could apply to taking a test in another subject.

8. Name at least three benefits of participating in a study group.

9. Describe at least three techniques for dealing with the thoughts connected to test anxiety.

10. Describe at least three techniques for dealing with the physical feelings connected to test anxiety.

Skills SNAPSHOT

Now that you've had some concrete experience with the strategies presented in this chapter, take a minute to reflect on your responses to the "Tests" section of the Discovery Wheel in Chapter 1. Expand on those responses by completing the following sentences.

PREPARING FOR TESTS

When studying for a test, the first thing I usually do is . . .

In addition, I . . .

TAKING TESTS

One strategy that helps me with objective tests (true/false and multiple choice) is . . .

One strategy that helps me with short-answer and essay tests is . . .

MANAGING TEST ANXIETY

On the day of a test, my level of confidence is generally . . .

If I feel stressed about a test, I respond by . . .

NEXT ACTION

I'll know that I've reached a new level of mastery with tests when . . .

To reach that level of mastery, the most important thing I can do next is to . . .

MASTER STUDENT PROFILE

chapter 6

■ Put it to Work
■ Quiz
■ Skills Snapshot
◀ ◀ ◀ ◀

Wali Shah

... is inspiring

As a new immigrant to Canada, Wali Shah had a hard time fitting in and finding his own voice, but in a few short years, he has gone from being an at-risk youth in Mississauga, to becoming the city's poet laureate.

He had fallen in with the wrong crowd and seen the sadness on his mother's face when he was arrested as a young teen. It was a teacher, Melanie Riley, who he credits with helping him turn his life around. Ms. Riley gave him a book by Tupac Shakur, *The Rose that Grew from Concrete*. Suddenly, he saw a way to share his own experiences with others through poetry. He saw the power of using narrative to connect to people.

"I was lucky to have the right teachers and mentorship; a lot of kids unfortunately don't," he said, adding that he wants to give that back through his poetry and speaking (Mirza, 2018, para.11).

Wali uses spoken word poetry to connect to others about the experience of being a new immigrant and minority youth just trying to fit in. As the poet laureate for Mississauga he acts as a literary ambassador for youth, helping to boost literary arts in his community, and is required to perform several original works at invited functions.

Wali has raised over $1 million dollars for the United Way through his public appearances and has been an ambassador for Bell "Let's Talk" about mental health.

In 2014, Wali was named one of the Top 20 under 20 by Plan Canada, in 2015 he was awarded a 3M National Student Fellowship, and in 2018 he was selected as one of 60 global youth changemakers to attend the Global Summit in Zurich Switzerland.

Now 23 years-old, Shah has completed his post-secondary education, graduating with an Honours BA in Sociology and Political Science. He intends to continue with his social activism through writing poetry and public speaking engagements. He believes that talking about mental health and diversity and promoting the arts for ethnically diverse communities is extremely important (Mirza, 2018).

As a change leader, Wali has only just begun to give back what others have given to him. "I want to help that one kid that was feeling like me," he says (Kopun, 2017, para. 21).

To find out more information on Wali, or to contact him, follow him on Twitter @LifeAsWali or visit his website, www.lifeaswali.com.

Sources: Kopun, F. (2017, May 7). "From troubled Mississauga teen to poet laureate." www.thestar.com. Accessed at www.thestar.com/news/gta/2017/05/07/from-troubled-mississauga-teen-to-poet-laureate.html; Mirza, M. (2018, July 15). "Mississauga's poet laureate Wali Shah talks about graduating, his past and what's to come." *Mississauga News*. Accessed at www.mississauga.com/news-story/8736011-mississauga-s-poet-laureate-wali-shah-talks-about-graduating-his-past-and-what-s-to-come.

Courtesy of Wali Shah. To find out more information on Wali, or to contact him, visit his website: www.wafloshah.com and follow him on Twitter! @waliFLOshah"

Wali Shah, a former at-risk student, becomes a creative force and social activist.

Thinking

mimagephotography/Shutterstock.com

WHAT if …

I could solve problems more creatively and make decisions in every area of life with more confidence?

WHY this chapter matters …

The ability to think creatively and critically helps you succeed in any course.

HOW to use this chapter …

Read, write, speak, and listen more effectively. Learn strategies to enhance your success in problem-solving. Apply thinking skills to practical decisions, such as choosing a major.

what is included …

do you have a minute?

Do a one-minute mental exercise to explore the relationship between thinking and happiness:

1. Think of an activity you would like to try, like painting, hot yoga, or meditation.

2. Close your eyes and imagine yourself engaged in the activity. What environment are you in? Are you with other people? How do you feel?

3. Open your eyes. What First Step could you take to explore the opportunity to actually do this activity at least once in the next month. Is there a club on campus you could explore or an organization in your community related to this activity?

4. Write down your ideas.

Being open to new experiences is the First Step to them actually happening. If you found this exercise useful, then consider making it a habit.

CRITICAL THINKING:
A survival skill

Society depends on persuasion. Advertisers want us to spend money on their products. Political candidates want us to "buy" their stands on the issues. Teachers want us to agree that their classes are vital to our success. Parents want us to accept their values. Authors want us to read their books. The business of persuasion has an impact on all of us.

A typical Canadian sees thousands of television commercials each year—not to mention the number of ads that are pushed toward us by the news feeds or social media sites we join. This leaves us with hundreds of choices about what to buy, where to go, and who to be. It's easy to lose our heads in the crosscurrent of competing ideas—unless we develop skills in critical thinking. When we think critically, we can make choices with open eyes. It has been said that human beings are rational creatures. Yet no one is born an effective thinker.

Critical thinking is a learned skill. It is an essential element of being a self-regulated learner and a master student. When we engage in critical thinking, we use reasoned, purposeful thinking toward self-directed goals (Halpern, 1999). We monitor and are self-reflective about the outcomes of our thought processes. In other words, critical thinking is another crucial element of metacognition, which serves the important function of directing the thinking process. It is an important part of effective decision-making, problem-solving, and argument analysis. You can learn critical thinking skills in a wide variety of courses, from how to use statistical analysis to solve real world problems to studying philosophy to learn argument analysis.

Critical thinking as thorough thinking

For some people, the term *critical thinking* has negative connotations. If you prefer, use *thorough thinking* instead. Both terms point to the same array of activities: sorting out conflicting claims, weighing the evidence, letting go of personal biases, and arriving at reasonable conclusions. This adds up to an ongoing internal conversation—a constant process, not a final product.

We live in a society that seems to value quick answers and certainty. This is often at odds with effective thinking. Thorough thinking is the ability to examine and re-examine ideas that might seem obvious. Such thinking takes time and the willingness to say three subversive words: "I don't know."

Thorough thinking is the basis for much of what you do in school—reading, writing, speaking, listening, note-taking, test-taking, problem-solving, and other forms of decision-making. Skilled students have strategies for accomplishing all these tasks. They distinguish between opinion and fact. They ask probing questions and make detailed observations. They uncover assumptions and define their terms. They make assertions carefully, basing them on sound logic and solid evidence. Almost everything that we call knowledge is a result of these activities. This means that critical thinking and learning are intimately linked.

Benefits of critical thinking

Critical thinking frees us from self-deception. It is the path to freedom from half-truths and deception. You have a right to question everything you hear, see, or read. Acquiring this ability is the major goal of postsecondary education.

One of the reasons that critical thinking is so challenging—and rewarding—is that we have the remarkable capacity to fool ourselves. Some of our ill-formed thoughts and half-truths have a source that hits a little close to home. That source is ourselves.

If you take a course in psychology, you might hear about the theory of **cognitive dissonance** (Cooper & Goren, 2007). This is a term for the tension we feel when we encounter a fact that contradicts our deeply held beliefs. To reduce the discomfort, we might deny the fact or explain it away with deceptive thinking.

For example, consider someone who stakes her identity on the fact that she is a valued employee. During a recession, she gets laid off. On her last day at work, she learns that her refusal to take part in on-the-job training sessions was the major reason that the company let her go. This fact contradicts her belief in her value. Her response: "I didn't need that training. I already knew that stuff anyway. Nobody at that company could teach me anything." A skilled critical thinker would go beyond such self-justifying statements and ask questions instead: "What training sessions did I miss? Could I have learned something from them? Were there any signs that I was about to be laid off, and did I overlook them? What can I do to prevent this from happening again?"

Master students are willing to admit the truth when they discover that their thinking is fuzzy, lazy, or based on false assumptions. These students value facts. When a solid fact contradicts a cherished belief, they are willing to change the belief.

Critical thinking promotes social change. Consider that the institutions in any society—courts, governments, schools, businesses—are the products of a certain way of thinking. Any organization draws its life from certain assumptions about the way things should be done. Before the institution can change, those assumptions need to be loosened up or reinvented. In many ways, the real location of an institution is inside our heads. All social movements—from LGBTQQ rights to rights for Indigenous peoples—come about through the work of engaged critical thinkers who actively participated in their communities and questioned what was going on around them. As critical thinkers, we strive to understand and influence the institutions in our society.

Critical thinking uncovers bias and prejudice. This is a First Step toward communicating with people of other races, backgrounds, nationalities, and cultures.

Critical thinking is essential for information literacy. Computer technology will usher in the age of the paperless office. Given the wide range of sources available to us on the Internet, critical thinking is essential for us to distinguish reliable sources from those that are deceptive at best, and malicious at worst. Our ability to determine the credibility of a source has become a critical skill in today's world.

Critical thinking reveals long-term consequences. Crises occur when our thinking fails to keep pace with reality. An example is the world's ecological crisis, which arose when people polluted the earth, air, and water without considering the long-term consequences. Imagine how different our world would be if our leaders had followed the First Nations practice of thinking of themselves as being the caretakers of the earth. Their thinking would then have focussed on the long-term impacts of environmental destruction.

Critical thinking is a skill that will never go out of style. Throughout history, half-truths, faulty assumptions, and other nonsense have at one time been commonly accepted as true. Here are some examples:

- People who touch toads will get warts.
- Women are incapable of voting intelligently.
- Humans evolved from chimpanzees.

The critical thinkers of history courageously challenged such ideas. They pointed out that—metaphorically speaking—the emperor had no clothes.

It's been said that human beings are rational creatures. Yet no one is born rational. Thorough critical thinking is a learned skill. Use the suggestions in this chapter to claim the thinking powers that are yours to develop. Critical thinking is one aspect of the master student that lives inside you. ✳

GETTING READY
for critical thinking

Antonio Guillem/Shutterstock.com

CRITICAL THINKING is a path to an intellectual adventure. Though there are dozens of possible approaches, the process can be boiled down to concrete steps.

One quality of a master student is the ability to ask questions that lead to deeper learning. Your mind is an obedient servant. It will deliver answers at the same level as your questions. Becoming a critical thinker means being flexible and asking a wide range of questions.

A psychologist named Benjamin Bloom identified six levels of thinking, known as Bloom's taxonomy. See Figure 7.1. He called them *educational objectives*, or goals for learning (Anderson & Krathwohl, 2001). Each level of thinking calls for asking and answering different kinds of questions.

LEVEL 1: Remembering

At this level of thinking, the key question is *Can I recall the key terms, facts, or events?* To prompt level 1 thinking, an instructor might ask you to do the following:

- List the nine steps of Muscle Reading.
- State the primary features of a mind map.
- Name the master student profiled in Chapter 6 of this book.

To study for a test with level 1 questions, you could create flash cards to review ideas from your readings and class notes. You could also read a book with a set of questions in mind and underline the answers to those questions in the text. Or, you could memorize a list of definitions so that you can recite them exactly.

Although remembering is important, this is a relatively low level of learning. No critical or creative thinking is involved. You simply recognize or recall something that you've observed in the past.

LEVEL 2: Understanding

At this level, the main question is *Can I explain this idea in my own words?* Often this means giving examples of an idea based on your own experience.

Suppose that your instructor asks you to do the following:

- Explain the main point of the Power Process: "Embrace the new."
- Summarize the steps involved in creating a concept map.
- Compare mind mapping with concept mapping, stating how they're alike and how they differ.

Other key words in level 2 questions are *discuss, estimate,* and *restate.* All of these are cues to go one step beyond remembering and to show that you truly *comprehend* an idea.

LEVEL 3: Applying

Learning at level 3 means asking, *Can I use this idea to produce a desired result?* That result might include completing a task, meeting a goal, making a decision, or solving a problem.

Some examples of level 3 thinking are listed here:

- Write an affirmation about succeeding in school, based on the guidelines in this text.
- Write an effective goal statement.
- Choose a mnemonic to remember the names of the Great Lakes.

Some key words in level 3 questions include *apply, solve, construct, plan, predict,* and *produce.*

LEVEL 4: Analyzing

Questions at this level boil down to this: *Can I divide this idea into parts or steps?* For example, you could do the following:

- Divide the steps of Muscle Reading into three major phases.

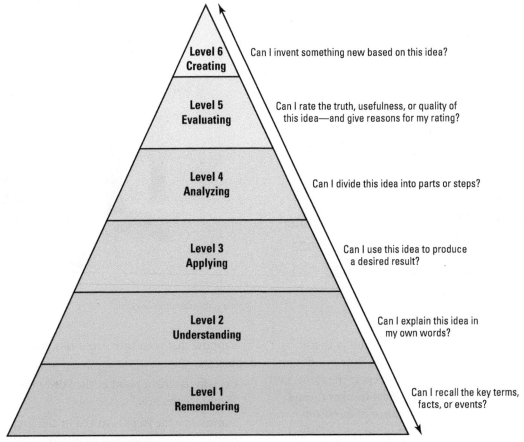

Figure 7.1 **Levels of Thinking**

The pyramid shows the levels of thinking, from bottom to top:

- **Level 6 / Creating** — Can I invent something new based on this idea?
- **Level 5 / Evaluating** — Can I rate the truth, usefulness, or quality of this idea—and give reasons for my rating?
- **Level 4 / Analyzing** — Can I divide this idea into parts or steps?
- **Level 3 / Applying** — Can I use this idea to produce a desired result?
- **Level 2 / Understanding** — Can I explain this idea in my own words?
- **Level 1 / Remembering** — Can I recall the key terms, facts, or events?

- Take a list of key events in the war in Afghanistan and arrange them in chronological order.
- Organize the 14 memory techniques from Chapter 3 into different categories.

Other key words in level 4 questions are *classify, separate, distinguish*, and *outline*.

LEVEL 5: Evaluating

Learning at level 5 means asking, *Can I rate the truth, usefulness, or quality of this idea—and give reasons for my rating?* This is the level of thinking you would use to do the following:

- Judge the effectiveness of an Intention Statement.
- Recommend the best method for taking lecture notes when an instructor talks fast.
- Rank the Power Processes in order of importance to you—from most useful to least useful.

Level 5 involves genuine critical thinking. At this level you agree with an idea, disagree with it, or suspend judgment until you get more information. In addition, you give reasons for your opinion and offer supporting evidence.

Some key words in level 5 questions are *critique, defend*, and *comment*.

LEVEL 6: Creating

To think at this level, ask, Can I invent something new based on this idea? For instance, you might do the following:

- Invent your own format for taking lecture notes.
- Prepare a list of topics that you would cover if you were teaching a student success course.
- Imagine that you now have enough money to retire and then write goals you would like to accomplish with your extra time.
- Create a PowerPoint® presentation based on ideas found in this chapter. Put the material in your own words, and use visual elements to enhance the points.

Creative thinking often involves analyzing an idea into parts and then combining those parts in a new way. Another source of creativity is taking several ideas and finding an unexpected connection among them. In either case, you are thinking at a very high level. You are going beyond agreement and disagreement to offer something unique—an original contribution of your own. Creative thinkers are able to synthesize and apply prior knowledge to new or unusual situations. Creative thinking is one of the key components of intelligence according to Robert Sternberg's theory of successful intelligence (Brown, Roediger, & McDaniel, 2014).

Questions for creative thinking often start with words such as adapt, change, collaborate, compose, construct, create, design, and develop. You might also notice phrases such as What changes would you make . . . ? How could you improve . . . ? Can you think of another way to . . . ? What would happen if . . . ?

Critical and creative thinking are exciting. The potential rewards are many, and the stakes are high. Your major decisions in life—from choosing a major to choosing a spouse—depend on your skills at critical and creative thinking.

All levels of thinking are useful. Notice that the lower levels of thinking (1 to 3) give you fewer options than the higher levels (4 to 6). Lower levels of thinking are sometimes about finding the "right" answer to a question. At levels 4, 5, and 6, you might discover several valid answers or create several workable solutions.

Also notice that the levels build on each other. Before you agree or disagree with an idea, make sure that you remember it accurately and truly understand it. Your understanding will go deeper if you can apply and analyze the idea as well. Master students stay aware of their current level of thinking. They can also move to other levels with a clear intention.

Remember that the highest levels of thinking call for the highest investments of time and energy. Also, moving from a lower level of thinking to a higher level often requires courage, along with an ability to tolerate discomfort. Give yourself permission to experiment, practise, and learn from mistakes.

The suggestions here will help you to deepen your skills at critical thinking. To learn more about creative thinking, see "Finding 'Aha!': Creativity fuels critical thinking" and "Ways to create ideas" later in this chapter. ✳

Becoming a
CRITICAL THINKER

Stripped to its essence, critical thinking means asking and answering questions. The four basic questions in the Learning Styles Applications in this book—*Why? What? How?* and *What if?*—are a powerful tool for thinking. As these questions take you through the cycle of learning, they can also guide you in becoming a critical thinker. This article offers a variety of tools for answering those questions. For more suggestions, see *Becoming a Critical Thinker* by Vincent Ryan Ruggiero (2015).

1 Why am I considering this issue? Critical thinking and personal passion go together. Begin critical thinking with a question that matters to you. Seek a rationale for your learning. Understand why it is important for you to think about a specific topic. You might want to arrive at a new conclusion, make a prediction, or solve a problem. By finding a personal connection with an issue, your interest in acquiring and retaining new information increases.

2 What are various points of view on this issue? Imagine Vladimir Putin, Tommy Douglas, and Mark Carney assembled in one room to choose the most desirable economic system. Picture Mahatma Gandhi, Lester B. Pearson, and General Roméo Dallaire lecturing at a U.N. conference on conflict resolution. Visualize Angela Merkel, Barack Obama, and Justin Trudeau in a discussion about distributing the world's resources equitably. When seeking out alternative points of view, let such events unfold in your mind.

Dozens of viewpoints exist on every important issue—reducing crime, ending world hunger, preventing war, educating our children, and countless other concerns. In fact, few problems allow for any single, permanent solution. Each generation produces its own answers to critical questions, based on current conditions. Our search for answers is a conversation that spans centuries. And on each question, many voices are waiting to be heard.

You can take advantage of this diversity by seeking out alternative views with an open mind. When talking to another person, be willing to walk away with a new point of view—even if it's the one you brought to the table, now supported with new evidence. After thinking thoroughly, you can adopt new perspectives or you can hold your viewpoint in a different way.

Examining different points of view is an exercise in analysis, which you can do with the suggestions that follow.

Define terms

Imagine two people arguing about whether an employer should limit extended healthcare benefits to members of a family. To one person, the word *family* means a mother, father, and children; to the other person, the word *family* applies to any long-term, supportive relationship between people who live together. Chances are, the debate will go nowhere until these people realize that they're defining the same word in different ways.

Conflicts of opinion can often be resolved—or at least clarified—when we define our key terms up front. This is especially true with abstract, emotion-laden terms such as *freedom, peace, progress,* or *justice.*

Look for assertions

A speaker's or writer's key terms occur in a larger context called an **assertion**. An assertion is a complete sentence that directly answers a key question. For example, consider this sentence: "Mastery means attaining a level of skill that goes beyond technique." This sentence is an assertion that answers an important question: How do we recognize mastery?

One path to critical thinking is tolerance for a wide range of opinions.

Look for at least three viewpoints

When asking questions, let go of the temptation to settle for just a single answer. Once you have come up with an answer, say to yourself, *Yes, that is one answer. Now what's another?* Using this approach can sustain honest inquiry, fuel creativity, and lead to conceptual breakthroughs. Be prepared: The world is complicated, and critical thinking is a complex business. Some of your answers might contradict others. Resist the temptation to have all of your ideas in a neat, orderly bundle.

Practise tolerance

One path to critical thinking is tolerance for a wide range of opinions. Taking a position on important issues is natural. When we stop having an opinion on things, we've probably stopped breathing.

The problem occurs when we become so attached to our current viewpoints that we refuse to consider alternatives. Many ideas that are widely accepted in Western cultures—for example, civil liberties for people of colour, same-sex marriage, and the right of women to vote—were once considered dangerous. Viewpoints that seem outlandish today might become widely accepted a century, a decade, or even a year from now. Remembering this can help us practise tolerance for differing beliefs and, in doing so, make room for new ideas that might alter our lives.

3 How well is each point of view supported?
Uncritical thinkers shield themselves from new information and ideas. As an alternative, you can follow the example of scientists, who constantly search for evidence that contradicts their theories. The following suggestions can help.

Look for logic and evidence

The aim of using logic is to make statements that are clear, consistent, and coherent. As you examine a speaker's or writer's assertions, you might find errors in logic—assertions that contradict each other or assumptions that are unfounded.

Also assess the evidence used to support points of view. Evidence comes in several forms, including facts, expert testimony, and examples. To think critically about evidence, ask questions like these:

- Are all or most of the relevant facts presented?
- Are the facts consistent with each other?
- Are facts presented accurately—or in a misleading way?
- Are enough examples included to make a solid case for the viewpoint?
- Do the examples truly support the viewpoint?
- Are the examples typical? That is, could the author or speaker support the assertion with other examples that are similar?
- Is the expert credible—truly knowledgeable about the topic?

Consider the source

Suppose you are reading an article on the problems of manufacturing cars powered by natural gas. It might have been written by an executive from an oil company. Check out the expert who disputes the connection between smoking and lung cancer. That "expert" might be the president of a tobacco company.

This is not to say that we should dismiss the ideas of people who have a vested interest in stating their opinions. Rather, we can take their self-interest into account as we consider their ideas.

Understand before criticizing

Polished debaters can sum up their opponents' viewpoints—often better than the people who support those viewpoints themselves. Likewise, critical thinkers take the time to understand a statement of opinion before agreeing or disagreeing with it.

Effective understanding calls for listening without judgment.

Effective understanding calls for listening without judgment. Enter another person's world by expressing her viewpoint in your own words. If you're conversing with that person, keep revising your summary until she agrees that you've stated her position accurately. If you're reading an article, write a short summary of it. Then scan the article again, checking to see if your synopsis is on target.

Watch for hot spots

Many people have mental "hot spots"— trigger topics that provoke strong opinions and feelings. Examples are abortion, gun control, animal rights, and the environment.

To become more skilled at examining various points of view, notice your own particular hot spots. Make a clear intention to recognize your feelings about these topics and to continue using critical thinking techniques to consider the feelings and opinions of others.

One way to cool down our hot spots is to remember that we can change or even give up our current opinions without giving up ourselves.

Be willing to be uncertain

Some of the most profound thinkers have practised the art of thinking by using a magic sentence: "I'm not sure yet."

Those are words that many people do not like to hear. Our society rewards quick answers and quotable sound bites. We're under considerable pressure to utter the truth in 10 seconds or less.

In such a society, it is courageous and unusual to take the time to pause, to look, to examine, to be thoughtful, to consider many points of view—and to be unsure. When a society adopts half-truths in a blind rush for certainty, a willingness to embrace uncertainty can move us forward.

4 What if I could combine various points of view or create a new one? Finding the truth is like painting a barn door by tossing an open can of paint at it. Few people who throw at the door miss it entirely. Yet no one can cover the whole door in a single toss.

People who express a viewpoint are seeking the truth. And no reasonable person claims to cover the whole barn door—to understand the whole truth about anything. Instead, each viewpoint can be seen as one approach among many possible alternatives. If you don't think that any one opinion is complete, combine different perspectives on the issue.

Create a critical thinking "spreadsheet"

When you consult authorities with different stands on an issue, you might feel confused about how to sort out, evaluate, and combine their points of view. To overcome confusion, create a critical thinking "spreadsheet." List the authorities across the top of a page and key questions down the left side. Then indicate each authority's answer to each question, along with your own answers.

For example, the spreadsheet in Figure 7.2 clarifies different points of view on the issue of whether to outlaw ultimate fighting.

	Medical doctor	Former ultimate fighter	Sports journalist	Me
Is ultimate fighting a sport?	No	Yes	Yes	Yes
Is ultimate fighting dangerous?	Yes	Yes	Yes	Yes
Is ultimate fighting more dangerous than other sports?	Yes	No	Yes	No
Can the risk of injury be overcome by proper training?	No	No	No	Yes

Figure 7.2 **A Critical Thinking "Spreadsheet"**
Source: Ruggiero, V. R. (2015). *Becoming a critical thinker*, 8E. © Heinle/Arts & Sciences, a part of Cengage Learning, Inc. Reproduced by permission. *www.cengage.com/permissions.*

You could state your own viewpoint by combining your answers to the questions in the spreadsheet: "I favour legalized ultimate fighting. While ultimate fighting poses dangers, so do other sports. And as with other sports, the risk of injury can be reduced when fighters get proper training."

Write about it

Thoughts can move at blinding speed. Writing slows down that process. Gaps in logic that slip by us in thought or speech are often exposed when we commit the same ideas to paper. Writing down our thoughts allows us to compare, contrast, and combine points of view more clearly—and therefore to think more thoroughly.

Notice your changing perspectives

Researcher William Perry (1970) found that students in higher education move through stages of

---

Four more questions for critical thinking

The four main questions presented in "Becoming a Critical Thinker" offer one approach to this skill. In their classic *How to Read a Book,* Mortimer Adler and Charles Van Doren offer another approach. They list four different questions to sum up the whole task of thinking critically about a body of ideas (Adler & Van Doren, 1972):

What is the writing or speech about as a whole? To answer this question, state the main topic in one sentence. Then list the related subtopics.

What is being said in detail, and how? List the main terms, assertions, and arguments. Also state what problems the writer or speaker is trying to solve.

Is it true? Examine the logic and evidence behind the ideas. Look for missing information, faulty information, and errors in reasoning. Also determine which problems were solved and which remain unsolved.

What of it? After answering the first three questions, prepare to change your thinking or behaviour as a result of encountering new ideas.

Attitudes of a critical thinker

The American Philosophical Association invited a panel of 46 scholars from Canada and the United States to come up with answers to the following two questions (Facione, 2013): "What is college/university-level critical thinking?" and "What leads us to conclude that a person is an effective critical thinker?" After two years of work, this panel concluded that critical thinkers share the attitudes summarized in the following chart.

Attitude	Sample statement
Truth-seeking	"Let's follow this idea and see where it leads, even if we feel uncomfortable with what we find out."
Open-minded	"I have a point of view on this subject, and I'm anxious to hear yours as well."
Analytical	"Taking a stand on the issue commits me to take some new action."
Systematic	"The speaker made several interesting points, and I'd like to hear some more evidence to support each one."
Self-confident	"After reading the book for the first time, I was confused. I'll be able to understand it after studying the book some more."
Inquisitive	"When I first saw that painting, I wanted to know what was going on in the artist's life when she painted it."
Mature	"I'll wait until I gather some more facts before reaching a conclusion on this issue."

intellectual development. Students in earlier stages of higher education tend to think there is only one correct viewpoint on each issue, and they look to their instructors to reveal that truth. Later, students acknowledge a variety of opinions on issues and construct their own viewpoints.

Monitor changes in your thinking processes as you combine viewpoints. Distinguish between opinions that you accept from authorities and opinions that are based on your own use of logic and your search for evidence. Also look for opinions that result from objective procedures (e.g., using the *Why? What? How?* and *What if?* questions in this article) as opposed to those from personal sources (using intuition or "gut feelings").

Remember that the process of becoming a critical thinker will take you through a variety of stages. Give yourself time, and celebrate your growing mastery. ✳

practising
CRITICAL THINKING

7-1

Applying Bloom's taxonomy to a higher level of thinking

Bloom's taxonomy (see Figure 7.1) describes six kinds of thinking: remembering, understanding, applying, analyzing, evaluating, and creating.

You can recall any suggestion from this book (**Level 1: Remembering**) and take that idea to a higher level of thinking. For example, the article "Motivation—I'm just not in the mood" (Chapter 1, "First Steps") includes this suggestion: "Ask for support." You could take this suggestion to **Level 2: Understanding** by adding personal examples:

It is easier to be motivated to succeed in school if I find classmates to study with at school. Not only do I find I study more when I have regular meetings with my study groups but I also learn a lot about teamwork, a skill that will be useful in my career after I graduate. Studying with others is also more fun than studying by myself. If I don't know whether study groups are available for my courses, I could always check with my instructor or with staff in our learning skills centre.

Now it's your turn. Choose another suggestion from this chapter (**Level 1: Remembering**) and think about it at **Level 2: Understanding**. In the space below, state the suggestion and write a brief paragraph that summarizes your higher-level thinking.

Note: If you'd like to demonstrate your thinking in another way—such as by making a drawing, building a model, or even writing a song—then discuss this with your instructor (Facione, 2013).

Source: Facione, Peter A. Critical thinking: What it is and why it counts. The latest version is available to students and faculty as a free download from *www.insightassessment.com.*

FINDING "AHA!":
Creativity fuels critical thinking

This article offers you a chance to practise two types of critical thinking: convergent thinking and divergent thinking. One focusses on finding a single solution to a problem, while the other asks you to consider as many viewpoints as possible.

Convergent thinking involves a narrowing-down process. Out of all the possible viewpoints on an issue or alternative solutions to a problem, you choose the one that is the most reasonable or that provides the most logical basis for action.

Some people see convergent thinking and critical thinking as the same thing. However, there's more to critical thinking. Before you choose among viewpoints, generate as many of them as possible. Open up alternatives and consider all of your options. Define problems in different ways. Keep asking questions and looking for answers. This opening-up process is called **divergent** (or *creative*) **thinking**. Creative thinking provides the basis for convergent thinking. In other words, one path toward having good ideas is to have *lots* of ideas. Then you can pick and choose from among them, combining and refining them as you see fit.

Choose when to think creatively

The key is to make conscious choices about what kind of thinking to do in any given moment. Generally speaking, divergent thinking is more appropriate in the early stages of planning and problem-solving. Feel free to dwell in this domain for a while. If you narrow down your options too soon, you run the risk of missing an exciting solution or neglecting a novel viewpoint. Convergent thinking is essential, and you should save it until you have plenty of options on the table.

Remember that divergent thinking and convergent thinking take place in a continuous cycle. After you've used convergent thinking to narrow down your options, you can return to divergent thinking at any time to generate new ones.

Cultivate "aha!"

Central to creative thinking is something called the "aha!" experience. Veteran Canadian journalist Robert Fulford has said, "Research is hard, writing is harder, but thinking is hardest of all." Aha! is the burst of creative energy heralded by the arrival of new, original thinking. It is the sudden emergence of an unfamiliar pattern, a previously undetected relationship, or an unusual combination of familiar elements. It is an exhilarating experience.

Aha! does not always result in a timeless poem or a Nobel Prize. It can be inspired by anything from playing a new riff on a guitar to figuring out why your car's fuel pump doesn't work. A nurse might notice a patient's symptom that everyone else missed. That's an aha! An accountant might discover a tax break for a client. That's an aha!

Follow through

The flip side of aha! is following through. Thinking is both fun and work. It is effortless and uncomfortable. It's the result of luck and persistence. It involves spontaneity and step-by-step procedures, planning and action, convergent and creative thinking.

Employers in all fields are desperately seeking those rare people who can find aha! and do something with it. The necessary skills include the ability to spot assumptions, weigh evidence, separate fact from opinion, organize thoughts, and avoid errors in logic. All of this can be demanding work. Just as often, it can be energizing and fun. ✷

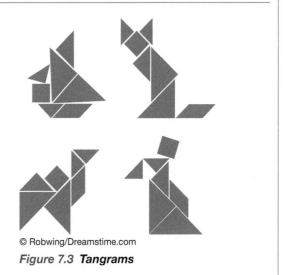
Ways to create
IDEAS

Anyone can think creatively. Use the following techniques to generate ideas about anything, whether you're studying math problems, remodelling a house, or writing a bestseller. With practice, you can set the stage for creative leaps, jump with style, and land on your feet with brand new ideas in hand.

Conduct a brainstorm

Brainstorming is a technique for finding solutions, creating plans, and discovering new ideas. When you are stuck on a problem, brainstorming can break through the stumbling block. For example, if you run out of money two days before payday every week, you can brainstorm ways to make your money last longer. You can brainstorm ways to pay for your education. You can brainstorm ways to find a job.

The purpose of brainstorming is to generate as many solutions as possible. Sometimes the craziest, most outlandish ideas, while unworkable in themselves, can lead to new ways to solve problems. Use the following steps to try out the brainstorming process:

- *Focus on a single issue or problem.* State your focus as a question. Open-ended questions that start with the words *what, how, who, where,* and *when* often make effective focussing questions.

- *Set a time limit* for your brainstorming session using the timer on your cellphone. Experiment with various lengths of time. Both short and long brainstorming sessions can produce powerful results.

- *Allow all answers.* Brainstorming is based on attitudes of permissiveness and patience. Accept every idea, no matter how wacky. If it pops into your head, put it down on paper. Quantity, not quality, is the goal. Avoid making judgments and evaluations during the brainstorming session.

- *Brainstorm with others.* Group brainstorming is a powerful technique. Assign one member of the group to write down solutions. Feed off the ideas of others and remember to avoid evaluating or judging anyone's ideas during the brainstorm.

- After your brainstorming session, *evaluate the results.* Toss out any truly crazy ideas, but not before you give them a chance.

Try brainwriting

Group brainstorming doesn't always work well to generate new ideas. Sometimes the person with the loudest voice dominates the discussion, or the person recording the ideas doesn't quite capture your thoughts. It can be intimidating at times to say your ideas out loud. And waiting to have your chance to talk can make you lose focus on what you were going to say or stop you from bothering to speak at all. One alternative is **brainwriting**.

In a six-person group, instead of saying ideas out loud, take five minutes for you and your group members to write three ideas at the top of a piece of paper. Try to keep your ideas short using keywords to express thoughts and try to be as specific as possible. After the five minutes, pass your sheet to another group member and each member reads what others have written. Use each set of ideas as a springboard for new ideas and write down three more ideas. Keep exchanging papers every five minutes until every member of the group has seen each sheet. In thirty minutes it is possible to generate 108 ideas (Litcanu, Prostean, Oros, & Mnerie, 2015).

After you have come up your lists of ideas, you can decide how to sort them (for example, by easiest to most difficult to implement, or least expensive to most

costly idea). Brainwriting is a great way to stimulate creativity while decreasing the pressure to respond to group norms. It also decreases "social loafing" since everyone is required to contribute. So next time your group gets stuck while trying to brainstorm a solution to a problem, try brainwriting instead.

Focus and let go

Focussing and letting go are alternating parts of the same process. Intense focus taps the resources of your conscious mind. Letting go gives your subconscious mind time to work. When you focus for intense periods and then let go for a while, the conscious and subconscious parts of your brain work in harmony. In doing so, you can produce the highest-quality results.

Focussing attention means being in the here and now. To focus your attention on a project, notice when you pay attention and when your mind starts to wander. And involve all of your senses. When you know the sights, sounds, and sensations you associate with being truly in focus, you'll be able to repeat the experience and return to your task more easily.

You might not be focussed all of the time. Be gentle with yourself when you notice that your concentration has lapsed. In fact, that might be a time to let go. "Letting go" means not forcing yourself to be creative. Practise focussing for short periods at first, then give yourself a break. Phone a friend. Get up and take a walk around the room or around your block, or do a little yoga or some simple exercises. Take a nap when you are tired. Thomas Edison took frequent naps. Then the light bulb clicked on.

Cultivate creative serendipity

The word **serendipity** was coined by the English author Horace Walpole from the title of an ancient Persian fairy tale, "The Three Princes of Serendip." The princes had a knack for making lucky discoveries. Serendipity is that knack, and it involves more than luck. It is the ability to see something valuable that you weren't looking for. History is full of serendipitous people. Country doctor Edward Jenner noticed "by accident" that milkmaids seldom got smallpox. The result was his discovery that mild cases of cowpox immunized them. Jenner used his discovery to create the smallpox vaccine. Penicillin was also discovered "by accident." Scottish scientist Alexander Fleming was growing bacteria in a laboratory petri dish. A spore of *Penicillium notatum*, a kind of mould, blew in the window and landed in the dish, killing the bacteria. Fleming isolated the active ingredient. A few years later, during World War II, penicillin saved thousands of lives. Had Fleming not been alert to the possibility, the discovery might never have been made.

pathdoc/Shutterstock.com

You can train yourself in the art of serendipity. First, keep your eyes open. You might find a solution to an accounting problem in a Saturday morning cartoon. You might discover a topic for your essay at the corner convenience store. Multiply your contacts with the world. Resolve to meet new people. Join a study or discussion group. Read. Go to plays, concerts, art shows, lectures, movies, and listen to podcasts. Then, expect discoveries. One secret for success is being prepared to recognize "luck" when you see it.

Keep idea files

We all have ideas. People who are viewed as creative are those who treat their ideas with care. That means not only recognizing ideas, but also recording them and following up on them. One way to keep track of ideas is to write them down on a pad of paper or use the note-taking application on your phone to record them.

Keep a journal. Journals don't have to be exclusively about your own thoughts and feelings. You can record observations about the world around you, conversations with friends, important or offbeat ideas—anything.

To fuel your creativity, read voraciously, including newspapers and magazines. Follow blogs or start your own and read news journals online. Use sites like *Delicious* or *Pinterest* to save and store browser bookmarks or sites. Use social networks to connect with fellow bloggers and to serve as a source of inspiration.

Safeguard your ideas, even if you're pressed for time. Jotting down four or five words is enough to capture the essence of an idea. You can write down or record one quotation in a minute or two.

Collect and play with data

Look from all sides at the data you collect. Switch your attention from one aspect to another. Examine each fact to avoid getting stuck on one particular part of a problem.

Turn a problem upside down by picking a solution first and then working backward. Ask other people to look at the data. Solicit opinions. Use your social networks to connect with others and to market your ideas.

Living with the problem invites a solution. Write down data, possible solutions, or a formulation of the problem on a notepad or your phone. Look at your ideas before you go to bed at night. Review them when you are waiting for the bus. Make them part of your life and think about them frequently.

Look for the obvious solutions or the obvious "truths" about the problem—then toss them out. Ask yourself: "Well, I know X is true, but if X were *not* true, what would happen?" Or ask the reverse: "If that *were* true, what would follow next?"

Put unrelated facts next to each other and invent a relationship between them, even if it seems absurd at first. In *The Act of Creation,* novelist Arthur Koestler

---

Creative ways for groups to get "unstuck"

Sometimes creative thinking dies in committee. People are afraid to disagree with a forceful leader and instead keep their mouths shut. Or a long-standing group ignores new members with new ideas. The result can be "group think," where no one questions the prevailing opinion. To stimulate creative thinking in groups, try these strategies:

Put your opinion on hold. If you're leading a meeting, ask other people to speak up first. Then look for the potential value in *any* idea. Think of the ideas as concepts to be elaborated on rather than pitches to be torn down. Avoid nonverbal language that signals a negative reaction, such as frowning or rolling your eyes.

Rotate group leadership. Ask group members to take turns. This strategy can work well in groups where people have a wide range of opinions.

Ask questions. Instead of giving immediate feedback to new ideas, ask questions. Probing questions are more likely to expand ideas rather than shutting down discussion.

Divide larger groups into several teams. People might be more willing to share their ideas in a smaller group. Try to limit group size to four to six members.

Start with a *positive* outcome in mind. Assume you will come up with the right idea in time. Use an appreciative inquiry approach to build on group members' strengths and ideas rather than immediately evaluating why an idea can't work.

Invite a guest expert. A fresh perspective from someone outside the group can spark an aha!

Set up a suggestion box. Let people submit ideas anonymously, in writing.

Review your notes regularly. Some amusing thought that came to you in November might be the perfect solution to a problem in March.

(1964) says that finding a context in which to combine opposites is the essence of creativity. Make imaginary pictures with the data. Condense it. Categorize it. Put it in chronological order. Put it in alphabetical order. Put it in random order. Order it from most to least complex. Reverse all of those orders. Look for opposites.

It has been said that there are no new ideas—only new ways to combine old ideas. Creativity is the ability to discover those new combinations.

Create while you sleep

A part of our mind works as we sleep. You've experienced this directly if you've ever fallen asleep with a problem on your mind and awakened the next morning with a solution. For some of us, the solution appears in a dream or just before falling asleep or waking up.

You can experiment with this process. Ask yourself a question as you fall asleep. Keep pencil and paper or your phone near your bed. The moment you wake up, begin writing or speaking and see if an answer to your question emerges.

There is a story about how Benjamin Franklin used this suggestion. Late in the evenings, as he was becoming drowsy, he would sit in his rocking chair with a rock in his right hand and a metal bucket on the floor beneath the rock. The moment he fell asleep, the rock would fall from his grip into the bottom of the bucket, making a loud noise that awakened him. Having placed a pen and paper nearby, he immediately wrote down what he was thinking. Experience taught him that his thoughts at this moment were often insightful and creative.

Refine ideas and follow through

Many of us ignore this part of the creative process. How many great money-making schemes have we had that we never pursued? How many good ideas have we had for short stories that we never wrote? How many times have we said to ourselves, "You know, what they ought to do is attach two handles to one of those things, paint it orange, and sell it to police departments. They'd make a fortune." And we never realize that we are "they."

Most schools now have a centre that supports student entrepreneurship. They provide mentors, potentially seed money, and workshops to assist students with taking their ideas to the next stage. So, find out if your school has an accelerator program. Don't wait to graduate to start the next great business—use the resources of your school to begin now.

Genius resides in the follow-through—the application of perspiration to inspiration. One powerful tool you can use to follow through is the Discovery and Intention Journal Entry system. First write down your idea in a Discovery Statement, and then write what you intend to do about it in an Intention Statement. You also can explore the writing techniques discussed in Chapter 8, "Communicating," as a guide for refining your ideas.

Create success strategies

Use creative thinking techniques to go beyond the pages of this book and create your own ways to succeed in school. Read other books on success. Interview successful people. Reflect on any of your current behaviours that help you do well in school. Change any habits that fail to serve you.

Trust the process

Learn to trust the creative process—even when no answers are in sight. We are often reluctant to look at problems if no immediate solution is at hand. We grow impatient and tend to avoid frustration by giving up altogether. Most of us do this to some degree with personal problems as well. If we are having difficulty with a relationship and don't see a quick resolution, we deny that the problem exists rather than facing up to it.

Trust that a solution will show up. Frustration and a feeling of being stuck are often signals that a solution is imminent.

Sometimes solutions break through in a giant AHA! More often they come in a series of little aha!s. Be aware of what your aha! moments look, feel, and sound like. That sets the stage for even more flights of creative thinking. ✳

Create on your feet

A popular trend in executive offices is the "stand-up" desk—a raised working surface at which you stand rather than sit.

Standing has advantages over sitting for long periods. You can stay more alert and creative when you're on your feet. One theory is that our problem-solving ability improves when we stand, due to increased heart rate and blood flow to the brain.

Standing is great for easing lower-back pain, too. Sitting aggravates the spine and its supporting muscles.

This is a technique with tradition. If you search the Web for stand-up desks, you'll find models based on desks used by Thomas Jefferson, Winston Churchill, and writer Virginia Woolf. Consider setting your desk up on blocks or getting an extension for your keyboard and monitor so that you can stand while writing, preparing speeches, or studying. Discover whether this approach works for you.

Courtesy of Karyn Olsen

practising
CRITICAL THINKING

7-2

Explore emotional reactions

Each of us has certain trigger topics—issues that generate strong emotional reactions. These topics may include bullying, racism, climate change, or decriminalizing prostitution. There are many other examples, varying from person to person. Examine your own trigger topics on a separate sheet of paper by writing a word or short phrase summarizing each issue about which you feel very strongly. Then describe what you typically say or do when each issue comes up in conversation.

After you have completed your list, think about what you can do to become a more effective thinker when you encounter one of these issues. For example, you could breathe deeply and count to five before you offer your own point of view. Or you might preface your opinion with an objective statement such as "There are many valid points of view on this issue. Here's the way I see it, and I'm open to your idea."

_____

_____

_____

_____

_____

DON'T FOOL YOURSELF:
15 common mistakes in logic

Logic is a branch of philosophy that seeks to distinguish between effective and ineffective reasoning. Students of logic look for valid steps in an *argument,* or a series of assertions. The opening assertions of the argument are the *premises,* and the final assertion is the *conclusion.*

Effective reasoning is not just an idle pastime for unemployed philosophers. Learning to think logically offers many benefits: When you think logically, you take your reading, writing, speaking, and listening skills to a higher level. You avoid costly mistakes in decision-making. You can join discussions and debates with more confidence, cast your election votes with a clear head, and become a better-informed citizen. People have even improved their mental health by learning to dispute illogical beliefs (Seligman, 2002).

Over the last 2,500 years, specialists in logic have listed some classic land mines in the field of logic—common mistakes that are called **fallacies**. These fallacies are included in just about every logic textbook. Following are fifteen examples. Knowing about them before you string together a bunch of assertions can help you avoid getting fooled.

1 Jumping to conclusions. Jumping to conclusions is the only exercise that some lazy thinkers get. This fallacy involves drawing conclusions without sufficient evidence. Take the bank officer who hears about an immigrant failing to pay back a loan. After that, the officer turns down all loan applications from immigrants. This person has formed a rigid opinion on the basis of hearsay. Jumping to conclusions—also called *hasty generalization*—is at work here.

Following are more examples of this fallacy:

- When I went to Mexico for spring break, I felt sick the whole time. Mexican food makes people sick.

- Google's mission is to "organize the world's information." Their employees must be on a real power trip.

- During a recession, more people go to the movies. People just want to sit in the dark and forget about their money problems.

© photos.com

2 Attacking the person. This mistake in logic is common at election time. An example is the candidate who claims during the campaign that her opponent has never wanted to really live in Canada. People who indulge in personal attacks are attempting an intellectual sleight of hand to divert our attention from the truly relevant issues.

3 Appealing to authority. A professional athlete endorses a brand of breakfast cereal. A famous musician features a beer company's product in a rock video. The promotional brochure for an advertising agency lists all of the large companies that have used its services.

In each case, the people involved are trying to win your confidence—and your dollars—by citing authorities. The underlying assumption is usually this: Famous people and organizations buy our product. Therefore, you should buy it too. Or: You should accept this idea merely because someone who's well known says it's true.

Appealing to authority is usually a substitute for producing real evidence. It invites sloppy thinking. When our only evidence for a viewpoint is an appeal to authority, it's time to think more thoroughly.

4 Pointing to a false cause. The fact that one event follows another does not necessarily mean that the two events have a cause-and-effect relationship. All we can actually say is that the events might be correlated. For example, as children's vocabularies improve, they can get more cavities. This does not mean that cavities are the result of an improved vocabulary. Instead, the increase in cavities is due to other factors, such as physical maturation and changes in diet or personal care.

5 Thinking in all-or-nothing terms. Consider these statements: Doctors are greedy. . . . You can't trust politicians. . . . Students these days are in school just to get high-paying jobs; they lack idealism. . . . Homeless people don't want to work.

These opinions imply the word *all.* They gloss over individual differences, claiming that all members of a group are exactly alike. They also ignore key facts, for instance, that some doctors volunteer their time at free medical clinics and that many homeless people are children who are too young to work. All-or-nothing thinking is one of the most common errors in logic.

6 Basing arguments on emotion. The politician who ends every campaign speech with flag waving and slides of him hugging babies is staking his future on appeals to emotion. So is the candidate who paints a grim scenario of the disaster and ruination that will transpire unless she is elected. Get past the fluff and histrionics to see if you can uncover any worthwhile ideas.

7 Using a faulty analogy. An **analogy** states a similarity between two things or events. Some arguments rest on analogies that hide significant differences. For instance, people who say if we ban alcohol advertising then pretty soon we will ban the advertising of eggs because they contain cholesterol which is a harmful substance. Is it really fair to compare alcohol to cholesterol in terms of being harmful substances?

8 Creating a straw man. The name of this fallacy comes from the scarecrows traditionally placed in gardens to ward off birds. A scarecrow works because it looks like a man. Likewise, a person can attack ideas that *sound like* his opponent's ideas but are actually absurd. For example, some members of Parliament attacked the law legalizing same-sex marriage by saying polygamy would be allowed if same-sex partners were allowed to legally marry. In fact, supporters of this bill proposed no such thing.

9 Begging the question. Speakers and writers beg the question when their colourful language glosses over an idea that is unclear or unproven. Consider this statement: *The criminal has committed the worst crime possible.* Anyone who makes such a statement "begs" (fails to answer) a key question: What is the worst crime possible?

10 Confusing fact and opinion. Facts are statements verified by direct observation or compelling evidence that creates widespread agreement. In recent years, for example, some politicians argued for tax cuts to corporations on the grounds that the Canadian economy needed to create more jobs. However, it's not a fact that tax cuts automatically create more jobs. This statement is almost impossible to verify by direct observation, and there's actually evidence against it.

11 Creating a red herring. When hunters want to throw a dog off a trail, they can drag a smoked red herring (or some other food with a strong odour) over the ground in the opposite direction. This distracts the dog, who is fooled into following a false trail. Likewise, people can send our thinking on false trails by raising irrelevant issues. Case in point: In 2008, some people who opposed the presidential campaign by U.S. senator Barack Obama emphasized his middle name: Hussein. This was an irrelevant attempt to link the senator to Saddam Hussein, the dictator and former ruler of Iraq.

12 Appealing to tradition. Arguments based on an appeal to tradition take a classic form: *Our current beliefs and behaviours have a long history; therefore, they are correct.* This argument has been used to justify the divine right of kings, feudalism, witch burnings, slavery, child labour, and a host of other traditions that are now rejected in most parts of the world. Appeals to tradition ignore the fact that unsound ideas can survive for centuries before human beings realize that they are being fooled.

13 Appealing to "the people." Consider this statement: Millions of people use Wikipedia as their main source of factual information. Wikipedia must be the best reference work in the world. This is a perfect example of the *ad populum* fallacy. (In Latin, that phrase means "to the people.") The essential error is assuming that popularity, quality, and accuracy are the same.

Appealing to "the people" taps into our universal desire to be liked and to associate with a group of people who agree with us. No wonder this fallacy is also called "jumping on the bandwagon." Following are more examples:

- Google is the most widely used Web browser. It must be the best one.
- Dan Brown's books, including The Da Vinci Code, did not sell as well as the Harry Potter books by J. K. Rowling. I guess we know who's the better writer.

You can refute such statements by offering a single example: Many Canadians once believed that women were inferior and therefore should not be allowed to vote. That did not make either belief right.

14 Distracting from the real issue. The fallacy of distracting from the real issue occurs when a speaker or writer makes an irrelevant statement and then draws a conclusion based on that statement. For example: *The most recent recession was caused by people who borrowed too much money and bankers who loaned too much money. Therefore, you should never borrow money to go to school.* This argument ignores the fact that a primary source of the recession was loans to finance housing—not loans to finance education. Two separate topics are mentioned, and statements about one do not necessarily apply to the other.

15 Sliding a slippery slope. The fallacy of sliding a slippery slope implies that if one undesired event occurs, then other, far more serious events will follow: *If we restrict our right to free speech, then all of our rights will soon be taken away. If people keep downloading music for free, pretty soon they'll demand to get everything online for free. I notice that more independent bookstores are closing; it's just a matter of time before people stop reading.* When people slide a slippery slope, they assume that different types of events have a single cause. They also assume that a particular cause will operate indefinitely. In reality, the world is far more complex. Grand predictions about the future often prove to be wrong.

Finding fallacies before they become a fatal flaw (bonus suggestions)

Human beings have a long history of fooling themselves. This article presents just a partial list of logical fallacies. You can prevent them and many more by following a few suggestions:

- When outlining a paper or speech, create a two-column chart. In one column, make a list of your main points. In the other column, summarize the

The problem of egocentric thinking

Egocentric thinking results from the unfortunate fact that humans do not naturally consider the rights and needs of others. We do not naturally appreciate the point of view of others, or the limitations in our own point of view. We become explicitly aware of egocentric thinking only if trained to do so. We do not naturally recognize our own egocentric assumptions, the egocentric way we use information, the egocentric way we interpret data, the source of our egocentric concepts and ideas, the implications of our egocentricity. We do not naturally recognize our self-serving perspective.

As humans we live with the unrealistic but confident sense that we have fundamentally figured out the way things actually are, and that we have done this objectively. We naturally believe in our intuitive perceptions, however inaccurate. Instead of using intellectual standards in thinking, we often use self-centred psychological standards to determine what to believe and what to reject. Here are the most commonly used psychological standards in human thinking.

"It's true because I believe it." Innate egocentrism: I assume that what I believe is true even though I have never questioned the basis for many of my beliefs.

"It's true because we believe it." Innate sociocentrism: I assume that the dominant beliefs of the groups to which I belong are true even though I have never questioned the basis for those beliefs.

"It's true because I want to believe it." Innate wish fulfillment: I believe in whatever puts me (or the groups to which I belong) in a positive light. I believe what "feels good," what does not require me to change my thinking in any significant way, what does not require me to admit I have been wrong.

"It's true because I have always believed it." Innate self-validation: I have a strong desire to maintain beliefs I have long held, even though I have not seriously considered the extent to which those beliefs are justified by the evidence.

"It's true because it is in my selfish interest to believe it." Innate selfishness: I believe whatever justifies my getting power, money, or personal advantage even though these beliefs are not grounded in sound reasoning or evidence.

Source: Paul, R., & Elder, L. (2008). *The miniature guide to critical thinking concepts and tools.* Dillon Beach, CA: The Foundation for Critical Thinking Press. Reprinted with permission.

evidence for each point. If you have no evidence for a point, a logical fallacy may be lurking in the wings.

- Go back to some of your recent writing—assigned papers, essay tests, journal entries, and anything else you can find. Look for examples of logical fallacies. Note any patterns, such as repetition of one

particular fallacy. Write an Intention Statement about avoiding this fallacy.

- Be careful when making claims about people who disagree with you. One attitude of a critical thinker is treating everyone with fairness and respect. ✳

Gaining skill at
DECISION-MAKING

We make decisions all of the time, whether we realize it or not. Even avoiding decisions is a form of decision-making. The student who puts off studying for a test until the last minute might really be saying, "I've decided this course is not important" or "I've decided not to give this course much time."

A planned decision-making style requires you to gather information and adopt a more systematic approach that requires you to balance logical reasoning and intuition. Decide right now to apply some of the following suggestions, and you can take your overall decision-making to new heights of effectiveness.

Recognize decisions
Decisions are more than wishes or desires. There's a world of difference between "I wish I could be a better student" and "I will take more powerful notes, read with greater retention, and review my class notes daily." Decisions are specific and lead to focussed action. When we decide, we narrow down. We give up actions that are inconsistent with our decision.

Establish priorities
Some decisions are trivial. No matter what the outcome, your life is not affected much. Other decisions can shape your circumstances for years. Devote more time and energy to the decisions with big outcomes.

Clarify your values
When you know specifically what you want from life, making decisions becomes easier. This is especially true when you define your values precisely and put them in

writing. Saying that you value education is fine. Now give that declaration some teeth. Note that you value lifelong learning as a chance to upgrade your career skills, for instance. That can make choosing next year's classes much easier.

Base your decisions on a life plan
The benefit of having long-term goals for our lives is that they provide a basis for many of our daily decisions. Being certain about what we want to accomplish this year and this month provides clarity to today's choices.

Choose an overall strategy
Every time you make a decision, you choose a strategy—even when you're not aware of it. Effective decision-makers can articulate and choose from among several strategies.

- *Find all of the available options and choose one deliberately.* This strategy can be the most time consuming. Save this strategy for times when you have a relatively small number of options, each of which leads to noticeably different results.

- *Find all of the available options and choose one randomly.* This strategy can be risky. Save it for times when your options are basically similar and fairness is the main issue.

- *Limit the options, then choose.* For example, when deciding which search engine to use on the Internet, visit many sites and then narrow the list down to two or three that you choose.

- *Choose to act on someone else's decision.* You use this strategy, for example, when you buy music based on a friend's recommendation.

Sometimes we face dilemmas—situations in which any course of action leads to undesirable consequences. In such cases, consider putting a decision on hold. Do nothing until the circumstances change, making one alternative clearly preferable to another. Waiting is especially useful if you find yourself in a negative mood, which can affect your ability to think clearly and creatively. Wait for the mood to pass, then assess your options.

Use intuition

Some decisions seem to make themselves. A solution pops into your mind and you gain newfound clarity. Using intuition is not the same as forgetting about the decision or refusing to make it. Intuitive decisions usually arrive after we've gathered the relevant facts and faced a problem for some time.

Act on your decision

There comes a time to move from the realm of discovery and intention to the arena of action. Action is a hallmark of a true decision.

Evaluate your decision

Hindsight can be a valuable source of insight. After you act on a decision, observe the consequences over time. Reflect on how well your decision worked and what you might have done differently. Look on each individual decision as a source of feedback that will improve your overall skill at decision-making.

Think choices

This final suggestion involves some creative thinking. Rather than making a decision, think about the word *choice*. Using the word *choice* frees up your thinking. When you *choose*, you express a preference for one option over others at this time. Choose for today, knowing that as you gain more wisdom and experience, you can choose again. ✳

Four ways to solve
PROBLEMS

There is a vast amount of literature on problem-solving techniques. Much of it can be traced to philosopher John Dewey, who devised these steps of effective problem-solving:

- Perceive a "felt difficulty" and state it clearly and concisely.

- Invent possible solutions.

- Rationally test each solution by anticipating its possible consequences.

- Act on the preferred solution, evaluate the consequences, and determine whether a new solution is needed (Dewey, 1910).

Much of what you'll read about problem-solving amounts to variations on Dewey's steps. Think of problem-solving as a process with four P's: Define the *problem,* generate *possibilities,* create a *plan,* and *perform* your plan.

Stone/Getty Images

1 **Define the problem.** To define a problem effectively, understand what a problem is—a mismatch between what you want and what you have. Problem-solving is all about reducing the gap between these two factors.

Tell the truth about what's present in your life right now, without shame or blame. For example: "I often get sleepy while reading my physics assignments, and after closing the book I cannot remember what I just read."

Next, describe in detail what you want. Go for specifics: "I want to remain alert as I read about physics. I also want to accurately summarize each chapter I read."

Remember that when we define a problem in limiting ways, our solutions merely generate new problems. This idea has many applications for success in college or university. An example is the student who struggles with note-taking. The problem, she thinks, is that her notes are too sketchy. The logical solution, she decides, is to take *more* notes, and her new goal is to write down almost everything her instructors say. No matter how fast and furiously she writes, she cannot capture all of the instructors' comments.

Consider what happens when this student defines the problem in a new way. After more thought, she decides that her dilemma is not the *quantity* of her notes but their quality. She adopts a new format for taking notes, dividing her notepaper into two columns. In the right-hand column, she writes down only the main points of each lecture. And in the left-hand column, she notes two or three supporting details for each point.

Over time, this student makes the joyous discovery that there are usually just three or four core ideas to remember from each lecture. She originally thought the solution was to take more notes. What really worked was taking notes in a new way.

2 Generate possibilities. Now put on your creative thinking hat. Open up. Brainstorm as many possible solutions to the problem as you can. As you generate possibilities, gather relevant facts. For example, when you're faced with a dilemma about what courses to take next term, get information on class times, locations, and instructors. If you haven't decided which summer job offer to accept, gather information on salary, benefits, and working conditions.

3 Create a plan. After rereading your problem definition and list of possible solutions, choose

the solution that seems most workable. Think about specific actions that will reduce the gap between what you have and what you want. Visualize the steps you will take to make this solution a reality and arrange them in chronological order. To make your plan even more powerful, put it in writing.

4 Perform your plan. This step gets you off your chair and out into the world. Now you actually *do* what you have planned. Ultimately, your skill in solving problems culminates in how well you perform your plan. Through the quality of your actions, you become the architect of your own success.

Define the **problem**	**What** is the problem?
Generate **possibilities**	**What if** there are several possible solutions?
Create a **plan**	**How** would this possible solution work?
Perform your plan	**Why** is one solution more workable than another?

When facing problems, experiment with these four P's. Also remember that any solution has the potential to create new problems. If that happens, cycle through the four P's of problem-solving again. ✳

"But I don't know what I want to do."
CHOOSING YOUR MAJOR

One decision that troubles many students in postsecondary education is the choice of a program of study or an academic major. Here is an opportunity to apply your skills at critical thinking, decision-making, and problem-solving. The following four suggestions can guide you through this process:

1 Discover options

Follow your interests

Perhaps you look forward to attending one of your classes and even like completing the assignments. This is a clue to your choice of major.

See if you can find lasting patterns in the subjects and extracurricular activities that you've enjoyed over the years. Look for a major that allows you to continue and expand on these experiences.

Also sit down with a notepad and brainstorm answers to the following questions:

- What do you enjoy doing most with your unscheduled time?

- Imagine that you're at a party and having a fascinating conversation. What is this conversation about?

- What kind of problems do you enjoy solving—those that involve people? Products? Ideas?

- What interests are revealed by your choices of reading material, blogs, and other entertainment?

- What would an ideal day look like to you? Describe where you'd be, who would be with you, and what activities you'd do. Do any of these visions suggest a possible major?

Questions like these can help determine what energizes you to finish the work of completing a major.

Consider your abilities

In choosing an academic program, ability counts as much as interest. In addition to considering what you enjoy, think about times and places when you excelled. List the courses that you aced, the work assignments that you mastered, and the hobbies that led to rewards

© Brian A Jackson/Shutterstock, © Yuri Arcurs/Shutterstock
© illustrart/Shutterstock

or recognition. Let your choice of a program of study reflect a discovery of your passions *and* potential.

Use formal techniques for self-discovery

Writing is a path to the kind of self-knowledge involved in choosing your major. Start with the exercises and Journal Entries in this book. Review what you've written, looking for statements about your interests and abilities.

Also consider questionnaires and inventories that are designed to correlate your interests with specific majors such as the Strong Interest Inventory and the Self-Directed Search. Your student services or careers office can give you more details about these and related inventories. Take several of them and meet with an advisor to interpret the results.

Remember that inventories can help you gain self-knowledge, and other people can offer valuable perspectives. However, what you *do* with all this input is entirely up to you.

Link to long-term goals

Your choice of a study program or major can fall into place once you determine what you want in life. Before you choose a major, back up to a bigger picture. List your core values, such as contributing to society, achieving financial security and professional recognition, enjoying good health, or making time for fun. Also write down specific goals that you want to accomplish five years, 10 years, or even 50 years from today.

Having a clear career goal gives you a powerful incentive for attending classes, taking part in discussions, reading textbooks, writing papers, and completing other assignments. When you see a clear connection between finishing school and creating the life of your dreams, the daily tasks of higher education become charged with meaning.

Studies indicate that the biggest factor associated with completing a degree in higher education is commitment to personal goals (Carlzon, 1989). A choice of academic major reflects those goals.

Ask other people

Key people in your life might have valuable suggestions about your choice of major. Ask for their ideas, and listen with an open mind. But don't feel pressured to choose a major or career that fails to interest you. If you make a choice based solely on the expectations of other people, you could end up with a major or even a career you don't enjoy.

Gather information

Check your school's catalogue or website for a list of available majors. Take a quick glance and highlight all the majors that interest you. Then talk to students who have declared them. Do you get excited about the chance to enroll in different majors? Pay attention to your "gut feelings."

Chat with instructors who teach courses in these areas, and ask for copies of their course syllabi. Go to the bookstore and browse required texts. Based on all this information, write a list of prospective programs of study. Discuss them with an academic advisor and someone at your school's career centre. Or if you can't find a major you like, see if taking an independent study program is possible.

Consider dual degrees

Many schools provide the opportunity to complete two degrees at the same time; you can, for example, combine the study of engineering with getting a business degree.

Combining two degrees can allow you to expand the skills you develop and provide you with some powerful credentials in the workplace. Completing a minor course of study in a complimentary area will also serve to enhance your career choices. So, if you are studying business, consider a minor in French. Proficiency in French could broaden your career options not just in Canada but also abroad.

Think critically about the link between your major and your career

Your career goals might have a significant impact on your choice of major. For an overview of career planning and an immediate chance to put ideas down on paper, see Chapter 12, "What's Next?"

You might be able to pursue a rewarding career by choosing among *several* different majors. Even students planning to apply for law school or medical school have flexibility in their choice of majors.

Remember that many students who choose an "impractical" major go on to prosper in their careers. According to the National Committee for Latin and Greek (2006), people who majored in classical civilizations and literature range from Ted Turner (founder of CNN) to Toni Morrison (winner of the Noble Prize for Literature) and J. K. Rowling (author of the Harry Potter novels).

2 Make a trial choice

Pretend that you have to choose a major today. Based on the options for a major that you have already discovered, write down the first three ideas that come to mind. Review the list for several minutes and then just choose one.

3 Evaluate your trial choice

When you've made a trial choice, take on the role of a scientist. Treat your choice as a hypothesis and then design a series of experiments to test it.

- Schedule meetings with instructors who teach courses in the program, asking about required course work and career options in the field.

- Discuss your trial choice with an academic adviser and a career counsellor.

- Enrol in a course related to your possible area of study. Remember that introductory courses might not give you a realistic picture of the workloads involved in advanced courses. Talk to upper year students in the program to learn more about the courses.

- Find an internship, service-learning experience, part-time job, or volunteer experience related to the program.

- Interview someone who works in a field related to the program of study or find out if your school has a job-shadowing program.

If these experiences confirm your choice of program of study, celebrate that fact. If they result in choosing a new program of study, celebrate that outcome as well. Also remember that higher education represents a safe place to test your choice of study programs—and to change your mind.

4 Choose again

Keep your choice of a major in perspective. There is probably no single "correct" choice. Your unique collection of skills is likely to provide the basis for majoring in several fields.

Odds are that you'll change your major at least once throughout your degree or diploma—and that you'll change careers several times during your life. One benefit of higher education is mobility. You gain the general skills and knowledge that can help you move into a new major or career field at any time.

Viewing a program of study as a one-time choice that determines your entire future can raise your stress levels. Instead, look at choosing a major as the start of a continuing path that involves discovery, choice, and passionate action. ✳

practising
CRITICAL THINKING

7-3

Make a trial choice of major

This exercise presents another method for choosing a major. Look at your school's academic calendar for a list of majors, and cross out all of the programs that you already know are not right for you. You will probably eliminate well over half the list.

Now scan the remaining majors. Next to the ones that definitely interest you, write "yes." Next to majors that you're willing to consider and are still unsure about, write "maybe."

Focus on your "yes" choices. See if you can narrow them down to three majors. List those here.

_____

_____

_____

_____

_____

_____

_____

_____

_____

_____

_____

_____

_____

_____

_____

_____

_____

Finally, write an asterisk next to the major that interests you most right now. This is your trial choice of major.

ASKING QUESTIONS:
Learning through inquiry

THINKING IS BORN of questions. Questions wake us up. Questions promote curiosity, and create new possibilities. Besides, instructors love them.

There's a chinese proverb: "Tell me and I forget; show me and I remember; involve me and I understand." Asking questions is a way to stay involved. One of the main reasons you are in school is to ask questions—a process called *inquiry-based learning*. This process takes you beyond memorizing facts and passing tests. Asking questions turns you into a lifelong learner. Master students know that asking good questions is just as important as being able to answer questions.

Questions have practical power. Asking for directions can shave hours off a trip. Asking a librarian for help can save hours of research time. Asking your academic counsellor a question can alter your entire education. Asking people about their career plans can alter *your* career plans.

Asking questions is also a great way to improve relationships with friends and co-workers. When you ask a question, you offer a huge gift to people—an opportunity for them to speak their brilliance and for you to listen to their answers.

Students often say, "I don't know what to ask." If you have ever been at a loss for what to ask, here are some ways to construct powerful questions about any subject you study in school, or about any area of your life that you choose to examine.

Ask about what's missing

One way to invent useful questions is to notice what's missing from your life and then ask how to supply it. For example, if you want to take better notes, you can write, "What's missing is skill in note-taking. How can I gain more skill in taking notes?" Or "What's missing is time. How do I create enough time in my day to actually do the things that I say I want to do?"

Begin a general question, then brainstorm endings

By starting with a general question and then brainstorming a long list of endings, you can invent a question that you've never asked before. For example:

What can I do when . . . ? What can I do when an instructor calls on me in class and I have no idea what

Monkey Business Images/Shutterstock.com

to say? What can I do when an instructor doesn't show up for class on time? What can I do when I feel overwhelmed with assignments?

How can I . . . ? How can I get just the kind of courses that I want? How can I expand my career options? How can I become much more effective as a student, starting today?

When do I . . . ? When do I decide on a program of study? When do I transfer to another school? When do I meet with an instructor to discuss an upcoming essay?

Ask what else you want to know

Many times you can quickly generate questions by simply asking yourself, "What else do I want to know?" Ask this question immediately after you read a paragraph in a book or listen to someone speak.

Start from the assumption that you are brilliant, and begin asking questions that can help you unlock your brilliance.

Let your pen start moving

Sometimes you can access a deeper level of knowledge by taking out your pen, putting it on a piece of paper, and writing down questions—even before you know *what* to write. Don't think. Just watch the paper and notice what appears. The results might be surprising. ✳

Asking questions

The art of asking questions is just as important to critical thinking as answering them. One eye-opening way to create questions is to write something you're sure of and simply put a question mark after it. (You might need to rephrase the question for grammatical sense.) The question you create can lead to others.

For example, someone might say, "I would never take a philosophy course." This person can write "I would never take a philosophy course?" That suggests other questions: "In what ways would taking a philosophy course serve my success in school?" "Could taking a philosophy course help me become a better writer?"

In the space below, write three statements that you accept with certainty. Then rephrase each statement as a question.

Statement #1:

_____

_____

_____

_____

_____

Question #1:

_____

_____

_____

_____

_____

Statement #2:

_____

_____

_____

_____

_____

Question #2:

_____

_____

_____

_____

_____

Statement #3:

_____

_____

_____

_____

Question #3:

_____

_____

_____

_____

THINK CRITICALLY ABOUT
information on the Internet

Sources of information on the Internet range from the reputable (e.g., Statistics Canada) to the flamboyant (e.g., the *National Enquirer*). People are free to post *anything* on the Internet, including outdated facts as well as intentional misinformation. The rise of social media networks that use filter bubbles has also contributed to an increase in people only seeing information or opinions that agree with their initial biases, potentially hiding other opinions from them. This has led to the rise of *fake news.*

Who posts fake news? It comes from a variety of sources including highly partisan news sources such as those who only post information that supports one point of view. It includes those who seek to influence public opinion by posting information that is a mixture of truth and fiction. Finally, it can come from commercially-driven sources that provide stories with no grounding in fact and whose goal is to direct web traffic in order to generate advertising income (Titcomb & Carson, 2018). One website that looks at media bias is *mediabiasfactcheck.com.*

Unlike newspaper, magazine, and book publishers who often employ fact checkers, editors, and lawyers to screen out errors and scrutinize questionable material before publication, authors of online sources might not have or choose to use these resources. Today more than ever before, you need to use your critical thinking skills of sound logic, credible evidence, and respect for your audience to assess the information you receive from news feeds, blogs, or any source online.

Distinguish between ideas and information

To think more powerfully about what you find on the Internet, consider the difference between information and ideas. Information refers to facts that can be verified by independent observers. Ideas are interpretations or opinions; they may or may not be based on facts. These include statements of opinion and value judgments. Several people with the same information might adopt different ideas based on that information. Don't assume that an idea is more current, reasonable, or accurate just because you find it on the Internet. Apply your critical thinking skills to all published material—print and online.

Look for overall quality

Examine the features of the website in general. Notice the effectiveness of the text and visuals as a whole. Also note how well the site is organized and whether you can navigate the site's features with ease. Look for the date that crucial information was posted, and determine how often the site is updated.

Next, take a more detailed look at the site's content. Examine several of the site's pages, and look for consistency of facts, quality of information, and competency with grammar and spelling. Are the links within the site easy to navigate?

Also evaluate the site's links to related Web pages. Look for links to pages of reputable organizations. Click on a few of those links. If they lead you to dead ends, you can safely conclude that the site you're evaluating is not updated often—a clue that it's not a reliable source for late-breaking information.

Look at the source

Think about the credibility of the person or organization that posts the website. Look for a list of author credentials and publications. Just because someone lists themselves as an authority on a topic doesn't mean that they are. Look at the sources they cite before you are willing to believe what you've read.

Notice evidence of bias or special interest. Perhaps the site's sponsoring organization wants you to buy a service, a product, or a point of view. This fact might suggest that the information on the site is not objective; it is therefore questionable.

The domain in the uniform resource locator (URL) for a website can give you clues about sources of information and possible bias. For example, distinguish among information from a for-profit commercial enterprise (URL ending in .com); a nonprofit organization (.org); a government agency (gc.ca); and a school, college, or university (.ca).

Note: Wikis (peer-edited sites) such as Wikipedia may not employ editors to screen out errors or scrutinize questionable material before publication. Wikis can be useful for a general introduction or background information. If an article or entry lists references, always check these sources yourself. Check with your instructor about whether you are allowed to cite Wikipedia articles when researching a paper or presentation. Also, be cautious about citing blogs, which often are not reviewed for accuracy.

Look for documentation

When you encounter an assertion on a Web page or some other Internet resource, note the types and quality of the evidence offered. Look for credible examples, quotations from authorities in the field, documented statistics, or summaries of scientific studies. ✳

journal entry 7-2

Discovery/Intention Statement

Reflect on Choosing a Major

Reflect for a moment on your experience with Practising Critical Thinking 7-3, "Make a trial choice of program of study." If you had already chosen a program of study, did it confirm that choice? Did you uncover any new or surprising possibilities?

I discovered that I . . .

_____

_____

_____

_____

_____

_____

_____

_____

Now consider the program that is your current top choice. Think of publications you expect to find, resources you plan to investigate, and people you intend to consult in order to gather more information about this specialization.

I intend to . . .

_____

_____

_____

_____

_____

_____

_____

_____

Plan to repeat this Journal Entry and Practising Critical Thinking 7-3 several times. You might find yourself researching several programs of study and changing your mind. That's fine. The aim is to start thinking about your program of study now.

Attitudes, affirmations, and
VISUALIZATIONS

"I have a bad attitude." Some of us say this as if we were talking about having the flu. An attitude is certainly as strong as the flu, but it isn't something we have to succumb to or accept. You can change your attitudes through regular practice with affirmations and visualizations.

Affirm it

An **affirmation** is a statement describing what you want. Affirmations can change your attitudes and behaviours. The most effective affirmations are personal, positive, and written in the present tense.

- **Present Tense.** Determine what you want, then describe yourself as if you already have it. To get what you want from your education, you could write, "I take full responsibility for my education. I learn with joy, and I use my experiences in each course to create the life that I want."

- **Positive.** Avoid words such as *not*, *never*, and *can't*. Instead of saying "I will not make mistakes while playing music," say "I will play music with joy and ease."

- **Personal and specific.** Use your own name. Involve all your senses—sight, sound, smell, taste, and touch. "I, Susan Smith, am a master student. I employ critical thinking when I ask questions in class."

Once you have written an affirmation, repeat it. Practise saying it out loud several times a day. Do this at a regular time, such as just before you go to sleep or just after you wake up. It's also effective to look in a mirror while saying the affirmation. Keep looking and repeating until you are saying your affirmation with conviction.

Visualize it

This technique complements affirmations. It's a favourite among athletes and performers. To begin, choose what you want to improve. Then describe in writing what it would look like, sound like, and feel like to have that improvement in your life.

Decide what you want to improve, and write down what it would look like, sound like, and feel like to have that improvement in your life.

If you are learning to play the piano, write down briefly what you would see, hear, and feel if you were playing skillfully. Once you have a sketch of what it would be like to be successful, practise it in your imagination. If you want to improve your basketball scoring technique, imagine how it feels when you toss the basketball and it swishes through the net. Feel the weight of the ball in your hand before you throw and then let it go. Each test the instructor hands back to you is graded A. Feel the smile on your face when you look at that grade. Practise at least once a day. Then wait for the results to unfold in your life. ✳

Attitude replacements

You can use affirmations to replace a negative attitude with a positive one. There are no limitations, other than your imagination and your willingness to practise. Here are some sample affirmations. Modify them to suit your individual hopes and dreams, and then practise them.

I, _____, am healthy.

I, _____, have abundant energy and vitality throughout the day.

I, _____, exercise regularly.

I, _____, work effectively with many different kinds of people.

I, _____, eat wisely.

I, _____, plan my days and use time wisely.

I, _____, have a powerful memory.

I, _____, take tests calmly and confidently.

I, _____, have a sense of self-worth that is independent of my test scores.

I, _____, fall asleep quickly and sleep soundly.

I, _____, am smart.

I, _____, am creative.

I, _____, am aware of and sensitive to other people's moods.

I, _____, have relationships that are mutually satisfying.

I, _____, work hard and contribute to other people through my job.

I, _____, know ways to play and have fun.

I, _____, focus my attention easily.

I, _____, like myself.

I, _____, am a worthwhile person even though I am _____.

I, _____, am relaxed in all situations, including _____.

I, _____, always live my life in positive ways for the highest good of all people.

CRITICAL THINKING

Reprogram your attitude

You can employ affirmations and visualizations to successfully reprogram your attitudes and behaviours. Use this exercise to change your approach to any situation in your life.

Step 1

Pick something in your life that you would like to change. It can be related to anything—relationships, work, money, or personal skills.

Describe briefly what you choose to change.

_____

_____

_____

_____

_____

_____

_____

Step 2

Add more details about the change you described in Step 1. Write down how you would like the change to come about. Be outlandish. Imagine that you are about to ask your fairy godmother for a wish that you know she will grant. Be detailed in your description of your wish.

_____

_____

_____

_____

_____

_____

_____

_____

Step 3

Use affirmations and visualizations to start yourself on the path to creating exactly what you wrote about in Step 2. Write at least two affirmations that describe your dream wish. Also, briefly outline a visualization that you can use to picture your wish. Be specific, detailed, and positive.

_____

_____

_____

_____

_____

_____

_____

Step 4

Put your new attitudes to work. Set up a schedule to practise them. Let the first time be right now. Then set up at least five other times and places that you intend to practise your affirmations and visualizations.

I intend to relax and practise my affirmations and visualizations for at least five minutes on the following dates and at the times and location(s) given.

Date	Time	Location
1.		
2.		
3.		
4.		
5.		

Step 5

Attitude change takes time. End this exercise by reflecting on your progress. Ask whether your practice of affirmations and visualization is actually changing the way that you speak and behave in daily life. You might want to change your affirmations and visualizations so that they're more detailed, positive, and vivid. Write down your revised versions.

POWERPROCESS

Embrace the new

Both creative thinking and critical thinking call on us to embrace the new. We can think critically about a new idea only if we're willing to *consider* it in the first place. And it's hard to create something original or change our behaviour if we insist on sticking with what's already familiar to us. All the game-changing devices in human history—from the wheel to the iPhone—happened only because their inventors were willing to embrace the new.

Embracing the new is more than just a nice idea. It's an essential skill for anyone who wants to survive and thrive in the work world. Your next career might be one that doesn't exist today. Think about certain job titles—*information architect, social media director, content strategist*—that came to life only in the twenty-first century. There are many more opportunities just waiting to be created.

When learning to embrace the new, start with the way you speak. Notice comments such as these: "That can't possibly be true." "That idea will never work." "We tried that last year and failed." Those statements represent the sound of a mind slamming shut.

Now consider replacing them with these: "What if that *were* true?" "How could we make that idea work?" "What could we do differently this time?"

To get the most value from this suggestion, remember that it's about more than being open to ideas. You can embrace the new on many levels: Be willing to think what you've never thought before, to say what you've never said before, to do what you've never done before. This is the essence of learning.

Also remember that embracing the new does *not* mean trashing the old. Adopting a new habit does not mean changing all your current habits. When you open up to unfamiliar ideas and experiences, you get to keep your core values. You can embrace change and still take a stand for what's important to you.

As you test new ideas and experiment with new strategies, keep those that work and let go of the rest. You might find that your current beliefs and behaviours work well with just a few tweaks. And in any case, you can go into the unknown with a known process—the cycle of discovery, intention, and action.

What's new is often going to stick around anyway. You have two basic options: Resist it or embrace it. The former is a recipe for frustration. The latter offers a fresh possibility in every moment.

Galyna Andrushko/Shutterstock.com

Put it to WORK

Strategies for creative and critical thinking can assist you in developing new products and services in the workplace. Some examples follow.

Iakov Filimonov/Shutterstock.com

State the obvious and go for the opposite

One way to generate a burst of creativity followed by critical thinking is to take an idea that seems obvious and state its opposite. Then see if you can find evidence to support the opposite idea.

This principle has been used with great success in business. An example comes from Jan Carlzon, former president of the Scandinavian Airline SAS. Carlzon questioned an "obvious" truth—that upper management in any company should make most of the decisions. He went for the opposite idea and allowed rank-and-file employees to make daily decisions that directly affected customers. If a customer got bumped from a flight, an SAS counter clerk could decide on the spot whether to pay the customer's hotel bill for the night or find the customer an alternative flight on a competitor's airline. After implementing this policy, SAS's business grew dramatically.

Find a smaller problem

You might feel overwhelmed with managing a complex, year-long project at work. One response is to give up—to quit. Another is to resign yourself to drudgery and dive into the project with a deep sigh.

A better alternative is to "find a smaller problem": Just divide a huge project into many small jobs. Rather than worry about the project as a whole, turn your full attention to a small, specific task until it is complete. Do the same with the next small task, and the next. Just handle the details, one after another, until the project is finished.

The role of planning is critical. "Find a smaller problem" is not a suggestion to fill your days with busywork. When you plan effectively, the small jobs you do are critical to the success of the bigger project.

Experiment with the decreasing options technique

The decreasing options technique (DOT) is a decision-making strategy. It allows you to rank a large pool of ideas created by groups of people in meetings. Before you put DOT into action, go to an office supply store and get a package of several hundred adhesive dots—small stickers that can be attached to a sheet of paper. Then follow these steps:

- *Ask meeting participants to brainstorm solutions to a problem.* Permit all ideas to be expressed. Don't edit them yet. To save time, ask participants to submit ideas before the meeting takes place. That way you can summarize and post ideas ahead of time.

- *Summarize each idea in a single word or phrase on a large sheet of paper.* Write letters that are big enough to be seen across the meeting room. Place only one idea on each sheet of paper.

- *Post the sheets where all meeting participants can see them.*

- *Do an initial review of the ideas.* Ask participants if they can eliminate some ideas as obviously unworkable. Also group similar ideas together and eliminate duplications.

- *"DOT" ideas.* Give each participant a handful of sticker dots. Then ask participants to go around the room and place an adhesive dot next to the ideas that they consider most important.

- *Discuss the most important ideas.* Stand back and review the ideas. The high-priority concerns of the group will stand out clearly as the sheets with the most dots. Now you can bring these important ideas to the discussion table.

You can also use the DOT method online with bulletin boards or virtual meetings. Participants can use email or networking software to post their ideas and manipulate computer graphics that look like sticker dots.

chapter 7

- Put it to Work
▶ ▶ ▶ ▶
- Skills Snapshot
- Master Student Profile

QUIZ

Name_____   Date____/____/____

1. List four questions that can guide you on your path to becoming a critical thinker.

2. Briefly describe one strategy for answering each question you listed in your response to Question 1.

3. For which types of activities are visualizations particularly effective?

4. Summarize the main steps in choosing a program of study or major.

5. According to the text, *critical thinking* and *thorough thinking* are two distinct and different activities. True or False? Explain your answer.

6. List the key question associated with each level of Bloom's taxonomy.

7. Give three reasons why brainwriting might be a more efficient strategy for group problem-solving than brainstorming.

8. Name at least one fallacy involved in this statement: "Everyone who's ever visited Toronto has agreed that it's the best city in the country."

9. List the four suggested steps for problem-solving and give an example of each step.

10. Why is breaking a big task down into smaller units important for getting your work completed?

Skills **SNAPSHOT**

Now that you've experimented with some new strategies for thinking, take a few minutes to revisit your responses to the "Thinking" section of the Discovery Wheel exercise earlier in the book. Then complete the following sentences.

CREATIVE AND CRITICAL THINKING

When I'm asked to come up with a topic for a paper or speech, the first thing I do is . . .

When I'm asked for my opinion about a political candidate, the first thing I take into account about the candidate is . . .

APPLIED THINKING

In declaring my major, the steps I plan to take include . . .

One of the biggest problems I face right now is . . .

To come up with a solution for this problem, I will . . .

I'll know that I've reached a new level of mastery with critical and creative thinking skills when . . .

To reach that level of mastery, the most important thing I can do next is to . . .

MASTER STUDENT PROFILE

Neil Pasricha
... is a positive thinker

NEW

sipaphotostwo/Newscom

Neil Pasricha is an author whose book *The Book of Awesome* became an international bestseller. His blog site has been named one of *PC* magazine's Top 100 Internet sites. At 8:00 a.m. in a downtown Tim Hortons, Neil Pasricha is already busy at his laptop, writing blog entry No. 535, describing how stretching as you wake up is awesome.

The little joys in life—and we do mean little: bakery air, popping bubble wrap, a really cold glass of water on a hot day—have preoccupied Pasricha, a Harvard MBA and former comedy writer, since he started the blog 1000awesomethings.com in 2008 to cheer himself up during a bleak period.

Boy, did it ever work. A self-described nerd with an office job in Mississauga, he won two Webby awards, the Oscars of the Internet, for his blog and *The Book of Awesome* was an #1 international bestseller for 142 weeks.

His blog—some entries are nostalgic, reflective, but always positive—now gets about 40,000 visits a day, more than 11 million hits in total. His email box is regularly packed with readers' messages, spilling out their woes and thanking him for lifting their spirits. "You made me realize the sun is still shining," wrote one woman.

"The response has been overwhelming," says Pasricha, 30. "I feel like the Pied Piper of happiness."

At Indigo Books and Music, Bahram Olfati, vice-president of adult trade, was skeptical at first about Pasricha's take on the subject. "That's my nature. C'mon, it's not so easy to be happy," says Olfati. Then he read it. "Staying in the shower an extra five minutes does make me happy. It is the little things," he laughs.

"Millions of blogs don't get picked up. The ones that do," says Olfati, "genuinely connect with people's feelings. The writers' personalities come through.

They're people you could easily become friends with."

"Walking here, as I approached the intersections, the red hand kept turning to walk without me breaking stride," says Pasricha, who lives downtown. "That's awesome. It was like the universe knew I was coming."

He extracts scraps of paper from his pocket, all scribbled with germs of ideas, and rapidly scrolls through his iPhone, revealing a stream of jotted-down thoughts.

"I'm really hyper, even before my coffee. Can you tell?"

In the universe of Pasricha, he was the kid with the thick Coke-bottle glasses growing up in Whitby. "I tried and quit so many sports." He writes about that too in his blog although he finds the upside of being face-smacked with a hard-kicked soccer ball (No. 893, Orange slices at half time). He remembers being a happy-go-lucky kid, friends with everyone, even the bullies.

At Queen's University, he studied commerce but loved writing for *Golden Words,* the school humour newspaper. He'd found his calling: comedy writer. But it became draining very quickly. "I realized this could never be my full time thing."

So he put on a business suit; did a marketing stint at Procter & Gamble, Toronto; ran a Quiznos franchise in Whitby; and took off for Harvard Business School. Somewhere in there, he got married.

And then Pasricha hit what he calls his "gloom and doom phase." His marriage was rocky, and his best friend emotionally unhinged. So what did he do?

"I decided I needed to look on the bright side of life." He went to his computer and started to write about a thousand—changed at the last second from a million—awesome things. No. 1000: Broccoflower, ". . . bizarre misfit child from two of nature's most hideous vegetables."

Followed soon by "The last crummy triangle in a bag of potato chips," "Getting grass stains," "Locking people out of the car and pretending to drive away," each entry a short essay. "Slowly I was finding myself in the posts," he explains.

His manner is more serious, more intense now. "I think you can choose to be happy," he says, leaning forward. "It's why 11 million people have visited the site. It's why people send me message after message, thanking me, saying, 'I needed this.'"

Has he always been such a positive thinker?

"You can call it that," he says flatly. "I think these are things we all think about. You go through six green lights in a row, you think 'awesome'. We all love snow days. They're truisms. I'm just the one saying, let's focus on the positive, we need it."

Source: White, Nancy J. (2010, April 14). "The 'awesome' blog is a huge hit: 40,000 Internet visits a day". *www.thestar.com*. Retrieved July 5, 2011 from *http://www.thestar.com/printarticle/795405*. Reprinted with permission.

Communicating

© Savageultralight/Shutterstock.com

what is included...

do you have a minute?

Gratitude for the good things that happen in our lives is an important component of happiness. Take a moment to think of three things you have today to feel gratitude for. Do this every day for the next week and write a Discovery Statement about the impact of this exercise on your life. Follow up with an Intention Statement about turning this type of thinking into a habit.

COMMUNICATING
creates our world

According to communication theorist Lee Thayer (1968), there are two basic life processes. One is acquiring and processing energy. The other is acquiring and processing information, also known as communication. From this point of view, communicating is just as fundamental to life as eating.

Through communication, we take raw impressions and organize them into meaningful patterns. With our senses, we perceive sights, sounds, and other sensations. However, none of our sense organs is capable of perceiving *meaning*. We create meaning by finding patterns in our sensations and communicating them.

Communication can be defined as the process of creating shared meaning. When two people agree about the meaning of an event, they've communicated. However, communication is a constant challenge. Each of us creates meaning in a way that is unique.

When people speak or listen, they don't exchange meaning. They exchange symbols—words, images, gestures. And symbols are open to interpretation. This means that communication is always flawed to some extent. We can never be sure that the message we send is the message that others receive. This challenge will only grow as social networking connects us to people around the world.

To be an effective communicator involves self-regulation. You need to be able to not just listen but also be reflective on your own communication behaviour. Sometimes it is not just *what* was said but *how* it was said.

Yet with practice we can overcome many of the difficulties inherent in human communication. That's what this chapter is all about. As you enhance your skills at listening, speaking, and writing, you can create a new world. ✳

journal entry 8-1

Discovery/Intention Statement

Commit to Create Value from This Chapter

Think of a time when you experienced an emotionally charged conflict with another person. Were you able to resolve this dispute effectively? If so, list below the strategies you used. If not, describe what you could have done differently.

I discovered that I...

_____

_____

_____

_____

Now scan this chapter for ideas that can help you get your feelings across more skillfully in similar situations. List at least four ideas here, along with the page numbers where you can read more about them.

Strategy   **Page number**

_____

_____

_____

_____

Describe an upcoming situation in which you intend to apply these techniques. If possible, choose a situation that will occur within the next week.

I intend to . . .

_____

_____

_____

_____

_____

COMMUNICATION:
Keeping the channels open

IN OUR DAILY contact with other people and the mass media, we are exposed to hundreds of messages. Yet the obstacles to receiving those messages accurately are numerous.

For one thing, only a small percentage of communication is verbal. We also send messages with our bodies and with the tone of our voices. Throw in a few other factors, such as a hot room or background noise, and it's a wonder we can communicate at all.

Written communication adds a whole other set of variables. When you speak, you supplement the meaning of your words with the power of body language and voice inflection. When you write, those nonverbal elements are absent. Instead, you depend on your skills at word choice, sentence construction, and punctuation to get your message across. The choices that you make in these areas can aid—or hinder—communication.

In communication theory (Figure 8.1), the term **noise** refers to any factor that distorts meaning. When noise is present, the channels of communication start to close. Noise can be external (a lawn mower outside

practising
CRITICAL THINKING
8-1

Practise sending or receiving

The purpose of this exercise is to help you slow down the pace of communication and clearly separate the roles of sending and receiving. Begin by applying the following steps to conversations on neutral topics. With some practice, you'll be ready to use this technique in situations that could escalate into an argument.

First, find a partner, and choose a topic for a conversation. Also set a time limit for doing this exercise. You will need someone to time the exercise for you. Then complete the following steps:

1. Sit back to back with your partner. Decide which one of you will talk first. The *sender* should speak for three minutes on the topic. The partner should listen without speaking until the sender's time is up.

2. When it is the partner or *receiver's* turn, she should first summarize what the *sender* said before she responds. She should take about a minute to summarize and then will have three minutes to talk on the topic. The partner should listen without speaking until it is his turn.

3. Next the original *sender* will summarize what the partner said for a minute and then again have three minutes to respond.

4. Keep switching roles until each of the partners has had at least three opportunities to speak. Remember to summarize what your partner said before you begin speaking and to not interrupt when the other person is talking.

After completing these steps, reflect on the experience. How well could you summarize what your partner said? What has this exercise taught you about your current skills as a speaker and listener?

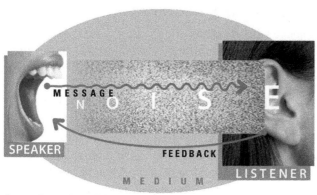

Source: Photos (mouth) © photos.com, (ear) © Andre Blais/Shutterstock

Figure 8.1 Communication Theory

a classroom) or internal (the emotions of the sender or receiver, such as speech anxiety). To a large extent, skillful communication means reducing noise and keeping channels open.

One powerful technique for doing these crucial things is to separate the roles of sending and receiving. Communication channels get blocked when we try to send and receive messages at the same time. Instead, be aware of when you are the receiver and when you are the sender. If you are receiving (listening or reading), just receive; avoid switching into the sending (speaking or writing) mode. When you are sending, stick with it until you are finished.

Communication works best when each of us has plenty of time to receive what others send *and* the opportunity to send a complete message when it's our turn. Communication is a two-way street. When someone else talks, just listen. Then switch roles so that you can be the sender for a while. Keep this up until you do a reasonably complete job of creating shared meaning. ✱

Choosing to **LISTEN**

OBSERVE A PERSON in a conversation who is not talking. Is he listening? Maybe. Maybe not. He might be preparing his response or daydreaming.

Listening is not easy. Doing it effectively requires concentration and energy. It's worth it. Listening well promotes success in school: more powerful notes, more productive study groups, and better relationships with students and instructors. Being an effective listener helps improve the sharing of information and leads to increased creativity and innovation. A skilled listener is appreciated by friends, family, and business associates. People love a good listener. Through skilled listening, you gain more than respect and insight into other people. You learn about the world and about yourself.

To be a good listener, choose to listen. Once you've made this choice, you can use the following techniques to be a more effective listener. These ideas are especially useful in times of high emotional tension.

Nonverbal listening

Much of listening is nonverbal. Here are six guidelines for effective nonverbal listening.

Through skilled listening, you gain more than respect. You gain insight into other people. You learn about the world and about yourself.

Be quiet

Silence is more than staying quiet while someone is speaking. Allowing several seconds to pass before you begin to talk gives the speaker time to catch his breath and gather his thoughts. He might want to continue. Someone who talks nonstop might fear he will lose the floor if he pauses.

If the message being sent is complete, this short break gives you time to form your response and helps you avoid the biggest barrier to listening—listening with your answer running. If you make up a response before the person is finished, you might miss the end of the message—which is often the main point.

In some circumstances, pausing for several seconds might be inappropriate. Ignore this suggestion completely when it is an emergency where immediate action is usually necessary.

Maintain eye contact

Look at the other person while she speaks. Doing so demonstrates your attentiveness and helps keep your mind from wandering. Your eyes also let you "listen" to body language and behaviour. When some of us avoid eye contact, not only do we fail to see—we fail to listen.

This idea is not an absolute. While maintaining eye contact is important in many cultures, people from some cultures are uncomfortable with sustained eye contact. Some individuals learn primarily by hearing; they can listen more effectively by turning off the visual input once in a while. Keep in mind the differences among people.

Display openness

You can communicate openness by means of your facial expression and body position. Uncross your arms and legs. Sit up straight. Face the other person and remove any physical barriers between you, such as a pile of books.

Send nonverbal acknowledgments

Let the speaker know periodically that you are still there. Words and nonverbal gestures of acknowledgment convey to the speaker that you are interested and that you are receiving his message. These include "Umhum," "OK," "Yes," and head nods.

These acknowledgments do not imply your agreement. When people tell you what they don't like about you, your head nod doesn't mean that you agree. It just indicates that you are listening.

Release distractions

Even when your intention is to listen, you might find your mind wandering. Thoughts about what *you* want to say or something you want to do later might claim your attention. There's a simple solution: Notice your wandering mind without judgment. Then bring your attention back to the act of listening.

You can also set up your immediate environment to release distractions. Turn off or silence your electronic devices. Send the message that your sole intention in the moment is to listen.

Suspend judgments

Listening and agreeing are two different activities. As listeners, our goal is to fully receive another person's message. This does not mean that we're obligated to agree with the message. Once you're confident that you accurately understand a speaker's point of view, you are free to agree or disagree with it. The key to effective listening is understanding *before* evaluating.

Verbal listening

Choose when to speak

When we listen to another person, we often interrupt with our own stories, opinions, suggestions, and comments. Consider the following dialogue:

"Oh, I'm so excited. I just found out that I've been nominated to be in *Who's Who in Canadian Musicians.*"

"Yeah, that's neat. My Uncle Elmer got into *Who's Who in Canadian Veterinarians.* He sure has an interesting job. One time I went along when he was treating a cow and you'll never believe what happened next...."

To avoid this kind of one-sided conversation, delay your verbal responses. This does not mean that you remain totally silent while listening. It means that you wait for an *appropriate* moment to respond.

Watch your nonverbal responses, too. A look of "Who cares!" from you can deter the other person from finishing his message.

Feed back meaning

Sometimes you can help the speaker clarify his message by paraphrasing it. This does not mean parroting what another person says. Instead, briefly summarize. Feed back what you see as the essence of that person's message: "Let me see if I understood what you said..." or "What I'm hearing you say is. . . ." (Psychotherapist Carl Rogers [1961] referred to this technique as **reflection**.) Often, the other person will say, "No, that's not what I meant. What I said was. . . ."

There will be no doubt when you get it right. The sender will say, "Yeah, that's it," and either continue with another message or stop sending when he knows you understand.

When you give feedback, be concise. This is not a time to stop the other person by talking on and on about what you think you heard.

Be aware of nonverbal messages and behaviour

You might observe that the speaker's body language seems to be the exact opposite of his words; for example, "I noticed you said you are excited, but you look bored."

Nonverbal behaviour can have different meanings, depending on the listener's cultural background. Someone who looks bored might simply be listening in a different way.

Listen for requests and intentions

An effective way to listen to complaints is to look for the request hidden in them.

"This class is a waste of my time" can be heard as "Please tell me what I'll gain if I participate actively in class." "The instructor talks too fast" might be asking "What strategies can I use to take notes when the instructor covers material rapidly?" We can even transform complaints into intentions. Take this complaint:

"The parking lot by the residences is so dark at night that I'm afraid to go to my car." This complaint can result in having a light installed in the parking lot.

Viewing complaints as requests gives us more choices. Rather than responding with defensiveness ("What does he know anyway?"), resignation ("It's always been this way and always will be"), or indifference ("It's not my job"), we can decide whether to grant the request (do what will alleviate the other's difficulty) or help the person translate his own complaint into an action plan.

Allow emotion

In the presence of full listening, some people will share things that they feel deeply about. They might even shed a few tears. If you feel uncomfortable when this happens, see if you can accept the discomfort for a little while longer. Emotional release can bring relief and trigger unexpected insights. Try to put yourself in the other person's shoes so you can feel what they are feeling. It's not easy to do but it is helpful to the person talking.

Ask for more

Full listening with unconditional acceptance is a rare gift. Many people have never experienced it. They are used to being greeted with resistance, so they habitually stop short of saying what they truly think and feel. Help them shed this habit by routinely asking, "Is there anything more you want to say about that?" This question sends the speaker a message that you truly value what she has to say.

Summarize what you have heard

At the end of every conversation summarize what you have heard. If you have made obligations about what you will do in the future, this summary will help to clarify responsibilities. For other interactions a summary statement will make individuals feel deeply heard. It conveys the feeling *you matter to me and what you say is worthwhile for me to hear.*

Take care of yourself

People seek good listeners, and there are times when you don't want to listen. You might be distracted with your own concerns. Be honest. Don't pretend to listen. You can say, "What you're telling me is important, and I'm pressed for time right now. Can we set aside another time to talk about this?" It's okay *not* to listen.

Stay open to the adventure of listening

Be willing to make the effort

To the untrained eye, listening looks passive: *I'm just going to listen while you talk.*

If you want to listen well, then experiment with the opposite idea. Think of listening as an active affair. See listening as something you can do. This alone can transform your experience of listening.

Avoid blocks to listening

There are several blocks to effective listening. Try to avoid these traps:

- *Rehearsing:* Rather than really listening, you spend your time rehearsing what you are going to say when the other person stops talking.

- *Mindreading:* You mistrust the person speaking, so you spend your time trying to decipher what they are saying and feeling rather than trusting their intentions.

- *Daydreaming:* You can't be bothered to listen to someone else so you go off in your own reveries rather than focussing on what is being said.

- *Identifying:* You refer everything the other person says back to your own experiences. If they tell you about feeling poorly because of having a cold, you think and talk about your own experiences with a cold.

- *Comparing:* You spend your time in conversation comparing yourself to the other person rather than listening—you focus on whether they are smarter, stronger, or better looking than you.

- *Filtering:* You listen only for information that is pertinent to you and forget about the rest.

- *Derailing:* You change the subject when you are uncomfortable or bored with the subject.

- *Placating:* You agree quickly to what the other person has said without allowing him to speak further, so you can move on to other topics.

- *Judging:* You spend your time evaluating what the other person is saying and dismissing things you disagree with.

- *Advising:* You offer advice without being asked and are very directive about what people should do; remember unsolicited advice may come across as condescending or even insulting.

Be willing to change

Receiving what another person has to say is an act of courage. Listening fully—truly opening yourself to the way another person sees the world—means taking risks. Your opinions may be challenged. You may be less certain or less comfortable than you were before.

Experience the rewards

Along with the risks of listening come the benefits. Listening in an unguarded way can take your relationships to a new depth and level of honesty. Deep listening can open up new possibilities for thinking, feeling, and behaving. And when you practise deep listening, other people are more likely to receive when it's your turn to send.

Using a different topic, try repeating Practising Critical Thinking 8-1 about sending and receiving, but this time face your partner, sitting a comfortable distance apart. You still should not interrupt your partner when she is speaking; but this time, try to ensure that you use your nonverbal listening skills. How does communication change when you use nonverbal cues like sending acknowledgments? How did the conversation feel this time? Was it any easier to summarize the information or to talk? Were you able to avoid the blocks to effective listening? To find out more about your listening skills, do the quiz at *www.mindtools.com/pages/article/listening-quiz.htm.* ✳

Choosing to **SPEAK**

YOU HAVE BEEN talking with people for most of your life, and you usually manage to get your messages across. There are times, though, when you don't. Often, these times are emotionally charged.

We all have this problem. Sometimes we feel wonderful or rotten or sad or scared, and we want to express it. Emotions can get in the way of the message. And although we can send almost any message by tears or laughter, usually words are better. Begin with a sincere intention to reach common ground with your listener. Then experiment with the suggestions below.

Replace "You" messages with "I" messages

It can be difficult to disagree with someone without him becoming angry or you becoming upset. When conflict occurs, we often make statements about the other person, or "You" messages:

"You make me mad."

"You must be crazy."

"You don't love me anymore."

This kind of communication results in defensiveness. He may respond like this:

"I don't care."

"No, *you* are crazy."

"No, *you* don't love *me!*"

"You" messages are hard to listen to. They suggest blame and demand rebuttal. Even praise starting with "You" can sometimes be ineffective. "You" messages just don't work.

When communication is emotionally charged, psychologist Thomas Gordon (1975) suggests that you consider limiting your statements to descriptions about yourself. Replace "You" messages with **"I" messages**.

"You make me mad" could be "I feel angry."

"You must be crazy" can be "I don't understand."

"You don't love me anymore" could become "I'm afraid we're drifting apart."

Suppose a friend asks you to pick her up at the airport. You drive 30 kilometres and wait for the plane. No friend. You decide your friend missed her plane, so you wait three hours for the next flight. No friend. Perplexed and worried, you drive home. The next day, you see your friend downtown.

"What happened?" you ask.

"Oh, I caught an earlier flight."

"You are a rude person," you reply.

Look for the facts, the observable behaviour. Everyone will agree that your friend asked you to pick her up, that she did take an earlier flight, and that you did not receive a call from her. But the idea that she is rude is not a fact—it's a judgment.

Your friend might go on to say this:

"I called your home and no one answered. My mom had a stroke and was rushed to Valley View Hospital. I caught the earliest flight I could get."

Your judgment no longer fits.

An "I" message can include any or all of the following five elements. Be careful when including the last two, since they can contain hidden judgments or threats.

Observations   Describe the facts—the indisputable, observable realities. Talk about what you—or anyone else—can see, hear, smell, taste, or touch. Avoid judgments, interpretations, or opinions. Instead of saying, "You're a slob," say, "The pan from last night's lasagna was still on the stove this morning."

Feelings   Describe your own feelings. It is easier to listen to "I feel frustrated" than to "You never help me." Stating how you feel about another's actions can be valuable feedback for that person.

Wants   You are far more likely to get what you want if you *say* what you want. If someone doesn't know what you want, he doesn't have a chance to help you get it. Ask clearly. Avoid demanding or using the word *need*. Most people like to feel helpful, not obligated. Instead of saying, "Do the dishes when it's your turn, or else!" say, "I want to divide the housework fairly."

Thoughts   Communicate your thoughts, and use caution. Beginning your statement with the word "I" doesn't make it an "I" message. "I think you are a slob" is a "You" judgment in disguise. Instead, say, "I'd have more time to study if I didn't have to clean up so often."

Intentions   The last part of an "I" message is a statement about what you intend to do. Have a plan that doesn't depend on the other person. For example, instead of "From now on we're going to split the dishwashing evenly," you could say, "I intend to do my share of the housework and leave the rest."

When you saw your friend, you might have said, "I waited and waited at the airport. I was worried about you. I didn't get a call. I feel angry and hurt. I don't want to waste my time. Next time, you can call me when your flight arrives, and I'll be happy to pick you up."

"I" messages don't judge. They don't invite the other person to counterattack with more of the same. "I" messages are also more accurate. They report our own thoughts and feelings.

At first, "I" messages might feel uncomfortable or seem forced. That's okay. With practice they will get easier.

Finally, repeat Practising Critical Thinking 8-1 again with a different topic. Again, sit facing your partner and continue to use nonverbal listening skills when your partner is talking. This time, when you summarize what the sender says, use "I" messages. Afterwards think about how including "I" messages changed the exchange between the two of you. When did you feel most listened to? Reflect on this exercise the next time you begin to debate a student in class. How could you make those exchanges more productive?

Remember that questions are not always questions

You've heard these "questions" before. A parent asks, "Don't you want to look nice?" Translation: "I wish you'd get a haircut, lose the blue jeans, and put on a tie."

We use questions that aren't questions to sneak our opinions and requests into conversations. "Doesn't it upset you?" means "It upsets me," and "Shouldn't we hang the picture over here?" means "I want to hang the picture over here."

Communication improves when we say, "I'm upset" and "Let's hang the picture over here."

Choose nonverbal messages

How you say something can be more important than what you say. Your tone of voice and gestures add up to a silent message. This message can support, modify, or contradict your words. Your posture, the way you dress, how often you shower, and even the poster hanging on your wall can negate your words before you say them.

Most nonverbal behaviour is unconscious. We can learn to be aware of it and choose our nonverbal messages. The key is to be clear about our intention and purpose. When we know what we want to say and are committed to getting it across, our inflections, gestures, and words work together and send a unified message.

Notice barriers to sending messages

Sometimes fear stops us from sending messages. We are afraid of other people's reactions, sometimes justifiably. Being truthful doesn't mean being insensitive to the impact that our messages have on others. Tact is a virtue; letting fear prevent communication is not.

Assumptions can also be used as excuses for not sending messages. "She already knows this," we tell ourselves.

Predictions of failure can be barriers to sending, too. "She won't listen," we assure ourselves. That statement might be inaccurate. Perhaps the other person senses that we're angry and listens in a guarded way. Or perhaps she is listening and sending nonverbal messages we don't understand.

It's easy to make excuses for not communicating. If you have a fear or some other concern about sending a message, be aware of it. Don't expect the concern to go away. Realize that you can communicate even with your concerns. You can choose to make them a part of the message: "I am going to tell you how I feel, and I'm afraid that you will think it's stupid."

Talking to someone when you don't want to could be a matter of educational survival. A short talk with an adviser, a teacher, a friend, or a family member might solve a problem that could jeopardize your education.

Speak candidly

When we brood on negative thoughts and refuse to speak them out loud, we lose perspective. And when we keep joys to ourselves, we diminish our satisfaction. A solution is to share regularly what we think and feel. Psychotherapist Sidney Jourard (1971) referred to such openness and honesty as *transparency* and wrote eloquently about how it can heal and deepen relationships.

Sometimes candid speaking can save a life. For example, if you think a friend is addicted to drugs, telling her so in a supportive, non-judgmental way is a sign of friendship.

This suggestion comes with a couple of caveats. First, there is a big difference between speaking candidly about your problems and complaining about them.

Complainers usually don't seek solutions. They just want everyone to know how unhappy they are. Instead, talk about problems as a way to start searching for solutions.

Second, avoid bragging. Other people are turned off by constant references to how much money you have, how great your partner is, or how much status your family enjoys. There is a difference between sharing excitement and being obnoxious.

Speak up!

Look for opportunities to practise speaking strategies. Join class discussions or clubs on campus that focus on speaking, like "Toastmasters." Start conversations about topics that excite you. Ask for information and clarification. Ask for feedback on your skills.

Also speak up when you want support. Consider creating a team of people who help one another succeed. Such a team can develop naturally from a study group that works well. Ask members if they would be willing to accept and receive support in achieving a wide range of academic and personal goals. Meet regularly to do goal-setting exercises from this book and brainstorm success strategies.

After you have a clear statement of your goals and a plan for achieving them, let family members and friends know. This can be a good way to keep motivated and it provides an understanding for when you may not be available to them. When appropriate, let them know how they can help. You may be surprised at how often people respond to a genuine request for support. ✳

practising
CRITICAL THINKING

8-2

Write an "I" message

First, pick something about school that irritates you. Then pretend that you are talking to a person who is associated with this irritation. In the space below, write down what you would say to this person as a "you" message.

_____

_____

_____

_____

Now write the same complaint as an "I" message. Include all of the elements suggested in "Five Ways to Say 'I.'"

_____

_____

_____

_____

_____

_____

Discovery/Intention Statement

Discover Communication Styles

The concept of *communication styles* can be useful when you want to discover sources of conflict with another person—or when you're in a conversation with someone from a different culture.

Consider the many ways in which people express themselves verbally. These characteristics can reflect an individual's preferred communication style:

- Extroversion—talking to others as a way to explore possibilities for taking action.

- Introversion—thinking through possibilities alone before talking to others.

- Dialogue—engaging in a discussion to hear many points of view before coming to a conclusion or decision.

- Debate—arguing for a particular point of view from the outset of a discussion.

- Openness—being ready to express personal thoughts and feelings early in a relationship.

- Reserve—holding back on self-expression until a deeper friendship develops.

- A faster pace of conversation—allowing people to speak quickly and forcefully while filling any gaps in conversation.

- A slower pace of conversation—allowing people to speak slowly and quietly while taking time to formulate their thoughts.

These are just a few examples of differences in communication styles. You might be able to think of others.

The point is that people with different communication styles can make negative assumptions about each other. For example, those who prefer fast-paced conversations might assume that people who talk slowly are indecisive. And people who prefer slower-paced conversations might assume that people who talk quickly are pushy and uninterested in anyone else's opinion.

Take this opportunity to think about your preferred communication styles and assumptions. Do they enhance or block your relationships with other people? Think back over the conversations you've had during the past week. Then complete the following sentences, using additional space as needed.

I discovered that I prefer conversations that allow me to . . .

_____

_____

_____

_____

_____

I discovered that I usually feel uncomfortable in conversations when other people . . .

_____

_____

_____

_____

_____

When people do the things listed in Item 2, I tend to make certain assumptions, such as . . .

_____

_____

_____

_____

_____

As an alternative to making the assumptions listed in Item 3, I intend to . . .

_____

_____

_____

_____

_____

Developing
EMOTIONAL INTELLIGENCE

In his book *Working with Emotional Intelligence*, Daniel Goleman (1995) defines emotional intelligence as a cluster of traits:

- *Self-awareness*—recognizing your full range of emotions and knowing your strengths and limitations.

- *Self-regulation*—responding skillfully to strong emotions, practising honesty and integrity, and staying open to new ideas.

- *Motivation*—persisting to achieve goals and meet standards of excellence.

- *Empathy*—sensing other people's emotions and taking an active interest in their concerns.

- *Skill in relationships*—listening fully, speaking persuasively, resolving conflict, and leading people through times of change.

Goleman concludes that "IQ washes out when it comes to predicting who, among a talented pool of candidates *within* an intellectually demanding profession will become the strongest leader" (pp. xiv-xv). At that point, **emotional intelligence** starts to become more important. In fact, recent research suggests that long-term career success is more determined by self-awareness, a key element of emotional intelligence, than by who you know (e.g., networking skills) and what you know (education or job skills; Williams, 2014).

If you're emotionally intelligent, you're probably described as someone with good "people skills." You're aware of your feelings. You act in thoughtful ways, show concern for others, resolve conflict, and make responsible decisions. Your emotional intelligence skills will serve you in school and in the workplace, especially when you collaborate on projects. Although much of our emotional intelligence is developed from our childhood experiences, it can be improved with effort and with assistance from others (Williams, 2014). You can deepen these skills with the following strategies.

Recognize three elements of emotion

Even the strongest emotion consists of just three elements: physical sensations, thoughts, and action. Usually

Hlib Marderosiants/Shutterstock.com

they happen so fast that you can barely distinguish them. Separating them out is a first step toward emotional intelligence.

Imagine that you suddenly perceive a threat—such as a supervisor who's screaming at you. Immediately your heart starts beating in double time and your stomach muscles clench (physical sensations). Then thoughts race through your head: *This is a disaster. She hates me. And everyone's watching.* Finally, you take action, which could mean staring at her, yelling back, or running away.

Name your emotions

Naming your emotions is a First Step to going beyond the "fight or flight" reaction to any emotion. The second that you attach a word to an emotion, you start to gain perspective. People with emotional intelligence have a rich vocabulary to describe a wide range of emotions. For example, do an Internet search with the key words *feeling list*. Read through the lists you find for examples of ways that you can name your feelings in the future.

Accept your emotions

Another step toward emotional intelligence is accepting your emotions—*all* of them. This can be challenging if you've been taught that some emotions are "good" while others are "bad." Be careful not to judge or edit how you feel but simply pay attention to the emotions and live with them for a little while. Emotions are complicated. They have many causes that are beyond your control, including what *other* people do. Because you do not choose your emotional reactions from moment to moment, you cannot be held morally responsible for them. However, you can be held responsible for what you *do* in response to any emotion. Learning how to reflect on your feelings is an important step in developing emotional intelligence.

Express your emotions

One possible response to any emotion is expressing it. The key is to speak without blaming others for the way you feel. The basic tool for doing so is using "I" messages.

Respond rather than react

The heart of emotional intelligence is moving from mindless reactions to mindful actions. See if you can introduce an intentional gap between sensations and thoughts on the one hand and your next action on the other hand. To do this more often, try these strategies:

- *Check in with your moods several times each day.* On a pad of paper, note the time of day and your emotional state at that point. Rate your mood on a scale of 1 (relaxed and positive) to 10 (very angry, very sad, or very afraid).
- *Write Discovery Statements.* In your journal, write about situations in daily life that trigger strong emotions. Describe these events—and your usual responses to them—in detail.
- *Write Intention Statements.* After seeing patterns in your emotions, you can consciously choose to behave in new ways. Instead of yelling back at the angry supervisor, for example, make it your intention to simply remain silent and breathe deeply until she finishes. Then say, "I'll wait to respond until we've both had a chance to cool down."

Make decisions with emotional intelligence

When considering a possible choice, ask yourself, "How am I likely to feel if I do this?" You can use "gut feelings" to tell when an action might violate your values or hurt someone. Think of emotions as energy. Anger, sadness, and fear send currents of sensation through your whole body. Ask yourself how you can channel that energy into constructive action. To find out more about your emotional intelligence you can complete a quiz by going to *www.extension .harvard.edu/professional-development/blog/assessing-your-emotional-intelligence-4-tools-we-love* or see also *www.mindtools.com/pages/article/ei-quiz.htm.* ✳

---

journal entry   8-3

Discovery/Intention Statement

Become More Self-Aware

Becoming self-aware requires you to self-reflect, and take time to get to know yourself. Think about what your top three strengths are and write them down. What are your values, and how do they influence your behaviour?

I discovered that. . . .

_____

_____

_____

_____

_____

Now think for a moment about what your weaknesses are and write them down three of them. What triggers, in terms of situations or people's behaviours, are most likely to make you uncomfortable? Choose a suggestion from this chapter, and describe how you will use it to learn about yourself so that you can take more control of those uncomfortable situations.

I intend to . . .

_____

_____

_____

_____

_____

_____

Managing
CONFLICT

Andrey_Popov/Shutterstock.com

CONFLICT IS NATURAL and happens in all our relationships. Conflict management is one of the most practical skills you'll ever learn. Here are strategies that can help.

The first five strategies below are about dealing with the *content* of a conflict—defining the problem, exploring viewpoints, and discovering solutions. The remaining strategies are about finding a *process* for resolving any conflict, no matter what the content.

To bring these strategies to life, think of ways to use them in managing a conflict that you face right now.

Focus on content

Back up to common ground
Conflict heightens the differences between people. When this happens, it's easy to forget how much we still agree with each other.

As a first step in managing conflict, back up to common ground. List all of the points on which you are *not* in conflict: "I know that we disagree about how much to spend on a new car, but we do agree that the old one needs to be replaced." Often, such comments put the problem in perspective and pave the way for a solution.

State the problem
Using "I" messages, as explained earlier in this chapter, state the problem. Tell people what you observe, feel, think, want, and intend to do. Allow the other people in a particular conflict to do the same.

Each person might have a different perception of the problem. That's fine. Let the conflict come into clear focus. It's hard to fix something unless people agree on what's broken.

Remember that the way you state the problem largely determines the solution. For example, "I need a new roommate" is a problem statement that dictates one solution. "We could use some agreements about who cleans the apartment" opens up more options, such as resolving a conflict about who will wash the dishes tonight.

State all points of view
If you want to defuse tension or defensiveness, set aside your opinions for a moment. Take the time to understand the other points of view. Sum up those viewpoints in words that the other parties can accept. When people feel that they've been heard, they're often more willing to listen.

Ask for complete communication
In times of conflict, we often say one thing and mean another. So before responding to what the other person says, use active listening. Check to see if you have correctly received that person's message by saying, "What I'm hearing you say is. . . . Did I get it correctly?"

Focus on solutions
After stating the problem, dream up as many solutions as you can. Don't hold back. Quantity—not quality—is the key. If you get stuck, restate the problem and continue brainstorming.

Next, evaluate the solutions you brainstormed. Discard the unacceptable ones. Talk about which solutions will work and how difficult they will be to implement. You might hit upon a totally new solution.

Choose one solution that is most acceptable to everyone involved, and implement it. Agree on who is going to do what by when. Then keep your agreements.

Finally, evaluate the effectiveness of your solution. If it works, great. If not, make changes or implement a new solution.

Focus on the future
Instead of rehashing the past, talk about new possibilities. Think about what you can do to prevent problems

in the future. State how you intend to change and ask others for their contributions to the solution.

Focus on process

Commit to the relationship

The thorniest conflicts usually arise between people who genuinely care for each other. Begin by affirming your commitment to the other person: "I care about you, and I want this relationship to last. So, I'm willing to do whatever it takes to resolve this problem." Also ask the other person for a similar commitment.

Allow strong feelings

Permitting conflict can also mean permitting emotion. Being upset is all right. Feeling angry is often appropriate. Crying is okay. Allowing other people to see the strength of our feelings can help resolve the conflict. This suggestion can be especially useful during times when differences are so extreme that reaching common ground seems possible.

Expressing the full range of your feelings can transform the conflict. Often what's on the far side of anger is love. When you express and release resentment, you might discover genuine compassion in its place.

Notice your need to be "right"

Some people approach conflict as a situation where only one person wins. That person has the "right" point of view. Everyone else loses.

When this happens, step back. See if you can approach the situation in a neutral way. Define the conflict as a problem to be solved, not as a contest to be won. Explore the possibility that you might be mistaken. There might be more than one acceptable solution. Let go of being "right," and aim for being effective at resolving conflict instead.

Sometimes this means apologizing. Conflict sometimes arises from our own errors. Others might move quickly to end the conflict when we acknowledge this fact and ask for forgiveness.

Be aware of triggers

Sometimes there are topics or behaviours that will trigger conflict in your relationships. Take a minute to analyze what you are really upset about. Is there something you are not getting that you want? Is there something you are scared of losing? Is your response to the conflict appropriate or exaggerated? Getting the answers to these questions may help you see the conflict in a whole new perspective.

Slow down the communication

In times of great conflict, people often talk all at once. Chances for resolving the conflict in this situation take a nosedive.

When everyone is talking at once, choose either to listen or to talk—not both at the same time. Just send your message. Or just receive the other person's message. Usually, this technique slows down the pace and allows everyone to become more level-headed.

To slow down the communication even more, take a break. Depending on the level of conflict, this might mean anything from a few minutes to a few days.

Communicate in writing

What can be difficult to say to another person face to face might be effectively communicated in writing. When people in conflict write letters or emails to each other, they automatically apply many of the suggestions in this article, such as slowing down the communication.

There is a drawback to this tactic, though: It's possible for people to misunderstand what you say in a letter, in an email, and especially in texts. To avoid further problems, make clear what you are *not* saying: "I am saying that I want to be alone for a few days. I am *not* saying that I want you to stay away forever." (Saying what you are *not* saying is often useful in face-to-face communication as well.)

Before you send your letter or email, put yourself in the shoes of the person who will receive it. Imagine how your comments could be misinterpreted, remembering that what you say will be permanently out there and can't be unsaid. Then rewrite your note, correcting any wording that might be open to misinterpretation. Another good strategy is to wait for your emotions to cool off before sending the email or letter.

On social media sites, be careful about "flaming"—sending incendiary comments that escalate the conflict rather than ease tensions. Model calming behaviour in your comments instead.

Maintain confidentiality

Deal directly with the person with whom you are in conflict. There is a tendency when we are upset to bring other people into the discussion. Venting to others will only complicate the issue and intensify the conflict. Even if the conflict happens in a public forum, such as on a social media site, try to deal with the person individually rather than drawing others into the issue.

Get an objective viewpoint

One way to get an objective viewpoint is to use a mediator—an objective, unbiased third party. Even an untrained mediator—as long as it's someone who is not a party to the conflict—can do much to decrease tension. The mediator's role is not to give advice but to keep the discussion on track and moving toward a solution.

Allow for cultural differences

People respond to conflict in different ways, depending on their cultural background. Some stand close, speak loudly, and make direct eye contact. Other people avert their eyes, mute their voices, and increase physical distance.

When it seems to you that other people are side-stepping or escalating a conflict, consider whether your reaction is based on cultural bias.

Agree to disagree

Sometimes we say all we have to say on an issue. We do all of the problem-solving we can do. We get all points of view across. And the conflict still remains, staring us right in the face.

Honest disagreements are a fact of life. We can peacefully coexist with other people—and respect them—even though we don't agree on fundamental issues. Conflict can be accepted even when it is not resolved.

See the conflict within you

Sometimes the turmoil we see in the outside world has its source in our own inner world.

When we're angry or upset, we can take a minute to look inside. Perhaps we are ready to take offense—waiting to pounce on something the other person said. Perhaps, without realizing it, we did something to create the conflict. Or maybe the other person is simply saying what we don't want to admit is true. A simple spot-check might help the conflict disappear right before our eyes. ✳

---

journal entry 8-4

Discovery/Intention Statement

Re-Create a Relationship

Think about one of your relationships for a few minutes. It can involve a parent, sibling, spouse, child, friend, hairdresser, or anyone else. In the space below, write down some things that are not working in the relationship. What bugs you? What do you find irritating or unsatisfying?

I discovered that . . .

_____

_____

_____

_____

_____

_____

_____

_____

_____

_____

_____

Now think for a moment about what you want from this relationship. More attention? Less nagging? More openness, trust, financial security, or freedom? Choose a suggestion from this chapter, and describe how you could use it to make the relationship work.

I intend to . . .

_____

_____

_____

_____

_____

_____

_____

_____

_____

_____

_____

_____

_____

Resolve conflicts with roommates

People who live together share a delicate bond. Relationships with even the best friends or closest relatives can quickly deteriorate over disagreements about who pays the bills or washes the dishes. Communication is the key to having a successful roommate relationship.

Your goal is to create harmony in your home so consider, for instance, adopting a policy about borrowing items. Lending your roommate a book or a tennis racket might seem like a small thing. Yet these small loans can become a sore point in a relationship if things get damaged. Some people have difficulty saying no and resent lending things. If so, keep borrowing to a minimum. Also, discuss some ground rules around respecting boundaries, such as playing loud music after one of your roommates has gone to bed.

If you are living off campus, you can prevent conflicts with roommates by negotiating written agreements. Check to see if you have an off-campus housing office at your school. If you do, chances are that on their website you will find a template for a roommate agreement.

Meet with your roommates to discuss the following:

- What will each of you pay for rent? Do roommates with smaller rooms pay less? Does the money get paid directly to the landlord by each of you or will one of you be responsible for delivering the total rent payment?

- What will you do about sharing belongings such as computers, audio and video equipment, food, or clothing?

Iakov Filimonov/Shutterstock.com

- How will you divide household chores? Who is responsible for keeping common areas clean?

- How will you create a study environment at home?

- Will you have quiet hours around exam times?

- How will you split household costs and make sure that bills get paid on time?

- How will you resolve conflicts when either of you thinks the other is not keeping the agreements?

Expand this list to include other issues that matter to you. Again, for maximum clarity, put your agreements in writing. Recognize that conflict is bound to happen from time to time and be prepared to negotiate a solution that works for everyone.

Five ways to say **NO...** gracefully

All your study plans can go down the drain when a friend says, "Time to party!" Sometimes, succeeding in school means replying with a graceful and firm *no*.

Students in higher education tend to have many commitments. Saying no helps you to prevent an overloaded schedule that compromises your health and grade point average. You can use these strategies to say no in a respectful way—gracefully.

1 Think critically about your assumptions. An inability to say no can spring from the assumption that you'll lose friends if you state what you really want. But consider this: If you cannot say no, then you are not in charge of your time. You've given that right to whoever wants to interrupt you. This is not a friendship based on equality. True friends will respect your wishes.

2 Plan your refusal. You might find it easier to say no when you don't have to grasp for words. Choose some key words and phrases in advance—for example, "I'd love to, but not today"; "Thanks for asking, but I have a huge test tomorrow and want to study"; or "I'd prefer not to do anything tonight; do you want to grab lunch tomorrow instead?"

When you refuse, align your verbal and nonverbal messages. Reinforce your words with a firm voice and a posture that communicates confidence.

3 Avoid apologies or qualifiers. People give away their power when they couch their *no*s in phrases such as "I'm sorry, but I just don't know if I want to" or "Would you get upset if I said no?"

You don't have to apologize for being in charge of your life. It's all right to say no.

ESB Professional/Shutterstock.com

4 Wait for the request. People who worry about saying no often give in to a request before it's actually been made. Wait until you hear a question. "Time to party!" is not a question. Nor is it a call to action. Save your response until you hear a specific request, such as "Would you go to a party with me?"

5 Remember that one *no* leads to another *yes*. *Yes* and *no* are complementary, not contradictory. Saying no to one activity allows you to say yes to something that's more important right now. Saying no to a movie allows you to say yes to outlining a paper or reading a textbook chapter. You can say an unqualified yes to the next social activity—and enjoy it more—after you've completed some key tasks on your to-do list. ✳

practising
CRITICAL THINKING

8-3

VIPs (very important persons)

Step 1
Under the column below titled "Name," write the names of at least seven people who have positively influenced your life. They might be relatives, friends, teachers, or perhaps persons you have never met. (Complete each step before moving on.)

Step 2
In the next column, rate your gratitude for this person's influence (from 1 to 5, with 1 being a little grateful and 5 being extremely grateful).

Step 3
In the third column, rate how fully you have communicated your appreciation to this person (again, 1 to 5, with 1 being not communicated and 5 being fully communicated).

Step 4
In the final column, put a "U" to indicate the persons with whom you have unfinished business (e.g., an important communication that you have not yet sent).

Name	Grateful (1–5)	Communicated (1–5)	U
1.			
2.			
3.			
4.			
5.			
6.			
7.			

Step 5
Now select two persons with "U's" beside their names and write each of them a letter. Express the love, appreciation, and joy you feel toward them. Tell them exactly how they have helped change your life and how glad you are that they did.

Step 6
You also have an impact on others. Write below the names of people whose lives you have influenced. Consider sharing with these people why you enjoy being a part of their lives.

_____

_____

_____

_____

_____

_____

Five steps to effective
COMPLAINTS

© woodsy/Shutterstock

SOMETIMES relationship-building involves making a complaint. Whining, blaming, pouting, kicking, and spitting usually don't get results. Here are five guidelines for complaining effectively.

1 Go to the source. Start with the person who is most directly involved with the problem. When you are in school that person is usually an instructor. Give this person the first chance to resolve an issue. Instructors usually appreciate feedback, and they can't read your mind to know when a problem occurs.

2 Present the facts without blaming anyone. Your complaint will carry more weight if you document the facts. Keep track of names and dates. Note what actions were promised and what results actually occurred.

3 Learn about other options. Schools have policies and procedures related to student complaints. Look for them in your school's catalogue and website.

At many schools you can talk to a student or staff ombudsperson—someone who is trained to help resolve conflicts between students and instructors. Those individuals are good resources for academic policies related to grade appeals and can give you good advice on how best to approach your instructor.

4 Ask for commitments. When you find someone who is willing to solve your problem, get him to say exactly what he is going to do and when.

5 Don't give up. Assume that others are on your team. Many people are out there to help you. State what you intend to do and ask for their partnership. ✳

Criticism really can be constructive

Although receiving criticism is rarely fun, it is often educational. Here are some ways to get the most value from it.

Avoid finding fault. When your mind is occupied with finding fault in others, you aren't open to hearing constructive comments about yourself.

Take criticism seriously. Some people laugh or joke in order to cover up their anger or embarrassment at being criticized. A humorous reaction on your part can be mistaken for a lack of concern.

React to criticism with acceptance. People often give feedback using the sandwich method—saying something nice (the bun), then areas for improvement (the meat), and then some praise again (more bun). Pay attention to all three parts. Sometimes people ignore the critical comments in the middle thinking two out of three positive comments is pretty good. Listen to critical comments openly—the meat is where your true learning will occur. But keep criticism in perspective. Avoid blowing the criticism out of proportion. The purpose of criticism is to provide you with feedback and to generate positive change.

Listen without defensiveness. You can't hear the criticism if you're busy framing your rebuttal.

COLLABORATING FOR SUCCESS:
Communicating in teams

Your experience in higher education will include group projects. These projects can be fun and rewarding. They can also fall flat and lead to frustration. To avoid the pitfalls that take teams down, develop some specific skills in communication.

Start with an attitude check

Students come to group projects with a wide range of attitudes. Some people dread working with a team. They get good grades on their own and prefer to study alone. When forced to join a group, they fear getting paired with a dominating leader, or a slacker who does no work and still gets credit. Those things can happen; however, group projects are here to stay. In the workplace, collaboration is the norm. Taking a project from a hazy idea to finished product requires the work of people with a variety of specialties and skills. Employers are looking for team players, not solo stars. If you can communicate well in groups, you're more likely to get the job you want and enjoy what you do.

There's a word that describes effective group work: synergy. Master students know about synergy firsthand. Groups of them experience it when they create results that none of them could achieve by working alone.

Define the team's purpose

To promote effective results, define your team's purpose, its expected results such as a presentation or paper, and describe how each member will be held accountable.

Effective team work requires you to implement many of the strategies described in Chapter 6, "Tests," when we talked about study groups. This includes having a planning meeting where you introduce yourself and exchange contact information. At that meeting you should spend time discussing what the results of the group work will look like. To define specific results ask yourselves four questions:

1. Why is this project being done?

2. What would a successful outcome for this project look like?

3. How are we going to create a bridge from our current reality to that successful outcome?

4. What if we truly made this outcome a high priority? What is the very next action that each of us would take to make it happen?

Once you define your outcome, get feedback from your instructor before you proceed.

At your meeting you should also decide how frequently the team will meet and set an agenda for the next meeting. You can use apps like *Doodle* to help you set meeting times.

Share roles

Similar to working in study groups, effective teams give everyone a role and rotate those roles from meeting to meeting. Typical roles include the *timer*, who keeps track of the clock to ensure that you are staying on schedule with your meeting agenda; the *leader*, who monitors the group's overall progress; and the *recorder*, who takes notes during meeting. Other roles, such as *technology specialist*, may be needed depending on the nature of the project. Giving everybody a chance to adopt a new role at different meetings will help broaden their skill set and discourage social loafing. Plan tasks and timelines.

Once your outcome and roles are clearly defined, create a step-by-step plan to actually get the work done. Answer these questions: *In order to produce our outcome, what's the very next action we need to take? What actions will follow that one? Who will take each action? By when?* One handy way to record the results of this discussion is to create a four-column chart:

Action	Assigned to	Due Date	Done

List your planned actions in order, along with a due date and person responsible for each one. When an action is completed, your group leader can check it off in the "Done" column.

Distribute a draft of this chart to your team and revise it until everyone agrees to it. Show the completed chart to your instructor or teaching assistant as well, and ask for feedback.

You can also use project management apps like *Trello* or *Basecamp* to keep you organized. These apps allow you to edit and store files in a common folder, keep a common calendar, share messages through text, voice, or email, share a common chat room, host Web meetings, or poll members in real time. Many of these apps let you send reminders to keep everyone on track.

Other tools like Google *Drive* or Microsoft's *OneDrive* provide online space where group members can work collaboratively on the project. One of the advantages of Google *Drive* is that all previous revisions of the document are available on the Web, so if you don't like an edit that was done you can always revert to a previous version.

A word to the wise about due dates: These are tricky. Students who are new to group work often underestimate the time they'll need to complete tasks. To prevent last-minute stress, start working on your project as soon as it's assigned. Also, plan to complete your group project several days before the assigned due date. This leaves your group with a cushion of extra time to deal with surprises and delays.

Ideas are tools

According to LaFasto and Larson (2002), authors of *When Teams Work Best*, the most common barrier to effective teamwork is an atmosphere of defensiveness.

Teams tend to fizzle when they create new ideas that team members greet with immediate skepticism or outright rejection: *This suggestion will never work. . . . That's just not the way we do things around here. . . . We can't break with tradition. . . .* These responses are examples of "groupthink," which happens when a team automatically rules out new ideas simply because they're . . . well, new.

Instead of automatically looking for what's wrong with a suggested idea, suggest that the team look for potential applications for that idea. Even a proposal that seems outlandish at first might become workable with a few modifications. In an empowered team, all ideas are welcome, problems are freely admitted, and any item is open for discussion.

Deal with challenges

Groups take time to gel. Don't expect yours to function perfectly right away. If conflicts develop between group members, view them as opportunities to develop your communication skills. The following suggestions will help.

Get the most from meeting time

Nothing drains energy from a group more than meetings that crop up at the last minute and waste everyone's time. If you're leading the group, be sure to give plenty of notice before meetings, and write up an agenda for each one. Keep it to three items, tops. To focus everyone's thinking, state each agenda item as a question to answer. Instead of listing "project schedule," for example, write, "When is a realistic time for our next meeting?"

Honing your leadership skills

You might be one of those students who complains every time they hear they have to do a group project, whether it is an essay or a group presentation. Instead, next time you have a group project, look at it as an opportunity to practise your best communication skills and, more importantly, to develop your own leadership skills. Keep in mind that in the workplace you will frequently be working in teams and, therefore, any leadership skills you develop as a student will be highly valued in the future. What are those skills? Kouzes and Posner (Marshall, 2009) suggest the five practices of good leaders:

1. Challenge the process—see new ways of acting in the world
2. Inspire a shared vision—get others to be committed to shared goals
3. Model the way—demonstrate the behaviour you would like to see in others
4. Enable others to act—facilitate collaborative behaviour
5. Encourage the heart—recognize and reward the accomplishments of others

You can start learning these practices through your work in groups, by taking leadership courses, and by working on these skills both inside and outside the classroom by participating in clubs and student government. All of these practices require you to have good emotional intelligence. View your group work as the First Step toward developing essential leadership skills.

When scheduling meetings, also set clear starting and stopping times. Then stick to them.

End each meeting by updating your list of planned actions. Make sure that each action is assigned to a specific person, with a clear due date. You'll know that meetings are working when the energy level in the group stays high and when people have clear commitments to take planned action before the next meeting.

A person who dominates the discussion in a meeting can prevent other group members from expressing their ideas. This is a common problem with group brainstorming. To prevent it, ask people to write up their ideas *before* a meeting. Gather these into one document and distribute it several days in advance. Then use this document to begin your discussion. ✳

USING SOCIAL NETWORKS
safely and responsibly

Social networks create value. Websites such as Facebook, Twitter, Instagram, and LinkedIn are known as places to share news, photos, and personal profiles. You can also use such sites to form study groups, promote special events, and make job contacts.

Activity in online communities can also have unexpected negative consequences. For some students, social networking takes time away from studying and activities that contribute to long-term goals. Comments made online can be hurtful and you may find that embarrassing details from your online profile can come back to haunt you years later, especially when you are looking for a job.

You can use simple strategies to stay in charge of your safety, reputation, and integrity when you connect with people online.

Post only what you want to be made public and permanent

The Internet as a whole is a public medium. This is true of its online communities as well. Post only the kind of information about yourself that you *want* to be made public.

> *Act today to protect the person that you want to be four or five years from now.*

Friends, relatives, university administrators, potential employers, and police officers might be able to access your online personal profile. Don't post anything that could embarrass you later and check to see that your friends haven't tagged you in any photos you wouldn't want shared. Act today to protect the person that you want to be four or five years from now. There is no way to delete information permanently from the Internet. Websites such as the Internet Archive and its "Wayback Machine" almost guarantee that anything you post online will stay online for a long time. Anyone with Internet access can take your words and images and post them on a website or distribute them via email to damage your reputation. In the virtual world, you never know who's following you.

To avoid unwanted encounters with members of online communities and identity theft, avoid posting the following:

- Personal information such as your home or school address, phone number, social insurance number, or birth date
- Your screen name for instant messaging
- Your class schedule
- Your financial information, such as bank account numbers, credit card numbers, or information about an eBay or PayPal account
- Information about places that you regularly go at certain times of the day
- Information about places you plan to visit or trips you plan to take in the future
- Provocative pictures or messages with sexual innuendo

- Pictures of yourself at school or at work
- To further protect your safety, don't add strangers to your list of online friends

Use similar caution and common sense when joining groups. Signing up for a group with a name like *Binge Drinking Forever* can have consequences for years to come. Also avoid flirting online—people may not be who they say they are.

Use privacy features

Many online communities offer options for blocking messages from strangers, including instant messages and friendship invitations. Several social networking sites allow you to create both private and public profiles. For specific instructions, look for a link on each site titled "Frequently Asked Questions," "Security Features," "Account Settings," or "Privacy Settings." For further protection, follow these suggestions:

- Review and update your list of followers or friends on a regular basis.
- Find out which third-party applications have permission to access and post on your profile. If you're not familiar with an application or are unsure about its privacy policies, revoke its access.

- Protect your profile with a secure password and change it frequently. For a password protection test, go to *howsecureismypassword.net*.
- Restrict the number of people that you "friend" or follow. Think twice about connecting with co-workers and supervisors.
- Check the address bar of your browser whenever you use a social networking site. Make sure the site address begins with *https*. This means that the site has built in an extra level of privacy and security.

Monitor your online presence

Use Google or another popular search engine to key in your name. This will reveal what another person, such as a potential employer, might see when he or she goes online to learn about you. If someone else has posted a fake profile in your name, this is one way to find out. Contact your school's information technology department or computer help desk for help in deleting such profiles.

Respect the privacy of others

Post photos of other people only with their permission. Also take care not to reveal confidential or potentially embarrassing information about the people in your network.

Cyberbullying

Using digital devices to bully other people is a serious concern in Canada. Research has found that about one-third to half of teens report being the target of online bullying (see *definetheline.ca*). Cyberbullying involves using digital devices to bully, harass, and intimidate others by spreading gossip, hacking into someone's account, and sending hurtful emails to others; tricking people into sharing personal information or revealing photos and then sharing that material with others via blogs or social media sites; and simply being mean by sharing spiteful jokes, stories, and online polls. Kids as young as eight can be bullied, but this behaviour tends to peak in the late teen years (*getcybersafe.gc.ca*). Although cyberbullying often starts with people saying "it was just a joke," it can end up having tragic consequences including people harming themselves and even committing suicide to get away from the bullying.

As we have become more used to employing digital devices to communicate, we may also have become less sensitive to the hurtful implications of our comments.

What can you do to stop cyberbullying? First, don't pass on messages you receive that you know would be hurtful to others. If you "like" such a message you are sending a powerful endorsement to the bully that his actions are okay. Also, because bullies don't directly see the impact of their actions on others, they may have less empathy for them and therefore engage in even more viscous attacks.

Define the Line, a research group at McGill University, states that it is important to develop digital citizenship skills where you recognize the good that comes through responsible use of the Internet and also the legal risks of your actions. You must learn to distinguish, for instance, the difference between teasing online and truly criminal behaviour (for example, understanding when sexting becomes the distribution of child pornography). Plus, you must learn how to protect yourself online so that you cannot be an easy target of cyberbullying. Learning to use the Internet in an ethical and socially responsible way is essential to us all. For more information on cyberbullying and how to prevent it go to the websites for Define the Line, Get Cyber Safe, or *prevnet.ca/bullying/cyber-bullying*.

Be cautious about meeting community members in person

Because people can give misleading or false information about themselves online, avoid meeting them in person. If you do opt for a face-to-face meeting, choose a public place, and bring along a friend you trust.

"Friend" people with care

You do not have to accept every friend request or "follow" every person who chooses to follow you.

Communicating with instructors

Many instructors will not connect with students in social networks, and some schools have policies to discourage this. Networks such as Facebook are by definition social websites. The relationship between students and instructors is professional—not social.

Report malicious content

If you find online content that you consider offensive or dangerous, report it to site administrators. In many online communities, you can do this anonymously. You can help prevent online forms of intolerance, prejudice, and discrimination. Set a positive counterexample by posting messages that demonstrate acceptance of diversity.

Remember netiquette

The word *etiquette* refers to common courtesy in interpersonal relationships. Its online equivalent is called **netiquette**—a set of guidelines for using computers, cellphones, or any other form of technology.

Certain kinds of exchanges can send the tone of online communications—including social networking, email messages, and blog postings—into the gutter. To promote a cordial online community, abide by the following guidelines:

- Fine-tune the mechanics. Proofread your message for spelling and grammar—just as you would a printed message. Some email programs have built-in spell-checkers as an optional tool. Give your readers the gift of clarity and precision. Use electronic communications as a chance to hone your writing skills.

- Avoid typing passages in ALL UPPERCASE LETTERS. This is the online equivalent of shouting.

- Remember that the message is missing the emotion. When you communicate online, the people who receive your email will miss out on voice inflection and nonverbal cues that are present in face-to-face communication. Without these cues, words can be easily misinterpreted. Reread your message before sending it to be sure you have clarified what you want to say and how you feel.

The cornerstone of netiquette is to remember that the recipient on the other end is a human being. Whenever you're at a keyboard or cellphone typing messages, ask yourself one question: "Would I say this to the person's face?" ✳

Text message etiquette—Five key points

1. **Keep it short.** Limit text messages to about 150 characters. That's two to three sentences. If you go longer, your phone might split the message in two or even drop the last few words. In addition, long texts can be confusing. Send an email or make a phone call instead.

2. **Double-check the outgoing number.** If a message intended for your boyfriend or girlfriend ends up going to your boss, the results could be alarming.

3. **At work, in class, and in other public places, set your phone on vibrate.** No one else wants to hear how many text messages you're getting.

4. **Keep the time in mind.** Save 2:00 a.m. text messages for special circumstances and your closest friends. A text can ring at the same volume as a phone call and wake people up.

5. **Make sure your message is appropriate for a text message.** Sometimes a phone call really is a better device for conveying information.

Three phases of
EFFECTIVE WRITING

EFFECTIVE WRITING is essential to your success. Papers, presentations, essay tests, email, social networking sites—and even the occasional text message—call for your ability to communicate ideas with force and clarity.

This section outlines a three-phase process for writing any essay or speech:

1. Getting ready to write
2. Writing a first draft
3. Revising your draft

PHASE 1: Getting ready to write

Schedule and list-writing tasks

You can divide the ultimate goal—a finished essay—into smaller steps that you can tackle right away. Estimate how long it will take to complete each step. Start with the date your essay is due and work backward to the present. Say that the due date is December 1 and you have about three months to write the essay. Schedule November 20 as your targeted completion date, plan what you want to get done by November 1, and then list what you want to get done by October 1. To help you plan your time, many schools have online assignment planners. They will help get you organized and send you email reminders to keep you on schedule. Check out what tools are available on your school's library website.

Follow your instructor's guidelines

This is really step 1. Do what your instructor has told you to do. This includes specific instructions. If she says compare two texts—compare two, not three. If he tells you to use a specific style guide, use it. Instructors often use a rubric to grade assignments. Ask to see the rubric and then use it as a guide for creating your paper. Don't lose marks needlessly by not following the guidelines.

Generate ideas for a topic

Speak it

To get ideas flowing, start talking. By putting your thoughts into words, you'll start thinking more clearly. To paraphrase

novelist E. M. Forster, "'Speak before you think' is creation's motto" (Wurman, Leifer, & Sume, 2001, p. 116).

Refine initial ideas

Select a topic and working title

It's easy to put off writing if you have a hard time choosing a topic. However, it is almost impossible to make a wrong choice at this stage. You can choose again later if you find the one you've chosen isn't working out.

Using your instructor's guidelines for the assignment, write down a list of topics that interest you. Write as many of these as you can think of in two minutes. Then choose one. To avoid getting stuck on this step, set a precise timeline: "I will choose a topic by 4:00 p.m. on Wednesday."

The most common pitfall is selecting a topic that's too broad. "Pierre Trudeau" is not a useful topic for your Canadian history essay. Instead, consider "Pierre

Trudeau's role during the October Crisis." Your topic statement can function as a working title.

Write a thesis statement

Clarify what you want to say by summarizing it in one concise sentence. This sentence, called a **thesis statement**, refines your working title. It also helps in making a preliminary outline.

You might write a thesis statement such as "Pierre Trudeau's actions as the prime minister should not have included invoking the War Measures Act during the October Crisis." A statement that's clear and to the point can make your essay easier to write. Remember, you can always rewrite your thesis statement as you learn more about your topic.

A thesis statement is different from a topic statement. Like newspaper headlines, a thesis statement makes an assertion or describes an action. It is expressed in a complete sentence, including a verb. "Diversity" is a topic. "Cultural diversity is valuable" is a thesis statement.

Consider your purpose

Effective writing flows from a purpose. Discuss the purpose of your assignment with your instructor. Also think about how you'd like your reader or listener to respond after considering your ideas. Do you want him to think differently, to feel differently, or to take a certain action?

Your writing strategy is greatly affected by how you answer these questions. If you want someone to think differently, make your writing clear and logical. Support your assertions with evidence. And if your purpose is to move the reader into action, explain exactly what steps to take and offer solid benefits for doing so.

To clarify your purpose, state it in one sentence. For example, "The purpose of this essay is to define the term *success* in such a clear and convincing way that I win a scholarship from a college."

Do initial research

At this stage, the objective of your research is not to uncover specific facts about your topic. That comes later. First, you want to gain an overview of the subject.

Discover the structure of your topic—its major divisions and branches. Say that you want to persuade the reader to vote for a certain candidate. You must first learn enough about this person to summarize his background and state his positions on key issues.

Outline

An outline is a kind of map. When you follow a map, you avoid getting lost. Likewise, an outline keeps you from wandering off the topic.

To start an outline, consider using the outlining features in your word processing software or you can do a search of the Internet for free outlining tools such as *Checkvist* or *Workflowy*—there are lots out there. These programs allow you to record and rearrange ideas on the screen, much the way you'd write on and shuffle index cards. There are also a number of mind-mapping tools, such as *MindMeister* or *Mindomo,* that allow you to develop your essay outline and that are also useful for doing collaborative projects.

Or you could gather a stack of index cards and brainstorm ideas you want to include in your essay. Write one phrase or sentence per card. Then experiment with the cards. Group them into separate stacks, each stack representing one major category. After that, arrange the stacks in order. Finally, arrange the cards within each stack in a logical order. Rearrange them until you discover an organization that you like.

After you write the first draft of your outline, test it. Make sure that each word relates directly to your statement of purpose.

Do in-depth research

You can find information about research skills in Chapter 4, "Reading." Chapter 5, "Notes," contains in-depth information on how to take notes while reading and on citation management software. Review those chapters before beginning the research necessary for your essay or speech. Use tools such as Google *Scholar* which lists scholarly sources, including journal articles, to search for sources. Enter some of the citations used in the texts in Google *Scholar* and then read the abstracts to see if those sources would be useful to you.

PHASE 2: Writing a first draft

IF YOU'VE planned your writing project and completed your research, you've already done much of the hard work. Now you can relax into writing your first draft.

Madhourse/Shutterstock

To create your draft, gather your notes and arrange them to follow your outline. Then write about the ideas in your notes. Write in paragraphs, one idea per paragraph. If you have organized your notes logically, related facts will appear close to each other. As you complete this task, keep the following suggestions in mind.

Ease into it

Some people find that it works well to forget the word *writing*. Instead, they ease into the task with activities that help generate ideas. You can free-associate, daydream, doodle, draw diagrams, visualize the event you want to describe, talk into a recording device—anything that gets you started.

Use free writing

Free writing, a technique championed by writing teacher Peter Elbow (1981), sends a depth probe into your creative mind. This is one way to bypass your internal censors, those little voices in your head that constantly say, "That sentence wasn't very good. Why don't you stop this before you get hurt?"

There's only one rule in free writing: Write without stopping. Set a time limit—say, 10 minutes—and keep your pencil in motion or your fingers dancing across the keyboard the whole time.

Give yourself permission to keep writing. Ignore the urge to stop and rewrite, even if you think what you've written isn't very good. There's no need to worry about spelling, punctuation, or grammar. It's okay if you stray from the initial subject. Just keep writing and let the ideas flow. Experiment with free writing as soon as your instructor assigns an essay.

Remember that the first draft is not for keeps

You can save quality for later, when you revise. Your goal at this point is simply to generate lots of material.

Don't worry about grammar, punctuation, or spelling as you write your first draft. Write as if you were explaining the subject to a friend. The purpose of a first draft is merely to have something to work with—period. For most of us, that's a heck of a lot better than facing a blank page. You will revise this rough draft several times, so don't be concerned if it seems rough or choppy.

Make writing a habit

The word *inspiration* is not in the working vocabulary for many professional writers. Instead of waiting for inspiration to strike, they simply make a habit of writing at a certain time each day. You can use the same strategy. Schedule a block of time to write your first draft. The very act of writing can breed inspiration.

Respect your deep mind

Part of the process of writing takes place outside our awareness. There's nothing mysterious about this. Many people report that ideas come to them while they're doing something totally unrelated to writing. Often this happens after they've been grappling with a question and have reached a point where they feel stuck. It's like the composer who said, "There I was, sitting and eating a sandwich, and all of a sudden this tune pops into my head." You can trust your deep mind. It's writing while you eat, sleep, and brush your teeth.

Get physical

Writing is physical, like running or playing tennis. You can move your body in ways that are in tune with the flow of your ideas. While working on the first draft, take breaks. Go for a walk. Speak or sing your ideas out loud. From time to time, practise relaxation techniques and breathe deeply.

PHASE 3: Revising your draft

Plan to revise a paper two or three times. Let each revised draft sit for three or four days. Schedule time for rewrites before you begin, and schedule at least one day in between revisions so that you can let the material sit. On Tuesday night, you might think your writing sings the song of beautiful language. On Wednesday, you will see that those same words, such as the phrase "sings the song of beautiful language," belong in the trash basket.

When you edit and revise, slow down and take a microscope to your work. One guideline is to allow 50 percent of writing time for planning, research, and writing the first draft. Then give the remaining 50 percent to revising.

An effective way to revise your essay is to read it out loud. When we read silently, the eyes tend to fill in the blanks in our own writing. The combination of voice and ears forces us to pay attention to the details.

Consider making an appointment to have your instructor go over the draft of your paper—just don't ask them to do this the night before the assignment is due. If your school has a writing centre, take your essay there for review. Another technique is to have a friend look over your essay. This is never a substitute for your own review, but a friend can often see mistakes that you miss. Keep in mind that any feedback they give you is about your work, not about you. Be open to the feedback you receive.

If you are asked to help other people with their assignments, try to find something positive to say first and then offer a specific suggestion such as "I think your paper would be even stronger if…"

Cut

Look for excess baggage. Avoid at all costs and at all times the really, really terrible mistake of using way too many unnecessary words, a mistake that some student writers often make when they sit down to write essays for the various courses in which they participate at the fine institutions of higher learning that they are fortunate enough to attend. (Example: The previous sentence could be edited to "Avoid unnecessary words.") Stay within the word limit that your instructor assigns.

Paste

In deleting passages, you've probably removed some of the original transitions and connecting ideas from your draft. The next task is to rearrange what's left of your essay or speech so that it flows logically. Look for consistency within paragraphs and for transitions from paragraph to paragraph and section to section.

If your draft doesn't hang together, reorder your ideas. Computers make it easy to edit your drafts and it is simple to move paragraphs around. If you are afraid

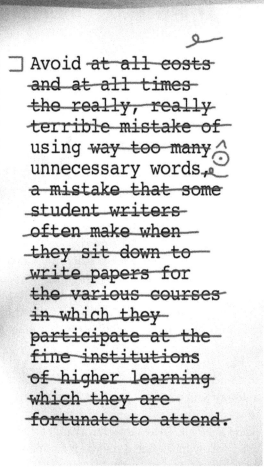

Tips for Master Students

Make your writing better

Use your four years of courses, and especially of essay writing, to make your writing better: more clean, clear and concise. It takes time, but it's so worth it.

Say you have a 2,000-word essay. Do the reading, work out your basic ideas, and then write a first draft. Don't worry if it's 2,500 words or even more. Now cut the essay down. Go through, read each sentence and ask of it: Are there words here that don't add anything but are just padding? Delete them. Doing this can easily shorten the essay by 10 to 15%. Now look at each paragraph and ask: Are there sentences here that just repeat what I've said before? Delete them too. Now look at the whole essay and ask: Is the space given a discussion proportional to its importance, either to the topic in general or to your specific argument about it? If not, shorten the paragraphs on what's peripheral and, if necessary, beef up the ones on what's central. On your main points, some repetition is okay.

Now do the whole thing again; that can take out another 10% or more. If you get good at this, your ideas will come through more powerfully, with fewer words as a filter between them and your readers. Your professors will appreciate this and reward you for it. You'll also be prepared for any career that requires communications skills, which is a whole lot of really good careers.

—Thomas Hurka, Jackman Distinguished Chair in Philosophical Studies at the University of Toronto (*Maclean's*, 2017)

Source: Advice for first-year students from Justin Trudeau (and 27 other people), by Maclean's, Maclean's, December 1, 2017.

of losing some great ideas, you can use the track changes function in your word processing system to mark your revisions in colour until you decide what will stay and what will go.

Fix

Now it's time to look at individual words and phrases.

In general, rely on nouns and verbs. Using too many adjectives and adverbs weakens your message and adds unnecessary bulk to your writing. Write about the details and be specific. Instead of writing *After making a timely arrival and perspicaciously observing the unfolding events, I emerged totally and gloriously victorious,* you can write to the point, as Julius Caesar did: *I came, I saw, I conquered.* Also, use the active rather than the passive voice. Instead of writing *A project was initiated,* write *The research team began a project.*

Define any terms that the reader might not know, putting them in plain English whenever you can. Check your paper for the type of truncated speech you would use when texting or instant messaging. Rewrite any examples of such informal language in full sentences.

Prepare

In a sense, any essay is a sales effort. If you hand in an essay with wrinkled jeans, its hair tangled and unwashed, and its shoes untied, your instructor is less likely to buy it. To avoid this situation, format your essay following accepted standards for margin widths, endnotes, title pages, and other details.

Ask your instructor for specific instructions on how to cite the sources used in writing your essay. Instructors tend to have specific requirements about which style you should use, so before you start documenting your references, ask which they prefer. Common style guides that are used include *MLA Handbook for Writers of Research Papers,* a book from the Modern Language Association, the *Publication Manual of the American Psychological Association* (APA), and the *Chicago Manual of Style.* Tools like *Citation Machine* can help you cite your references correctly according to the appropriate style guide. Most of these guides will be available to you electronically through your library. If you "cut and paste" material from a Web page directly into your essay, be sure to place that material in quotation marks and cite the source. (This process is dealt with in more detail later in the chapter, in the section "Academic integrity: Avoiding plagiarism.")

Just because it's on the Web doesn't mean it's true.

And before citing an online reference, check to see that the source is truly an authority on the subject. Just because it's on the Web doesn't mean it's true.

Proof

As you ease down the homestretch, read your revised essay one more time. This time, go for the big picture and look for

- A clear thesis statement
- Sentences that introduce your topic, that guide the reader through the major sections of your essay, and that summarize your conclusions
- Details—such as quotations, examples, and statistics—that support your conclusions
- Lean sentences that have been purged of needless words
- Plenty of action verbs and concrete, specific nouns

Finally, look over your essay with an eye for spelling and grammar mistakes. Use the spell-check function of your word processing program carefully. Check under tools to make sure you have the Canadian dictionary activated.

Again, most schools have a writing centre to assist you with your work. For at least your first few assignments, try seeking their help in proofreading your work. When you're through proofreading, take a minute to savour the result. You've just witnessed something of a miracle—the mind attaining clarity and resolution. That's the aha! in writing. Follow your instructor's specific instructions on how to submit the paper. ✳

Discovery Statement

Take a First Step Against Writing Anxiety

This Journal Entry is for people who avoid writing. As with any anxiety, you can approach writing anxiety by accepting it fully. Realize that it's all right to feel anxious about writing. Others have shared this feeling, and many people have worked with it successfully.

Begin by telling the truth. Describe exactly what happens when you start to write. What thoughts or images run through your mind? Do you feel any tension or discomfort in your body? Where? Let the thoughts and images come to the surface without resistance. Complete the following statement.

When I begin to write, I discover that I . . .

ACADEMIC INTEGRITY:
Avoiding plagiarism

'YOU'VE COPIED ALL THIS OFF THE INTERNET...'

© Grizelda/CartoonStock

HIGHER EDUCATION consists of a community of scholars who trust one another to speak and write with integrity. Plagiarism undermines this trust. The consequences of plagiarism are therefore serious and can range from a failing grade to expulsion from school.

Using another person's words, ideas, or pictures without properly citing the source is called plagiarism. This is a real concern for anyone who writes, including students. Plagiarism amounts to stealing someone else's work and claiming it as your own—the equivalent of cheating on a test.

There are many tools that instructors can use to determine whether the words in a paper are your own. For example, *Turnitin* is electronic plagiarism-checking software that instructors can use to compare your paper with a gigantic database of online papers and digital resources. So don't get caught cheating; instead learn how to cite your sources correctly.

Plagiarism can be unintentional. Some students don't understand the research process. Sometimes they leave writing until the last minute and don't take the time to organize their sources of information. Also, some people are raised in cultures where identity is based on group membership rather than individual achievement. These students may find it hard to understand how an individual can own creative work. Remember, however, that even accidental plagiarism can lead to a lowered grade and other penalties.

Most course outlines include a written statement on plagiarism. Read this document carefully and ask questions about *anything* you don't understand.

The basic guideline for preventing plagiarism is to cite a source for any fact or idea that is new to you. These include words and images created by another person. The overall goal is to clearly distinguish your own work from the work of others. A secondary goal is to give enough information about your sources so that they are easy for your reader to find. There are several ways to ensure that you meet both of these goals consistently.

Know the perils of "paper mills"

A big part of the problem of plagiarism is misuse of the Internet. Anyone with a computer can access thousands of Web pages on a given topic. Images and text from those sources are easily copied and pasted into another document. Technology makes it easy to forget that some information is free for the taking—and some is privately owned.

A quick Web search will uncover hundreds of online businesses called paper mills that sell term papers, essays, and book reports. These services are based on plagiarism. Students who use these services might answer, "When I buy a paper online, it's not plagiarism. I paid for those words, so now they're mine." But in fact, those words were still created by someone else. Plagiarism is more than merely copying words from another source: It's turning in thoughts and work that you did not produce.

Identify direct quotes

If you use a direct quote from another writer or speaker, put that person's words in quotation marks. Be careful not to copy and paste information directly from the Internet into your notes. *This is the same as taking direct quotes from your source.* To avoid plagiarism, identify such passages by enclosing them in quotation marks.

Paraphrase carefully

Paraphrasing means restating the original passage in your own words, usually making it shorter and simpler. Students who copy a passage word for word and then just rearrange or delete a few phrases are running a serious risk of plagiarism. Consider this paragraph:

> *Higher education also offers you the chance to learn how to learn. In fact, that's the subject of this book. Employers value the person who is a "quick study" when it comes to learning a new job. That makes your ability to learn a marketable skill.*

Following is an improper paraphrase of that passage:

> *With higher education comes the chance to learn how to learn. Employers value the person who is a "quick study" when it comes to learning a new job. Your ability to learn is a marketable skill.*

A better paraphrase of the same passage would be this one:

> *The author notes that when we learn how to learn, we gain a skill that is valued by employers.*

You must cite a source for paraphrases, just as you do for direct quotes.

When you use the same sequence of ideas as one of your sources—even if you have not paraphrased or directly quoted—cite that source.

Summarize carefully

For some of your notes, you may simply want to summarize your source in a few sentences or paragraphs. To do this effectively,

- read your source several times for understanding.
- put your source away; then write a summary in your own words.
- in your summary, include only the author's major points.
- check your summary against your source for accuracy.
- cite the source of your facts in the summary unless they are common knowledge—such as the capital of Canada being Ottawa.
- cite more rather fewer sources than necessary—better to err on the side of caution and cite extra sources than to cite too few.

Identify distinctive terms and phrases

Some ideas are closely identified with their individual creators. Students who present such ideas without

mentioning the individual are plagiarizing. This is true even if they do not copy words, sentence structure, or overall organization of ideas.

For example, the phrase "seven habits of highly effective people" is closely linked to Stephen Covey, author of several books based on this idea. A student might write a paper titled "Habits of Effective People," using words, sentences, and a list of habits that differ completely from Covey's. However, the originality of this student's thinking could still be called into question. This student would be wise to directly mention Covey in the paper and acknowledge Covey's idea that effectiveness and habits are closely linked. Backing up your statements with references will strengthen your arguments.

Note details about each source

Identify the source of any material that you quote, paraphrase, or summarize. For books, details about each source include the author, title, publisher, publication date, location of publisher, and page number. For articles from print sources, record the article title and the name of the magazine or journal as well. If you found the article in an academic or technical journal, also record the volume and number of the publication. A librarian can help identify these details.

If your source is a Web page, record as many identifying details as you can find—author, title, sponsoring organization, URL, publication date, and revision date. Use citation management software to make this task easier (see Chapter 5, "Notes," for more details).

Allow time to do your own research

Good research, like good writing, takes time. It is not something that you can do the night before the assignment is due. Instead, allow for time to reread and reflect on the facts you gather. This creates conditions for genuine understanding and original thinking. Also, your paper should reflect your own voice and your original thoughts. A paper composed of a string of even correctly cited facts will not be rated as highly as one where your own ideas and thoughts are presented coherently.

In particular, take the time to do these things:

- Read over all your notes and think about what you might write.
- Summarize major points of view in your own words on your topic, noting points of agreement and disagreement.
- Look for connections in your material—ideas, facts, and examples that occur in several sources.
- Note direct answers to your main research question and provide supporting research.
- Revise your thesis statement, based on discoveries from your research.

- Put all your notes away and write informally about what you want to say about your topic.

Submit only your own work

At the end of the day, plagiarism is cheating and takes away from the value of your degree or diploma. You've spent a lot on your education so don't throw it away. You get out of your education only what you put into it—so write your own assignments. Don't put your education at risk. ✳

Did you **know that …?**

In 2017, Sheridan College became the first postsecondary institution in Canada to have their musical theatre play, "Come from Away," nominated for seven Tony Awards. Written by Irene Sankoff (whose degree from York was in psychology) and David Hein, the play was developed and incubated by Sheridan's Canadian Music Theatre Project but who would expect it would be a hit on Broadway. You never know where your writing will take you (Sheridan, 2017).

Mastering public
SPEAKING

SOME PEOPLE tune out during a speech. Just think of all the times you have listened to instructors, lecturers, politicians, and others. Remember all the wonderful daydreams you have had during their speeches.

DON MACKINNON/AFP/Getty Images

Your Audiences are like you. The way you plan and present your speech can determine the number of audience members who will stay with you until the end. Polishing your speaking and presentation skills can also help you think on your feet and communicate clearly. These are skills that you can use in any course and in any career you choose.

You can learn a lot about effective speaking simply by observing other speakers. Besides hearing *what* they say, notice *how* they present themselves. Creating a presentation is much like writing a paper. Divide the project into three phases:

1. Preparing your presentation
2. Delivering your presentation
3. Reflecting on your presentation

PHASE 1: Preparing your presentation
Start from your passions

If your instructor allows you to choose the topic of presentation, then choose one that you find interesting.

Imagine that the first words in your presentation will be "I'm here to talk to you because I feel passionately about. . . ." How would you complete the sentence? Turn your answer into your main topic.

Analyze your audience

Developing a speech is similar to writing a paper. Begin by writing out your topic, purpose, and thesis statement. Then carefully consider how you will present your material to your specific audience by using the strategies in Table 8.1.

Organize your presentation

List three to five questions that your audience members are likely to ask and then organize your talk around it. Consider the length of your presentation. Plan on delivering about 100 words per minute. Time yourself as you practise your presentation. Aim for a lean presentation—enough words to make your point but not so many as to make your audience restless. Leave your listeners wanting more. For good examples of speeches,

Table 8.1 Tailor Your Topic to Your Audience

If your topic is new to listeners . . .	Explain why your topic matters to them.
	Relate the topic to something that listeners already know and care about.
	Define any terms that listeners might not know.
If listeners already know about your topic . . .	Acknowledge this fact at the beginning of your speech.
	Find a narrow aspect of the topic that may be new to listeners.
	Offer a new perspective on the topic, or connect it to an unfamiliar topic.
If listeners are likely to disagree with your thesis . . .	Tactfully admit your differences of opinion.
	Reinforce points on which you and your audience agree.
	Build credibility by explaining your qualifications to speak on your topic.
	Quote expert figures that agree with your thesis—people whom your audience is likely to admire.
	Explain that their current viewpoint has costs for them, and that a slight adjustment in their thinking will bring significant benefits.
If listeners may be uninterested in your topic . . .	Explain how listening to your speech can help them gain something that matters deeply to them.
	Explain ways to apply your ideas in daily life.

© Cengage Learning

use your browser to find some TED Talks from expert presenters. Think about how they hook the audience into their topic and how they present their material.

There are typically three sections to a speech—similar to an essay, there is an introduction, body, and conclusion.

Write the introduction

Rambling speeches with no clear point or organization put audiences to sleep. Solve this problem with your introduction. The following introduction, for example, reveals the thesis and exactly what's coming. The speech will have three distinct parts, each in logical order:

Dogfighting is a cruel sport. I intend to describe exactly what happens to the animals, tell you who is doing this, and show you how you can stop this inhumane practice.

Whenever possible, talk about things that hold your interest. Include your personal experiences and start with a hook! Consider this introduction to a speech on the subject of world hunger:

I'm very honoured to be here with you today. I intend to talk about malnutrition and starvation. First, I want to outline the extent of these problems, then I will discuss some basic assumptions concerning world hunger, and finally I will propose some solutions.

You can almost hear the snores from the audience. Following is a rewrite:

More people have died from hunger in the past five years than have been killed in all of the wars, revolutions, and murders in the past 150 years. Yet there is

enough food to go around. I'm honoured to be here with you today to discuss solutions to this problem.

Most people pay attention to at least the first few seconds of a speech, so you need to catch their attention right from the start by highlighting your main points.

Draft your introduction and then come back to it after you've written the rest of your speech. In the process of creating the main body and conclusion, your thoughts about the purpose and main points of your speech might change. You might even want to write the introduction last.

Write the body

The body of your speech is the content, which accounts for 70 to 90 percent of most speeches. In the body, you develop your ideas in much the same way that you develop a written essay.

Be careful about using humour in your speech. You run the risk of offending someone. If you aren't naturally funny, this is not the time to practise your stand-up comedy routine.

Transitions are especially important. Give your audience a signal when you change points, using meaningful pauses and verbal emphasis as well as transitional phrases: "On the other hand, until the public realizes what is happening to children in these countries. . . ." or "The second reason hunger persists is. . . ."

In long speeches, recap from time to time and preview what's to come. Use facts, descriptions, expert opinions, and statistics to hold your audience's attention.

Write the conclusion

At the end of the speech, summarize your points and draw your conclusion. You started with a bang; now finish with drama. The first and last parts of a speech are the most important. Make it clear to your audience when you've reached the end. Avoid endings such as "This is the end of my speech." A simple standby is "So in conclusion, I want to reiterate three points: First. . . ." When you are finished, stop talking.

Create speaking notes

Some professional speakers recommend writing out your speech in full, then putting key words or main points on a few numbered index cards. As you finish the information on each card, move it to the back of the pile. Write information clearly and in letters large enough to be seen from a distance.

The disadvantage of the index card system is that it involves card shuffling. Some speakers prefer to use standard outlined notes. You can include your speaking points in large font, so they are easy to read within *PowerPoint*®, and this is also a simple way to keep track of what slide you are on. Another option is mind mapping. Even an hour-long speech can be mapped on one sheet of paper. You can also use memory techniques to memorize the outline of your speech.

Create supporting visuals

Presentations often include visuals such as slides created with presentation software such as *PowerPoint*®, *Keynote*®, or *Prezi*. These visuals can reinforce your main points and help your audience understand how your presentation is organized. Remember to include your reference sources in your presentation. This includes your sources of both visual and textual material.

Use visuals to *complement* rather than *replace* your speaking. If you use too many visuals—or visuals that are too complex—your audience might focus on them and forget about you. Here are guidelines to help you use presentation software to full advantage:

- Ask your instructor whether it's acceptable to use technology in your presentation.

- Use fewer visuals rather than more. Save them for illustrations, photos, charts, and concepts that are hard to express in words. For a 15-minute presentation, a total of five to 10 slides is enough.

- Check to make sure the illustrations are easy for the audience to see no matter where they are sitting in the room.

- Limit the amount of text on each visual. Three points per slide is plenty. Stick to key words presented in short sentences or phrases, and in bulleted or numbered lists.

- Use a consistent set of plain fonts that are large enough for all audience members to see.

- Avoid using more than two fonts, and avoid UPPERCASE letters.

- Stick with a simple, coherent colour scheme. Use light-coloured text on a dark background, or dark text on a light background.

Regardless of which presentation software you use, remember to make a backup copy of your presentation and email it to yourself.

Manage your fear of public speaking

Even skilled speakers can panic at the thought of getting up in front of an audience. You may not be able to eliminate fear of public speaking entirely, but you can take steps to reduce and manage it.

Prepare thoroughly

Research your topic thoroughly. Knowing your topic inside and out can create a baseline of confidence. To make a strong start, memorize the first four sentences that you plan to deliver, and practise them many times. Delivering them flawlessly when you're in front of an audience can build your confidence for the rest of your speech.

Accept your physical sensations

You've probably experienced physical sensations that are commonly associated with stage fright: dry mouth, a pounding heart, sweaty hands, muscle jitters, shortness of breath, and a shaky voice. One immediate way to deal with such sensations is to simply notice and accept them. Actually, a little anxiety is important for a good presentation. If you go in sounding bored with what you are talking about, chances are your presentation will fall flat. Even Lady Gaga gets nervous about her performances (Cain, 2013).

Focus on content, not delivery

Michael Motley (1998), a professor at the University of California–Davis, distinguishes between two orientations to speaking. People with a **performance orientation** believe that the speaker must captivate the audience by using formal techniques that differ from normal conversation. In contrast, speakers with a **communication orientation** see public speaking simply as an extension of one-to-one conversation. The goal is not to perform but to communicate your ideas to an audience in the same ways that you would explain them to a friend.

Adopting a communication orientation can reduce your fear of public speaking. Instead of thinking about yourself, focus on your message. Your audiences are more interested in *what* you have to say than in *how* you say it. Forget about giving a "speech." Just give people valuable ideas and information that they can use.

Use your "speaker's voice"

When you practise, do so in a loud voice. Your voice sounds different when you talk loudly, and this can be unnerving. Get used to it early on.

Making the grade in group presentations

When preparing group presentations, you can use three strategies for making a memorable impression.

Get organized. As soon as you get the assignment, determine everyone's role in the presentation and exchange contact information. Schedule specific times and places for planning, researching, writing, and practising your presentation.

At your first meeting, write a to-do list including all of the tasks involved in completing the assignment and the due dates for when things must be done. Distribute tasks fairly, paying attention to the strengths of individuals in your group. For example, some people excel at brainstorming while others prefer researching. However, make sure everyone shares a cohesive view of the whole project so that you can produce a unified presentation. This is the time to sort out your different perspectives (Petty, 2010).

As you get organized, remember how your presentation will be evaluated. If the instructor doesn't give marking criteria, create your own.

One powerful way to get started is to define clearly the topic and thesis, or main point, of your presentation. Then, support your thesis by looking for the most powerful facts, quotations, and anecdotes you can find.

Get coordinated. You need to capture your audience's attention in the first minute so take time to think about how you are going to engage them in this topic—what is your hook? Doing a presentation is a lot like telling a story, so get your audience interested and engaged from the first slide.

Do at least one rehearsal. Coordinate your presentation so that you have planned transitions between individual speakers. Practise making those transitions smooth. It can be as simple as "Next Jennifer will discuss . . ."

All group members should stay engaged and alert during the presentation even when it isn't their turn to present. You'll look more professional to the instructor. Also, if you are keeping track, it is possible to save a struggling classmate if he needs you to step in during his part of the presentation.

Practise using visuals such as flipcharts, posters, or presentation software. To give visuals their full impact, make them appropriate for the room where you will present. Make sure that text is large enough to be seen from the back of the room. Try to get one member to create the presentation slides so that the materials that you present look well integrated. At the end of the presentation, make sure you have a closing summary—don't just end with "That's it." Presentations that get top scores take teamwork and planning.

Celebrate success. Take the time to celebrate the group's hard work after the class. Thank everyone for their contributions to the presentation. You've all put in the effort, now take the time to mark your success.

Practise your presentation. The key to successful public speaking is practice, practice, practice. In addition, over-preparation is a key to dealing with presentation anxiety.

Practise in the room in which you will deliver your speech

Hear what your voice sounds like over a sound system. If you can't practise your speech in the actual room, at least visit the site ahead of time. Also make sure that the materials you will need, such as a computer and screen, will be available when you want them. Have a backup plan, such as printed copies of your slides, prepared in case of any technical glitches.

Make a recording

Make a recording of your presentation with your device. Use it while you practise, then view the finished recording to evaluate your presentation.

Listen for repeated phrases

Examples include *you know, kind of,* plus any little *uh's, umm's,* and *eh's.* To get rid of these, tell yourself that you intend to notice every time they pop up in your daily speech. When you hear them, remind yourself that you don't use those words anymore.

Keep practising until you know your material inside and out

Don't read word for word from your presentation slides. The slides should contain only bullet points. You need to elaborate on those points in your speech. Nothing is more boring than a speaker who reads word for word from her slides so be prepared to present without looking at them. Practise your presentation until you could deliver it in your sleep, then run through it a few more times.

PHASE 2: Delivering your presentation

Before you begin, get the audience's attention. If people are still filing into the room or adjusting their seats, they're not ready to listen. Begin when all eyes are on you. Start speaking slowly until you feel comfortable with your audience. Add in more gestures as you begin to relax.

Dress for the occasion

The clothing you choose to wear on the day of your presentation delivers a message that's as loud as your words. Consider your audience and then choose a wardrobe based on the impression you want to make.

Project your voice

When you speak, talk loudly enough to be heard. Try to project your voice in an engaging manner, crafting your speech to the needs of the audience.

Give out handouts

If you have handouts, give them out before or after the speech so that you avoid wasting time or so that you don't distract your audience from your key messages.

Maintain eye contact

It is easier for the audience to listen to someone when that person is looking at them. Find a few friendly faces around the room and imagine that you are talking to each of those people individually.

Notice your nonverbal communication

Be aware of what your body is telling your audience. Contrived or staged gestures will look dishonest. Be natural.

Keep track of the time

You can increase the impact of your words by keeping track of the time during your speech. Better to end early than run late. The conclusion of your speech is what is likely to be remembered, and you might lose this impact if people are looking at the clock.

Pause strategically

Beginners sometimes feel that they have to fill every moment with the sound of their voices. Release that expectation. Give your listeners a chance to make notes and absorb what you say.

PHASE 3: Reflecting on your presentation

Review and reflect upon your performance. Did you finish on time? Did you cover all of the points you intended to cover? Was the audience attentive? Did you handle any nervousness effectively? Be as kind to yourself as you would be to someone else after a presentation. In addition to noting areas for improvement, note what you did well. Congratulate yourself on getting up in front of an audience and completing your presentation.

Welcome feedback from others. Most of us find it difficult to hear criticism about our speaking. Be aware of resisting such criticism and then let go of your resistance. Listening to feedback will increase your skill. ✳

The persuasive presentation

You might create a speech with the aim of changing the way your audience thinks or feels about a topic. Think critically about the complexity of this task. Consider your audience's *attitude system*, which has three key elements:

- *Attitudes* involve feelings of approval or disapproval.
- *Beliefs* reflect what people know—or think they know—about a topic.
- *Values* are broad, enduring principles that guide our behaviours.

Of these three elements, values are often the most resistant to change. In addition, people generally seek consistency in their attitudes, beliefs, and values.

This situation suggests a strategy for persuasion. Instead of trying to change your audience's values, see if you can persuade your audience members that one of their attitudes or beliefs *contradicts* their values. Then you can present a new attitude or belief that restores consistency to their attitude system.

Say that you are preparing to speak to a politically conservative audience about a gun registry system managed by the federal government. This proposal is not always popular with conservatives. However, many members of this political group also value law and order legislation. You could create a speech arguing that the gun control registry helps keep Canadians safe.

To analyze the audience for your next speech, create a list of attitudes, beliefs, and values to consider. To organize your thinking, fill in the following chart.

Next, circle any attitudes or beliefs that contradict your audience's values. Then, in the space below, brainstorm and write down a new attitude or belief that you can propose, along with some key evidence for it.

_____

_____

_____

_____

_____

_____

_____

_____

_____

_____

_____

_____

_____

Audience attitudes toward your topic	Audience beliefs about your topic	Audience values related to your topic

Employ your word

The person you are is, in large part, a result of the agreements you make. Others know who you are by your words and your commitments. And you can learn who you are by observing which commitments you choose to keep and which ones you choose to avoid.

Relationships are built on agreements. When we break a promise to be faithful to a spouse, to help a friend move to a new apartment, or to pay a bill on time, relationships are strained.

The words we use to make agreements can be placed onto several different levels. We can think of each level as one rung on a ladder—the ladder of powerful speaking. As we move up the ladder, our speaking becomes more effective.

The lowest rung on the ladder is *obligation*. Words used at this level include *I should, he ought to, someone had better, they need to, I must,* and *I had to.* Speaking this way implies that something other than ourselves is in control of our lives. When we live at the level of obligation, we speak as if we are victims.

The next rung up is *possibility*. At this level, we examine new options. We play with new ideas, possible solutions, and alternative courses of action. As we do, we learn that we can make choices that dramatically affect the quality of our lives. We are not the victims of circumstance. Phrases that signal this level include *I might, I could, I'll consider, I hope to,* and *maybe.*

From possibility, we can move up to *preference*. Here we begin the process of choice. The words *I prefer* signal that we're moving toward one set of possibilities over another, perhaps setting the stage for eventual action.

Above preference is a rung called *passion*. Again, certain words signal this level: *I want to, I'm really excited to do that,* and *I can't wait to.*

Action comes with the next rung— *planning*. When people use phrases such as *I intend to, my goal is to, I plan to,* and *I'll try like mad to,* they're at the level of planning. The Intention Statements you write in this book are examples of planning.

The highest rung on the ladder is *promising*. This is where the power of your word really comes into play. At this level, it's common to use phrases such as these: *I will, I promise to, I am committed,* and *you can count on it.* Promising is where we bridge from possibility and planning to action. Promising brings with it all of the rewards of employing your word.

Put it to WORK

chapter 8

◄◄◄◄
■ Quiz
■ Skills Snapshot
■ Master Student Profile

The techniques described in this chapter have direct applications in the workplace.

Monkey Business Images/Shutterstock.com

Research on why college and university grads don't get hired consistently shows that their problem isn't *not* having top notch computer or technical skills; rather, it is their lack of communication and interpersonal skills (White, 2013). It is having these so-called "soft skills" that makes all the difference in who gets chosen for a job. Employers want workers who are good team players, and have strong critical thinking, problem-solving, and verbal communication skills.

The ability to write is also in demand. To verify this, scan job postings and notice how many of them call for it. Proposals, reports, email messages, Web pages, and other documents are essential to the flow of ideas and information. People without writing skills can only influence people through direct contact. If you can write a persuasive memo, however, your ideas can spread to hundreds of people. Most new products and services—especially those that involve high budgets—begin with a written proposal.

Use storytelling techniques

During a job search, emphasize your communication skills. Talk about times when you demonstrated these skills in work and academic experiences. In particular, draw on one of the most powerful forms of human communication—stories. In essence, a story is a series of events that occur when a person faces a significant problem and solves it. Practise talking about your experiences with this definition in mind.

Develop conversation skills

One of the most practical communication skills you can develop is the ability to hold one-on-one conversations. In the workplace, you will regularly meet new co-workers, customers, and clients. The ability to put people at ease through "small talk" makes you valuable to an employer. In a business context, this is a high-level skill that depends on the ability to listen closely, suspend judgment, and sympathize with another person's experiences.

Develop complex communication skills

In their book *The New Division of Labor: How Computers Are Creating the Next Job Market*, Frank Levy and Richard J. Murname (2004) emphasize the value of **complex communication**. This is the ability to acquire information, explain it, and persuade co-workers that your explanation implies a definite course of action. A supervisor who wants her employees to adopt a new procedure needs complex communication skills. So does an engineer who submits a new prototype for a software app, a marketing manager who wants her company to develop a new product, and a salesperson who confronts a skeptical customer.

Complex communication is required for any job that involves direct teaching, persuasion, or negotiation. People who develop this set of skills are less likely to lose their jobs due to automation or outsourcing. Start now by seizing every opportunity to write papers and make presentations that persuade people to adopt new ideas and take action on them.

Edit your writing for the workplace

Jakob Nielsen (2000), author of *Designing Web Usability: The Practice of Simplicity*, suggests that effectively written Web pages are

- *Concise*—free of needless words and organized so that the main point of each section and paragraph comes at the beginning.

- *Scannable*—prepared with subheadings and visuals that allow readers to skim and quickly find what they need.

- *Objective*—packed with credible facts and free of "hype"—vague or exaggerated claims presented without evidence.

- These three guidelines can assist you in all forms of business writing.

Manage conflict within teams

If you get into a personal conflict with a co-worker, reread the article "Managing conflict" and choose a suggestion to apply. Simply by remembering to separate the processes of sending and receiving, you can immediately improve your relationships with both supervisors and employees.

Now create a career connection of your own

Review this chapter, looking for a suggestion that you will commit to use while working or looking for a job. In a sentence or two, describe exactly what you plan to do and the primary benefit you want to gain. For example, "I will join a site for professional networking, such as *LinkedIn*. Developing an online profile for this site will give me a head start on creating my resumé."

State your strategy and desired benefit in the space below:

_____

_____

_____

_____

_____

QUIZ

Name_____   Date____/____/____

1. What type of tools can you use to work on group assignments together?

2. One suggested guideline for nonverbal listening is to respond frequently to the speaker. True or False? Explain your answer.

3. The suggested techniques for verbal listening include which of the following?
   (a) Parrot exactly what another person says.
   (b) Pay attention to the speaker's words and not the emotions behind the words.
   (c) Always put your own concerns aside in order to listen attentively.
   (d) Look for the requests hidden in complaints.

4. "You always interrupt when I talk!" is a complaint. An effective way to restate this as a request is
   (a) "You almost always interrupt when I talk."
   (b) "You sometimes interrupt when I talk."
   (c) "Why do you interrupt me?"
   (d) "Please let me finish speaking before you talk."

5. List the five parts of an "I" message (the five ways to say "I").

6. Describe three blocks to effective listening.

7. The fact that a disagreement is getting worse means that there's little hope for conflict resolution. True or False? Explain your answer.

8. Which of the following is an effective thesis statement? Explain your answer.
   (a) Two types of thinking.
   (b) Critical thinking and creative thinking go hand in hand.
   (c) The relationship between critical thinking and creative thinking.
   (d) Creativity, critical thinking, and success.

9. Define *plagiarism* and explain ways to avoid it.

10. What characteristic distinguishes the top five rungs of the ladder of powerful speaking from the bottom rung?

Skills SNAPSHOT

Take a few minutes to revisit your responses to the "Communicating" section of the Discovery Wheel exercise in Chapter 1. Reflect on the progress you've made, and clarify your intentions to develop further mastery. Then complete the following sentences.

DISCOVERY

My score on the Communicating section of the Discovery Wheel was . . .

When I feel angry with people, the way I usually express it is to . . .

I would describe my current level of emotional intelligence as . . .

INTENTION

The suggestion from this chapter that can help me most with listening is . . .

The suggestion from this chapter that can help me most with speaking is . . .

The suggestion from this chapter that can help me most with writing is . . .

I'll know that I've reached a new level of mastery with my communication skills when . . .

ACTION

To reach that level of mastery, the most important thing I can do next is to . . .

To take the suggestions I just listed and put them into practice, the three new habits I will adopt next are . . .

MASTER STUDENT
PROFILE

chapter 8

■ Put it to Work
■ Quiz
■ Skills Snapshot
◀ ◀ ◀ ◀

Billy-Ray Belcourt
… is grounded.

For Billy-Ray Belcourt, poetry is the "language of everyday life" that can create "a sort of connectivity" between him and people he might not otherwise meet.

It has also brought him acclaim, as the Canadian winner of this year's $65,000 Griffin Poetry Prize, one of the world's richest awards for a poetry book.

Belcourt, 23, says he's trying "to bring to light" experiences of Indigenous people who are also from the LGBTQ community.

"I am both Indigenous and queer," he says. "To even tell that story is already to break through the sound barrier of Canadian history."

Belcourt, who is from Driftpile Cree Nation in Alberta and is a student at the University of Alberta in Edmonton, says he wants Canada to be a country where "a whole host of marginalized peoples aren't called marginalized anymore."

And it would be a country, he says, where "we actually can love and desire things outside of ourselves and pursue goals—career goals, educational goals, political goals—in a way that doesn't ratchet up our vulnerability."

Source: "Just watch them: 10 young Canadians who are making their mark in their communities and beyond." CBC News, June 30, 2018. Accessed at *https://newsinteractives.cbc.ca/longform/canada-day-10-young-canadians*.

Billy-Ray is an award-winning poet, educator and Rhodes Scholar. He is the 2018 Pierre Elliott Trudeau Foundation Scholar in English and Film Studies at the University of Alberta.

Diversity

Rawpixel.com/Shutterstock.com

what is included ...

do you have a minute?

Expand your universe by exploring the opportunities you have to learn more about yourself and the world around you right now at your school.

1. Go to your school's website and find out whether you have an alternative spring break program and consider applying.

2. Visit your school's Indigenous student services and find out when they are having a public event that you can attend.

3. Stand up against bullying and attend your school's "Pink Shirt Day." If your school doesn't have this event, consider starting one.

Waking up to
DIVERSITY AND INCLUSION

Working and living with people from different racial, religious, or ethnic backgrounds or sexual orientation, including those with different abilities, allow us to enjoy more success at school, on the job, and in our neighbourhood communities. Sharing in this success means learning new ways to think, speak, and act. Learning about diversity opens up myriad possibilities—an education in itself. Developing an inclusive approach to diversity is imperative as we move toward global citizenry in our increasingly connected world. Respecting the inherent dignity and worth of everyone is key to success everywhere.

Diversity in Canada

Canada is a mosaic of people from many different cultures and ethnicities. Canadians belong to over 250 specific ethnocultural groups including those of Indigenous origins (Ballingall, 2017). Statistics Canada (2017e) population projections suggest that by 2036 the proportion of Canadians who are foreign-born could reach between 24.5 percent and 30 percent with 57 percent of this population being born in Asia. By that time, between 39 percent and 49 percent of Canadians under 15 will be foreign-born themselves or have a parent who was not born in Canada. Immigrants aren't expected to assimilate when they move to Canada, but rather to add their cultures into the mix.

According to World Population Review (2018), Toronto has the second-highest percentage of foreign-born residents of all world cities after Miami. Toronto is one of the world's most diverse cities, with no single overwhelmingly dominant culture or nationality. Results from Census 2016 revealed that more than half of Torontonians identified as visible minorities. This is an increase from 2011 when 47 percent identified as a visible minority. The largest group of visible minorities in Toronto are South Asians (13 percent), followed next by Chinese (11 percent) and black (9 percent; Whalen, 2017).

Our country welcomed 1.2 million new immigrants between 2011 and 2016, with South Asians being the largest visible minority group at 25.1 percent of

the total. Another 20.5 percent of visible minorities are Chinese, while 15.6 percent are black (Grenier, 2017). Based on Statistics Canada (2017f) population projection scenarios, the overwhelming majority of immigrants (more than 91 percent) will continue to live in urban areas—specifically Toronto, Montreal, and Vancouver. Today 22 percent of Canadians are immigrants; this is the highest percentage in 85 years (Whalen, 2017).

We live in a world where Naheed Nenshi, whose parents immigrated from Tanzania, became the mayor of Calgary; where Michäelle Jean, a refugee from Haiti, became the Governor General of Canada; and where Drake, an African Canadian from Toronto, could become a mega rapper, songwriter, and entrepreneur. These individuals set examples of diversity in leadership that inspire many. Prepare to apply your own leadership skills in a multicultural world.

What does this mean to you? You are living in the right country at the right time to experience the world's diversity by simply walking down the street. Our diversity and commitment to **equity** and inclusion makes this a great country to learn about yourself and the world around you.

Discussions of diversity often focus on characteristics commonly linked to race—differences in skin tone, facial features, and hair texture. But grouping people according to such differences is arbitrary. We could just as easily classify them on the basis of height, weight, foot size, fingernail length, or a hundred other physical traits.

In this chapter, the word **diversity** refers to differences of any type. From this perspective, diversity can be compared to an iceberg. Only the top of an iceberg is visible; most of it is hidden under water. Likewise, only a few aspects of diversity are visible, such as obvious differences in physical appearance, language, social and economic background, and behaviour. Much remains hidden from our awareness—different ideas about relationships, decision-making, and problem-solving; different assumptions about the meaning of love and duty, beauty and friendship, justice and injustice; and

Diversity in Canada

- Over 80 percent of Canadians live in urban areas (Statistics Canada, 2017h).

- Half of all same-sex couples in Canada are living in Montreal, Toronto, Ottawa-Gatineau, and Vancouver (Statistics Canada, 2017g).

- 10 percent of the student population of Thompson Rivers University is Indigenous in origin (Lewingon, 2017).

- 4.9 percent of the Canadian population is Indigenous, an increase of 42.5 percent since 2006 and a growth rate more than 4 times the non-Indigenous population (Grenier, 2017).

- 6 percent of the population of Nunavut say they have no religion, with the most common religion being the Anglican faith (Statistics Canada, 2011c).

- Over 14 percent of Canadians have a physical disability, with pain and mobility disabilities being the most common (Statistics Canada, 2011d).

- In 2016, the Black population in Canada increased to over one million. This visible minority group comprised 15.6 percent of the visible minority population (Statistics Canada, 2017e).

- More than 60 percent of new immigrants come from Asia (including the Middle East). Africa has now surpassed Europe as the second largest source of new immigrants, increasing to 13.4 percent (Grenier, 2017).

- If current trends continue, from 55.7 percent to 57.9 percent of all immigrants will be born in Asia by 2036 (Statistics Canada, 2017f).

much more. Moving from diversity to **inclusion** is a goal we all share. An inclusive approach to diversity requires us to respect and appreciate individual differences and to empower people to bring their authentic selves to the table in the workplace and classroom.

Intercultural competence

This chapter is titled "Diversity" because that term is widely accepted. You might gain more value from thinking about **intercultural competence** instead. This term reminds us that even in the most culturally sensitive environment, people can fail at understanding each other and working toward shared goals. Intercultural competence refers to the ability "to look at the world through different eyes" (Bennett, Bennett, & Allen, 2003, p. 244). It requires far more than becoming knowledgeable about other cultures. It is having a combination of skills, knowledge, and awareness.

The Truth and Reconciliation Commission (TRC) had as its mandate to inform all Canadians about the injustices and harm suffered by the Indigenous peoples in the over 100 years when they were removed from their homes and sent to Indian residential schools. One of the calls to action of the report of the TRC (2015) was to build on our capacity as Canadians for intercultural understanding, empathy, and mutual respect. Developing intercultural competence will help us all

support the TRC calls to action. For more on the TRC, go to *www.trc.ca/websites/trcinstitution/index.php?p=3*.

To develop intercultural competence, you must be a self-reflective, self-aware learner. You also need to develop cultural knowledge and challenge your own cultural assumptions and true acceptance of cultural differences. To become more culturally aware, you'll need to interact with individuals from diverse cultures for an extended period of time, working collaboratively together toward shared goals and taking the time to learn about the history of each group. As part of global citizenship, cultural awareness is important for all of us. To assess your current cultural competency, go to *www .coloradoedinitiative.org/wp-content/uploads/2015/10/ cultural-competence-self-assessment-checklist.pdf*.

You'll learn the most by stepping outside your comfort zone and taking risks. Get involved in a study group or campus organization with people from backgrounds different than your own. Take advantage of study abroad programs. Students who engage in such programs typically comment that they feel more culturally aware, and have a greater openness to difference and a better sense of their own identity (Canadian Bureau for International Education, 2018). Keep asking yourself, "What is the next action I could take to live and work more effectively in our global village?" The answers could change your life. ✳

Circles of identity

One way to begin to think about inclusion is to "identify who we are (and who we aren't) as individuals and as a group in relation to those who wield power in our society" (Arnold, Burke, James, Martin, & Thomas, 1991, p. 87). In Figure 9.1 you can see a set of circles.

1. With a partner, go around each item in the circle and on the *inner* circle identify which group you believe is dominant in society in terms of social identity in Canada. For instance, English might be the language you would write in the language category. The blank slot is there in case you want to identify one more category (such as being born inside or outside of Canada) you think is important to consider.

2. On your own, go around the *outer* circle and, as you feel comfortable, label your own identity in the outside circle.

3. Self-reflection: Consider how many categories you have as an individual that are different than the dominant circle—these categories are areas of power conferred by society. Are there categories in which you can change your identity? Are there others where you cannot? Think about which can be changed and which can't; for example, you can change where you live, but you can't change your race. What do you think are the implications for those whose identity matches or does not match the dominant categories of the inner circle? Which part of yourself do you sometimes feel necessary to submerge to be a successful student (Arnold et al., 1991)?

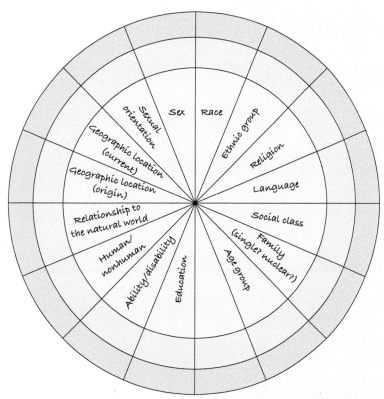

"Circles of Identity" from Arnold, R., Burke, B., James, C., Martin, D., & Thomas, B., eds., *Educating for a Change* (Toronto: Between the Lines, 1991) 88. Reprinted by permission of Between the Lines.

Figure 9.1 Circles of Identity

Discovery/Intention Statement

Commit to Create Value from This Chapter

Briefly describe an incident in which you felt excluded from a group because you differed in some way from the other people. This difference could be any kind, such as hair length, style of clothing, political affiliation, religion, skin colour, sexual orientation, age, gender, economic status, or accent.

I discovered that I . . .

_____

_____

_____

_____

_____

_____

_____

Now, think about the opposite scenario. Recall a time when you felt included in a group of people, even though the group was diverse. Describe this incident as well.

I discovered that I . . .

_____

_____

_____

_____

_____

_____

_____

_____

Finally, scan this chapter for ideas that could help you change situations like the first one you described above to an environment more like the second. List at least five ideas that you intend to explore in more detail, along with their associated page numbers.

Strategy   **Page number**

_____

_____

_____

_____

_____

_____

_____

_____

_____

_____

_____

_____

_____

_____

_____

_____

_____

DIVERSITY IS REAL—
and valuable

WE HAVE ALWAYS lived with people of different races and cultures. Many of us come from families who immigrated to Canada just recently or one or two generations ago. The things we eat, the tools we use, and the words we speak are a cultural tapestry woven by many different peoples.

ValeStock/Shutterstock.com

Think about a common daily routine. A typical Canadian citizen awakens in a bed (an invention from the Near East). After dressing in clothes (often designed in Italy), she slices a banana (grown in Honduras) onto her bowl (made in China) of cereal, and brews coffee (shipped from Nicaragua). After breakfast, she reads the morning newspaper (printed by a process invented in Germany, on paper, which was first made in China). She then puts on her headphones (made from components manufactured in Japan, China, and Korea) and listens to music (possibly performed by a band from Cuba).

Multiculturalism refers to ethnic diversity—and many other kinds of diversity as well. As anthropologist Dorothy Lee (1959) tells us, culture is simply one society's solutions to perennial human problems, such as how to worship, celebrate, resolve conflict, work, think, and learn. **Culture** is a set of learned behaviours—a broader concept than race, which refers to the biological makeup of people. Big "C" Culture can be thought of as the formal culture. This would include famous figures from history, great works of literature and art, and formal institutions (political and social) associated with a particular society or group of people. Little "c" culture is related to characteristics of everyday living, such as what people wear or eat and what is viewed as appropriate behaviour (Bennett, Bennett, & Allen, 2003).

It is the little "c" culture that can be particularly important but difficult to learn. There are the cultures of men and women; heterosexual, homosexual, and bisexual people; and older and younger people. There are differences in culture between urban and rural dwellers, between able-bodied people and those with disabilities, and between people from two-parent families, people from single-parent families, and people from same-sex families. There are social classes based on differences in standards of living. Diversity in religion is a factor, too; this can be especially difficult to accept, since many people identify strongly with their religious faith.

Multiculturalism refers to the co-existence of diverse cultures, including racial, ethnic, and religious groups with diverse ways of thinking, communication styles, cultural norms and values.

People can differ in countless ways—race, gender, ethnic group, sexual orientation, and more. The suggestions offered in this chapter can help you respond effectively to the many kinds of diversity you'll encounter. Higher education can help reinforce an attitude of tolerance, open-mindedness, and respect for individual differences.

Discrimination is also real

The ability to live with diversity is now more critical than ever. Racism, sexism, homophobia, and other forms of discrimination still exist, even in educational settings.

Indigenous students, for example, often do not feel welcome on our campuses; this sense of exclusion is one reason why only about half of 25- to 64-year-old Indigenous people have a postsecondary qualification compared to two-thirds of non-Indigenous people (Statistics Canada, 2011b). This is a slowly changing statistic as more effort is being made to Indigenize curriculum, incorporating more Indigenous content in courses and including more Indigenous approaches to assessment as recommended in the Truth and Reconciliation Commission's Calls to Action. Colleges and universities are making more effort to provide Indigenous students with special programs, such as elders on campus to help students feel more comfortable in this educational setting.

The Canadian Human Rights Commission investigates complaints of discrimination and fosters public understanding and adherence to the principles of the Human Rights Act.

Consider how you would respond to these situations:

- Members of a sociology class are debating the merits of social welfare in Canada. The instructor calls on an Indigenous student and says, "Tell us. What's the First Nations perspective on this issue anyway?" Here the student is being stereotyped as a spokesperson for his entire ethnic group.

- Students in a mass media communications class are learning to think critically about television programs. They're talking about a situation comedy set in an urban high school. "Man, they really whitewashed that show," says one student. "It's mostly about inner-city kids, but they didn't show anybody getting into trouble, doing drugs, or joining gangs." The student's comment perpetuates common racial stereotypes.

- On the first day of the term, students taking English composition enter a class taught by a professor from India. One of the students asks the professor, "Am I in the right class? Maybe there's been a mistake. I thought this was supposed to be an English class." The student assumed that only people with white skins are qualified to teach English courses.

The United Nations defines **racism** as a theory of races hierarchy that presumes that one race is superior to others. Racism can be seen when groups or individuals adopt unfair policies and at times outright hostility to other social or ethnic groups. The operating assumption behind racism is that differences mean deficits.

Diversity is invaluable

Higher education can help reinforce an attitude of tolerance, open-mindedness, and respect for individual differences.

When racism lives, we all lose—even those groups with social and political power. We lose the ability to make friends and to function effectively on teams. We crush human potential. People without the skills to bridge cultures are already at a disadvantage.

Higher education offers a chance to change this. Academic environments can become cultural laboratories—places where people of diverse races and cultures can meet in an atmosphere of tolerance. Students who create alliances outside their immediate group are preparing to succeed in both school and work.

Synergy is the idea that the whole is more than the sum of its parts. Consider some examples: A symphony orchestra consists of many different instruments; when played together, their effect is multiplied many times. A football team has members with different specialties; when their talents are combined, they can win a league championship.

Today, we are waking up not only to the *fact* of diversity but also to the *value* of diversity. Biologists tell us that diversity of animal species benefits our ecology. The same idea applies to the human species. Through education, our goal can be to see that we are all part of a complex world—that our own culture is different from, not better than, others. Knowing this, we can stop saying, "This is the way to work, learn, relate to others, and view the world." Instead, we can say, "Here is the way I have been doing it. I would also like to see your way."

The fact of diversity also represents opportunity in the workplace. Understanding cultural differences—local and international—will help you to embrace others' viewpoints, which can lead to profitable solutions. Organizations that are attuned to diversity are more likely to prosper in the global marketplace. Look at the annual list of Canada's Best Diversity Employers and you will see many names you recognize, from Bell Canada, which offers enhanced mental health benefits for employees, to Home Depot, which supports people with disabilities. TD Bank Group has regional LGBTQQ employee resource groups and has an active Pride Network with over 3,000 members. General Motors Canada has a Supplier Diversity Council, which works specifically with recognized women-owned and minority businesses in North America. Check out Canada's Best Diversity Employers website to see the complete list of annual winners at *www.canadastop100.com/diversity*.

Accepting diversity does not mean ignoring the differences among cultures so that we all become the same. Instead, we can become more like a mosaic—a piece of art in which each element maintains its individuality yet blends with others to form a harmonious whole.

The more you can embrace diversity, the more friends you can make in school and the better prepared you'll be for the workforce of the 21st century. If you plan to pursue a career in healthcare, for example, you can prepare to work with patients from many ethnic, religious, racial, sexual orientation, and ability groups. If you choose to start a business, you can prepare to sell to customers from many demographic groups. And if you plan to teach, you can prepare to assist every student who walks into your classroom.

Learning to live with diversity is a process of returning to "beginner's mind"—a place where we question our biases and assumptions. It takes courage to dwell in beginner's mind—courage to go outside the confines of our own culture and world view. It can feel uncomfortable at first. Yet there are lasting rewards to gain. Research shows that students who interact more frequently with those who are different than themselves grow more in terms of interpersonal development and cognition than those who don't (Schreiner, 2010b). But to be truly successful, you want to be able to have a greater ability to interact sensitively across a wide variety of cultures. You all have school in common, so use this opportunity to meet new people and explore other points of view.

As you read the following articles, look within yourself. This chapter aims to help you examine your own biases. With self-awareness, you can go beyond them.

Building relationships
ACROSS CULTURES

COMMUNICATING WITH PEOPLE of other cultures is a learned skill—a habit. According to Stephen R. Covey (1989), author of *The Seven Habits of Highly Effective People*, a habit is the point at which desire, knowledge, and skill meet. Desire is about wanting to do something. Knowledge is understanding what to do. And skill is the ability to do it.

Desire, knowledge, and skill are equally important for bridging gaps in cultural understanding. This article speaks to the first two factors—*desire* and *knowledge*—and also provides suggestions for gaining *skill*.

Start with self-discovery

The first step to developing diversity skills is to learn about yourself and understand the lenses through which you see the world. One way to do this is to intentionally switch lenses; that is, to consciously perceive familiar events in a new way.

For example, think of a situation in your life that involved an emotionally charged conflict among several people. Now mentally put yourself inside the skin of another person in that conflict. Ask yourself, "How would I view this situation if I were that person?" You can also learn by asking, "What if I were a person of the opposite gender? Or if I were a member of a different racial or ethnic group? Or if I were older or younger?"

Do this exercise consistently, and you'll discover that we live in a world of multiple realities. There are many different ways to interpret any event—and just as many ways to respond, given our individual differences.

Also reflect on how people can have experiences of privilege *and* prejudice. For example, someone might tell you that he's more likely to be promoted at work because he's white and male—*and* that he's been looked down upon because he lives in a trailer park.

See if you can recall incidents such as these from your own life. Think of times when you were favoured because of your gender, race, or age—and times when you were excluded or ridiculed based on one of those same characteristics. In doing this, you'll discover ways to identify with a wider range of people.

Learn about other cultures

Back up your desire with knowledge. People from different cultures read differently, write differently, think differently, eat differently, and learn differently than you do. Knowing this, you can be more effective with your classmates, co-workers, and neighbours.

One key to understanding communication styles is to look for several possible interpretations of any behaviour. Here are some examples:

- Consider the hand signal that signifies *OK* to many Canadians—thumb and index finger forming a circle. In France, that signal denotes the number zero. In Japan, it is a symbol for money. And in Brazil, it is considered an obscene gesture.

- When Canadians see a speaker who puts her hands in her pockets, they seldom attribute any meaning to this behaviour. But in many countries—such as Germany, Indonesia, and Austria—this gesture is considered rude.

- During a conversation, you might prefer having a little distance between yourself and another person. But both gender and culture influence how close people might sit during conversation.

- In much of Canadian culture, you are supposed to look at individuals directly when you talk to them. However, this is not true of many Aboriginal peoples or people from many Asian cultures.

These examples could be extended to cover many areas—posture, physical contact, facial expressions, and more. And the various ways of interpreting these behaviours are neither right nor wrong. They simply represent differing styles in making meaning out of what we see.

You might find yourself fascinated by the communication styles that make up a particular culture. Consider learning as much about that culture as possible. Immerse yourself in it. Read novels, see plays, go to concerts, listen to music, look at art, take courses, and learn the language.

Look for differences between individualist and collectivist cultures

Individualist cultures flourish in Canada, the United States, and Western Europe. If your family has deep roots in one of these areas, you were probably raised to value personal fulfillment and personal success. You received recognition or rewards when you stood out from your peers by earning the highest grades in your class, scoring the most points during a basketball season, or demonstrating another form of individual achievement.

In contrast, collectivist cultures value cooperation over competition. Group progress is more important than individual success. Credit for an achievement is widely shared. If you were raised in such a culture, you probably place a high value on your family and were

taught to respect your elders. Collectivist cultures dominate Asia, Africa, and Latin America.

In short, individualist cultures often emphasize "I"; collectivist cultures tend to emphasize "we." Forgetting about the differences between them can strain a friendship or wreck an international business deal.

If you were raised in an individualist culture, here are some suggestions to help you work well with someone from a collectivist culture:

- *Remember that someone from a collectivist culture may place a high value on "saving face."* This idea involves more than simply avoiding embarrassment. This person may *not* want to be singled out from other members of a group, even for a positive achievement. If you have a direct request for this person or want to share something that could be taken as a personal criticism, save it for a private conversation.

- *Respect titles and last names.* Although Canadians often like to use first names immediately after meeting someone, in some cultures this practice is acceptable only among family members. Especially in work settings, use last names and job titles during your first meetings; for example, Professor Thompson or Dean Kimila. Allow time for informal relationships to develop.

- *Put messages in context.* For members of collectivist cultures, words convey only part of an intended message. Notice gestures and other nonverbal communication as well.

If you were raised in a collectivist culture, you can creatively "reverse" the above list:

- Keep in mind that direct questions from a Canadian student or co-worker are meant not to offend but only to clarify an idea.

- Don't be surprised if you are called by a nickname, if no one asks about your family, or if you are rewarded for a personal achievement.

- In social situations, remember that indirect cues might not get another person's attention.

- Practise asking clearly and directly for what you want.

Reach out

If carrying out any of these suggestions feels awkward, don't give up. By intentionally expanding your comfort zone over time, you can break down social barriers and gain a new level of ease at being with people.

A more formal option is to arrange an intergroup dialogue—a "*facilitated*, face-to-face meeting between students from two or more social identity groups that have a history of conflict or potential conflict" (Nagda & Zúñiga, 2003). Examples are Christians and Muslims, blacks and whites, and people with disabilities and those without disabilities. The goal is sustained and meaningful conversation about controversial issues. Groups typically gather with a skilled facilitator for two-hour meetings over 6 to 12 weeks.

Look for common ground

Students in higher education—no matter what their cultural background—often find that they worry about many of the same things—including tuition bills, the quality of the residence food, and the shortage of on-campus parking spaces. More important, our fundamental goals as human beings—such as health, physical safety, and economic security—cross culture lines.

The key is to honour the differences among people while remembering what we have in common. Intercultural competence is not just about our differences—it's also about our similarities. On a biological level, less than 1 percent of the human genome accounts for visible characteristics such as skin colour. In terms of our genetic blueprint, we are more than 99 percent the same (Szalavitz, 2001).

Speak and listen with cultural sensitivity

After first speaking with someone from another culture, don't assume that you've been understood or that you fully understand the other person. Cultures differ dramatically in terms of who is responsible for understanding a message, the speaker or the listener. In **low context cultures** such as Canada, the United States, and Scandinavia, the onus is on the speaker to explicitly convey the message to the listener, whereas in **high context cultures** such as Japan and Mediterranean countries, it is up to the listener to get the implicit message from the speaker (Dimitrov, 2009).

For Canadians, this means that speakers from high context cultures may sound vague or secretive; they might wonder why the speaker doesn't just get to the point. Speakers from high context cultures assume that the listener has the same background knowledge of the topic and therefore the listener should be able to figure out what the speaker is trying to communicate. All cultures vary on the continuum from high to low context and there may even be differences within a culture based on the person's age or gender. In the classroom, differences between individuals from high versus low context cultures may lead to challenges in communication between students and their instructors.

If you're speaking with someone who doesn't understand English well, keep in mind the following ideas:

- Speak slowly, distinctly, and patiently.
- To clarify your statement, don't repeat individual words over and over again. Restate your entire message with simple, direct language and short sentences.
- Avoid slang and figures of speech.
- English courses for non-native speakers often emphasize written English, so write down what you're saying.
- Stay calm, and avoid sending nonverbal messages that you're frustrated.

Keep in mind that just because someone speaks with an accent does not mean they do not understand English perfectly. If you're unsure about how well you're communicating, ask questions: "I don't know how to make this idea clear for you. How might I communicate better?" "When you look away from me during our conversation, I feel uneasy. Is there something else we need to talk about?" "When you don't ask questions, I wonder if I am being clear. Do you want any more explanation?" Questions such as these can get cultural differences out in the open in a constructive way.

Look for individuals, not group representatives

Sometimes the way we speak glosses over differences among individuals and reinforces stereotypes. For example, a student worried about her grade in math expresses concern over "all those Asian students who are skewing the class curve." Or a white music major assumes that her Caribbean classmate knows a lot about reggae music. We can avoid such errors by seeing people as individuals—not spokespersons for an entire group.

Find a translator, mediator, or model

People who move with ease between two or more cultures can help us greatly. Diane de Anda (1984), a professor at the University of California, Los Angeles, speaks of three kinds of people who can communicate across cultures. She calls them **translators, mediators**, and **models**.

A *translator* is someone who is truly bicultural—a person who relates naturally to both people in a mainstream culture and people from a contrasting culture. This person can share her own experiences in overcoming discrimination, learning another language or dialect, and coping with stress.

Mediators are people who belong to the dominant or mainstream culture. Unlike translators, they might not be bicultural. However, mediators value diversity and are committed to cultural understanding. Often they are teachers, counsellors, tutors, mentors, or social workers.

Models are members of a culture who are positive examples. Models include students from any racial or cultural group who participate in class and demonstrate effective study habits. Models can also include athletes, community leaders, and entertainers. Drake is a current example of a model; his philanthropy has included donating $50,000 to a student in Miami for school.

Your school might have people who serve these functions, even if they're not labelled translators, mediators, or models. Some schools have mentor or "bridge" programs that pair new students with teachers or peers of the same race or culture. Ask your international student services or student counselling services about such programs.

Develop support systems

Many students find that their social adjustment affects their academic performance. Students with strong support systems—such as families, friends, churches, self-help groups, and mentors—are using a powerful strategy for success in school. As an exercise, list the support systems that you rely on right now. Also list new support systems you could develop.

Support systems can help you bridge culture gaps. With a strong base of support in your own group, you can feel more confident in meeting people outside that group.

Be willing to accept feedback

Members of another culture might let you know that some of your words or actions had a meaning other than what you intended. For example, perhaps a comment that seems harmless to you is offensive to them. And they may tell you directly about it.

Avoid responding to such feedback with comments such as "Don't get me wrong," "You're taking this way too seriously," or "You're too sensitive." Instead, listen without resistance. Open yourself to what others have to say. Remember to distinguish between the *intention* of your behaviour and its actual *impact* on other people. Then take the feedback you receive, and ask yourself how you can use it to communicate more effectively in the future.

You can also interpret such feedback positively—a sign that others believe you can change and that they see the possibility of a better relationship with you.

If you are new at responding to diversity, expect to make some mistakes along the way. As long as you approach people in a spirit of tolerance, your words and actions can always be changed.

Speak up against discrimination

You might find yourself in the presence of someone who tells a racist joke, makes a homophobic comment, or utters an ethnic slur. When this happens, you have a right to state what you observe, share what you think, and communicate how you feel. Depending on the circumstance, you might say,

- "That's a stereotype, and we don't have to fall for it."
- "Other people are going to take offence at that. Let's tell jokes that don't put people down."

Did you **know that …?**

Pink Shirt Day was started by teenagers in Nova Scotia to support a grade nine male student who was being bullied. They started a global anti-bullying movement that has now spread to over 180 countries. To learn more about Pink Shirt Day go to *www.pinkshirtday.ca*.

- "I realize that you don't mean to offend anybody, but I feel hurt and angry by what you just said."
- "I know that a gay person told you that story, but I still think it's homophobic and creates an atmosphere that I don't want to be in."

This kind of speaking may be the most difficult communicating you ever do. However, in choosing not to speak, you give the impression that you agree with biased speech.

In response to your candid comments, many people will apologize and express their willingness to change. Even if they don't, you can still know that you practised integrity by aligning your words with your values.

Change the institution

None of us lives in isolation. We all live in systems, and these systems do not always tolerate diversity. As a student, you might see people of colour ignored in class. You might see people of a certain ethnic group passed over in job hiring or underrepresented in school organizations. And you might see gay and lesbian students ridiculed or even threatened with violence. One way to stop these actions is to point them out.

You can speak more effectively about what you believe by making some key distinctions. Remember the following:

- **Stereotypes** are errors in thinking—inaccurate ideas about members of another culture.
- **Prejudice** refers to positive or negative feelings about others based on stereotypes.
- **Discrimination** takes places when stereotypes or prejudice get expressed in policies and laws that undermine equal opportunities for all cultures.

The *Canadian Charter of Rights and Freedoms*, as well as the written policies of educational institutions, bans racial and ethnic discrimination. Most institutions have formal procedures that protect students against such discrimination. Find out what those procedures are and use them, if necessary.

In recent history, students have fuelled much social change. When it comes to ending discrimination, you are in an environment where you can make a difference. Run for student government. Write for school publications. Speak at rallies. Express your viewpoint. This is training for citizenship in a multicultural world. ✳

practising
CRITICAL THINKING

Becoming a culture learner

To learn about other cultures in depth, actively move through the cycle of learning described by psychologist David Kolb (and explained more fully in "Learning styles: Discovering how you learn" in Chapter 1). This exercise, which has three parts, illustrates one way to apply the cycle of learning. Use additional space as needed to complete each part.

Part 1: Concrete experience

Think of a specific way to interact with people from a culture different than your own. For example, attend a meeting for a campus group that you normally would not attend. Or sit in a campus cafeteria with a new group of people.

In the space below, describe what you will do to enhance your experience of a different culture. If you are working in the print textbook, use extra paper if necessary.

_____

_____

_____

_____

_____

Part 2: Reflective observation

Describe the experience you had while doing Part 1 of this exercise. Be sure to separate your observations—what you saw, heard, or did—from your interpretations. In addition, see if you can think of other ways to interpret each of your observations.

Use the table provided for this part of the exercise. An example is included to get you started.

Part 3: Abstract conceptualization

Next, see if you can refine your initial interpretations and develop them into some informed conclusions about your experience in Part 1. Do some research about other cultures, looking specifically for information that can help you understand the experience. (Your instructor and a librarian can suggest ways to find such information.) Whenever possible, speak directly to people of various cultures. Share your observations from Part 1, and ask for *their* interpretations.

Reflect on the information you gather. Does it reinforce any of the interpretations you listed in Part 2? Does it call for a change in your thinking? Summarize your conclusions in the space below.

_____

_____

_____

_____

_____

_____

_____

_____

Observation	Your Initial Interpretation	Other Possible Interpretations
For 30 minutes starting at noon on Tuesday, I sat alone in the northeast section of the cafeteria in our student union. During this time, all of the conversations I overheard were conducted in Mandarin.	I sat alone because the Mandarin-speaking students did not want to talk to me. They are unfriendly.	The Mandarin-speaking students are actually friendly. They were just not sure how to start a conversation with me. Perhaps they thought I wanted to eat alone or study. Also, I could have taken the initiative to start a conversation.

Overcome stereotypes with
CRITICAL THINKING

Consider assertions such as "Students like to drink heavily," "People who speak English as a second language are hard to understand," and "Most of the people who live in the Maritimes are on welfare."

These are examples of stereotyping—generalizing about a group of people based on the behaviour of isolated group members. Stereotypes are a potent source of intellectual error. They are signals that we need to shift our thinking skills into high gear—to demand evidence, examine logic, and insist on accurate information.

The word *stereotype* originally referred to a method used by printers to produce duplicate pages of text. This usage still rings true. When we stereotype, we gloss over individual differences and assume that every member of a group is the same.

Stereotypes infiltrate every dimension of human individuality. People are stereotyped on the basis of their race, nationality, physical or mental abilities, ethnic group, religion, political affiliation, geographic location, job, age, gender, IQ, height, or hobby. You name it. We stereotype people based on everything from the colour of their hair to the year of their car.

Stereotypes have many possible sources: fear of the unknown, uncritical thinking, and negative encounters between individual members of different groups. Whatever their cause, stereotypes abound.

In themselves, generalizations are neither good nor bad. In fact, they are essential. Mentally sorting people, events, and objects into groups allows us to make sense of the world. But when we consciously or unconsciously make generalizations that rigidly divide the people of the world into "us" versus "them," we create stereotypes and put on the blinders of prejudice.

You can take several steps to free yourself from stereotypes.

Look for errors in thinking

Here are some of the most common errors:

- **Selective perception.** Stereotypes can literally change the way we see the world. If we assume that homeless people are lazy, for instance, we tend to notice only the examples that support our opinion. Stories about homeless people who are too young or too ill to work will probably escape our attention.

- **Self-fulfilling prophecy.** When we interact with people based on stereotypes, we set them up in ways that confirm our thinking. For example, when people of colour were denied access to higher education based on stereotypes about their intelligence, they were deprived of opportunities to demonstrate their intellectual gifts.

- **Self-justification.** Stereotypes can allow people to assume the role of a victim and to avoid taking responsibility for their own lives. An unemployed white male might believe that affirmative action programs are making it impossible for him to get a job—even as he overlooks his own lack of experience or qualifications.

Create categories in a more flexible way

Stereotyping has been described as a case of "hardening of the categories." Avoid this problem by making your categories broader. Instead of seeing people based on their skin colour, you could look at them on the basis of their heredity. (People of all races share most of the same genes.) Or you could make your categories narrower. Instead of talking about "religious extremists," look for subgroups among the people who adopt a certain religion. Distinguish between groups that advocate violence and those that shun it.

Test your generalizations about people through action

You can do this by actually meeting people of other cultures. It's easy to believe almost anything about certain groups of people as long as we never deal directly with individuals. Inaccurate pictures tend to die when people from various cultures study together, work together, and live together. Consider joining a school or community organization that will put you in contact with people of other cultures. Your rewards will include a more global perspective and an ability to thrive in a multicultural world.

Be willing to see your own stereotypes

The Power Process "Notice your pictures and let them go" (Chapter 4) can help us to dispel our stereotypes. One belief about ourselves that many of us can shed is this: "I have no pictures about people from other cultures." Even people with the best of intentions can harbour subtle biases. Admitting this possibility allows us to look inward even more deeply for stereotypes. Every time that we notice inaccurate pictures buried in our minds and let them go, we each take a personal step toward embracing diversity. *

STUDENTS WITH DISABILITIES:
Know your rights

EQUAL OPPORTUNITY for people with disabilities is the law. The federal Employment Equity Act of 1995 was created to protect equal opportunity in the workplace for people with disabilities.

Ask for what you want

Students with disabilities used to face a restricted set of choices in school. For instance, many had trouble specializing in subjects—engineering, science, or medicine—that called for using technical equipment. New technology—computers and calculators operated with voice commands and other adaptive devices—has changed that. Students with disabilities can now choose from almost any course or program of study offered in postsecondary education.

Instructors with even the best of intentions can forget about promoting learning for people with disabilities. To protect your rights, speak up. Ask for what you want. Begin with the suggestions about being assertive in Chapter 8, "Communicating," using "I" messages and listening actively. Those strategies can help you succeed in school. So can the following.

Use available resources

A wealth of resources already exists to support your success in education. To begin with, check into services offered by your province. Provincial governments often provide funds for education or they can help you find that money. Provincial ministries of education can guide you to services. In addition, the Learning Disabilities Association of Canada (*www.ldac-acta.ca*)

Monkey Business Images/Shutterstock.com

offers help in placing employees with learning or physical disabilities. The Canadian National Institute for the Blind offers those with vision loss help finding employment through CareerConnect Canada. Many other organizations are there to help you.

If you need an academic accommodation, such as being allowed to have extra time on exams, first identify yourself to the Services for Students with Disabilities office within your institution. This office is part of student services at most colleges or universities. Your school will ask you to document that you have a disability and need academic accommodation. This documentation might include a written evaluation from a physician, psychologist, or other professional who has worked with you.

The services to ask about include the following:

- Permits that allow you to park closer to classrooms
- Note-taking services
- Lecture transcriptions
- Textbook-reading services and textbooks with voice-reading functionality
- Sign language interpreters
- Help in selecting courses and registering for classes
- Assistants for laboratory courses in science
- Shuttle buses for transportation between classes
- Closed captioning for instructional television programs
- TTY/TDD devices for students with hearing impairments
- Assistance with taking tests
- Accessible residence rooms

Use technology to your advantage

If you have a disability, then gain as many computer skills as possible. Also set up your computer to promote your success. For example, find out how to do the following:

- Enlarge the cursor and adjust its blink rate.
- Enlarge all fonts and icons.
- Zoom in on all or a portion of the screen image.
- Adjust the screen display to remove all colour and render images in black and white or grey-scale.
- Use voice recognition rather than the keyboard for menu options.
- Turn on text-to-speech capabilities so that a computer-generated voice reads menu options, alerts, and Web pages out loud.
- Choose a keyboard layout that's more convenient for typing with one hand or finger.

To access such features in the Windows operating system, select the Windows Control Panel or use the Accessibility Wizard. In Mac OS X, click on the Apple menu in the upper-left corner of the screen and select "System Preferences." In the System Preferences panel, click "Accessibility." Your Office for Services for Students with Disabilities can assist you with using technology productively.

Speak assertively

Tell instructors when it's appropriate to consider your disability. If you use a wheelchair, for example, ask for

---

Planning for success: What students with learning disabilities need to know

There are more and more students with learning disabilities attending postsecondary education. The majority of these students choose to attend community colleges. Students with learning disabilities can impact their college success in several ways. If you have a learning disability (LD), it is important to connect with your school's Learning Services or Disabilities Office before classes begin and get an accommodation plan in place. Many students begin postsecondary courses without the accommodations that they used in high school, but after a while most find that they require the accommodations. An accommodation plan will help students with learning disabilities have an even playing field. Accommodations make learning accessible for students with LD by providing the supports students need to acquire the course information and demonstrate their knowledge.

It is essential for students with LD to communicate regularly with their professors and instructors. Students will benefit from explaining to the instructor what accommodations they find most helpful and why. Instructors are aware of students' rights to accommodations but do not necessarily understand learning disabilities or the impact of the accommodations for the individual student.

Planning and managing time is important for all students, but especially important for students with LD. This means breaking up reading, studying, and assignments into manageable segments so that the accumulation of work is not overwhelming. Breaking down assignments into smaller sections and using a calendar to set a time frame for the completion of each section is one way to approach the volume of work. Students also need to organize their time so that they know when assignments are due and tests are scheduled. Being proactive in planning helps keep things from creeping up unexpectedly. Most schools offer workshops in time management, stress management, assignment writing, etc. Students with LD can successfully complete postsecondary education—having supports in place and using effective strategies are keys to this success.

Kathyrn Hansen, Instructor, St. Clair College

Courtesy of Kathryn Hansen

appropriate transportation on field trips. If you have a visual disability, request that instructors speak as they write on the chalkboard. Also ask them to use high-contrast colours and to write legibly.

Plan ahead

Meet with your Counsellor for Students with Disabilities to design an educational plan—one that takes your needs into account. Ask for recommendations for instructors before registering for classes. Interview prospective instructors and sit in on their classes. Express an interest in the class, ask to see a course outline, and discuss any adjustments that could help you complete the course. Some of the services you request might take extra time to deliver. Allow for possible delays as you plan your schedule. If you are on a large campus and have a physical disability, consider how far apart the classrooms are and how easy it is to move from building to building in the winter.

Ask for appropriate treatment

The Office for Services for Students with Disabilities will let instructors know what accommodations you need while ensuring the confidentiality of any details you may have shared with them. It is not necessary for you to discuss personal details with your instructors.

Follow up when necessary

If the academic accommodation that you requested is not working for you, tell your advisor in the Disability Office right away. Talk to the person who helped set up the accommodation or your academic counsellor about trying another accommodation. If necessary, schools usually have grievance procedures for resolving conflicts about the services you're receiving. Most schools have an ombudsperson who can be a good resource on how to deal with any grievance you might have.

Take care of yourself

Many students with chronic illnesses or disabilities find that rest breaks are essential. If this is true for you, write such breaks into your daily or weekly plan. A related suggestion is to treat yourself with respect. If your health changes in a way that you don't like, avoid berating yourself. Even when you do not choose the conditions in your life, you can choose your attitude toward those conditions.

It's important to accept compliments and periodically review your accomplishments in school. Fill yourself with affirmation. As you educate yourself, you are attaining mastery. ✳

DEALING WITH
sexism and sexual harassment

HARASSMENT OCCURS in schools and workplaces. Nearly all of incidents of harassment are illegal or violate organizational policies.

Heidi Besen/Shutterstock.com

In Canada today, women make up the majority of first-year students in postsecondary education, yet they still encounter bias based on gender.

This bias can take many forms. For example, instructors might gloss over the contributions of women. Students in philosophy class might never hear of a woman named Hypatia, an ancient Greek philosopher and mathematician. Those specializing in computer science might never learn about Rear Admiral Grace Murray Hopper, who pioneered the development of a computer language named COBOL. And your art history textbook might not mention the Canadian painter Emily Carr.

Although men also can be subjects of **sexism** and **sexual harassment**, women are more likely to experience this form of discrimination. Even the most well-intentioned people might behave in ways that discriminate against or discount women. Sexism is a factor when the following situations occur:

- Instructors use only masculine pronouns—*he, his,* and *him*—to refer to both men and women.

- Career counsellors hint that careers in mathematics and science are not appropriate for women.

- Students pay more attention to feedback from a male teacher than from a female teacher.

- Women are not called on in class, their comments are ignored, or they are overly praised for answering the simplest questions.

Students who are LGBTQQ are far more likely to experience either verbal, physical, or sexual harassment than their peers. Transgender students are even more vulnerable to these attacks. A study of Canadian high school students found that 74 percent of transgender students reported being verbally harassed about their gender expression (Taylor & Peter et al., 2011). Students who are members of both a sexual minority and a visible minority or Indigenous group experience a "double whammy." They are harassed for both their gender orientation and their ethnicity. All LGBTQQ students report high levels of sexual harassment (between 33 and 49 percent).

Many kinds of behaviour—both verbal and physical—can be categorized as sexual harassment. This includes unwelcome sexual conduct. Examples of such conduct are found in a school setting:

- Sexual touching or advances
- Any other unwanted touch
- Unwanted verbal intimacy
- Online sexual bullying
- Displaying or distributing sexually explicit materials
- Sexual gestures or jokes
- Pressure for sexual favours
- Talking about personal sexual activity
- Spreading rumours about someone's sexual activity or rating someone's sexual performance.

The feminist and gay movements have raised awareness about discrimination against women and sexual and gender minorities. We can now respond to sexism and harassment in the places we live, work, and go to school. Here are some specific strategies.

Point out sexist language and behaviour

When you see examples of sexism or harassment, point them out. Your message can be more effective if you use "I" messages instead of personal attacks, as explained in Chapter 8, "Communicating." Indicate the specific statements and behaviours that you consider sexist.

Keep in mind that men can also be subjected to sexism, ranging from antagonistic humour to exclusion from jobs that have traditionally been done by women.

Address homophobic language when you hear it. When you hear comments like "She throws like a girl" or name-calling, let the person know that's not okay with you.

Observe your own language and behaviour

Looking for sexist behaviour in others is effective. Detecting it in yourself can be just as powerful. Write a Discovery Statement about specific comments that could be interpreted as sexist. Then notice if you say any of these things. Ask people you know to point out occasions when you use similar statements. Follow up with an Intention Statement that describes how you plan to change your speaking or behaviour.

Use language that is gender inclusive—say *children* rather than *boys and girls* or *people* rather than *men or women*. Respect everyone's right to be addressed by the pronoun they prefer.

Avoid making assumptions about people's sexual orientation based upon their appearance.

Encourage support for women and gender and sexual minorities

Through networks, women can work to overcome the effects of sexism. Strategies include study groups for women, women's job networks, and professional organizations such as Women in Small Businesses. Check your school calendar and library to see if any of these services are available at your school.

Attend workshops on LGBTQQ issues or start a discussion group so you can become more knowledgeable about issues which affect sexual and gender minorities.

Set limits

Women, value yourselves. Recognize your right to an education without the distraction of inappropriate and invasive behaviour. Trust your judgment about when your privacy or your rights are being violated. Decide now what kind of sexual comments and actions you're uncomfortable with—and refuse to put up with them.

Take action

If you are sexually, physically, or verbally harassed, take action.

The *Canadian Charter of Rights and Freedoms*, part of the Constitution Act of 1982, protects the interests of Canadians by providing a way to challenge abuses of basic rights and freedoms. It prohibits gender discrimination and all forms of harassment.

Even the most well-intentioned people might behave in ways that discriminate against or discount women.

Since education is a provincial jurisdiction, the most direct route for students to deal with sexual harassment is through their academic institution or their provincial Human Rights Commission. These commissions administer the provincial human rights codes that provide guarantees and remedies for those who have been sexually harassed or discriminated against.

Many provinces have adopted new legislation around sexual violence and harassment; for example, Ontario's Bill 132, "The Sexual Violence and Harassment Plan Act," and British Columbia's Bill 23, "Sexual Violence and Misconduct Policy Act," which mandates that all employers, including colleges and universities, investigate and address occurrences of sexual harassment. This includes ensuring that investigations are handled in a timely fashion and that they have a transparent process about reporting. Information about your campus policy about sexual harassment and violence should be available on your school's website. ✳

journal entry 9-2

Discovery Statement

Reflect on the Quality of a Recent Conversation

Read the Power Process "Choose your conversations and your community," later in this chapter. Then in the space below, describe the circumstances of a conversation you had today and summarize its content.

_____

_____

_____

_____

_____

_____

_____

Now reflect on this conversation. Determine whether it aligned with your values and goals.

I discovered that . . .

_____

_____

_____

_____

_____

_____

_____

_____

_____

Word associations

Write down the first words that come to mind when you hear the terms listed below. Do this now.

musician

_____

_____

_____

homeless people

_____

_____

hockey players

_____

_____

software engineers

_____

_____

disabled person

_____

retired person

_____

_____

mature student

_____

_____

_____

Next, exchange your responses to this exercise with a friend. Did you discover stereotypes or other examples of bias? What counts as evidence of bias? Summarize your answers here.

_____

_____

_____

_____

_____

_____

_____

_____

_____

_____

_____

_____

_____

_____

_____

_____

_____

_____

_____

_____

_____

_____

_____

POWER PROCESS

Choose Your Conversations and Your Community

Andrey_Popov/Shutterstock.com

Conversations can exist in many forms. One form involves people talking out loud to each other. At other times, the conversation takes place inside our own heads, and we call it *thinking*. Our observations about communications have three implications that wind their way through every aspect of our lives.

One implication is that conversations exercise incredible power over what we think, feel, and do. They shape our attitudes, our decisions, our opinions, our emotions, and our actions. If you want clues as to what a person will be like tomorrow, listen to what she's talking about today.

Second, given that conversations are so powerful, it's amazing that few people act on this fact. Most of us swim in a constant sea of conversations, almost none of which we carefully and thoughtfully choose.

The real power of this process lies in a third discovery: We can choose our conversations. Certain conversations create real value for us. They give us fuel for reaching our goals. Other conversations distract us from what we want. They might even create lasting unhappiness and frustration.

Suppose that you meet with an instructor to ask about some guidelines for writing a term paper. He launches into a tirade about your writing skills. This presents you with several options. One possibility is to talk about what a jerk the instructor is and give up on the idea of learning to write well. Another option is to refocus the conversation on what you can do to improve your writing skills, such as working with a writing tutor or taking a basic composition class. These two sets of conversations will have vastly different consequences for your success in school.

Another important fact about your conversations is that they are dramatically influenced by the people you associate with. If you want to change your attitudes about almost anything—prejudice, politics, religion, humour—choose your conversations by choosing your community. Spend time with people who speak about and live consistently with the attitudes you value. Use conversations to change habits and create new options in your life. It's as simple as choosing the next article you read or the next topic you discuss with a friend.

Begin applying this Power Process today. Start choosing your conversations, and watch what happens.

Put it to WORK

Talk about intercultural competence

In the workplace, the term *intercultural competence* is starting to replace the term *diversity skills*. The reason is simple: It's one thing to create a workplace that includes people of various cultural backgrounds. It's another thing to create a workplace where all those people feel welcome. During job interviews, be prepared to give evidence of your intercultural competence. Talk about cooperative learning projects with diverse members—and how you involved everyone on the team.

Expect differences

Most of us unconsciously judge others by a single set of cultural standards—our own. That can lead to communication breakdown. Consider some examples:

- A man in Costa Rica works for a company that's based in Canada and has offices around the world. He turns down a promotion that would take his family to Manitoba. This choice mystifies the company's executives. But the man has grandparents who are in ill health, and leaving them behind would be taboo in his country.

- A Caucasian woman from Toronto travels to Mexico City on business. She shows up promptly for a 9:00 a.m. meeting and finds that it starts 30 minutes late and goes an hour beyond its scheduled ending time. She's entered a culture with a flexible sense of time.

- An American executive schedules a meeting over dinner with people from his company's office in Italy. As soon as the group orders food, the executive launches into a discussion of his agenda items. He notices that his co-workers from Italy seem unusually silent and wonders whether they feel offended. He forgets that they come from a culture where people phase in to business discussions slowly—only after building a relationship through "small talk."

To prevent misunderstandings, remember that culture touches every aspect of human behaviour, ranging from the ways that people greet each other to the ways they resolve conflict. Expecting differences upfront helps you keep an open mind.

Use language with care

Even people who speak the same language can use simple words that can be confusing to others. For instance, giving someone a "mickey" can mean pulling a practical joke—or slipping a drug into someone's drink. We can find it tough to communicate simple observations, let alone abstract concepts.

You can help by communicating simply and directly. When meeting with people who speak English as a second language,

© shaunl/iStockphoto

think twice before using figures of speech or slang expressions. Stick to standard English and enunciate clearly. Fight the common urge to speak louder. Speak slowly and clearly, not loudly.

Also remember that nonverbal language differs across cultures. For example, people from India shake their head from side to side to indicate agreement, not disagreement.

Put messages in context

When speaking to people of another culture, you might find that words carry only part of an intended message. In many countries, strong networks of shared assumptions form a context for communication. As an example, people from some Asian and Arabic countries might not include every detail of an agreement in a written contract. These people often place a high value on keeping verbal promises. Spelling out all the details in writing might be considered an insult. Knowing such facts can help you prevent and resolve conflicts in the workplace.

Now create a career connection of your own

Review this chapter, looking for a suggestion that you will commit to using while working or looking for a job. In a sentence or two, describe exactly what you plan to do and the primary benefit you want to gain; for example, "I will go on an alternative spring break where I travel and work with people from other cultures. I will begin to develop my intercultural communication skills."

State your strategy and desired benefit in the space below.

_____

_____

_____

_____

_____

QUIZ

chapter 9

■ Put it to Work
◄ ◄ ◄ ◄
■ Skills Snapshot
■ Master Student Profile

Name_____   Date____/____/____

1. Explain the differences among *stereotypes*, *prejudice*, and *discrimination* as defined in the text.

2. Give two examples of differences between individualist and collectivist cultures.

3. List three strategies for communicating across cultures.

4. Explain the difference between *self-fulfilling prophecy* and *self-justification* when it comes to detecting stereotypes.

5. Define the terms *translator*, *mediator*, and *model* as explained in this chapter.

6. Describe at least one way to overcome stereotypes with critical thinking.

7. Explain a strategy for taking charge of the conversations in your life.

8. You are part of a class discussion and find that one of the students responds quite tersely to a question from the instructor. When asked why we build dams for hydroelectricity, the student responds, "Geography." The short response may be because the student is from
   (a) high context culture
   (b) low context culture
   (c) high power culture
   (d) low power culture

9. Rewrite the following sentence so that it is gender neutral: "Any writer can benefit from honing his skill at observing people."

10. What are three things that students with learning disabilities can do to enhance their success in school?

Skills **SNAPSHOT**

Now that you've reflected on the ideas in this chapter and experimented with some new strategies, revisit your responses to the "Diversity" section of the Discovery Wheel exercise in Chapter 1. Then complete the following sentences.

QUESTIONING ASSUMPTIONS

The racial, ethnic, and gender stereotypes that I've heard include . . .

If I talk to people who express such stereotypes, I will respond by . . .

BRIDGING CULTURES

When I meet someone whose beliefs or customs differ in a major way from mine, my first reaction is . . .

Other ways I could respond to such differences include . . .

NEXT ACTION

I'll know that I've reached a new level of mastery with diversity when . . .

To reach that level of mastery, the most important thing I can do next is to . . .

MASTER STUDENT
PROFILE

chapter 9

■ Put it to Work
■ Quiz
■ Skills Snapshot
◄ ◄ ◄ ◄

Brielle Beardy-Linklater
… is breaking down barriers

Brielle Beardy-Linklater is forthright about her desire to improve conditions for First Nations people—even if that means doing it with a take-no-prisoners attitude.

"Years of systemic oppression and facing racism and transphobia on a daily basis has made me that way," she explains. "No one was really apologetic about that, so I'm not afraid to say what I need to say to help people thrive. This is all about lifting up other people."

Beardy-Linklater believes politics is the best way to solve many socio-economic issues, like poverty, which disproportionately affect First Nations communities.

"Who better to advocate on behalf of those factors, than someone who's lived them … and continues to live them," said Beardy-Linklater.

In the past, she's worked with the New Democratic Party in Manitoba. She has decided to run for office for the party in 2020.

"It's about Indigenous people going into a political atmosphere, and taking your space and reclaiming it. It's the only way to do it."

As a transgender woman she says: "I would be breaking a mould, definitely."

But Beardy-Linklater has already broken that mold. She was one of 338 Daughters of the Vote, a competition which selected one young woman to fill every seat in the House of Commons as a way of marking the 100th anniversary of women receiving the vote.

She made history of her own that day, becoming the first transgender woman to take a seat in Parliament, a moment she says was a huge honour.

"It's about Indigenous people going into a political atmosphere, and taking your space and reclaiming it. It's the only way to do it."

For Beardy-Linklater, being Indigenous means something incredibly special.

"I am a testament to survival," she says. "We are a really strong people. We have such values of love and community."

She would prefer to see those values acknowledged and honoured, instead of the celebration of Canada's 150th anniversary.

"The country was founded on the colonization of Indigenous people, so it is very difficult for me to celebrate that," she explains.

Beardy-Linklater hopes the next 150 years for Canada will see more collaboration on tackling the issues affecting Indigenous people, as well as better education, employment, and economic opportunities.

"I really feel like something is changing. We're seeing it. Something is happening, I definitely feel it."

Source: Sapurji, S, Karapita, M., & Alex, C. (n.d.). I am Indigenous. *CBC News.* Accessed at *http://www.cbc.ca/news2/interactives/i-am-indigenous-2017/beardy-linklater.html.* Reprinted with permission.

Material republished with the express permission of: Winnipeg Sun, a division of Postmedia Network Inc.

Brielle Beardy-Linklater is determined to become an agent of change. "I consider myself a political activist, of the radical variety," says the Cree woman from Thompson, Manitoba.

Money

ilona.shorokhova/Shutterstock.com

what is included . . .

do you have a minute?

Take a minute right now to search your school's website for the location, phone number, and email address of the financial aid office. Make an appointment to meet with someone in that office to find out more about bursaries or grants that might be available to you.

THE END
of money worries

leungchopan/Shutterstock.com

"I can't afford it" is a common reason that students give for dropping out of school. "I don't know how to pay for it" or "I don't think it's worth it" are probably more accurate ways to state the problem.

Money produces more unnecessary conflict and worry than almost anything else. And it doesn't seem to matter how much money a person has. People who earn $10,000 a year never have enough. People who earn $100,000 a year also say that they never have enough.

Let's say they earned $1 million a year. Then they'd have enough, right? Not necessarily.

Most money problems result from spending more than is available. It's that simple, even though we often do everything we can to complicate the problem.

The solution also is simple: *Don't spend more than you have.* If you are spending more than you have, then increase your income, decrease your spending, or do both. This idea has never won a Nobel Prize in Economics, but you won't go broke applying it.

Money management may be based on a simple idea, but there is a big incentive for us to make it seem more complicated than it really is. If we don't understand money, then we don't have to be responsible for it. After all, if you don't know how to change a flat tire, then you don't have to be the one responsible for fixing it.

Using the strategies in this chapter could help you to have financial peace of mind. That's a bold statement— perhaps even an outrageous one. But what if it's true? Approach this idea with an open mind. Then experiment with it, using your own life as the laboratory.

This chapter can benefit you even during a recession. Although the state of the overall economy matters as well, your financial fate depends far more on the small choices you make every day about spending and earning money.

The strategies you're about to learn are not complicated. In fact, they're not even new. The strategies are all based on the cycle of discovery, intention, and action that you've already practised with the Journal Entries in this book. With these strategies and the abilities to add and subtract, you have everything you need to manage your money.

journal entry · 10-1

Discovery/Intention Statement

Commit to a New Experience of Money

Reflect on your overall experience of money. List any statements you've made about your money during the last month—anything from "I never have enough" to "I have some extra money to invest, and I'm wondering where to put it." Write your statements here.

When speaking about my money, I discovered that I . . .

_____

_____

_____

_____

_____

Scan this chapter with an eye for strategies that could help you increase your income, decrease your expenses, or both. List three money strategies that you'd like to use right away.

I intend to . . .

_____

_____

_____

_____

_____

There are three main steps in money management:

1. Tell the truth about how much money you have and how much you spend (discovery).

2. Commit to living within your means by spending less than you earn (intention).

3. Apply the suggestions for earning more money, spending less money, or both (action).

If you do these three things consistently, you can eventually say goodbye to most money worries.

For example, the single habit of paying off your entire credit card balance each month might be enough to transform your financial life.

This chapter about money does not tell you how to become a millionaire, though you can certainly adopt that as a goal if you choose. Instead, the following pages reveal what many millionaires know—ways to control money instead of letting money control you. ✳

practising
CRITICAL THINKING

10-1

The Money Monitor/Money Plan

Many of us find it easy to lose track of money. It likes to escape when no one is looking. And usually, no one *is* looking. That's why the simple act of noticing the details about money can be so useful—even if this is the only idea from the chapter that you ever apply.

Use this exercise as a chance to discover how money flows into and out of your life. The goal is to record all the money you receive and spend over the course of one month. This sounds like a big task, but it's simpler than you might think. Besides, there's a big payoff for this action. With increased awareness of income and expenses, you can make choices about money that will change your life. Here's how to begin.

1. Review the sample money monitor form (Figure 10.1) and make copies of the blank form (Figure 10.2)

Make photocopies of Figure 10.2 to use each month. The form helps you do two things. One is to get a big picture of the money that flows in and out of your life. The other is to plan specific and immediate changes in how you earn and spend money.

2. Keep track of your income and expenses

Use your creativity to figure out how you want to carry out this step. The goal is to create a record of exactly how much you earn and spend each month. Use any method that works for you. And keep it simple. Following are some options:

Save all receipts and file them. Every time you buy something, ask for a receipt. Then stick it in your wallet, purse, or pocket. When you get home, make notes about the purchase on the receipt. Then file the receipts in a folder labelled with the current month and year. Every time you get a paycheque during that month, save the stub and add it to the folder. Detailed receipts will help you later on when you file taxes, categorize expenses (e.g., food and entertainment), and check your purchases against credit card statements.

Use personal finance software. Learn to use *Quicken* or a similar product that allows you to record income and expenses on your computer and to sort them into categories. Many schools provide student finance apps to help you make the calculation of what it will cost you to go to school. These interactive calculators can help you determine the real cost of completing specific programs. Ask about this when you visit the campus financial aid office. There are also a number of budgeting apps available online.

Use online banking services. Take advantage of the online records that the bank is already keeping for you. Every time you transfer money, use a debit card, or make a deposit, the transaction will show up online. You can log in to your account on your device a view these transactions at any time. Many banks also provide free budgeting tools to help you increase your consciousness of what you are really spending. Ask your bank what tools they have available to assist you.

Experiment with several of the above options. After experimenting with these options, settle into one that feels most comfortable to you. Or create a method of your own. Use an Excel spreadsheet perhaps. Anything will work, as long as you end each month with an *exact and accurate* record of your income and expenses.

Sample Money Monitor/Money Plan
Month_____ Year_____

Income	This Month	Next Month	Expenses	This Month	Next Month
Employment	500		Books and Supplies		
Grants	100		Car Maintenance		
Interest from Savings			Car Payment		
Loans	300		Clothes		
Scholarships/bursaries	100		Deposits into Savings Account		
			Eating Out	50	–
			Entertainment	50	–
			Gas	100	
			Groceries	300	+
			Insurance (Car, Life, Home)		
			Internet	50	
			Laundry	20	
			Phone	55	
			Rent/Mortgage Payment	400	
			Tuition and Fees		
			Utilities	50	
Total Income	1000		Total Expenses	1075	–

Figure 10.1 Sample Money Monitor/Money Plan

3. On the last day of the month, fill out your Money Monitor/Money Plan

Pull out a blank Money Monitor/Money Plan. Label it with the current month and year. Fill out this form using the records of your income and expenses for the month.

Notice that the left column of the Money Monitor/Money Plan includes categories of income and expenses. (You can use the blank rows for categories of income and expenses that are not already included.) Write your total for each category in the middle column.

For example, if you spent $300 at the grocery store this month, write that amount in the middle column next to

Groceries. If you work a part-time job and received two pay-cheques for the month, write the total in the middle column next to *Employment*. See the sample Money Monitor/Money Plan on the next page for more examples.

Split expenses when necessary. For example, you might make one payment each month to pay the balance due on your credit card. The purchases listed on your credit card bill might fall into several categories. Total your expenses in each category, and list them separately. Suppose that you used your credit card to pay for a music streaming service, purchase a sweater, pay for three restaurant meals, and buy two tanks of gas for your car. Write the fee for the online streaming service next to

Money Monitor/Money Plan
Month_____ Year_____

Income	This Month	Next Month	Expenses	This Month	Next Month
Employment			Books and Supplies		
Grants			Car Maintenance		
Interest from Savings			Car Payment		
Loans			Clothes		
Scholarships/bursaries			Deposits into Savings Account		
			Eating Out		
			Entertainment		
			Gas		
			Groceries		
			Insurance (Car, Life, Home)		
			Internet		
			Laundry		
			Phone		
			Rent/Mortgage Payment		
			Tuition and Fees		
			Utilities		
Total Income			Total Expenses		

Figure 10.2 **Money Monitor/Money Plan Form**

Entertainment. Write the amount you paid for the hoodie next to *Clothes*. Write the total you spent at the restaurants next to *Eating Out*. Finally, write the total for your gas stops next to *Gas*.

Now look at the column on the right of the Money Monitor/ Money Plan. This column is where the magic happens. Review each category of income and expense. If you plan to reduce your spending in a certain category during the next month, write a minus sign (–) in the far right column. If you plan a spending increase in any category next month, write a plus sign (+) in the far right column. If you think that a category of income or expense will remain the same next month, leave the column blank.

Look again at the sample Money Monitor/Money Plan. This student plans to reduce her spending for clothes, eating out, and entertainment (which includes her subscription for streaming music). She plans to increase the total she spends on groceries. She figures that even so, she'll save money by cooking more food at home and eating out less.

4. After you've filled out your first Money Monitor/ Money Plan, take a moment to congratulate yourself

You have actively collected and analyzed the data needed to take charge of your financial life. No matter how the numbers add up, you are now in conscious control of your money. Repeat this exercise every month. It will keep you on a steady path to financial freedom.

No budgeting required

Notice one more thing about the Money Monitor/ Money Plan: It does not require you to create a budget. Budgets—like diets—often fail. Many people cringe at the mere mention of the word *budget*. To them it is associated with scarcity, drudgery, and guilt. The idea of creating a budget conjures up images of a penny-pinching Ebenezer Scrooge shaking a bony, wrinkled finger at them and screaming, "You spent too much, you loser!"

That's not the idea behind the Money Monitor/Money Plan. In fact, there is no budget worksheet for you to complete each month. And no one is pointing a finger at you. Instead of budgeting, you simply write a plus sign or a minus sign next to each expense or income category that you *freely choose* to increase or decrease next month. There's no extra paperwork, no shame, and no blame.

journal entry 10-2

Discovery/Intention Statement

Reflect on Your Money Monitor/Money Plan

Now that you've experimented with the Money Monitor/ Money Plan process, reflect on what you're learning. To start creating a new future with money, complete the following statements.

After monitoring my income and expenses for one month, I was surprised to discover that . . .

When it comes to money, I am skilled at . . .

When it comes to money, I am *not* so skilled at . . .

I could increase my income by . . .

I could spend less money on . . .

After thinking about the most powerful step I can take right now to improve my finances, I intend to . . .

Supporting yourself
IN SCHOOL

For many people, finding a way to increase income is the most appealing way to fix a money problem. This approach is reasonable, but it has a potential problem: When income increases, many people continue to spend more than they make. This means that money problems persist, even at higher incomes.

To avoid this problem, manage your expenses no matter how much money you make.

If you do succeed at controlling your expenses over the long term, then increasing your income is definitely a way to build wealth. Among the ways to make more money are to focus on your education, consider financial aid, work while you're in school, and do your best at every job.

Focus on your education

Your most important assets are not your bank accounts, your car, or your house—they are your skills. As Henry Ford said, "The only real security that a person can have in this world is a reserve of knowledge, experience, and ability. Without these qualities, money is practically useless" (Fordcarz.com, 2011).

That's why your education is so important. Right now, you're developing knowledge, experience, and abilities that you can use to create income for the rest of your life.

Once you graduate and land a job in your chosen field, continue your education. Look for ways to gain additional skills or certifications that lead to higher earnings and more fulfilling work assignments.

Consider financial aid

Student bursaries, government grants, and loans can play a major role in your postsecondary education success by freeing you up from having to work full-time or even part-time. Many students are eligible for a Canada Student Loan or Grant. When you apply for your provincial financial aid program, you will automatically be assessed for the Canada Student Loan (CSL) program. Low-income students are eligible for up to $3,000 in grant funding for full-time study and $1,800 for part-time study (Ottaway, 2018). For more information about

wavebreakmedia/Shutterstock.com

either the CSL program or provincial financial aid programs, go to the Government of Canada Student Loans website (*www.canada.ca/en/services/jobs/education/ student-financial-aid/student-loan.html*). Each province has a different student assistance program, so check out your province's program to see what benefits you might be eligible for.

If you live in Alberta and are Indigenous, you may be eligible for an Indigenous Career Award for up to $4,000 an academic year for postsecondary programs (*https://studentaid.alberta.ca/scholarships/alberta -scholarships/indigenous-careers-award.aspx*).

Even if you are an international student, you may qualify for an emergency loan or for a bursary. Your financial aid office or international student centre should be able to tell you what options you might have.

For both international and domestic students, it is important to visit your financial aid offices for counselling, should you find yourself in financial need. They are there to support your success.

File your taxes

Many students don't file taxes because they don't owe any money. However, if you don't file taxes, you won't get a tax return and more important you won't get the GST/HST credit. If you have a modest income, as most students do, you'll receive at least $248 over 12 months—but only if you file a tax return. This free money may be augmented by provincial credits as well.

You can claim a tuition tax credit against any income you might have. If your income is low, you can transfer that credit to your parent, grandparent, or spouse. You'll need to get a T2202A form as proof of enrollment from your school.

In addition, you can claim moving expenses if you moved more than 40 kilometres to go to your school or for work (Cestnick, 2018). You may also be able to claim moving costs if you moved home in the summer to work. The deduction for moving expenses has some restrictions but it is definitely worth looking into. You can also claim childcare expenses if you are enrolled either full- or part-time in postsecondary education. So, you could get extra money in your pocket by just filing your taxes.

Work while you're in school

If you work while you're in school, you earn more than money. You gain experience, establish references, interact with a variety of people, and make contact with people who might hire you in the future. And regular income in any amount can make a difference in your monthly cash flow.

If you are in financial need, you may be eligible for a work study program. Check out the website of your financial aid services to see how you can apply. Many students work part-time jobs while attending school. Work and school don't have to conflict, especially if you plan carefully (see Chapter 2, "Time"). Working up to 15 hours a week can, in fact, help to increase your time management skills while also giving you needed real-world experience. However, working more than 15 hours can have a negative impact on your likelihood of completing your program (Pascarella & Terenzini, 2005) and also on your opportunities to get involved with campus activities such as clubs.

Check into career and job placement services at your school for job listings. Using these resources can greatly increase your job options.

Most jobs are never advertised. In fact, a key source of information about new jobs is people—friends, relatives, co-workers, and fellow students. Tell all of them that you're looking for a job.

In addition, make a list of several places where you would like to work. Then go to each place on your list, and tell someone that you would like a job. If you're told that no jobs are currently available, not a problem—ask

to be considered for future job openings. Leave a resumé. Then check back periodically.

Some part-time jobs are made just for students. Serving or delivering food may not be glamorous, but the tips can make a real difference in your monthly income. Although the tips can be good working in bars and restaurants, find out how late you have to work, as the job may interfere with your ability to get to that early morning class. Other jobs, such as working the reference desk at the campus library or monitoring the front desk in a residence, can offer quiet times that are ideal for doing some extra studying. Working on-campus has other advantages. First, your employer is more willing to move your work schedule around to accommodate your classes. And you also won't be wasting valuable time commuting to your workplace.

Another option is to start your own business. Consider a service you could offer—anything from lawn mowing to computer consulting. Students can boost their incomes in many other ways, such as running errands, giving guitar lessons, walking pets, and housesitting. Charge reasonable rates, provide impeccable service, and ask your clients for referrals.

Self-employment during higher education can blossom into amazing careers. For example, Mike Lazaridis co-founded the tech company BlackBerry, previously called Research in Motion (RIM), while still an undergraduate at the University of Waterloo. He is credited with changing the profile of scientific research in Canada with his founding of the Perimeter Institute.

Do your best at every job

Once you get a job, make it your intention to excel as an employee. A positive work experience can pay off for years by leading to other jobs, recommendations, and contacts.

To maximize your earning power, keep honing your job-hunting and career-planning skills. You can find a wealth of ideas on these topics in Chapter 12, "What's Next?"

Finally, keep things in perspective. If your job is lucrative and rewarding, great. If not, remember that almost any job can support you in becoming a master student and reaching your educational goals. ✳

Protect your money online

Avoid scams   Con artists have been around ever since money was invented. Today, they're active online, looking for high-tech ways to peddle their schemes. Don't fall for them. One strategy is called *phishing*. It works like this: You receive an email that looks as if it came from a bank or credit card company. The email asks you to verify your account number, PIN, password, social insurance number, or other private information by clicking on a link.

If you get such a message, trash it. No reputable business asks for this kind of information via email. Call the bank or company directly if you are unsure. People who forget this fact set themselves up for identity theft.

Guard your money data   To prevent other security breaches when managing money, regularly monitor your online bank accounts:

- Keep account information—including your social insurance number—private.
- For money transactions, use websites with addresses (URLs) that begin with *https://* rather than *http://*. The extra *s* stands for *secure*, meaning that any data you send will be encrypted and virtually impossible to steal.
- Check the lower right-hand corner of your browser for an icon that looks like a closed lock. This also indicates a secure site.
- Don't manage your money on public computers. Other users could see your information displayed on the screen and watch the keyboard as you type in passwords.
- Don't let your Web browser store passwords and other log-in information for sites that you use to manage money. People who know how to access this information could hack into your accounts. Clear your browsing history periodically.
- Guard your PIN when you enter it to make online purchases.

- Take any financial documents you print out or receive in the mail and shred them before throwing them away.

Prevent identity theft   If someone learns your social insurance number, credit card numbers, or bank account numbers, that person could get access to your money and negatively affect your credit rating. Students often own multiple devices on which their personal information is stored making them more susceptible to identity theft. To prevent this problem, be very careful of using public Wi-Fi. Don't ever use public Wi-Fi to access your banking information. Be careful to set your privacy settings on social media sites so that others cannot access vital information about you.

Use different usernames and passwords for each of social media and banking accounts. Use a strong password whenever you pay bills or buy something online. Such a password will look like a string of random characters to anyone but you. To create a strong password, make it at least eight characters long, and include a combination of letters, numbers, and symbols. Choose characters from across the entire keyboard rather than characters that are located close together. Also consider using a *passphrase*—several words with a symbol between each word. Choose a phrase that's easy for you to remember but difficult for anyone else to guess.

Save your passwords in an encrypted vault or use a password manager App, such as *LastPass*. Whatever you do, don't write down your passwords on paper!

Keep your social insurance card in a secret place. If any of your confidential information is stolen, file a police report right away. Also contact your bank and credit card companies. Afterward, keep checking your bank statements and credit card bills to make sure that problem has stopped. For more help, go online to the RCMP identity theft and identity fraud site at *www.rcmp-grc.gc.ca/scams-fraudes/id-theft-vol-eng.htm*

SPEND LESS
money

Controlling your expenses is something you can do right away, and it's usually easier than increasing your income. Use ideas from the following list, and invent more of your own.

Think before you spend

Look to big-ticket items

When you look for places to cut expenses, start with the items that cost the most. Choices about where to live, for example, can save you thousands of dollars. Sometimes a place a little farther from campus will be much less expensive. You can also keep your housing costs down by finding a roommate. Offer to do repairs or maintenance in exchange for reduced rent. Pay your rent on time, and treat property with respect.

Another high-ticket item is a car. Take the cost of buying or leasing and then add expenses for parking, insurance, repairs, gas, maintenance, and tires. You might find that it makes more sense to car share, walk, bike, use public transportation, and call for an occasional taxi ride. Check to see if a transit or bus pass is included in your student fees—you may not need a car at all.

Check to see if your cost of tuition includes a health, dental, or medical plan. If you are already covered under your parents' plan, then don't waste money by failing to opt out of your school's plan on time.

Use Figure 10.2, "The Money Monitor/Money Plan Form" earlier in the chapter, to discover the main drains on your finances. Then focus on one or two areas where you can reduce spending while continuing to pay your fixed monthly bills, such as rent and tuition.

Look to small-ticket items

Reducing or eliminating the money you spend on low-cost purchases can make the difference between saving money and going into debt. For example, $5 spent at the coffee shop every day adds up to $1,825 over a year.

Ask for student discounts

Movie theatres, restaurants, bars, shopping centres, and other businesses sometimes discount prices for students. Also go to your bank, and ask whether you can open a low-cost student chequing and savings account with online banking. Go online to check your balances weekly so that you avoid overdraft fees. Consider investing in cards like the International Student Identity Card (www.isic.org/). For only $20 it provides full-time students with 40,000 discounts on travel, goods, and services all over the globe.

Do comparison shopping

Prices vary dramatically. Shop around, wait for off-season sales, and use coupons. Check out second-hand stores, thrift stores, and garage sales. You can find "pre-owned" clothes, furniture, sports equipment, audio equipment, and computer hardware in retail stores and on the Internet. Go online to *kijiji.ca* to see what you can find—there are even things for free.

Wait to buy textbooks

Lots of students buy all their textbooks new in the first week of class. Most schools have a used book store that can significantly reduce your book costs. Or look online for discounts. If you are planning on selling your books at the end of the year, try to keep them in good condition so you get the most money for them. Also, there is usually at least one copy of a textbook available in the library. Wait a couple of weeks to figure out what you really need before you make these costly purchases. You need to buy only required, not recommended, texts. Again, check to see if copies of recommended books are in the library.

Postpone purchases

If you feel like going shopping, leave your credit card at home. Look at all the possibilities. Then go home and make your decision when you don't feel pressured. When you are ready to buy, wait a week, even if the salesperson pressures you. What seems like a necessity today may not even cross your mind the day after tomorrow.

Spend wisely

Be aware of quality

The cheapest product is not always the least expensive over the long run. Sometimes, a slightly more expensive item is the best buy because it will last longer. Remember, there is no correlation between the value of something and the amount of money spent to advertise it. Carefully inspect things you are considering buying, and see if they are well made.

Save money on eating and drinking

This single suggestion could significantly lower your expenses. Instead of hitting a restaurant or bar, head to the grocery store. Fresh fruits, fresh vegetables, and whole grains are not only better for you than processed food; they also cost less.

Cooking for yourself doesn't need to take much time if you do a little menu planning. Create a list of your five favourite home-cooked meals. Learn how to prepare them. Then keep ingredients for these meals always on hand. To reduce grocery bills, buy these ingredients in bulk. When you have time, make large quantities and freeze the extra in individual servings for easy meals in the future.

If you live in a residence, review the different meal plans you can buy. Some schools offer meal plans for students who live off campus. These plans reduce the cost of eating while you're on campus.

Lower your phone bills

If you use a cellphone, pull out a copy of your latest bill. Review how many minutes you used last month. Perhaps you could get by with a less expensive phone, fewer minutes, fewer text messages, and a cheaper plan.

Do an Internet search on *cellphone plan comparison* and see if you could save money by switching providers. Also consider a family calling plan, which might cost less than a separate plan for each person. In addition, consider whether you need a home phone (a land line) *and* a cellphone. Dropping the home phone could save you money right away. You can even use apps like *WhatsApp* to make long distance calls for free. This can be far cheaper than using your phone, and for international students it is great to be able to both talk to and see your family if they have a computer too!

Go "green"

To conserve energy and save money on utility bills, turn out the lights when you leave a room. Keep windows and doors closed in winter. In summer, keep windows open early in the day to invite lots of cool air into your living space. Then close up the apartment or house to keep it cool during the hotter hours of the day. Leave air-conditioning set at 21°C or above. In cool weather, dress warmly and keep the house at 19°C or less. In hot weather, take shorter, cooler showers.

Unplug any electric appliances that are not in use. Appliances like microwaves, audio systems, and cellphone chargers use energy when plugged in even when they're not in use. Also, plug computer equipment into power strips that you can turn off while you sleep.

Find out if you have a smart meter measuring your use of electricity. If you do, find out how the time of use can affect your billing. It may cost almost twice as much to run the washing machine during peak hours as it does during off-peak hours.

Explore budget plans for monthly payments that fluctuate, such as those for heating your home. These plans average your yearly expenses so you pay the same amount each month.

Pay cash

To avoid interest charges, deal in cash or direct debit from your back account. If you don't have the cash, don't buy. Buying on credit makes it more difficult to monitor spending. You can easily bust next month's money plan with this month's credit card purchases.

Notice what you spend on "fun"

Blowing your money on fun is fun. It is also a fast way to blow your savings. When you spend money on entertainment, ask yourself what the benefits will be and whether you could get the same benefits for less money. You can read magazines for free at the library, for example. Your school probably has movie nights along with concerts, and athletic events that can keep you entertained at a low cost.

Use the envelope system

After reviewing your monthly income and expenses, put a certain amount of cash each week in an envelope labelled *Entertainment/Eating Out*. When the envelope is empty, stop spending money on these items for the rest of the week. If you use online banking, see if you can create separate accounts for various spending categories. Then deposit a fixed amount of money into each of those accounts. This is an electronic version of the envelope system.

It's easy to feel flush with money when your student aid comes in but remember how long it has to last. Put your student aid in a separate account, and transfer a set amount each month from it into the account you use. Use the envelope system to prevent overspending. You don't want to get stuck at the end of year with not enough money for food.

Make lifestyle choices that reflect who you are

You are a student right now so don't expect to have the lifestyle you'll have once you finish your education. This usually means living within limited means and therefore not living in your dream apartment. Consider living at home one more year—it will really help you to save money. Try to keep connected with friends who have a strong commitment to their studies. It will make focussing on school easier and help you not to get distracted from what really counts—finishing school. Having a realistic plan for personal, academic, and financial goals will help make the time spent on post-secondary education less stressful. So, take the time to assess why you are at school and why that matters, and make financial choices accordingly.

Use the money you save to prepare for emergencies and reduce debt

If you apply strategies such as those listed above, you might see your savings account swell nicely. Congratulate yourself. Then choose what to do with the extra money. To protect yourself during tough times, create an emergency fund. Then reduce your debt by paying more than the minimum on credit card bills and loan payments. ✳

practising
CRITICAL THINKING

10-2

Show me the money

See if you can use *Becoming a Master Student* to create a financial gain that is many times more than the cost of the book. Scan the entire text, and look for suggestions that could help you save money or increase income in significant ways; for example,

- Use suggestions for career planning and job hunting in Chapter 12, "What's Next?" to find your next job more quickly—and start earning money sooner.

- Use suggestions from this chapter to reduce your monthly expenses and fatten up your savings account.

- Use suggestions for goal setting from Chapter 2, "Time," to create a detailed plan for acquiring a skill that will facilitate your getting a higher-paying job.

Write your ideas for creating more money from your experience of this book.

Managing money during
TOUGH TIMES

THE BIGGEST FACTOR in your long-term financial well-being is your own behaviour. Taking informed action is a way to cut through financial confusion and move beyond fear. An added benefit: The habits that help you survive tough times will also help you manage money when the economy rebounds.

wavebreakmedia/Shutterstock.com

Start by completing Figure 10.2 "Money Monitor/ Money Plan Form" earlier in this chapter. This exercise will give you the details about what you're spending and earning right now. With that knowledge, you can choose your next strategy from among the following.

Pay yourself first

David Chilton, the author of *The Wealthy Barber* (1989), has "pay yourself first" as one of his primary rules. What he suggests is that you automatically deposit money into a savings account as soon as you are paid (Roseman, 2009). So, if you have a part-time job, get into the habit of putting away a portion of every paycheque. In fact, Chilton would suggest putting aside 10 percent of each paycheque.

Spend less and save more

The less you spend, the more money you'll have on hand. Use that money to pay your monthly bills, pay off your credit cards, and create an emergency fund to use in case you lose your job or a source of financial aid.

Author Suze Orman recommends three actions to show that you can reduce spending at any time: (1) do not spend money for one day, (2) do not use your credit card for one week, and (3) do not eat out for one month. Success with any of these strategies can open up your mind to other possibilities for spending less and saving (Orman, 2009).

Pay off your credit cards

If you have more than one credit card with an outstanding balance, then find out which one has the highest interest rate. Put as much money as you can toward paying off that balance while making the minimum payment on the other cards. Repeat this process until all unpaid balances are erased.

Invest only after saving

The stock market is only for money that you can afford to lose. Before you speculate, first save enough money to live on for at least six months in case you lose your source of income. Then, consider what you'll need over the next five years to finish your schooling and handle other major expenses. Save for these expenses before taking any risks with your money.

Think about your next job

During an economic crisis, you can get laid off even if you're a star employee. Prepare for this situation now. Create a career plan that describes the next job you want, the skills that you'll develop to get it, and the next steps you'll take to gain those skills. Stay informed about the latest developments in your field. Find people who are already working in this area, and contact them for information interviews.

Research unemployment benefits

Unemployment benefits have limits and may not replace your lost wages. However, they can cushion the blow of losing a job while you put other strategies in place. To learn about the types of unemployment benefits that are available, go to the Service Canada website and search for unemployment benefits.

Talk to your financial aid office

All schools have financial aid officers who can help you with your budget; they often have emergency loans they can offer.

Get help that you can trust

Avoid debt consolidators that offer schemes to wipe out your debt. What they don't tell you is that their fees are high, and that using them can lower your credit rating. Turn instead to Credit Counselling Canada at *www.creditcounsellingcanada.ca*. On its website you can check out your credit rating. Review the report you receive for accuracy.

Use food banks

Many schools have food banks, or your student services offices should be able to tell you where the local food bank is located. It's easier to solve your other money problems if you are not hungry. So go to the food bank if you need it. When you have more money, you can donate back to the food bank.

Choose your money conversations

When the economy tanks, the news is filled with gloomy reports and dire predictions. Remember that reports are constantly competing for your attention. Sometimes they use gloom-and-doom headlines to boost their ratings. Keep financial news in perspective. Recessions can be painful. And they eventually end. Our economy will continue to reward people who create valuable new products and services.

To manage stress, limit how much attention you pay to fear-based articles and programs. You can do this even while staying informed about news. Avoid conversations that focus on problems. Instead, talk about ways to take charge of your money and open up job prospects. Even when the economy takes a nosedive, there is always at least one more thing you can do to manage stress and get on a firmer financial footing.

When tough times happen, use them as a chance to embrace the truth about your money life rather than resist it. Live from conscious choice rather than unconscious habit. Learning to live within your means is a skill that can bring financial peace of mind for the rest of your life. ✳

Take charge of your
CREDIT

A good credit rating will serve you for a lifetime. With this asset, you'll be able to borrow money anytime you need it. A poor credit rating, however, can keep you from getting a car or a house in the future. You might also have to pay higher insurance rates, and you could even be turned down for a job.

To take charge of your credit, borrow money only when truly necessary. If you do borrow, make all of your payments, and make them on time. This is especially important for managing credit cards and student loans.

Use credit cards with caution

The government of Canada has a handy website that explains how to choose the right credit card. Go to

Loveischiangrai/Shutterstock.com4

www.canada.ca/en/financial-consumer-agency/services/ credit-cards.html to find out more information about how to choose the right credit card for you. Cards differ greatly in terms of interest rates, rewards, and annual fees. In particular, check out the credit card comparison tool (*https://itools-ioutils.fcac-acfc.gc.ca/CCCT-OCCC/SearchFilter-eng.aspx*) that allows you to see just how much you'll pay for the privilege of having that credit card.

A credit card is compact and convenient. That piece of plastic seems to promise peace of mind. Low on cash this month? Just whip out your credit card, slide it across the counter, and relax. Your worries are over—that is, until you get the bill. Credit cards often come with a hefty interest rate—sometimes as high as 30 percent.

Many students are carrying high amounts of credit card debt, with costs that can soar over time. Suppose that a student owes $7,000 on a credit card with an annual rate of 18.9 percent. Also, suppose that he pays only the minimum balance due each month and charges nothing else to the account. He'll need to make payments for 16 years and pay $7,173 in interest (O'Malley, 2008). Credit cards do offer potential benefits, of course. Having one means that you don't have to carry around a chequebook or large amounts of cash, and they're pretty handy in emergencies. Getting a card is one way to establish a credit rating. Some cards offer rewards, such as frequent flier miles and car rental discounts.

Used unwisely, however, credit cards can create a debt that takes decades to repay. This debt can seriously delay other goals—paying off student loans, financing a new car, buying a home, or saving for retirement.

Use the following strategies to take control of your credit cards:

Pay off the balance each month

An unpaid credit card balance is a sure sign that you are spending more money than you have. To avoid this outcome, keep track of how much you spend with credit cards each month. Pay off the card balance each month, on time, and avoid finance or late charges.

If you do accumulate a large credit card balance, go to your bank and ask about ways to get a loan with a lower interest rate. Use this loan to pay off your credit cards. Then promise yourself never to accumulate credit card debt again.

Scrutinize credit card offers

Beware of cards offering low interest rates. These rates are often only temporary. After a few months, they could double or even triple. Also look for annual fees, late fees, and other charges buried in the fine print.

Be especially wary of credit card offers made to students. Remember that the companies who willingly dispense cards on campus are not there to offer an educational service. They are in business to make money by charging you interest.

Avoid cash advances

Due to their high interest rates and fees, credit cards are not a great source of spare cash. Even when you get cash advances on these cards from an ATM, it's still borrowed money. As an alternative, get a debit card tied to a chequing account, and use that card when you need cash on the go.

Check statements against your records

File your credit card receipts each month. When you get the bill for each card, check it against your receipts for accuracy. Mistakes in billing are rare, but they can happen. In addition, checking your statement reveals the interest rate and fees that are being applied to your account.

Use just one credit card

To simplify your financial life and take charge of your credit, use only one card. Choose one with no annual fee and the lowest interest rate. Consider the bottom line and be selective.

Protect your credit score

Whenever you apply for a loan, the first thing a lender will do is check your credit score. With a poor credit score, it can be hard to get a new credit card or to buy a car when you need one for a new job. Here's how to protect your credit score:

- Pay all your bills on time.
- Hold on to credit cards that you've had for a while.
- Avoid applying for new credit cards.
- Pay off your credit card balance every month—especially for the cards that you've had the longest.
- If you can't pay off the entire balance, then pay as much as you can above the minimum monthly payment.
- Never charge more than your limit.
- Avoid using a credit card as a source of cash.
- Avoid any actions that could lead a credit card company to reduce your credit limit.

Manage student loans

Higher education is one of the best investments you can make. The Conference Board of Canada states that without a doubt those who invest in a diploma or degree will outperform and out-earn those who do not have a credential from a postsecondary institution (Pittis, 2017). But you don't have to go broke to get that education. You can make that investment with the lowest debt possible. The Government of Canada website provides a tremendous amount of information on how to apply for loans and scholarships. If you haven't done it already, check out *www.canlearn.ca.*

TD bank offers 20 scholarships for community leadership worth up to $70,000 to students in the last year of high school or attending CEJEP (in Quebec). Scholarships are offered to students by many companies; these will reward your academic and personal achievements. Check out *scholarshipscanada.com*.

About half of students graduate with some debt—approximately $14,000 for a college degree and $26,000 for a bachelor's (Hansen, 2017). But keep in mind that the cost is still no more than buying a car. A car's value constantly decreases over time while the benefit of having your diploma or degree will continue to pay dividends over your entire lifetime.

Choose schools with costs in mind

In addition to choosing schools on the basis of reputation, consider how much they cost and the financial aid packages that they offer. Tuition fees vary from province to province so check out schools in other provinces. By moving away for your education, you just might broaden your experiences and pay less than going to a school in your own province.

Check the availability of awards

Schools differ widely in the number of scholarships, grants, and bursaries they offer, so check to see what one-time and continuing awards are available through your financial aid office or your office of awards, scholarships, and bursaries. Scholarships, grants, and bursaries are the best to receive as you don't need to repay them when you graduate. Scholarships are given on the basis of academic achievement, whereas grants and bursaries are awarded on a combination of financial need plus other attributes, such as academic achievement, athletic ability, or some special skills. Bursaries may be offered if you are a first-generation student (the first in your family to go on to postsecondary education) or if, for instance, you are in specific programs such as Women in Technology. Literally thousands of scholarships are available to students; but to receive them, you need to apply and meet their criteria and deadlines. Even those based on academic achievement don't require you to be a brainiac—so take the time and apply. Two websites that can give information about what scholarships are available Canada-wide are *yconic. com* and *scholarshipscanada.com*. You should apply if you qualify, even if you fear you may not be the best candidate; many of these scholarships are never awarded because students haven't applied for them.

Students with disabilities can find out what awards are available to them by going to *www.disabilityawards .ca*. On this website, you can also find out about Canada

practising CRITICAL THINKING 10-3

Education by the hour

Determine exactly what it costs you to go to school. Fill in the blanks below using totals for a semester, quarter, or whatever term system your school uses.

Note: Include only the costs that relate directly to going to school. For example, under "Transportation," list only the amount that you pay for gas to drive back and forth to school—not the total amount you spend on gas for a semester.

Tuition	$_____
Books	$_____
Fees	$_____
Transportation	$_____
Clothing	$_____
Food	$_____
Housing	$_____
Entertainment	$_____
Other expenses (e.g., insurance, Internet, and childcare)	$_____
Subtotal	$_____
Salary you could earn per term if you weren't in school	$_____
Total (A)	$_____

Now figure out how many classes you attend in one term. This is the number of your scheduled class periods per week multiplied by the number of weeks in your school term. Put that figure below:

Total (B)   _____

Divide the **Total (B)** into the **Total (A)**, and put that amount here:

$_____

This is what it costs you to go to one class, one time.

Describe your responses to discovering this figure. Also list anything you will do differently as a result of knowing the hourly cost of your education.

_____

_____

_____

_____

student loans available for students with permanent disabilities.

First Nations and Inuit students may be eligible for financial assistance from the Post-Secondary Student Support Program (*www.aadnc-aandc.gc.ca/eng/110010 0033679/1100100033680*). Sponsorship covers tuition, cost of living, books, and travel. You may also be eligible for other forms of financial assistance. Your band office, Inuit designated organization, Indigenous Services Canada, or Indigenous and Northern Affairs Canada (INAC) regional office should be able to assist you with finding out about sponsorship.

Avoid debt when possible

The surest way to manage debt is to avoid it altogether. If you do take out loans, borrow only the amount that you cannot get from other sources—scholarships, grants, employment, gifts from relatives, and personal savings. Private bank loans or personal lines of credit require you to repay the amount while you are still in school while money received from the Canada Student Loan program does not require you to repay until after you graduate. In addition, interest is not accrued on Canada Student Loans for full-time students until graduation.

Set a target date for graduation and stick to it. The fewer years you go to school, the lower your debt.

Shop carefully for loans

Go to the financial aid or awards office of your school to find out more about what government loans you might be eligible for. The Canada Student Loan program is available for all Canadian students, except those from Québec, Nunavut, and the Northwest Territories. In those cases, the province and the territories have their own financial assistance program. Again, the government website CanLearn (*www.canlearn.ca*) can provide vital information about how to apply in your province or territory. When you apply for a Canada Student Loan, you are automatically assessed for a grant which is the portion that is non-repayable. The CanLearn loan repayment calculator will tell you how much you should expect to budget to pay back your federal or provincial

loans on a monthly basis depending upon the length of time you wish to take to pay the loan off. This is a useful step to take before you start accruing debt. You may not want to pay off debt for many years after you graduate, and the repayment calculator may help you to consider other sources of funding such as a part-time job.

Once you are out of school for six months, you will need to begin paying back your student loans. However, the Repayment Assistance plan allows graduates to delay paying back any Canada Student Loans they receive until they are earning more than $25,000 annually; this plan also covers the interest on the loan until then (Ottaway, 2018). In addition, you can claim a tax credit for any interest paid on your CSL. If your income is too low to use the credit, you can take it forward for up to five years. You have up to 10 years to repay your CSL.

Many provincial programs offer grants that may cover your full tuition. In Ontario those with family income less than $50,000 are eligible for free tuition. There is an Ontario Student Assistance Program (OSAP) calculator on the first page of the website (*www.ontario.ca/page/osap-ontario-student-assistance -program*) that can give you an idea of how much you will receive in loans and grants. Plus, in Ontario you don't have to begin paying back your loans until you make $35,000 a year.

Interest rates for the different student loan programs vary from province to province, from no interest in several of the Maritime provinces to prime plus 1% in Ontario (Moore, 2017). The Canada Student Loan interest rate is prime plus 2.5%.

Paying back your student loan is essential. If you are found to be delinquent on your student loan, this will have a very negative impact on your credit rating. If you are having difficulties making your loan payment, go to your bank and student loan administrator to figure out what you can do. A recent study of university graduates found that 58 percent expected to graduate with more than $20,000 in debt and 21 percent expected that they would owe more than $40,000 (Habib, 2013). So manage your money well and borrow only what you really need. ✳

If you're in trouble . . .

Financial problems are common. Solve them in ways that protect you for the future.

Get specific data.   Complete Figure 10.2 "The Money Monitor/Money Plan Form" included earlier in this chapter.

Be honest with creditors.   Determine the amount that you are sure you can repay each month, and ask the creditor if that would work for your case.

Go for credit counselling.   Most cities have agencies with professional advisors who can help straighten out your financial problems.

Change your spending patterns.   If you have a history of overspending (or under-earning), change *is* possible. This chapter is full of suggestions.

Keep your money secure.   To prevent other security breaches when managing money, regularly monitor online bank accounts. Use websites with an address that begins with *https://* rather than *http://*. The '*s*' stands for secure, meaning that the data you send will be encrypted.

Common credit terms

Annual fee—a yearly charge for using a credit card, sometimes called a *membership fee* or *participation fee*.

Annual percentage rate (APR)—the interest that you owe on unpaid balances in your account. The APR equals the periodic rate times the number of billing periods in a year.

Balance due—the remaining amount of money that you owe a credit card company or other lender.

Balance transfer—the process of moving an unpaid debt from one lender to another lender.

Bankruptcy—a legal process that allows borrowers to declare their inability to pay their debts. People who declare bankruptcy transfer all their assets to a court-appointed trustee and create a plan to repay some or all of their borrowed money. Bankruptcy protects people from harassment by their creditors but lowers their credit scores.

Credit score—a three-digit number that reflects your history of repaying borrowed money and paying other bills on time. This number ranges from 300 to 850. The higher the number, the better your credit rating.

Default—state of a loan when the borrower fails to make required payments or otherwise violates the terms of the agreement. Default may prompt the creditor to turn the loan over to a collection agency, which can severely harm the borrower's credit score.

Finance charge—the total fee for using a credit card, which includes the interest rate, periodic rate, and other fees. Finance charges for cash advances and balance transfers can be different than finance charges for unpaid balances.

Grace period—a period of time when no interest is charged on a purchase if the credit card user pays off the entire balance due. When there is no grace period, finance charges apply immediately to a purchase.

Interest rate—an annual fee that borrowers pay to use someone else's money, normally a percentage of the balance due.

Minimum payment—the amount you must pay to keep from defaulting on an account; usually 2 percent of the unpaid balance due.

Payment due date—the day that a lender must receive your payment—*not* the postmarked date or the date you make a payment online. Check your statements carefully, as credit card companies sometimes change the due dates.

Periodic rate—an interest rate based on a certain period of time, such as a day or a month.

Money for the
FUTURE

Start saving now

You can begin saving now even if you are in debt and living in a residence on a diet of macaroni. Saving now helps you establish a habit that will pay off in the future.

Create an emergency fund

Take some percentage of every paycheque you receive, and immediately deposit that amount in a savings account. Again, start by saving 10 percent of your income. Then see if you can increase that amount over time. Put those savings in a Tax Free Savings Account (TFSA) and watch your savings grow.

The first purpose of this savings account is to have money on hand for surprises and emergencies—anything from a big repair bill to a sudden job loss. For peace of mind, have an emergency fund equal to at least six months of living expenses. Once you have that amount in place, save for longer-term goals. Examples are a car, a child's education, or a house.

Invest carefully

Investing in stocks, corporate bonds, and mutual funds can be risky. Do so only if you regularly save money and pay off the full balance on your credit cards each month. Even then, only invest money that you can afford to lose.

Successful investing requires extensive homework. Educate yourself by taking a class about personal finance and getting coaching from an independent, certified financial planner. No matter how you choose to invest, put time on your side. Invest as much as you can—keeping in mind the tips above—and invest as early as you can.

Join a car-sharing service

A car is a lousy investment. The minute you drive it off the dealer's lot, it loses value. If you must buy a car, keep the costs as low as possible. Reduce interest charges by sticking to a three-year loan rather than extending it to four or five years. Check out certified, pre-owned cars. These are used cars that come with a warranty from the manufacturer, not the car dealer. Don't lease cars as there is no return on your investment whatsoever.

Rather than buying a car, consider a car-sharing service. With car-sharing services you typically pay a membership fee and then are charged a fee for the length of time you have the vehicle. Different rules exist: With a

---

Education is worth it

Education is one of the few things you can buy that will last a lifetime. Once you have a degree, no one can take it away. That makes your education a safer investment than real estate, gold, oil, diamonds, or stocks. As was mentioned in the Introduction, getting an education leads to more than a good job; it leads to better health, greater job satisfaction, and better civic and community engagement. It also leads to your living longer, makes you less likely to participate in crime, and helps you to become a better parent (Pittis, 2017).

In short, education is a good deal for you and for society. It's worth investing in it periodically throughout your life to update your skills, reach your goals, and get more of what you want in life.

---

membership to Car2Go, for example, you are able to pick the car up in one place and drop it off in another; with Zipcar, you must pick it up and drop it back in the same neighbourhood. It has been suggested that if you drive less than 9,700 kilometres a year, it is cheaper to share a car than to own (Tchir, 2017).

You might want to check out other types of sharing/lending/swapping services for items such as clothes.

Save on insurance

Protect your assets by getting insurance for your home, car, and life. If you live in an apartment, get renters' insurance.

Find an independent insurance agent who can help you with all these policies. Ask about discounts for buying more than one policy from the same insurance company. Also ask if you can lower your premiums by raising your deductibles.

Many schools offer an extended healthcare plan (in addition to provincial coverage) for their students. Find out what's available on your campus. Keep in mind that, if you are already covered on an equivalent health care plan (e.g., with your parents or spouse), there usually is an opt-out date when you can withdraw from the student healthcare plan. You want to avoid paying twice for the same coverage. ✳

Your learning styles and
YOUR MONEY

Why What How What if

IfH/Shutterstock.com; © Scott Maxwell/LuMaxArt/Shutterstock/Image used with the permission of the Bank of Canada; © Sebastian Kaulitzki/Shutterstock; © Marina Krasnorutskaya/Shutterstock; Tom Wang/Shutterstock.com

"Learning styles: Discovering How You Learn" (in Chapter 1, "First Steps") explains four learning styles—unique ways of perceiving and processing our experiences. You can see these different styles at work in the ways that people spend and earn money.

For example, some people buy quickly once they find a product or service that connects to something they care about deeply (*active experimentation*). Others take the time to shop around and compare prices before they spend much (*reflective observation*). Some people are curious about how the stock and bond markets work and will take the time to analyze the field (*abstract conceptualization*). Others want to jump right in and experiment with ways to make more money (*concrete experience*).

When you face a financial decision, ask the following four questions. They will help you gain the benefits of using each learning style to make a more balanced choice.

Ask: *Why* **am I considering spending this money?** We buy when we see something to be gained. This could involve a small benefit, such as spending a couple of dollars on pop to satisfy your thirst. Or it could be a larger benefit, like spending thousands of dollars on a car to satisfy your desire for convenience and mobility. Before you hand over your cash or credit card, be clear about what you want to gain.

Ask: *What* **are the facts I need to know?** The answer to this question is useful even with small purchases. In the case of pop, for example, check out the ingredients on the label. Then think about whether you want to put that stuff in your body. If you're buying a car, find out

exactly how much it will cost beyond the sticker price. If you plan to borrow money, research the available options. Your bank or credit union may offer a better interest rate than the car dealer. Or maybe a relative would consider giving you a no-interest loan.

Ask: *How* **would this purchase affect my life?** Many purchases come with a cost that goes beyond money. That pop might come with hidden costs—excess sugar and calories. Buying or renting a bigger house could tie you into higher payments. And that might require you to work more hours or see less of your family. When you spend your time, energy, and money for one purpose, those resources are not available for other purposes.

Ask: *What if* **I could get the same benefit without spending money?** You could save a couple dollars, reduce calories, *and* quench your thirst by using a water fountain instead of buying an overpriced drink. You could get around town *and* save thousands of dollars by using public transportation and paying for an occasional taxi ride. And you could gain more living space by building a small addition to your current home, or by simply cleaning out some cluttered rooms. Before you spend a dime, ask whether you can get the same benefit for no money down—or no money at all. ✳

Money management

The money management articles in this chapter are based on three core ideas:

- Money problems have a simple source: You spend more than you have.

- The solution to money problems is also simple: Spend less than you have.

- You can implement this solution with three broad strategies: Increase your income, decrease your expenses, or both.

In this exercise, you will think critically about these statements by completing the following four steps:

1. First, test the logic of these assertions. Are they clear? Are they consistent with one another? And are they based on sound assumptions?

   For example, the first assertion is based on the assumption that problems can have a single cause. You might argue that this is simplistic and that most problems have more than one cause.

   Summarize your thinking about the logic of the three assertions in the space below:

   _____
   _____
   _____
   _____
   _____
   _____
   _____
   _____
   _____
   _____
   _____
   _____
   _____
   _____
   _____
   _____

2. Next, consider the evidence for these assertions. See if you can think of examples to support them. Also see if you can think of any counter-examples. For instance, you might be able to list money problems that are not due to spending more than you have.

Summarize your evidence for and against the three assertions here:

_____
_____
_____
_____
_____
_____
_____
_____
_____

3. The third assertion states three broad financial goals that you could adopt: Increase your income, decrease your expenses, or both. Think about whether these goals imply actions that you could reasonably take. For example, could you actually decrease your expenses by finding a cheaper place to live or by spending less on entertainment?

   In the space below, summarize your ideas about whether you can truly apply the main strategies in this chapter:

   _____
   _____
   _____
   _____
   _____
   _____
   _____

4. Finally, if you agree to act on the strategies in this chapter, write a specific intention and take action. Also make a note on your calendar to return to this exercise in one month and assess the results. Did you carry through on your planned action? If so, do the results support or contradict the assertions listed above?

   Summarize your ideas in the space below:

   _____
   _____
   _____
   _____
   _____
   _____
   _____
   _____
   _____

Risk Being a Fool

A master student has the courage to take risks. And taking risks means being willing to fail sometimes—even being willing to be a fool. This idea can work for you because you already are a fool.

Don't be upset. All of us are fools at one time or another. There are no exceptions. If you doubt it, think back to that stupid thing you did just a few days ago. You know the one. Yes ... *that* one. It was embarrassing, and you tried to hide it. You pretended you weren't a fool. This happens to everyone.

We are all fallible human beings. Most of us, however, spend too much time and energy trying to hide our foolhood. No one is really tricked by this—not even ourselves. It's okay to look ridiculous while dancing. It's all right to sound silly when singing to your kids. Sometimes it's okay to be absurd. It comes with taking risks.

This Power Process comes with a warning label: Taking risks does *not* mean escaping responsibility for our actions. "Risk being a fool" is not a suggestion to get drunk at a party and make a fool of yourself. It is not a suggestion to fool

around or do things badly. Mediocrity is not the goal.

The point is that mastery in most activities calls for the willingness to do something new, to fail, to make corrections, to fail again, and so on.

"Risk being a fool" means that foolishness—along with courage, cowardice, grace, and clumsiness—is a human characteristic. We all share it. You might as well risk being a fool because you already are one, and nothing in the world can change that. Why not enjoy it once in a while?

There's one sure-fire way to avoid any risk of being a fool, and that's to avoid life. The writer who never finishes a book will never have to worry about getting negative reviews. The centre fielder who sits out every game is safe from making any errors. And the comedian who never performs in front of an audience is certain to avoid telling jokes that fall flat. The possibility of succeeding at any venture increases when we're comfortable with making mistakes—that is, with the risk of being a fool.

© Daly and Newton/Jupiter Images

Put it to WORK

Strategies from *Becoming a Master Student* can help you succeed in your career, as well as in school. To start discovering how suggestions in this chapter apply to the workplace, reflect on the following case study.

Vijit Ramcha graduated from college during a recession and felt lucky to land a job within a month after leaving school. He'd done an internship at a small non-profit organization and was inspired by the sense of mission that its employees showed. He then began working full-time for the same organization as an accountant.

On Vijit's first day, his supervisor laid out the hard news about the organization's finances. Its primary source of income was a single funder—a foundation created by a local family. The economic downturn had delivered a hard blow to just about everyone's investment portfolio, and the foundation had decided to reduce its upcoming grant to Vijit's organization by 40 percent. To make ends meet, Vijit's supervisor now wanted to reduce their organization's expenses by 10 percent each month during the first quarter of the new fiscal year.

Vijit rose to the challenge. He was full of suggestions: Ask vendors for discounts. Rent out a rarely used conference room in the organization's office. Ask employees to take a temporary wage cut rather than lay off anyone. Put off doing a major upgrade of the organization's computer system.

"Those are all useful ideas," said Vijit's supervisor. "And, they're all focussed on the short term. Let's back up a minute and get a bigger picture. We've been through hard times in the past, and we'll make it through the current recession. The question is, How can we start planning for the next recession *before* it arrives?"

Both Vijit and his supervisor demonstrated money strategies that are presented in this chapter: Reduce expenses. Postpone purchases. List some other short-term strategies that might be useful to Vijit's organization:

_____

_____

_____

Dragon Images/Shutterstock.com

What would you say in response Vijit's supervisor's question: "How can we start planning for the next recession *before* it arrives?"

_____

_____

_____

_____

Like Vijit, you might get a job that requires preparing budgets, making financial forecasts, and adjusting income and expenses to meet an organization's financial goals. The ability to handle such tasks successfully is called *workplace financial literacy*. To get the most from your education, plan to develop this form of literacy. Following are some strategies to consider:

● Think about the ways you'll be handling money in your chosen career.

● Find out more by interviewing people who work in your field and asking them about how they handle money on the job.

● After listing the financial skills you need, consider which courses you'll take to develop them.

● Look for work-study assignments and internships that can help you to develop financial skills.

● Throughout your career, keep track of the positive outcomes you produce at work, including financial successes. Summarize these results in a sentence or two. Add them to your resumé.

QUIZ

chapter 10

■ Put it to Work
◄ ◄ ◄ ◄
■ Skills Snapshot
■ Master Student Profile

Name_____   Date____/____/____

1. List five sources of money to help students pay for their educations.

2. Describe at least three ways to decrease your expenses while you are in school.

3. How can you avoid getting into financial trouble when you use credit cards?

4. The text asserts that investing in your education is safer than investing in real estate, gold, oil, or stocks. List the reasons given for this assertion.

5. What does it cost you to go to school for one year? Create a list of possible expenses. For three items, suggest at least one way expenses can be reduced.

6. A First Step approach to managing money is to
   (a) Admit that you probably don't have enough money.
   (b) Admit that money management is complicated.
   (c) Tell the truth about how much money you have and how much you spend.
   (d) All of the above.
   (e) None of the above.

7. State three ways that you can ensure your credit rating remains in a healthy state as you progress through your postsecondary education.

8. Power Process: "Risk Being a Fool" suggests that sometimes you should take action without considering the consequences. True or False? Explain the answer.

9. Describe three strategies for increasing your income.

10. List three ways to make online transactions more secure.

chapter 10

- Put it to Work
- Quiz
- ▶ ▶ ▶ ▶
- Master Student Profile

Skills SNAPSHOT

Now that you've reflected on the ideas in this chapter and experimented with some new strategies, revisit your responses to the "Money" section of the Discovery Wheel exercise in Chapter 1. Think about the most powerful action you could take in the near future toward financial mastery. Complete the following sentences.

MANAGING INCOME AND EXPENSES

Right now my main sources of income are . . .

My three biggest expenses each month are . . .

One monthly expense that I could reduce right away is . . .

To begin reducing this expense, I could . . .

PAYING FOR SCHOOL

I plan to graduate by (month and year) . . .

I plan to pay for my education next year by . . .

TAKING THE NEXT ACTION

I'll know that I've reached a new level of mastery with money when . . .

To reach that level of mastery, the most important thing I can do next is to . . .

MASTER STUDENT
PROFILE

chapter 10

■ Put it to Work
■ Quiz
■ Skills Snapshot
◀ ◀ ◀ ◀

Régine Chassagne & Edwin Farnham Butler
. . . are caring

© Simone Joyner/Stringer/Getty Images

Musically, Arcade Fire has always prided themselves in making it up as they go along—fidèle to the feeling, but not the rules. But there is a larger plan.

Since 2005, the group has raised more than $1 million for development work in the Western hemisphere's poorest nation. Recently, Chassagne and Dominique Anglade, a Montréal businesswoman and childhood friend, formed their own charity, Kanpe (Creole for "stand up"). Working with *Partners in Health (PIH)*, an international NGO, and Fonkoze, a Haitian micro-lending organization, Kanpe is set to launch a concerted attack on the roots of poverty in one island community, shepherding 300 families to economic and physical health. The budget for the three-year project is $2 million. The band has pledged to match every dollar raised, up to a million, from their own pockets. In March, in between award shows, they'll all travel together to Haiti to check out the work that has already begun, and get their own hands dirty.

On the surface, at least, they seem like an unlikely pair. Edwin Farnham Butler III, 30, the lanky eldest son of a blue-blood New Englander and a Joni Mitchell-style California musician, raised in Texas, and diminutive Régine Chassagne, the 33-year-old francophone daughter of Haitian refugees who washed up on Montréal's south shore.

They met at the McGill Faculty of Music in 2000. She was studying vocals and playing recorder in a medieval ensemble. He wasn't in school—although he did study comparative Biblical Scripture for a time—just haunting the corridors, looking for a drummer for his then more-notional-than-actual band. Their paths crossed again at an art opening where Chassagne was singing with a jazz band. They got together a few nights later to play music and wrote a tune, Headlights Look Like Diamonds, that ended up on Arcade Fire's first EP in 2003, the year they married.

Chassagne taught herself to play piano at age four. Growing up in a close-knit household, song was always a part of daily life, but it was only after an undergrad degree in communications at Concordia, and her mother's untimely death, that she ever dared to breathe her dream of performing. Her parents had come to Montréal in the early 1970s, after meeting in the States. Régine's mother fled Haiti when she returned home from market one day to find her cousins and friends had been murdered. Her dad left after his father was taken away by the Tonton Macoutes and executed. As new Canadians, both worked hard to establish themselves—he taught math, she worked as a secretary and at a daycare. But Haiti remained the country of all their imaginations. "Growing up, I never went there," says Chassagne. "It wasn't a possibility financially, and especially with

Both musicians are part of the Indie rock band Arcade Fire, which has won numerous musical awards (including a Grammy, several Junos, and two Brits). They received the Juno humanitarian award in 2016. They are committed to giving back to others by working with Partners in Health in Haiti.

my mom—she still had nightmares. She wanted to forget about it."

Even before [their first trip to Haiti], Arcade Fire had been raising money for Partners in Health, tacking on a charity surcharge—one dollar, one euro or one pound—to every ticket sold. The "biggest no-brainer thing we ever did," as Win calls it, has so far collected almost US$1 million. At shows, he gives a short spiel about the organization, and PIH volunteers are always on hand to pass out literature. During the most recent tour, 5,500 fans signed up for its "Stand with Haiti" campaign.

They still control, or as Chassagne prefers to say, "direct" their own business, paying their way in the studio, on video shoots and the road. But there have been small concessions to stardom, like the manager they share with Björk and Paul McCartney. Butler swears things haven't changed that much. "Our day-to-day life is identical, except for not sweating the electrical bill as much. We still have the same crap in our house; the old chairs, and the stool I fished out of the dumpster."

[Arcade Fire is] a band that's trying to change the world, without letting it change them.

Source: Gatehouse, J. (2011, February 21). Their main act: Arcade Fire doesn't chase fame. *Maclean's*. Reprinted with permission.

Health

what is included …

javi_indy/Shutterstock.com

WHAT if …

I could meet the demands of daily life with energy and optimism to spare?

WHY this chapter matters …

Success in higher education calls for a baseline of physical and emotional well-being.

HOW you can use this chapter …

Maintain your physical and mental energy. Enhance your self-esteem. Make decisions about alcohol and other drugs in a way that supports your success.

do you have a minute?

Take a minute to think about how you take care of yourself. Reflect on what food you use to fuel your body, what exercise you do to maintain it, and how do you nourish your spirit to maintain good mental health. Write a Discovery Statement about how you currently take care of yourself. Follow up with an Intention Statement about what you will do in the next week to enhance your self-care. For example, will you take a walk in nature, eat more vegetables, or visit your campus rec centre? Think about what works for you and just do it.

Wake up to
HEALTH

Some people see health as just a matter of common sense. These people might see little value in reading a chapter about health. After all, they already know how to take care of themselves. Yet *knowing* and *doing* are two different things. Health information does not always translate into healthy habits.

We expect to experience health challenges as we age. Even youth, though, is no guarantee of good health. Over the last three decades, obesity among young adults in Canada has tripled. Twenty-seven percent of young adults smoke (Statistics Canada, 2018a). And the leading causes of death among 20- to 24-year-olds are unintentional injuries, suicide, cancer, and homicide (Statistics Canada, 2018b).

As a student, your success in school is directly tied to your health. Lack of sleep and exercise have been associated with lower grade point averages among undergraduate students. So have alcohol use, tobacco use, gambling, and chronic health conditions (University of Minnesota, 2007). And any health habit that undermines your success in school can also undermine your success in later life.

On the other hand, you can adopt habits that sustain your well-being. One study found that people lengthened their lives by an average of 14 years by adopting just four habits: staying tobacco-free, eating more fruits and vegetables, exercising regularly, and drinking alcohol in moderation, if at all (Khaw et al., 2008).

Health also hinges on a habit of exercising some tissue that lies between your ears—the organ called your brain. One path to greater health starts not with new food or a new form of exercise, but with new ideas.

Consider the power of beliefs. Some of them create barriers to higher levels of health: "Your health is programmed by your heredity." "Some people are just low on energy." "Healthy food doesn't taste very good." "Over the long run, people just don't change their habits." Be willing to test these ideas and change them when it serves you.

journal entry 11-1

Discovery Statement

Take a First Step Toward Good Health

This structured Discovery Statement allows you to look closely at your health. If you look and feel healthy, understanding your body better can help you be aware of what you're doing right. If you are not content with your present physical or emotional health, you might discover some ways to adjust your personal habits and increase your sense of well-being.

Complete the following statements in the space provided. As with the Discovery Wheel exercise in Chapter 1, the usefulness of this Journal Entry will be determined by your honesty and courage.

Eating

1. What I know about the way I eat is . . .
2. What I would most like to change about my diet is . . .
3. My eating habits lead me to be . . .

_____

_____

_____

_____

_____

_____

Exercise

1. The way I usually exercise is . . .
2. The last time I did 20 minutes or more of heart/lung (aerobic) exercise was . . .
3. As a result of my physical conditioning, I feel . . .
4. And I look . . .
5. It would be easier for me to work out regularly if I . . .
6. The most important benefit for me in exercising more is . . .

_____

_____

_____

_____

_____

_____

_____

_____

Substances

1. My history of cigarette smoking is . . .
2. An objective observer would say that my use of alcohol is . . .
3. In the last 10 days, the number of alcoholic drinks I have had is . . .
4. My use of cannabis is . . .
5. I would describe my use of coffee, energy drinks, pop, and other caffeinated drinks as . . .
6. I have used the following illegal drugs in the past week: . . .
7. When it comes to drugs, what I am sometimes concerned about is . . .
8. I take the following prescription drugs:

_____

_____

_____

_____

_____

_____

_____

_____

_____

Relationships

1. Someone who knows me fairly well would say I am emotionally . . .
2. The way I look and feel has affected my relationships by . . .
3. My use of drugs or alcohol has been an issue with the following people . . .
4. The best thing I could do for myself and my relationships would be to . . .

_____

_____

_____

_____

_____

_____

Sleep

1. The number of hours I sleep each night is . . .
2. On weekends I normally sleep . . .
3. I have trouble sleeping when . . .
4. Last night I . . .
5. The quality of my sleep is usually . . .

_____

_____

_____

_____

_____

In general

1. What concerns me more than anything else about my health is . . .
2. Looking back at my responses to this exercise, I feel . . .

_____

_____

_____

_____

_____

People often misunderstand what the word *health* means. This word is similar in origin to *whole, hale, hardy,* and even *holy.* Implied in these words are qualities that most of us associate with healthy people: alertness, vitality, vigour. Healthy people meet the demands of daily life with energy to spare. Illness or stress might slow them down for a while, but then they bounce back. They know how to relax, create loving relationships, and find satisfaction in their work.

Perhaps *health* is one of those rich, multilayered concepts that we can never define completely. That's okay. In the end, your definition of *health* comes from your own experience. The proof lies not on these pages but in your life—in the level of health that you create, starting now. You have two choices. You can remain unaware of habits that have major consequences for your health. Or you can become aware of current habits (discovery), choose new habits (intention), and take appropriate action.

Health is a choice you make every moment, with each action that you take. Wake up to this possibility by experimenting with the suggestions in this chapter. ✳

Choose your
FUEL

It's a cliché, and it's true: You are what you eat. What you eat can have immediate and long-term effects on your performance as a student. That giant jelly dough-nut can make you drowsy within minutes. A steady diet of jelly doughnuts can affect the amount of energy you have available to meet and juggle the demands of classes, family members, jobs, extracurricular activities, and other commitments.

Start with widely accepted guidelines

There have been hundreds of books written about nutrition. One says don't drink milk. Another says the calcium provided by milk is an essential daily nutrient. Although such debate seems confusing, take comfort. There's actually wide agreement about how to fuel your-self for health.

Nutritional guidelines have been developed by Health Canada, in Canada's Food Guide. Though you might be able to find a more healthful diet, you can do well by following these guidelines.

Avoid fad diets

If you are overweight, avoid people who make claims about a quick fix. Even if that "Lose 20 pounds in 20 days!" diet works at first, you're likely to gain the weight back. Fad diets just don't work! As you hear people debate the next low-carbohydrate or low-fat diet, watch out. A large-

Mauro Matacchione/Shutterstock.com

scale study of over 600 individuals who followed either a low-fat or low-carbohydrate diet for 12 months found no significant difference in the amount of weight loss (Hull, 2018). They also didn't lose very much weight over the course of the year. In addition, as is typical with diets, 21 percent of the participants dropped out of the study before the end of the year.

The formula for weight loss is simple, though not always easy: Eat better food, eat less food, and exercise regularly. To find safe weight loss and nutrition pro-grams, visit your doctor or student health service. Go online to the Heart and Stroke Foundation (*www.heartandstroke.ca*) for good advice about how to lose weight healthily. Look for a program that provides peer support.

Limit fast foods

Fast foods can be tempting, especially if you're pressed for time. When eaten consistently, these foods can expand your waistline and drain your budget. A medium pop, large order of fries, and double cheeseburger can pack over 1,500 calories and 60 grams of fat.

About 26 percent of Canadians are obese, which is significantly less than the rate of obesity for Americans; but we are quickly catching up (Ferreras, 2017). Our love affair with fast food and our inactivity contributes to that figure.

To save money and promote health, prepare meals at home and centre them on whole grains, legumes, fruits, and vegetables; as well, reduce portions. See Figure 11.1 for examples of a serving for each food group in Canada's Food Guide. For your recommended number of servings per day and for more information on eating well, see the complete Food Guide at *www.canada.ca/ en/health-canada/services/food-nutrition/canada-food -guide/get-your-copy.html.* ✳

Eating well with
CANADA'S FOOD GUIDE

1 Emphasize vegetables and fruits in your diet. Vegetables and fruit generally have little to no fat, and they are rich in vitamins and minerals. Dark green and orange vegetables, such as broccoli, romaine lettuce, spinach, carrots, squash, and sweet potatoes, are especially vitamin rich, as are orange fruits such as oranges and cantaloupes. Eat at least one orange and one dark green vegetable every day. Choose recipes for vegetables and fruits that have no added fat, salt, or sugar. Try to eat vegetables and fruits more often than drinking juice.

A recent update to the Canada Food Guide suggests that most Canadians need to shift toward eating more plant-based foods and less red meat.

2 Choose grain products. Ensure at least half of your grain products, such as barley, oats, quinoa, and brown rice are whole grain. These products are rich in complex carbohydrates and fibre, as well as some vitamins and minerals. Whole grain pasta and whole grain breads are also good additions to your diet.

3 Choose lower-fat milk and alternatives. This includes skim, 1 percent, and 2 percent milk or fortified soya beverages if you do not drink milk. Lower-fat milk and alternatives provide the same healthy protein and calcium as full-fat ones. Try to choose foods that contain unsaturated fat, such as nuts, avocados, and seeds rather than saturated foods, such as cheeses or butter.

4 Have meat alternatives often. Try to eat beans, tofu, and lentils often. Some fat is important in a healthy diet, but most Canadians eat too much fat. Go for lean cuts of meat and fish. Trim off visible fat before cooking. Try baking, broiling, roasting, or microwaving instead of frying. Beans, peas, and lentils contain protein, are low in fat, and can increase your intake of fibre. Eat at least two servings of fish, such as char, herring, mackerel, salmon, sardines, and trout, each week[*].

5 Drink water regularly and enjoy a variety of foods. Eating is one of life's great pleasures. Don't hesitate to try new things and expand your food horizons. Eating a variety of foods from each of the food groups is the best way to make sure your body gets all the nutrients it needs.

Try to limit your intake of foods and beverages that are high in calories, fat, salt (sodium), or sugars—foods such as cakes, muffins, French fries, nachos, alcohol, pop, and energy drinks. The trip to your local coffee bar

[*]Health Canada provides advice for limiting exposure to mercury from certain types of fish. Refer to *www.healthcanada.gc.ca* for the latest information.

What is One Food Guide Serving?
Look at the examples below.

Figure 11.1 *Examples of Canada's Food Guide Servings*

can be laden with calories too. The next time you reach for a white chocolate mocha or caramel frappé, ask yourself if it is worth getting a third of your daily calories in just one drink.

To determine what nutrients or how much sugar or fats are in prepared foods, read the labels on products. Many fast food restaurants post the number of calories for each menu item (in some provinces, such as Ontario, they're required to do so by law). Use that information to make wise choices. Eating less processed or prepared food will decrease your consumption of salt (sodium), saturated fats, and sugars. Consuming less salt can reduce your chances of developing high blood pressure. Canada's Food Guide is being revised so check on the Health Canada website for updates.

For most adults, moderate alcohol consumption means no more than one drink per day. Excessive drinking is a serious risk to health and safety.

6 Eat foods from diverse cultures. Eating healthily doesn't mean giving up food from the many cultures we grew up in. With over 250 different ethnocultural groups in our country, there are many ways to eat well and continue with all our food traditions, including the traditions and culture of our Indigenous peoples.

7 Achieve and maintain a healthy body weight by enjoying regular physical activity and healthy eating. Healthful eating and regular physical activity are both important to staying well. You should aim to maintain a healthy body weight, which will help you to stay active and lower your risk of health problems. Make physical activity part of your daily routine—it is recommended that adults accumulate at least 2½ hours of moderate to vigorous physical activity each week and that children and youth accumulate at least 60 minutes per day. Being active not only helps you keep a healthy weight, but it also strengthens your heart, lungs, and muscles. Find ways to be active that you enjoy and that suit your own schedule and lifestyle. ✳

Prevent and treat eating disorders

Eating disorders affect many students. These disorders involve serious disturbances in eating behaviour. Examples are excessive preoccupation with calories, compulsive exercising, or extreme reduction of food intake, as well as an irrational concern about body shape or weight. Women are much more likely to develop these disorders than men.

Bulimia involves cycles of binge eating and forced purges. A person with this disorder might gorge on a pizza, doughnuts, and ice cream and then force herself to vomit. Or she might compensate for overeating with excessive use of laxatives, enemas, or diuretics.

Anorexia nervosa is a potentially fatal illness marked by self-starvation, either through extended fasts or by eating only one food for weeks at a time (National Eating Disorder Information Centre, 2014a).

Eating disorders are not due to a failure of willpower. Instead, these are illnesses in which harmful patterns of eating take on lives of their own.

Eating disorders can lead to many complications, including life-threatening heart conditions and kidney failure. Many people with eating disorders also struggle with depression, substance abuse, and anxiety.

These disorders require immediate treatment to stabilize health. Treatment is usually followed by continuing medical care, counselling, and medication to promote a full recovery.

University and college students, particularly women, are at risk for developing eating disorders (National Eating Disorder Information Centre, 2014b). A recent Government of Canada survey found that 1.5 percent of young women between the ages of 15 and 24 had an eating disorder (National Eating Disorder Information Centre, 2014b). Moving away from home, making the transition to college life, and fear of the famous "Frosh 15" (15 pounds often gained in the first year) can all lead to stress.

Most campuses have some type of peer-mentoring or support programs that can help you meet new people and make you feel more at ease in this new environment. Don't be afraid to reach out for help if you need it. If you're worried that you have an eating disorder, visit a doctor or student health services. If you live in residence, speak to the residence assistant or don. If you see signs of an eating disorder in someone else, express your concern with "I" messages as explained in Chapter 8, "Communicating." For more information, contact the National Eating Disorder Information Centre toll free at 1-866-633-4220, or go online to the National Eating Disorders Information Centre at *www.nedic.ca* or the Eating Disorders Association of Canada *www.edac-atac.ca*.

Choose to
EXERCISE

oneinchpunch/Shutterstock.com

Our bodies need to be exercised. The world ran on muscle power back in the era when we had to hunt down a woolly mammoth every few weeks and drag it back to the cave. Now we can grab a burger at a drive-thru window. Today we need to make a special effort to exercise.

Choosing to exercise can lift your mood, increase your stamina, strengthen your bones, stabilize your joints, and help prevent heart disease. It can also reduce your risk of high blood pressure, diabetes, and several forms of cancer. If you do resistance training—such as weight machines or elastic-band workouts—you'll strengthen your muscles as well. For a complete fitness program, add stretching exercises to enjoy increased flexibility (Brody, 2006).

Exercise also promotes brain fitness, and it reduces the symptoms of depression and anxiety. It also helps to prevent heart attack, diabetes, and several forms of cancer (Harvard Medical School, 2008). Exercise also refreshes your body and your mind. If you're stuck on a math problem or blocked on writing a paper, take an exercise break. Chances are that you'll come back with a fresh perspective and some new ideas.

If you get moving, you'll create lean muscles, a strong heart, and an alert brain. You don't have to train for the Olympics, however. And if the word *exercise* turns you off, think *physical activity* instead. Here are some things you can do:

Stay active throughout the day

Countries like Canada are activity poor—in other words, we don't walk a lot. Not surprisingly, there is a high correlation between lack of activity and obesity (Ferreras, 2017). So, do your heart a favour by walking some extra blocks. Take the stairs instead of riding elevators. Park a little farther from work or school and walk the extra distance. (Be sure to take safety precautions if doing so alone at night.) For an extra workout, climb two stairs at a time.

An hour of daily activity is ideal, but do whatever you can. Use a fitness tracker app or device to record your activity. Most people aim for at least 10,000 steps a day so track your steps to see how well you are doing. Some activity is better than none.

No matter what you do, ease into it. For example, start by walking briskly for at least 15 minutes every day. Increase that time gradually, and add a little jogging.

Adapt to your campus environment

Look for exercise facilities on campus. You have paid for these facilities in your student fees, so get your money's worth. Search for classes in cardio fitness, swimming, volleyball, basketball, golf, spinning, and other sports. Intramural sports are another option. School can be a great place to get in shape.

Do what you enjoy

Stay active over the long term with aerobic activities that you enjoy. You might enjoy cycling, kickboxing, yoga, Pilates, Zumba fitness classes, or mountain climbing. Check out your school's recreational facilities to see what courses they offer.

Vary your routine

Find several activities that you enjoy, and rotate them throughout the year. Your main form of activity during winter might be dancing, aquafit, or snowboarding. In summer, you could switch to outdoor sports. Whenever possible, choose weight-bearing activities such as walking, running, or stair-climbing.

Did you **know that …?**

> You can get a great workout on campus without even going to the campus recreation centre? Just climb a few extra stairs. At Vancouver Island University, there are 409 steps from the top to the bottom of its Nanaimo campus—now that's a Stairmaster! ("50 little-known facts," 2017)

Get active early

Consider working out first thing in the morning. Then it's done for the day. Make it part of your daily routine, just like brushing your teeth.

Exercise with other people

Making exercise a social affair can add a fun factor and raise your level of commitment.

Look for gradual results

It will take a while to get in shape so be patient. Find some activity you love and start to develop a routine of being active. It will make a difference over time.

Before beginning any vigorous exercise program, consult a healthcare professional. This is critical if you are overweight, in poor condition, or a smoker, or if you have a history of health problems. ✳

Choose to
REST

In addition to requiring activity, human bodies need sufficient periods of rest. A lack of rest can decrease your immunity to illness and impair your performance in school.

As a student, you might be tempted to cut back drastically on your sleep once in a while. All-nighters to study for exams or catch up on a lengthy reading assignment are common for some students. Unfortunately, staying up all night will leave you bleary-eyed for your exam and therefore decrease your performance; it will also exhaust you for other necessary work. If you find you are indulging in all-nighters often, read Chapter 2 for some time management ideas. Depriving yourself of sleep is a choice you can and should avoid.

Promote sound sleep

Sometimes, getting to sleep isn't easy, even when you feel tired. If you have trouble falling asleep, experiment with the following suggestions:

- Exercise daily. For many people, this promotes sounder sleep. However, finish exercising several hours before you want to go to sleep.
- Avoid lengthy naps during the daytime.
- Monitor your caffeine intake, especially in the afternoon and evening.
- Avoid using alcohol to feel sleepy. Drinking alcohol late in the evening can disrupt your sleep during the night.
- Make tomorrow's to-do list before you go to sleep so you won't lie there worrying that tomorrow you'll forget about something you need to do.

Dmitry A/Shutterstock.com

- Develop a sleep ritual—a regular sequence of calming activities that end your day. You might take a warm bath and do some light reading. Turn off all screens (cellphones, tablets, etc.) at least one hour before you go to bed.
- Keep your sleeping room cool.
- Sleep in the same place each night. When you're there, your body gets the message "It's time to go to sleep."
- Practise relaxation techniques while lying in bed. A simple one is to count your breaths and release distracting thoughts as they arise.
- Get up and study or do something else until you're tired.
- See a doctor if sleeplessness persists.

How much sleep is enough? Probably more than you are currently getting. The 2016 American College Health Association survey, which included students from twenty Ontario universities, found that 28.8 percent of Canadian students reported that sleep difficulties interfered with their academic performance. Lack of sleep can interfere with your memory, your concentration, and your ability to stay awake in class. The solution is a good night's sleep. ✳

Ways to change a
HABIT

Dean Drobot/Shutterstock.com; © Alberto Zornetta/Shutterstock;
Evgeniia Freeman/Shutterstock.com

Consider a new way to think about the word *habit*. Imagine for a moment that many of our most troublesome problems and even our most basic traits are just habits.

That expanding waistline that is blamed on a partner's cooking—maybe that's just a habit called overeating.

Procrastination, stress, and money shortages might just be names that we give to collections of habits—scores of simple, small, repeated behaviours that combine to create a huge result. The same goes for health, wealth, love, and many of the other things that we want from life.

One way of thinking about success is to focus on habits. Behaviours such as failing to complete reading assignments or skipping class might be habits leading to an outcome that "couldn't" be avoided—dropping out of school. When you confront a behaviour that undermines your goals or creates a circumstance that you don't want, consider a new attitude: It's just a habit. And it can be changed.

One change in behaviour that seems insignificant at first can have effects that ripple throughout your life. A recent book that reinforces this idea is *The Power of Habit: Why We Do What We Do in Life and in Business* by Charles Duhigg (2012). He has looked at how habits are formed and how they can be changed. In particular, Duhigg examines the neuroscience behind habits. Habits he suggests affect the behaviour not just of individuals but also of organizations and even societies. Habits shape the choices we make on a daily basis almost as much as our conscious thoughts and they do so for a reason: It takes less mental energy to do things automatically than to think through every action that we take. Think about when you learned to drive. Initially every action required conscious attention, from turning out of the driveway, to signalling before pulling into traffic. Eventually these actions became automatic, and some days you can't even recall your trip home from school. Scary as this might seem, our ability to be able to chunk sequences of actions together, like always turning off the stove after the KD is cooked, allows us to act more efficiently in the world.

Duhigg talks about "the habit loop." This is where a cue in the environment, such as a slot machine with flashing lights, consistently leads to a behavioural routine, pulling the lever on the machine, that results in a reward, the rush of adrenaline you feel as you wait to see if you won or not. The more this loop is repeated, the more the sequence of behaviour becomes automatic. Lots of habits are good for us, like automatically putting toothpaste on our toothbrushes in the morning, but others, like gambling or overeating, need to be changed if we want to live healthy, well-balanced lives.

To change a habit, you need to change one or all of the elements in the routine. After interviewing hundreds of people, psychologists James Prochaska, John Norcross, and Carlo DiClemente (1994) identified stages that people typically go through when adopting a new behaviour. These stages take people from *contemplating* a change and making a clear *determination* to change, to taking *action* and *maintaining* the new behaviour. Following are ways to help yourself move successfully through each stage.

Tell the truth

Telling the truth about any habit—from chewing our fingernails to cheating on exams—frees us. Without taking this step, our efforts to change might be as ineffective as rearranging the deck chairs on the *Titanic*. Telling the truth allows us to see what's actually sinking the ship.

When we admit what's really going on in our lives, our defences are down. We're open to accepting help from others. The support we need to change the habit has an opportunity to make an impact.

Choose and commit to a new behaviour

It often helps to choose a new habit to replace an old one. First, make a commitment to practise the new habit. If, as Duhigg (2012) states, habits are repeated patterns of behaviour, then we need to practise the new behaviour as much as possible. Tell key people in your life about your decision to change. Set up a plan for when and how. Answer questions such as these: When will I apply the new habit? Where will I be? Who will be with me? What will I be seeing, hearing, touching, saying, or doing? Exactly how will I think, speak, or act differently?

Take the student who always snacks when he studies. Each time he sits down to read, he positions a bag of potato chips within easy reach. For him, opening a book is a cue to start chewing. Snacking is especially easy, given the place he chooses to study: the kitchen. He decides to change this habit by studying at a desk in his bedroom instead of at the kitchen table. And every time he feels the urge to bite into a potato chip, he sips a glass of water instead.

Affirm your intention

You can pave the way for a new behaviour by clearing a mental path for it. Before you apply the new behaviour, rehearse it in your mind. Mentally picture what actions you will take and in what order.

You can act as if your intention is already a reality, as if the new habit is already a part of you. Experience the change you want to see—today. In some cases, this might be enough to change the old habit completely.

Start with a small change

You can sometimes rearrange a whole pattern of behaviours by changing one small habit. If you have a habit of always being late for class, and if you want to change that habit, be on time for one class. As soon as you change the old pattern by getting ready and arriving on time at one class, you'll likely find yourself arriving at all of your classes on time. You might even start arriving everywhere else on time. Duhigg suggests that changing one pattern of behaviour or habit—what he calls a "keystone habit"—can be vital in allowing you to change other habits.

Get feedback and support

This is a crucial step and a point at which many plans for change break down. It's easy to practise your new behaviour with great enthusiasm for a few days. After the initial rush of excitement, however, things can get a little tougher. We begin to find excuses for slipping back into old habits: "One more cigarette won't hurt." "I can get back to my diet tomorrow." "It's been a tough day. I deserve this beer."

One way to get feedback is to bring other people into the picture. They might be friends or family, or you might require the more focussed support you can get from a support group. Ask others to remind you that you are changing your habit. If you want to stop an old behaviour, such as cramming for exams, it often works to tell everyone you know that you intend to stop. Support from others can be as simple as a quick phone call: "Hi. Have you started that outline for your research paper yet?"

You are probably the most effective source for your own support and feedback. Figure out a way to monitor your progress from charts to graphs to journals.

Practise, practise, practise—without self-judgment

Repetition is the key way for behaviour to become habitual. This idea is key to changing habits. Act on your intention. If you fail or forget, let go of any self-judgment. Just keep practising the new habit and allow whatever time it takes to make a change.

Then you need to figure out the reward you will give yourself for changing the behaviour. At school it can feel natural to reward yourself for studying for two hours by having a snack—a bad habit in itself—so think about what else you can do instead. It may be that you allow yourself to play a favourite video game or to go for a run. Remember that Duhigg (2012) states that to change the habit you have to break that "habit loop." Once you understand ways to change one habit, you understand ways to change almost any habit. ✳

Dean Drobot/Shutterstock.com

Daniel Kirkegaard Mouritsen/ Shutterstock.com

Choose
MENTAL HEALTH

The number of students in higher education who have mental health problems is steadily increasing (Pang, 2017). According to the 2016 American College Health Association survey, 44.4 percent of Ontario students reported that they have felt "so depressed it was difficult to function." They also found that 13 percent reported seriously considering suicide with 18.4 percent of those surveyed saying they had been "diagnosed or treated" by a professional for anxiety (Max & Waters, 2018, pg. 3). Not only have suicide rates risen but there has been an 86% increase in substance abuse (Cribb, 2017). So, if you are feeling depressed, stressed out, or anxious, you are not alone. There are strategies and resources you can use to stave off stress as you get your education.

Most colleges and universities have adopted new strategic plans to address student mental health and wellness. According to educational leaders, Wilson and Ono (2017), postsecondary schools have a special role to play in reducing the stigma that stops many students from seeking help. They recognize that the sooner students seek help the sooner they can start to heal.

The transition from high school to postsecondary education can be challenging and lead to mental health difficulties (MacDonald, 2017). One organization, Jack.org, was created to educate students and their families about mental health. Formed after Eric Windeler's son Jack, a first-year student, died by suicide, the organization seeks to train and support youth leaders to facilitate the discussion around mental health. There are many local chapters of this organization. Check the website to see if your school is involved in ending the stigma associated with mental health. Peer leaders are crucial to the success of such programs. The website also provides resources about mental health issues.

Mental health includes many factors: your skill at managing stress, your ability to build loving relationships, your capacity to meet the demands of school and work, and your beliefs about your ability to succeed. People with mental illness have thoughts, emotions, or behaviours that consistently interfere with these areas of life.

You can take simple and immediate steps to prevent mental health problems or cope with them if

wavebreakmedia/Shutterstock.com

they do occur. Remember that strategies for managing test-related stress can help you manage *any* form of stress (See "Let go of test anxiety" in Chapter 6). Here are some other suggestions to promote your mental health.

Take care of your body

Your thoughts and emotions can get scrambled if you go too long feeling hungry or tired. According to Dr. Richard Kadison, the chief of the Mental Health Service at Harvard University, lack of sleep is a huge issue in making college students feel stressed out. He says that most college and university students only sleep 6½ hours a night (Kadison & Foy DiGeronimo, 2004). That is just not enough. So, if you are starting to feel stressed out, check how much sleep you are getting. And follow the suggestions in this chapter for eating, exercise, and sleep.

Solve problems

Although you can't "fix" a bad feeling in the same way that you can fix a machine, you can choose to change a situation associated with that feeling. There might be a problem that needs a solution. You can use feeling bad as your motivation to solve that problem.

Sometimes an intense feeling of sadness, anger, or fear is related to a specific situation in your life. Describe the problem. Then brainstorm solutions and choose one to implement. Reducing your course load, cutting back on hours at work, getting more financial aid, delegating a task, or taking some other concrete action might solve the problem and help you feel better.

Stay active

A related strategy is to do something—*anything* that's constructive, even if it's not a solution to the specific problem. For example, mop the kitchen floor. Clean out your dresser drawers. Iron your shirts. This sounds silly, but it works. You, not your emotions, are in control.

The basic principle is that you can separate emotions from actions. It is appropriate to feel miserable when you do. It's normal to cry and express your feelings. But it is also possible to take action: to go to class, study, work, eat, even though you are not feeling great. Unless you have a diagnosable problem with anxiety or depression, you can and should continue your normal activities until the negative feeling passes.

Share what you're thinking and feeling

There are times when negative thoughts and emotions persist even after you take appropriate action. Tell a family member or friend about those feelings. This is a powerful way to gain perspective. The simple act of describing a problem can sometimes reveal a solution or give you a fresh perspective.

Curtail your use of social media

Recent research suggests that students today have higher expectations of themselves than previous generations (Hrvatin, 2018). Social media sites like Instagram and Facebook can increase the pressure students face to be perfect and to be successful. When everyone else's life looks perfect, it is easy to be too hard on yourself. Rather than comparing yourself to others on social media, take a break and talk to a friend face to face.

Focus on one task at a time

It's easy to feel stressed if you dwell on how much you have to accomplish this year, this term, this month, or even this week. One solution is to plan to implement the suggestions in Chapter 2, "Time."

Remember that an effective plan for the day does two things. First, it clarifies what you're choosing *not* to do today. (Tasks that you plan to do in the future are listed on your calendar or to-do list.) Second, an effective plan reduces your day to a series of concrete tasks—such as making phone calls, going to classes, running errands, or reading chapters—that you can do one at a time.

If you feel overwhelmed, just find the highest-priority task on your to-do list. Do it with total attention until it's done. Then go back to your list for the next high-priority task. Do *it* with total attention. Savour the feeling of mastery and control that comes with crossing each task off your list.

Manage stress

Three-quarters of Canadians, regardless of age, report they feel stressed out at least once a month, and 43 percent feel really stressed more than once a week (Canadian Mental Health Association, 2011). Luckily, stress levels do decrease as you get older, with 87 percent of 18- to 24-year-olds saying they feel stressed out at least once a month compared to only 56 percent of over 65-year-olds; however, school environments can be especially stressful.

Stress is not always harmful. It can result from pleasant experiences as well as unpleasant ones. The excitement of a new term—new classes, new instructors, new classmates—can be fun and stressful at the same time. Oddly enough, your body perceives excitement in almost the same way that it perceives fear. Both emotions produce rapid heart rates, increased adrenalin flow, and muscle contractions. Both emotions produce stress.

Stress, at appropriate times and at manageable levels, is normal and useful. It can sharpen our awareness and boost our energy just when we need it the most. Work is a major source of stress, yet many (41 percent) report that the stress from work actually has a positive impact on their performance. And most individuals felt that their employer was effective at dealing with workplace stress. Companies like Starbucks and Manulife have greatly increased their mental health benefits in response to the demands from their employees (Cribb, 2017).

When stress persists or becomes excessive, however, it is harmful. Chances are your stress level is too high if you consistently experience any of the following symptoms: panic attacks, depression; low productivity; strained relationships at work or home; health problems such as an upset stomach, nausea, shortness of breath, and a low energy level; a pattern of avoiding tasks; insomnia; feeling burned out at home or at work; feeling tense, nervous, or fearful.

Stress has both mental and physical components. The mental components include thoughts that promote fear and anxiety; the physical components include illnesses and muscle tension.

The fact that these elements are all part of stress points to several broad strategies for managing it:

- *Deal with the problem.* Sometimes an intense feeling of sadness, anger, or fear is related to a specific situation in your life. The Canadian Mental Health Association (2011) suggests that the first step is to identify the cause of the stress, brainstorm solutions, and take steps to solve the problem. With school, the issue is often mounting homework, so make sure your own procrastination isn't adding to your stress levels. Go back over Chapter 2 again to see how you can use your time more wisely to get the work done.

- *Deal with stressful thoughts by releasing irrational beliefs.* According to Seligman (1998) and other cognitive psychologists, stress results not from events in our lives but from the way we *think* about those events. If we believe that people should always behave in exactly the way we expect them to, for instance, we set ourselves up for stress. Noticing these beliefs and replacing them with more rational ones (e.g., *I can control my own behaviour but not the behaviour of others*) can reduce stress significantly.

- *Deal with stressful thoughts by releasing them altogether.* Meditation offers a way to release distressing thoughts. While meditating, you simply notice your thoughts as they arise and pass—without reacting to them. Eventually, your stream of thinking slows down. You might even find that it comes to a complete stop while at the same time you remain alert and aware. This is a state of deep relaxation that might also yield life-changing insights. You can find meditation instruction through health maintenance organizations, YMCAs, and community centre education programs.

- *Counter the physical element of stress.* Options include breathing exercises, relaxation techniques, yoga, and therapeutic bodywork such as massage. Some schools offer classes in these subjects. Regular physical exercise is another key ingredient when you are feeling stressed (Paterson, 2002). Go for a walk or work out at the gym the next time tension causes stress.

- *Develop better self-regulation of your behaviours.* Sometimes it is hard to stay focussed on long-term goals and it is easy to give in to distractions. However, research has found that students who are better at paying attention to the tasks at hand are happier and experience less stress (Barseghian, 2013). Revisit Chapter 1, "First Steps," to see how developing your metacognitive skills can help you to reduce the stress in your life.

- *Use this book.* It includes relaxation and breathing exercises. Many of the Power Processes and the techniques for letting go of test anxiety can also help you manage stress.

Stress is a part of life; it is how you deal with it that counts!

Find resources on or off campus

Although making the transition from high school to university can feel overwhelming at times, postsecondary schools also provide the opportunity to help you move from languishing to flourishing (Kostouros, & Bennet, 2017). You are not alone. You are surrounded by an engaged academic community and campus resources to support your success.

When should you seek help? Whenever problems with your thinking, moods, or behaviours consistently interfere with your ability to sleep, eat, go to class, work, or create positive relationships.

Sometimes you just can't fix the problem on your own. A family doctor can refer you to a mental health professional if it seems appropriate. The student health centre is not just for treating colds, allergies, and flu symptoms. Counsellors at the health centre are trained to help students deal with adjustment to campus, changes in mood, academic problems, and drug abuse and dependence. Students with anxiety disorders, clinical depression, bipolar disorder, and other diagnoses might get referred to a psychiatrist or psychologist who works on or off campus. The referral process can take time, so seek help right away. Your tuition helps to pay for these services. It's smart to use them now.

When should you seek help? Whenever problems with your thinking, moods, or behaviours consistently interfere with your ability to sleep, eat, go to class, work, or create positive relationships. Talk to your doctor about a screening for depression if you've felt despondent and have had little interest or pleasure in doing things for two weeks straight.

These guidelines can help you now and they can also work after you graduate. Promoting mental health is a skill to use for the rest of your life.

The Canadian Mental Health Association has a list of 10 apps you can access to help you manage your well-being (*https://bhn.cmha.ca/news/top-10-mental-health-apps*). Your goal is to find strategies to improve your own self-care. Another app that can help you is *HealthyMinds*. It is designed to help you cope with stress and to give you a tool to manage mental wellness. The app includes a daily mood tracker and tips on dealing with stress. It helps you to develop problem-solving strategies and resilience to deal with emotional issues. A good website for resources and interactives is *Mindyourmind.ca*; if you are looking for resources on everything from transitioning to college or university to building positive self-esteem, this website is designed specifically with students in mind. Another good website for students was developed by the Canadian Mental Health Association (*www.sj.cmha.ca/youreducation/introduction.html*). This website will help you find a support network and set you up for success in college and university. It has a separate section for the challenges of mature students and higher education. Finally, some provinces offer helplines for postsecondary students. ✳

You've got support

As you make the transition to college or university, there are a lot of things to consider—and one of the most important is your mental health. About 1 in 5 Canadians will experience mental illness and many of these first appear between the ages of 16 and 25—the ages when young people are attending college or university (Wilson & Ono, 2017). If you already know that you have a mental illness, your first step to ensure continued care is to connect with healthcare providers at your school. It's a good idea to connect with disability or accessible learning services at your school if you also need academic or other accommodations.

Some people will experience the beginning of a mental illness when they are away at school; many people will experience mental health distress because of things like grief or homesickness. Most campuses have several services to help you through these difficult times—no problem is too small to merit support. Get connected with these services so that you don't have to go through it alone.

Everyone will experience some stress related being a first-year student. Make a plan to take care of yourself in four important areas:

1. Body: Prioritizing sleep and regular physical activity sets you up to handle all the demands, changes, and stresses of being a student.

2. Heart: Making and maintaining good relationships builds a circle of support to celebrate the good times and help in the challenging times.

3. Spirit: Nurture your spirit by engaging in activities that make daily life meaningful. Make time for your religious or spiritual practices, being in nature, or volunteering your time with causes that allow you to put your values into action.

4. Feelings: You are the expert on your own wellness and your first job is to notice when you start to feel overwhelmed, sad, or isolated. Make a commitment to reach out for support when you notice a change in the way you normally feel or act.

Dr. Susan Rodger, Psychologist, & Dr. Melanie-Anne Atkins, Wellness Coordinator, Western University

National Online Resources:

Transitions: Making the most of your campus experience. Free resources at *http://teenmentalhealth.org/product/transitions*

First Nations and Inuit mental health and wellness: *www.canada.ca/en/indigenous-services-canada/services/first-nations-inuit-health/health-promotion/mental-health-wellness.html*, or call 1(855) 242-3310.

Crisis Services Canada: *Suicide prevention and support. www.crisisservicescanada.ca* or call 1(833) 456-4566

Government of Canada: Mental health support, *www.canada.ca/en/public-health/services/mental-health-services/mental-health-get-help.html*

For provincial mental health services, go to *www.ctvnews.ca/health/mental-health-care-in-canada-where-to-find-help-1.3767445*

Courtesy of Susan Rodger and Melanie-Anne Atkins

journal entry 11-2

Discovery/Intention Statement

Choose to be Healthy

For three minutes, brainstorm things you can do during the next month to improve the ways that you fuel, move, rest, and observe your body. Write your ideas in the space below. Use additional space if needed.

I discovered that I . . .

_____

_____

_____

_____

Next, pick three ideas that you can begin to use or practise this week. Write an Intention Statement below about how and when you intend to use these ideas.

I intend to . . .

_____

_____

_____

_____

_____

_____

EMOTIONAL PAIN
is not a sickness

EMOTIONAL PAIN has gotten a bad name. This type of slander is undeserved. There is nothing wrong with feeling bad. It's okay to feel miserable, depressed, sad, upset, angry, dejected, gloomy, or unhappy.

It might not be pleasant to feel bad, but it can be good for you. Often, the appropriate way to feel is bad. When you leave a place you love, sadness is natural. When you lose a friend or lover, misery might be in order. When someone treats you badly, it is probably appropriate to feel angry. Our feelings are what make us human and the goal of good mental health is not to suppress our feelings but, in fact, to be open to them.

Feeling bad for too long can be a problem, though. If depression, sadness, or anger persists, get help. Otherwise, allow yourself to experience these emotions. They're usually appropriate and necessary for personal growth. In fact, feeling rotten can be a cue to us that something is wrong in our lives that we need to address.

When a loved one dies, it is necessary to grieve. The grief might appear in the form of depression, sadness, or anger. There is nothing wrong with extreme emotional pain. It is natural, and it doesn't have to be fixed.

When feeling bad becomes a problem, it is usually because you didn't allow yourself to feel bad at the outset. So, the next time you feel rotten, go ahead and feel rotten. The feeling will pass—and probably more quickly if you don't fight it or try to ignore it.

Allowing yourself to feel bad might even help you get smarter. Harvey Jackins (1991), a psychotherapist, bases his work on this premise. Jackins believes that when people fully experience and release their emotions, they also remove blocks to their thinking and clear a path for profound personal insights. And Daniel Goleman (1995), author of *Emotional Intelligence,* asserts that

being attuned to feelings can lead to sounder personal decisions. Following are some good ways to feel bad.

Don't worry about reasons
Sometimes we allow ourselves to feel bad only if we have a good reason; for example, "Well, I feel very sad, but that is because I just found out my best friend is moving to Europe." It's all right to know the reason why you are sad, but it is also fine not to know. You can feel bad for no apparent reason. The reason doesn't matter.

Connect with people
Talking to people is a way of healing. Do things with other people. Include old friends. Make new friends. If friends and family members can't help, see a counsellor at your campus health centre.

Reassure others
Sometimes other people—friends or family members, for example—have a hard time letting you feel bad. They might be worried that they did something wrong and they want to make it better. They want you to quit feeling bad. Tell them you will. Assure them that you will feel good again, but that for right now, you just want to feel bad.

Remember that pain passes
Emotional pain does not last forever. Often it ends in a matter of weeks. There's no need to let a broken heart stop your life. Although you can find abundant advice on the subject, just remember a simple and powerful idea: This, too, shall pass. ✳

SUICIDE
is no solution

While preparing for and entering higher education, people typically face major changes. The stress that they feel can lead to an increase in depression, anxiety, and, very occasionally, attempted suicide. So, let's talk about the danger signals for suicide.

Recognize danger signals

- *Talking about suicide.* People who attempt suicide often talk about it beforehand. They might say, "I just don't want to live anymore." Or "I want you to know that no matter what happens, I've always loved you." Or "Tomorrow night at 7:30 I'm going to end it all."

- *Planning for it.* People planning suicide will sometimes put their affairs in order. They might close bank accounts, give away or sell precious possessions, or make or update a will. They might even develop specific plans on how to kill themselves.

- *Having a history of previous attempts.* Some estimates suggest that up to 50 percent of the people who kill themselves have attempted suicide at least once before.

- *Dwelling on problems.* Expressing extreme helplessness or hopelessness about solving problems can indicate that someone might be considering suicide.

- *Feeling depressed.* Although not everyone who is depressed attempts suicide, almost everyone who attempts suicide feels depressed.

Take prompt action

In Canada, suicide is the leading cause of premature death (Centre for Suicide Prevention, 2011). If you suspect that someone you know is considering suicide, do whatever it takes to ensure the person's safety. If you are living in residence, talk to the residence staff. It is not up to you to solve the other student's problems, though. Let the troubled person know that you will persist in connecting her to those who can help, until you are certain that she's safe. Any of the following actions can help:

- *Take it seriously.* Taking suicidal comments seriously is especially important when you hear them from young adults. Over 13 percent of Canadian undergraduate students report having seriously considered suicide (American College Health Association, 2016). Suicide threats are more common in this age group and might be dismissed as "normal." Err on the side of being too careful rather than on the side of being negligent.

- *Listen fully.* Encourage the person at risk to express thoughts and feelings appropriately to you or, more importantly, to a trained counsellor. If she claims that she doesn't want to talk, be inviting, be assertive, and be persistent. Be totally committed to listening.

- *Speak powerfully.* Let the person at risk know that you care. Trying to talk someone out of suicide or minimizing problems is generally useless. Acknowledge that problems are serious and that they can be solved. Point out that suicide is a permanent solution to a temporary problem—and that help is available on campus and in the community.

- *Get professional help.* Suggest that the person see a mental health professional. If they resist seeking help, get others involved, including the depressed person's family, residence staff, or other school personnel.

- *Remove access to drugs, guns, and razors.*

- *Handle an emergency.* If a situation becomes a crisis, do not leave the person alone. Call a crisis hotline, 911, or a social service agency. If necessary, take the person to the nearest hospital emergency room, clinic, or police station.

Take care of yourself

If you ever begin to think about taking your own life, remember that you can apply any of the above suggestions to yourself. For example, look for warning signs and take them seriously. Seek out someone you trust and tell this person how you feel. If necessary, make an appointment to see your doctor or a counsellor and ask someone to accompany you. When you're at risk, you deserve the same compassion that you'd willingly extend to another person.

Find out more on this topic from the Centre for Suicide Prevention website at *suicideinfo.ca*. ✳

Choose to STAY SAFE

Most schools are relatively safe. While on campus, you might feel insulated from the outside world and believe that you have special protection. The vast majority of Canadian students report feeling safe on campus during the day (American College Health Association, 2016). Nighttime, though, brings with it another perspective, with 61.7 percent of males and only 30 percent of females stating they feel safe on campus (American College Health Association, 2016). For LGBTQQ students, even daytime doesn't feel safe: 64 percent of these students reporting they do not feel safe in their schools, particularly in gender-segregated spaces such as washrooms or change rooms (Taylor & Peter et al., 2011).

Take general precautions

Three simple actions can significantly increase your personal safety. One is to always lock doors when you're away from home. If you live in a residence, follow the policies for keeping the front doors secure. Don't let an unauthorized person walk in behind you. If you commute to school or have a car on campus, keep your car doors locked.

The second action is to avoid walking alone, especially at night. Many schools offer a foot patrol service where students will walk with you to your car or residence. Use them. As a backup, carry enough spare cash for a taxi ride.

Third, plan for emergencies. Look for emergency phones along the campus routes that you normally walk. If you have a cellphone, you can always call 911 for help.

Also, be willing to make that call when you see other people in unsafe situations. For example, you might be at a party with a friend who drinks too much and collapses. In this situation, some underage students might hesitate to call for help. They fear getting charged with illegal alcohol possession. Don't make this mistake. Every minute that you delay calling 911 puts your friend at further risk.

Lesbian, Gay, Bisexual, Transgendered, Queer, Questioning (LGBTQQ) Students

If you are an LGBTQQ student, you are more at risk for **homophobic bullying** and hate crimes. Statistics Canada recently found that youth are most likely to be involved

Marc Bruxelle/Getty Images

in hate crimes than other age groups, and that more than half the hate crimes motivated by sexual orientation were violent (Toronto Police Service, 2018). In fact, hate crimes based on sexual orientation rose by 25 percent in a single year in Canada (Theobold, 2018).

Many schools have a "Positive Space" program (Algonquin College, 2018) in which volunteers (including students, staff, and faculty) provide support to LGBTQQ campus members. One of the goals of the program is to make us all more aware of the **transphobia**, **heterosexism**, and **homophobia** that occur in our schools and society. Positive Space program volunteers participate in training and typically identify themselves by placing a sticker on their office or residence room doors. Find out if your school has such a program and, if not, consider starting one. Whether you are gay or straight, we all are responsible for creating a safe school environment.

If your school has not adopted gender neutral bathrooms (bathrooms that are open to any gender) start a campaign for them. This will help demonstrate your support for trans and gender non-conforming students at your school.

There are many organizations available to support LGBTQQ members, such as Egale Canada Human Rights Trust (*https://egale.ca*); PFLAG Canada (*www.pflagcanada.ca*), which offers peer-to-peer support; and the LGBT Youth Line (*www.youthline.ca*), which provides peer counselling.

Prevent sexual assault

The rise of the #Metoo movement has shown how widespread sexual violence is within our society. You need to know how to prevent sexual assault while you're on campus. This problem could be more common at your school than you think. Ontario, Nova Scotia, Manitoba, and British Columbia all have legislation that requires colleges and universities to have a policy for dealing with occurrences of sexual violence and to collect information on sexual assaults at their institutions (Chiose, 2018). *Our Turn* is a student movement that was formed to address sexual violence on campus. It represents 14 different schools across the country and provides a scorecard on each school's sexual violence policies.

People often hesitate to report sexual assault for many reasons, such as fear, embarrassment, and concerns that others won't believe them.

Both women and men can take steps to prevent sexual assault from occurring in the first place:

- Get together with a group of people for a tour of the campus. Make a special note of danger spots, such as unlit paths and unguarded buildings. Keep in mind that sexual assault can occur during daylight and in well-lit places.

- Be aware that the first few weeks of school is when students are particularly vulnerable to attacks.

- Ask if your school has a foot patrol service for people taking evening classes. If you do take an evening class, ask if there are security officers on duty before and after the class.

- Take a course or seminar on self-defence and sexual assault prevention. To find these courses, check with your student counselling service, community education centre, or local library.

If you are sexually assaulted, get medical care right away. Go to the nearest rape crisis centre, hospital, student health service, or police station. Also, arrange for follow-up counselling. It's your decision whether to report the crime. Filing a report does not mean that you have to press charges. And if you do choose to press charges later, having a report on file can help your case.

Date rape—the act of forcing sex on a date—is a common form of sexual assault among college students. Date rape is sexual assault. It is a crime.

Drugs such as Rohypnol (flunitrazepam) and GHB (gamma-hydroxybutyrate) have been used in date sexual assault. These drugs, which can be secretly slipped into a drink, reduce resistance to sexual advances and produce an effect similar to amnesia. People who take these drugs might not remember the circumstances that led to their being sexually assaulted. To protect yourself when you are out, don't leave your drinks unattended, and don't let someone else get drinks for you.

Decide what kind of sexual relationships you want. Then set firm limits, and communicate them clearly and assertively.

Take further steps to protect yourself from sexual assault. Decide what kind of sexual relationships you want. Then set firm limits, and communicate them clearly and assertively. Make sure that your nonverbal messages match your verbal message. If someone refuses to respect your limits, stay away from that person.

Also make careful decisions about using alcohol or drugs. Know your limit and stay within it. Be wary of dates who get drunk or high. Consider providing your own transportation on dates. Avoid going to secluded places with people you don't know well. Forcing someone to have sex is **never** acceptable. You have the right to refuse to have sex with anyone—dates, your partner, your fiancée or fiancé, or your spouse.

Watch out for other safety concerns

Accidents due to unsafe conditions and behaviours can lead to disability and even death. Here are ways you can greatly reduce the odds of accidents:

- Don't drive after drinking alcohol or using psychoactive drugs.

- Drive with the realization that other drivers may be preoccupied, intoxicated, or careless. Be a defensive driver.

- Make sure poisons are clearly labelled.

- Keep stairs, halls, doorways, and other pathways clear of shoes, toys, newspapers, and other clutter.

- Don't smoke in bed.

- Don't let candles burn unattended.

- Keep children away from hot stoves. Turn pot handles inward.

- Check electrical cords for fraying, loose connections, or breaks in insulation. Don't overload extension cords.

- Keep a fire extinguisher handy.

- Install smoke detectors where you live and work. Most run on batteries that need occasional replacement. Follow the manufacturer's guidelines.

- Watch for ways that an infant or toddler could suffocate. Put away or discard small objects that can be swallowed, old refrigerators or freezers that can act as airtight prisons, unattended or unfenced swimming pools, kerosene heaters in tightly closed rooms, and plastic kitchen or clothing bags. ✳

CHOOSE SEXUAL HEALTH:
Prevent infection

Sexual health is more than the absence of disease—it involves creating a state of well-being about our sexuality, not just physically but also spiritually, culturally, and psychologically. To develop healthy relationships, it is important to be able to communicate openly and clearly about sex and sexuality. This can be difficult for all students, but for LGBTQQ students in particular this can be hard because they are likely to have heard negative slurs or experienced rejection. These negative experiences can lead to the need for students to hide their sexual orientation (Public Health Agency of Canada, 2014). You still hear students saying, "That's just so gay" (Taylor & Peter et al., 2011). Students who are heterosexual, or straight, may underestimate the impact of these words on LGBTQQ students. In fact, there is a price being paid for all these words as LGBTQQ youth are more likely than their straight peers to experience bullying, depression, homophobic victimization, and substance abuse.

Recent research in the Toronto District School Board found that students who identified as non-heterosexual came out at about 15 or 16 years of age (PHAC, 2010). But college and university is still a time where we are all answering the "who am I" questions, one of which will revolve around our sexuality. Sexuality isn't simple. Some of us are predominantly heterosexual—physically and emotionally attracted to the opposite sex. Some of us are predominantly homosexual (gay or lesbian), and some are bisexual (attracted to both men and women).

Sexual orientation differs from gender identity. Orientation is about who we are emotionally and physically attracted to, whereas gender identity is about our inner sense of being male or female. Individuals who are transgendered have a gender identity that doesn't match their outward appearance.

Some Aboriginal people prefer to use the term *two-spirited* rather than transgender, gay, lesbian, or bisexual. Again, sexuality is complicated. Wherever you are on the sexuality continuum, learning more about sexual and gender minorities can help us all to create healthier communities.

Gustavo Frazao/Shutterstock.com

Choices about sex can be life altering. Sex is a basic human drive, and it can be wonderful. In certain conditions, sex can also be hazardous to your health. It pays to be clear about the pitfalls, including sexually transmitted infections and unwanted pregnancies.

Technically, anyone who has sex is at risk of getting a **sexually transmitted infection (STI)**. Without treatment, some of these diseases can lead to blindness, infertility, cancer, heart disease, or even death. Sometimes there are no signs or symptoms of an STI; the only way to tell if you're infected is to be tested by a healthcare professional.

STIs, which include sexually transmitted viruses, are often spread through body fluids that are exchanged during sex—semen, vaginal secretions, and blood. Some STIs, such as herpes and genital warts, are spread by direct contact with infected skin. Human immunodeficiency virus (HIV) can be spread in other ways as well.

There are more than 25 kinds of STIs, including chlamydia, gonorrhea, syphilis, genital warts, genital herpes, and trichomoniasis. Hepatitis can also be spread through sexual contact. STIs are the most common contagious diseases in North America, and the incidence is on the rise. The two most common STIs in Canada are HPV (human papillomavirus) and chlamydia (Racco, 2017). In addition, human papillomavirus (HPV) is an extremely common STI; more than 70% of sexually active men and women will acquire HPV at least once in their lives (Public Health Agency of Canada, 2017).

HPV is a sexually transmitted virus that leads to genital warts in men and women; it can also lead to cervical cancer in women. Often individuals with HPV have no symptoms at all. There is no cure for HPV although the warts can be removed. There are now at least three HPV vaccines for women (Gardasil, Gardasil 9, and Cervarix). Gardasil 9 is also used as a vaccine for males (Health Canada, 2017a). Because HPV can lead to precancerous lesions and cancer of the cervix, it is imperative that women who are sexually active have regular Pap tests. It has been found in studies of university women that up to 25 percent have HPV (Society of Obstetricians and Gynecologists of Canada, 2010).

Chlamydia is also very prevalent among Canadian youth and, like HPV, often asymptomatic. However, if left undiagnosed it can cause significant health problems, including infertility in women (SOGC, 2010). It can easily be cured with a single dose of antibiotics.

HIV is one of the most serious STIs, and it is different from the others in several respects. HIV is the virus that causes acquired immune deficiency syndrome (AIDS). AIDS is the last stage of HIV infection. A person with AIDS has an immune system that is weakened to the point of having difficulty fighting off many kinds of infections and cancers.

Someone infected with HIV might feel no symptoms for months—sometimes years. Many times, those who are spreading HIV don't even know that they have it.

HIV/AIDS is not transmitted solely through unprotected sexual contact. It can be transmitted by shared needles or equipment used to inject drugs. The virus can also be passed from an infected pregnant woman to her fetus during pregnancy or delivery, or through breastfeeding after delivery.

Although gay men and men who have sex with other men are the majority of those who have HIV infections in Canada (53 percent of the estimated 75,500 living with HIV in 2014), it is becoming increasingly common among individuals who inject drugs and those who come from countries where HIV is endemic (Public Health Agency of Canada, 2011). Twenty-two percent of the individuals with HIV are women. In Canada, it has been found that a disproportionate percentage of those living with HIV are Aboriginal persons (9 percent) (Public Health Agency of Canada, 2014).

Public hysteria and misinformation about HIV/AIDS still flourish. You cannot get HIV/AIDS from touching, kissing, hugging, food, coughs, mosquitoes, toilet seats, hot tubs, or swimming pools.

Being infected with HIV is not a death sentence. There are medical treatments that can slow down the rate at which HIV weakens the immune system.

Syda Productions/Shutterstock.com

Some of the illnesses associated with AIDS can be prevented or treated, although AIDS itself is not curable. Some people live with HIV for years without developing AIDS, and people with AIDS might live for years after developing the condition. As with other chronic illnesses, early detection and early entry into medical care offer more options for treatment and a longer life.

STIs other than AIDS and herpes can be cured, if treated early. Prevention is better. Remember these guidelines:

- **Abstain from sex.** Abstain for sex or have sex exclusively with one person who is free of infection and has no other sex partners. This is the only way to be absolutely safe from STIs.

- **Use condoms.** Male condoms are thin latex membranes stretched over the penis prior to intercourse. They prevent semen from entering the partner's body. Both women and men can carry them and insist that they be used. Use a condom every time you have sex, and for any type of sex—oral, vaginal, or anal. Use latex condoms—not lambskin or polyurethane. While condoms can be effective, they are not guaranteed to work all of the time. Condoms can break, leak, or slip off. In addition, condoms cannot protect you from STIs that are spread by contact with herpes sores or warts.

- **Stay sober.** People are more likely to have unsafe sex when drunk or high.

- **Get screened for STIs.** See a doctor to get checked for STIs. As part of your annual checkup, make sure you talk to your doctor about STIs. Make sure to have a Pap test if you are a sexually active woman. Both men and women can easily be checked for HIV and chlamydia. If you have sex with several different people, get checked for STIs even if you have no symptoms. The more people you have sex with, the greater your risk. You are at risk even if you have sex only once with one person who is infected.

- **Talk about STIs.** Ask sex partners if they have an STI. Tell your partner if you have one.

- **Get vaccinated.** Vaccines are available for HPV and Hepatitis B. Ask your doctor.

- **Recognize the symptoms of STIs.** Symptoms include swollen glands with fever and aching; itching around the vagina; vaginal discharge; pain during sex or when urinating; sore throat following oral sex; anal pain after anal sex; sores, blisters, scabs, or warts on the genitals, anus, tongue, or throat; rashes on the palms of your hands or soles of your feet; dark urine; loose and light-coloured stools; and unexplained fatigue, weight loss, and night sweats.

- **Do not share needles.** Sharing needles or other paraphernalia with other drug users spreads STIs.

- **Take action soon after you have sex.** Urinate soon after you have sex and wash your genitals with soap and water.

Note: Do not use spermicides containing nonoxynol-9. Also avoid lubricants, condoms, and other sex products with nonoxynol-9. At one time, researchers thought that this ingredient could help prevent STIs. New studies indicate that nonoxynol-9 can irritate the vagina and cervix, which actually increases the risk of STIs.

If you think you have an STI, call your medical healthcare professional, student health service, or local public health clinic. Seek counselling and further testing to find out if you are really infected. Early entry into treatment might prevent serious health problems. To avoid infecting other people, abstain from sex until you are treated and cured. ✳

Men, consider your health

In a poll conducted by Louis Harris and Associates, researchers found that one in three men did not have a doctor whom they saw regularly for medical advice. This might be one reason why life expectancy for men averages six years less than for women (Sandman, Simantov, & An, 2000).

If you're a man, consider doing your part to reverse this trend. Here are some suggestions (Agency for Healthcare Research and Quality, 2003): Have your cholesterol checked at least every five years, starting at age 35. If you smoke or have diabetes, or if heart disease runs in your family, start having your cholesterol checked at age 20.

- Have your blood pressure checked at least every two years.
- Conduct regular self-examinations for testicular cancer. According to the National Cancer Institute, this disease

occurs most often in men between the ages of 15 and 34. If detected early, this cancer is highly treatable. Search online for testicular self-exam instructions.

- Begin regular screening for colorectal cancer starting at age 50. Your doctor can help you decide which test is right for you.
- Have a test to screen for diabetes if you have high blood pressure or high cholesterol.
- Talk to your doctor to see whether you should be screened for sexually transmitted diseases, such as HIV.
- Talk to your doctor about the possible benefits of prostate cancer screening—a prostate-specific antigen (PSA) test or digital rectal examination (DRE).
- Have your body mass index (BMI) calculated to screen for obesity.

CHOOSE SEXUAL HEALTH:
Protect against unwanted pregnancy

You and your partner can avoid unwanted pregnancy. This is not a complete list of options, so be sure to supplement it with information from your medical healthcare professional.

Total abstinence and sterilization are the most effective methods of birth control. Other methods can fail. Also, many forms of birth control do not protect against STIs.

Abstinence

Abstinence is choosing not to have intercourse. Abstinence as a means of birth control is guaranteed, but only when it is practised without exception.

You might feel pressured to change your mind about this choice, but many people exist happily without sexual intercourse.

Hormonal methods

Hormonal methods can be used to prevent pregnancy. These methods work by preventing ovulation, fertilization, or implantation of a fertilized egg. The birth control pill is a synthetic hormone that "tells" a woman's body not to release eggs. To be effective, it must be taken as directed by your doctor or pharmacist. Birth control pills must be prescribed by a medical healthcare professional; the type of pill and the dose needed vary from one woman to the next. Side effects sometimes include slight nausea, breast tenderness, weight gain from water retention, and moodiness. This is the most commonly used form of birth control used by Canadian women (Statistics Canada, 2015). The failure rate (the number of pregnancies expected) as listed by the Centers for Disease Control and Prevention is nine per 100 women (Centers for Disease Control and Prevention, 2017a).

Some women choose not to take the pill due to increased risks of heart disease, including high blood pressure, blood clots, and breast or endometrial cancer. If you have a history of any of these conditions, talk to your doctor before taking the pill. If you are over age 35 and smoke, also talk to your doctor before using this form of birth control.

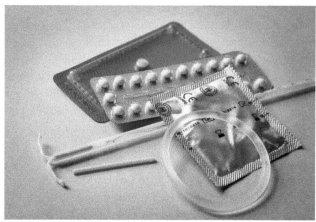

B. BOISSONNET/BSIP/ageFotostock

A *contraceptive injection* (Depo-Provera) into the buttocks or arm muscle is administered by a doctor or nurse every three months. This hormone prevents pregnancy by decreasing ovulation, preventing sperm from reaching the egg, and preventing a fertilized egg from implanting in the uterus. Unlike the pill, this method requires little effort: Women simply need an injection every three months. Failure rates are typically 6 percent. Side effects can include irregular periods, weight gain, and breast tenderness.

The *hormonal vaginal contraceptive ring* (NuvaRing) releases the hormones progestin and estrogen from a ring placed inside the vagina and around the cervix. A woman removes the ring during her period and then puts in a new ring. The typical failure rate is 9 percent.

The *patch* is a method available by prescription in Canada since 2004 (SOGC, 2010). Similar to the birth control pill, it stops women's ovaries from releasing eggs. The advantage of this method is that a new patch only needs to be administered weekly rather than daily like the pill. You put on a new patch each week for three consecutive weeks and then have a patch-free week prior to starting the cycle again. The typical failure rate is 9 percent. Some negatives are side effects like skin irritation, and no protection against STIs. However, for women who have trouble remembering to take the pill daily, the patch may be a good alternative.

Intrauterine devices

An *intrauterine device* (IUD) is a small metal or plastic device that is inserted in the uterus and left there for 1 to 10 years. It prevents fertilized eggs from developing. Side effects might include heavier menstrual flow, anaemia, pelvic infection, perforation of the cervix or uterus, increased risk of pelvic inflammatory disease, abnormal bleeding, cramps, or septic abortion. They have a failure rate of less than one percent making it one of the most effective birth control methods available (Centers for Disease Control and Prevention, 2017a).

Barrier methods

Several methods of birth control create barriers that prevent sperm from reaching a woman's egg. All barrier methods are less effective methods of preventing pregnancies than hormonal methods and IUDs. When used carefully and consistently, *male condoms* offer a safe method of birth control with a failure rate of 18 percent. Latex condoms work the best for reducing the risk of STIs. They can only be used once. Do not use condoms with oil-based lubricants such as petroleum jelly, lotions, or baby oil, all of which can lead to breakage.

Female condoms help keep sperm outside of the body. Like male condoms they help reduce the risk of STIs and have a typical failure rate of 21 percent. They are lubricated and placed inside the woman's vagina. Carefully follow the instructions about when to insert the female condom. Use a new condom each time you have sex. Do not use a female condom and a male condom at the same time.

Another method is the *sponge*. This is a soft disk made of polyurethane that contains nonoxynol-9—a spermicide (chemical that kills sperm). To use a sponge, a woman runs it under water and then places it inside her vagina to cover the cervix (the opening to the womb). If you choose to use the sponge, ask your doctor for instructions on when to remove it after you have intercourse. This method is not very effective on its own (with a failure rate of 12 percent for those who have never given birth and up to 24 percent for those who have given birth) and should only be used with other birth control methods such as condoms. Keep in mind that nonoxynol-9 can irritate tissue in the vagina and anus with frequent use. This makes it easier for STIs to enter the body. Remember also that some women are sensitive to nonoxynol-9 so the sponge is not an option for them.

Another barrier method is the *diaphragm*. A diaphragm is a shallow rubber dome that is covered with a spermicide (sperm-killing cream) and inserted in the vagina. It fits over the cervix, which is the opening of the uterus, and prevents sperm from getting to the egg. A trained medical healthcare professional must measure and fit the diaphragm. It must be inserted before intercourse and left in place for six to eight hours after intercourse. It is more than 80 percent effective.

The *cervical cap* is a soft rubber cup that fits snugly around the cervix. Available by prescription only, it is also used with spermicide. Wearing it for more than 48 hours is not recommended due to a low risk of toxic shock syndrome. Its failure rate is similar to the diaphragm.

Foams, creams, tablets, suppositories, and *jellies* are chemicals that are placed in the vagina before intercourse and prevent sperm from getting to the egg. Their failure rate is high— typically 28 percent. They should be used in conjunction with other barrier methods such as diaphragms, cervical caps, or condoms.

Calendar Method

This is often called the *rhythm method.* It involves avoiding intercourse during ovulation. The problem with this method is that it is difficult to know for sure when a woman is ovulating. There are no side effects to this method, but as it is often difficult to predict ovulation, it is more likely to lead to pregnancy than any other method with a failure rate of 25 percent.

Emergency contraceptives

When women have vaginal sex without using birth control, or when they use birth control that fails, they can take "morning-after" pills. These pills are taken in two doses, 12 hours apart. The pills release hormones that stop ovulation or stop sperm from fertilizing an egg. This method works best when the pills are taken within 72 hours after sex. They do not require a doctor's prescription but are usually kept behind the counter in pharmacies.

Permanent methods

Some birth control methods are only for people who do not want ever to have children or want to stop having children. One method is surgical sterilization. For women this means clipping shut, or cutting and cauterizing the fallopian tubes (where eggs travel to the uterus to implant). Men get a vasectomy, which prevents sperm from entering the penis by severing and sealing the vas deferens (the tubes from the testes). Sperm can stay in a man's body for about three months after surgery, so it is important to use another form of birth control during this time, and until a fertility test verifies no presence of sperm.

Women can also be sterilized without surgery. The doctor inserts an implant (Essure) that causes scar tissue to form in the fallopian tubes. Until the scarring appears—usually in about three months—another form of birth control is needed.

Where to get birth control

You can buy condoms, sponges, and spermicides over the counter at a store. Other birth control devices require a prescription from a doctor.

Note: Withdrawal does not work

Withdrawal happens when a man takes his penis out of the woman's vagina before he has an orgasm. Don't rely on this method for birth control. It requires extraordinary self-control. In addition, men can release some sperm before they have an orgasm. This can lead to pregnancy. Unfortunately, after the birth control pill and male condoms, this is the third most prevalent form of birth control used by postsecondary students according to the National College Health Assessment survey (33%; American College Health Association, 2016). In addition to a high rate of failure, the withdrawal method also does not prevent the spread of infection from an STI.

Evaluate birth control methods

Be sure you know how to use your chosen method of birth control. A doctor might assume that you already have this knowledge. If you don't, ask questions freely. More information about birth control can be found at *www.plannedparenthood.org*. Remember that some methods require practice and special techniques. For example, male condoms have an inside and outside surface, and they work best when there's a little space left at the tip for fluid.

Effectiveness rates can only be estimated. The estimates depend on many factors—for example, the health of the people using them, their number of sex partners, and how often they have sex. *Remember, the best method is the one you consistently use.* ✳

journal entry 11-3

Intention Statement

Choose to Break a Habit

Choose one habit related to protecting your body that you would like to change immediately. Below, write an Intention Statement about changing this habit so that your body can begin experiencing greater health today.

   I intend to . . .

_____

_____

_____

ALCOHOL, CANNABIS, TOBACCO, and DRUGS: The facts

The truth is that getting high can be fun. In our culture, and especially in our media, getting high has become synonymous with having a good time. Even if you don't smoke, drink, or use other drugs, you are certain to come in contact with people who do.

For centuries, human beings have devised ways to change their feelings and thoughts by altering their body chemistry. The Chinese were using cannabis 5,000 years ago. Herodotus, the ancient Greek historian, wrote about a group of people in Eastern Europe who threw cannabis on hot stones and inhaled the smoke.

We might take care of ourselves when we see that the costs of using a substance outweigh the benefits.

Today we are still a drug-using society. Of course, some of those uses are therapeutic and lawful, including drugs that are taken as prescribed by a doctor. The problem comes when we turn to drugs as *the* solution to any problem, even before seeking professional guidance.

We live in times when reaching for instant comfort via chemicals is not only condoned—it is encouraged. If you're bored, tense, or anxious, you can drink a can of beer, smoke weed, down a glass of wine, or light up a cigarette.

Binge drinking

Whether you call it "getting hammered" or "getting wasted," binge drinking can take a terrible toll on your health. **Binge drinking** involves drinking a lot of alcohol quickly—four drinks if you are a woman, five if you are a man (Spears, 2017). More than 40 percent of young Canadians aged 20–24 report that they have been binge drinking 12 times or more in the last year (Canadian Mental Health Association, n.d.). And males are even more likely than females to engage in binge drinking.

Mixing alcohol with energy drinks is an even worse idea as those who do are more likely to engage in risky behaviours such as unprotected sex or driving a vehicle than those who drink alcohol alone (Centers for Disease Control and Prevention, 2017b).

Kumar Sriskandan/Alamy Stock Photo

Why does binge drinking matter? When you drink quickly you get drunk, and drunkenness leads to impaired judgment; you might engage in behaviour that will be extremely embarrassing the next day. If you are a guy, you are far more likely to engage in other reckless behaviours like driving too fast or getting into fights. More importantly, binge drinking can lead to alcohol poisoning and can permanently damage your liver and your brain. It also increases the odds of developing cancer and becoming an addict to alcohol.

Rather than binge drinking, you should drink slowly and intersperse alcohol with other non-alcoholic drinks. Regardless of how fast you drink alcohol, it still takes about an hour a drink for your body to process the alcohol. Drinking coffee won't make a difference. Chugging beer—bad idea. So, before you prime to go out to a bar on a Thursday, think about all that you are putting at risk.

Using cannabis and other drugs

Since October 27, 2018, cannabis use in Canada has been legal. Just because it is legal doesn't mean it is good for you. With Canadian youth leading the world in their use of cannabis or marijuana (Barton, 2017), you need to find out more about what the impact of using this drug is on you. Recent research

Some facts . . .

In Canada, substance abuse and addiction take a heavy toll on postsecondary students (Table 11.1). Research performed by the American College Health Association (2016) reports these repercussions of substance abuse:

Table 11.1 **Effects of Substance Abuse and Addiction**

Alcohol use	Alcohol is the most frequently used drug. About a third of university students drink more than 15 drinks a week—a level that puts them at greater risk for health-related problems.
Academic problems	Eighteen percent of students reported they had missed a class because they had a hangover and 4.9 percent suggested drinking alcohol had significantly affected their academic performance such as receiving a lower grade on an exam.
Drunk driving	12.1 percent of students reported driving under the influence of alcohol in the last 30 days.
Unsafe sex	23.5 percent had unprotected sex in the last 12 months.
Memory problems	29.2 percent of students who reported drinking in the last 12 months had an episode where they did not remember where they were or what they did.
Death	Among fatally injured drivers, 46 percent had some alcohol in their blood and 39 percent had over the legal blood alcohol limit.
Assault	One in four students reported having been physically assaulted by a person who had been drinking. Men are far more likely than women to get into physical fights or in trouble with the police as a result of drinking.
Drug use	18.6 percent of students reported using cannabis (marijuana) in the last 30 days. Almost 11 percent of students reported using prescription drugs not prescribed to them within the last 12 months.
Suicidal thoughts	Five percent of students stated that they had seriously considered suicide when drinking alcohol.
Other	37.1 percent of students indicated that they did something they later regretted when they were drinking alcohol.

For more information on addiction, contact the Centre for Addiction and Mental Health or go online to *www.camh.ca*.

has found that even casual use of this drug impacts the cognitive development of youth under 25 (Hudes, 2018). Cannabis seems to have a particularly negative effect on intelligence for those who started using it in their teens. Teen use of cannabis has also been linked to the later development of schizophrenia. Daily use of cannabis in youth significantly decreases the likelihood of ever finishing a university degree (Baron, 2017). So, when you consider self-medicating to relax after an exam, think about the long-term effects on your brain and on your life.

You can pick from a large selection of illegal drugs on the street; but if you do, you are taking an enormous risk. With the rise of street drugs being laced with Fentanyl, the result of taking those drugs could be death. Fentanyl is an extremely strong pain killer—40 times stronger than heroin. It is a leading cause of accidental overdoses (Stevenson, 2016). Overdose signs include severe sleepiness, trouble breathing, clammy skin, and the person being unresponsive. If you think someone is experiencing a drug overdose, it is imperative that you immediately call 911. The EMTs may administer another drug called Naloxone, which can temporarily reverse the effects of fentanyl, if used in time. Canada enacted the Good Samaritan Drug Overdose Law in 2017 to encourage individuals to help others who need assistance. Even if you are in possession of an illegal drug yourself, you will not be charged if you are trying to assist someone who could be in danger (Health Canada, 2017b).

Abusing alcohol or drugs

Substance abuse is the compulsive use of a chemical in alcohol or drugs resulting in negative consequences. People can also relate to food, gambling, money, sex, and even work in compulsive ways.

I wouldn't bet on it

When we think of gamblers, we probably picture men around a table in a dark and smokey back room or some old guy hanging around the race track. In fact, take a look in the mirror, because the new face of gambling could be yours. Over 60 percent of undergraduates report having bet money on at least one gambling activity in the last year (Adlaf, Demers, & Gliksman, 2005). Types of activities that they engaged in ranged from lotteries (51 percent) to slot and video lotteries (22.7 percent) to sports betting (10.8 percent). Males are particularly likely to engage in sports betting (19.4 percent of men versus 4.0 percent of women). Over 5 percent of undergrads report gambling weekly. There are provincial differences, too, with the Atlantic provinces having the highest percentage of gamblers (72 percent) compared to British Columbia (56.8 percent).

Gambling is often seen as a low-risk activity, with even 10-year-olds being given a "scratch and win card" as a birthday present. But we know that a small percentage of students (about 6–8 percent) are at risk of developing a severe gambling problem (International Centre for Youth Gambling, 2018). Gambling problems ensue when individuals are unable to stop gambling and they are unable to set limits on the time or money devoted to this activity. Men are twice as likely as women to be at risk for gambling problems; they are far six times more likely to have moderate to severe gambling problems (Adlaf, Demers, & Gliksman, 2005).

Georgejmclittle/Shutterstock.com

The International Centre for Youth Gambling and High Risk Behaviours at McGill University was founded because of the recent surge in compulsive gambling among youth worldwide. The growth of online gambling makes it possible to be gambling literally anytime and anywhere. If you want to see if you have a problem with your gambling behaviour, go to *www.youthgambling.com* or to *www .problemgambling.ca/gambling-help*.

If gambling is starting to interfere with getting your schoolwork done or attending class, or if it is causing problems with friends or family, then it is time to seek help. Speak to school counsellors, or look up the many resources, such as Gamblers Anonymous (*www.gamblersanonymous.org/ ga*) or the Ontario Problem Gambling Helpline, which has service available 24 hours a day.

Some people will stop abusing a substance or activity when the consequences get serious enough. Other people can't stop. They continue their self-defeating behaviours, no matter what the consequences are for themselves, their friends, or their families. At that point, the problem goes beyond abuse. It's addiction. The health costs of substance addiction can include overdose, infection, and lowered immunity to disease—all of which can be fatal.

Long-term excessive drinking, for example, damages every organ system in the human body. To find out more about how your drinking compares to others your age, go to Check Your Drinking at *www.checkyourdrinkingu.net/ cyd/CYDScreenerP1_0.aspx* or to the Alcohol Help Center at *www.alcoholhelpcenter.net.*

Addiction to tobacco also has detrimental health effects, effects that will be no surprise to you. Each year, 37,000 Canadians die from the effects of cigarette smoking. One of the highest rates of smoking occurs in 20- to 24-year-olds (27 percent)—your demographic (Statistics Canada, 2018a). About half of all smokers will die from illnesses related to smoking. Smoking shortens your life span by eight to 10 years, as compared to others who have never smoked (Canadian Cancer Society, 2018b). And everyone—not just the smoker—is affected by second-hand smoke, from children and other adults in the home, to pets. All are at risk for developing cancer and other respiratory illnesses (Canadian Cancer Society, 2018b).

Lectures about why it's important to avoid excessive alcohol consumption and drug abuse can be pointless. Ultimately, you won't take care of your bodies because a textbook says you should. You might take care of yourself when you see that the costs of using a substance outweigh the benefits. You choose. It's your body.

Acknowledging that alcohol, tobacco, and other drugs can be fun infuriates a lot of people who might assume that this is the same as condoning their use. The point is this: People are more likely to abstain when they're convinced that using these substances leads to more pain than pleasure over the long run. ✳

Addiction: How do I know . . .?

People who have problems with drugs and alcohol are great at hiding that fact from themselves and from others. It is also hard to admit that a friend or loved one might have a problem.

The purpose of this exercise is to give you an objective way to look at your relationship with drugs or alcohol. There are signals that indicate when drug or alcohol use has become abusive or even an addiction. This exercise can also help you determine if a friend might be addicted.

Answer the following questions quickly and honestly with "yes," "no," or "n/a" (not applicable). If you are concerned about someone else, rephrase each question using that person's name.

_____ Are you uncomfortable discussing drug abuse or addiction?

_____ Are you worried about your own drug or alcohol use?

_____ Are any of your friends worried about your drug or alcohol use?

_____ Have you ever hidden from a friend, spouse, employer, or co-worker the fact that you were drinking? (Pretended you were sober? Covered up alcohol breath?)

_____ Do you sometimes use alcohol or drugs to escape lows rather than to produce highs?

_____ Have you ever gotten angry when confronted about your use?

_____ Do you brag about how much you consume? ("I drank her under the table.")

_____ Do you think about or do drugs when you are alone?

_____ Do you store up alcohol, drugs, cigarettes, or caffeine (in coffee or pop) to be sure you won't run out?

_____ Does having a party almost always include alcohol or drugs?

_____ Do you try to control your drinking so that it won't be a problem? ("I drink only on weekends now." "I never drink before 5:00 p.m." "I drink only beer.")

_____ Do you often explain to other people why you are drinking? ("It's my birthday." "It's my friend's birthday." "It's the May 24 weekend." "It sure is a hot day.")

_____ Have you changed friends to accommodate your drinking or drug use? ("She's okay, but she isn't excited about getting high.")

_____ Has your behaviour changed in the last several months? (Marks down? Lack of interest in a hobby? Change of values or of what you think is moral?)

_____ Do you drink or use drugs to relieve tension? ("What a day! I need a drink.")

_____ Do you have medical problems (stomach trouble, malnutrition, liver problems, anaemia) that could be related to drinking?

_____ Have you ever decided to quit drugs or alcohol and then changed your mind?

_____ Have you had any fights, accidents, or similar incidents related to drinking or drugs in the last year?

_____ Has your drinking or drug use ever caused a problem at home?

_____ Do you envy people who go overboard with alcohol or drugs?

_____ Have you ever told yourself you can quit at any time?

_____ Have you ever been in trouble with the police after or while you were drinking?

_____ Have you ever missed school or work because you had a hangover?

_____ Have you ever had a blackout (a period you can't remember) after drinking?

_____ Do you wish that people would mind their own business when it comes to your use of alcohol or drugs?

_____ Is the cost of alcohol or other drugs taxing your budget or resulting in financial stress?

_____ Do you need increasing amounts of the drug to produce the desired effect?

_____ When you stop taking the drug, do you experience withdrawal?

_____ Do you spend a great deal of time obtaining and using alcohol or other drugs?

_____ Have you used alcohol or another drug when it was physically dangerous to do so (e.g., when driving a car or working with machines)?

_____ Have you been arrested or had other legal problems resulting from the use of a substance?

Now count the number of questions you answered with "yes." If you answered "yes" five or more times, talk with a professional. Five "yes" answers does not necessarily mean that you are addicted. It does point out that alcohol or other drugs are adversely affecting your life. Talk to someone with training in recovery from chemical dependency. Do not rely on the opinion of anyone who lacks such training.

If you filled out this questionnaire about another person and you answered "yes" five or more times, your friend might need help. You probably can't provide that help alone. Seek out a counsellor or a support group such as Al-Anon. Call the local Alcoholics Anonymous chapter to find out about an Al-Anon meeting near you.

From dependence
TO RECOVERY

The technical term for drug addiction is drug dependence. This disease is defined by the following:

- *Loss of control*—continued substance use or activity in spite of adverse consequences
- *Pattern of relapse*—vowing to quit or limit the substance use and continually failing to do so
- *Tolerance*—the need to take increasing amounts of a substance to produce the desired effect
- *Withdrawal*—signs and symptoms of physical and mental discomfort or illness when the substance is taken away (Hasin et al., 2013)

This list can help you determine whether dependence is a barrier for you right now. The items above can apply to anything from cocaine use to compulsive gambling.

If you have a problem with dependence in any form, get help. Consider the following suggestions.

Dragon Images/Shutterstock.com

Use responsibly

Show people that you can have a good time without alcohol or other drugs. If you do choose to drink, consume alcohol with food. Pace yourself. Take time between drinks.

Avoid promotions that encourage excess drinking. "Ladies Drink Free" nights are especially dangerous. Women are affected more quickly by alcohol, making them targets for sexual assault. Also stay out of games that encourage people to guzzle. Drinking games like "Neknominate" can be lethal to your health. And avoid people who make fun of you for choosing not to drink.

Admit the problem

People with active addictions are a varied group—rich and poor, young and old, successful and unsuccessful. Often these people do have one thing in common: They are masters of denial. They deny that they are unhappy. They deny that they have hurt anyone. They are convinced that they can quit any time they want. They sometimes become so adept at hiding the problem from themselves that they die.

Pay attention

Whenever you use alcohol or another drug, do so with awareness. Then pay attention to the consequences.

Make a deliberate decision rather than acting out of habit or under pressure from others.

Look at the costs

There is always a trade-off. Drinking 10 beers might result in a temporary high, and you will probably remember that feeling. No one feels great the morning after consuming 10 beers, but it seems easier to forget pain. Often people don't notice how bad alcoholism, drug addiction, or other forms of substance abuse make them feel.

Take responsibility for recovery

Nobody plans to become an addict. If you have pneumonia, you can recover without guilt or shame. Approach an addiction in yourself or others in the same way. You can take responsibility for your recovery without blame, shame, or guilt.

Get help

Many people find that they cannot treat addiction on their own. Addictive behaviours are often symptoms of an illness that needs treatment.

You can take responsibility for your recovery without blame, shame, or guilt.

Two broad options exist for getting help with addiction. One is the growing self-help movement. The other is formal treatment. People recovering from addiction often combine the two.

Many self-help groups are modelled after Alcoholics Anonymous. AA is made up of recovering alcoholics and addicts. These people understand the problems of abuse firsthand, and they follow a systematic, 12-step approach to living without the substance they are addicted to. This is one of the oldest and most successful self-help programs in the world. Chapters of AA welcome people from all walks of life, and you don't have to be an alcoholic to attend most meetings. Programs based on AA principles exist for many other forms of addiction as well.

Some people feel uncomfortable with the AA approach. Other resources exist for these people, including private therapy and group therapy. Also investigate organizations such as the Centre for Addiction and Mental Health, Women for Sobriety, the Secular Organizations for Sobriety, and Rational Recovery Systems. Use whatever works for you.

Treatment programs are available in almost every community. They might be residential (you live there for weeks or months at a time) or outpatient (you visit several hours a day). Find out where these treatment centres are located by calling a doctor, a mental health professional, or a local hospital.

Alcohol and drug treatments are now covered by many private health insurance programs. If you don't have additional insurance, it is usually possible to arrange some other payment program. Cost is no reason to avoid treatment.

Get help for a friend or family member

You might know someone who uses alcohol or other drugs in a way that can lead to serious and sustained negative consequences. If so, you have every right to express your concern to that person. Wait until the person is clear-headed and then mention specific incidents. For example: "Last night you drank five beers when we were at my apartment, and then you wanted to drive home. When I offered to call a cab for you instead, you refused." Also, be prepared to offer a source of help, such as the phone number of a local treatment centre. ✳

---

journal entry 11-4

Discovery/Intention Statement

Choose a New Level of Health

Review your responses to Journal Entry 11-1: "Take a First Step toward better health" earlier in the chapter. This Discovery Statement asked you to reflect on your current state of health. Review what you wrote. Then summarize your top three health concerns.

I discovered that . . .

_____

_____

_____

If you've read the preceding articles, you've learned about ways to choose good health in a variety of areas—by eating, exercising, sleeping, protecting your mental health, and staying safe. In the space below, list some suggestions that could help you respond positively to your top health concerns:

I discovered that . . .

_____

_____

_____

Next, choose one of the above suggestions that you would like to use immediately. Write an Intention Statement about turning this behaviour into a daily habit:

I intend to . . .

_____

_____

_____

Finally, introduce some accountability. Share your Intention Statement with someone else. Consider asking this person to check in with you during the next month and ask how your plan to adopt a new habit is going.

Note: You can use the above process to change your behaviour—discovery, intention, and action with accountability—and adopt *any* new habit.

practising
CRITICAL THINKING

Applying Bloom's taxonomy

This exercise involves thinking at all six levels of Bloom's taxonomy described in the article "Becoming a critical thinker" in Chapter 7, "Thinking."

Note: If you'd like to keep your responses to this exercise confidential, then write on separate paper.

Do you **remember** your response to the Journal Entry that opened this chapter? If not, take a minute to review what you wrote.

Now, after reading and completing the exercises in this chapter, do you **understand** your current level of health in a different way? Explain your answer:

_____

_____

_____

_____

Also take a minute to page through this chapter again and review the suggested strategies for protecting your health. List five strategies that you'd like to **apply**:

_____

_____

_____

_____

_____

Next, **analyze** your current level of health in more detail. If a statement does not apply to you, then skip it. As with the Discovery Wheel, the usefulness of this writing will be determined by your honesty and courage.

Eating

What I know about the way I eat is . . .

_____

_____

What I would most like to change about my diet is . . .

_____

_____

My eating habits lead me to be . . .

_____

_____

Exercise

The way I usually exercise is . . .

_____

_____

The last time I did 20 minutes or more of heart/lung (aerobic) exercise was . . .

_____

_____

As a result of my physical conditioning, I feel . . .

_____

_____

And I look . . .

_____

_____

It would be easier for me to work out regularly if I . . .

_____

_____

The most important benefit for me in exercising more is . . .

_____

_____

Substances

My history of cigarette smoking is . . .

_____

_____

An objective observer would say that my use of alcohol is . . .

_____

_____

In the last 10 days, the number of alcoholic drinks I have had is . . .

_____

_____

I would describe my use of coffee, pop, energy drinks, and other caffeinated drinks as . . .

_____

_____

An objective observer would say my use of cannabis is . . .

_____

_____

I have used the following illegal drugs in the past week:

_____

When it comes to drugs, what I am sometimes concerned about is . . .

_____

_____

I take the following prescription drugs:

_____

_____

Relationships

Someone who knows me fairly well would say I am emotionally . . .

_____

_____

The way I look and feel has affected my relationships by . . .

_____

My use of drugs or alcohol has been an issue with the following people . . .

_____

_____

The best thing I could do for myself and my relationships would be to . . .

_____

_____

Sleep

The number of hours I sleep each night is . . .

_____

On weekends I normally sleep . . .

_____

_____

I have trouble sleeping when . . .

_____

_____

Last night I . . .

_____

_____

The quality of my sleep is usually . . .

_____

In light of your analysis, go back to the five strategies you listed earlier. **Evaluate** them by considering the aspect of your health that is most important to you right now. Then choose one strategy that you will definitely commit to use during the next 30 days. Describe that strategy below, making sure it is an action that you can take immediately:

_____

_____

_____

_____

_____

_____

_____

Finally, experiment with the idea that your health is something that you **create** over the long term. Write a larger health-related goal—one that could make a big difference in the quality of your life over the next year. Also list the actions you will take to achieve that goal:

_____

_____

_____

_____

_____

_____

_____

_____

_____

_____

Be smoke free

If you don't smoke now, don't start!

If you do smoke, there is no magic formula for becoming tobacco-free. However, you can take steps to succeed sooner rather than later. Although many young people have switched from smoking cigarettes to e-cigarettes or vapes, the long-term effects of using such products are not known. Be cautious about using these unregulated products. If you are thinking about quitting, the American Cancer Society and the Canadian Cancer Society offer the following suggestions.

Make a firm choice to quit. All plans for quitting depend on this step. If you're not ready to quit yet, then admit it. Take another look at how smoking affects your health, finances, and relationships.

Set a date. Choose a "quit day" within the next month that's close enough for a sense of urgency—and time to prepare. Consider a date with special meaning, such as a birthday or anniversary. Let friends and family members know about the big day.

Get personal support. Involve other people. Sign up for a quit smoking class. Attend Nicotine Anonymous or a similar group.

Consider medication. Medication can double your chances of quitting successfully (American Cancer Society, 2018). Options include bupropion hydrochloride (Zyban) and varenicline (Champix), for which you need a prescription from your doctor, as well as the nicotine patch, gum, nasal spray, inhaler, and lozenge that are available without a prescription at the drugstore.

Prepare the environment. Right before your quit day, get rid of all cigarettes and ashtrays at home and at work. Stock up on oral substitutes such as sugarless gum, candy, and low-fat snacks like veggies, unbuttered popcorn, and fresh fruit. Don't worry about minor weight gain. You would need to gain 80 to 100 pounds to negate the many health benefits of stopping smoking.

Write out a quit plan. The plan should include your quit date, the supports you have, and the quit aids you will use. Post it on the fridge or your mirror where you are likely to look at it often. The website of the smokers' helpline (*smokershelpline.ca*) contains sample worksheets as part of their self-help guides, or call the smokers' helpline during the day if you want a trained coach to help you develop a personalized help plan (1-877-513-5333).

Drink fluids. Drink a lot of fluids, especially water, to help rid your system of nicotine. Avoid caffeine and alcohol. Caffeine will make you antsy so keep away from it.

Be active. Ride your bike or go for a run. Being physically active helps to relieve stress, helps your metabolism, and will help you stop thinking of smoking.

Deal with cravings for cigarettes. Distract yourself with exercise or another physical activity. Breathe deeply. Tell yourself that you can wait just a little while longer until the craving passes. Even the strongest urges to smoke will pass. Avoid alcohol use, which can increase cravings.

Learn from relapses. If you break down and light up a cigarette, don't judge yourself. Quitting often requires several attempts. Think back over your past plans for quitting and how to improve on them. Every relapse contains a lesson about how to succeed next time.

For more information go to the Health Canada guide for tips that can help you develop an action plan: *www.canada.ca/en/health-canada/services/publications/healthy-living/road-quitting-guide-becoming-non-smoker-young-adults.html* or contact the Smokers helpline.

POWERPROCESS

Surrender

Life can be magnificent and satisfying. It can also be devastating.

Sometimes there is too much pain or confusion. Problems can be too big and too numerous. Life can bring us to our knees in a pitiful, helpless, and hopeless state. A broken relationship with a loved one, a sudden diagnosis of cancer, total frustration with a child's behaviour problem, or even the prospect of several long years of school are situations that can leave us feeling overwhelmed—powerless.

In these troubling situations, the first thing we can do is to admit that we don't have the resources to handle the problem. No matter how hard we try and no matter what skills we bring to bear, some problems remain out of our control. When this is the case, we can tell the truth: "It's too big and too mean. I can't handle it."

Desperately struggling to control a problem can easily result in the problem's controlling us. Surrender is letting go of being the master in order to avoid becoming the slave.

Many traditions make note of this idea. Western religions speak of surrendering to God. Hindus say surrender to the Self. Members of Alcoholics Anonymous talk about turning their lives over to a Higher Power. Agnostics might suggest surrendering to the ultimate source of power. Others might speak of following their intuition, their inner guide, or their conscience.

In any case, surrender means being receptive to help. Once we admit that we're at the end of our rope, we open ourselves up to receiving help. We learn that we don't have to go it alone. We find out that other people have faced similar problems and survived. We give up our old habits of thinking and behaving as if we have to be in control of everything. We stop acting as general manager of the universe. We surrender. And that creates a space for something new in our lives.

Surrender is not "giving up." It is not a suggestion to quit and do nothing about your problems. Giving up is fatalistic and accomplishes nothing. You have many skills and resources. Use them. You can apply all of your energy to handling a situation and still surrender at the same time. Surrender includes doing whatever you can in a positive, trusting spirit. So let go, keep going, and recognize when the true source of control lies beyond you.

MJTH/Shutterstock.com

Put it to WORK

Strategies from *Becoming a Master Student* can help you succeed in your career, as well as in school. To discover how suggestions in this chapter can apply to the workplace, reflect on the following case study.

Iakov Filimonov/Shutterstock.com

For weeks David had been bothered by aching muscles, loss of appetite, restless sleep, and fatigue. Eventually he became so short-tempered and irritable that his wife insisted he get a checkup.

Now, sitting in the doctor's office, David barely noticed when Theresa took the seat beside him. They had been good friends when she worked in the front office at the plant. He hadn't seen her since she left three years ago to take a job as a customer service representative. Her gentle poke in the ribs brought him around. Within minutes they were talking freely.

"You got out just in time," he told her. "Since the reorganization, nobody feels safe. It used to be that as long as you did your work, you had a job. Now they expect the same production rates even though two guys are now doing the work of three. We're so backed up that I'm working 12-hour shifts 6 days a week. Guys are calling in sick just to get a break."

"Well, I really miss you guys," she said. "In my new job, the computer routes the calls, and they never stop. I even have to schedule my bathroom breaks. All I hear the whole day are complaints from unhappy customers. I try to be helpful and sympathetic, but I can't promise anything until I get my boss's approval. Most of the time I'm caught between what the customer wants and company policy. The other reps are so uptight and tense they don't even talk to one another. We all go to our own little cubicles and stay there until quitting time. No wonder I'm in here with migraine headaches and high blood pressure."

David and Theresa are using a powerful strategy to promote health—talking about how they feel with a person they trust. List three other strategies that might be useful to them:

_____

_____

_____

Imagine that you suggested those three strategies to David and Theresa. They responded, "Those are good ideas, but we can't get relief from stress until our working conditions change. And that's up to our supervisors, not us." How would you respond to them?

_____

_____

_____

Consider these other strategies for staying healthy under pressure.

Ask for change

Use your skill with "I" messages (see Chapter 8, "Communicating") to make suggestions and ask for specific changes in working conditions. If your employer conducts a survey of workers' satisfaction with their jobs, answer honestly and completely—especially if responses are kept anonymous.

Deal with depression

Untreated depression costs the economy as much as heart disease or AIDS. However, many employees don't report symptoms of depression. They worry about confidentiality in the workplace and about paying for treatment. Yet confidential and free or low-cost help is often available through employee assistance plans. Find out whether your employer offers such a plan.

Check the full range of your health benefits

In addition to screening and treatment for depression, your employee health benefits might include screenings for other conditions, paid time off for medical appointments, and massages. Set up a meeting with someone at work who can explain all the options available to you.

QUIZ

Name_____   Date____/____/____

1. Explain three ways you can respond effectively if someone you know threatens suicide.

2. The strategies suggested for dealing with stress do *not* include
   (a) Release irrational beliefs.
   (b) Use breathing and relaxation exercises.
   (c) Cut back on exercising.
   (d) Consider therapeutic bodywork such as massage.
   (e) Check with your student health service.

3. How is the Power Process "Surrender" different from giving up?

4. A person infected with HIV might have no symptoms for months—sometimes years. True or False? Explain your answer.

5. Explain why LGBTQQ students might be more at risk on campus than other students? What can you do to help?

6. List at least three dietary guidelines that can contribute to your health.

7. One of the suggestions for dealing with addiction is "Pay attention." This implies that it's okay to use drugs, as long as you do so with full awareness. True or False? Explain your answer.

8. Name at least three methods for preventing unwanted pregnancy.

9. What are two of the impacts of using cannabis on youth under the age of 25?

10. The article "Emotional pain is not a sickness" suggests that sometimes it helps to allow yourself to feel bad for a while. What is the point behind this idea?

Skills SNAPSHOT

Now that you've reflected on the ideas in this chapter and experimented with some new strategies, revisit your responses to the "Health" section of the Discovery Wheel exercise in Chapter 1. Think about the most powerful action you could take in the near future toward mastery in this area of your life. Complete the following sentences.

DISCOVERY

To monitor my current level of health, I look for specific changes in . . .

After reading and doing this chapter, my top three health concerns are . . .

INTENTION

My top three intentions for responding to these concerns are . . .

I'll know that I've reached a new level of mastery with health when . . .

NEXT ACTION

To reach that level of mastery, I intend to . . .

At the end of this course, I would like my Health score on the Discovery wheel to be . . .

MASTER STUDENT
PROFILE

chapter 11

■ Put it to Work
■ Quiz
■ Skills Snapshot
◀◀◀◀

Clara Hughes
. . . is courageous

Clara Hughes was already in the history books as the only Canadian to win medals in both the Summer and Winter Olympic Games. The wide-smiling former Winnipegger became the darling of the sports world (and the country) with her drive, ambition, and athletic prowess.

Now she's a hero for another reason. When Hughes decided to disclose her two-year battle with depression, she put a familiar face onto the stigma of mental illness. She, in the parlance of the business, normalized the disease.

When we spoke this week, she described her descent into despair. "I tended to internalize things," she said. "I thought I should be tough enough to deal with it."

She wasn't and she couldn't, and so she got help. She deserves kudos for her candour from the hundreds of thousands of Canadians affected by mental illness and those who love them.

"Clara has so much admiration for doing this. I think in the mental health field she deserves a medal," says Tara Brousseau, executive director of the Mood Disorders Association of Manitoba. "She's giving strength."

Anyone who has spent time skittering their way around the edge of depression's abyss understands the strength Hughes' disclosure took. The battle back to wellness required similar guts. Hughes doesn't sugar-coat her experiences.

She felt let down after the 1996 Olympics. She attributed it to a normal post-Olympics deflation. But it didn't

stop and she was crying all the time and sleeping too much and gaining weight and wanted to quit cycling.

In fact, she did quit, unsure whether she'd ever come back.

"I knew I couldn't go on like this. After I quit, I still didn't feel better. It progressed to something I had never experienced before," she said. Depression does that, disguising itself as the blues, winding tendrils of doubt and self-loathing around the sufferer. Obstacles become insurmountable. Self-worth, even for an Olympic champion, vanishes.

Hughes reached out, first to her now-husband. She talked to a doctor. She switched up her diet and changed her training schedule. She fought with the drive and single-mindedness that earned her those medals.

"I had to change my thinking. I'd look at my competitors and think they were probably training harder. I still like to revert to that to train way too hard and way too much."

She didn't require medication. She knows she's lucky there, that many people with depression need drugs and therapy and crossed fingers to get them across the abyss.

"Medication was an option," she said. "I just wanted to see if I could change things in my life. I wanted to try to get through it without being medicated. I think it's different for everyone."

She's right. It is different for everyone. And everyone with clinical depression has suffered the advice of the

George Pimentel/Getty Images

An extraordinary athlete who has been named an Officer of the Order of Canada. Clara is heavily involved in charity work, including Right to Play, an organization that provides youth with the opportunity to learn through sport and discover the merits of physical activity.

unknowing, people who think they should just cheer up, count their blessings, be glad it's not cancer and generally stop and smell the roses.

There are no roses when depression has you in its unforgiving grip. Depression is one of the cancers of the mind. It can be fatal, although some people insist that's a personal choice.

It's not.

Hughes came back, of course. That's why she has those extra medals in speed-skating and the endorsement contracts that allow her to train and, through Bell Canada, to get the word out on mental illness. Lucky her. Lucky us.

Because if you think of [people with mental illness] as weak, as people who just need to snap out of it, look at Clara Hughes. Canadian sports has never had anyone like her, with the medals in two sports and the grit and the never-ending desire to compete.

The mental health community has never had anyone like her, either. In Hughes, they have proof illness can strike any of us, that even the strongest competitor can be felled. She has given face and voice and hope for the silently shamed.

If that's not worth a medal, I don't know what is.

Source: Reynolds, Lindor. (2011, February 14) Hughes adds new triumph: Erase stigma attached to mental illness." *The Winnipeg Free Press*. Reprinted with permission.

chapter 12

What's Next?

© Hxdbzxy/Shutterstock.com

what is included ...

do you have a minute?

Seize this moment to do something that will create a positive future for yourself:

- Visit your entrepreneurship centre and find out when and where you can pitch your ideas for the next great business.

- Go online to your school's website and look for information about the career centre.

- Make an appointment with your academic advisor to find out about study abroad programs.

WHAT if ...

I could begin creating the life of my dreams—starting today?

WHY this chapter matters ...

You can use the techniques introduced in this book and this chapter to set and achieve goals for the rest of your life.

HOW you can use this chapter ...

Choose the next steps in your education and career. Highlight your continuing success on resumés and in interviews. Experience the joys of contributing. Use a Power Process that enhances every technique in this book.

Now that you're done—
BEGIN

If you used this book fully—if you actively participated in reading the contents, writing the journals, doing the practising critical thinking exercises, completing the learning styles applications, and applying the suggestions—you have had quite a journey.

Recall some high points of that journey. The first half of this book is about the nuts and bolts of education—the business of acquiring knowledge. It helps prepare you for making the transition to postsecondary education and suggests that you take a First Step by telling the truth about your skills and setting goals to expand them. Also included are guidelines for planning your time, making your memory more effective, improving your reading skills, taking useful notes, and succeeding at tests. All of this activity prepares you for another aim of education—generating new knowledge and creating a unique place for yourself in the world. Meeting this aim leads you to the topics in the second half of this book: thinking for yourself, enhancing your communication skills, embracing diversity, and living with vibrant health. All are steps on the path of becoming a master student. Now what? What's the next step?

As you answer these questions, remember that the process of experimenting with your life never ends. At any moment, you can begin again.

Consider the possibility that you can create the life of your dreams. Your responses to the ideas and critical thinking exercises in this book can lead you to think new thoughts, say new things, and do what you never believed you could do. If you're willing to master new ways to learn, the possibilities are endless. This message is more fundamental than any individual tool or technique you'll ever read about.

There are people who scoff at the suggestion that they can create the life of their dreams. These people have a perspective that is widely shared. Please release it.

If this sounds like a pitch for the latest recreational drug, it might be. That drug is adrenalin, and your body generates it automatically when you are learning, growing, taking risks, and discovering new worlds inside and outside your skin. The world is packed with possibilities for master students. If you excel in adventure, exploration, discovery, and creativity, you will never lack for opportunities.

One of the first articles in this book is about transitions. You are about to make another transition—not only to another chapter of this book but also to the next chapter of your life. Each article in this chapter is about creating your future through the skills you've gained in this course. Use the following pages to choose what's next for you. ✳

journal entry 12-1

Discovery/Intention Statement

Revisiting What You Want and How You Intend to Get It

Review the Power Process "Discover What You Want" in the Introduction. Then complete the following sentences with the first thoughts that come to mind.

From my life, I have discovered that I want . . .

_____

_____

_____

_____

_____

To get what I want from my life, I intend to . . .

_____

_____

_____

_____

_____

_____

" . . . use the following suggestions
TO CONTINUE . . . "

Go to talks on campus

Most schools will have frequent talks by speakers from different industries. This is a great opportunity for you to find out what careers in those areas are all about. You can also network with potential employers. To find out when you have speakers or employers on campus, check out your career or employment centre.

Take a workshop

Schooling doesn't have to stop at graduation, and it doesn't have to take place on a campus. In most cities, there are a variety of organizations that sponsor ongoing workshops, covering topics from cosmetology to cosmology. Use workshops to learn skills, to enhance your resumé, to understand the world, to network, and to discover yourself. You can be trained in cardiopulmonary resuscitation (CPR), attend a lecture on developing nations, or take a course on assertiveness training. Become a lifelong learner.

Read, watch, and listen

Ask friends and instructors what they are reading. Sample a variety of blogs, podcasts, newspapers, and magazines. None of them has all of the truth; most of them have a piece of it. You can use a newsreader to stay informed so that when your favourite websites are updated you receive a list of the headlines with summaries. A common web-based feed reader is Feedly (*https://feedly.com/i/welcome*). Often you can subscribe to a specific news feed by clicking on a button on the website. Record your most exciting discoveries in an idea file.

Take an unrelated class

Sign up for a class that is totally unrelated to your program of study. If you are studying business, take a physics course. If you are going to be a doctor, take an English course. Take a course that will help you develop new computer skills and expand your possibilities for online learning.

You can discover a lot about yourself and your intended future when you step out of old patterns. In addition to formal courses offered at your school, check

© Michael Atkinson

into local community education courses. These offer a low-cost alternative that poses no threat to your marks.

Travel

See the world. Visit new neighbourhoods. Travel to other countries. Explore. Find out what it looks like inside buildings that you normally have no reason to enter, museums that you never found interesting before, cities that are out of the way, forests and mountains that lie beyond your old boundaries, and far-off places that require planning and saving to reach. Find out about study abroad opportunities, or if your school offers an Alternative Spring Break program. Combine your passion for travel with a desire to contribute to the world. Consider volunteering with Habitat for Humanity or other volunteer agencies.

Get counselling

Solving emotional problems is not the only reason to visit a counsellor, therapist, or psychologist. These people are excellent resources for personal growth. You can use counselling to look at and talk about yourself in ways that might be uncomfortable for anyone except a trained professional. Counselling offers a chance to focus exclusively on yourself, something that is usually not possible in normal social settings. Most schools also provide free career counselling. When you want to start exploring your career options, these counsellors are wonderful people to consult.

Continue your education online

Supplement your courses by taking a free course online through venues like the Khan Academy (*www .khanacademy.org*) or a MOOC (a massive open online course) such as those offered by MIT open courseware (*https://ocw.mit.edu/index.htm*) or Simon Fraser University (*www.class-central.com/university/sfu*).

Find a mentor—or become one

Seek the counsel of experienced people you respect and admire. Use them as role models. If they are willing, ask them to be sounding boards for your plans and ideas. Many people are flattered to be asked.

You can also become a mentor. Many schools offer peer-mentoring programs through student services. Both being mentored and being a mentor can teach you valuable leadership skills and knowledge of other cultures. If you want to perfect your skills as a master student, teach them to someone else. Volunteering in your writing centre or international student centre will allow you to develop your own communication skills while you provide needed services to others. In addition to being able to document these experiences in your resumé, many students form lifelong friendships with those they tutor or mentor.

Redo this book

Start by redoing one chapter or maybe just one exercise. If you didn't get everything you wanted from this book, it's not too late.

You can also reread and redo portions that you found valuable. As you plan your career and hunt for jobs, you might find that the Put It to Work articles in each chapter acquire new meaning. Redo the quizzes to test your ability to recall certain information. Redo the critical thinking exercises that were particularly effective for you. They can work again. Many of the exercises in this book can produce a different result after a few months. You are changing, and your responses change, too.

The Discovery Wheel can be useful in revealing techniques you have actually put into practice. You can also repeat the Journal Entries. If you keep your own journal, refer to it as you rewrite the Journal Entries in this book.

As you redo this book or any part of it, reconsider techniques that you skimmed over or skipped before. They might work for you now. Modify the suggestions or add new ones. Redoing this book can refresh and fine-tune your study habits.

Another way to redo this book is to retake your student success course. People who do this often say that the second time is much different from the first. They pick up ideas and techniques that they missed the first time around and gain deeper insight into things they already know. ✳

Create your
CAREER NOW

THERE'S AN OLD SAYING: "If you enjoy what you do, you'll never work another day in your life." If you clearly define your career goals and your strategy for reaching them, you can plan your education effectively and create a seamless transition from school to the workplace.

sirtravelalot/Shutterstock.com

Career planning involves continuous exploration. There are dozens of effective paths to planning your career. You can begin your career-planning adventure now by remembering the following ideas.

You already know a lot about your career plan

When people learn study skills and life skills, they usually start by finding out things they don't know. That means discovering new strategies for taking notes, reading, writing, managing time, and the other subjects covered in this book.

Career planning is different. You can begin by realizing how much you know right now. You've already made many decisions about your career. This is true for young people who say, "I don't have any idea what I want to be when I grow up." It's also true for those who change career in midlife.

Consider the student who can't decide if he wants to be a cost accountant or a tax accountant and then jumps to the conclusion that he is totally lost when it comes to career planning. It's the same with the student who doesn't know if he wants to be a veterinary assistant or a nurse.

These people forget that they already know a lot about their career choices. The person who couldn't decide between veterinary assistant and nursing had already ruled out becoming a lawyer, computer programmer, or teacher. He just didn't know yet whether he had the right bedside manner for horses or for people. The person who was debating tax accounting versus cost

accounting already knew he didn't want to be a doctor, playwright, or taxi driver. He did know he liked working with numbers and balancing books.

In each case, these people have already narrowed their list of career choices to a number of jobs in the same field—jobs that draw on the same core skills. In general, they already know what they want to be when they grow up.

Use the GROW model to explore career options

This is a simple four-step model that has been used successful for years by career planners and can help simplify your career planning (Yates, 2013).

1. *G = Goal* You already know that goal planning is the key to success. Start with your dream career and then narrow it down by stating both broad and specific goals you would like to achieve. Your dream might be to start an environmentally sound bicycle touring company. A broad goal might be that you'd like to spend more time outside in nature. A specific goal might be you'd like to work in a company that allows you to use your social media skills on a daily basis.

2. *R = Reality* Size up your current situation. Reflect on questions like these: What is your current situation? How do your career possibilities align with your values? What is most important to you in your next job? What skills and knowledge do you currently have? What do you need to develop? Can you think about a successful school project you

Discover your career

Find a long list of occupations. One source is *The Career Handbook,* Second Edition, a Canadian government publication available online. Check out the part of the website called *Classification Structure by Skill Type* (*http://noc.esdc.gc.ca/ English/CH/ClassificationStructure.aspx?ver=06&ch=03*). Under each skill type, such as Health Occupations, they list a number of different careers, such as dental hygienist, and provide a brief description. This is a long list of occupations so keep scrolling down each page to look at the variety of careers available and to read the descriptions. Using index cards, write down about 100 randomly selected job titles, one title per index card. Sort through the cards and divide

them into two piles. Label one pile "Careers I've Definitely Ruled Out for Now." Label the other pile "Possibilities I'm Willing to Consider."

Keep resorting the "Possibilities I'm Willing to Consider" pile until you narrow it down to five in the "Possibilities" pile. Click on the job title to read the descriptors for each of those five occupations and write down what is the appeal for each choice. Think about how well your skills and interests match each job description. Go back and rank the five choices from One ("This job would be fabulous right now") to Five ("I might consider this job at some point in the future").

This is the start of your career adventure.

---

have had and how the skills you developed could be applied in your future job?

3. *O = Options and obstacles* Brainstorm a list of potential career options that might be open to you at this time. Once you have created that list, narrow down your options by considering the pros and cons of each option. Listen to your gut here. Your dream job might be professional ice-climber, but how realistic is this if you have a terminal fear of heights? Consider what obstacles might stand in your way of achieving your dream job and if you have any avenues for overcoming those barriers. Do you need to expand your computing skills or other skills prior to applying for your dream position?

4. *W = Way forward* Now you need to set your plan in motion. What are the specific next steps you will take to achieve your goal? Try to be as concrete as you can at this point, specifying a time frame for action. Be realistic in developing these next steps.

Your career is a choice, not a discovery

Many people approach career planning as if they were panning for gold. They keep sifting through the dirt, clearing the dust, and throwing out the rocks. They are hoping to strike it rich and discover the perfect career.

Other people believe that they'll wake up one morning, see the heavens part, and suddenly know what

they're supposed to do. Many of them are still waiting for that magical day to dawn.

You can approach career planning in a different way. Career planning can be the bridge between your dreams and the reality of your future. Instead of seeing a career as something to discover, you can see it as something you choose. You don't find the right career. You create it.

There's a big difference between these two approaches. In Chapter 1, "First Steps," we talked about the difference between growth mindset and fixed mindset. Thinking that there's only one "correct" choice for your career can lead to a lot of anxiety: "Did I choose the right one?" "What if I made a mistake?" It's what those with a fixed mindset say. If you are afraid of getting it wrong, you will also limit the possibility of getting it right.

Instead, look at your career through a growth mindset, something that requires you to invest effort and energy in to determine your pathway. Viewing your career as your creation helps you relax. Instead of anguishing over finding the right career, you can stay open to possibilities. You can choose one career today, knowing that you can choose again later.

One caution is in order. Choosing your career is not something to do in an information vacuum. Rather, choose after you've done a lot of research. That includes research into yourself—your skills and interests—and a thorough knowledge of what careers are available.

Tips for Master Students

After all of the data have been gathered, there's only one person who can choose your career: you. This choice does not have to be a weighty one. In fact, it can be like going into your favourite restaurant and choosing from a menu that includes all of your favourite dishes. At this point, it's difficult to make a mistake. Whatever your choice, you know you'll enjoy it.

You have a world of choices

Our society offers a limitless array of careers. You no longer have to confine yourself to a handful of traditional categories, such as business, education, government, or manufacturing. The number of job titles is expanding so rapidly that we can barely keep track of them.

In addition, people are constantly creating new goods and services to meet emerging needs. For instance, there are people who work as *event planners*, helping people organize their weddings, anniversaries, graduations, and other ceremonies. Being a *Professional blogger* is a great way to combine your love of writing and an engaging personality with social media savvy. If you have a unique brand story, this could be the job for you. A *social media coordinator* works with a company to ensure the company is appropriately profiled on social media sites by managing a company's profile and coordinating the digital strategy. This could be a good way to put your social media skills to use. *Clinical informatics specialists* allow clinicians, like lab technologists, to apply their clinical knowledge and skills to developing effective IT applications, like telehealth, for other clinical users. *Professional organizers* will walk into your home or office and advise you on managing time and paperwork. And *life coaches* will assist you in setting and achieving goals relating to your career or anything else. None of these jobs existed 20 years ago!

The global marketplace creates even more options for you. Your customers or clients could be located in Calgary or China, Prince Edward Island or Panama. Your skills in thinking globally and communicating with a diverse world could help you create a new product or service for a new market—and perhaps a career that does not even exist today.

Plan by naming names

One key to making your career plan real, and ensuring that you can act on it, is naming. Go back over your plan to see that you include specific names whenever they're called for:

- *Name your job.* Take the skills you enjoy using and find out which jobs use them. What are those jobs called? List them. Note that the same job might have different names.

- *Name your company—the agency or organization you want to work for.* If you want to be self-employed or start your own business, name the product or service you'd sell. Also list some possible names for your business. If you plan to work for others, name the organizations or agencies that are high on your list. For example, if you want to work for company with excellent diversity programs, create a list of these companies (check out Canada's Best Diversity Employers for ideas for companies that have exceptional programs for diversity and inclusion at *www.canadastop100.com/diversity*).

- *Name your contacts.* Take the list of organizations you just compiled. What people in these organizations are responsible for hiring? List those people and contact them directly. If you choose self-employment, list the names of possible customers or clients. All of these people are job contacts. Don't forget that the Web has some great networking tools, like *LinkedIn* (*www.linkedin.com*) and *Monster.ca*, that allow you meet others who are in industries you might be interested in.

- *Name your location.* Ask if your career choices are consistent with your preferences about where to live and work. For example, someone who wants to make a living as a studio musician might consider living in a large city such as Toronto or New York. This contrasts with the freelance graphic artist who conducts his business mainly by phone or email. He might be able to live anywhere and still pursue his career.

Now expand your list of contacts by brainstorming with your family and friends. Come up with a list of names—anyone who can help you with career planning and job-hunting. Write down each of the names in a spiral-bound notebook or in a file you keep on your mobile device.

Next, call the key people on your list. After you speak with them, make brief notes about what you discussed. Also jot down any actions you agreed to take, such as a follow-up call.

Consider everyone you meet a potential member of your job network and be prepared to talk about what you do. Develop an "elevator pitch"—a short statement of your career goal that you can share easily with your contacts; for example, "After I graduate, I plan to work in the travel business. I'm looking for an internship in a travel agency for next summer. Do you know of any agencies that take interns?"

Describe your ideal lifestyle

In addition to choosing the content of your career, you have many options for integrating work into the context of your life. You can work full-time. You can work part-time. You can commute to a cubicle at a major corporate office. Or you can work at home and take the 30-second commute from your bedroom to your desk.

Close your eyes. Visualize an ideal day in your life after graduation. Vividly imagine the following:

- Your work setting
- Your co-workers
- Your calendar and to-do list for that day
- Other sights and sounds in your work environment

This visualization emphasizes the importance of finding a match between your career and your lifestyle preferences—the amount of flexibility in your schedule, the number of people you see each day, the variety in your tasks, and the ways that you balance work with other activities.

Consider self-employment

Instead of joining a thriving business, you could create one of your own. If the idea of self-employment seems far-fetched, consider that as a student, you already *are* self-employed. You are setting your own goals, structuring your time, making your own financial decisions, and monitoring your performance. These are all transferable skills that you could use in becoming your own boss. Many successful businesses—including Facebook and BlackBerry—were started by college students. Check to see if your school has any entrepreneurship programs that provide start-up funding to budding businesses; many colleges and universities do, such as Humber College's LaunchPad program or the McGill Dobson Centre for Entrepreneurship.

Test your career choice—and be willing to change

Career-planning materials and counsellors can help you. Read books about careers and search for career-planning websites. Ask career counsellors about skills assessments that can help you discover more about your skills and identify jobs that call for those skills. Take career-planning courses and workshops sponsored by your school. Visit the

career planning and job placement offices on campus in your first year of study—don't wait until you are graduating to make use of these excellent and free resources.

Once you have a career choice, translate it into workplace experience.

- Contact people who are actually doing the job you're researching, and ask them a lot of questions about what it's like (an *information interview*). This is a great way to gain insider's knowledge about a field and also to network with potential employers for after graduation.
- Choose an internship, field placement, or volunteer position in a field that interests you. Many times, employers are more willing to hire you once they have seen you on the job; and by working in the field, you have the opportunity to see if this is the correct job for you.
- Get a part-time or summer job in your career field. The more work experience you have, the more likely a potential employer will consider you for similar jobs upon graduation. So, when thinking about part-time or summer employment, don't look just at the paycheque you will be receiving; rather, look to see how the position will allow you to broaden your work skills and knowledge.

If you find that you enjoy meeting the people who are in your field of work or a work placement, then you've probably made a wise career choice. And the people you meet are possible sources of recommendations, referrals, and employment in the future. If you did *not* enjoy your experiences, celebrate what you learned about yourself. Now you're free to refine your initial career choice or go in a new direction.

Career planning is not a once-and-for-all proposition. Career plans are made to be changed and refined as you gain new information about yourself and the world.

Career planning never ends. If your present career no longer feels right, you can choose again—no matter what stage of life you're in. The process is the same, whether you're choosing your first career or your fifth.

Remember your purpose

While digging deep into the details of career planning, take some time to back up to the big picture. Listing skills, researching jobs, writing resumés—all of this is necessary and useful. At the same time, attending to these tasks can obscure our broadest goals. To get perspective, we can go back to the basics—a life purpose.

Create your career plan—now

Write your career plan. Now. Start the process of career planning, even if you're not sure where to begin. Your response to this exercise can be just a rough draft of your plan, which you can revise and rewrite many times. The point is to get your ideas in writing.

The final format of your plan is up to you. You might include many details, such as the next job title you'd like to have, the courses required for your major, and other training that you want to complete. You might list companies to research and people that could hire you. You might also include target dates to complete each of these tasks.

Another option is to represent your plan visually through flowcharts, timelines, mind maps, or drawings. You can generate these by hand or by using computer software.

For now, experiment with career planning by completing the following sentences. When answering the first question below, write down what comes to your mind first. The goal is to begin the process of discovery. You can always change direction after some investigation.

1. The career I choose for now is . . .

_____

_____

_____

2. The major steps that will guide me to this career are . . .

_____

_____

_____

3. The immediate steps I will take to pursue this career are . . .

_____

_____

_____

Your deepest desire might be to see that hungry children are fed, to make sure that beautiful music keeps getting heard, or to help alcoholics become sober. When such a large purpose is clear, smaller decisions about what to do are often easier.

A life purpose makes a career plan simpler and more powerful. It cuts through the stacks of job data and employment figures. Your life purpose is like the guidance system for a rocket. It keeps the plan on target while revealing a path for soaring to the heights (Ellis, Lankowitz, Stupka, & Toft, 2003). ✳

Tips for Master Students

Don't be afraid to stray from your path

My advice is this: don't be afraid to stray from your strict path. Take a gap year. Find your passion. If your calling changes, follow it; then pursue it until you're living it every day.

—Marc Kielburger, co-founder of WE, graduate of Harvard and Oxford universities, and Rhodes Scholar (*Maclean's*, 2017)

Sample
CAREER PLANS

Following are some examples of mind maps, pie charts, and lists that you can use to visually represent your career plan. *

Figure 12.1 **Mind Map**
A mind map that links personal values to desired skills that could be used in a variety of careers

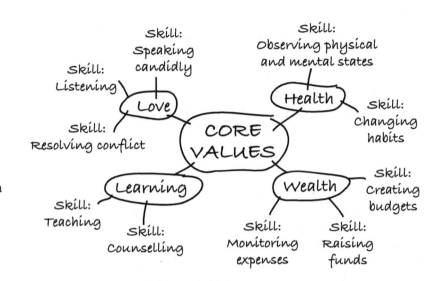

Figure 12.2 **Pie Chart**
A pie chart summarizing the amounts of time devoted to career-related activities

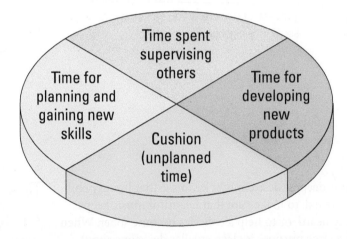

Figure 12.3 **List**
A list of career goals sorted by priority. In this case, each goal is assigned a number from 1 to 100. Higher numbers denote higher priority.

- Consult career services office on law school options (100)
- Prepare rigorously for LSAT and do well (100)
- Get into top-10 law school (95)
- Get position as editor on *Law Review* (90)
- Graduate in top of class at law school (85)
- Work in provincial court as a crown attorney (80)
- Use my position and influence to gain political contacts (75)
- Found private law firm focussed on protection of workers' rights (70)
- Win major lawsuits in defence of human rights in the workplace (60)
- Leave law practice to travel to developing countries in aid of refugees for two years (60)
- Found international agency for protection of human rights (50)
- Win the Nobel Prize (30)

Discover your
EMPLOYABILITY SKILLS

In chapter 1, "First Steps," we talked about how the Conference Board of Canada (2010) has produced *Employability Skills 2000+,* a list of essential skills to enter, stay in, and progress in the world of work. Review the list, assess your current skills, and consider which ones you still need to develop. Keep in mind that no matter what career you settle on, more than 70 percent of jobs require some form of postsecondary education (Ontario Ministry of Training, Colleges and Universities, 2010).

Fundamental skills

Communicate

- Read and understand information in a variety of forms.
- Write and speak so others pay attention and understand.
- Ask good questions and listen openly to other points of view.
- Share information using a range of information and communications technologies.
- Use scientific, technological, and mathematical skills to explain or clarify ideas.

Manage information

- Locate, gather, and organize information using appropriate technology and information systems.
- Access, analyze, and apply knowledge and skills from various disciplines.

Use numbers

- Decide what needs to be measured or calculated.
- Observe and record data using appropriate tools and technology.
- Make estimates and verify calculations.

Think and solve problems

- Assess situations and identify problems.
- Examine situations from a variety of perspectives.
- Identify the root cause of a problem.
- Be creative and innovative in exploring possible solutions.
- Easily use technology, science, and math as part of problem-solving and decision-making.
- Evaluate solutions to make recommendations or decisions.
- Implement solutions and act on opportunities.
- Review solutions to ensure that they work and make improvements if necessary.

Personal management skills

Demonstrate positive attitudes and behaviours

- Deal with people, problems, and situations with honesty, integrity, and personal ethics.
- Exhibit good self-esteem and confidence in your abilities.
- Recognize your own and other people's good efforts.
- Demonstrate a healthy lifestyle.
- Show interest, initiative, and effort.

Be responsible

- Set goals and priorities balancing work and personal life.
- Plan and manage time, money, and other resources.
- Assess, weigh, and manage risk.
- Show accountability for your own actions and those that you work with.
- Demonstrate social responsibility and be accountable for your actions and the actions of your group.

Be adaptable

- Be innovative and resourceful, identifying alternative ways to get a job done.
- Work well individually or as part of a group.
- Be capable of multi-tasking or working on several projects at once.
- Be open to change.
- Learn from mistakes and accept feedback and change.
- Cope with uncertainty.

Learn continuously

- Assess personal strengths and areas for development.
- Embrace lifelong learning.
- Continuously assess your strengths and needs for growth.
- Set, plan, and achieve your own learning goals.
- Identify and access learning sources and opportunities.

Work safely

- Be aware of personal and group health and safety practices.
- Act in accordance with the above.

Teamwork skills

Work with others

- Recognize and respect people's diversity, individual differences, and perspectives.
- Be knowledgeable about group dynamics, ensure that you are respectful of team members and supportive of their ideas.
- Focus on clearly articulated team goals.

- Accept and provide constructive feedback to team members.
- Motivate your team to high performance.
- Contribute to a team by sharing information and expertise.
- Understand the role of conflict in a group and manage it to reach solutions.

Participate in projects and tasks

- Plan, design, and execute a project from start to finish, developing a plan with well-defined objectives and outcomes.
- Review, revise, and test plans.
- Ensure quality standards are upheld.
- Utilize appropriate technology and tools for the task at hand.
- Monitor the success of a project, seek feedback, and identify ways to improve. ✷

Source: Conference Board of Canada. (2000). Employability skills 2000+ Brochure 2000 E/F. Ottawa: The Conference Board of Canada.

practising
CRITICAL THINKING

12-3

Assess your employability skills

In reading the Conference Board of Canada list of employability skills, identify
Three areas of strength that you have:

1. _____

2. _____

3. _____

Three areas that you need to improve:

1. _____

2. _____

3. _____

Think about how you might gain those needed skills by taking courses, by involvement in clubs or other activities, or through volunteer work or self-study. Select three methods you will use to improve your skills.

1. _____

2. _____

3. _____

Jumpstart your career with
TRANSFERABLE SKILLS

WHEN MEETING with an academic advisor, some students say, "I've just been taking courses in arts and humanities. I haven't got any marketable skills." Think again.

Few words are as widely misunderstood as *skill*. Defining it carefully can have an immediate and positive impact on your career planning.

Two kinds of skills

One dictionary defines *skill* as "the ability to do something well, usually gained by training or experience." Some skills—such as the ability to repair fibre optic cables or do brain surgery—are acquired through formal schooling, on-the-job training, or both. These abilities are called *work-content skills*. People with such skills have mastered a specialized body of knowledge needed to do a specific kind of work.

However, there is another category of skills that we develop through experiences both inside and outside the classroom. We may never receive formal training to develop these abilities. Yet they are key to success in the workplace. These are *transferable skills*. Transferable skills are the kind of abilities that help people thrive in any job—no matter what work-content skills they have.

Perhaps you've heard someone described this way: "She's really smart and knows what she's doing, but she's got lousy people skills." People skills—such as *listening* and *negotiating*—are prime examples of transferable skills. These are often considered to be soft skills and may be overlooked by graduates who often think that, to be successful, they need more content skills (like learning one more computer program). Their lack of challenging employment is probably far more related to these so-called soft skills.

Succeeding in many situations

Transferable skills are often invisible to us. The problem begins when we assume that a given skill can only be used in one context, such as being in school or working at a particular job. Thinking in this way places an artificial limit on our possibilities. As an alternative, think about the things you routinely do to succeed in

school. Analyze your activities to isolate specific skills. Then brainstorm a list of jobs where you could use the same skills.

Consider the task of writing an essay. This calls for many skills:

- *Planning*—setting goals for completing your outline, first draft, second draft, and final draft
- *Managing time* to meet your writing goals
- *Interviewing* people who know a lot about the topic of your essay
- *Researching* using the Internet and campus library to discover key facts and ideas to include in your essay
- *Writing* to present those facts and ideas in an original way
- *Editing* your drafts for clarity and correctness

Now consider the kinds of jobs that draw on these skills.

For example, you could transfer your skill at writing essays to a possible career in journalism, technical writing, or advertising copywriting.

You could use your editing skills to work in the field of publishing as an online magazine or book editor.

Interviewing and research skills could help you enter the field of market research. And the abilities to plan, manage time, and meet deadlines will help you succeed in all the jobs mentioned so far.

Use the same kind of analysis to think about transferring skills from one job to another job. For example, if you work part-time as an administrative assistant at a computer dealer that sells a variety of hardware and software, you probably take phone calls from potential customers, help current customers solve problems using their computers, and attend meetings where your co-workers plan ways to market new products. You are developing skills at *selling, serving customers,* and *working on teams* that could help you land a job as a sales representative for a computer manufacturer or software developer.

The basic idea is to take a cue from the word *transferable*. Almost any skill you use to succeed in one situation can *transfer* to success in another situation.

The concept of transferable skills creates a powerful link between postsecondary education and the work world. Skills are the core elements of any job. While taking any course, list the specific skills you are developing and how you can transfer them to the work world. Almost everything you do in school can be applied to your career—if you consistently pursue this line of thought.

Ask four questions to identify your transferable skills

To experiment further with this concept of transferable skills, ask and answer four questions.

1 Why identify my transferable skills? Getting past the "I-don't-have-any-skills" syndrome means that you can approach job-hunting with more confidence. As you uncover these hidden assets, your list of qualifications will grow as if by magic. You won't be padding your resumé. You'll simply be using action words to tell the full truth about what you can do.

Identifying your transferable skills takes a little time. And the payoffs are numerous. A complete and accurate list of transferable skills can help you land jobs that involve more responsibility, more variety, more freedom to structure your time, and more money.

Transferable skills also help you thrive in the midst of constant change. Technology will continue to upgrade. Ongoing discoveries in many fields could render current knowledge obsolete. Jobs that exist today may disappear in a few years, only to be replaced by entirely new ones. Your keys to prospering in this environment are transferable skills—those that you can carry from one career to another.

2 What are my transferable skills? Discover your transferable skills by reflecting on key experiences. Recall a time when you performed at the peak of your ability, overcame obstacles, won an award, gained a high mark, or met a significant goal. List the skills you used to create those successes.

In each case, remember that the word skill points to something that you do. In your list of transferable skills, start each item with an action verb such as budget or coach or consult. Or use a closely related part of speech—budgeting or coaching.

For a more complete picture of your transferable skills, describe the object of your action. Perhaps one of the skills on your list is organizing. This could refer to organizing ideas, organizing people, or organizing objects in a room. Specify the kind of organizing that you like to do.

3 How do I perform these skills? You can bring your transferable skills into even sharper focus by adding adverbs—words that describe *how* you take action. You might say that you edit *accurately* or learn *quickly*.

In summary, you can use a three-column chart to list your transferable skills.

Verb	Object	Adverb
Organizing	Records	Effectively
Serving	Customers	Courteously
Coordinating	Special events	Efficiently

Add a specific example of each skill to your list, and you're well on the way to an engaging resumé and a winning job interview.

As you list your transferable skills, focus on the skills that you most enjoy using. Then look for careers and jobs that directly involve those skills.

4 What if I could expand my transferable skills? In addition to thinking about the skills you already have, consider the skills you'd like to acquire. Describe those skills in detail and list experiences that can help you develop them. Let your list of transferrable skills grow and develop as you do. ✳

65 transferable skills

There are literally hundreds of transferable skills. To learn more transferable skills and which occupations they match, go to the Canadian government website *Working in Canada*. On the website, fill in a checklist of your skills and knowledge and get some ideas about which occupations match up with those skill sets (*www.jobbank.gc.ca/skillsandknowledge?action=search_form*). If you are particularly interested in the skilled trades and technology field, go to *Skills Competencies Canada* (*www.skillscompetencescanada.com/en/*), and check out the website of this non-profit organization. There you'll find tools for discovering your skills and matching them to specific occupations. Additional information on careers and job-hunting is available online through *CanadianCareers.com,* which is a great website that lists valuable information about labour market trends plus essential information about marketing yourself.

Rate yourself on each of the eight skill areas (on a one to five scale where a five means you're great at these skills and a one means you need improvement). Reflect on the areas where improvement is still needed and consider what steps you will take to improve, from rereading a chapter of this book to signing up for a free online course in this area. Write an intention statement outlining your next steps for continuing to develop these skills.

Self-discovery and self-management skills (_____ /5)

1. Assessing your current knowledge and skills
2. Seeking out opportunities to acquire new knowledge and skills
3. Choosing and applying learning strategies
4. Showing flexibility by adopting new attitudes and behaviours

For more information about self-discovery skills, review the Introduction to this book and Chapter 1.

Time-management skills (_____ /5)

1. Scheduling due dates for project outcomes
2. Scheduling time for goal-related tasks
3. Choosing technology and applying it to goal-related tasks
4. Choosing materials and facilities needed to meet goals
5. Designing other processes, procedures, or systems to meet goals
6. Working independently to meet goals
7. Planning projects for teams
8. Managing multiple projects at the same time
9. Monitoring progress toward goals
10. Persisting in order to meet goals
11. Delivering projects and outcomes on schedule

For more information about time-management skills, review Chapter 2.

Reading skills (_____ /5)

1. Reading for key ideas and major themes
2. Reading for detail
3. Reading to synthesize ideas and information from several sources
4. Reading to discover strategies for solving problems or meeting goals
5. Reading to understand and follow instructions

For more information about reading skills, review Chapter 4.

Note-taking skills (_____ /5)

1. Taking notes on material presented verbally, in print, or online
2. Creating pictures, graphs, and other visuals to summarize and clarify information
3. Organizing information and ideas in digital and paper-based forms
4. Researching by finding information online or in the library
5. Gathering data through field research or working with primary sources

For more information about note-taking skills, review Chapter 5.

Test-taking and related skills (_____ /5)

1. Assessing personal performance at school or at work
2. Using test results and other assessments to improve performance
3. Working cooperatively in study groups and project teams
4. Managing stress
5. Applying scientific findings and methods to solve problems
6. Using mathematics to do basic computations and solve problems

For more information about this group of skills, review Chapters 3, 6, and 11.

(continued)

Thinking skills (_____ /5)

1. Thinking to create new ideas, products, or services
2. Thinking to evaluate ideas, products, or services
3. Evaluating material presented verbally, in print, or online
4. Thinking of ways to improve products, services, or programs
5. Choosing appropriate strategies for making decisions
6. Choosing ethical behaviours
7. Stating problems accurately
8. Diagnosing the sources of problems
9. Generating possible solutions to problems
10. Weighing benefits and costs of potential solutions
11. Choosing and implementing solutions
12. Interpreting information needed for problem-solving or decision-making

For more information about thinking skills, review Chapter 7.

Communication skills (_____ /5)

1. Assigning and delegating tasks
2. Coaching
3. Consulting
4. Counselling
5. Editing publications
6. Giving people feedback about the quality of their performance
7. Interpreting and responding to nonverbal messages
8. Interviewing people
9. Leading meetings
10. Leading project teams
11. Listening fully (without judgment or distraction)
12. Preventing conflicts (defusing a tense situation)
13. Resolving conflicts
14. Responding to complaints
15. Speaking to diverse audiences
16. Writing
17. Editing

For more information about communication skills, review Chapters 8 and 9.

Money skills (_____ /5)

1. Monitoring income and expenses
2. Raising funds
3. Decreasing expenses
4. Estimating costs
5. Preparing budgets

For more information about money skills, review Chapter 10.

Recognize your skills

This exercise about discovering your skills includes three steps. Before you begin, gather at least 100 index cards and a pen or pencil. Or open up a computer file and use any software that allows you to create lists. Allow about one hour to complete the exercise.

STEP 1

List recent activities. Recall your activities during the past week or month. To refresh your memory, review your responses to "The Time Monitor" exercise in Chapter 2. (You might even benefit from doing that exercise again.)

List as many of these activities as you can. (If you're using index cards, list each item on a separate card.) Include work-related activities, school activities, and hobbies. Spend 10 minutes on this step.

STEP 2

List rewards and recognitions. Next, list any rewards you've received, or other recognition of your achievements, during the past year. Examples include scholarship awards, athletic awards, recognitions for volunteer work, or specific praise at work or in class. Allow 10 minutes for this step as well.

STEP 3

List work-content skills. Now review the two lists you just created. Then take another 10 minutes to list any specialized areas of knowledge needed to do those activities, win those awards, and receive those recognitions.

These areas of knowledge indicate your *work-content skills*. For example, tutoring a French class requires a working knowledge of that language.

List all of your skills that fall into this category, labelling each one as "work-content."

STEP 4

List transferable skills. Go over your list of activities one more time. Spend 10 minutes looking for examples of *transferable skills*—those that can be applied to a variety of situations. For instance, giving a speech or working as a salesperson in a computer store requires the ability to persuade people. Tuning a car means that you can attend to details and troubleshoot.

List all your skills that fall into this category, labelling each one as "transferable."

STEP 5

Review and plan. You now have a detailed picture of your skills. Review all the lists you created in the previous steps. See whether you can add any new items that occur to you.

Save your lists in a place where you can easily find them again. Plan to update all of them at least once each year. Your lists will come in handy for writing your resumé, preparing for job interviews, and doing other career-planning tasks.

Build an irresistible
RESUMÉ

Jamie Grill/Blend Images/Getty Images

A resumé is much more than a list of your qualifications. This document says a lot about who you are, what you love to do, and how you contribute to the world by using your skills. You can gain a lot from thinking about those things now, even if you don't plan to apply for a job in the near future. Start *building* your resumé now, even if you don't plan to *use* one for a while.

Build your resumé from a skills perspective

According to one perspective, there's no need to think about a resumé until your last term in school. At that time, you go to a career planning workshop or two, check the job listings, and start sending out applications. And if you don't land a job—well, you can always go back to school.

Instead of this rather undirected approach, take a skills perspective. Ask one question about every experience you have in higher education: *How will this help me develop a valuable skill?* Remembering this question will help you choose courses, instructors, and extracurricular activities with a new level of clarity. Then, when it's your time to send out a resumé, you'll be ready to demonstrate your mastery.

An education is much more than a grade point average and list of course credits. The whole point is to become a new and improved version of yourself. Graduating means being able to *do* things that you could not do when you started school.

Today you can start developing the ability to think critically, speak persuasively, and write clearly. You can learn to work on teams, solve complex problems, innovate, and act with integrity. These are skills that allow you to prosper in the workplace and find your place in a global economy. From this perspective, a resumé is something that you build during your whole time in higher education.

Start building skills for your ideal resumé early

To get the most from your education, think about the resumé you want to have when you graduate. With that vision of the person you want to be, choose the skills that you want to gain.

If you've actively participated with this course and this book, then you've got a head start. Reread your responses to the Journal Entries and exercises throughout this book. Also review the articles in this chapter about values, transferable skills, and choosing your career.

With those insights fresh in mind, start planning. Write goals to develop specific skills. Then list the actions you will take to continue to develop those skills. Add reminders of these actions to your to-do list and calendar so that you can actually achieve your goals.

Many of your plans will involve taking courses. In addition, look for ways to gain and use skills outside the classroom. Sign up for internships and community service-learning projects related to your major. Find part-time jobs related to your career plan. Seize every opportunity to take theories and test them in the work world. These experiences will help you develop an expertise, build a job network, and make a seamless transition to your next career.

Remember the reason for a resumé

When you *do* write a resumé to apply for a job, approach it as a piece of persuasive writing—not a dry recitation of facts or a laundry list of previous jobs. The key purpose of your resumé is to get you to the next step in the hiring process.

There is no formula for a great resumé. Employers have many different preferences for what they want to see. Just remember that an effective resumé states how you can benefit a potential employer. Second, it offers evidence that you can deliver those benefits.

Make sure that every word in your resumé serves those goals.

To write an effective resumé, consider your audience. Picture a person who has several hundred resumés to plow through, and almost no time for that task. She may spend only 20 seconds reviewing each resumé before making a decision about who to call for interviews. This means that you want to make it as easy as possible for her to find the most important information. Format the resumé in order that it is visually easy to scan.

Remember to be concise. Try to keep the length of the resumé to one to two pages unless you have plenty of work experience. But don't neglect to include critical experiences you have had like starting your own YouTube channel or volunteer work specifically related to the position you are apply for.

Your goal is to get past the first cut. Neatness, organization, and correct grammar and punctuation are essential. Remember that a resumé is a marketing tool—this is not the time to be modest about your skills and accomplishments. Meet these goals, and then make an even stronger impression with the following strategies.

Use this resumé checklist

The following suggestions will guide you through one common resumé format:

- *Let people know how to contact you.* Start your resumé with contact information. This includes your name, phone number, email address, and mailing address. If you have a website or a LinkedIn profile, add the links as well. Make sure that your email address, voice mail greeting, online presence, and LinkedIn convey a professional image.

- *Highlight your experience.* Follow your objective with the body of your resumé. One common heading is "experience." Write this section carefully. Here is where you give a few relevant details about your past jobs, listed in order starting with your most recent position. This is the heart of a *chronological* resumé. An alternative to the chronological format is the *functional* resumé. It highlights your skills, strengths, and personal achievements rather than past jobs. This format might be useful for people with limited experience or gaps in their work history. Try to use wording or key verbs that match the language found in the job posting.

- *Highlight your education.* A second common heading for the body of a resumé is "education." List any degree that you attained beyond high school, along with honours, awards, and significant activities. If you are currently enrolled in classes, note

that as well. Include your planned degree and date of graduation.

- *Include references.* Many resumés end with a line such as "references are available on request." Before you add this statement, make sure that you can deliver a list of people who have already agreed to write a reference for you. Ask for their permission and current contact information.

- *Write so that the facts leap off the page.* Whenever possible, use phrases that start with an action verb: "*supervised* three people," "*generated* leads for sales calls," "*wrote* speeches and *edited* annual reports," "*designed* a process that reduced production expenses by 20 percent." Active verbs refer directly to your skills. Make them relevant to the job you're seeking, and tie them to specific accomplishments whenever possible. Be prepared to discuss these accomplishments during a job interview.

- *Cut the fluff.* Leave out information that could possibly eliminate you from the hiring process and send your resumé hurtling into the circular file. Avoid boilerplate language—stock wording or vague phrases such as "proven success in a high-stress environment," "highly motivated self-starter," or "a demonstrated capacity for strategic thinking."

- *Get feedback.* Ask friends and family members if your resumé is persuasive and easy to understand. Also get feedback from someone at your school's career counselling centre. Revise your resumé based on their comments. Then revise some more. Create succinct prose that will intrigue a potential employer enough to call you for an interview.

- *Take charge of your online resumé.* While you're writing a resumé, take a break to check your online presence. Type your name into an Internet search engine such as Google and see what results you get. These search results make up your online resumé. Employers will check social networking sites such as Facebook, LinkedIn, and Twitter to learn about you. Review your posts, photos, videos, and files on all social networks you have joined, deleting inappropriate content that you would not want an potential employer to see as well as unsubscribing from any inactive social network accounts. Be mindful as you post future content. Add updates about your academic achievements, extracurricular activities, and internships.

- *Use social networking to actively support your job search.* For example, start a Twitter stream about topics related to your major and career plan. Link your followers to useful articles, and start following people who are working in your chosen field.

Stock Rocket/Shutterstock.com

Round out your resumé with a portfolio

Photographers, contractors, and designers regularly show portfolios filled with samples of their work. Today, employers and educators increasingly see the portfolio as a tool that's useful for everyone. Some schools require students to create them, and some employers want to see a portfolio before they hire. When you create your portfolio, experiment with a four-step process:

1 Collect and catalogue artifacts. An *artifact* is any object that's important to you and that reveals something about yourself. Examples include awards, recommendation letters, job descriptions for positions you've held, writing samples, presentations, articles about projects you've done, lists of grants or scholarships you've received, programs from performances you've given, and transcripts of your grades. Your portfolio can also include photographs, audio or video recordings, websites, or representations of anything else you've created.

To save hours when creating your portfolio, start documenting your artifacts now, if you haven't already. Record the "five W's" about each one: *who* was involved with it, *what* you did with it, *when* it

was created, *where* it was created, and *why* the artifact is important to you. Update this information as you collect new artifacts. Whenever possible, manage this information with a computer, using word-processing or database software.

2 Plan your portfolio. When you're ready to create a portfolio for a specific audience, write your purpose—for example, to demonstrate your learning or to document your work experience as you prepare for a job interview.

Also think about your audience—the people who will see your portfolio. Predict what questions they will ask and make sure that you have included an answer in your portfolio. Screen artifacts with your purpose and audience in mind. If a beautiful artifact fails to meet your purpose or fit your audience, leave it out for now.

3 Assemble your portfolio. Assemble your portfolio according to your plan. Include a table of contents, overview, or summary at the start of the portfolio, title and captions for each artifact, and an index.

4 Present your portfolio. You may be asked to do this at the interview so practise how you would do this, in front of friends or, if possible, those in your career field. Consider how you will highlight your best artifacts especially those which make you stand out from other candidates.

5 Put your portfolio online. Consider presenting your portfolio online in the form of a personal website with an online portfolio or ePortfolio of your work. ePortfolios serve the same purpose as your paper portfolios but are likely to reach a wider audience as you can send a link to it to potential employers. Find out if your school's learning management system has an ePortfolio tool. This can be useful particularly if you can export your ePortfolio after you graduate. Your ePortfolio contains digital artifacts of your work that may be difficult to capture on paper like videos, images, blog entries, and hyperlinks. In both an online and a paper portfolio, you want to make sure that the artifacts in your portfolio contain your best work and illustrate your development over time. Consider the organization of the ePortfolio, as potential viewers may be viewing it without you being there to guide them through it. An ePortfolio is a dynamic tool and a great way for you to reflect upon your own learning. It can be reorganized and updated as needed.

See your resumé as a work in progress

To create an effective resumé, plan to revise it regularly. Save a copy on your device in a file you can update. See which version of your resumé leads to the most interviews.

Look at a lot of sample resumés, especially from people in your career field. There is no ideal format for a resumé. Just focus on doing what works. Many examples can be found on the Internet. You will find resumé tips for college students and graduates at this site: *https://www.thebalancecareers.com/resume-examples-for-college-students-and-graduates-2063553*

Take advantage of the many apps out there that can help you build a great resumé. These include *Online CV* (*https://www.visualcv.com/*), and *Resume Maker - Pro CV* (*https://download.cnet.com/Resume-Maker-Pro-CV-Designer/3000-2064_4-77136878.html*). Many of these sites also help you write a cover letter.

You can combine your resumé with other job-search strategies. If you just send out resumés and neglect to make personal contacts, you will be disappointed with the results. Instead, research companies and do information interviews. Contact potential employers directly—even if they don't have a job opening at the moment. Find people in organizations who have the power to hire you. Then use every job contact you have to introduce yourself to those people and schedule an interview. To get the most from your resumé, use it to support a variety of job-hunting strategies. ✳

Fine-tune your cover letter

Remember the primary question in an employer's mind: What do you have to offer us? Using a three-part structure can help you answer this question.

1. Gain attention   In your first sentence, address the person who can hire you and grab that person's attention. Make a statement that appeals directly to his self-interest. Write something that moves a potential employer to say, "We can't afford to pass this person up. Call her right away to set up an appointment."

To come up with ideas for your opening, complete the following sentence: "The main benefits that I can bring to your organization are. . . ." Another option: "My work experience ties directly to several points mentioned in your job description. First, ..."

Perhaps someone the employer knows told you about this job opening. Mention this person in your opening paragraph, especially if he or she has a positive reputation in the organization.

2. Build interest   Add a fact or two to back up your opening sentence. If you're applying for a specific job opening, mention that job. If you're not, then offer an idea that will intrigue the employer enough to respond anyway. Another option is to give a summary of your key qualifications for a specific job. Briefly refer to your experience and highlight a few key achievements.

3. Take care of business   Refer the reader to your resume. Mention that you'll call at a specific point to follow up. Then make good on your promise.

And don't forget . . .

- Whenever possible, address your letter to a specific person. Make sure to use this person's correct title and mailing address, and spell the name correctly. If you cannot find a specific name, then address your letter to "Dear Hiring Manager for [name of the position]."

- Use a simple typeface that is easy to read.

- Tailor each letter you write to the specific company and position you are applying for. Sending a "stock letter" implies that you don't really care about the job.

- Thank your reader for his time and consideration.

Use job interviews to
"HIRE" AN EMPLOYER

THE LOGICAL outcome of your career plan is a focussed job hunt.

Job interviews are times for an employer to size up applicants and screen most of them out. The reverse is also true: Interviews offer you a chance to size up potential employers. Careful preparation and follow-up can help you get the information—and the job—that you want. Use your applications for summer or part-time work as an opportunity to hone your job-searching skills.

Searching for jobs

Mention the phrase *job-hunting*, and many people envision someone browsing through dozens of job postings on websites, sending out hundreds of resumés, or enlisting the services of employment agencies to find job openings and set up interviews.

Unfortunately, this often doesn't work. Across all fields, the majority of job openings are not listed on the Internet or in newspaper want ads. Most jobs come about through our contacts or the networks we are involved in. Posting a resumé on a website will not automatically lead to job offers. For an effective job search, you need to view the Internet and online job postings as just one resource. Websites such as *CareerBuilder.ca*, *Glassdoor.ca*, *Monster.ca*, *jobpostings.ca*, *Workopolis.com*, and *Brazen.com* are great places to find information about companies, jobs, potential salaries, and job searching strategies. *Careeroptionsmagazine.com* is website which offers career advice and has ads for top Canadian employers.

Many employers turn to online help—wanted listings, resumés, and employment agencies only as a last resort. When they have positions to fill, they prefer instead to hire people they already know. Employers also listen closely when friends, family members, and co-workers recommend someone *they* know.

Remembering this can help you overcome frustration, tap the hidden job market, and succeed more often at getting the position you want. One powerful source of information about new jobs is people. Ask around.

© Andrey_Popov/Shutterstock.com

Tell everyone—friends, relatives, co-workers, and fellow students—that you want a job.

Richard Bolles (2018), author of *What Color Is Your Parachute? A Practical Manual for Job-Hunters and Career-Changers*, recommends the following steps in job-hunting:

- Discover which skills you want to use in your career, and which jobs draw on the skills you want to use.
- Interview people who are doing the kind of jobs you'd want to do.
- Research companies on the Internet that you'd like to work for, and find out what kinds of problems they face on a daily basis. Check out their profile on LinkedIn.
- Identify your contacts—a person at each one of these companies who has the power to hire you.
- Arrange an interview with that person, even if the company has no job openings at the moment.

- Stay in contact with the people who interviewed you, knowing that a job opening can occur at any time (Taylor, 2009).

Notice that getting an interview comes toward the bottom of the above list—*after* you take the time to discover a lot about yourself and the work world. Those are keys to unlocking the hidden job market.

Start building your network—now

Networking is often described as the most effective way to get a job. Start by sharing your career plans with friends, relatives, neighbours, co-workers, students, instructors, and advisors. Basically, your network includes *anyone* who can hire you or refer you to an employer.

It's never too early to start building your network. Look for student and professional organizations that relate to your career plan. Attend your campus career fairs. Most colleges and universities host career fairs for summer and permanent jobs. This is a great way to start building your networking skills—and remember even if you don't apply this year for a position with a company, next year when you do, it is easier to apply if you can mention in your cover letter you met the employer last year at the fair. Many students have business cards printed to hand out to potential employers at fairs and other networking events so that it is easier to follow up your discussions later—again, employers tend to be more prone to hiring people they have met. Check with your career centre's website to see when these events are occurring on your campus. Keep a list of the employers you have met and brief notes about what you discussed.

Also begin networking online. Having a Web presence can be an asset during your job search—it's an opportunity to stand out from the pack. Consider starting a blog and writing a post every two weeks or so. Focus your posts on topics related to your career plan. Search for blogs by people with similar interests and add constructive comments to their posts. Through LinkedIn you can build your networks, join groups, and get endorsements for your skills and knowledge. The first step is to create a LinkedIn profile. (Go to *https://ca.linkedin.com/company/canada*.) Your LinkedIn profile is also a great way to highlight your experience and accomplishments.

The Internet can be a double-edged sword for job hunters, as employers also use it to find out information about job candidates. When employers search online to find information about you, not only may they find the information about your accomplishments and experience that you want them to find, but they may find information about your network, including groups and organizations you're associated with; so ensure that these are associations that reflect well on you as a job candidate. Consider carefully where you leave your online footprint.

The bottom line: When you want a job, tell everyone—especially people who have the power to hire you. This sets the stage for getting interviews.

Before you go to the interview

To get the most from your interviews, learn everything you can about each organization that interests you by searching the Internet. See if your target company has a profile on LinkedIn. Speak to a reference librarian on campus about good sources of information or ask the people in your campus's career centre.

Before you interview for a job at any organization, learn about

- the organization's products and services
- major developments in the organization during the past year
- directions that the organization plans to go during the upcoming year
- names of the organization's major divisions
- names of people who could hire you
- the types of jobs they offer

Next, prepare for common questions. Many interviewers are concerned about your job readiness (how much will they have to teach you before you can do the job) and how well you will fit their organization (for instance, if they take a team-based approach to work, they will want to know if you thrive in this type of environment).

You need to consider how you would answer questions related to job readiness and job fit. Think about personal characteristics that make you a good match for the job. Also describe your skills as the they relate to the job description and specific examples of how you have used those skills in the past to create positive results. Write down your main talking points and practise your answers until you sound prepared without delivering canned answers.

For extra practice, prepare answers for the following:

Tell me about yourself. For interviewers, this prompt serves several purposes. It encourages you to open up and tests your ability to think on your feet. A skilled interviewer will pay as much attention to *how* you answer the question as to *what* you say. Focus on the top two to three things that you want the interviewer to recall about you. Talk about aspects of your education and experience that most qualify you for the job. Do *not* give the story of your life.

What are your weaknesses? Interviewers want to know that you have enough self-awareness to spot your limitations. By planning in advance, you will be prepared to share a weakness that points to one of your strengths. For example, you might be slow to complete some tasks because you show a high level of attention to detail. At the same time, declare your intention to improve.

Why should I hire you? The full version is *Why should I hire you instead of any of the other people who are applying for this job?* Take a cue from the field of advertising, and develop your "unique selling proposition." This is the main thing that sets you apart from other job applicants. Focus on a key benefit that you can deliver—one that's unusual or distinctive. Begin your answer with a reference to the interviewer's organization. For example, mention a current development such as a new product, service, or initiative. Then talk specifically about how you can enhance that new development.

If you plan to bring examples of work from your portfolio, contact the employer ahead of time to find out how many people will be at the interview so you can bring the correct number of copies.

Also plan to dress appropriately for your interview. Don't choose clothing that will clash with an employer's or organization's expectations.

Round out your preparation by reviewing the Power Process: "Be it," found later in this chapter. To convince an employer that you can do a job, first convince yourself. Be authentic. Start from a conviction that you already *are* an excellent candidate and that the job connects with your values. Your passion and personality counts as much as any prepared answer.

During the interview

Plan to arrive early for your interview and observe the people in the workplace. See whether you can "read" the company culture by making informal observations.

Just before the interview begins, remind yourself that you have one goal—to get the *next* interview. The top candidates for a job often talk to several people in a company.

When you meet the interviewer, do three things right away: smile, make eye contact, and give a firm handshake. Nonverbal communication creates a lasting impression.

After making small talk, the interviewer will start asking questions. Draw on the answers you've prepared. At the same time, respond to the *exact* questions that you're asked speaking naturally and being aware of how long you are speaking.

Avoid answers that are too brief or too long. Respond to each question for a minute or two. If you have more to say, end your answer by saying, "Those are the basics. I can add more if you want."

A skilled interviewer will allow time for *you* to ask questions about the company. Use this time to your full advantage. Some things to ask about include what a typical day looks like or possibilities for more training.

Remember during the interview that the Employment Equity Act and the Canadian Human Rights Act are there to protect you from discrimination, based on your race, ethnic background, gender, or sexual orientation, in all aspects of the workplace from hiring to firing. If you feel your rights were violated in the interview, check with the Canadian Human Rights Commission by calling 1-888-643-3304 or go to their website *www.chrc-ccdp.ca.*

Save questions about benefits, salary, and vacation days for the second interview. When you get to that point, you know that the employer is interested in you. You might have leverage to negotiate. Preparing for salary negotiation can immediately increase your income by hundreds or sometimes thousands of dollars particularly over the course of your career. Even if you are in an entry-level position, it may be possible to start above the base; so be prepared in the second interview to ask for what you think you deserve. Included in your negotiations may be a discussion of the benefits package and vacation time, so think about what you would like.

Be sure to find out the next step in the hiring process and when it will take place. Also ask interviewers for their business cards and how they want you to follow up (by phone call or email).

If you're truly interested in the job and feel comfortable with the interviewer, ask one more question: "Do you have any concerns about hiring me?" Listen carefully to the reply. Then respond to each concern in a polite way.

After the interview

Congratulate yourself for getting as far in the hiring process as an interview. Write a Discovery Statement that describes your strengths, along with what you learned about your potential employer. Also write an Intention Statement about ways to be more effective during your next interview.

Now comes follow-up. This step can give you the edge that leads to a job offer.

Pull out the business cards from the people who interviewed you. Send an email thanking them for the interview and the opportunity to discuss their company. Briefly remind them why you are a good fit to the position. Do this within two business days after the interview. If you talked to several people at the same company, then write a different note to each one.

Also alert your references that they might get a contact from the interviewers.

Within five business days, find a reason to contact the interviewer again. For example, email a link to an interesting article and explain how it might be useful. If you have a website with a blog, let them know about a recent post. Reinforce the value you will bring to their team.

If you have permission to make contact by phone, also do so within 10 business days of the interview.

If you get turned down for the job after your interview, don't take it personally. Every interview is a source of feedback about what works—and what doesn't work—in contacting employers. Use that feedback to interview more effectively next time. Remember it takes grit or perseverance to job-hunt. Look at the job search process as just one more opportunity to show your metal.

Each person you talked to is now a member of your network. This is true even if you do not get a job offer. Follow up by asking interviewers to keep you in mind for future job openings. Using this approach, you gain from every interview, no matter what the outcome. ✳

practising
CRITICAL THINKING

12-6

Do something you can't

Few significant accomplishments result from people sticking to the familiar. You can accomplish much more than you think you can. Doing something you think you can't involve taking risks. This exercise has three parts. Complete this exercise on a separate piece of paper.

Part 1

Select something that you have never done before, that you don't know how to do, that you are fearful of doing, or that you think you probably can't do.

Perhaps you've never learned to play an instrument, or you've never run a marathon. Be smart. Don't pick something that will hurt you physically, such as flying from a third-floor window.

Part 2

Do it. Of course, this is easier said than done. This exercise is not about easy. It is about discovering capabilities that stretch your self-image.

To accomplish something that is bigger than your self-perceived abilities, use any of the tools you have gained from this book. Develop a plan. Divide and conquer. Stay focussed. Use outside resources. Let go of self-destructive thoughts.

Summarize the tools you will use.

Part 3

Write about the results of this exercise.

Top 10 tips to help ensure a successful job search

1. **Access your school's career centre.**

   - Attend career counselling workshops, employer recruitment events, career fairs, and opportunities for skill development.

2. **Start early.**

   - Don't wait until the term before graduation to begin. Career planning is a process and it can't be done successfully overnight.

   - The earlier you start thinking about your career goals and planning for employment after graduation, the more successful you will be in getting the job you want.

3. **Know yourself.**

   - Making good career choices requires you to have a solid understanding of your skills, interests, personality, and values.

   - If you aren't clear on who you are and what your needs are in terms of your career, consider taking a career assessment, which can help clarify some of these areas.

4. **Do your research.**

   - Learn all that you can about the industries, companies, and job roles that are part of the labour market. Start by browsing company or government websites.

   - Talk to people who are doing the type of work that you are interested in. This is called *information interviewing* and is a highly effective way to assess your fit for different roles and organizations.

5. **Get away from the computer.**

   - Do not restrict your job search to the Internet and online job search postings.

   - Approximately 20 percent of employment opportunities are posted, which means that 80 percent are part of the hidden job market.

   - So, spend 20 percent of your time looking for opportunities online and the remaining 80 percent of your time actually meeting people.

6. **Network, network, network.**

   - A successful job search begins with networking, which is the primary way to access the hidden job market.

   - Talk to everyone about your job search.

7. **Think broadly.**

   - Don't let your major dictate or limit the type of work that you consider; even if a job isn't directly related to your degree or diploma, there is a good chance that you will be able to demonstrate to an employer that you do, in fact, have the skills necessary to do the work.

8. **Customize your resumé and cover letter.**

   - Use the job posting to customize your documents according to the specific skills requested, and show a potential employer why you're the best candidate for the job.

9. **Practise, practise, practise.**

   - Successfully interviewing is a skill and, like any skill, it is perfected through practise.

   - Ask if your career centre provides opportunities for students to practise their interview skills. If not, you can also practise on your own with friends or family, or even in front of a mirror.

10. **Be strategic.**

    - All experience is good experience, but being *strategic* about the activities you participate in as a student is even better.

    - Think about where you want to go career-wise, and then actively participate in paid and unpaid opportunities that will help you develop the *skills* necessary for your career choice.

Dr. Kim Miller
Career Counsellor

Courtesy of Kim Miller

Surviving your first day
ON A NEW JOB

You've landed a new job. Congratulations! Well-meaning people may advise you to "just be yourself" when you show up for your first day of work. The following checklist offers more specifics.

Dress the part
To make a positive impression, put special effort into looking your best on your first day. Think back to what people in the office were wearing when you showed up for your job interview. Then dress at that level or slightly above it.

Arrive early
Don't underestimate the power of this simple suggestion. Arriving late for your first day of work sends mixed messages. To you, it may be a simple mistake. Your supervisor might interpret it as being careless or having an "attitude."

Notice your "nonverbal"
Remember to shake hands firmly and say hello in a friendly voice. Make eye contact and smile. Make sure your cellphone is turned off or on vibrate.

Start decoding the culture
Even if you graduated from school with a straight-A average—a real accomplishment—your new co-workers are not likely to know or care. Your task on your first day is to start adapting to this environment rather than remaking it.

Keep your eyes open. Notice when people arrive for work, how they greet each other, when they leave for lunch, how often they take breaks, how they make requests, and when they go home. Look for clues to the workplace culture: the unwritten rules that seem to shape peoples' behaviour.

Take notes
During your first day, you'll cover lots of details. First, there's the obvious stuff—where to sit, where to park, where to eat, where to make photocopies, where to take breaks. Then there's higher-level stuff, such as phone numbers, and user IDs and passwords for Internet access. Be prepared to copy down the details.

Minerva Studio/Shutterstock.com

Pack a briefcase or messenger bag
Companies tend to push paper at new employees—brochures, forms, maps, manuals, and more. When you receive these things, look at them for a few seconds then place the papers in a professional-looking folder or briefcase. Take these handouts home to read.

Go easy on yourself
Notice whether there's a self-critical voice in your head that's saying something like this: "You're not fooling anyone—you really have no idea what you're doing here." No one else hears that voice. In this competitive job market, they hired you because you have what it takes to succeed—try to demonstrate the confidence they have in you. To really shine as a new employee, focus on your people skills. If you demonstrate that you're willing to listen and learn, you'll have done good work on your first day. ✳

Did you **know that ...?**

There are academic programs in beer making offered at several colleges and universities across Canada, such as Niagara College and Kwantlen Polytechnic University. It is possible to combine your interests with your studies, so check out the possibilities when you're considering the next steps in your journey.

Choosing schools . . .
AGAIN

CHANGING TO A different school involves making a decision that will have a major impact on your education. This is true at many points in postsecondary education—whether you're first choosing a university program, or transferring from a community college to a university, or choosing a graduate school or a post-degree diploma at a college.

kitty/Shutterstock.com

Chances are you will attend more than one postsecondary institution throughout your life, whether you choose to return to school to acquire new career skills or because you just want to continue to expand your mind. Lifelong learning is the norm for Canadians, with more and more of them engaging in furthering their education after high school. Selecting the school that has the best fit for you requires that you learn a bit more about what is out there. The options today are endless—from face-to-face classes to online programs to hybrid courses. Figuring out what works best for you means taking the time to learn more about the postsecondary opportunities that are available.

Know key terms

As you begin researching your next school, take a few minutes to review some key terms:

Undergraduate university degree program. Offers three- or four-year academic studies at university that lead to degrees such as Bachelor of Arts (B.A.), Bachelor of Science (B.S.), or Bachelor of Commerce (B.Comm.) degrees.

Four-year applied college degree program. Offers the best of both worlds: the practical, technical strengths of a college education and the theoretical foundation of a bachelor's degree.

Joint college/university collaborative program. Offers a collaborative learning environment that involves taking courses at both the college and university levels.

Post-diploma/post-graduate/post-certificate program. Builds on knowledge and experience gained through previous postsecondary study and may result in an additional diploma, certificate, or degree. Often includes some hands-on experience in the workplace through internships or practicum.

Co-op program. Offers in-school training through scheduled periods of employment in related industries within the academic year, often paid and required for graduation. These programs are offered at both colleges and universities.

Apprenticeship program. Provides provincial certification in a trade after completing provincial training requirements; usually includes 75 to 90 percent learning time on-the-job and the remaining 10 to 25 percent in the classroom (Industry Training Authority, 2017).

Gather information

To find out more about your new school, you need to do research. Go online and look at the school websites; write to request the school's viewbook. Go to *campusstarter.com* to get a complete list of college and university programs in Canada plus links to the school websites. The *Globe Campus* at *www.globecampus.ca*

provides in-depth articles on Canadian colleges and universities. Talk to the school's recruitment officers, academic counsellors, and other staff members. If you can talk to students who have gone to the school you are considering, that is another great source of information.

Find out if there are any college fairs happening in your city. From Halifax to Vancouver, university fairs are held annually in many of Canada's major cities and are a great way to comparison shop on the spot. Both *Maclean's* magazine, through its annual rankings of universities, and *The Globe and Mail*'s University Report Card can give you more information to consider in making your choice.

You might also want to check to see if the institution has participated in the *National Survey of Student Engagement (NSSE)*. *NSSE* measures students' participation in activities, both inside and outside the classroom, that lead to deep learning (Pascarella, Seifert, & Blaich, 2010). Take a look and see whether students feel there is a high degree of student–faculty interaction or opportunities for experiential education. This again could provide an important benchmark for you to use to compare institutions you might be considering attending. Institutions that have participated in NSSE often list their outcomes on their websites. Finally, take the time to visit your top two or three picks and look for the place that feels right to you. Use your research to find out more about key factors such as the following:

- **Number of students.** Large Canadian universities can have a full-time student body numbering 50,000 or more. Smaller universities, colleges, and vocational schools might have fewer than 1,000 students, with most somewhere in between. According to the University Report Card, a survey produced annually by *The Globe and Mail*, larger universities are often considered impersonal and lacking in school spirit. Smaller colleges often score higher with students in terms of personal attention and quality of education but are criticized for problems with student services and poor campus facilities, such as inadequate libraries.

- **Class sizes.** Large educational institutions might enrol 800 in an introductory course. At smaller institutions, classes might number between 20 and 30 people, especially in specialized courses. Within a single school class sizes can vary between course levels and departments. Ask how often you can expect to have smaller classes, particularly in the upper-year courses.

- **Contact with instructors.** Schools vary concerning who they have teaching their classes. Some classes may be taught by part-time faculty who are experts in their field or by full-time faculty who spend a lot of their time doing research. Other classes may be taught by a graduate teaching assistant who is just learning to teach. If you value close contact with your instructors, this is a crucial factor to investigate, especially at the graduate level.

- **Work integrated learning (WIL).** Look to see if there are opportunities for WIL at the college or university. Currently about 2/3 of college graduates and ½ of university graduates participate in some form of WIL—field placements, internships, co-ops, practicums, or service-learning placements. Having some form of WIL as part of your program of study leads to greater likelihood of being hired and higher salaries (Sattler, 2011). Many employers want a minimum of two years work experience even for entry level jobs. Opportunities to apply what you learn in the classroom can greatly enhance your educational experience. In addition, participating in WIL is a great way to determine if this is the job for you and to get your foot in the door of a company. The availability of study abroad programs can also greatly deepen the learning experience. Schools should be able to tell you if the work experiences are paid or unpaid, or for study abroad, if bursaries are available.

- **Admissions criteria.** Institutions may have open access policies or they may be highly competitive in who they admit. Find out by looking at their admission policies.

- **Availability of degrees.** Community colleges and vocational-technical schools commonly offer diplomas or certificates. For university grads, community college diplomas are often a way to gain applied skills that lead directly to employment (Belford, 2009). Most college programs include some type of experiential education component, such as internships or co-op placements, that employers value. Other colleges and universities generally offer four-year degrees, such as the Bachelor of Arts (B.A.) or Bachelor of Science (B.S.). Many larger educational institutions also offer graduate programs, leading to master's and doctoral degrees, or specialized degrees in law, medicine, or dentistry.

- **Costs.** Tuition fees at Canadian colleges and universities vary, with the average cost at about $6,500 per year for a full-time student; however, professional degrees such as dentistry tend to have significantly higher fees. Other costs include books, materials, housing, health insurance, student fees, and laboratory fees.

- **Location.** The educational institution you choose may be composed primarily of commuter students or it may be residential in nature. This can greatly

Don't be afraid to change directions

When I left high school in the '70s, I had a dream of being a rock star. I attended the music program at Humber College before taking to the road in a band with a few friends. It was quickly apparent to me that I lacked the talent necessary to be successful as a musician. I figured that perhaps I could go to the university and use my music background to become a music teacher. Standing in line to register for classes—yep, standing in line—I had second thoughts and decided to take a few psychology courses until I "got things figured out." I finished that undergraduate degree and followed it with an MSc at McMaster, a PhD at Auburn and a post-doc at Purdue. Clearly the path one starts on can take many twists and turns. My message here is simple: it's okay if you are not sure about your path. Explore your options and don't be afraid to change directions. Everything you do adds to your experience. Nothing is ever lost.

—Daniel J. Weeks, president and vice-chancellor at University of Northern British Columbia (*Maclean's*, 2017)

colour your experience of postsecondary education. Take this opportunity to try something new and to explore Canada.

- **Diversity.** This term can apply to faculty members as well as students. Today most large Canadian universities have a highly diverse student body in terms of race, nationality, religion, culture, language, and sexual orientation.

Dig up other key facts

Gather the facts about your current academic profile. This includes marks, courses completed, degrees attained, and grade point average (GPA). Check course equivalents at your new institution with a registrar or an admissions office. Since no two educational institutions offer the same curriculum, determining which of your courses are accepted is often a matter of interpretation. Keep a folder of syllabuses from your courses; they can be useful when transferring credits.

After totalling the costs of attending an educational institution, check on the financial aid that is available to you.

Choose your new school

If you follow the above suggestions, you'll end up with stacks of publications and pages of notes. As you sort through all this information, remember that your impressions of a school will go beyond a dry list of facts.

Also pay attention to your instincts and intuitions—your "gut feelings" of attraction to one school or hesitation about another. These impressions can be important to your choice. Allow time for such feelings to emerge.

You can also benefit from putting your choice of schools in a bigger context. Consider the purposes, values, and long-term goals you've generated by doing the exercises and Journal Entries in this book. Consider which school is most likely to support the body of discoveries and intentions that you've created.

As you choose your new school, consider the needs and wishes of your family members and friends. Ask for their guidance and support. If you involve them in the decision, they'll have more stake in your success.

At some point, you'll just choose a school. Remember that there is no one "right" choice. You could probably thrive at many schools—perhaps even at your current one. Use the suggestions in this book to practise responsibility for yourself. Take charge of your education no matter which school you attend.

Succeed at your new school

Be willing to begin again

Some students approach a transfer with a "been there, done that" attitude. Having enrolled in higher education before, they assume that they don't need the orientation, academic counselling, or other student services available at their new school.

Consider an alternative. Since your tuition and fees cover all these services, you might as well take advantage of them. By doing so, you could uncover opportunities that you missed while researching schools. At the very least, you'll meet people who will support your transition.

Your prior experience in higher education gives you strengths. Acknowledge them, even as you begin again at your new school. While celebrating your past accomplishments, you can explore new paths to student success.

Connect to people

At your new school, you'll be in classes with people who have already developed social networks. To avoid feeling left out, seek out chances to meet people. Join study groups, check out extracurricular activities, and consider volunteering for student organizations. Making social connections can ease your transition to a new academic environment. ✳

CONTRIBUTING:
The art of giving back or paying forward

THE TECHNIQUES AND suggestions in these pages focus on ways to get more out of school and out of life. If they remain unused, the techniques and strategies in this book make no difference in all this. However, *you* can make a difference. By working with and for others, you can contribute to a new future for our planet.

Our interdependence calls for contributing

Every day we depend on contributing. We stake our lives on the compassion of other people. When we drive, we depend on others for our lives. If a driver in an oncoming lane should cross into our lane, we might die. People everywhere are growing more interdependent. A decrease in oil prices gives businesses everywhere a shot in the arm. A tsunami in Japan can cause widespread devastation and lead to the slowing down of automobile manufacturing in Canada.

In this interdependent world, there is no such thing as win/lose. If others lose, their loss directly affects us. If we lose, it is more difficult to contribute to others. The only way to win and to get what we want in life is for others to win, also.

Besides, contributing means getting involved with other people. This is one way to break the ice in a new community and meet people with interests similar to your own. If you want to build community, then contribute.

FrameStockFootages/Shutterstock.com

You can start to experience the advantages of contributing right now. Don't wait for disasters to motivate your volunteerism. The world will welcome your gifts of time, money, and talent.

How you can begin contributing

When you've made the decision to contribute, the next step is knowing how. There are ways to contribute in your immediate surroundings. Visit a neighbour, take a family member to a movie, offer to tutor a roommate, or participate in an alternative spring break program where you volunteer abroad. Your school will probably host a volunteer fair at the start of the school year. Check online for local sites in your area (search for "volunteer" and your city). Volunteering gives you a way to contribute to society and it allows you to explore possible career choices. Consider the following organizations, for starters. ✳

Purpose of the organization/ Group/Event	Sample organizations
Mentoring youth	Girl Guides, Boy Scouts, Big Brothers, Big Sisters, Junior Achievement, your church, an elementary school
Environmental issues	The Canadian Environmental Network, Greenpeace, World Wildlife Fund
Human rights	Amnesty International, Pen Canada
To serve others	Kiwanis, Lions, Rotary International, WE, Habitat for Humanity
Poverty	Oxfam, CARE, The Hunger Project, local food banks
Health and well-being	Canadian Cancer Society, Canadian National Institute for the Blind (CNIB), Heart and Stroke, Canadian Women's Health Network, Canadian Aids Society, or local hospice or nursing homes
Multicultural issues	Centre for Race and Culture, National Organization of Immigrant and Visible Minority Women of Canada, and local multicultural groups
Disaster relief	Canadian Red Cross, Doctors Without Borders, Engineers Without Borders
Local arts	Local museums, art galleries, festivals
Mental health issues	Canadian Mental Health Association, Centre for Addiction and Mental Health (CAMH), Canadian Schizophrenia Society, Jack.org, local distress centres
LGBTQQ issues	PFLAG Canada, the Trevor Project, Pink Shirt Day, Pride Day celebrations
Children internationally	Plan International, WE.org
Animal rights	Animal Welfare Foundation of Canada, Animal Alliance of Canada, local Humane Societies

practising
CRITICAL THINKING

12-7

List your strengths, skills, and competencies

Make a list of the strengths, skills, and competencies you have developed in the past year.

_____

_____

_____

_____

Now go online and research two national and two local non-profit organizations or agencies that might make use of your strengths, skills, and competencies. Record their Web addresses and describe what you could do as a volunteer for them.

_____

_____

_____

_____

_____

_____

_____

_____

_____

Make a commitment to volunteer at least one day in the coming month for one of the organizations you have listed.

I promise to commit my time

_____

COMMUNITY SERVICE-LEARNING
The art of learning by contributing

As part of a community service-learning project for a sociology course, students volunteer at a community centre for older adults. For another service-learning project, history students interview people in seniors' residences about their immigration to Canada.

Meanwhile, arts students work collaboratively on a community-based cultural production. Photography students facilitate digital photography workshops for teens in the downtown core. Other students learn about nutritional health issues and youth and then create a curriculum that can be delivered in the classroom to youth.

These examples of actual projects from the Canadian Alliance for Community Service-Learning demonstrate the working premise of service-learning—that volunteer work and other forms of contributing can become a vehicle for postsecondary education.

Service-learning projects generally include three elements: meaningful community service, a formal academic curriculum, and time for students to reflect on what they learn from service. That reflection can include speeches, journal writing, and essays.

Service-learning creates a win/win scenario. For one thing, as a student you gain the satisfaction of contributing. You also gain experiences that can guide your future career choices and help them develop job skills.

At the same time, community service-learning adds a valuable resource with a handsome return on investment to the community. You can participate in a service-learning project as part of a course you take (look for experiential learning opportunities), as part of campus-led alternative spring break program, through campus service-learning days, or through external organizations such as *Me to We Social Enterprises*.

When you choose a community service-learning project, consider these suggestions:

Work with a community agency that has experience with students. Make sure that the agency has liability insurance to cover volunteers.

© Douglas Keddy, The University of Western Ontario

Handle logistics. Integrating service-learning into your schedule can call for detailed planning. If your volunteer work takes place off campus, arrange for transportation and allow for travel time.

Reflect on your service-learning project with a tool you've used throughout this book—the Discovery and Intention Journal Entry system. Write Discovery Statements about what you want to gain from service-learning and how you feel about what you're doing. Follow up with Intention Statements about what you'll do differently for your next volunteer experience.

Let your participation in a service-learning project be the first step to continued involvement in making change in the community you live in. "Be the Change" you want to see in the world. As you do, you'll be gaining valuable skills and knowledge that you can apply in the workplace. ✳

DEFINE YOUR VALUES,
align your actions

ONE KEY WAY to choose what's next in your life is to define your values. Values are the things in life that you want for their own sake. Values influence and guide your choices, including your moment-by-moment choices of what to do and what to have. Your values define who you are and who you want to be.

Some people are guided by values that they automatically adopt from others or by values that remain largely unconscious. These people could be missing the opportunity to live a life that's truly of their own choosing.

Investing time and energy to define your values is a pivotal suggestion in this book. In fact, *Becoming a Master Student* is based on a particular value system that underlies suggestions given throughout the book. This system includes these values:

- Focussed attention
- Grit
- Responsibility
- Integrity
- Risk-taking
- Contributing

You'll find these values and related ones directly stated in the Power Processes throughout the text:

Discover what you want (Introduction) is about the importance of living a purpose-based life.

Ideas are tools (Chapter 1) points to the benefits of being willing to experiment with new ideas.

Persist (Chapter 2) expresses the value of sticking with tasks even when the going gets tough.

Love your problems (and experience your barriers) (Chapter 3) is about seeing difficulties as opportunities to develop new skills.

Notice your pictures and let them go (Chapter 4) is about adopting an attitude of open-mindedness.

I create it all (Chapter 5) is about taking responsibility for our beliefs and behaviours.

Detach (Chapter 6) reminds us that our core identity and value as a person does not depend on our possessions, our circumstances, or even our accomplishments.

Embrace the new (Chapter 7) is about being willing to try new ideas or activities while holding on to your core values.

Employ your word (Chapter 8) expresses the value of making and keeping agreements.

Choose your conversations and your community (Chapter 9) reminds us of the power of language, and that we can reshape our lives by taking charge of our thoughts.

Risk being a fool (Chapter 10) is about courage—the willingness to take risks for the sake of learning something new.

Surrender (Chapter 11) points to the value of human community and the power of asking for help.

Be it (Chapter 12) is specifically about the power of attitudes—the idea that change proceeds from the inside out as we learn to see ourselves in new ways.

In addition, most of the study skills and life skills you read about in these pages have their source in values. The Time Monitor/Time Plan exercise, for example, calls for focussed attention. Even the simple act of sharing your notes with a student who missed a class is an example of contributing.

As you begin to define your values, consider those who have gone before you. In creeds, scriptures, philosophies, myths, and sacred stories, the human race has left a vast and varied record of values. Be willing to look everywhere, including sources that are close to home. The creed of your local place of worship might eloquently describe some of your values—so might the mission statement of your school, company, or club. Another way to define your values is to describe the qualities of people you admire.

Although defining your values is powerful, it doesn't guarantee any results. You must translate your values into behaviour. To achieve your goals, take actions that align with your values. ✳

journal entry 12-2

Discovery/Intention Statement

Revisiting Your Discovery Wheel

The purpose of this Journal Entry is to (1) review both of the Discovery Wheels you completed in this book, (2) summarize your insights from doing them, and (3) declare how you will use these insights to promote your continued success in school.

Again, a lower score on the second Discovery Wheel does not necessarily indicate decreased personal effectiveness. Instead, the lower score could result from increased honesty and greater self-awareness.

	Chapter 1	Chapter 12
Attitude	_____	_____
Time	_____	_____
Memory	_____	_____
Reading	_____	_____
Notes	_____	_____
Tests	_____	_____
Thinking	_____	_____
Communicating	_____	_____
Diversity	_____	_____
Money	_____	_____
Health	_____	_____
Purpose	_____	_____

Comparing the Discovery Wheel in this chapter with the Discovery Wheel in Chapter 1, I discovered that I . . .

_____

_____

_____

_____

_____

_____

_____

In the next six months, I intend to review the following articles from this book for additional suggestions I could use:

_____

_____

_____

_____

_____

_____

practising
CRITICAL THINKING 12-8

This book shouts, "Use me!"

Becoming a Master Student is designed to be used for years. The success strategies presented here are not likely to become habits overnight. There are more suggestions than can be put into action immediately. Some of what is discussed might not apply to your life right now, but might be just what you could use in a few months.

Plan to keep this book and use it again. Imagine that your book has a voice. (Visualize the mouth.) Also imagine that it has arms and legs. (Visualize them.)

Now picture your book sitting on a shelf or table that you see every day. Imagine a time when you are having trouble in school and struggling to be successful as a student. Visualize your book jumping up and down, shouting, "Use me! Read me! I might have the solution to your problem, and I know I can help you solve it."

This is a memory technique you can use to remind you to use any resource. Sometimes when you are stuck, all you need is a small push or a list of possible actions. At those times, hear your book shout, "Use me!"

The Discovery Wheel: Coming full circle

This book doesn't work. It is worthless. Only you can work. Only you can make a difference and use this book to become a more effective student.

The purpose of this book is to give you the opportunity to change your behaviour. The fact that something seems like a good idea doesn't necessarily mean that you will put it into practice. This exercise gives you a chance to see what behaviours you have changed on your journey toward becoming a master student.

Answer each question quickly and honestly. Record your results on the Discovery Wheel in Figure 12.4. Only after filling out the new Discovery Wheel should you compare it with the one you completed in Chapter 1.

The scores on this Discovery Wheel indicate your current strengths and weaknesses on your path toward becoming a master student. The last Journal Entry in this chapter provides an opportunity to write about how you intend to change. As you complete this self-evaluation, keep in mind that your commitment to change allows you to become a master student. *Your scores might be lower here than on your earlier Discovery Wheel.* That's OK. Lower scores might result from increased self-awareness and honesty, and other valuable assets.

Note: The online version of this exercise does not include number ratings, so the results will be formatted differently than described here. If you did your previous Discovery Wheel online, do it online again. This will help you compare your two sets of responses more accurately.

5 points	This statement is always or almost always true of me.
4 points	This statement is often true of me.
3 points	This statement is true of me about half the time.
2 points	This statement is seldom true of me.
1 point	This statement is never or almost never true of me.

1 Attitude

_____ I enjoy learning.

_____ I understand and apply the concept of multiple intelligences.

_____ I connect my courses to my purpose for being in school.

_____ I make a habit of assessing my personal strengths and areas for improvement.

_____ I am satisfied with how I am progressing toward achieving my goals.

_____ I use my knowledge of learning styles to support my success in school.

_____ I am willing to consider any idea that can help me succeed in school—even if I initially disagree with that idea.

_____ I regularly remind myself of the benefits I intend to get from my education.

_____ **Total Score: Attitude**

2 Time

_____ I set long-term goals and periodically review them.

_____ I set short-term goals to support my long-term goals.

_____ I write a plan for each day and each week.

_____ I assign priorities to what I choose to do each day.

_____ I plan regular recreation time.

_____ I adjust my study time to meet the demands of individual courses.

_____ I have adequate time each day to accomplish what I plan.

_____ I plan review time so that I don't have to cram before exams.

_____ **Total Score: Time**

③ Memory

_____ I am confident of my ability to remember.

_____ I can remember people's names.

_____ At the end of a lecture, I can summarize what was presented.

_____ I apply techniques that enhance my memory skills.

_____ I can recall information when I'm under pressure.

_____ I remember important information clearly and easily.

_____ I can jog my memory when I have difficulty recalling.

_____ I can relate new information to what I've already learned.

_____ **Total Score: Memory**

④ Reading

_____ I preview and review reading assignments.

_____ When reading, I ask myself questions about the material.

_____ I underline or highlight important passages when reading.

_____ When I read textbooks, I am alert and awake.

_____ I relate what I read to my life.

_____ I select a reading strategy to fit the type of material I'm reading.

_____ I take effective notes when I read.

_____ When I don't understand what I'm reading, I note my questions and find answers.

_____ **Total Score: Reading**

⑤ Notes

_____ When I am in class, I focus my attention.

_____ I take notes in class.

_____ I am aware of various methods for taking notes and choose those that work best for me.

_____ I distinguish important material and note key phrases in a lecture.

_____ I copy down material that the instructor writes on the chalkboard or overhead projector.

_____ I can put important concepts into my own words.

_____ My notes are valuable for review.

_____ I review class notes within 24 hours.

_____ **Total Score: Notes**

⑥ Tests

_____ I use techniques to manage stress related to exams.

_____ I manage my time during exams and am able to complete them.

_____ I am able to predict test questions.

_____ I adapt my test-taking strategy to the kind of test I'm taking.

_____ I understand what essay questions ask and can answer them completely and accurately.

_____ I start reviewing for tests at the beginning of the term.

_____ I continue reviewing for tests throughout the term.

_____ My sense of personal worth is independent of my test scores.

_____ **Total Score: Tests**

⑦ Thinking

_____ I have flashes of insight and often think of solutions to problems at unusual times.

_____ I use brainstorming to generate solutions to a variety of problems.

_____ When I get stuck on a creative project, I use specific methods to get unstuck.

_____ I see problems and tough decisions as opportunities for learning and personal growth.

_____ I am willing to consider different points of view and alternative solutions.

_____ I can detect common errors in logic.

_____ I construct viewpoints by drawing on information and ideas from many sources.

_____ As I share my viewpoints with others, I am open to their feedback.

_____ **Total Score: Thinking**

⑧ Communicating

_____ I am candid with others about who I am, what I feel, and what I want.

_____ Other people tell me that I am a good listener.

_____ I can communicate my upset and anger without blaming others.

_____ I can make friends and create valuable relationships in a new setting.

_____ I am open to being with people I don't especially like in order to learn from them.

_____ I can effectively plan and research a large writing assignment.

_____ I create first drafts without criticizing my writing, then edit later for clarity, accuracy, and coherence.

_____ I know ways to prepare and deliver effective speeches.

_____ **Total Score: Communicating**

9 Diversity

_____ I am aware of my biases and am open to understanding people from other cultures, nationalities, and ethnic groups.

_____ I build rewarding relationships with people from other backgrounds.

_____ I can point out examples of discrimination and sexual harassment and effectively respond to them.

_____ I am learning ways to thrive with diversity—attitudes and behaviours that will support my career success.

_____ I can effectively resolve conflict with people from other cultures.

_____ My writing and speaking are free of sexist and homophobic expressions.

_____ I can recognize bias and discrimination in the media.

_____ I use technology in a way that enriches my life and supports my success.

_____ **Total Score: Diversity**

10 Money

_____ I am in control of my personal finances.

_____ I can access a variety of resources to finance my education.

_____ I am confident that I will have enough money to complete my education.

_____ I take on debts carefully and repay them on time.

_____ I have long-range financial goals and a plan to meet them.

_____ I make regular deposits to a savings account.

_____ I pay off the balance on credit card accounts each month.

_____ I can have fun without spending money.

_____ **Total Score: Money**

11 Health

_____ I have enough energy to study and still fully enjoy other areas of my life.

_____ If the situation calls for it, I have enough reserve energy to put in a long day.

_____ The food I eat supports my long-term health.

_____ The way I eat is independent of my feelings of self-worth.

_____ I exercise regularly to maintain a healthful weight.

_____ My emotional health supports my ability to learn.

_____ I notice changes in my physical condition and respond effectively.

_____ I am in control of any alcohol or other drugs I put into my body.

_____ **Total Score: Health**

12 Purpose

_____ I see learning as a lifelong process.

_____ I relate school to what I plan to do for the rest of my life.

_____ I learn by contributing to others.

_____ I have written a career plan and update it regularly.

_____ I am gaining skills to support my success in the workplace.

_____ I take responsibility for the quality of my education and my life.

_____ I live by a set of values that translates into daily actions.

_____ I am willing to accept challenges even when I'm not sure how to meet them.

_____ **Total Score: Purpose**

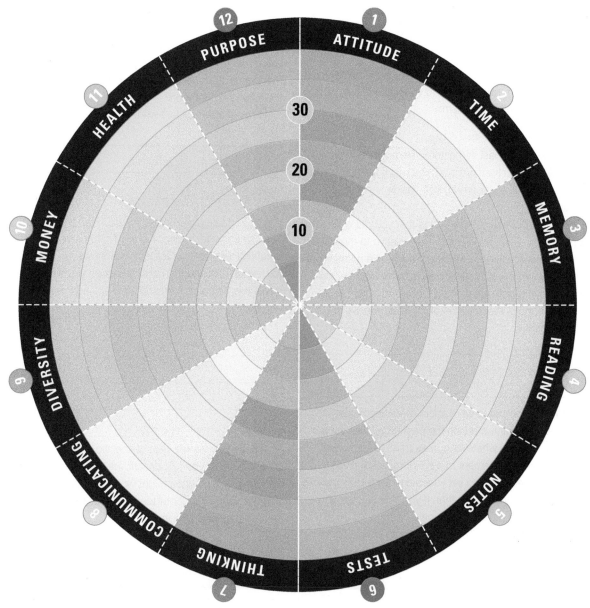

Figure 12.4 **Your Discovery Wheel**

© Cengage Learning

Filling in your Discovery Wheel.

Using the total score from each category, shade in each section of the Discovery Wheel.
Use different colours, if you want. For example, you could use green to denote areas you want to work on.
When you have finished, complete Journal Entry 12-2.

Create your next semester or term

This exercise offers a chance to celebrate your successes during the past term—and to think in specific ways about what you want to create next term.

Part 1: Update your First Step

Looking back on this past semester or term, you might be surprised at how quickly it went by. You might also be surprised at how much you learned, both inside and outside the classroom.

In the space below, list three things that you did well during the current term. Perhaps you took the initiative to meet a new person or created an effective way to take notes in class. Write down any success that you find personally significant, no matter how small it might seem to others. If you are working in the printed version of this text, you will need additional paper.

1. _____

2. _____

3. _____

Now take a moment to write about three things that did not go as well as you wanted during the past term. Give yourself permission to explore whatever comes to mind—anything from a simple embarrassment to a major mistake. If you missed a class because you set your alarm for 7 p.m. instead of 7 a.m., you can write about that. If you failed a test, you might describe that experience as well.

As you practise truth-telling, remember to keep it light. It's fine to acknowledge slip-ups and to laugh at yourself as you do.

1. _____

2. _____

3. _____

Part 2: Determine what you want next

You've come a long way since first setting foot on campus. Now consider where you want to go next term. Brainstorm some intentions in several areas of your life. Then channel them into some new behaviours.

Do this activity by building on the writing you did in Part 1 of this exercise. Reflect on ways to maintain or expand on the successes you listed. Also consider ways to change or prevent some of the experiences you didn't like.

Determine what you want from academics. For instance, you could set a goal to raise your average to a specific number, or to declare your major by a certain date. Complete the following sentence.

In my academic life, I want to . . .

_____

_____

_____

Now consider your social life. Perhaps you want to resolve a conflict with an instructor or roommate. Or you might want to deepen a connection with someone you already know and make this person a friend for life. Put such goals in writing by completing the following sentence.

In my social life, I want to . . .

_____

_____

_____

Finally, brainstorm a list of specific actions you can take to meet the goals you just described. Write these actions below. Reflect on which ones might work best for you and record them in your calendar or to-do list. For more suggestions on goal setting, see Chapter 2.

_____

_____

_____

_____

_____

_____

_____

_____

_____

_____

_____

Be It

Use this Power Process to enhance all of the techniques in this book.

Consider that most of our choices in life fall into three categories. We can do the following:

- Increase our material wealth (what we have)
- Improve our skills (what we do)
- Develop our "being" (who we are)

Many people devote their entire lifetime to the first two categories. They act as if they are "human havings" instead of human beings. For them, the quality of life hinges on what they have. They devote most of their waking hours to getting more—more clothes, more cars, more relationships, more degrees, more trophies. "Human havings" define themselves by looking at the circumstances in their lives—what they have.

Some people escape this materialist trap by adding another dimension to their identities. In addition to living as "human havings," they also live as "human doings." They thrive on working hard and doing everything well. They define themselves by how efficiently they do their jobs, how effectively they raise their children, and how actively they participate in clubs and organizations. Their thoughts are constantly about methods, techniques, and skills.

In addition to focussing on what we have and what we do, we can also focus on our being. That last word describes how we see ourselves.

All of the techniques in this book can be worthless if you operate with the idea that you are an ineffective student. You might do almost everything this book suggests and still never achieve the success in school that you desire.

Instead, picture yourself as a master student right now. Through higher education, you are simply gaining knowledge and skills that reflect and reinforce this view of yourself. Change the way you see yourself. Then watch your actions and results shift as if by magic.

Remember that "Be It" is not positive thinking or mental cheerleading. This Power Process works well when you take a First Step—when you tell the truth about your current abilities. The very act of accepting who you are and what you can do right now unleashes a powerful force for personal change.

If you can first visualize where you want to be, if you can go there in your imagination, if you can "be it" today, then you set yourself up to succeed.

If you want it, be it.

Put it to WORK

Plan for change

Even the most brilliant people can fall flat when predicting trends in business and the workplace. Case in point: Thomas Watson, founder of IBM, said, "I think there's a world market for about five computers" (Isaac, 2007).

Still, you can benefit from making predictions about changes in the workplace that affect your own employment opportunities. Keep up to date with breaking changes as you decide what's next in your career. This is easier to do than ever before, thanks to resources mentioned throughout this book:

- *The Internet.* Use your skills in searching the Internet to find websites devoted to your field. Start by keying your job title into a search engine such as Google. Also search for career-related listservs—programs that distribute email messages to groups of people with similar interests.

- *News Media.* Read the business sections of *The Globe and Mail* and *The Wall Street Journal,* for example. Almost all newspapers and general interest magazines, such as *Maclean's* and *Business Week*, have online editions.

- *Professional associations.* People in similar jobs like to band together and give each other a heads-up on emerging trends, which is one reason professional associations have been formed. These range from the Canadian Medical Association to the Chartered Professional Accountants of Canada. There's bound to be one for people in your field. Ask colleagues and search the Internet. (Note: Almost all associations have websites and publish newsletters or trade magazines online.)

- *Conferences and conventions.* Many professional associations sponsor annual meetings. Here's where you can meet people face-to-face and use your networking skills. Print and online publications are powerful sources of news, but sometimes nothing beats plain old schmoozing.

Make yourself indispensable

Look for ways to excel at your job by building relationships, becoming a rock-star collaborator, and consistently delivering results. Whenever possible, exceed your work-related goals. These are strategies for surviving layoffs and increasing job security.

Keep your career plan alive

Write your career goals on index cards or sticky notes. Post these in places where you can't miss them—your desk, your bathroom mirror, your car. Put your vision for the future in front of your face.

Evan Lorne/Shutterstock.com

Use technology to power your job search

Social networking sites such as *LinkedIn* are designed for you to connect with employers. Create a professional profile on these sites and build a network of contacts. Begin this process now. Develop relationships over time, well before you start applying for jobs.

Remember that you can use Facebook, Twitter, and similar sites for professional purposes. Use their search functions to find companies that interest you—and names of people within those companies who could hire you. After "following" these people for a while and establishing a friendly online connection, you might be able to send them a direct message. In addition, search for blogs related to your career interests. Pay special attention to blogs that include job listings.

Consider launching your own professional blog. Include an online resumé and articles with useful content for people in your field. Be prepared to add new content weekly, or even daily, especially during your job search.

Now create a career connection of your own

Review this chapter, looking for at least one suggestion that you will commit to use while working or looking for a job. In a sentence or two, describe exactly what you plan to do and the primary benefits you want to gain. For example, "I will register for workshops and seminars that help me keep my skills up to date. This will help me stay in the career of my choice."

State your strategies and desired benefits in the space below:

_____

_____

_____

_____

_____

QUIZ

Name_____ Date____/____/____

1. According to the text, you can create a career plan through the process of "naming names." True or False? Explain your answer.

2. Explain how work *content skills* and *transferable skills* differ. Give one example of each kind of skill.

3. Explain how career planning can be a process of choosing instead of a process of discovery.

4. List three suggestions for designing an effective service-learning project.

5. Describe the three main types of life choices explained in the Power Process: "Be It."

6. List at least three ways you can used social media to help you with your job search.

7. If your scores are lower on the Discovery Wheel the second time you complete it, that means your study skills have not improved. True or False? Explain your answer.

8. Contributing to others does *not* involve
   (a) telling people what is best for them
   (b) finding out what people want or need
   (c) determining if you can help people get what they want
   (d) giving your time, talent, or money
   (e) making sure that you experience satisfaction, as well

9. Describe a flaw associated with the typical job-hunting strategy of looking through help wanted advertisements. Suggest an alternative approach to job-hunting.

10. List at least four ways that you can continue on your path of becoming a master student after completing this book.

chapter 12

- ■ Put it to Work
- ■ Quiz
- ▶ ▶ ▶ ▶
- ■ Master Student Profile

Skills **SNAPSHOT**

Jerry Seinfeld told one aspiring comedian that "the way to be a better comic was to create better jokes and the way to create better jokes was to write every day" (Isaac, 2007). Seinfeld also revealed his own system for creating a writing habit: He bought a big wall calendar that displayed the whole year on one page. On each day that he wrote jokes, Seinfeld marked a big red "X" on the appropriate day on the wall calendar. He knew that he'd established a new habit when he looked at the calendar and saw an unbroken chain of "Xs."

So much of success boils down to changing habits. Take a snapshot of your habits as they exist today, after reading and doing this book. Then take the next step toward mastery by committing to a specific action in the near future.

DISCOVERY

During this course, it has been my intention to change the following habits . . .

I would describe my skill at changing those habits as . . .

INTENTION

Three habits that I am committed to changing in the future are . . .

NEXT ACTION

Of the three habits listed above, the one I would like to focus on next is . . .

To experience a new level of mastery at making this habit change, I will . . .

MASTER STUDENT
PROFILE

chapter 12

■ Put it to Work
■ Quiz
■ Skills Snapshot
◄ ◄ ◄ ◄

Craig Kielburger
...is a selfless visionary

© FilmMagic/Getty Images

My grandfather came to Canada from Romania just before the Second World War, already in debt after buying his boat ticket on borrowed dime.

In one sense, the journey was a foolish risk, but I prefer to think of it as selfless and idealistic.

My grandfather didn't come to Canada for his own sake. He came here so that his son, my father, would have a better life.

Some say there is no uniquely Canadian identity, that our multicultural fabric is too varied to establish a common thread. I disagree. My grandfather came to a country that celebrates diversity, embraces strife with compassion and respects selfless idealism.

Canada hasn't always lived up to these ideals. In fact, at times we have failed considerably during our history, which is full of dark passages, including grave injustices against aboriginal peoples.

As we prepare to mark 150 years since Confederation, we look to the past as a learning experience, and to the future to aspire to be better. "WE" is the country's largest youth service organization, and we're betting on the selfless idealism of a new generation. We want to ensure that every Canadian child serves their local and global communities.

I am proud to unveil "WE"—our name and our philosophy. WE provides people with the tools to create positive change at home and around the world.

Above all, WE means recognizing that we're part of a larger community, and that our daily choices have an impact on that community. While so many news outlets, politicians and world leaders seem content

to divide, it's crucial that Canada raises its next generation to think "WE." After all, Canada was the first country in the world to adopt an official policy of multiculturalism. We strive for diversity and inclusion, with social safety nets, equality and democracy. These systems are not perfect, but at their best they embody Canadians' desire to help our neighbours.

To be Canadian is to be selfless. We are idealists who believe there's more that unites us than divides us.

We want to empower Canada's youth to uphold these values by acting on their selfless ideals.

Our WE Schools program offers experiential service learning that helps students develop the life skills for success. And WE Schools is partnering with the Canadian government to create a national service program that will engage our future leaders in volunteer service.

I believe that service learning is the future of education, prepping students with real-life skills in response to real-world issues. Tools gained through service—communication, organization, project management, and complex problem solving—are preparation for entrepreneurs.

Canada must instill the same sense of wonder at our great country that my grandfather had years ago. It's time to usher in the next generation of selfless idealists—for the next 150 years.

Source: Kielburger, Craig. (2016, October 13). Craig Kielburger looks ahead to the next 150 years. *The Globe and Mail*. Accessed at *https://www.theglobeandmail.com/life/giving/craig-kielburger-looks-head-the-next-150-years/article32350561*.

Craig is a *New York Times* bestselling author who has written 12 books. He co-founded WE Charity, which has lifted more than one million people from poverty. He is an MBA graduate with 15 honorary doctorates, and has been awarded by the World Economic Forum and Roosevelt Institute. His purpose is helping others discover their purpose. Craig lives in Toronto with his wife, Leysa, and son, Hilson.

Glossary

Academic tenacity The ability to work hard to achieve long-term education goals even in the face of setbacks. p. 9

Acronyms Words created from the initial letters of a series of words. Can be used as a mnemonic device. p. 125

Affirmation Positive assertion. p. 255

Analogy A similarity between two things or events. p. 243

Anorexia nervosa A physical and emotional illness that leads individuals to severely restrict the food they eat and to have distorted beliefs about their body image. This is a potentially life-threatening eating disorder. p. 365

Assertion A complete sentence that directly answers a key question. p. 232

Binge drinking The consumption of large quantities of alcohol over a short time period—four drinks for women and five for men. p. 384

Blocked practice A study strategy where the student solves similar problems repeatedly. p. 195

Brainstorming A technique for finding solutions, creating plans, and discovering new ideas. Typically used in groups, brainstorming involves people spontaneously trying to generate many potential solutions to problems. p. 237

Brainwriting A creativity technique where groups of individuals generate potential solutions to problems by silently writing down their ideas on paper, sharing their written ideas with others, and using the ideas of their group members to inspire potential solutions to problems. p. 238

Bulimia An eating disorder where normal or near-normal weight adults eat excessively and then use methods such as self-induced vomiting or laxatives to prevent weight gain. p. 365

Cognition Everything that goes on inside your brain—thinking, perceiving, and learning. p. 54

Cognitive dissonance The term used for the tension we feel when we encounter a fact that contradicts our deeply held beliefs. To reduce the discomfort, we might deny the fact or explain it away with deceptive thinking. p. 228

Communication The process of creating shared meaning. p. 265

Communication orientation Seeing public speaking simply as an extension of one-to-one conversation. p. 298

Complex communication The ability to acquire information, explain it, and persuade co-workers that your explanation implies a definite course of action. p. 303

Concept map A diagram in which you draw circles or boxes in a hierarchical fashion and then create links between related ideas. These crosslinks are particularly important. The starting point is often a focus question from which you can branch off. p. 118

Consolidation The memory process when information moves from short-term memory to long-term memory. p. 117

Convergent thinking A narrowing-down process in choosing the most reasonable viewpoint on an issue or solution to a problem. p. 236

Culture A set of learned behaviours and beliefs that characterize a particular group. p. 313

Decode Reactivate neurons that wired together in the past; part of the memory process. p. 109

Deductive reasoning Reasoning from the general to the particular. p. 53

Deep learning In-depth understanding to learn the connections between concepts. p. 115

Discovery Statements A record of what you are learning about yourself as a student—both strengths and weaknesses. Discovery Statements can also be declarations of your goals, descriptions of your attitudes, statements of your feelings, transcripts of your thoughts, and chronicles of your behaviour. p. 5

Discrimination The unfair or unjust treatment of a group of people, often based on race, age, sex, or ability. p. 318

Divergent thinking (also called creative thinking.) The process of generating as many solutions/ideas as possible. p. 236

Diversity Differences of any type. p. 309

Eating disorder Serious disturbances in eating behaviours, such as overeating or extreme reduction of food intake. p. 365

Elaboration Consciously encoding new information by asking yourself questions such as, How does this connect to what I previously learned? or How is this idea similar to what I already know? or When can I use this new idea or technique? p. 117

Emotional intelligence An ability to validly reason with emotions and to use emotions to enhance thought. Recognizing and responding to feelings in skillful ways. Often referred to as "people skills." p. 274

Encode Store information as links between active neurons; part of the memory process. p. 109

Encoding error A mistake that happens during the process of encoding data or learning. p. 110

Equity Being fair and impartial to everyone. p. 309

Extrinsic motivation Motivation when you do tasks or activities for external rewards or to avoid a punishment. p. 61

Fallacies Common mistakes in logic. p. 242

Fixed mindset The concept that your abilities are determined by your genetic predisposition and that you either have a specific talent or you don't. It is the belief that effort doesn't make a difference in influencing the degree to which your talents are manifested. p. 56

Generation A study strategy where you try to anticipate the solution to a problem before being shown the answer. p. 214

Graphic organizer Visual representation of ideas or concepts. p. 118

Grit Perseverance. Those with grit find it easier to maintain their focus on their goals even in the face of serious obstacles and therefore are more likely to achieve long-term goals than those who lack grit. p. 9

Growth mindset The concept that your abilities, such as intelligence or creativity, are determined to a large degree by the effort you put into developing them. p. 9

Heterosexism A system of attitudes, bias, and discrimination that favours heterosexual relationships. p. 376

High context culture A culture where it is up to the listener to get the implicit message from the speaker; e.g. Japan. p. 317

Higher-order thinking skills Thinking that requires manipulation of information and ideas in ways that transform their meaning and implications. For example, synthesizing or hypothesizing to arrive at a conclusion. p. 122

Homophobia A range of negative attitudes including prejudice, fear, and antipathy toward lesbian and gay, and sometimes bisexual and transgendered, people. p. 376

Homophobic bullying Bullying that is based on negative beliefs or prejudices towards people who are perceived to be or who are actually gay. p. 376

"I" messages A technique for communicating when strong emotions might get in the way of the message. Replace "you …" accusations with "I feel" messages that report your own thoughts and feelings. p. 270

Intention Statements Your commitment to do a specific task or take a certain action. An intention arises out of your choice to direct your energy toward a particular goal. p. 5

Intercultural competence The ability "to look at the world through different eyes"; a combination of skills, knowledge, and awareness of other cultures. p. 310

Illusion of knowing When you feel you have mastered new content or concepts but you actually have not; a failure of metacognition. It happens when you are unable to judge correctly your understanding of new concepts or material. p. 195

Inclusion The development of policies and practices that reinforce equity and access, leading to the social inclusion of everyone. p. 310

Interleaved practice Studying by mixing together several subjects or several skills rather than studying one subject at a time. In studying math, for example, students would mix or interleave solving different problem types in one study session. p. 194

Intrinsic goals Objectives that are motivated by internal needs such as the internal satisfaction of doing a good job. p. 61

Intrinsic motivation Motivation from doing a task or activity just for the pleasure of doing it and not for any external reward. p. 61

Learning goals Goals that focus on an internal need to develop competence in a particular area for your own self-improvement; also called mastery goals. p. 79

Learning style Differences in how people prefer to perceive and process information. p. 40

Learning transfer The ability to take what you have been learning and apply it to a new situation or task. p. 117

Loci A synonym for place. Describes a system to create visual associations with familiar locations. p. 126

Long-term memory Our permanent memory store. p. 112

Low context culture A culture where the onus is on the speaker to explicitly convey the message to the listener; e.g. Canada. p. 317

Lower-order thinking skills Receiving or reciting factual information or using rules and algorithms. p. 122

Massed practice Occurs when there is only a short interval between study or practice sessions. p. 194

Mastery Attaining a level of skill that goes beyond technique. p. 8

Mastery goals Learning objectives that focus on the development of competence and task mastery to self-set standards; also known as learning goals. p. 79

Mediator In cross-cultural communication, someone who belongs to the dominant or mainstream culture and who is committed to cultural understanding. p. 317

Metacognition Thinking about thinking, learning about learning. The ability to stand "above" your mental processes—to observe them and to take conscious control of them. p. 54

Mind maps Visual patterns that can serve as a framework for recalling information. They work on both verbal and nonverbal levels, contain lists and sequences, and show relationships. Main ideas are directly connected to a central topic and unlike concept maps the ideas are not cross linked to other topics (they have a single parent). p. 173

Mindset Your philosophy for living and how you view the world. p. 56

Mnemonic devices Tricks that can increase your ability to recall information. p. 125

Model In cross-cultural communication, a model is a member of a culture who is a positive example. p. 317

Motivation The willingness to do something, and the reasons a person has for behaving a certain way. p. 61

Multiculturalism The coexistence of diverse cultures, including racial, ethnic and religious groups with diverse ways of thinking, communication styles, cultural norms, and values. p. 313

Multiple intelligences Gardner's theory of intelligences states that people have different kinds of intelligences. People do not have just one, but use many different intelligences including musical, interpersonal, spatial-visual, and linguistic intelligences. p. 58

Netiquette Common courtesy guidelines for online interpersonal relationships. p. 287

Neural traces Paths in the brain. p. 112

Neuron A specialized cell that is part of the body's nervous system. p. 109

Noise A term used in communication theory to refer to any internal or external factor that distorts meaning. p. 266

Performance goals Short-term goals that are focussed on your own performance relative to the performance of other individuals. p. 78

Performance orientation Belief that the speaker must captivate the audience by using formal techniques that differ from normal conversation. p. 298

Plagiarism Using another person's words, ideas, or pictures without giving proper credit. p. 182

Prejudice An unfavourable opinion, based on stereotypes, about a particular group of people. p. 318

Primacy-recency effect Suggests that we remember most easily the first and last items in any presentation. p. 144

Procrastination Putting off doing something, delaying an action until a later time. p. 63

Proposition A statement linking a new concept to a concept that you already understand; a statement of the relationship between two or more concepts. p. 118

Racism A theory of races hierarchy that presumes that one race is superior to others. p. 314

Reflection Listening, then summarizing what the person says. p. 268

Selective perception The tendency to notice only the stereotypes that support our opinion. p. 320

Self-actualization Realizing your talents and living up to your fullest potential. p. 18

Self-directed learner Learner who shows independence and accountability in setting goals and defining what is worthwhile to learn. p. 185

Self-discipline Controlling your feelings in order to overcome weaknesses; the ability to reject instant gratification in service of a greater goal. p. 61

Self-efficacy Belief in your ability to determine the outcomes of events, especially the outcomes that are strongly influenced by your own behaviour. p. 76

Self-fulfilling prophecy When we set people up in ways that confirm common stereotypes; an error in thinking that often leads to prejudice. p. 320

Self-justification The tendency in stereotypical thinking for someone to assume the role of a victim and avoid taking responsibility for their own lives. p. 320

Self-regulation Ability to set specific goals, monitor your own progress toward those goals, and regularly change your behaviour to produce the desired results. p. 9

Serendipity Something valuable that you weren't looking for. p. 238

Sexism A belief that one sex, typically women, is less able than the other. p. 324

Sexual harassment Unwelcome sexual advances or offensive remarks in the workplace, residence, or educational setting. p. 324

Sexually transmitted infections (STIs). Infections or diseases that are spread through sexual contact, particularly, oral and anal sex and vaginal intercourse. p. 378

Shallow processing Where the information is stored in the brain according to surface features like the shape of the letters or the sound of the words. p. 115

Spaced practice Occurs when you distribute your studying over a period of time. p. 117

Short-term memory The system in your brain that works to temporarily store and manage information. p. 112

Stereotype The assumption that every member of a group is the same. p. 318

Synthesis Combining individual facts into a meaningful whole; an aspect of metacognition. p. 142

Thesis statement One concise sentence that summarizes the content of an essay or speech. p. 289

Translators In cross-cultural communication, a "bicultural" person—someone who relates naturally to people in a mainstream and a contrasting culture. p. 317

Transphobia Discrimination against transsexual or transgender people. p. 376

Willpower The inner strength to make decisions and carry out tasks, regardless of resistance. p. 61

Working memory The part of memory used to plan and carry out behaviours; includes short-term memory and the processing mechanisms that allow us to use the short-term memory store. p. 109

References

A

Adlaf, E. M., Demers, A., and Gliksman, L. (2005) *Canadian Campus Survey 2004.* Toronto, Canada: Centre for Addiction and Mental Health.

Adler, M., & Van Doren, C. (1972). *How to read a book: The classic guide to intelligent reading.* New York, NY: Simon and Schuster.

Agency for Healthcare Research and Quality. (2003). *Men, stay healthy at any age.* Retrieved from http://www.ahrq.gov/ppip/healthymen.htm/

Algonquin College. (2018). *Positive space program.* Retrieved from http://www.algonquincollege.com/counselling/resources/positive-space-workshops/

Allen, D. (2001). *Getting things done: The art of stress-free productivity.* New York, NY: Penguin.

American Cancer Society. (2018). *Prescription drugs to help you quit tobacco.* Retrieved from https://www.cancer.org/healthy/stay-away-from-tobacco/guide-quitting-smoking/prescription-drugs-to-help-you-quit-smoking.html

American College Health Association. (2016). *National college health assessment II: Undergraduate students reference group data report, 2016.* Baltimore, MD: Author

American Psychological Association. (1994). *Diagnostic and statistical manual of psychoactive substance abuse disorders.* Washington, D.C.: American Psychological Association.

Anderson, L. W., & Krathwohl, D. R. (2001). *A taxonomy for learning, teaching and assessing: A revision of Bloom's taxonomy of educational objectives.* New York, NY: Addison, Wesley, Longman.

Arnold, R., Burke, B., James, C., Martin, D., & Thomas, B. (1991). *Educating for a change.* Toronto: Between the Lines Press.

Arthur, N., & Flynn, S. (2013). International students' views of transition to employment and immigration. *The Canadian Journal of Career Development, 12*(1), 28–37.

B

Bain, K. (2012). *What the best college students do.* Cambridge, MA: The Belknap Press of Harvard University Press.

Ballingall, A. (2017, October 25). A majority of Torontonians now identify themselves as visible minorities. *The Star.* Retrieved from https://www.thestar.com/news/gta/2017/10/25/a-majority-of-torontonians-now-identify-themselves-as-visible-minorities-census-shows.html

Bandura, A. (1994). Self-efficacy. In V. S. Ramachaudran (Ed.), *Encyclopedia of Human Behavior* (vol. 4, pp. 71–81). New York, NY: Academic Press.

Barseghian, T. (2013, February 20). How to foster grit, tenacity and perseverance: An educators' guide. *KQED News.* Retrieved from http://ww2.kqed.org/mindshift/2013/02/20/how-to-foster-grit-tenacity-and-perseverance-an-educators-guide/

Barton, A. (2017, June 5). Your kid's brain on pot: The real effect of marijuana on teens. *The Globe and Mail.* Retrieved from https://www.theglobeandmail.com/life/health-and-fitness/health/your-kids-brain-on-pot-the-real-effects-of-marijuana-on-teens/article21127612/

Beck, B. L., Koons, S. R., & Milgrim, D. L. (2000). Correlates and consequences of behavioural procrastination: The effects of academic procrastination, self-consciousness, self-esteem and self-handicapping. *Journal of Social Behavior and Personality, 15*(5), 3–13.

Belford, T. (2009, November 16). Cultivating the new work force. *The Globe Campus.* Retrieved from http://www.globecampus.ca/in-the-news/globecampusreport/cultivating-the-new-work-force/

Bell, K.E., & Limber, J. E. (2010). Reading skill, textbook marking and course performance. *Literacy Research and Instruction, 49,* 56–67.

Bennett, J. M., Bennett, M. J., & Allen, W. (2003). Developing intercultural competence in the language classroom. In D. L. Lange & R. M. Paige (Eds.), *Culture as the core: Perspectives on culture in second language learning* (pp. 237–270). Greenwich, CT: Information Age Publishing.

Bernstein, D. A., Penner, L. A., Clarke-Stewart, A., & Roy, E. J. (2006). *Psychology.* Boston, MA: Houghton Mifflin.

Bohart, A. (2005). *Master student guide to academic success.* Boston, MA: Houghton Mifflin.

Bolles, R. N. (2018). *What color is your parachute? A practical manual for job-hunters and career-changers.* Berkeley, CA: Ten Speed Press.

Bonner, J. M., & Holliday, W. G. (2006, October). How college students engage in note-taking strategies. *Journal of Research in Science Teaching, 43*(8), 786–818.

Brazeau, G. A. (2006, April 15). Handouts in the Classroom: Is note taking a lost skill? *American Journal of Pharmaceutical Education, 70*(2), 38.

Brenza, A. (2016). 7 Habits of super-productive people. *Huffington Post.* Retrieved from http://www.huffingtonpost.com/prevention/7-habits-of-super-productive-people_b_8637820.html?ir=Healthy+Living

Bresciani, M. J., Duncan, A. J., & Hui Cao, L. (2010). Embracing the ambiguity: Twelve considerations for holistic time management. *About Campus, 15*(5), 17–21.

Brody, J. (2006, September 12). Exercise = weight loss, except when it doesn't. *New York Times.* Retrieved from http://www.nytimes.com/2006/09/12/health/nutrition/12brody.html/

Brown, P.C., Roediger III, H.L., & McDaniel, M.A. (2014). *Make it stick: The science of successful learning.* Cambridge, MA: The Belknap Press of Harvard University Press.

Brownlow, S., & Reasinger, R. D. (2000). Putting off until tomorrow what is better done today: Academic procrastination as a function of motivation toward college work. *Journal of Social Behavior and Personality, 15*(5), 15–34.

Burmester, A. (2017, June 5). Working memory: How you keep things "in mind" over the short term. *Scientific American.* Retrieved from https://www.scientificamerican.com/article/working-memory-how-you-keep-things-ldquo-in-mind-rdquo-over-the-short-term/

Buzan, T. (1993). *The mind map book: How to use radiant thinking to maximize your brain's untapped potential.* New York, NY: Plume Penguin.

C

Cain, S. (2013, February 1). Public speaking for introverts: 6 essential tips. *Duarte.* Retrieved June 1, 2014, from http://www.duarte.com/blog/author/susan-cain/

Canadian Bureau for International Education. (2018). *A world of learning: Canada's performance and potential in international education.* Retrieved from https://cbie.ca/media/facts-and-figures/

Canadian Cancer Society. (2018a). *Smoking shortens lives.* Retrieved from http://www.cancer.ca/en/prevention-and-screening/reduce-cancer-risk/make-healthy-choices/live-smoke-free/smoking-shortens-lives/?region=on

Canadian Cancer Society. (2018b). What is second hand smoke and how does it affect you. Retrieved from http://www.cancer.ca/en/prevention-and-screening/reduce-cancer-risk/make-healthy-choices/live-smoke-free/what-is-second-hand-smoke/?region=on

Canadian Mental Health Association. (2011, February 10). *2001 Canadian mental health survey.* Retrieved from http://www.cmha.ca/bins/content_page.asp?cid=5-34-212-213&lang=1/

Canadian Mental Health Association (n.d.) *Partying and getting drunk.* Retrieved from https://www.camh.ca/en/health-info/guides-and-publications/partying-and-getting-drunk

Carlzon, J. (1989). *Moments of truth.* New York, NY: HarperCollins.

Carr, N. (2017, October 6). How smartphones highjack our minds. *The Wall Street Journal.* Retrieved from https://www.wsj.com/articles/how-smartphones-hijack-our-minds-1507307811

Carter, C. (2008). *Keys to effective learning: developing powerful habits of mind* http://webcat2.library.ubc.ca/vwebv/holdingsInfo?searchId=734009&recCount=20&recPointer=0&bibId=3705951&searchType=7. Upper Saddle River, NJ: Pearson Prentice Hall.

Centers for Disease Control and Prevention. (2017a). *Contraception: How effective are birth control methods.* Retrieved from https://www.cdc.gov/reproductivehealth/contraception/index.htm

Centers for Disease Control and Prevention. (2017b). *Fact sheets-Alcohol and Caffeine.* Retrieved from https://www.cdc.gov/alcohol/fact-sheets/caffeine-and-alcohol.htm

Centre for Suicide Prevention. (2011). Retrieved from http://www.suicideinfo.ca/csp/assets/FacingtheFacts.pdf/

Cestnick, T. (2018, March 29). How students can put more money in their pockets at tax time. *The Globe and Mail.* Retrieved from https://www.theglobeandmail.com/investing/personal-finance/taxes/article-how-students-can-put-more-money-in-their-pockets-at-tax-time/

Charbonneau, L. (2014, September 9). A glance at Canada's postsecondary education standings. *University Affairs.* Retrieved from https://www.universityaffairs.ca/opinion/margin-notes/a-glance-at-canadas-postsecondary-education-standings/

Chen, Q., & Yan, Z. (2016). Does multitasking with mobile phones affect learning? A review. Computers in Human Behavior, 54, 34–42.

Chilton, D. B. (1989). The wealthy barber: The common sense guide to successful financial planning. Toronto: Stoddart.

Chiose, S. (2018, May 4). Sexual assault policies have students asking: Are these new systems any better than the courts? *The Globe and Mail.* https://www.theglobeandmail.com/canada/article-sexual-assault-policies-at-universities-have-students-asking-are/

Conference Board of Canada. (2010, November 10). *Employability Skills.* Retrieved from http://www.conferenceboard.ca/topics/education/learning-tools/employability-skills.aspx/

Conference Board of Canada. (2000). *Employability skills 2000+* Brochure 2000 E/F. Ottawa: The Conference Board of Canada.

Cooper, J., & Goren, A. (2007). Cognitive dissonance theory. In R. Baumeister & K. Vohs (Eds.), *Encyclopedia of social psychology* (pp. 150–153). Thousand Oaks, CA: SAGE Publications, Inc. doi: http://dx.doi.org/10.4135/9781412956253.n86

Covey, S. R. (1989, 1990). *The seven habits of highly effective people: Restoring the character ethic.* New York, NY: Simon & Schuster.

Cribb, R. (2017, May 29). Demand for youth mental health services is exploding. How universities and business are scrambling to react. *The Star.* Retrieved from https://www.thestar.com/news/canada/2017/05/29/youth-mental-health-demand-is-exploding-how-universities-and-business-are-scrambling-to-react.html

Cuseo, J. (n.d.). *Academic-support strategies for promoting student retention and achievement during the first year of college. University of Ulster Office of Student Transition and Retention.* Retrieved from http://www.ulst.ac.uk/star/data/cuseoretention.htm#peestud

D

Dean, J. (n.d.). *Jeremy Dean's making habits, breaking habits.* Retrieved from http://www.spring.org.uk/images/Making-Habits-Breaking-Habits-by-Jeremy-Dean-ChapOne.pdf

de Anda, D. (1984). *Bicultural socialization: Factors affecting the minority experience.* Washington, DC: National Association of Social Workers.

Define the line: Clarifying the blurred line between cyberbullying and digital citizenship. Retrieved July 23, 2014, from definetheline.ca

Dewey, J. (1910). *How we think.* Boston, MA: Heath.

Dimitrov, N. (2009). *Western guide to mentoring graduate students across cultures.* London, ON: Teaching Support Centre Purple Guides.

Duckworth, A. (2016). *Grit: The power of passion and perseverance.* New York, NY: Scribner.

Duckworth, A. L., & Eskreis-Winkler, L. (2013). True Grit. *Psychological Science.* Retrieved from http://www.psychologicalscience.org/observer/true-grit

Duckworth, A. L., Peterson, C., Matthews, M. D., & Kelly, D. R. (2007). Grit: Perseverance and passion for long-term goals. *Personality Processes and Individual Differences, 92,* 1087.

Duckworth, A. L., & Seligman, M. E. P. (2005). Self-discipline outdoes IQ in predicting academic performance of adolescents. *Psychological Science, 16,* 939–944.

Duhigg, C. (2012). *The power of habit: Why we do what we do in life and business.* New York, NY: Random House.

Dunlosky, J., Marsh, E. J., Rawson, K. A., Natahn, M. J., & Willingham, D. T. (2013). Improving students' learning with effective learning techniques: Promising directions from cognitive and educational psychology. *Psychological Science in the Public Interest, 14,* 4–58.

Dweck, C. S. (2006). *Mindset: The new psychology of success.* New York, NY: Random House.

Dweck, C. S., Walton, G. M., & Cohen, G. L. (2014). *Academic tenacity: Mindsets and skills that promote life-long learning.* Retrieved from https://ed.stanford.edu/sites/default/files/manual/dweck-walton-cohen-2014.pdf

E

Elbow, P. (1981). *Writing with power: Techniques for mastering the writing process.* New York, NY: Oxford University Press.

Elliot, A. J., Dweck, C. S., & Yeager, D. S. (2017). *Handbook of Competence and Motivation.* New York, NY: The Guilford Press.

Ellis, D. (2006). *From master student to master employee.* Boston, MA: Houghton Mifflin.

Ellis, D. (2006) *Master student guide to academic success.* Boston, MA: Houghton Mifflin.

Ellis, D. (1998). *Creating your future.* Boston, MA: Houghton Mifflin Company.

Ellis, D., & Lankowitz, S. (1995). *Human being: a manual for happiness, health, love, and wealth.* Rapid City, SD: Breakthrough Enterprises.

Ellis, D., Lankowitz, S., Stupka, E., & Toft, D. (2003). *Career planning* (3rd ed.). Boston, MA: Houghton Mifflin Company.

Ericsson, K. A., Prietula, M. J., & Cokely, E. T. (2007, July–August). The making of an expert. *Harvard Business Review.* Retrieved from https://hbr.org/2007/07/the-making-of-an-expert

F

Facione, P. A. (2013). *Critical thinking: What it is and why it counts.* California Academic Press. Retrieved from https://www.nyack.edu/files/CT_What_Why_2013.pdf

Ferreras, J. (2017, July 13). Canada ranks among the world's more overweight countries, and this study may have shown why. *Global News.ca.* Retrieved from https://globalnews.ca/news/3595135/canada-fattest-countries-activity-inequality/

Fordcarz.com. (n.d.). *Henry Ford Quotations.* Retrieved from www.fordcarz.com/henry_ford_quotes.htm/

Fried, C. B. (2008). In-class laptop use and its effects on student learning. *Computers and Education, 50,* 906–914.

G

Gardner, H. (1993). *Frames of mind: The theory of multiple intelligences.* New York, NY: Basic Books.

Gatehouse, J. (2011, February 21). Their main act: Arcade Fire doesn't chase fame. *Maclean's, 124*(6), 44.

Gates, G. S. (1917). Recitation as a factor in memorizing. *Archives of Psychology, 6*(40).

Get Cyber safe (2018). Retrieved from http://www.getcybersafe.gc.ca

Gillett, R., Feloni, R., & Lutz, A. (2016). *33 Famous people who failed before they succeeded.* Retrieved from http://www.businessinsider.com/famous-people-who-failed-before-they-succeeded-2016-10/

Glater, J. D. (2006, May 18). Colleges chase as cheats shift to higher tech. *New York Times.* Retrieved from http://www.nytimes.com/2006/05/18/education/18cheating.html/

Goleman, D. (1995). *Emotional intelligence: Why it can matter more than IQ.* New York, NY: Bantam.

Gordon, T. (1975). *Parent effectiveness training: The tested way to raise responsible children.* New York, NY: New American Library.

Graybiel, A. (2014). *How the brain makes and breaks habits.* Retrieved from http://www.scientificamerican.com/article/how-the-brain-makes-and-breaks-habits/

Grenier, E. (2017). 21.9% of Canadians are immigrants, the highest share in 85 years. *CBC.ca.* Retrieved from http://www.cbc.ca/news/politics/census-2016-immigration-1.4368970

Gustavson, D. E., & Miyake, A. (2017). Academic procrastination and goal accomplishment: A combined experimental and individual differences investigation. *Learning and Individual Differences, 54,* 160–172.

H

Habib, M. (2013, October 22). Can you afford university? *The Globe and Mail.* Retrieved from http://www.theglobeandmail.com/news/national/education/canadian-university-report/can-you-afford-university/article14948509/

Hallowell (2006). Crazy busy: Overstretched, overbooked, and about to snap. New York, NY: Ballantine.

Halpern, D. (1999). Teaching for critical thinking: Helping college students develop the skills and dispositions of a critical thinker. *New Directions for Teaching and Learning, 80,* 69–74.

Hansen, J. (2017, September). 'It's a big stress': how to deal with student debt that keeps piling up. CBC News. Retrieved from http://www.cbc.ca/news/business/post-secondary-student-debt-1.4295476

Harvard Medical School. (2008, October 14). *HEALTHbeat: 20 no-sweat ways to get more exercise.* Boston, MA: Harvard Health Publications.

Hasin, D. S., O'Brien, C. P., Auriacombe, M., Borges, G., Bucholz, K., Budney, A., ... & Schuckit, M. (2013). DSM-5 criteria for substance use disorders: recommendations and rationale. *American Journal of Psychiatry, 170*(8), 834–851.

Hayes, Steven C. (2004). *Get out of your mind and into your life: The new acceptance and commitment therapy.* Oakland, CA: New Harbinger.

Health Canada (2017a). Human papillomavirus (HPV). Retrieved from https://www.canada.ca/en/public-health/services/diseases/human-papillomavirus-hpv.html

Health Canada (2017b). Good Samaritan drug overdose act becomes law in Canada. Retrieved from https://www.canada.ca/en/health-canada/news/2017/05/good_samaritan_drugoverdoseactbecomeslawincanada.html

Health Canada. (2011). *Eating well with Canada's Food Guide.*

Health Canada. (n.d.). *Human papilloma virus.* Retrieved from http://www.hc-sc.gc.ca/hl-vs/iyh-vsv/diseases-maladies/hpv-vph-eng.php

Hebb, D. (2001). In D. J. Siegel, Memory: An overview. *Journal of the American Academy of Child and Adolescent Psychiatry 40*(9), 997–1011.

Hodges, L. C. (2015). Teaching undergraduate science: A guide to overcoming obstacles to student learning. Sterling VA: Stylus Publishing.

Hrvatin, V. (2018, January 4). Students are feeling more pressure than ever to be perfectionist and social media may be to blame. *National Post*. Retrieved from http://nationalpost.com/news/world/students-are-feeling-more-pressure-than-ever-to-be-perfectionists-and-social-media-may-be-to-blame

Hudes, S. (2018, May 14). Alberta colleges, universities wrestle with the issue of cannabis on campus. *Calgary Herald*. Retrieved from http://calgaryherald.com/news/local-news/alberta-post-secondary-schools-wrestle-with-issue-of-cannabis-on-campus?utm_source

Hull, M. (2018, February 21). Low-fat versus low-carb? Major study concludes: It doesn't matter for weight loss. *Examine.com*. Retrieved from https://examine.com/nutrition/low-fat-vs-low-carb-for-weight-loss/

I

Industry Training Authority. (2017). *Apprenticeships basics*. Retrieved from http://www.itabc.ca/about-apprentices/apprenticeship-basics

International Centre for Youth Gambling. (2018). *Adolescents: Myths and facts*. Retrieved from http://www.youthgambling.com/

Isaac, B. (2007). Jerry Seinfeld's productivity secret. *Lifehacker*. Retrieved from http://www.lifehacker.com/software/motivation/jerry-seinfelds-productivity-secret-281626.php/

J

Jackins, H. (1991). *The benign reality*. Seattle, WA: Rational Island.

Jourard, S. (1971). *The transparent self*. New York, NY: Van Nostrand.

K

Kabat-Zin, J. (2001). *Full catastrophe living: How to cope with stress, pain and illness using mindfulness meditation*. London, UK: Piatkus Books.

Kadison, R., & Foy DeGeronimo, T. (2004). *College of the overwhelmed: The campus mental health crisis and what to do about it*. Toronto, ON: John Wiley & Sons Canada Ltd.

Kang, S. H. K. (2016). Spaced repetition promotes efficient and effective learning: Policy implications for instruction. *Behavioral and Brain Sciences, 3*, 12-19.

Karpicke, J. D., & Blunt, J. R. (2011, January 20). Retrieval practice process produces more learning than elaborative studying with concept mapping. *Science Express*. Retrieved from http://science.sciencemag.org/content/331/6018/772

Khaw, K.-T., Wareham, N., Bingham, S., Welch, A., Luben, R., & Day, N. (2008). Combined impact of health behaviours and mortality in men and women: The EPIC-Norfolk Prospective Population Study. *PLoS Medicine. 5*(11). Retrieved from http://www.plosmedicine.org/article/info:doi/10.1371/journal.pmed.0050012/

Kielburger, C. (2016, October 13). Craig Kielburger looks ahead to the next 150 years. The Globe and Mail. Accessed at https://www.theglobeandmail.com/life/giving/craig-kielburger-looks-head-the-next-150-years/article32350561.

Knowles, M. (1984). Andragogy in action. San Francisco, CA: Jossey-Bass.

Koestler, A. (1964). *The act of creation*. New York, NY: Dell.

Kolb, A. Y. & Kolb, D. A. (2005). Learning styles and learning spaces: Enhancing experiential learning in higher education. *Academy of Management Learning & Education, 4*, 193–212.

Kolb, D. A. (1984). *Experiential learning: Experience as the source of learning and development*. Englewood Cliffs, NJ: Prentice-Hall.

Kostouros, P., & Bennett, D. (2017). Caring about post-secondary student self-care. *Transformative Dialogues, 10*(3) 1–13.

L

LaFasto, F., & Larson, C. (2002). *When teams work best*. Thousand Oaks, CA: Sage Publications.

Lakein, A. (1996). *How to get control of your time and your life*. New York, NY: New American Library.

Lamb, C. (2016, June 23). New president to help alumni find their voices. *Western News*. Retrieved from http://news.westernu.ca/2016/06/new-president-help-alumni-find-voices

Larmar, S., & Lodge, J. (2014). Making sense of how I learn: Metacognitive capital and the first year university student. *The International Journal of the First Year in Higher Education, 5*(1), 93-105.

Law, A., & Stock, R. (2017). Learning approach and its relationship to type of media use and frequency of media-multitasking. *Active Learning in Higher Education*, doi: 10.1177/1469787417735612.

Lee, D. (1959). *Freedom and culture*. Englewood Cliffs, NJ: Prentice-Hall.

Leopold, C., & Leutner, D. (2015). Improving students' science comprehension through metacognitive self-regulation when applying learning strategies. *Metacognition and Learning, 10*, 313–346. doi: 10.1007/s11409-014-9130-2

Levy, F., & Murname, R. J. (2004). *The new division of labor: How computers are creating the next job market*. Princeton, NJ: Princeton University Press.

Lewingon, J. (2017). Truth and education. *Maclean's*. Retrieved from https://archive.macleans.ca/issue/20171101

Lien, M.-C., Ruthruff, E., & Johnston, J. C. (2005). Attentional limitations in doing two tasks at once: The search for exceptions. *Current Directions in Psychological Science, 15*(2), 89–93.

Life Literacy Canada. (2018). *Adult literacy facts*. Retrieved from https://abclifeliteracy.ca/workplace-literacy-facts

Litcanu, M., Prosten, O., Oros, C., & Mnerie, A. V. (2015). Brainwriting vs. brainstorming case study for power engineering education. *Procedia-Social and Behavioural Sciences, 191*, 387–390.

Livingstone, D. W., & Raykov, M. (2013). Adult learning trends in Canada: Basic findings of the WALL 1998, 2004, and 2010 Surveys. Center for the Study of Education and Work. Retrieved from http://wall. oise. utoronto. ca/Adult-Learning-Trends-in-Canada-2013.pdf

Locke, E. A. (2004). Goal setting theory and its applications to the world of business. *Academy of Management Executive, 18*(4), 130–133.

M

MacDonald, G. (2017, August 17). For some students the transition to university can be hard on mental health. *The Globe and Mail.* Retrieved from https://www.theglobeandmail.com/life/parenting/back-to-school/the-transition-to-university-can-be-hard-on-mental-health/article36003286/

Maclean's. (2017, December 1). Advice for first-year students from Justin Trudeau (and 27 other people). *Maclean's.* Retrieved from http://www.macleans.ca/education/28-things-i-wish-id-known-in-first-year/

Mager, R. (1975). *Preparing instructional objectives.* Belmont, CA: Fearon.

Mann, L. (2016). Procrastination revisited: A commentary. *Australian Psychologist, 51,* 47–51. doi:10.1111/ap.12208

Marshall, S. M. (2009). The student leadership challenge: Five practices for exemplary leaders. *Journal of College Student Development, 50,* 245–247.

Maslow, A. H. (1971). *The farther reaches of human nature.* New York, NY: Viking.

Max, A., & Waters, R. (2018). *Breaking down barriers: Mental health and Canadian post-secondary students.* Canadian Alliance of Student Associations, Ottawa Canada.

Mayo Clinic. (2007, September 11). Generalized anxiety disorder. *Mayo Clinic.* Retrieved from http://www.mayoclinic.com/health/generalized-anxiety-disorder/DS00502/DSECTION=symptoms/

McGregor, J., Symonds, W. C., Foust, D., Brady, D., & Herbst, M., (2006, July 10). How failure breeds success. *Business Week.* Retrieved from http://www.businessweek.com/magazine/content/06_28/b3992001.htm/

McKinney, M. (2006). *Overcome procrastination.* Retrieved from http://www.successfulacademic.com/book_review_pro/

McLaren, D. (2009, November 17). On campus it's hip to be mature. *The Globe and Mail.* Retrieved from https://www.collegesontario.org/news/colleges-in-the-news/On-campus-its-hip-to-be-mature.html

McMaster, G. (2018, February 22). Rhodes scholarship just the beinning for rising Indigenous star. Folio. Retrieved from https://www.folio.ca/rhodes-scholarship-just-the-beginning-for-rising-indigenous-star/

Meier, A., Reinecke, L., & Meltzer, C. E. (2016). "Facebocrastination"? Predictors of using Facebook for procrastination and its effects on students' well-being. *Computers in Human Behavior, 64,* 65-76. Retrieved from http://dx.doi.org/10.1016/j.chb.2016.06.011 0747-5632

Misra, R., & McKean, M. (2000). College students' academic stress and its relation to their anxiety, time management, and leisure satisfaction. *American Journal of Health Studies, 16*(1), 41.

Moore, R. (2006). The importance of admission scores and attendance to first-year performance. *Journal of the First-Year Experience & Students in Transition, 18,* 105–125.

Moore, S. (2017). Student loan costs in 2017: What will you pay? [Web log post] Retrieved from https://proliteracy.ca/blogpost/student-loans-costs-in-2017-what-will-you-pay

Motley, M. T. (1998). *Overcoming your fear of public speaking: A proven method.* New York, NY: Houghton Mifflin.

Mueller, P. A., & Oppenheimer, D. M. (2014). The pen is mightier and the keyboard: Advantages of longhand over laptop note taking. *Psychological Science, 25*(6), 1159–1168. doi: 10.1177/0956797614524581

N

Nagda, B. R. A., & Zúñiga, X. (2003). Fostering meaningful racial engagement through intergroup dialogues. *Group Processes & Intergroup Relations, 6*(1), 111–128.

National College Health Assessment from CACUSS. (2016). Retrieved June 23, 2014, from http://www.cacuss.ca/_Library/documents/NCHA-II_WEB_SPRING_2013_CANADIAN_REFERENCE_GROUP_EXECUTIVE_SUMMARY.pdf

National Committee for Latin and Greek. (2006, March 5). Retrieved May 1, 2018, from http://www.acha-ncha.org/docs/ncha-ii%20spring%202016%20canadian%20reference%20group%20executive%20summary.pdf

National Eating Disorder Information Centre. (2014a). *Clinical definitions.* Retrieved from http://nedic.ca/node/806#Anorexia%20Nervosa

National Eating Disorder Information Centre. (2014b). *Statistics.* Retrieved from http://nedic.ca/know-facts/statistics

Nielsen, J. (2000). *Designing web usability: The practice of simplicity.* San Francisco, CA: New Riders Publishing.

Novak, J., & Gowin, D. B. (1984). *Learning how to learn.* Cambridge, UK: Cambridge University Press.

O

O'Malley, M. (2008). Educating undergraduates on using credit cards. *SallieMae.* Retrieved from http://www.nelliemae.com/library/cc_use.html/

Ontario Ministry of Training, Colleges and Universities. (2010). *Change your world: Achieve your dreams.* Retrieved from http://www.tcu.gov.on.ca/yourfuture/index.html

Orman, S. (2009). *Suze Orman's 2009 action plan.* New York, NY: Spiegel & Grau.

Ottaway, C. (2018). Want free university? Changes to OSAP, Canada Student grants could help. *Maclean's.* Retrieved from http://www.macleans.ca/education/university/want-free-university-changes-to-osap-canada-student-grants-could-help/

P

Pang, W. (2017). Universities see spike in students seeking mental health help. *The Globe and Mail.* Retrieved from https://www.theglobeandmail.com/news/national/education/peace-of-mind-universities-see-spike-in-students-seeking-mental-health-help/article36637574/

Park, N., Peterson, C., & Seligman, M. (2004). Strengths of character and well-being. *Journal of Social and Clinical Psychology, 24*(5), 603–619.

Pascarella, E. T., Seifert, T. A., & Blaich, C. (2010). How effective are the NSSE benchmarks in predicting important educational outcomes? *Change, 42*(1), 16–22.

Pascarella, E. T., & Terenzini, P. T. (2005). *How college affects students: A third decade of research,* Volume 2. San Francisco, CA: Jossey-Bass.

Paterson, R. J. (2002). *Your depression map.* Oakland, CA: New Harbinger Publications.

Patterson, R. W., & Patterson, R. M. (2017). Computers and productivity: Evidence from laptop use in college. *Economics of Education Review, 57,* 66–79.

Pauk, W., & Owens, R. J. Q. (2005). *How to study in college* (8th ed.). Boston, MA: Houghton Mifflin.

Paul, R., & Elder, L. (2008). *The miniature guide to critical thinking concepts and tools.* Dillon Beach, CA: The Foundation for Critical Thinking Press.

Perry, W. G. Jr. (1970). *Forms of intellectual and ethical development in the college years: A scheme.* New York, NY: Holt, Rinehart, & Winston.

Petty, A. (2010, April 16). 9 Tips for nailing the classroom group project presentation. *Art Petty.com.* Retrieved June 1, 2014, from http://artpetty.com/2010/04/16/9-tips-for-nailing-the-classroom-group-project-presentation/

Pineño, O., & Miller, R. R. (2005). Primacy and recency effects in extinction and latent inhibition: A selective review with implications for models of learning. *Behavioural Processes, 69,* 223–235.

Pintrich, P. R., Smith, D. A., Garcia, T., & McKeachie, W. J. (1993). Reliability and predictive validity of the motivated strategies for learning questionnaire (MSLQ). *Educational and Psychological Measurement, 53,* 801–813.

Pittis, D. (2017, September 12). Yes, post-secondary education makes you rich but that may not be the best part. *CBC.ca.* Retrieved from http://www.cbc.ca/news/business/education-canada-economics-1.4268921

Prevnet: Promoting relationships and eliminating violence network. Retrieved July 23, 2014, from http://www.prevnet.ca/bullying/cyber-bullying

Prochaska, J. O., Norcross, J. C., & DiClemente, C. C. (1994). *Changing for good.* New York, NY: Avon.

Public Health Agency of Canada. (2017). *Human papillomavirus.* Retrieved from https://www.canada.ca/en/public-health/services/infectious-diseases/sexual-health-sexually-transmitted-infections/human-papillomavirus-hpv.html

Public Health Agency of Canada. (2014a). *Summary: Estimates of HIV incidence, prevalence and proportion undiagnosed in Canada, 2014.* Surveillance and Epidemiology Division, Professional Guidelines and Public Health Practice Division, Centre for Communicable Diseases and Infection Control, Public Health Agency of Canada, 2015. Retrieved from http://www.catie.ca/sites/default/files/2014-HIV-Estimates-in-Canada-EN.pdf

Public Health Agency of Canada. (2014b). *Questions and answers: Sexual orientation in schools.* Retrieved from https://www.canada.ca/en/public-health/services/infectious-diseases/sexual-health-sexually-transmitted-infections/reports-publications/questions-answers-schools.html

Public Health Agency of Canada. (n.d.). *Leading causes of death, Canada, 2008, males and females combined.* Retrieved from http://www.phac-aspc.gc.ca/publicat/lcd-pcd97/table1-eng.php/

Pychyl, T. A. (2010). *The procrastinator's digest: A concise guide to solving the procrastination puzzle.* Canada: Howling Pines Publishing.

Pychyl, T. A., Morin, R. W., & Salmon, B. R. (2000). Procrastination and the planning fallacy: An examination of the study habits of university students. *Journal of Social Behavior and Personality, 15*(5), 135–150.

R

Racco, M. (2017). *Why STI rates are going steadily up in Canada.* Retrieved from https://globalnews.ca/news/3797824/why-sti-infection-rates-are-steadily-going-up-in-canada/

Reynolds, L. (2011, February 14). Hughes adds new triumph: Erase stigma attached to mental illness. *The Winnipeg Free Press.*

Rico, G. (1983). *Writing the natural way.* Los Angeles, CA: J. P. Tarcher.

Rogers, C. (1969). *Freedom to learn.* Columbus, OH: Merrill.

Roseman, E. (2009, December 16). Roseman: Carney's debt warning a shot of common sense. *The Star.* Retrieved from http://www.yourhome.ca/homes/realestate/article/739287/

Rosen, C. (2008). The myth of multitasking. *The New Atlantis, 20,* 105–110.

Rudow, H. (2017). Exploring motivation among college students. *Counselling Today.* Retrieved from https://ct.counseling.org/2013/09/exploring-motivation-among-college-students/

Ruggiero, V. R. (2015). *Becoming a critical thinker* (8th ed.). Stamford CT: Cengage Learning.

S

Sana, F., Weston, T., & Cepeda, N. J. (2013). Laptop multitasking hinders classroom learning for both users and nearby peers. *Computers & Education, 62,* 24–31.

Sandman, D., Simantov, E. & An, C. (2000). Out of touch: American men and the health care system. *The Commonwealth Fund, 2000.* Retrieved from https://www.usrf.org/breakingnews/Men_out_of_touch.pdf

Sapadin, L., & Maguire, J. (1997). *It's about time! The six styles of procrastination and how to overcome them.* New York, NY: Penguin.

Sapurji, S, Karapita, M., & Alex, C. (n.d.). I am Indigenous. *CBC News.* Accessed at http://www.cbc.ca/news2/interactives/i-am-indigenous-2017/beardy-linklater.html.

Sattler, P. (2011). *Work-integrated learning in Ontario's postsecondary sector.* Toronto: Higher Education Quality Council of Ontario.

Scharff, L., Draeger, J., Verpoorten, D., Devlin, M., Dvorakova, L. S., Lodge, J. M., & Smith, S. (2017). Exploring metacognition as support for learning transfer. *Teaching & Learning Inquiry, 5*(1), 1–14, 1–8. http://dx.doi.org/10.20343/teachlearninqu.5.1.6

Schreiner, L. (2010a). Thriving in the classroom. *About Campus, 15*(3), 2–10.

Schreiner, L. (2010b). Thriving in community. *About Campus, 15*(4), 2–11.

Seligman, M. E. P. (2002). *Authentic happiness: Using the new positive psychology to realize your potential for lasting fulfillment.* New York, NY: Simon and Schuster.

Seligman, M. E. P. (1998). *Learned optimism.* New York, NY: Pocket Books.

Shepard, L. A. (2016, October 5). Teenage scientist captures Arctic ice melt on film. *Nexus Media. Popular Science.* Retrieved from https://www.popsci.com/teenage-scientist-captures-arctic-ice-melt-on-film

Sheridan College. (2017, May 2). *Sheridan makes history with Tony Award nomination for* Come From Away. *Sheridan.* Retrieved from www.sheridancollege.ca/news-and-events/news/sheridan

-makes-history-with-tony-award-nomination-for-come
-from-away

Siegel, D. J. (2001). Memory: An overview. *Journal of the American Academy of Child and Adolescent Psychiatry, 40*(9) 997–1011.

Sirois, F. M., & Pychyl, T. (2013). Procrastination and the priority of short-term mood regulation: Consequences for future self. *Social and Personality Psychology Compass, 7*(2), 115-127.

Society of Obstetricians and Gynaecologists. (2010). *The Society of Obstetricians and Gynaecologists of Canada.* Retrieved from https://sogc.org.

Spears, T. (2017). *Just how bad is binge drinking?* Retrieved from https://bodyandhealth.canada.com/news/chealth/35146?newssource=0

Sperounes, S. (2010, December 30). Hootenannies and hallelujahs: 25 years of k.d. lang. *Edmonton Journal.* Retrieved from http://www.edmontonjournal.com/entertainment/Hootenannies+hallelujahs+years+lang/3998975/story.html

Statistics Canada. (2018a). *Smokers, by age group.* Retrieved from https://www150.statcan.gc.ca/t1/tbl1/en/tv.action?pid=1310009610

Statistics Canada. (2018c). *Leading cause of death, Total population, by age group.* https://www150.statcan.gc.ca/t1/tbl1/en/tv.action?pid=1310039401&pickMembers%5B0%5D=2.6&pickMembers%5B1%5D=3.1

Statistics Canada. (2017a). *Does education pay? A comparison of earnings by level of education in Canada and its provinces and territories.* Retrieved from http://www12.statcan.gc.ca/census-recensement/2016/as-sa/98-200-x/2016024/98-200-x2016024-eng.cfm

Statistics Canada. (2017b). *Postsecondary enrolments degree programs, all programs, STEM programs, by sex, 2010 and 2015.* Retrieved from https://www.statcan.gc.ca/daily-quotidien/171207/t001c-eng.htm

Statistics Canada. (2017c). *Postsecondary enrolments, by student status, country of citizenship and sex.* Retrieved from http://www5.statcan.gc.ca/cansim/a26?lang=eng&id=4770031

Statistics Canada. (2017d). *Postsecondary enrolments by field of study.* Retrieved from https://www.statcan.gc.ca/daily-quotidien/161123/t002b-eng.htm

Statistics Canada (2017e). *Immigration and ethnocultural diversity: Key results from the 2016 census.* Retrieved from https://www.statcan.gc.ca/daily-quotidien/171025/dq171025b-eng.htm?HPA=1

Statistics Canada (2017f). *Immigration and diversity: Population projections for Canada and its regions, 2011–2036.* Retrieved from https://www.statcan.gc.ca/pub/91-551-x/91-551-x2017001-eng.htm

Statistics Canada (2017g). *Census in brief: Same-sex couples in Canada 2016.* Retrieved from https://www12.statcan.gc.ca/census-recensement/2016/as-sa/98-200-x/2016007/98-200-x2016007-eng.cfm

Statistics Canada (2017h). *Canada goes urban.* Retrieved from https://www150.statcan.gc.ca/n1/pub/11-630-x/11-630-x2015004-eng.htm

Statistics Canada (2016). *Study: International Students in Canadian Universities, 2005/2005 to 2013/2014.* Retrieved from http://www.statcan.gc.ca/daily-quotidien/161020/dq161020e-eng.htm

Statistics Canada. (2015). *Oral contraceptive use among women aged 15 to 49: Results from the Canadian Health Measures Survey.* Retrieved from https://www150.statcan.gc.ca/n1/pub/82-003-x/2015010/article/14222-eng.htm

Statistics Canada (2011a). *The 10 leading causes of death, 2011.* Retrieved from https://www.statcan.gc.ca/pub/82-625-x/2014001/article/11896-eng.htm

Statistics Canada (2011b). *The educational attainment of aboriginal peoples in Canada.* Retrieved from http://www12.statcan.gc.ca/nhs-enm/2011/as-sa/99-012-x/99-012-x2011003_3-eng.cfm

Statistics Canada (2011c). *Selected religions, for Canada, provinces and territories.* Retrieved from http://www12.statcan.ca/english/census01/products/highlight/religion/Page.cfm?Lang=E&Geo=PR&View=1a&Code=62&Table=1&StartRec=1&Sort=2&B1=Canada&B2=1/

Statistics Canada. (2011d, May 25). *Canadians in context—People with disabilities.* Retrieved from http://www4.hrsdc.gc.ca/.3ndic.1t.4r@-eng.jsp?iid=40/

Stevenson, V. (2016, March 22). Youth the face of fentanyl awareness campaign. *The Star.* Retrieved from https://www.thestar.com/news/gta/2016/03/22/youth-the-face-of-fentanyl-awareness-campaign.html

Subrahmanyam, K., Michikyan, M., Clemmons, C., Carrillo, R., Uhls, Y. T., & Greenfield , P. M.(2013). Learning from paper, learning from screens: Impact of screen reading and multi-tasking conditions on reading and writing among college students. *International Journal of Cyber Behavior, Psychology and Learning, 3*(4), 1–27.

Svinicki, M. D., & McKeachie, W. J. (2014). *McKeachie's teaching tips: Strategies, research, and theory for college and university teachers.* Belmont, CA: Wadsworth Cengage Learning.

Svinicki, M. D. (2004). *Learning and motivation in the postsecondary classroom.* Bolton, MA: Anker Publishing.

Sweet, C., Blythe, H., & Carpenter, R. (2017, August 22). Mind mapping: A technique for metacogntition. *Teaching with metacognition.* 1–4. Retrieved from http://www.improvewithmetacognition.com/mind-mapping-technique-metacognition/

Szalavitz, M. (2001, March 2). Race and the genome. *Howard University Human Genome Center.* Retrieved from http://www.genomecenter.howard.edu/article.htm/

T

Taylor, L. C. (2009, March 09). Bad English barrier to job: Survey. *The Star.* Retrieved from http://www.thestar.com/printarticle/598636

Taylor, C. & Peter, T., with McMinn, T. L., Elliott, T., Beldom, S., Ferry, A., Gross, Z., Paquin, S., & Schachter, K. (2011). *Every class in every school: The first national climate survey on homophobia, biphobia, and transphobia in Canadian schools.* Final report. Toronto, ON: Egale Canada Human Rights Trust.

Taylor, P. (2011, January 13). Writing about fears before the tests boosts students' grades, study. *The Globe and Mail.* Retrieved from http://license.icopyright.net/user/viewFree.act?fuid=MTE0MTc5Nzk%3D/

Tchir, J. (2017). Is car-sharing really cheaper than owning or renting? *The Globe and Mail.* Retrieved from https://www.theglobeandmail.com/globe-drive/culture/commuting/is-car-sharing-really-cheaper-than-owning-or-renting/article26565669/

Thayer, L. (1968). Communication—Sine qua non of the behavioral sciences. In David L. Arm (Ed.), *Vistas in science*. Albuquerque, NM: University of New Mexico.

Theobold, C. (2018). Reported hate crime against sexual minorities sees spike in Canada. *The Star*. Retrieved from https://www.thestar.com/edmonton/2018/04/25/hate-crimes-in-canada-based-on-sexual-orientation-rose-25-per-cent-in-a-single-year-with-most-incidents-involving-violence.html

Thompson, C. (2005, October 16). Meet the lifehackers. *New York Times*. Retrieved January 24, 2011, from http://www.nytimes.com/2005/10/16/magazine/16guru.html

Titcomb, J., & Carson, J. (2018). Fake news: What exactly is it—and how can you spot it? *The Telegraph*. Retrieved from http://www.telegraph.co.uk/technology/0/fake-news-exactly-has-really-had-influence/

Toronto Police Service. (2018). *Report homophobic violence, period*. Retrieved February 12, 2011, from http://www.torontopolice.on.ca/rhvp/

Truth and Reconciliation Commission. (2015). *Truth and Reconciliation Commission of Canada: Calls to action*. Retrieved from www.trc.ca/websites/trcinstitution/File/2015/Findings/Calls_to_Action_English2.pdf

U

University of Minnesota. (2007). *Health and academic performance: Minnesota undergraduate students*. Retrieved from https://boynton.umn.edu/sites/boynton.umn.edu/files/2017-09/HealthAcademicPerformanceReport_2007.pdf

V

van der Meer, J., Jansen, E., & Torenbeek, M. (2010). 'It's almost a mindset that teachers need to change': first-year students' need to be inducted into time management. *Studies in Higher Education, 35*(7), 777–791.

W

Whalen, J. (2017). Census 2016: More than half of Torontonians identify as visible minorities. Retrieved from http://www.cbc.ca/news/canada/toronto/census-visible-minorities-1.4371018

White, M. (2013, November 10). The real reason new college grads can't get hired. *Time.com*. Retrieved June 1, 2014, from http://business.time.com/2013/11/10/the-real-reason-new-college-grads-cant-get-hired/

Williams, R. (2014, January 1). The biggest predictor of career success? Not skills or education—but emotional intelligence. *Financial Post*. Retrieved June 17, 2014, from http://business.financialpost.com/2014/01/01/the-biggest-predictor-of-career-success-not-skills-or-education-but-emotional-intelligence/

Wilson, M., & Ono, S. (2017). Students are not fragile flowers: We must care about their mental health. *The Globe and Mail*. Retrieved from https://www.theglobeandmail.com/opinion/students-are-not-fragile-flowers-we-must-care-about-their-mental-health/article36498798/

Wong, L. (2003). *Essential study skills*, 4th ed. Boston, MA: Wadsworth Cengage.

World Population Review (2018). Toronto population 2018. Retrieved from http://worldpopulationreview.com/world-cities/toronto-population/

Wurman, R. S. (1989). *Information anxiety*. New York, NY: Doubleday.

Wurman, R. S., Leifer, L., & Sume, D. (2001). *Information anxiety #2*. Indianapolis, IN: Que.

Y

Yates, J. (2013). *The career coaching handbook*. New York, NY: Taylor and Francis.

Z

Zúñiga, X. (2009). Fostering intergroup dialogue on campus: Essential ingredients. *Diversity Digest*. Retrieved from http://www.diversityweb.org/Digest/W98/fostering.html/

50 little-known facts about Canadian universities. (2017, June). *University Affairs*. Retrieved from www.universityaffairs.ca/feature-50-little-known-facts-canadian-universities-text/

Index